Frommer's®

South Florida

with the best of Miami & the Keys

7th Edition

by Lesley Abravanel

WILEY

Wiley Publishing, Inc.

ABOUT THE AUTHOR

Lesley Abravanel is a freelance journalist and a graduate of the University of Miami School of Communication. When she isn't combing South Florida for the latest hotels, restaurants, and attractions, she is on the lookout for vacationing celebrities and covers them in her weekly nightlife and gossip column, "Velvet Underground," in the *Miami Herald.* She is a contributor to *Business Traveler, Time Out,* all three illustrious supermarket tabloids, and is the author of *Florida For Dummies, Frommer's Florida,* and *Frommer's Portable Miami.*

Published by:

WILEY PUBLISHING, INC.

111 River St.
Hoboken, NJ 07030-5774

ISBN 978-0-470-63235-2 (paper); ISBN 978-0-470-91710-7 (ebk); ISBN 978-0-470-41371-5 (ebk); ISBN 978-0-470-94347-2 (ebk)

Editor: Stephen Bassman
Production Editor: Katie Robinson
Cartographer: Nick Trotter
Photo Editor: Richard Fox
Production by Wiley Indianapolis Composition Services
Front cover photo: Red mangrove tree in Key Biscayne National Park © Marc Muench / Alamy Images.
Back cover photo: Art Deco houses on Ocean Drive in Miami © Walter Bibikow / John Arnold Images Ltd. / Alamy Images.

For information on our other products and services or to obtain technical support, please contact our Customer Care Department within the U.S. at 877/762-2974, outside the U.S. at 317/572-3993 or fax 317/572-4002.

Wiley also publishes its books in a variety of electronic formats. Some content that appears in print may not be available in electronic formats.

Manufactured in the United States of America

5 4 3 2 1

CONTENTS

LIST OF MAPS

ACKNOWLEDGMENTS

Thanks to all the intrepid publicists out there, for whom no question is an inane one. Hair dryers in rooms? Wi-Fi vs. high speed Internet? I needed it now, and you gave it to me when I asked for it. Well, most of you did. Thanks to my husband, the Swede, for trekking through the long state of Florida and for insight and entertainment. Most of all, thanks to my parents for convincing me that Florida really would be a good experience. Seventeen years later, I admit it: They were right.

—Lesley Abravanel

HOW TO CONTACT US

In researching this book, we discovered many wonderful places—hotels, restaurants, shops, and more. We're sure you'll find others. Please tell us about them, so we can share the information with your fellow travelers in upcoming editions. If you were disappointed with a recommendation, we'd love to know that, too. Please write to:

Frommer's South Florida with the Best of Miami & the Keys, 7th Edition
Wiley Publishing, Inc. • 111 River St. • Hoboken, NJ 07030-5774
frommersfeedback@wiley.com

AN ADDITIONAL NOTE

Please be advised that travel information is subject to change at any time—and this is especially true of prices. We therefore suggest that you write or call ahead for confirmation when making your travel plans. The authors, editors, and publisher cannot be held responsible for the experiences of readers while traveling. Your safety is important to us, however, so we encourage you to stay alert and be aware of your surroundings. Keep a close eye on cameras, purses, and wallets, all favorite targets of thieves and pickpockets.

FROMMER'S STAR RATINGS, ICONS & ABBREVIATIONS

Every hotel, restaurant, and attraction listing in this guide has been ranked for quality, value, service, amenities, and special features using a **star-rating system.** In country, state, and regional guides, we also rate towns and regions to help you narrow down your choices and budget your time accordingly. Hotels and restaurants are rated on a scale of zero (recommended) to three stars (exceptional). Attractions, shopping, nightlife, towns, and regions are rated according to the following scale: zero stars (recommended), one star (highly recommended), two stars (very highly recommended), and three stars (must-see).

In addition to the star-rating system, we also use **seven feature icons** that point you to the great deals, in-the-know advice, and unique experiences that separate travelers from tourists. Throughout the book, look for:

Special finds—those places only insiders know about

Fun facts—details that make travelers more informed and their trips more fun

Best bets for kids and advice for the whole family

Special moments—those experiences that memories are made of

Places or experiences not worth your time or money

Insider tips—great ways to save time and money

Great values—where to get the best deals

The following **abbreviations** are used for credit cards:

AE	American Express	DISC Discover	V Visa
DC	Diners Club	MC MasterCard	

TRAVEL RESOURCES AT FROMMERS.COM

Frommer's travel resources don't end with this guide. Frommer's website, **www.frommers. com**, has travel information on more than 4,000 destinations. We update features regularly, giving you access to the most current trip-planning information and the best airfare, lodging, and car-rental bargains. You can also listen to podcasts, connect with other Frommers. com members through our active-reader forums, share your travel photos, read blogs from guidebook editors and fellow travelers, and much more.

THE BEST OF SOUTH FLORIDA

A week in Miami is not unlike watching an unbelievable reality show, only this time it's actually *real*. Miami: the city where Jennifer Aniston went "public" with her romance to rocker John Mayer, where troubled British pop star Amy Winehouse married her incarcerated husband, and where the paparazzi camps out for days, hoping to catch a glimpse of something or someone fabulous. It's where former U.S. President Bill Clinton kibitzes with the head of a top modeling agency at a St. Tropez–ish beach club, and where Janet Reno, Ben Affleck, and Matt Damon throw politically driven dance and cocktail parties at a South Beach nightclub. And about those unbelievable reality shows: A few have filmed here lately, too. Just ask the Kardashians. But that's just a small sample of the surreal, Fellini-esque world that exists way down here at the bottom of the map. Nothing in Miami is ever what it seems.

What used to be a relatively sleepy beach vacation destination has awakened from its humid slumber, upped its tempo, and finally earned its place in the Blackberries and iPhones of cutting-edge jet-setters worldwide. But don't be fooled by the hipper-than-thou, celebrity-drenched playground known as South Beach. While the chic elite do, indeed, flock to Miami's coolest enclave, it is surprisingly accessible to the average Joe, Jane, or José. Especially during the economic downturn, when there were indeed bargains to be had. For every Philippe Starck–designed, bank account–busting boutique hotel on South Beach (one actually refused to lower its prices during the evil recession despite the fact that rooms were empty), there's a kitschy, candy-coated Art Deco one that's much less taxing on the pockets. For each Pan-Mediterranean-Asian

Florida

G U L F   O F

M E X I C O

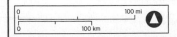

haute cuisine restaurant, there's always the down-home, no-nonsense Cuban bodega offering hearty food at ridiculously cheap prices.

Beyond the whole glitzy, *Us Weekly*-meets-beach-blanket-bacchanalia-as-seen-on-TV, Miami has an endless number of sporting, cultural, and recreational activities to keep you entertained. Its sparkling beaches are beyond compare. Plus, it has excellent shopping and nightlife activities, including ballet, theater, and opera (as well as all the celebrity-saturated hotels, restaurants, bars, and clubs that have helped make Miami so famous).

One thing you'll notice about Miami is the number of construction cranes dotting the skyline, languishing there as the last remnants of a real estate boom that has since crashed. For now, we take pride in watching the already majestic skyline take a new shape, albeit with empty, multimillion-dollar condos that many describe as soulless.

Leave Miami, be it for the Keys, the Gold Coast, or the Treasure Coast, and you'll expose yourself not only to more UV rays, but to a world of cultural, historical, and sybaritic surprises where you can take in a spring baseball game, walk in the footsteps of Hemingway, get up-close and personal with the area's sea life, soak up the serenity of unspoiled landscapes, catch the filming of *CSI: Miami* or a big-budget Hollywood flick, and much more.

Forget what you've heard about South Florida being "Heaven's Waiting Room." That slogan is as passé as the concept of early-bird dinners (which you can still get—they just no longer define the region). In fact, according to some people, South Florida *is* heaven.

FROMMER'S FAVORITE SOUTH FLORIDA EXPERIENCES

o **Driving Along Florida A1A:** This oceanfront route, which runs north up Miami Beach, through Sunny Isles and Hollywood, and into Fort Lauderdale (starting at Ocean Dr. and First St. in Miami and merging onto Collins Ave. before running north), embodies the essence that is South Florida. From time-warped hotels steeped in Art Deco kitsch to multimillion-dollar modern high-rises, A1A is one of the most scenic, albeit heavily trafficked, roads in all of Florida.

o **Airboat Ride Through the Outskirts of the Everglades:** Unfettered by jet skis, cruise ships, and neon bikinis, the Everglades are Florida's outback, resplendent in their swampy nature. The Everglades are best explored either by slow-moving canoes that really get you acquainted with your surroundings or via an airboat that can quickly navigate its way through the most stubborn of saw grass while providing you with an up-close and personal (as well as fun) view of the land's inhabitants, from alligators and manatees to raccoons and Florida panthers. See p. 252.

o **Dining at Garcia's on the Miami River:** Some consider dining on the Miami River to be industrial chic; others consider it seedy in a *Miami Vice* sort of way. However you choose to look at it, by all means *do* look at it; the sleepy Miami River is nestled below the sweeping downtown Miami skyline, reminding you that even though you're in a major metropolis, things in this often-frenetic city are capable of slowing down to a more soothing pace. See p. 149.

o **Getting the Juice at El Palacio de los Jugos:** For the true, frenetic, cacophonous Miami Cuban experience, this is the place to go, where heaps of gloriously greasy fare and sort of healthy fresh squeezed juices have people coming in packs. See p. 155.

o **Joe's Stone Crab Restaurant:** You *will* wait in line at Miami Beach's landmark spot for crab, but it's never dull, and the cacophony of mostly Northeastern U.S. accents and the occasional celebrity will keep you entertained until you are seated for your feast of crustacean. Dip medium, large, or jumbo crab into a tasty mustard-mayo sauce or just mustard, and save room for Key lime pie. Open October through May only. See p. 121.

o **Midnight Snacking at Versailles:** This iconoclastic, gaudy Cuban diner in the heart of Miami's Little Havana is humming with the buzz of old-timers reminiscing about pre-Castro Cuba, local politicos trying to appease them, and a slew of detached people there only for the fantastically cheap and authentic Cuban fare. Much like its French namesake in whose image it's been literally mirrored, Miami's Versailles provides a palatial view of Miami's ever-changing Cuban landscape. See p. 156.

o **Sunset Cocktails at Smith & Wollensky:** Say bon voyage to the mega ships sailing out of Government Cut from this, one of the best waterfront vantage points in all of Miami. See p. 124.

o **Learning to Salsa:** If the only salsa you're familiar with is the kind you put on your tacos, get over to Bongo's Cuban Café, the hottest salsa club north of Havana, where Miami's most talented salsa dancers will teach you how to move your two left feet in the right direction. See p. 232.

o **Relishing the View from Bill Baggs Cape Florida State Park:** You haven't truly seen South Florida until you've checked out the view from the southern point of Key Biscayne. Whether it's the turquoise water or the sight of Stiltsville—seven still-inhabited aquatic cabins dating back to the 1930s, perched smack in the middle of the Biscayne Channel—it may take a little coercing to get you to leave. See p. 187.

o **Scuba Diving in the Treasure Coast:** They don't call it the Treasure Coast for nothing, you know. Three popular artificial reefs off Hutchinson Island provide excellent scenery for divers of any level. The **USS Rankin,** sunk in 120 feet of water in 1988, lies 7 miles east-northeast of the St. Lucie Inlet. **Donaldson Reef** consists of a cluster of plumbing fixtures sunk in 58 feet of water. **Ernst Reef,** made from old tires, is a 60-foot dive located 4½ miles east-southeast of the St. Lucie inlet.

o **Burgers at Le Tub:** This former 1959 Sunoco gas station was transformed into a kitschy waterfront oasis whose resplendent scenery is almost secondary to the decor: old toilet bowls, bathtubs, and sinks—seriously. Not the least bit as gross as it sounds, Le Tub also has the best hamburgers, chili, a 4am closing time, and a strict "no children" policy. See p. 355.

o **Discovering Your Inner Flipper at the Dolphin Research Center:** Learn to communicate with and touch, swim, or play with the mammals at the nonprofit Dolphin Research Center in Marathon Key, home to a school of approximately 15 dolphins. See p. 269.

o **Eyeing the Estates on Palm Beach:** The winter playground for the *Lifestyles of the Rich and Famous* set, Palm Beach is lined with jaw-dropping palatial estates. Though many of them are hidden behind towering shrubbery, head south on South County Road, from Brazilian Avenue, where you will see some of the most opulent homes ever built. Make sure someone holds the steering wheel if you're driving, because you *will* do a double take. See chapter 13.

o **Water Taxiing Through the Intracoastal Waterway:** The waterway that connects the natural bays, lagoons, and rivers along Florida's East Coast snakes around from the Florida-Georgia border all the way to the port of Miami. A ride through the Fort Lauderdale Intracoastal provides a sublime view of million-dollar waterfront houses. See p. 336.

o **Unleashing Your Inner Gourmand in Miami's Design District:** Turns out, the home of high-end furniture showrooms and interior design firms is also home to some of Florida's most lauded eateries—Michael's Genuine Food & Drink, Sra. Martinez, Pacific Time. Some tapas with your tapestries, perhaps?

o **Channeling Andy Warhol in Miami's Wynwood Arts District:** After waiting patiently for this arty, funky area to hit its comeuppance, Miami's hipsters and artists have finally been rewarded with this still raw neighborhood of galleries, studios, and even a few cool bars, lounges, and restaurants that exude that New York City SoHo–meets–Meatpacking District vibe.

o **Sundays at Alabama Jack's:** There is nothing like hanging out, chugging a cheap beer, chowing down on amazing conch fritters, and watching a bunch of sauced octogenarians dressed like extras from *Hee Haw* line-dancing to incredible live country music, all in a Sunday's afternoon. Even better is the spectacular waterfront setting that makes you truly appreciate why you're in Florida in the first place. See p. 266.

> ## Impressions
>
> *What could be better than to sit on the beach playing cards in my shirt-sleeves in January?*
> —Anonymous Miami Beach resident

best BEACHES

o **For Tranquillity: Matheson Hammock Park Beach** (© 305/665-5475) in South Miami features an enclosed man-made lagoon that is flushed naturally by the tidal action of the adjacent Biscayne Bay. The serene beach is surrounded by the bay's warm, calm waters and a backdrop of tropical hardwood forest. See p. 71.

The beach at **Bahia Honda State Park** (© 305/872-2353) in Bahia Honda Key is one of the nicest and most peaceful in Florida, located amid 635 acres of nature trails and even a portion of Henry Flagler's railroad. See p. 287.

o **For Watersports: Hobie Beach** (© 305/361-2833), located on the south side of Key Biscayne's Rickenbacker Causeway, is one of the most popular beaches for watersport enthusiasts, featuring jet ski, sailboat, windsurfing, and sailboard rentals; shade, if necessary, from the Australian pine; and a sublime view of the picturesque downtown Miami skyline. See p. 170.

o **For People-Watching: Lummus Park Beach** (© 305/673-7714) is world renowned, not necessarily for its pristine sands, but for its more common name of **South**

Beach. Here, seeing, being seen, and, at times, the obscene, go hand in hand with the sunscreen and beach towels. See p. 170.

Not nearly as scenic, but still heavily populated, **Fort Lauderdale Beach** (© 954/468-1597) is the site of many a bacchanalian Spring Break, Frankie and Annette, and now, an eclectic—albeit calmer—mix of young, buff beach bums. See p. 332.

o **For Nature Lovers: MacArthur Beach** (© 561/624-6950; www.macarthur beach.org), in West Palm Beach, is considered by many nature enthusiasts to be the most beautiful nature park in South Florida, with a nice stretch of beach set against a lush and diverse background of foliage, plus a state-of-the-art nature center and renowned sea turtle awareness program.

o **For Nude Sunbathing:** For that all-over tan, the place to be is the north end of **Haulover Beach** (© 305/944-3040), nestled between the Intracoastal Waterway and the ocean. A gay, nude beach is also there, as is an area for nude volleyball. See p. 171.

o **For Seclusion:** The producers of *Survivor* could feasibly shoot their show on the ultra-secluded, picturesque, and deserted **Virginia Key** (© 305/361-2749), on Key Biscayne, where people go purposely not to be found. See p. 172.

John U. Lloyd Beach State Park (© 954/923-6711) in Dania Beach is unfettered by high-rise condos, T-shirt shops, and hotels, and remains intact with an untouched shoreline surrounded by a canopy of Australian pine to ensure that your seclusion is, indeed, highly guarded. See p. 334.

o **For Gay Beachgoers:** South Beach's **12th Street Beach** (© 305/673-7714) is the beach of choice for gay residents and travelers who come to show off just how much time they've spent in the gym, and, of course, catch up on the latest gossip and upcoming must-attend parties and events. Oftentimes, this beach is the venue for some of the liveliest parties South Beach has ever seen. See p. 172.

o **For Kids:** Miami's **Crandon Park Beach** (© 305/361-5421) is extremely popular for families with kids because of the shallow water created by a neighboring sandbar. Convenient parking, picnic areas, a winding boardwalk, eco-adventure tours, and a multiethnic mix of families grilling, dancing, and relaxing are the benchmarks of this beach. See p. 170.

best HOTEL BETS

o **Best Historic Hotel:** With a guest registry that reads like a who's who of history crossed with an engrossing whodunit, Miami's monumental, Mediterranean Revivalist–style **Biltmore Hotel** (© 800/727-1926 or 305/445-1926) opened its doors in 1926. Guests ranging from Al Capone to the duke and duchess of Windsor loved the stately hotel so much that they never left, so say those who claim the hotel is haunted. Ghosts aside, this national landmark boasts the largest hotel pool in the continental United States as well as a 300-foot bell tower modeled after the Cathedral of Seville. See p. 106.

A close second is Palm Beach's landmark **The Breakers** (© 888/273-2537), built in 1896 by Standard Oil Company magnate Henry Flagler. See p. 379.

o **Best Cheap-Chic Hotel:** West Palm Beach's **Hotel Biba** (© 561/832-0094) is a funky, single-story, converted 1940s motor lodge–turned–boutique hotel featuring an oversized swimming pool, Asian gardens with sitting areas, a reflection pond, and the ultrahip Biba Bar. Rooms start at $100. See p. 382.

The Catalina Hotel & Beach Club (South Beach; ☎ **877/SOBEGRP** [762-3477] or 305/674-1160): Affordable and hip, the Catalina is a retro fab stay with stylish rooms, Swedish Tempur-Pedic mattresses, a hot bar, and VIP hookups at all the clubs in South Beach. See p. 88.

o **Best Hotel Transformation:** In its past life, Miami's **Hotel Urbano** (☎ **888/384-2997**) was a Hampton Inn. Today, it's a hip, 65-room boutique art hotel that's the antithesis of its former identity. See p. 105.

o **Best Celebrity-Saturated Hotel: The W South Beach** (South Beach; ☎ **305/938-3000**): Although it's hardly the first in the chain of hip, trendy hotels, the W South Beach is considered the brand's signature showpiece and for good reason. All 312 rooms in this visually arresting, Bali–meets–Miami Beach resort boast ocean views and all the trappings of modern hipster society. The hotel's bar and restaurant scene are among the city's hottest thanks to a celebrity clientele who flock to Mr. Chow and Wall nightclub. The **W Fort Lauderdale** (☎ **954/414-8200**) isn't too shabby on celeb sightings either, hosting everyone from Pamela Anderson to the Real Housewives of [insert your favorite city or county here]. And for, dare we say, publicity-shy celebs, the low-key, luxurious **Brazilian Court Hotel** in Palm Beach (☎ **954/655-7740**) is very Beverly Hills. See p. 81.

o **Best Out-of-Place Bed-and-Breakfast:** Located on the outskirts of gritty, bustling downtown Miami is the historic **Miami River Inn** (☎ **800/468-3589** or 305/325-0045), housed in five restored clapboard buildings dating back to 1906. By the looks of this place, you could swear you were somewhere in New England—until you step out for a breath of the balmy air. See p. 105.

o **Best Hotel in a League of Its Own: Jules' Undersea Lodge** (☎ **305/451-2353**) in Key Largo really gives you the low-down on the full Keys experience by requiring all guests to scuba 30 feet underwater to get to their rooms, which are literally located under the sea, in the mangrove habitat of Emerald Lagoon. See p. 276.

o **Best Art Deco Hotel:** The **Raleigh Hotel** (☎ **800/848-1775** or 305/534-6300) in Miami is the reigning diva of Deco, dating back to 1940. It features one of the most photographed palm-lined swimming pools, reminiscent of the days of Esther Williams. See p. 85.

o **Best Spa Hotel: The Standard** (☎ **305/673-1717**) in Miami Beach is a wholly holistic experience located right on Biscayne Bay. In addition to dolphin sightings, there are Turkish hammams, an outdoor yoga lounge, and even a mud lounge where getting dirty was never so cleansing. See p. 86.

o **Best Hotel Lobby:** A tough call between the dreamy *Alice in Wonderland*–meets–South Beach sleek at **Mondrian** (☎ **305/672-2662**), the luxe living-room-style lobby of the **W South Beach** (☎ **305/938-3000**) with its tufted leather ottomans, dark wood floors and velvet curtains, and the **W Fort Lauderdale** (☎ **954/414-8200**) in which you can look up and see into the pool, for better or for worse. See p. 77, p. 81, and p. 343.

o **Best Hotel Pool: The Raleigh** (☎ **305/534-6300**) always wins this one for its most photogenic Esther Williams–era pool, but we'd also give props to downtown Miami's **Viceroy** (☎ **866/720-1991**) and Coral Gables' **Biltmore** (☎ **800/727-1926** or 305/445-1926) if just for sheer size alone. See p. 85.

- **Best Beach Hotel:** Miami's **Ritz-Carlton, South Beach** (℃ **800/241-3333** or 786/276-4000) is a lot more than just a drop in the sand thanks to its DiLido Beach Club, providing stellar food, drink, entertainment, and beach toys whenever and wherever you feel like it. Coming in at a close second is its Key Biscayne sibling, **The Ritz-Carlton, Key Biscayne** (Key Biscayne; ℃ **800/241-3333** or 305/365-4500). See p. 78.

  Two hotels with outstanding off-property beach hotels are the **Boca Raton Resort** (℃ **888/495-BOCA** (2622) or 561/447-3000), whose recently revamped beach club features a half-mile of private beach, watersports activities, pool, bar and restaurant; and the **Brazilian Court Hotel & Beach Club** (℃ **561/655-7740**), featuring private beach, pool, food, drink, and spa services. See p. 363 and p. 378.

- **Best Inexpensive Hotel:** It's hard to find a hotel on South Beach with both good value and excellent service, but the **Chesterfield Hotel, Suites & Day Spa** (South Beach; ℃ **305/673-3767**) delivers as one of Miami's best bargains as well as coolest hotels. See p. 88.

  In Key West, the **Grand Guesthouse** (℃ **888/947-2630** or 305/294-0590), despite its name, will not leave you with a huge tab at the end of your stay. The rooms in this hotel are bright and airy and the proprietor works hard to keep you happy. See p. 317.

- **Best Hotel in an Empty Condo:** The **Viceroy** (Miami; ℃ **866/720-1991**): Amidst the staid buildings in Miami's so-called financial district lies this tastefully trendy, edgy Kelly Wearstler–designed hotel whose crown jewels are the mammoth pool deck and 50th floor restaurant, lounge and lap pool. See p. 104.

- **Best for Families:** On South Beach, the **Loews** (℃ **800/23-LOEWS** [235-6397] or 305/604-1601) is known for its Loews Loves Kids program of activities for kids and kids at heart including Dive-in Movies at the pool, salsa lessons, and bingo. See p. 77.

  In Fort Lauderdale, **Marriott's Harbor Beach** (℃ **800/222-6543** or 954/525-4000) has a Beachside Buddies program for children ages 5 to 12, offering half-day and all-day children's activities that range from seashell collecting to hula-hoop contests. See p. 341.

  The **Boca Raton Resort & Club** (℃ **888/495-BOCA** (2622) or 561/447-3000) has activity programs designed for distinct age groups. Upon registering children in the program, each parent is given a beeper with a 60-mile radius so that each may be contacted by the children at any time. See p. 363.

- **Best Hotel for Foodies:** The **Fontainebleau,** in Miami Beach (℃ **305/538-2000**) has not one, but three star-chef-helmed restaurants: Scott Conant's **Scarpetta,** Alfred Portale's **Gotham Steak,** and Alan Yau's **Hakkasan,** the first Michelin-starred haute Chineserie outside of the U.K. The **Boca Raton Resort & Club** (℃ **561/447-3000**) is another gourmand's favorite, with South Florida's only offering from Iron Chef Masaharu Morimoto in the form of the **Morimoto Sushi Bar** as well as a branch of NYC ice cream parlor **Serendipity** and Meat Packing District landmark, **Old Homestead.** See p. 97 and p. 363.

- **Best for Romance:** Imagine an intimate haven on your own private island and you've got **Little Palm Island** (℃ **800/343-8567** or 305/872-2524), located just 3 miles offshore in the Florida Keys, accessible only by boat or seaplane, and quite possibly the closest thing to paradise, with only one telephone on the entire island. See p. 290.

Although it's 2 blocks from Duval Street—Bourbon Street South—**The Gardens Hotel** (© 800/526-2664 or 305/294-2661) is Key West's most romantic, Eden-istic hideaway that's worlds away from the madness. See p. 308.

In Palm Beach, modeled after a quaint English inn, the **Chesterfield Hotel** (© 800/243-7871 or 561/659-5800) is absolutely seductive, thanks in part to its sexy, sultry Leopard Lounge, its cozy fireside library, and Churchill's Cigar Room. See p. 380.

best DINING BETS

o **Best for Celebrating a Big Deal: Prime One Twelve** on Miami Beach (© 305/532-8112) is where everyone from Gorbachev and Clinton to Madonna and Beyoncé come to satisfy their carnivorous sides with fare such as $25 Kobe beef hot dogs, dried sticks of bacon at the bar in lieu of peanuts, and, if you must cheat, the best truffle-infused macaroni and cheese you'll ever eat. See p. 123.

o **Best Romantic Restaurant: Casa Tua,** in South Beach (© 305/673-1010), offers exquisite Italian cuisine in a Mediterranean villa that's hidden from the street with lush landscaping and an iron gate, resplendent outdoor garden, cozy Hamptons-esque dining room, communal kitchen, and intimate upstairs lounge and patio. See p. 119.

o **Best Waterfront Dining:** It's a tossup between Biscayne Bay and the Atlantic Ocean, but whichever you prefer, there are two restaurants that provide front-row seats to both. The Mandarin Oriental Hotel's global fusion restaurant, **Azul** (© 305/913-8538), faces the Miami skyline and beautiful, tranquil Biscayne Bay, while **Garcia's** (© 305/375-0765) faces the scenic Miami River. Tough decisions, but both are winners. See p. 144 and p. 149.

In Hollywood and Fort Lauderdale, some of the most direct waterfront dining is on the Intracoastal, not the ocean. **Taverna Opa** (© 954/576-1630), **China Grill** (© 954/759-9950), and **Le Tub** (© 954/931-9425) all have fantastic Intracoastal views. See p. 229, p. 119, and p. 355.

Louie's Backyard in Key West (© 305/294-1061) offers Caribbean cuisine and one of the best views of the Gulf you'll ever have. See p. 319.

o **Best Restaurant Not Worth the Wait for a Table:** The legendary South Florida institution known as **Joe's Stone Crab Restaurant,** in Miami Beach (© 305/673-0365), refuses to take reservations, but that doesn't stop people from clawing their way into the restaurant for a table—despite a wait that's often in excess of 3 hours. Thing is, if only they knew about **Joe's Take Away,** directly next door, the only thing they'd be waiting for is seconds. See p. 121.

o **Best Cuban Restaurant:** There's always a debate on who has the best, most authentic Cuban cuisine, but for those of you who have never been to Havana, Miami's **Versailles,** in Little Havana (© 305/444-0240), is *the* quintessential Cuban diner, featuring enormous portions at paltry prices. For an even more frenetic, freshly squeezed Cuban dining experience, check out **El Palacio de los Jugos** (© 305/221-1615) See p. 156 and p. 155.

o **Best Old School Steakhouse:** Miami's **Capital Grille** (© 305/374-4500) may be part of a chain, but its dry-aged steaks are still a cut above the rest. See p. 144. In addition to **Prime One Twelve** (see above), which is quickly on its way to becoming an old-school South Beach steakhouse at last, **BLT Steak** on South

Beach (☏ 305/673-0044), **Bourbon Steak** in Aventura (☏ 305/279-6600) and **Christy's** in Coral Gables (☏ 305/446-1400), are other top carnivorous choices. See p. 118, p. 142, and 160.

○ **Sexiest Restaurant: Hakkasan,** at the Fontainebleau on Miami Beach (☏ 305/573-3355), brings an exotic, authentic Asian vibe to a place where even Italian restaurants serve sushi. The custom silk light fixtures from Paris separated by screens of dark walnut, elaborate latticework, and hand-carved decorative teak panels illuminated by washes of dimmed lighting give way to a very exotic, erotic Kama Sutra vibe. See p. 136.

○ **Best Sunday Brunch: Michael's Genuine Food & Drink** (Design District; ☏ 305/573-5550) could win every one of our "best of" categories thanks to its locally sourced, organic seasonal cuisine, out-of-control desserts, buzzy bar scene and colorful crowd of foodies, hipsters, celebrities and assorted culinary dignitaries, but this brunch is truly in a category of its own. In a few words: kimchi Benedict and strawberry and *yuzu* Pop-Tarts. See p. 149.

At the stately Biltmore Hotel in Coral Gables, **Palme d'Or** (☏ 305/913-3201) rolls out a regal buffet that's good enough to feed royalty. Delray Beach's **Sundy House Restaurant** (☏ 561/272-5678) features a gourmet all-you-can-eat $40 brunch *including* alcoholic beverages—an unheard-of value that comes complete with a stunning outdoor garden setting. See p. 161 and p. 364.

○ **Best View: Garcia's Seafood Grille & Fish,** in Miami (☏ 305/375-0765), is all about gritty-chic, located on the Miami River, where tugboats and cargo ships slink by as you indulge in fresh fish under the glow of the brilliant downtown skyline hovering above. See p. 149. On South Beach, **Smith & Wollensky** (☏ 305/673-2800) has views of Fisher Island, Government Cut, and the occasionally passing cruise ship. See p. 124. **Le Tub** (☏ 954/931-9425) may not be considered fine dining, but when you sink your teeth into one of their incredible burgers while overlooking the Intracoastal, nothing could be finer. See p. 355.

○ **Best People-Watching:** The **News Cafe,** in South Beach (☏ 305/538-6397), practically invented the sport of people-watching, encouraging its customers to sit at an outdoor table all day if they want, lingering over the passing parades of people while sipping a cappuccino. Lincoln Road's Euro-fabulous **Segafredo Espresso** cafe (☏ 305/673-0047), provides a front-row seat to the hordes of people who parade along the pedestrian mall. See p. 134 and p.228.

○ **Best Comfort Food: Big Pink,** in Miami Beach (☏ 305/532-4700), serves kitsch in large doses, featuring TV dinners served in compartmentalized trays. It's fun and funky, and the food's pretty good, too. For Cuban comfort fare for those whose grandmothers do not hail from Cuba: **Versailles** (☏ 305/444-0240) in Little Havana. For upscale comfort food including some of the best fried chicken and braised short ribs, well, ever, Michelle Bernstein's Biscayne Boulevard standout **Michy's** (☏ 305/759-2001) is the place to eat and be seen. See p. 128, p. 156, and p. 147.

○ **Best Tapas:** Star chef Michelle Bernstein of Michy's fame pays homage to her Latin roots at **Sra. Martinez** (☏ 305/573-5474), an upscale tapas restaurant housed in an historic post office. This isn't just meat and cheese either. Among the standouts: a sea urchin sandwich pressed and grilled with some soy-ginger butter. Ole! See p. 148.

o **Best Italian Food:** Miami Beach's **Macaluso's** (℡ 305/604-1811) would make Tony Soprano very proud of his Italian heritage, thanks to Chef Michael's expertly prepared Staten Island–meets–SoHo cuisine. Also stellar on South Beach, **Sardinia** (℡ 305/531-2228), where the wood-burning oven churns out some fabulous and creative fare hailing from its Italian namesake. See p. 131 and p. 126. For Little Italy in Coral Gables, **Randazzo's** (℡ 305/448-7002) is a knockout. For a taste of Tuscany in Fort Lauderdale or Boca Raton, people swear by **Casa D'Angelo** (℡ 954/564-1234) and its Southern Italian accents. **Café Martorano,** in Fort Lauderdale (℡ 954/561-2554), is where the cast of the former hit show *The Sopranos* eats when they're in town. Fugheddaboutit. See p. 163 and p. 348.

o **Best Mexican:** The fresh, authentic Mexican fare at **Baja Cafe,** in Boca Raton (℡ 561/394-5449), will have you swearing off Taco Bell forever. See p. 368. And the gourmet Mexican fare in Fort Lauderdale's lauded **Eduardo de San Angel** (℡ 954/772-4731) is *Like Water for Chocolate* and from the gods. See p. 350.

o **Best Haute Cuisine:** Star chef Daniel Boulud's **Café Boulud** at the Brazilian Court Hotel and Beach Club in Palm Beach (℡ 561/655-6060) is sublime. Chef Zach Bell carries out his boss's signature French dishes with ease, grace, and skill that's unparalleled in these parts. See p. 382.

o **Best Discovery in the Treasure Coast Since Gold: 11 Maple Street** in Jensen Beach (℡ 772/334-7714) serves farm-raised meats and vegetables in this cozy New American find that some foodies say is the best in Palm Beach County, hands down.

o **Best Sushi:** Sunny Isles' stellar **NAOE** (℡ 305/947-6263) has a Hollywood vibe and serves up sushi with star-power. See p. 142.

o **Best Seafood: Sunfish Grill,** in Pompano Beach (℡ 954/788-2434), is simple, unpretentious, and consistently serves the freshest fish in town—any which way you desire. See p. 142.

   In Miami, **The River Seafood and Oyster Bar** (Downtown Miami; ℡ 305/530-1915), **Area 31** (Miami; ℡ 305/424-5234), and **Garcia's Seafood Grille & Fish** (Downtown Miami; ℡ 305/375-0765), are three of your best catches.

o **Kitschiest Dining: Anthony's Runway 84** (℡ 954/467-8484) in Fort Lauderdale is pure *Goodfellas* kitsch, complete with mirrored walls, servers and waiters who all seem to be named Tony, and a cheesy '70s airliner theme—the bar is even crafted out of plane fuselage. This is a good place to dine family style. See p. 350. For those with a morbid appetite, **Heart Stoppers Sports Grill** (℡ 561/276-5554) in Delray Beach serves its Artery Cloggers (also known as burgers) on gurneys with IV poles and seats you in wheelchairs. See p. 368.

THE REST OF THE BEST

o **Best Museum:** A collector's dream come true, Miami's **Wolfsonian** is a treasure trove of miscellany (a matchbook that once belonged to the King of Egypt) and artifacts hailing from the propaganda age of World War II. See p. 182.

o **Best Cultural Experience:** A walk through **Little Havana** is a fascinating study in the juxtaposition and fusion of two very vibrant cultures in which pre-Castro Cuba is as alive and well as the McDonald's right next door. See p. 153.

o **Best Snorkeling Spot: Looe Key National Marine Sanctuary,** Bahia Honda State Park. With 5.3 square miles of gorgeous coral reef, rock ledges up to 35 feet tall, and a colorful and motley marine community, you may never want to come up for air. See p. 289.

o **Best Public Golf Course:** Miami's **Biltmore Golf Course,** Biltmore Hotel. If it's good enough for former President Clinton, it's good enough for those of you who don't travel with a bevy of Secret Service agents. But the real question is: Are *you* good enough for the course? The 6th hole is notoriously difficult, with distracting water hazards among other difficulties. Nonetheless, it's an excellent course with a picture-postcard setting. See p. 200.

o **Best Dive Bar: Jose Cuervo Underwater Bar.** In May 2000, the legendary tequila company celebrated Cinco de Mayo by submerging an actual, $45,000 full-size bar and six stools about 600 feet off South Beach's First Street beach. For expert divers, this bar is more than your average watering hole. See p. 196.

o **Best Place to Satisfy Your Morbid Curiosity: The Mystery, Mayhem and Vice Crime Bus Tour.** Not that we're implying anything here, but Miami is a haven for people like O. J. Simpson and, at one time, Al Capone. It's a place where shady characters come to reinvent themselves. However, at times, they also tend to reincriminate themselves. See the spots where some of these criminals fell off the wagon—it's morbidly delicious. See p. 193.

o **Best Offbeat Experience:** Although it's little more than a tropical shantytown, **Jimbo's,** located at the tip of Virginia Key, is consistently fantastic, with no-frills smoked fish, beer out of the bucket, and colorful locals, all of which make it the best offbeat and off-the-beaten-track experience in South Florida. See p. 158.

SOUTH FLORIDA IN DEPTH

Since the roaring '20s, South Florida has been a playground for the rich, famous, and freezing. But the area has been inhabited for at least 10 centuries, making its stereotypical blue hairs seem downright young. Par for the course, South Florida's history is an illustrious and rich one.

THE LAND & ITS PEOPLE

Because the population of South Florida is largely confined to a strip of land between the Atlantic Ocean and the Everglades, the Miami Urbanized Area (that is, the area of contiguous urban development) is about 110 miles long (north to south), but never more than 20 miles wide, and in some areas only 5 miles wide (east to west). South Florida is longer than any other urbanized area in the United States except for the New York metropolitan area. It was the eighth most densely populated urbanized area in the United States in the 2000 Census. As of the 2000 Census, the urbanized area had a land area of 1,116 square miles, with a population of 4,919,036, for a population density of 4,407.4 per square mile. Miami and Hialeah (the second largest city in the metropolitan area) had population densities of more than 10,000 per square mile. The Miami Urbanized Area was the fifth largest urbanized area in the United States in the 2000 Census, ahead of the Dallas–Fort Worth–Arlington, Texas, Urbanized Area.

In 2006, the area, including Fort Lauderdale and Palm Beach, had an estimated 5,463,857 persons, of which 1,671,398 live in unincorporated areas. Considering that the area has an urban population of 4,919,036, only 544,821 residents live outside of the urban area, meaning that *at least* 1,126,577 persons live in urban unincorporated areas, but the number is actually higher. Palm Beach County was added to the Miami–Fort Lauderdale metropolitan area for the first time in 2000, giving it a considerable boost in population and in ranking among U.S. metropolitan areas.

Fast forward to 2009, however, and the only boost Florida experienced was one in the amount of foreclosures, coming in second only to California. As a result of the abysmal economy, loss of jobs, and loss of homes, for the first time in over 60 years, the state experienced a net loss of approximately 58,000 people. In fact, in 2009 more people moved out of Florida than moved in. According to Mark Wilson, president of the Florida Chamber of Commerce, the state, once the fifth cheapest state to live in, had become the 14th most *expensive*. Some optimists predict a positive trend for long-term growth in the state. The job forecast, however, is expected, according to economists, to remain dismal until 2012.

As we wait for the economy to rebound, we realize there are other pressing issues to be dealt with. Scientists have observed changes in Florida consistent with the early effects of global warming: retreating and eroding shorelines, dying coral reefs, saltwater intrusion into inland freshwater aquifers, an upswing in forest fires, and warmer air and sea-surface temperatures. As glaciers melt and warming waters expand, sea levels will rise anywhere from 8 inches to 2½ feet over the next century. In Florida, seawater will advance inland as much as 400 feet in low-lying areas, flooding shoreline homes and hotels, limiting future development, and eroding the state's beloved beaches. People aren't kidding when they say that one day, Florida will be underwater.

On a more positive note, some say this perceived global warming threat has been greatly exaggerated. Though preliminary research raised concerns that warmer ocean temperatures would lead to more frequent hurricanes, scientists now discount this theory. Nevertheless, global warming may increase hurricanes' maximum intensity, which will serve to exacerbate a natural cyclical trend toward more severe storms—a trend likely to persist for the next 25 to 40 years.

A LOOK AT THE PAST
Prehistoric South Florida

Fourteen thousand years ago, Florida would have made an ideal location for the show *Land of the Lost*—that is, if there were actually dinosaurs down here. Not so much. During the age of dinosaurs, the Florida peninsula was underwater and did not exist as a land mass. Therefore, no dinosaur remains were ever deposited in Florida.

However, in 1998, archaeologists discovered a slew of artifacts in downtown Miami in an area now known as The Miami Circle. With origins dating back at least 2,000 years, it was discovered that the artifacts belonged to the Calusa or Tequesta tribes.

Paleo-Indians got here by crossing over to North America from Asia. Most of their activity was around the watering holes, sinkholes, and basins in the beds of modern rivers.

Paleo-Indian culture was eventually replaced by, or evolved into, the Early Archaic culture. There were now more people in Florida, and as they were no longer tied to a few water holes in an arid land, they left their artifacts in many more locations.

The Early Archaic period evolved into the Middle Archaic period around 5000 B.C. People started living in villages near wetlands, and favored sites may have been occupied for multiple generations. The Late Archaic period started around 3000 B.C., when Florida's climate had reached current conditions and the sea had risen close to its present level. People now lived everywhere there were fresh or saltwater wetlands. Many people lived in large villages with purpose-built mounds. Fired pottery appeared in Florida by 2000 B.C. By about 500 B.C., the Archaic culture that had been fairly uniform across Florida began to fragment into regional cultures.

The post-Archaic cultures of eastern and southern Florida developed in relative isolation, and it is likely that the peoples living in those areas at the time of first European contact were direct descendants of the inhabitants of the areas in late Archaic times. The cultures of the Florida Panhandle and the north and central Gulf coast of the Florida peninsula were strongly influenced by the Mississippian culture, although there is continuity in cultural history, suggesting that the peoples of those cultures were also descended from the inhabitants of the Archaic period. Cultivation of maize was adopted in the Panhandle and the northern part of the peninsula, but was absent or very restricted in the tribes that lived south of the Timucua-speaking people (that is, south of a line approximately from present-day Daytona Beach to a point on or north of Tampa Bay).

NATIVE AMERICANS Spanish explorers of the early 16th century were likely the first Europeans to interact with the native population of Florida. The first documented encounter of Europeans with Native Americans of the United States came with the first expedition of Juan Ponce de León to Florida in 1513, although he encountered at least one native that spoke Spanish. In 1521, he encountered the Calusa Indians, who established 30 villages in the Everglades and successfully resisted European colonization.

The Spanish recorded nearly 100 names of groups they encountered, ranging from organized political entities such as the Apalachee, with a population of around 50,000, to villages with no known political affiliation. There were an estimated 150,000 speakers of dialects of the Timucua language, but the Timucua were organized only as groups of villages, and did not share a common culture. Other tribes in Florida at the time of first contact included the Ais, Calusa, Jaega, Mayaimi, Tequesta, who lived on the southeast coast of the Everglades, and Tocobaga. All of these tribes diminished in numbers during the period of Spanish control of Florida.

At the beginning of the 18th century, tribes from areas to the north of Florida—supplied, encouraged, and occasionally accompanied by white colonists from the Province of Carolina—raided throughout Florida, burning villages, killing many of the inhabitants, and carrying captives back to Charles Towne to be sold as slaves. Most of the villages in Florida were abandoned and the survivors sought refuge at St. Augustine, or in isolated spots around the state. Some of the Apalachee eventually reached Louisiana, where they survived as a distinct group for at least another century.

The few surviving members of these tribes were evacuated to Cuba when Spain transferred Florida to the British Empire in 1763. The Seminole, originally an offshoot of the Creek people who absorbed other groups, developed as a distinct tribe in Florida during the 18th century, and are now represented in the Seminole Nation of Oklahoma, the Seminole Tribe of Florida, and the Miccosukee Tribe of Indians of Florida.

SPANISH RULE   Once Ponce de León laid his eyes on Florida in 1513, a slew of competitive Conquistadors made futile efforts to find gold there and colonize the region. The first to establish a fort in Florida were the French, actually, but it was ultimately destroyed by the Spanish, who introduced Christianity, horses, and cattle to the region. Unfortunately they also introduced diseases and Conquistador brutality, which ultimately decimated Indian populations. Eager to expand its own American colony collection, Britain led several raids into Florida in the 1700s to overthrow Spanish rule. Among the most notable Spaniards in Florida included the aforementioned Ponce de León; Hernando de Soto, the most ruthless of the explorers whose thirst for gold led to the massacre of many Indians; Panfilo de Narvaez, whose quest for El Dorado—the land of gold—landed him in Tampa Bay; and Pedro Menendez de Aviles, who founded St. Augustine after defeating the French.

BRITISH RULE   The Brits weren't interested in gold—they were all about Florida's bounty of hides and furs and they'd stop at nothing to get them. After taking control in 1763, the Brits divided Florida into two. Because Florida was subsidized by the English, Floridians remained loyal to Mother England during the American Revolution—that is, until the Spanish returned and regained West Florida in 1781 and, 2 years later, East Florida. During the Spanish re-conquest, American slaves fled to Florida, causing major turmoil between Spain and the U.S. Combined with Indian raids in the north and an Indian alliance with runaway slaves, Florida was, well, a mess, until General Andrew Jackson invaded Spanish Florida, captured Pensacola, and occupied West Florida. Then Florida was a disaster. Jackson's invasion kicked off the First Seminole War in 1817. Finally, to settle Spain's $5 million debt to the U.S., all Spanish land east of the Mississippi, including Florida, was ceded to the U.S. in 1819.

AMERICAN RULE   Florida became an organized territory of the United States on March 30, 1822. The Americans merged East Florida and West Florida (although the majority of West Florida was annexed to Orleans Territory and Mississippi Territory), and established a new capital in Tallahassee, conveniently located halfway between the East Florida capital of St. Augustine and the West Florida capital of Pensacola. The boundaries of Florida's first two counties, Escambia and St. Johns, approximately coincided with the boundaries of West and East Florida, respectively.

At this time, the plantation system was adopted by north Florida and because the settlers wanted the best possible land, the federal government tried moving all Indians west of the Mississippi, resulting in the Second and Third Seminole Wars. When Abraham Lincoln was elected president in 1860, Florida became the third state to secede from the Union. Florida saw little action during the Civil War—its main role was to supply beef and salt to the Confederates. The state got off easy for a change.

After meeting the requirements of Reconstruction, including amendments to the U.S. Constitution, Florida was readmitted to the United States on July 25, 1868.

MIAMI   It wasn't long after Florida became the 27th state in the union (in 1845) that Miami began to emerge as a city—or somewhat one. During the war, the U.S. created Fort Dallas on the north bank of a river that flowed through southern Florida. When the soldiers left, the fort became the base for a small village established by William H. English, who dubbed it Miami, from the Indian word *Mayami,* meaning "big water."

In 1822, the Homestead Act offered 160 acres of free land to anyone who would stay on it for at least 5 years. Edmund Beasley bit and in 1868 moved into what is now Coconut Grove. Two years later, William Brickell bought land on the south bank of the Miami River and Ephraim Sturtevant took over the area called Biscayne. In 1875, his daughter Julia Tuttle visited him and fell in love with the area, although not returning for another 16 years, when she would further transform the city.

In the meantime, Henry Flagler, who made a $50 million fortune working with John Rockefeller in the Standard Oil Company, came to Florida in the late 1800s because he thought the warm weather would help his wife's frail health. After moving to the area, he built a railroad all the way down the east coast of Florida, stopping in each major town to build a hotel. Another railway honcho, Henry Plant, laid his tracks from Jacksonville to Tampa.

When her husband died in 1886, Julia Tuttle decided to leave Cleveland for Florida and asked Plant to extend his railroad to Miami. Plant declined, so Tuttle went to Flagler, whose own railroad stopped 66 miles away in what is now known as Palm Beach. Flagler laughed at Tuttle's request, saying he didn't see what Miami had to offer in terms of tourism.

After a devastating winter that killed all crops north of the state, Tuttle sent Flagler a bounty of orange blossoms to prove that Miami did, indeed, have something to offer. After Tuttle agreed to give Flagler some of her land along with William Brickell's, Flagler agreed to extend the railway. When the first train arrived in Miami on April 15, 1896, all 300 (!) of the city's residents showed up to see it. Miami had arrived and newspapers and magazines began touting the city as "the sun porch of America, where winter is turned to summer."

FLORIDA KEYS No one knows exactly when the first European set foot on one of the Florida Keys, but as exploration and shipping increased, the islands became prominent on nautical maps. The nearby treacherous coral reefs claimed many lives. The chain was eventually called "keys," also attributed to the Spanish, from *cayos*, meaning "small islands." In 1763, when the Spanish ceded Florida to the British in a trade for the port of Havana, an agent of the King of Spain claimed that the islands, rich in fish, turtles, and mahogany for shipbuilding, were part of Cuba, fearing that the English might build fortresses and dominate the shipping lanes.

The British realized the treaty was ambiguous, but declared that the Keys should be occupied and defended as part of Florida. The British claim was never officially contested. Ironically, the British gave the islands back to Spain in 1783, to keep them out of the hands of the United States, but in 1821 all of Florida, including the necklace of islands, officially became American territory.

Many of the residents of Key West were immigrants from the Bahamas, known as Conchs (pronounced "Conks") who arrived in increasing numbers after 1830. Many were sons and daughters of Loyalists who fled to the nearest crown soil during the American Revolution.

In the 20th century many residents of Key West started referring to themselves as "Conchs," and the term is now generally applied to all residents of Key West. In 1982, Key West, and the rest of the Florida Keys, briefly declared its "independence" as the Conch Republic in a protest over a United States Border Patrol blockade. This blockade was set up on U.S. 1 where the northern end of the Overseas Highway meets the mainland at Florida City. This blockade was in response to the Mariel

Boatlift. A 17-mile traffic jam ensued while the Border Patrol stopped every car leaving the Keys, supposedly searching for illegal aliens attempting to enter the mainland United States. This paralyzed the Florida Keys. The Conch Republic Independence Celebration—including parades and parties—is celebrated every April 23.

THE EVERGLADES Thanks to the work of the Everglades' foremost supporter, Ernest F. Coe, Congress passed a park bill in 1934. Dubbed by opponents as the "alligator and snake swamp bill," the legislation stalled during the Great Depression and World War II. Finally, on December 6, 1947, President Harry Truman dedicated the Everglades National Park. In that same year, Marjory Stoneman Douglas first published *The Everglades: River of Grass*. She understood its importance as the major watershed for South Florida and as a unique ecosystem.

FORT LAUDERDALE Fort Lauderdale is named after a series of forts built by the United States during the Second Seminole War. However, development of the city did not begin until 50 years after the forts were abandoned at the end of the conflict. Three forts named "Fort Lauderdale" were constructed; the first was at the fork of the New River, the second at Tarpon Bend, and the third near the site of the Bahia Mar Marina. The forts took their name from Major William Lauderdale, who was the commander of the detachment of soldiers who built the first fort.

The area in which the city of Fort Lauderdale would later be founded was inhabited for more than 1,000 years by the Tequesta Indians. Contact with Spanish explorers in the 16th century proved disastrous for the Tequesta, as the Europeans unwittingly brought with them diseases to which the native populations possessed no resistance, such as smallpox. For the Tequesta, disease, coupled with continuing conflict with their Calusa neighbors, contributed greatly to their decline over the next 2 centuries. By 1763, there were only a few Tequesta left in Florida, and most of them were evacuated to Cuba when the Spanish ceded Florida to the British in 1763, under the terms of the Treaty of Paris, which ended the Seven Years' War. Although control of the area changed between Spain, England, the United States, and the Confederate States of America, it remained largely undeveloped until the 20th century.

It was not until Frank Stranahan arrived in the area in 1893 to operate a ferry across the New River, and the Florida East Coast Railroad's completion of a route through the area in 1896, that any organized development began. The city was incorporated in 1911, and in 1915 was designated the county seat of newly formed Broward County.

Fort Lauderdale's first major development began in the 1920s, during the Florida land boom. The 1926 Miami Hurricane and the Great Depression of the 1930s caused a great deal of economic dislocation. When World War II began, Fort Lauderdale became a major U.S. Navy base, with a Naval Air Station to train pilots, radar and fire control operator training schools, and a Coast Guard base at Port Everglades.

After the war ended, service members returned to the area, spurring an enormous population explosion, which dwarfed the 1920s boom. Today, Fort Lauderdale is a major yachting center, one of the nation's largest tourist destinations, and the center of a metropolitan division with 1.8 million people.

PALM BEACH   Palm Beach County was created in 1909. It was named for its first settled community, Palm Beach, in turn named for the palm trees and beaches in the area. The county was carved out of what was then the northern half of Dade County. The southern half of Palm Beach County was subsequently carved out to create the northern portion of Broward County in 1915. Henry Flagler was instrumental in the county's development in the early 1900s with the extension of the Florida East Coast Railway through the county from Jacksonville to Key West. After Flagler came Addison Mizner, an architect with a flair for Mediterranean styles. You can blame or thank Mizner for all those pink houses. As Palm Beach became a haven for the über-rich, it also became a political focal point and was one of the counties at the center of the 2000 U.S. presidential election recount controversy, and ended up turning the state in favor of George W. Bush by 537 votes.

TREASURE COAST   The name "Treasure Coast" is derived from a number of Spanish galleons (especially those of the 1715 Spanish treasure fleet) that wrecked off the coast during the 17th and 18th centuries. Artifacts from these ships are still being recovered today, by both amateur and professional treasure-hunters.

For 2 centuries, Spain sent fleets twice a year to collect treasure from her New World colonies. In 1715, 11 Spanish ships crashed into the treacherous reefs off the Florida coast. The survivors swam to the beaches but the violent winds sucked many back into the water. Daybreak found more than 700 men missing, with wreckage and bodies scattered across 30 miles.

The senior surviving officer ordered a damaged lifeboat repaired, and then sent the chaplain and a young pilot for help. Three days later they landed 120 miles to the north.

The Spanish attempted to salvage the treasure for the next 4 years; however, the hazards of sharks, barracudas, buccaneers, and Indians led them to abandon the operation. Records indicate that only 30 percent of the treasure was recovered; the rest lay buried in the sands of the Treasure Coast.

Modern South Florida

South Florida today is a fascinating study in, well, everything. It seems as if the state is always in the news for *something,* and with this timeline, you'll understand why.

o **1980**   Race riots tear apart Miami. The Mariel Boatlift brings 140,000 Cubans to Florida. The Miami Seaquarium celebrates its 25th anniversary.

o **1983**   Thirty-eight overseas highway bridges from Key Largo to Key West are completed under the Florida Keys Bridge Replacement Program.

o **1984**   The Miami Metro Rail, the only inner-city, elevated rail system in Florida, begins service in May.

o **1986**   Treasure hunter Mel Fisher continues to salvage vast amounts of gold and silver from his discovery of the Spanish galleon Nuestra Senora de Atocha, which sank in 1622 during a hurricane off Key West. The television series Miami Vice continues to capture the nation's imagination, revitalizing interest and tourism for South Florida.

o **1987**   U.S. Census Bureau estimates indicate that Florida has surpassed Pennsylvania to become the fourth most populous state in the nation. The ranking will not become official until the bureau publishes its report in early 1988. It is predicted that Florida will be the third most populous state by the year 2000.

- **1990** Panama's governor Manuel Noriega is brought to Miami in January for trial on drug charges. Joe Robbie, Miami Dolphins founder, dies in January.
- **1991** Queen Elizabeth II visits Miami. Five Navy bombers found by treasure salvagers are determined not to be the "Lost Squadron" of Bermuda Triangle fame that went down in 1945 off the coast of Florida. Miami and Denver are awarded new national Major League Baseball franchises. The 1990 Federal Census puts Florida's population at 12,937,926, a 34% increase from 1980.
- **1992** Homestead and adjacent South Florida are devastated on August 24 by the (then) costliest natural disaster in American history, Hurricane Andrew, demanding billions in aid. There were 58 deaths directly or indirectly related to Andrew. The hurricane destroyed 25,000 homes and damaged 10,000 others. Twenty-two thousand federal troops were deployed. Shelters housed 80,000 persons.

  Among African Americans elected to Congress was Carrie Meek of Miami. Sixty-six in 1993, her political career saw her elected first to the Florida House of Representatives, next the Florida Senate, and then the U.S. House of Representatives.
- **1993** Janet Reno, state attorney for Dade County (Miami) for 15 years, is named attorney general of the U.S. by President Bill Clinton; Reno is the first woman to so serve in U.S. history. Although a pro-choice Democrat, she managed to win reelection four times in a conservative stronghold, the last time without opposition.
- **1996** Miami turns 100.
- **2000** Florida became the battleground of the controversial 2000 U.S. presidential election, when a count of the popular votes held on Election Day was extremely close and mired in accusations of fraud and manipulation. Subsequent recount efforts degenerated into arguments over mispunched ballots, "hanging chads," and controversial decisions by Florida Secretary of State Katherine Harris and the Florida Supreme Court. Ultimately, the United States Supreme Court ended all recounts and let stand the official count by Harris, which was accepted by Congress.
- **2003** The Florida Marlins win the World Series.
- **2004** George W. Bush wins the presidential election again. His brother Jeb celebrates in Florida's State Capitol.
- **2006** The Miami Heat win the NBA championships.
- **2007** Jeb Bush vacates the governor's office, which is taken over by Charlie Crist.
- **2008** Florida continues to be one of the fastest growing states in the country. The economy still depends greatly on tourism, but expanding industries in business and manufacturing are strengthening its growth potential. State leaders are working on problems created due to huge population increases and environmental concerns.
- **2009** In October 2009, Florida, along with California and Nevada, posted the highest foreclosure rates in the country. To make matters worse, unemployment rates in the state skyrocketed to over 11%. For the first time in over 60 years, Florida experienced a population decline.

○ **2010** Like the calm after the storm, South Florida ekes carefully out of its economic slumber. If funds from the Travel Promotions Act aren't enough to drive tourism, LeBron James' move to the Miami Heat is seen in some circles as the panacea to all economic problems. A massive spill of oil from a BP oil rig in the Gulf raises fears of sullied coastlines (one charter boat company in the Keys sued the oil company for even creating the "perception" of oil from the spill), though no such effects are evident as of July 2010.

RECOMMENDED BOOKS, MOVIES & MUSIC

South Florida—and Florida in general—is an author's dream come true. In this state of much diversity (read: bizarre characters, to say the least), inspiration is practically hanging from the palm trees.

Fiction

○ **The Perez Family** (W. W. Norton & Co. Inc.) by Christine Bell—Cuban immigrants from the Mariel Boatlift exchange their talents for an immigration deal in Miami (also a 1995 movie by Mira Nair).

○ **Miami, It's Murder** (Avon) by Edna Buchannan—Miami's Agatha Christie keeps you in suspense with her reporter protagonist and her life as an investigative crime solver in Miami.

○ **To Have and Have Not** (Scribner) by Ernest Hemingway—One of the many must-reads by Key West's most famous resident.

○ **In Cuba I Was a German Shepherd** (Grove Press), by Ana Menendez—Stories of people who gather in Little Havana to lament the loss of the good old days.

○ **Naked Came the Manatee** (Ballantine Books) by Carl Hiassen—Thirteen *Miami Herald* writers contributed to this hilarious story about the discovery of Castro's head.

○ **Killing Mister Watson** (Vintage Books USA) by Peter Matthiessen—A fascinating story about the settlement of the Everglades and the problems that ensued.

○ **The Yearling** (Collier MacMillan Publishers) by Marjorie Kinnan Rawlings—A classic about life in the Florida backwoods.

○ **Seraph on the Suwanee** (Harper Perennial) by Zora Neale Hurston—A novel about turn-of-the-century Florida "white crackers."

○ **Nine Florida Stories** (University Press of Florida) by Marjory Stoneman Douglas—The beloved Florida naturalist's fictional take on Florida, set in a scattering of settings—Miami, Fort Lauderdale, the Tamiami Trail, the Keys, the Everglades—and revealing the drama of hurricanes and plane crashes, of kidnappers, escaped convicts, and smugglers.

○ **Rum Punch** (Harper Torch), by Elmore Leonard—The story of a stewardess, bail bondsman, and gun runner in Palm Beach County.

○ **Swim to Me** (Algonquin Books) by Betsy Carter—A wacky novel set in Weeki Wachee about a shy teenager who finds her purpose at the mermaid-happy theme park.

- **Tourist Season** (Warner Books), by Carl Hiaasen—Hiaasen is at his darkest, funniest, and finest in this book about a newspaper columnist who kills off tourists on a quest to return Florida to its long gone, unfettered, pristine state.

Nonfiction

- **Fool's Paradise: Players, Poseurs and the Culture of Excess in South Beach** (Crown), by Steven Gaines—A New Yorker's love/hate take on America's alleged Riviera.
- **Miami Babylon: Crime, Wealth and Power—A Dispatch from the Beach** (Simon & Schuster), by Gerald Posner—The name says it all about this investigative look at the sybaritic paradise that is Miami.
- **Miami** (Vintage) by Joan Didion—An intriguing compilation of impressions of the Magic City.
- **Miami, the Magic City** (Centennial Press) by Arva Moore Parks—An authoritative history of the city.
- **The Everglades: River of Grass** (Pineapple Press) by Marjory Stoneman Douglas—Eco-maniacs will love this personal account of the treasures of Florida's most famous natural resource.
- **Celebration USA: Living in Disney's Brave New Town** (Holt Paperbacks) by Douglas Frantz and Catherine Collins—An eye-opening true story about living in Disney's "model town."

Movies Filmed in Florida

- Clarence Brown's **The Yearling** (1946) based on novel by M.K. Rawlings
- John Huston's **Key Largo** (1948) based on novel by Hemingway (gangsters, hurricanes, and Bogey and Bacall)
- Harry Levin's **Where the Boys Are** (1960) (spring break in Fort Lauderdale)
- John Schlesinger's **Midnight Cowboy** (1969) based on novel by James Leo Herlihy
- Ernest Lehman's **Portnoy's Complaint** (1972) based on novel by Philip Roth (Jewish culture)
- Lawrence Kasdan's **Body Heat** (1981) (crime)
- Ron Howard's **Cocoon** (1985) based on novel by David Saperstein (retirees)
- Tim Burton's **Edward Scissorhands** (1990) (modern fairy tale filmed in Dade City and Lakeland)
- Mike Nichols' **Birdcage** (1996) (South Beach comedy)
- Andrew Bergman's **Striptease** (1996) based on novel by Carl Hiassen
- John Singleton's **Rosewood** (1997) based on historic Rosewood massacre (African-American culture)
- Victor Nunez's **Ulee's Gold** (1997) (Panhandle family drama)
- Peter Weir's **The Truman Show** (1998) (sci-fi in Seaside)
- Spike Jonze's **Adaptation** (2002) loosely based on Susan Orleans' *The Orchid Thief*
- Patty Jenkins' **Monster** (2003) biopic of serial killer Aileen Wournos
- Taylor Hackford's **Ray** (2004) biopic of musician Ray Charles, born in Florida

- David Frankel's **Marley & Me** (2008) based on the best selling novel of the same name by a former Fort Lauderdale *Sun Sentinel* reporter
- Jason Reitman's **Up in the Air** (2009) starring George Clooney as a frequent flyer who comes through MIA and the Miami Airport Hilton

Music of South Florida

The Miami recording industry did not begin with Gloria Estefan's Miami Sound Machine, contrary to popular belief. In fact, some major rock albums were recorded in Miami's Criteria Studios. Among them: *Rumours* by Fleetwood Mac and *Hotel California* by The Eagles. Long-time local music entrepreneur Henry Stone and his label, TK Records, created the local indie scene in the 1970s. TK Records produced the R&B group KC and the Sunshine Band along with soul singers Betty Wright, George McCrae, and Jimmy "Bo" Horne, as well as a number of minor soul and disco hits, many influenced by Caribbean music. In the 2000s, Miami has seen an enormous rap boom in the form of Daddy Yankee, Pitbull, Rick Ross, and more.

Cuisine of South Florida

Before Florida started evolving into a bona fide gastronomic destination, one respected by eaters and chefs alike, when one used the word *food* in the same sentence as *The Sunshine State,* one of two things may have come to mind—oranges and early bird. And while both still play a very important role in the state's reputation, pop culturally or otherwise, there's a lot more to Florida food than just citrus and $3.99 prime rib, and as the locavore craze continues in which people prefer to eat or cook with only local ingredients, the following list of foods indigenous to the state can be considered the holy grail for Florida gourmands. If it's true Florida cuisine you are looking for, these are the ingredients you'll want to have, whether in some fancy, five star fusion restaurant or a hands on sea shanty with ice cold beer, paper napkins, and plastic cutlery.

- Avocado
- Starfruit
- Coconut
- Key lime
- Kumquat
- Hearts of palm
- Mango
- Papaya
- Passion fruit
- Spiny lobster
- Stone crabs

As for the unofficial term "Florida Cuisine," it can mean many things, but we suppose Floribbean, the fusion of Caribbean and Latin flavors with the aforementioned local Florida flavors, says it best, especially down in South Florida and in Tampa where the Latin influences are so enormous. Some food snobs shudder at the term and prefer the phrase New World Cuisine, the product of Miami-based chef Norman Van Aken. But it's all semantics. Think crack conch chowder with orange, saffron, and coconut. Or spiny lobster salad with mango.

But Florida cuisine really does vary by region. The farther north you go, the closer to the Deep South you are, and instead of Latin influences, you'll see more of a Southern comfort twist on Florida cuisine—a locally caught fish with, say, hush puppies and collard greens. Or, gator tail with grits and butter. Over on the Gulf Coast, you tend to see a lot of smoked fish, most commonly mullet, in many incarnations but most ubiquitously as a dip or spread eaten with crackers and, if you dare, hot sauce. Near Lake Okeechobee, the fish is usually catfish, and it's almost always fried.

The following is a good, but by no means comprehensive, list of typical (or atypical, rather) South Florida cuisine:

o **Cuban Sandwiches** (also known as *medianoche,* translation: "at midnight"): some say they were originated in Miami, others say Tampa, but wherever it was, it's a delicious combo of ham, roasted pork, Swiss, pickles, mustard, and, depending on where you are, sometimes salami on crispy, crusty, toasted "Cuban bread," whose origin is still questionable.
o **Grouper Sandwiches:** Or pretty much any fish (snapper, mahimahi, pompano, and so on) sandwich, though grouper is the Ryan Seacrest of Florida fish, appearing on many menus in many incarnations, from grilled and fried to blackened or jerked.
o **Mango Salsa:** A Floribbean staple much like ketchup is to BBQ.
o **Conch Fritters:** Fried balls of chewy conch, usually found in the Keys or anywhere where there's water views.
o **Key Lime Pie:** Made from those luscious limes found, yes, in the Keys, these pies are everywhere throughout the region, and everywhere claims to have the best. You be the judge.
o **Hearts of Palm Salad:** Often found in old school $6.99 prime rib, steak, and lobster houses, though often found in chichi eateries as well.

PLANNING YOUR TRIP TO SOUTH FLORIDA

3

Although some say parts of Florida (namely Miami) are out of this world—or of another world, or more specifically, like being in another country—thankfully, Florida, last we checked, is still part of the United States. And whether you plan to spend a day, a week, 2 weeks, or longer in the Sunshine State, you'll need to make many "where," "when," and "how" choices before leaving your home. As for the where, well, that's a toughie. With no time and budget constraints, we'd tell you go cover it all—the Keys, Miami, Everglades, Gold Coast, Treasure Coast and Southwest Florida. But that's up to you. How to get to Florida? We recommend almost every and any way except hitchhiking. Walking would be pretty ambitious, too. And now to the when. That's the biggest question we get. As South Florida shifts from a seasonal to a more year-round destination, there's always a good time to visit. Really. Even during Hurricane Season (Jun 1–Nov 30), when prices are lower, crowds are thinner, and hurricanes are (knock on wood) often elusive. When temperatures freeze elsewhere, that's when Florida starts sinking further into the ocean as crowds flock to the state for deep thawing and the state feels, well, heavier. For those who love heat, humidity, and sweating, summertime is the ideal time to visit and saves you a trip to the sauna. But with global warming, cooling, freezing, and whatnot, when it comes to temperatures these days, it's anyone's guess. What's not a guessing game is whether or not to visit in general. You bought the book, so what are you waiting for?

For additional help in planning your trip and for more on-the-ground resources in South Florida, please turn to "Fast Facts," on p. 387.

WHEN TO GO

To a large extent, the timing of your visit will determine how much you'll spend—and how much company you'll have—once you get to South Florida. That's because room rates can more than double during so-called high seasons, when countless visitors flock to Florida.

The weather determines the high seasons (see "Climate," below). In subtropical South Florida, high season is in the winter, from mid-December to mid-April, although if you ask tourism execs, the high season is now creeping longer into spring and even, in some parts, summer. On the other hand, you'll be rewarded with incredible bargains if you can stand the heat, humidity, and daily rain storms of a South Florida summer between June and early September.

Hurricane Season runs from June to November, and, as seen in 2005, the most active hurricane season on record, and 2009, the quietest, you never know what can happen. Pay close attention to weather forecasts during this season and always be prepared. See "Weather" under "Fast Facts: South Florida," p. 392.

Presidents' Day weekend in February, Easter week, Memorial Day weekend, the Fourth of July, Labor Day weekend, Thanksgiving, Christmas, and New Year's are busy throughout the state.

South Florida's so-called shoulder season is April through May, and September through November, when the weather is pleasant throughout Florida and the hotel rates are considerably lower than during the high season. If price is a consideration, these months of moderate temperatures and fewer tourists are the best times to visit.

See the accommodations sections in the chapters that follow for specifics on the local high, shoulder, and off seasons.

CLIMATE   Contrary to popular belief, South Florida's climate is subtropical, not tropical. Accordingly, Florida sees more extremes of temperatures than, say, the Caribbean islands.

Spring, which runs from late March to May, sees warm temperatures throughout Florida, but it also brings tropical showers.

Summer in Florida extends from May to September, when it's hot and very humid throughout the state. If you're in an inland city during these months, you may not want to do anything too taxing when the sun is at its peak. Coastal areas, however, reap the benefits of sea breezes. Severe afternoon thunderstorms are prevalent during the summer heat (there aren't professional sports teams here named Lightning and Thunder for nothing), so schedule your activities for earlier in the day, and take precautions to avoid being hit by lightning during the storms. Those storms, by the way, often start out fierce and end with a rainbow and sunshine, so don't worry; just don't stand under a tree or on a golf course during the main act.

Autumn—about September through November—is a great time to visit, as the hottest days are gone and the crowds have thinned out. Unless a hurricane blows through, November is usually Florida's driest month. These days, however, one can never predict 100% sunshine. June through November is Hurricane Season here, but even if one threatens, the National Weather Service closely tracks the storms and gives ample warning if there's need to evacuate coastal areas.

Winter can get a bit nippy throughout the state and in recent years, downright freezing. Although snow is rare, the end of 2009 saw flakes falling as north as Pensacola and as south as Kendall in South Miami. Speaking of cold in Miami, locals have been known to whip out the coats, hats, and boots when the temperature drops below 80. The "cold snaps" usually last only a few days in the southern half of the state, however, and daytime temperatures should quickly return to the 70s (20s Celsius). Again, that was before all the El Niño, La Niña, global warming took effect, so whenever you travel to Florida, bring a jacket. Even in summertime you may need it indoors when air conditioning reaches freezing temperatures.

For up-to-the-minute weather info, tune into cable TV's Weather Channel or check out its website at www.weather.com.

Miami's Average Monthly High/Low Temperatures & Rainfall

	JAN	FEB	MAR	APR	MAY	JUNE	JULY	AUG	SEPT	OCT	NOV	DEC
High (°F)	76	77	80	83	86	88	89	90	88	85	80	77
High (°C)	24	25	27	28	30	31	32	32	31	29	27	25
Low (°F)	60	61	64	68	72	75	76	76	76	72	66	61
Low (°C)	16	16	18	20	22	24	24	24	24	22	19	16
Rain (in.)	2.0	2.1	2.4	3.0	5.9	8.8	6.0	7.8	8.5	7.0	3.1	1.8

Calendar of Events

For an exhaustive list of events beyond those listed here, check http://events.frommers.com, where you'll find a searchable, up-to-the-minute roster of what's happening in cities all over the world.

JANUARY

FedEx Orange Bowl Championship (☏ **305/341-4700;** www.orangebowl.org), Miami. Football fanatics flock down to the big Orange Bowl game (taking place not at the recently razed Orange Bowl in seedy downtown, but at the much more savory Dolphins Stadium) on New Year's Day, featuring two of the year's best college football teams. Call early if you want tickets; they sell out quickly. First week of January.

Polo Season (☏ **561/793-1440;** www.palmbeachpolo.com), Palm Beach. Join the crisp and clean Ralph Lauren–clad polo fanatics (including stars and socialites) at the Palm Beach Polo and Country Club for polo season. Begins in early January.

Key West Literary Seminar (☏ **888/293-9291;** www.keywestliteraryseminar.org),

Key West. Literary types have a good reason to put down their books and head to Key West. This 3-day event features a different theme every year, along with a roster of incredible authors, writers, and other literary types. The event is so popular it sells out well in advance, so call early for tickets. Second week of January.

Art Deco Weekend (☏ **305/672-2014;** www.mdpl.org), South Beach. Gain a newfound appreciation for the Necco-wafered Art Deco buildings, Deco furniture, history, and fashion at this weekend-long festival of street fairs, films, lectures, and other events. Mid- to late January.

FEBRUARY

Everglades City Seafood Festival (☏ **239/695-2561;** www.evergladesseafoodfestival.com), Everglades City. What seems like schools of fish-loving people flock down to Everglades City for a 2-day feeding frenzy in which Florida delicacies from stone crab to gator tails are served from shacks and booths on the outskirts of this quaint Old Florida town. Free admission, but you pay for the food you eat, booth by booth. First full weekend in February.

Coconut Grove Arts Festival (📞 305/447-0401; www.coconutgroveartsfest.com), Coconut Grove. Florida's largest art festival features over 300 artists who are selected from thousands of entries. Possibly one of the most crowded street fairs in South Florida, the festival attracts art lovers, artists, and lots of college students who seem to think this event is the Mardi Gras of art fairs. Presidents' Day weekend.

Miami International Boat Show (📞 954/441-3231; www.miamiboatshow.com), Miami Beach. If you don't like crowds, beware, as this show draws a quarter of a million boat enthusiasts to the Miami Beach Convention Center. Some of the world's priciest megayachts, speedboats, sailboats, and schooners are displayed for purchase or for gawking. Mid-February.

South Beach Wine & Food Festival (📞 877/762-3933; www.sobewineandfoodfest.com), South Beach. A 3-day celebration featuring some of the Food Network's best chefs, who do their thing in the kitchens of various restaurants and at events around town. In addition, there are tastings, lectures, seminars, and parties that are all open to the public—for a price, of course. Last weekend in February.

Miami International Film Festival (📞 877/888-MIFF [6433]; www.miamifilmfestival.com), Miami. Though not exactly Cannes, the Miami Film Festival, sponsored by the Film Society of America, is an impressive 10-day celluloid celebration, featuring world premieres of Latin American, domestic, and other foreign and independent films. Actors, producers, and directors show up to plug their films and participate in Q&A sessions with the audiences. End of February to early March.

MARCH

Winter Party (📞 305/538-5908; www.winterparty.com), Miami Beach. Gays and lesbians from around the world book trips to Miami as far as a year in advance to attend this weekendlong series of parties and events benefiting the Dade Human Rights Foundation. Travel arrangements can be made through Different Roads Travel, the event's official travel company, by calling 📞 888/ROADS-55 (762-3755), ext. 510. Early March.

Grand Prix of Miami (📞 866/409-RACE [7223]; www.homesteadmiamispeedway.com), Homestead. A little bit of Daytona in Miami, the Grand Prix is a premier racing event, attracting celebrities, Indy Car drivers, and curious spectators who get a buzz off the smell of gasoline. Get tickets early, as this event sells out quickly. Early to mid-March.

Calle Ocho Festival (📞 305/644-8888; www.carnavalmiami.com), Little Havana. What Carnaval is to Rio, the Calle Ocho Festival is to Miami. This 10-day extravaganza, also called Carnaval Miami, features a lengthy block party spanning 23 blocks, with live salsa music, parades, and, of course, tons of savory Cuban delicacies. Those afraid of mob scenes should avoid this party at all costs. Mid-March.

Winter Music Conference (📞 954/563-4444; www.wmcon.com), Miami. A massive dance, electronic and techno-music industry gathering featuring DJs, musicians, execs and artists from around the world all on a mission to promote their sounds. Rather than taking place in a convention hall, however, WMC takes over Miami's clubs, lounges, hotels and restaurants where spin doctors of all genres wheel, deal and perform. Sometimes live. Many events are open to the public. Mid-March.

Sony Ericsson Open (☎ **866/725-5472;** www.sonyericssonopen.com), Key Biscayne. Roddick, Nadal, Federer, and the Williams sisters are only a few of the Grand Slammers who appear at this, one of the world's foremost tennis tournaments. Tickets for the semifinals and finals are hard to come by, so order early. End of March.

APRIL

Conch Republic Independence Celebration (☎ **305/296-0213;** www.conchrepublic.com), Key West. A 10-day party celebrating the day the Conch Republic seceded from the union. Events include a kooky bed race and drag queen race to minigolf tournaments, cruiser car shows and booze, lots of it. Late-April.

World Cup Polo Tournament (☎ **305/538-3809;** www.miamipolo.com), South Beach. The last tournament of the polo season, this event draws the diamond-studded mallet set who gather on the sands of South Beach one more time in the name of scene and sport. Mid-April.

Sunfest (☎ **561/659-5980;** www.sunfest.com), West Palm Beach. Sleepy downtown West Palm comes alive at the end of April for this street fair and concert, featuring big-name entertainment, food stands, a youth fair, and hordes of people. Admission charges are reasonable, but, unless there's someone performing whom you must see, not always worth the price. Stick to the free nontented area on Clematis Street for excellent people-watching.

Air Lauderdale (☎ **954/241-0395;** www.airlauderdale.com), Fort Lauderdale. A two-day spectacle featuring top military and civilian pilots showing off in the sky as spectators crane their necks along 4 miles of the city's beach. Previously known as the Air and Sea Show, the event has been known to attract millions of people, so air and space at this event is a premium. Late April.

Miami Gay & Lesbian Film Festival (☎ **305/534-9924;** www.mglff.com), Miami Beach. This 10-day event is the Sundance of festivals for gay and lesbian films and filmmakers. It features an impressive roster of independent and commercial films, plus appearances by some of the films' directors, actors, and writers. Late April, early May.

JULY

Lower Keys Underwater Music Fest (☎ **800/872-3722**), Looe Key. When you hear the phrase "the music and the madness," you may think of this amusing aural aquatic event in which boaters head out to the underwater reef at the Looe Key Marine Sanctuary, drop speakers into the water, and pipe in all sorts of music, creating a disco-diving spectacular. Considering the heat at this time of year, underwater is probably the coolest place for a concert. Early July.

Hemingway Days Festival (☎ **305/294-4440**), Key West. The legendary author is alive and well—many times over—at this celebration of the literary world's most famous Papa, to which eerily accurate Hemingway clones flock in the hopes of winning the big look-alike contest. Late-July.

AUGUST/SEPTEMBER

These months are possibly the most scorching, which is why event planners try to avoid it altogether. Your best bet? Try the beach, pool, or anywhere with air-conditioning.

OCTOBER

Columbus Day Regatta, Miami. On the day that Columbus discovered America, the party-hearty discover their fellow Americans' birthday suits, as this bacchanalia encourages participants in the so-called regatta (there is a boat race at some point during the day, but most people are too preoccupied to notice) to strip down to their bare necessities and party at the sandbar in the middle of Biscayne Bay. You may not need a bathing suit, but you will need a boat to get out to where all the action is. Consider renting one on Key Biscayne, which is the closest to the sandbar. Second weekend of October.

Fort Lauderdale International Boat Show (© **954/764-7642**), Fort Lauderdale. The world's largest boat show, this one's got boats of every size, shape, and status symbol displayed at the scenic Bahia Mar marina and four other locations in the area. Traffic-phobes beware. Mid-October.

Fantasy Fest (© **305/296-1817**; www.fantasyfest.net), Key West. Mardi Gras takes a Floridian holiday as the streets of Key West are overtaken by wildly costumed revelers who have no shame and no parental guidance. This weeklong, hedonistic, X-rated Halloween party is not for children 17 and under. Make reservations in Key West early as hotels tend to book up quickly during this event. Last week of October.

NOVEMBER

South Florida International Auto Show (© **305/947-5950**), Miami Beach. Cars are everywhere—literally—at this massive auto show, displaying the latest and most futuristic modes of transportation on the market. Try to take public transportation or call a cab to get to this gridlocked event. Early November.

Ford 400 NASCAR Sprint Cup Series Championship (© **866/409-RACE** [7223] or 305/230-5200; www.homesteadmiamispeedway.com), Homestead. World-class racing takes place on Miami's world-class 344-acre motor sports complex. Rev your engines early for tickets to this event. Mid-November.

Miami Book Fair International (© **305/237-3258**), Miami. Bibliophiles, literati, and some of the world's most prestigious and prolific authors descend upon downtown Miami for a weeklong homage to the written word, which also happens to be the largest book fair in the United States. The weekend street fair is the best attended of the entire event, in which regular folk mix with wordsmiths such as Tom Wolfe, Nora Ephron, Salman Rushdie, and Jane Smiley while indulging in snacks, antiquarian books, and literary gossip. All lectures are free but fill up quickly, so get there early. Mid-November.

White Party Week, Miami and Fort Lauderdale. This weeklong series of parties to benefit AIDS research is built around the main event, the White Party, which takes place at Villa Vizcaya and sells out as early as a year in advance. Philanthropists and celebrities such as Calvin Klein and David Geffen join thousands of white-clad, mostly gay men (and some women) in what has become one of the world's hottest and hardest-to-score party tickets. Thanksgiving week.

DECEMBER

Art Basel Miami Beach (www.artbaselmiamibeach.com), Miami Beach/Design District. Switzerland's most exclusive art fair and the world's most prominent collectors fly south for the winter and set up shop on South Beach and in the Design District with thousands of exhibitions, not to mention cocktail parties, concerts, and containers—as in shipping—that are set up on the beach and transformed into makeshift galleries. First or second weekend in December.

Seminole–Hard Rock Winterfest Boat Parade (© **954/767-0686**; www.winterfestparade.com), Fort Lauderdale. People who complain that the holiday season just isn't as festive in South Florida as it is in colder parts of the world haven't been to this spectacular boat parade along the Intracoastal Waterway. Forget decking the halls. At this parade, the decks are decked out in magnificent holiday regalia as they gracefully—and boastfully—glide up and down the water. If you're not on a boat, the best views are from waterfront restaurants or anywhere you can squeeze in along the water. Mid-December.

ENTRY REQUIREMENTS

Passports

Virtually every air traveler entering the U.S. is required to show a passport. All persons, including U.S. citizens, traveling by air between the United States and Canada, Mexico, Central and South America, the Caribbean, and Bermuda are required to present a valid passport. **Note:** U.S. and Canadian citizens entering the U. S. at land and sea ports of entry from within the Western Hemisphere must now also present a passport or other documents compliant with the Western Hemisphere Travel Initiative (WHTI; see www.getyouhome.gov for details). Children 15 and under may continue entering with only a U.S. birth certificate, or other proof of U.S. citizenship.

For information on how to get a passport, go to **"Passports,"** under **"Fast Facts: South Florida,"** p. 390—the websites listed provide downloadable passport applications as well as the current fees for processing passport applications. For an up-to-date, country-by-country listing of passport requirements around the world, go to the "Foreign Entry Requirement" Web page of the U.S. Department of State at **http://travel.state.gov**. International visitors can obtain a visa application at the same website. **Note:** Children are required to present a passport when entering the United States at airports. More information on obtaining a passport for a minor can be found at http://travel.state.gov.

It is advised to always have at least one or two consecutive blank pages in your passport to allow space for visas and stamps that need to appear together. It is also important to note when your passport expires. Many countries require your passport to have at least 6 months left before its expiration in order to allow you into the destination.

Visas

For specifics on how to get a visa, go to **"Visas,"** under **"Fast Facts: South Florida,"** p. 392.

The U.S. State Department has a **Visa Waiver Program (VWP)** allowing citizens of the following countries to enter the United States without a visa for stays of up to 90 days: Andorra, Australia, Austria, Belgium, Brunei, Czech Republic, Denmark, Estonia, Finland, France, Germany, Hungary, Iceland, Ireland, Italy, Japan, Latvia, Liechtenstein, Lithuania, Luxembourg, Malta, Monaco, the Netherlands, New Zealand, Norway, Portugal, San Marino, Singapore, Slovakia, Slovenia, South Korea, Spain, Sweden, Switzerland, and the United Kingdom. (**Note:** This list was accurate at press time; for the most up-to-date list of countries in the VWP, consult http://travel.state.gov/visa.) Even though a visa isn't necessary, in an effort to help U.S. officials check travelers against terror watch lists before they arrive at U.S. borders, visitors from VWP countries must register online through the Electronic System for Travel Authorization (ESTA) before boarding a plane or a boat to the U.S. Travelers must complete an electronic application providing basic personal and travel eligibility information. The Department of Homeland Security recommends filling out the form at least 3 days before traveling. Authorizations will be valid for up to 2 years or until the traveler's passport expires, whichever comes first. Currently, there is no fee for the online application. **Note:** Any passport issued on or after October 26, 2006, by a VWP country must be an **e-Passport** for VWP travelers to be eligible to enter the U.S. without a visa. Citizens of these nations also need to present a round-trip air or cruise ticket upon arrival. E-Passports contain computer chips capable of storing biometric information, such as the required digital photograph of the holder. If your passport doesn't have this feature, you can still travel without a visa if the valid passport was issued before October 26, 2005, and includes a machine-readable zone; or if the valid passport was issued between October 26, 2005, and October 25, 2006, and includes a digital photograph. For more information, go to **http://travel.state.gov/visa**. Canadian citizens may enter the United States without visas, but will need to show passports and proof of residence.

Citizens of all other countries must have (1) a valid passport that expires at least 6 months later than the scheduled end of their visit to the U.S.; and (2) a tourist visa.

Customs

WHAT YOU CAN BRING INTO THE U.S.

Every visitor 21 years of age or older may bring in, free of duty, the following: (1) 1 U.S. quart of alcohol; (2) 200 cigarettes, 50 cigars (but not from Cuba), or 3 pounds of smoking tobacco; and (3) $100 worth of gifts. These exemptions are offered to travelers who spend at least 72 hours in the United States and who have not claimed them within the preceding 6 months. It is forbidden to bring into the country almost any meat products (including canned, fresh, and dried meat products such as bouillon, soup mixes, and so on). Generally, condiments including vinegars, oils, pickled goods, spices, coffee, tea, and some cheeses and baked goods are permitted. Avoid rice products, as rice can often harbor insects. Bringing fruits and vegetables is prohibited since they may harbor pests or disease. International visitors may carry in or out up to $10,000 in U.S. or foreign currency with no formalities; larger sums must be declared to U.S. Customs on entering or leaving, which includes filing form CM 4790. For details regarding U.S. Customs and Border Protection, consult your nearest U.S. Embassy or consulate, or **U.S. Customs** (www.customs.gov).

WHAT YOU CAN TAKE HOME FROM SOUTH FLORIDA:

For information on what you're allowed to bring home, contact one of the following agencies:

U.S. Citizens: U.S. Customs & Border Protection (CBP), 1300 Pennsylvania Ave., NW, Washington, DC 20229 (℡ **877/287-8667;** www.cbp.gov).

Canadian Citizens: Canada Border Services Agency, Ottawa, Ontario, K1A 0L8 (℡ **800/461-9999** in Canada, or 204/983-3500; www.cbsa-asfc.gc.ca).

U.K. Citizens: HM Customs & Excise, Crownhill Court, Tailyour Road, Plymouth, PL6 5BZ (℡ **0845/010-9000;** from outside the U.K., 020/8929-0152; www.hmce.gov.uk).

Australian Citizens: Australian Customs Service, Customs House, 5 Constitution Ave., Canberra City, ACT 2601 (℡ **1300/363-263;** from outside Australia, 612/6275-6666; www.customs.gov.au).

New Zealand Citizens: New Zealand Customs, The Customhouse, 17–21 Whitmore St., Box 2218, Wellington, 6140 (℡ **04/473-6099** or 0800/428-786; www.customs.govt.nz).

Medical Requirements

Unless you're arriving from an area known to be suffering from an epidemic (particularly cholera or yellow fever), inoculations or vaccinations are not required for entry into the United States.

GETTING THERE & AROUND

Getting to South Florida

BY PLANE

Most major domestic airlines fly to and from many Florida cities. Choose from **American, Continental, Delta, United,** and **US Airways.** Of these, Delta and US Airways have the most extensive network of commuter connections within Florida (see "Getting Around," below).

Several so-called no-frills airlines—with low fares but few, if any, amenities—also fly to Florida. The biggest and best is **Southwest Airlines,** which has flights from many U.S. cities to Fort Lauderdale, Jacksonville, Orlando, Tampa, and Panama City.

Others flying to Florida include **AirTran; JetBlue; Virgin America; Frontier Airlines;** and **Spirit.**

The major airports in South Florida are **Miami International Airport (MIA), Fort Lauderdale Hollywood International Airport (FLL),** and **Palm Beach International Airport (PBI).**

Tip: When booking airfare to Miami, consider flying into the Fort Lauderdale Hollywood International Airport for considerably cheaper fares. The airport is only a half-hour from downtown Miami.

Internet resources such as **Travelocity** (www.travelocity.com) and **Expedia** (www.expedia.com) make it easy to compare prices and purchase tickets.

BY CAR

Although four major roads run to and through Miami—I-95, S.R. 826, S.R. 836, and U.S. 1—chances are you'll reach Miami and the rest of South Florida by way of I-95. This north-south interstate is South Florida's lifeline and an integral part of the region. The highway connects all of Miami's different neighborhoods, the airport, the beaches, and all of South Florida to the rest of the country. Miami's road signs are notoriously confusing and notably absent when you most need them. Think twice before you exit from the highway if you aren't sure where you're going: Some exits lead to unsavory neighborhoods.

Other highways that will get you to Florida include I-10, which originates in Los Angeles and terminates at the tip of Florida in Jacksonville, and I-75, which begins in North Michigan and runs through the center of the state to Florida's west coast.

Florida law allows drivers to make a right turn on a red light after a complete stop, unless otherwise indicated. In addition, all passengers are required to wear seat belts, and children 3 and under must be securely fastened in government-approved car seats.

See "Getting Around," beginning on p. 35, for more information about driving in Florida and the car-rental firms that operate here.

International visitors should note that insurance and taxes are almost never included in quoted rental car rates in the U.S. Be sure to ask your rental agency about additional fees for these. They can add a significant cost to your car rental.

Getting There & Around | PLANNING YOUR TRIP TO SOUTH FLORIDA

Most car rental companies in Florida require that you be 25, but if not, there's a hefty surcharge applied to renters 21 to 24 years old.

BY TRAIN

Amtrak (© **800/USA-RAIL** [872-7245]; www.amtrak.com) offers train service to Florida from both the East and West coasts. It takes some 26 hours from New York to Miami, and 68 hours from Los Angeles to Miami. Amtrak's fares aren't much less—if not more—than many of the airlines' lowest fares.

Amtrak's **Silver Meteor** and **Silver Star** both run twice daily between New York and either Miami or Tampa, with intermediate stops along the East Coast and in Florida. Amtrak's Thruway Bus Connections are available from the Fort Lauderdale Amtrak station and Miami International Airport to Key West; from Tampa to St. Petersburg, Treasure Island, Clearwater, Sarasota, Bradenton, and Fort Myers; and from Deland to Daytona Beach. From the West Coast, the **Sunset Limited** runs three times weekly between Los Angeles and Orlando. It stops in Pensacola, Crestview (north of Fort Walton Beach and Destin), Chipley (north of Panama City Beach), and Tallahassee. Sleeping accommodations are available for an extra charge.

If you intend to stop along the way, you can save money with Amtrak's **Explore America** (or All Aboard America) fares, which are based on three regions of the country.

Amtrak's **Auto Train** runs daily from Lorton, Virginia (12 miles south of Washington, D.C.), to Sanford, Florida (just northeast of Orlando). You ride in a coach while your car is secured in an enclosed vehicle carrier. Make your train reservations as far in advance as possible.

BY BUS

Greyhound (© **800/231-2222**; www.greyhound.com) has over 50 stops within the state of Florida and over 2,400 service locations in North America. While buses aren't the fastest way to get to Florida, it can be the most economical.

BY BOAT

While you can't hop on a cruise ship to Florida, you can from Florida with major cruise ports located in Miami, Port Everglades, Cape Canaveral, and Tampa.

Getting Around

Having a car is the best and easiest way to see South Florida's sights or to get to and from the beach. Public transportation is available only in the cities and larger towns, and even there, it may provide infrequent or inadequate service. When it comes to getting from one city to another, cars and planes are the ways to go

BY PLANE

The commuter arms of **Continental, Delta,** and **US Airways** provide extensive service between Florida's major cities and towns. Fares for these short hops tend to be reasonable.

Cape Air flies between Key West and Naples, which means you can avoid backtracking to Miami from Key West if you're touring the state. (You can also take a 3-hour boat ride between Key West and Fort Myers Beach, Naples, or Marco Island.) **Collins Aviation** connects Fort Lauderdale with Marathon.

Some large airlines offer transatlantic or transpacific passengers special discount tickets under the name **Visit USA,** which allows mostly one-way travel from one U.S. destination to another at very low prices. Unavailable in the U.S., these discount tickets must be purchased abroad in conjunction with your international fare. This system is the easiest, fastest, cheapest way to see the country.

BY CAR

If you're visiting from abroad and plan to rent a car in Florida, keep in mind that foreign driver's licenses are usually recognized in the U.S., but you should get an international one if your home license is not in English.

Jacksonville is about 350 miles north of Miami and 500 miles north of Key West, so don't underestimate how long it will take you to drive all the way down the state. The speed limit is either 65 mph or 70 mph on the rural interstate highways, so you can make good time between cities. Not so on U.S. 1, U.S. 17, U.S. 19, U.S. 41, and U.S. 301; although most have four lanes, these older highways tend to be heavily congested, especially in built-up areas.

Every major car-rental company is represented here, including **Alamo, Avis, Budget, Dollar, Enterprise, Hertz, National,** and **Thrifty.**

State and local **taxes** will add as much as 20% to your final bill. You'll pay an additional $2.05 per day in statewide use tax, and local sales taxes will tack on at least 6% to the total, including the statewide use tax. Some airports add another 35¢ per day and as much as 10% in "recovery" fees. You can avoid the recovery fee by picking up your car in town rather than at the airport. Budget and Enterprise both have numerous rental locations away from the airports. But be sure to weigh the cost of transportation to and from your hotel against the amount of the fee.

Competition is so fierce among Florida rental firms that most have now stopped charging **drop-off fees** if you pick up a car at one place and leave it at another. Be sure to ask in advance if there's a drop-off fee.

To rent a car, you must have a valid **credit card** (not a debit or check card) in your name, and most companies require you to be at least 25 years old. Some also set maximum ages and may deny cars to anyone with a bad driving record. Ask about requirements and restrictions when you book, in order to avoid problems once you arrive.

BY TRAIN

International visitors can buy a **USA Rail Pass,** good for 15, 30, or 45 days of unlimited travel on **Amtrak** (© **800/USA-RAIL** [872-7245]; www.amtrak.com). The pass is available online or through many overseas travel agents. See Amtrak's website for the cost of travel within the western, eastern, or northwestern United States. Reservations are generally required and should be made as early as possible. Regional rail passes are also available.

BY BUS

Greyhound (© **800/231-2222;** www.greyhound.com) is the sole nationwide bus line. International visitors can obtain information about the **Greyhound North American Discovery Pass.** The pass, which offers unlimited travel and stopovers in the U.S. and Canada, can be obtained from foreign travel agents or through www.discoverypass.com.

MONEY & COSTS

THE VALUE OF THE U.S. DOLLAR VS. OTHER POPULAR CURRENCIES

US$	C$	£	€	A$	NZ$
1	1.026	0.66	0.73	1.094	1.42

Frommer's lists exact prices in the local currency. The currency conversions quoted above were correct at press time. However, rates fluctuate, so before departing consult a currency exchange website such as **www.oanda.com/convert/classic** to check up-to-the-minute rates.

The easiest way to pay for almost everything in South Florida is with a credit card. MasterCard and Visa credit and debit cards are accepted almost everywhere. American Express, Diners Club, and Discover cards are also accepted, although not as widely as MasterCard and Visa.

The best way to get cash while you're traveling in South Florida is to use your debit or credit cards at ATMs. Of the big national banks, **First Union Bank** and **Bank of America** have offices with ATMs throughout Florida.

How much money you spend on a Florida vacation will depend on your own desires and choices, when you go, and most definitely *where* you go. The state has a wide range of accommodations, from some of the country's most luxurious and expensive beachfront resorts to no-frills but friendly mom-and-pop motels sitting right by the beach. If you can do without the luxuries, you needn't spend a fortune.

Tourism is Florida's biggest industry, and the economic law of supply and demand dictates that the prices of hotel rooms are highest during the seasons when tourists invade Florida: the winter months in the southern half of the state, the summer months up north.

See "When to Go," earlier in this chapter, for details on Florida's high, low, and in-between seasons.

Beware of hidden credit-card fees while traveling. Check with your credit or debit card issuer to see what fees, if any, will be charged for overseas transactions. Recent reform legislation in the U.S., for example, has curbed some exploitative lending practices. But many banks have responded by increasing fees in other areas, including fees for customers who use credit and debit cards while out of the country—even if those charges were made in U.S. dollars. Fees can amount to 3% or more of the purchase price. Check with your bank before departing to avoid any surprise charges on your statement.

STAYING HEALTHY

South Florida doesn't present any unusual health hazards for most people. Folks with certain medical conditions, such as liver disease, diabetes, and stomach ailments, however, should avoid eating raw **oysters,** which can carry a natural bacterium linked to severe diarrhea, vomiting, and even fatal blood poisoning. Cooking kills the bacteria, so if in doubt, order your oysters steamed, broiled, or fried.

Florida has millions of **mosquitoes** and invisible biting **sand flies** (known as "no-see-ums"), especially in the coastal and marshy areas. Fortunately, neither insect carries malaria or other diseases. Keep these pests at bay with a good insect repellent.

WHAT THINGS COST IN SOUTH FLORIDA	$
Taxi from the airport to downtown Miami	22.00
Double room, moderate	175.00
Double room, inexpensive	100.00
Three-course dinner for one without wine, moderate	25.00–50.00
Bottle of beer	3.00–6.00
Bottle of Coca-Cola	1.00–4.00
Cup of coffee	1.50–5.00
1 gallon/1 liter of premium gas	2.61/0.69
Admission to most museums	10.00–20.00
Admission to most national parks	5.00–7.00

It's especially important to protect yourself against **sunburn.** Don't underestimate the strength of the sun's rays down here, even in the middle of winter. Use a sunscreen with a high protection factor and apply it liberally. Limit your exposure to the sun, especially during the first few days of your trip and thereafter from 11am to 2pm. Remember that children need more protection than do adults.

If You Get Sick

Hospitals are as ubiquitous in South Florida as palm trees. If you're in a major city, you'll have no problem and even if you're not, you'll be near enough to a facility that will provide adequate health care.

We list additional **emergency numbers** in "Fast Facts," p. 389.

CRIME & SAFETY

While tourist areas in Florida are generally safe, you should always stay alert. This is particularly true in the larger cities, such as Miami, Orlando, Tampa, and St. Petersburg. If you're in doubt about which neighborhoods are safe, ask your hotel's front-desk staff or the area's tourist office.

Remember also that hotels are open to the public, and in a large hotel, security may not be able to screen everyone entering. Always lock your room door. Don't assume that, once inside your hotel, you are automatically safe and no longer need to be aware of your surroundings.

SPECIALIZED TRAVEL RESOURCES

In addition to the destination-specific resources listed below, please visit Frommers.com for other specialized travel resources.

LGBT Travelers

The editors of *Out and About,* a gay and lesbian newsletter, have described Miami's **South Beach** as the "hippest, hottest, most happening gay travel destination in the world." Today, however, **Fort Lauderdale**—where gays own more than 20 motels, 40 bars, and numerous other businesses—steals its rainbow-colored crown. For many years, that could also be said of **Key West,** which still is one of the country's most popular destinations for gays.

You can contact the **Gay, Lesbian & Bisexual Community Services of Central Florida,** 946 N. Mills Ave., Orlando, FL 32803 (© **407/228-8272;** www. glbcc.org), whose welcome packets usually include the latest issue of the *Triangle,* a quarterly newsletter dedicated to gay and lesbian issues, and a calendar of events pertaining to the gay and lesbian community. Although not a tourist-specific packet, it includes information and ads for the area's gay and lesbian clubs.

Watermark, P.O. Box 533655, Orlando, FL 32853 (© 407/481-2243; fax 407/ 481-2246; www.watermarkonline.com), is a biweekly tabloid newspaper covering the gay and lesbian scene, including dining and entertainment options, in Orlando, the Tampa Bay area, and Daytona Beach.

The **International Gay and Lesbian Travel Association** (**IGLTA;** © **800/ 448-8550** or 954/776-2626; www.iglta.org) is the trade association for the gay and lesbian travel industry, and offers an online directory of gay- and lesbian-friendly travel businesses and tour operators.

Travelers with Disabilities

Florida is exceptionally accommodating to those with special needs. In addition to special parking set aside at every establishment, out-of-state vehicles with disability parking permits from other states can park in these spots. Florida state law and the ADA require guide dogs be permitted in all establishments and attractions, although some ride restrictions do apply. For the hearing impaired, TDD service is available by dialing 711 via the Florida Relay Service. There are several resources for the disabled traveling within Florida, including special wheelchairs with balloon tires provided free of charge at many Florida beaches. For the best information on traveling with disabilities, go to www.visitflorida.com/articles/florid-able.

Family Travel

South Florida is chock-full of kid-friendly hotels, attractions, and restaurants. When visiting the Keys, be sure to check that the hotel or inn allows children, as many do not. Look for the "Kids" icon throughout this book.

You may also want to consult *The Unofficial Guide to Florida with Kids* as well as *How to Take Great Trips with Your Kids* (The Harvard Common Press), which is full of good general advice that can apply to travel anywhere.

Most Florida hotels and restaurants are willing, if not eager, to cater to families traveling with children. Many hotels and motels let children age 17 and younger stay free in a parent's room. (Be sure to ask when you reserve.)

At the beaches, it's the exception rather than the rule for a resort not to have a children's activities program. (Some will even mind the youngsters while the parents enjoy a night off!) Even if they don't have a children's program of their own, most will arrange babysitting services.

Recommended family travel websites include **Family Travel Forum** (www. familytravelforum.com), a comprehensive site that offers customized trip planning; **Family Travel Network** (www.familytravelnetwork.com), an online magazine providing travel tips; and **TravelWithYourKids.com** (www.travelwithyourkids.com), a comprehensive site written by parents for parents, offering sound advice for long-distance and international travel with children. To locate accommodations, restaurants, and attractions that are particularly kid-friendly, look for the "Kids" icon throughout this guide.

Senior Travel

With one of the largest retired populations of any state, Florida offers a wide array of activities and benefits for seniors. Don't be shy about asking for discounts, but always carry some kind of identification, such as a driver's license, that shows your date of birth. Mention the fact that you're a senior when you make your travel reservations. In most cities, people over the age of 60 qualify for reduced admission to theaters, museums, and other attractions, as well as discounted fares on public transportation.

Members of **AARP,** 601 E. St. NW, Washington, DC 20049 (🕐 **888/687-2277;** www.aarp.org), get discounts on hotels, airfares, and car rentals. Anyone older than 50 can join.

The U.S. National Park Service offers an **America the Beautiful—National Park and Federal Recreational Lands Pass—Senior Pass** (formerly the **Golden Age Passport**), which gives seniors 62 years or older lifetime entrance to all properties administered by the National Park Service—national parks, monuments, historic sites, recreation areas, and national wildlife refuges—for a one-time processing fee of $10. The pass must be purchased in person at any NPS facility that charges an entrance fee. Besides free entry, the America the Beautiful Senior Pass also offers a 50% discount on some federal-use fees charged for such facilities as camping, swimming, parking, boat launching, and tours. For more information, go to www.nps.gov/fees_passes.htm or call 🕐 **888/467-2757.**

Many reliable agencies and organizations target the 50-plus market. **Exploritas** (🕐 **800/454-5768;** www.exploritas.org) arranges worldwide study programs for those ages 55 and older. **ElderTreks** (🕐 **800/741-7956** or 416/558-5000 outside North America; www.eldertreks.com) offers small-group tours to off-the-beaten-path or adventure-travel locations, restricted to travelers age 50 and older.

RESPONSIBLE TOURISM

Florida's biggest attraction isn't Disney, but rather its natural resources. Thanks to some of the state's initiatives, keeping Florida green is becoming second nature. The Florida Green Lodging program, for instance, is a voluntary initiative of the Florida Department of Environmental Protection that designates and recognizes lodging facilities making a commitment to conserving and protecting Florida's natural resources. As of February 19, 2010, there were 621 designated Florida Green Lodging properties. In order to be considered for membership in this very exclusive, green group, motels, hotels, and resorts must: educate customers, employees and the public on conservation; participate in waste reduction, reuse, recycling, water conservation, and energy efficiency; and provide eco-friendly transportation. The designation is valid for three years from the date of issue and all properties are required to submit environmental performance data every year as well as implement at least two new environmental practices from any of the six areas of sustainable operations. For a list of these properties, go to www.dep.state.fl.us/greenlodging/lodges.htm.

GENERAL RESOURCES FOR green travel

In addition to the resources for Florida listed above, the following websites provide valuable wide-ranging information on sustainable travel.

o **Responsible Travel** (www.responsibletravel.com) is a great source of sustainable travel ideas; the site is run by a spokesperson for ethical tourism in the travel industry. **Sustainable Travel International** (www.sustainabletravelinternational.org) promotes ethical tourism practices, and manages an extensive directory of sustainable properties and tour operators around the world.

o **Carbonfund** (www.carbonfund.org), **TerraPass** (www.terrapass.org), and **Cool Climate** (http://coolclimate.berkeley.edu) provide info on "carbon offsetting," or

offsetting the greenhouse gas emitted during flights.

o **"Green" Hotels Association** (www.greenhotels.com) recommends green-rated member hotels around the world that fulfill the company's stringent environmental requirements. **Environmentally Friendly Hotels** (www.environmentallyfriendly hotels.com) offers more green accommodation ratings.

o **Volunteer International** (www.volunteerinternational.org) has a list of questions to help you determine the intentions and the nature of a volunteer program. For general info on volunteer travel, visit **www.volunteer abroad.org** and **www.idealist.org**.

Ecotourism isn't just a trendy catchphrase when it comes to tourism in Florida. The Florida Fish and Wildlife Conservation Commission estimates that outdoor activities have almost a $10 billion impact on the state's economy. The Everglades alone is an ecotourism hot spot where responsible tourism isn't an option but a mandatory requirement for anyone visiting or working there. In fact, in 2010, the Comprehensive Everglades Restoration Plan reinvigorated a restoration plan that will return some lands previously squandered for development to their formerly pristine, natural conditions. For a directory of sustainable, eco-conscious tourism, try *EcoFlorida Magazine* or its blog at http://ecoflorida.blogspot.com.

Contrary to popular belief, when it comes to responsible tourism in Florida it is, indeed, easy being green.

SPECIAL INTEREST & ESCORTED TRIPS

Special Interest Trips

Diving, boating and sailing, camping, canoeing and kayaking, fishing, golfing, tennis—you name it, South Florida has it. These and other activities are described in the outdoor-activities sections of the following chapters, but here's a brief overview of some of the best places to move your muscles, with tips on how to get more detailed information.

The **Florida Sports Foundation,** 2390 Kerry Forest Pkwy., Ste. 101, Tallahassee, FL 32309 (© **850/488-8347;** fax 850/922-0482; www.flasports.com), publishes free brochures, calendars, schedules, and guides to outdoor pursuits and spectator sports throughout Florida. I've noted some of its specific publications in the sections below.

For excellent color maps of state parks, campgrounds, canoe trails, aquatic preserves, caverns, and more, contact the **Florida Department of Environmental Protection,** Office of Communications, 3900 Commonwealth Blvd., Tallahassee, FL 32399 (© **850/245-2118;** www.dep.state.fl.us). Some of the department's publications are mentioned below.

The Great Outdoors

BIKING & IN-LINE SKATING   Florida's relatively flat terrain makes it ideal for bicycling and in-line skating. You can bike right into **Everglades National Park** along the 38-mile-long Main Park Road. Many towns and cities have designated routes for cyclists, skaters, joggers, and walkers, such as the paved pathways along Fort Lauderdale Beach and **Ocean Drive** on South Beach.

BOATING & SAILING   With some 1,350 miles of shoreline, it's not surprising that Florida is a boating and sailing mecca. In fact, you won't be anyplace near the water very long before you see flyers and other advertisements for rental boats and sailboat cruises. Many of them are mentioned in the chapters that follow.

Key West keeps gaining prominence as a world sailing capital. *Yachting* magazine sponsors the largest winter regatta in America here each January, and smaller events take place regularly.

The prestigious **Annapolis Sailing** (www.annapolissailing.com) has a base in Marathon in the Keys.

Florida Boating & Fishing, available for free from the Florida Sports Foundation (see the introduction to this section, above), is a treasure trove of tips on safe boating; state regulations; locations of marinas, hotels, and resorts; marine products and services; and more.

CAMPING   Florida is literally dotted with RV parks (if you own such a vehicle, it's the least expensive way to spend your winters here). But for the best tent camping, look to Florida's national preserves and 110 state parks and recreation areas. Options range from luxury sites with hot-water showers and cable TV hookups, to primitive island and beach camping with no facilities whatsoever.

Top spots include **Bill Baggs Cape Florida State Park,** on Key Biscayne in Miami. Down in the Keys, the oceanside sites in **Long Key State Park** are about as nice as they get.

In each of these popular campgrounds, reservations are essential, especially during the high season. Each of Florida's state parks take bookings up to 11 months in advance.

The **Florida Department of Environmental Protection,** Division of Recreation and Parks, Mail Station 535, 3900 Commonwealth Blvd., Tallahassee, FL 32399-3000 (© **850/245-2118;** www.dep.state.fl.us), publishes an annual guide of tent and RV sites in Florida's state parks and recreation areas.

Pet owners, note: Pets are permitted at some—but not all—state park beaches, campgrounds, and food service areas. Before bringing your animal, check with the department or the individual park to see if your pet will be allowed. And bring your pet's rabies certificate, which is required.

For private campgrounds, the **Florida Association of RV Parks & Campgrounds,** 1340 Vickers Dr., Tallahassee, FL 32303 (© **850/562-7151;** fax 850/562-7179; www.floridacamping.com), issues an annual *Camp Florida* directory with locator maps and details about its member establishments in the state.

CANOEING & KAYAKING   Canoers and kayakers have almost limitless options for discovery here: picturesque rivers, sandy coastlines, marshes, mangroves, and gigantic Lake Okeechobee. Exceptional trails run through several parks and wildlife preserves, including **Everglades National Park** and **Briggs Nature Center,** on the edge of the Everglades near Marco Island.

Based during the winter at Everglades City, on the park's western border, **North American Canoe Tours, Inc.** (© **239/695-3299;** www.evergladesadventures. com), offers weeklong guided canoe expeditions through the Everglades.

Thirty-six creek and river trails, covering 950 miles altogether, are itemized in the excellent free *Canoe Trails* booklet published by the Florida Department of Environmental Protection, Office of Communications, 3900 Commonwealth Blvd., Tallahassee, FL 32399 (© **850/245-2118;** www.dep.state.fl.us).

Specialized guidebooks include *A Canoeing and Kayaking Guide to the Streams of Florida: Volume 1, North Central Florida and Panhandle,* by Elizabeth F. Carter and John L. Pearce; and *Volume 2, Central and Southern Peninsula,* by Lou Glaros and Doug Sphar. Both are published by Menasha Ridge Press (www.menasharidge.com).

ECO-ADVENTURES   If you don't want to do it yourself, you can observe Florida's flora and fauna on guided field expeditions—and contribute to conservation efforts while you're at it.

The **Sierra Club,** the oldest and largest grass-roots environmental organization in the U.S., offers eco-adventures through its Florida chapters. Recent outings have included canoeing or kayaking through the Everglades, hiking the Florida Trail in America's southernmost national forest, camping on a barrier island, and exploring the sinkhole phenomenon in North-Central Florida. You do have to be a Sierra Club member, but you can join at the time of the trip. Contact the club's national outings office at 85 Second St., 2nd Floor, San Francisco, CA 94105-3441 (© **415/977-5500;** www.sierraclub.org).

The Florida chapter of the **Nature Conservancy** has protected 578,000 acres of natural lands in Florida and presently owns and manages 36 preserves. For a small fee, you can join one of its field trips or work parties that take place periodically throughout the year; fees vary from year to year and event to event, so call for more information. Participants get a chance to learn about and even participate in the preservation of the ecosystem. For details on all the preserves and adventures, contact the Nature Conservancy, Florida Chapter, 222 S. Westmonte Dr., Ste. 300, Altamonte Springs, FL 32714 (© **407/682-3664;** fax 407/682-3077; www.nature. org).

A nonprofit organization dedicated to environmental research, the **Earthwatch Institute,** 3 Clocktower Place, Ste. 100 (P.O. Box 75), Maynard, MA 01754 (© **800/776-0188** or 978/461-0081; www.earthwatch.org), has excursions to survey dolphins and manatees around Sarasota and to monitor the well-being of the whooping cranes raised in captivity and released in the wilds of Central Florida.

Another research group, the **Oceanic Society,** Fort Mason Center, Building E, San Francisco, CA 94123 (© **800/326-7491** or 415/441-1106; fax 415/474-3395; www.oceanic-society.org), also has Florida trips among its expeditions, including manatee monitoring in the Crystal River area, north of Tampa.

FISHING In addition to the amberjack, bonito, grouper, mackerel, mahimahi, marlin, pompano, redfish, sailfish, snapper, snook, tarpon, tuna, and wahoo running offshore and in inlets, Florida has countless miles of rivers and streams, plus about 30,000 lakes and springs stocked with more than 100 species of freshwater fish. Indeed, Floridians seem to fish everywhere: off canal banks and old bridges, from fishing piers and fishing fleets. You'll even see them standing alongside the Tamiami Trail (U.S. 41) that cuts across the Everglades—one eye on their line, the other watching for alligators.

Anglers 16 and older need a license for any kind of saltwater or freshwater fishing, including lobstering and spearfishing. Licenses are sold at bait-and-tackle shops around the state and online at www.fl.wildlifelicense.com/start.php.

The **Florida Department of Environmental Protection,** 3900 Commonwealth Blvd., Tallahassee, FL 32399-3000 (© **850/245-2118;** www.dep.state. fl.us), publishes the annual *Fishing Lines,* a free magazine with a wealth of information about fishing in Florida, including regulations and licensing requirements. It also distributes free brochures with annual freshwater and saltwater limits. And the Florida Sports Foundation (see the introduction to this section, above) publishes *Florida Fishing & Boating,* another treasure trove of information.

GOLF Florida is the unofficial golf capital of the United States. But one thing is for certain: Florida has more golf courses than any other state—more than 1,150 at last count, and growing. I picked the best for chapter 1, but suffice it to say that you can tee off almost anywhere, anytime there's daylight. It's a rare town in Florida that doesn't have a municipal golf course—even Key West has 18 great holes.

Greens fees are usually much lower at the municipal courses than at privately owned clubs. Whether public or private, greens fees tend to vary greatly, depending on the time of year. You could pay $150 or more at a private course during the high season, but less than half that when the tourists are gone. The fee structures vary so much that it's best to call ahead and ask, and always reserve a tee time as far in advance as possible.

You can learn the game or hone your strokes at one of several excellent golf schools in South Florida including **Jimmy Ballard's** school at the Ocean Reef Club on Key Largo or at the **PGA National Resort & Spa** in Palm Beach Gardens where they live, breathe, and eat golf.

You can get information about most Florida courses, including current greens fees, and reserve tee times through **Tee Times USA,** P.O. Box 641, Flagler Beach, FL 32136 (© **888/GOLF-FLO** [465-3356] or 386/439-0001; www.teetimesusa. com), which publishes a vacation guide with many stay-and-play golf packages.

Florida Golf, published by the Florida Sports Foundation (see the introduction to this section, above), lists every course in Florida. It's the state's official golf guide and is available from Visit Florida (www.visitflorida.com).

Golfer's Guide magazine publishes monthly editions covering most of Florida. It is available free at local visitor centers and hotel lobbies, or you can contact the magazine at 2 Park Lane, Ste. E, Hilton Head Island, SC 29928 (© **800/864-6101** or 843/842-7878; fax 843/842-5743; www.golfersguide.com).

You can also get more information from the **Professional Golfers' Association (PGA),** 400 Ave. of the Champions, Palm Beach Gardens, FL 33418 (© **800/633-9150;** www.pga.com); or from the **Ladies Professional Golf Association (LPGA),** 100 International Golf Dr., Daytona Beach, FL 32124 (© **904/254-6200;** www.lpga.com).

More than 700 courses are profiled in *Florida Golf Guide,* by Jimmy Shacky (Open Roads Publishing), available at bookstores for $20.

SCUBA DIVING & SNORKELING Divers love the Keys, where you can see magnificent formations of tree-size elk-horn coral and giant brain coral, as well as colorful sea fans and dozens of other varieties, sharing space with 300 or more species of rainbow-hued fish. Reef diving is good all the way from Key Largo to Key West, with plenty of tour operators, outfitters, and dive shops along the way. Particularly worthy are **John Pennekamp Coral Reef State Park** in Key Largo, and **Looe Key National Marine Sanctuary** off Big Pine Key. *Skin Diver* magazine picked Looe Key as the number-one dive spot in North America. Also, the clearest waters in which to view some of the 4,000 sunken ships along Florida's coast are in the Middle Keys and the waters between Key West and the Dry Tortugas. Snorkeling in the Keys is particularly fine between Islamorada and Marathon.

Over on the Treasure Coast, which didn't earn its name for nothing, you'll find an underwater bounty of shipwrecks, reefs, and dive sites.

If you want to keep up with what's going on statewide, you can subscribe to the monthly magazine *Florida Scuba News* (© **904/783-1610;** www.scubanews.com). You might also want to pick up a specialized guidebook. Some good ones include *Coral Reefs of Florida,* by Gilbert L. Voss (Pineapple Press; www.pineapple press.com); and *The Diver's Guide to Florida and the Florida Keys,* by Jim Stachowicz (Windward Publishing).

TENNIS Year-round sunshine makes Florida great for tennis. There are some 7,700 places to play throughout the state, from municipal courts to exclusive resorts. Some municipal facilities equal expensive resorts, except they're free or close to it. Some retired professionals even have their own tennis centers, including Chris Evert in Boca Raton.

The three hard courts and seven clay courts at the **Crandon Tennis Association,** 6702 Crandon Blvd. (© **305/365-2300**), get crowded on weekends because they're some of Miami's most beautiful. You'll play on the same courts as Lendl, Graf, Evert, McEnroe, Roddick, Nadal, Federer, and other greats; this is the venue for one of the world's biggest annual tennis events, the Sony Ericsson Open. There's a pleasant, if limited, pro shop, plus many good pros. Only four courts are lighted at night, but if you reserve at least 48 hours in advance, you can usually take your pick. Hard court fees are $4 per person, per hour during the day; $6 per person, per hour at night. Clay court fees are $7 per person, per hour during daytime only. Grass courts are $11 per person, per hour during daytime only. The courts are open daily from 8am to 9pm.

Famous as the spot where Chris Evert got in her early serves, the **Jimmy Evert Tennis Center,** 701 NE 12th Ave. (off Sunrise Blvd.), Fort Lauderdale (© **954/828-5378**), has 18 clay and three hard courts (15 lighted). Her coach and father, James Evert, still teaches young players here, though he is very picky about whom he'll accept. Nonresidents of Fort Lauderdale pay $7.50 an hour per person before 5pm and $9 an hour per person after 5pm.

SUGGESTED SOUTH FLORIDA ITINERARIES

4

Contrary to popular belief, South Florida isn't just Miami. There's the Keys, the Everglades, the Gold Coast, the Treasure Coast and, well, you get the picture. Set your sights on what you want to do and see the most, and simply unwind.

The range of possible itineraries is endless; what we've suggested below is a very full program covering Florida over a **2-week period.** If possible, you should extend your time—2 weeks is not really enough time if you plan to actually explore the Sunshine State, but if you plan to veg out on a beach, then it's plenty of time—or cut out some of the destinations suggested. You can always tack on one itinerary to the next. We've done our best to keep it geographically viable and logical. Whatever you finally decide to do, we highly recommend that you at least include a stop at one of Florida's natural wonders, be it the beaches, the Everglades, or the Keys.

Important: Should limited time force you to include only the most obvious stops in your itinerary, you will invariably make contact with only those who depend on you to make a living, which regrettably could leave you with a frustrated sense that Florida is one big, long tourist trap. This is why it is so important to *get off the beaten tourist track*—to experience the wacky, the kitschy, the stunning, the baffling, and the fascinating people, places, and things that make Florida an incredible destination.

BEACHY KEEN SOUTH FLORIDA IN 1 WEEK

South Florida's beaches have been more photographed—we think—than Paris Hilton. In addition to the sand and sparkling waters of the Atlantic, the beaches have various personalities, from laid back and remote to year-round MTV *Spring Break*. It may be fun to get a taste of all of these, if not for an hour or two at a time.

Suggested South Florida Itineraries

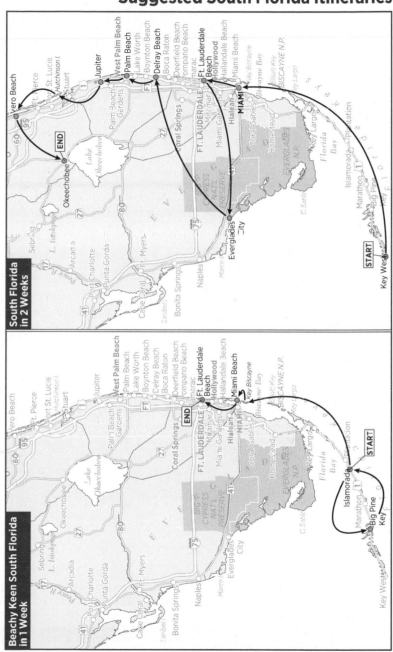

Day 1: Arrive in Islamorada ★★★

Check into the **Cheeca Lodge and Spa** and take in the panoramic ocean views. Park yourself on a chair and enjoy one of the Florida Keys' best—and only—private beaches. Waste no time making a dinner reservation for an outside table on the upstairs verandah at **Pierre's,** where you must, *must,* try the Florida Keys Hogfish Meuniere. After dinner, park yourself on the beach at the **Morada Bay Café** and listen to some live music while sipping a piña colada.

Day 2: Bahia Honda State Park ★★★

Just an hour south of Islamorada is one of South Florida's most resplendent beaches. Spend the day on the 524-acre park and lose yourself in the mangroves, beach dunes, and tropical hammocks. Not in the mood to spend all day in the park? Go be one with nature and check out the National Key Deer Refuge where you'll catch a glimpse of the most famous residents of the Lower Keys, or go snorkeling at the Looe Key National Marine Sanctuary where you'll see over 150 varieties of coral and the most magnificent tropical fish found outside an animated Disney flick. Head back to Cheeca and have dinner at the Atlantic's Edge for serious seafood and locally grown, organic produce, or the Green Turtle Inn, where authentic, gourmet Florida Keys cooking comes with a serious sense of humor. See p. 287.

Day 3: To Key Biscayne ★★

Take the scenic, sleepy, and often slow-moving Overseas Highway north to Key Biscayne, make a fish-dip stop at rustic Alabama Jack's, and check into the Ritz-Carlton Key Biscayne. On this, the southernmost barrier island on the Atlantic coast, you will be able to beach hop until the sun goes down. For the party people, Crandon Park Beach is the place to be, with 2 miles of beach and lots of salsa emanating from various sunbathers' boom boxes. Grab some much-needed peace and quiet at Bill Baggs Cape Florida State Park where you will forget you're in Miami, thanks to the miles of nature trails and completely unfettered beach. Do lunch at the park's charming Lighthouse Café before heading over to Virginia Key and Jimbo's, the place where *Flipper* was filmed and old Florida cracker-style houses serve as a backdrop to a beachfront bacchanal.

Days 4 & 5: South Beach/Miami Beach ★★★

Going to "the beach" takes on a totally different meaning when you're on South Beach. Not only does it mean sunbathing on Lummus Park Beach, also known as South Beach, for a cornucopia of half-naked beautiful people, but also enjoying the surrounding sights, sounds, and tastes of the area's bars, restaurants, shops, hotels, and Art Deco relics. There's a plethora of places to stay, whether you're on a budget or are willing to splurge; and best of all, the beach is free and a great place to crash and watch the sun set after spending the night out in the clubs!

Days 6 & 7: Swanky & Annette—also known as Fort Lauderdale Beach ★★★

Your dad may have spent Spring Break here with his frat buddies when the Beatles were just a random group of country bumpkins from Liverpool, but if he saw it now, he'd be completely surprised. Sure, the beach is beautiful, clean—no dogs allowed except on a special pet beach nearby—and visible from A1A, but the surrounding

More Suggested South Florida Itineraries

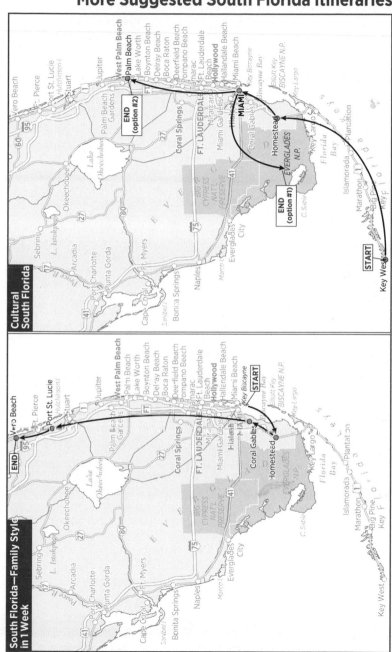

Cultural South Florida

START — Key West
END (option #1) — EVERGLADES N.P.
END (option #2) — Palm Beach
MIAMI

South Florida—Family Style in 1 Week

START — Key Biscayne
END — Vero Beach

area—the infamous Fort Lauderdale Strip—has matured into a sophisticated cafe society with outdoor eateries, bars, and more. If you must enter a beer-drinking contest, however, we're sure you'll find one nearby. Don't miss a cruise through the Venice of America, a scenic, informative and convenient way to make your way from one end of the strip to another. See p. 332.

SOUTH FLORIDA IN 2 WEEKS

Consider this tour a South Florida sampler. We've custom-built an itinerary that will provide you with a local's-eye view of some of the best diversions So Flo is known for. Whether you're into being a beach bum or a beachcomber, a club hopper or someone who prefers to swing a club, a nature lover or people-watcher—there's something for everyone on this tour.

4

Days 1 & 2: Arrive in Key West ★★★

After arriving in the so-called Conch Republic, or Margaritaville if you will, plan to spend at most a day or two here. A full day on the 4×2-mile island is plenty for exploring, but if you're into doing the Duval Bar Crawl, you may want to leave yourself with a day to recover from that inevitable hangover. Focus most of your sightseeing energy on Old Town, where you'll see stunning, restored Victorian-style homes; lush, tropical greenery; and the old Bahama Village. Make sure not to miss the sunset celebration at Mallory Square and, if possible, do dinner at **Blue Heaven** in the Bahama Village. Then hit the Duval Street bars if you're so inclined. The next day, either spend the day relaxing at your hotel pool—we recommend the **Gardens Hotel** or **Simonton Court** for a true Key West experience—or explore the Historic Seaport and all its shops and Key West kitsch. See p. 292.

Day 3: Miami: Coral Gables, Little Havana & South Beach ★★★

Take the 3-hour drive on the Overseas Highway to **Miami**—one of the most scenic drives you'll ever take, albeit sometimes a boring one. If you've seen it before, just fly. Make a pit stop in Coral Gables where you can either get a bite to eat on **Miracle Mile** or cool off in the **Venetian Pool.** If you like what you see, check into the historic **Biltmore Hotel.** If not, make sure to at least see the hotel and then continue on to SW Eighth Street, otherwise known as **Calle Ocho,** the heart of Little Havana. Either take an organized walking tour or go it on your own. A tour is recommended for those who are interested in the history of the neighborhood. If not, peruse the cigar stores, the old men playing dominoes in Domino Park, and buy an old Cuban phone book at Little Havana to Go. Grab a Cuban coffee at **Versailles** and then head north to South Beach and watch the cruise ships leave from **Smith & Wollensky.** Spend the night in the trendy South of Fifth area at the **Hotel St. Augustine,** known for its sublime spa bathroom, or for a real spa hotel on the bay, **The Standard,** which is anything but. See p. 86.

Day 4: South Beach ★★★

Wake up early and catch the sunrise on the beach. Have breakfast at the Front Porch Café. Stake your claim on the sand and spend the morning on the beach or check out the original Miami supermodel: the Art Deco District via a walking tour. Hit Lincoln Road for lunch. Try **David's Café** for a delicious, inexpensive Cuban feast. Shop along Lincoln and Collins avenues before having a cocktail at the **Rose Bar at the Delano Hotel.** Walk that drink off out back on the paved path along the beach and stop at the delightfully deco **Raleigh** for an old-fashioned cocktail or freshly muddled mojito. Return to your own hotel for a disco nap; wake up around 9pm. Have dinner at **Prime One Twelve** if you can score a reservation (if not, try the equally sublime, yet lower key **Red the Steakhouse** around the corner), and then hit the clubs: **Wall, Mansion, Cameo,** and **SET.** If you're still up for the boogie, hop in a cab and head to **LIV** at the **Fontainebleau.** Grab a late night snack at **La Sandwicherie** or the **11th St. Diner** and then crash at your hotel.

Day 5: From South Beach to Fort Lauderdale ★★

Have breakfast and watch the club kids coming home from the night before at **Front Porch Café** or the **Big Pink.** Get in the car and take A1A north—the scenic route. Hit the Hollywood Beach Broadwalk, our version of Atlantic City without the casinos. If you're hungry for lunch, have the world's best burger at **Le Tub.** Continue along A1A until you reach the famous Fort Lauderdale strip. Take a break at the world-famous **Elbo Room** and watch the action on the beach. If you can't, uh, elbow your way to the bar there, consider cocktails at Beach Place where spectacular views of the ocean make it okay to go to a chain restaurant on vacation. Spend the night at the **Riverside Hotel** on Las Olas Boulevard or, for a trendier stay, the **W Fort Lauderdale.**

Day 6: Sand, Seminoles & Santana ★★

Hit the famous Fort Lauderdale Beach, where Frankie and Annette used to play beach blanket bingo. Then take a bit of a diversion and head west to the **Seminole Hard Rock Hotel and Casino** where you may catch a concert by a Billboard-charting artist or even Jerry Seinfeld; hit the jackpot on one of the hundreds of slot machines (the hotel claims it pays out $12.9 million daily!); try your hand at black-jack and poker; or relax by the pool which is almost as nice, if not nicer, than the one at the Hard Rock Hotel in Vegas. See p. 346. Also check out the **Seminole Okalee Indian Village and Museum,** at the Seminole Hard Rock Hotel & Casino, 5716 Seminole Way, Hollywood (*©* **954/797-5551;** www.semtribe.com) before heading over and out to spot signs of real wildlife in the Everglades.

Days 7 & 8: Seminole Indian Reservation & Everglades National Park ★★★

Travel 45 minutes west on I-75 to the Seminole Indian Reservation, which encompasses over 69,000 acres of the Everglades' Big Cypress Swamp. Hop on a swamp buggy at the **Billie Swamp Safari** to see hogs, bison, 'gators, and deer. Continue west to Everglades City, check into the **Ivey House B&B,** and ask owners Sandee and David if they can hook you up with a special, insiders' tour of the 'Glades.

Days 9 & 10: The Palm Beaches ★★

Skip Boca Raton unless you feel like hitting the Town Center mall and head directly to Delray Beach, where its Atlantic Avenue is full of stores, restaurants, bars, and clubs. Check into the **Sundy House** and peruse the hotel's Taru Gardens. The next

HOLLYWOOD SOUTH—celebrities' SOUTH BEACH (& BEYOND)

It's not that ironic that the French Riviera is now billing itself as a European South Beach. Between all the jet-setters, celebrities, rock stars, and magazine stories on the place, it's about time! Some people come to South Florida just for a taste of this fabulous life. This is not an itinerary per se, but the following tips will help you plan a busy social schedule so you don't miss out on a Paris or Diddy sighting.

Haute Hotels Wherever you decide to stay, it won't matter, because if you're looking for celebrities on South Beach, you'll end up spying most of them by the end of your trip. We suggest you do breakfast at the Blue Door Restaurant at the Delano, where you may catch a glimpse of Jamie Foxx sunbathing by the wading pool. Linger as long as you are able to before heading next door to the Raleigh, where you may find *Vogue* editor Anna Wintour hiding behind her sunglasses and sipping an iced tea at the pool. Grab some lunch if you're hungry or wait until you go next door to the Shore Club, where Nobu acts as the hotel's resident star magnet, a place where Britney Spears always stops when in town. Hit Lincoln Road and see if you can spot J-Lo. If you don't, she's probably at the Bal Harbour Shops, so you may want to go there. For early evening cocktails, head to The Setai, where Jay Z, Beyoncé, Bono, and Lenny Kravitz have all partied. Take your drink either at the bar indoors or outside by the pool. Next door at the W South Beach, young Hollywood rules, and you may have to Google some of your sightings to discover you're downing a beer next to the 'tween star from the *Twilight* series. For a mature caliber of celebrity, head to Mr Chow where the A-listers dine on exorbitant Chinese food. For a little *Gossip Girl* with your sunset cocktail, the Mondrian on South Beach's bayside is command central for celebrity-studded cocktail chatter. For so-called reality star sightings as well as the possible Lindsay Lohan or Fergie sighting, the Gansevoort South and its STK Miami, Philippe and Plunge rooftop pool are the places to check. Hit the Ritz-Carlton South Beach for a nightcap, where some of the *Desperate Housewives* have stayed. Off of South Beach, you'll probably spot the likes of

day, do not miss the **Morikami Museum and Japanese Gardens** before moving on to West Palm Beach where you should check into the **Hotel Biba** and do a little antiques shopping in downtown West Palm. At night, check out the clubs and restaurants in downtown West Palm, on Clematis Street. Make sure to have a beer and enjoy the view at **Bradley's.**

Day 11: From Mar-A-Lago to the Moon—Well, Jupiter, at Least ★★

Spend the morning driving around Palm Beach proper, making sure to stop and catch a glimpse of Donald Trump's palatial **Mar-A-Lago.** Stop by **Worth Avenue** to see the ladies with little dogs who lunch and shop. It's the Rodeo Drive of South

Miley Cyrus and Lady Gaga at the Fontainebleau, Tom Cruise and Katie Holmes, J-Lo, or Janet Jackson, either at the Viceroy on Brickell, the Mandarin Oriental on Brickell Key, the Four Seasons Miami and, on Key Biscayne, the Ritz-Carlton Key Biscayne. For details on Miami hotels, see p. 69.

Stars & Bars Keeping in mind that you can go to any of these places on any given night, some clubs do have specific nights that are better than others in terms of crowds and celebs. On Monday night clubs are usually at rest, so hit the hotel bars at the W South Beach, the Gansevoort South, Mondrian, Delano, Shore Club, and Setai. Tuesday night, head to the Lenny Kravitz–designed Florida Room below the Delano. Thursday night, check out Skybar and Set, where you're likely to run into everyone from Mary J. Blige and her famous friends to Simon Cowell, Randy Jackson, and Ryan Seacrest. On Friday, head to Cameo, where Matt Damon actually met his wife, Luciana, who was a cocktail waitress there. On Saturday it's all about LIV, where any celeb who's in town will stop by—if not for the evening, at least for one drink.

On Saturday, Mansion's hot, but even hotter is WALL, the new club at the W South Beach, where a keen eye may spot an A-lister lounging in or dancing on a banquette. Sunday afternoon, thankfully, is the day of pool parties—Shore Club, Viceroy, and Mondrian all have one—where you can lounge by the pool along with the likes of a chart topping rapper to a starlet on *Beverly Hills, 90210* revisited. On any given night you may run into Bono or Lou Reed at Ted's Hideaway or Mac's Club Deuce, two of Miami's beloved dive bars. For details on Miami's nightlife, see p. 222.

Eating It Up (Stars Eat, Too) Among the places you'll find celebs stuffing their faces: Asia de Cuba; Mr Chow; Philippe; Macaluso's; Nobu; Nemo; The Restaurant at the Setai; DeVito South Beach; The Blue Door; Barton G. The Restaurant; Prime One Twelve; Azul; Michael's Genuine Food & Drink; Eos; Scarpetta; Hakkasan; Burger & Beer Joint; News Café; China Grill; and, we kid you not, La Sandwicherie, the late-night sandwich bar across the street from Club Deuce. For more on Miami's dining scene, see p. 114.

Florida, truly, and you can't miss the people-watching there. For an actual glimpse inside a Palm Beach manse, go to the **Flagler Museum** where you can explore Whitehall, Standard Oil tycoon Henry Flagler's wedding present to his third wife. Go back to reality and head toward Jupiter, the home of Burt Reynolds. Check into the **Ritz-Carlton Palm Beach.** See p. 380.

Days 12 & 13: The Treasure Coast

You may not find gold in your exploration of the Treasure Coast but you will find **Jonathan Dickinson State Park on Hutchinson Island,** where you should rent a canoe and explore the plethora of botanical treasures. If you're into snorkeling and diving and feel like delving deeper, check out the most popular artificial reef in the area, **the USS *Rankin,*** an old WWII ship that was sunk in 1988, located 7 miles east-northeast of the St. Lucie Inlet. Check into the Hutchinson Island Marriott Beach Resort and Marina and consider taking the ***Loxahatchee Queen*** for a 2-hour tour of the area. Next, head to Vero Beach and Sebastian for a taste of old Florida. Sports fans will want to check out Dodgertown despite the fact that no major league team currently Springs there. Check into the completely unique **Driftwood Resort** or, for music fans, Gloria Estefan's oceanfront **Costa d'Este Beach Resort** where the only rhythm that's gonna get you is that of the waves gently swishing on the ocean. If not, check into the **Vero Beach Hotel and Club** and do dinner at the **Ocean Grill** if your budget allows. If not, The Beachside Restaurant at the Palm Court Resort is a great spot for blue-plate specials and, for NY-style pizza, **Nino's** can't be beat.

Day 14: Lake Okeechobee or Bust?

If you can't extend your trip to include a side trip to Lake Okeechobee, consider it for next time. In the meantime, fly home out of either Palm Beach International Airport, 35 miles south of Vero Beach, or the Melbourne International Airport, which is less than 35 miles north of Vero Beach.

SOUTH FLORIDA, FAMILY STYLE, IN 1 WEEK

Despite a thriving nightlife and sometimes R-rated (or worse) sensibility—and dress code (or lack thereof)—South Florida is definitely a kid-friendly destination. While we don't recommend you taking the little ones to South Beach, there are tons of other places that are family friendly and won't have the kids screaming that they wish they were at Disney World!

Days 1 & 2: Key Biscayne ★★★

The **Ritz-Carlton Key Biscayne** has fabulous children's programs, not to mention pretty cool diversions for adults, too. Spend a day checking out the resorts, and then skip the **Miami Seaquarium**—unless the kids want to swim with the dolphins—and spend the day at the **Marjory Stoneman Douglas Biscayne Nature Center** where the entire family can explore an ancient fossil tidal pool. If there's time left, check out the **Bill Baggs Cape Florida State Park** and rent a hydrobike. See p. 99.

Days 3 & 4: Coral Gables ★★★ & South Miami ★★

Get an early start and head south to Homestead's legendary **Coral Castle.** After the kids tire of seeing this wacky attraction, grab lunch at the family-friendly, family-run Mexican mainstay, **El Toro Taco.** On your way to Coral Gables, make a stop at **Miami Metro Zoo or Monkey Jungle** depending on your preference in animals, and then clean off that stinky animal scent with a splash in Coral Gables's resplendent, refreshing **Venetian Pool.** If you're up for it, check out **Vizcaya Museum and Gardens** and/or the **Miami Science Museum.** After working up an appetite, take the kids for a big dinner at **Rio's Churrascaria,** where they'll enjoy holding up their signs when they're ready to eat more meat!

Days 5 & 6: Miami–Port St. Lucie ★★★

Before leaving Miami, make sure to stop at the **Miami Children's Museum** where the kids can spend a few hours channeling their inner grown up in a bona fide TV and recording studio. If they'd rather see animal antics, head across the causeway to **Jungle Island.** Grab a TV dinner at the G-rated **Big Pink** on South Beach and then hit the road to Vero Beach and check into the **Club-Med Sandpiper** on the St. Lucie River, where there are four different children's clubs for ages 4 months all the way up to 13 years. En route to Vero, you may want to take the kids to West Palm Beach's whimsical **Playmobil Fun Park** or on a safari through **Lion Country Safari** and then grab lunch at **Tom's Place for Ribs.** See p. 385.

Day 7: Vero Beach ★★★

As if Club Med doesn't have enough for the family to do—or not do—you may want to take the kids out to **Disney's Vero Beach Resort,** which is situated on 71 acres of beach and features that Disney vibe the kids may be in the mood for at this point!

GETTING TO KNOW MIAMI

Apropos jokes about bad drivers, Grandma forgetting to shut off her turn signal, and traffic nightmares aside, Miami is a fascinating city to explore, be it by foot, bike, scooter, boat, or car. Because of its larger-than-life persona, Miami may seem a lot bigger than it really is, but although the city comprises many different neighborhoods, it's really not that difficult to learn the lay of the land. Much like the bodies beautiful on Ocean Drive, the Magic City is a tidy package that's a little less than 2,000 square miles.

5

ORIENTATION
Arriving

Originally carved out of scrubland in 1928 by Pan American Airlines, **Miami International Airport (MIA)** has become 2nd in the United States for international passenger traffic and 10th in the world for total passengers. Despite the heavy traffic, the airport is quite user-friendly and not as much of a hassle as you'd think. You can change money or use your ATM card at Bank of America, located near the exit. Visitor information is available 24 hours a day at the **Miami International Airport Main Visitor Counter,** Concourse E, second level (② **305/876-7000**). Information is also available at **www.miami-airport.com**. Because MIA is the busiest airport in South Florida, travelers may want to consider flying into the less crowded **Fort Lauderdale Hollywood International Airport (FLL)** (② **954/359-1200**), which is closer to north Miami than MIA, or the **Palm Beach International Airport (PBI)** (② **561/471-7420**), which is about 1½ hours from Miami.

GETTING INTO TOWN

Miami International Airport is about 6 miles west of downtown and about 10 miles from the beaches, so it's likely you can get from the plane to your hotel room in less than half an hour. Of course, if you're arriving from an international destination, it will take more time to go through Customs and Immigration.

BY CAR All the major car-rental firms operate off-site branches reached via shuttles from the airline terminals. See the "Rentals" section, under "Getting Around," on p. 62, for a list of major rental companies in Miami. Signs at the airport's exit clearly point the way to various parts of the city, but the car-rental firm should also give you directions to your destination. If you're arriving late at night, you might want to take a taxi to your hotel and have the car delivered to you the next day.

BY TAXI Taxis line up in front of a dispatcher's desk outside the airport's arrivals terminals. Most cabs are metered, though some have flat rates to popular destinations. The fare should be about $20 to Coral Gables, $25 to downtown, and $35 to South Beach, plus tip, which should be about 15% (add more for each bag the driver handles). Depending on traffic, the ride to Coral Gables or downtown takes about 15 to 20 minutes, and to South Beach, 20 to 25 minutes.

BY VAN OR LIMO Group limousines (multipassenger vans) circle the arrivals area looking for fares. Destinations are posted on the front of each van, and a flat rate is charged for door-to-door service to the area marked.

SuperShuttle (☎ 305/871-2000; www.supershuttle.com) is one of the largest airport operators, charging between $10 and $50 per person for a ride within the county. Its vans operate 24 hours a day and accept American Express, MasterCard, and Visa. This is a cheaper alternative to a cab (if you are traveling alone or with one other person), but be prepared to be in the van for quite some time, as you may have to make several stops to drop passengers off before you reach your own destination. SuperShuttle also has begun service from Palm Beach International Airport to the surrounding communities. The door-to-door, shared-ride service operates from the airport to Stuart, Fort Pierce, Palm Beach, and Broward counties.

> ## Words to Live By
>
> *I figure marriage is kind of like Miami; it's hot and stormy, and occasionally a little dangerous . . . but if it's really so awful, why is there still so much traffic?*
> —Sarah Jessica Parker's character, Gwen Marcus, in *Miami Rhapsody*

Private limousine arrangements can be made in advance through your local travel agent. A one-way meet-and-greet service should cost about $50. Limo services include **Aventura Limousine** (☎ 800/944-9886) and **Limo Miami** (☎ 305/742-5900).

BY PUBLIC TRANSPORTATION Public transportation in South Florida is a major hassle bordering on a nightmare. Painfully slow and unreliable, buses heading downtown leave the airport only once per hour (from the arrivals level), and connections are spotty, at best. It could take about 1½ hours to get to South Beach via public transportation. Journeys to downtown and Coral Gables, however, are more direct. The fare is $2, plus an additional 50¢ for a transfer. For those heading to South Beach from the airport, a new bus route, the Airport-Beach Flyer Route, provides direct express service from MIA to Miami Beach and costs $2.35. With only one minor stop en route, the trip to the beach takes about a half-hour. Not bad.

Visitor Information

The most up-to-date information is provided by the **Greater Miami Convention and Visitor's Bureau,** 701 Brickell Ave., Ste. 700, Miami, FL 33131 (© **800/933-8448** or 305/539-3000; fax 305/530-3113). Several chambers of commerce in Greater Miami will send out information on their particular neighborhoods.

If you arrive at the Miami International Airport, you can pick up visitor information at the airport's main visitor counter on the second floor of Concourse E. It's open 24 hours a day.

Always check local newspapers for special events during your visit. The city's only daily, the *Miami Herald,* is a good source for current-events listings, particularly the "Weekend" section in Friday's edition. Even better is the free weekly alternative paper the *Miami New Times,* available in bright red boxes throughout the city.

Information on everything from dining to entertainment in Miami is available on the Internet at www.miami.citysearch.com, www.citysbest.aol.com/south-florida, www.miaminewtimes.com, www.miami.com, and www.miamiherald.com.

City Layout

Miami seems confusing at first, but quickly becomes easy to navigate. The small cluster of buildings that make up the downtown area is at the geographical heart of the city. In relation to downtown, the airport is northwest, the beaches are east, Coconut Grove is south, Coral Gables is west, and the rest of the city is north.

FINDING AN ADDRESS Miami is divided into dozens of areas with official and unofficial boundaries. Street numbering in the city of Miami is fairly straight-forward, but you must first be familiar with the numbering system. The mainland is divided into four sections (NE, NW, SE, and SW) by the intersection of Flagler Street and Miami Avenue. Flagler divides Miami from north to south, and Miami Avenue divides the city from east to west. It's helpful to remember that avenues generally run north-south, while streets go east-west. Street numbers (1st St., 2nd St., and so forth) start from here and increase as you go farther out from this intersection, as do numbers of avenues, places, courts, terraces, and lanes. Streets in Hialeah are the exceptions to this pattern; they are listed separately in map indexes.

Getting around the barrier islands that make up Miami Beach is easier than moving around the mainland. Street numbering starts with First Street, near Miami Beach's southern tip, and goes up to 192nd Street, in the northern part of Sunny Isles. As in the city of Miami, some streets in Miami Beach have numbers as well as names. When listed in this book, both name and number are given.

The numbered streets in Miami Beach are not the geographical equivalents of those on the mainland, but they are close. For example, the 79th Street Causeway runs into 71st Street on Miami Beach.

STREET MAPS It's easy to get lost in sprawling Miami, so a reliable map is essential. The **Trakker Map of Miami,** available at most bookstores, is a four-color accordion map that encompasses all of Dade County. Some maps of Miami list streets according to area, so you'll have to know which part of the city you are looking for before the street can be found.

The Neighborhoods in Brief

South Beach–The Art Deco District South Beach's 10 miles of beach are alive with a frenetic, circuslike atmosphere and are center stage for a motley crew of characters, from eccentric locals, seniors, snowbirds, and college students to gender benders, celebrities, club kids, and curiosity seekers. Individuality is as widely accepted on South Beach as Visa and MasterCard.

Bolstered by a Caribbean-chic cafe society and a sexually charged, tragically hip nightlife, people-watching on South Beach (1st St.–23rd St.) is almost as good as a front-row seat at a Milan fashion show. But although the beautiful people do flock to South Beach, the models aren't the only sights worth drooling over. The thriving Art Deco District within South Beach has the largest concentration of Art Deco architecture in the world (in 1979, much of South Beach was listed in the National Register of Historic Places). The pastel-hued structures are supermodels in their own right—only *these* models improve with age.

Miami Beach In the fabulous '50s, Miami Beach was America's true Riviera. The stomping ground of choice for the Rat Pack and notorious mobsters such as Al Capone, its huge self-contained resort hotels were vacations unto themselves, providing a full day's worth of meals, activities, and entertainment. Then in the 1960s and 1970s, people who fell in love with Miami began to buy apartments rather than rent hotel rooms. Tourism declined, and many area hotels fell into disrepair.

However, since the late 1980s and South Beach's renaissance, Miami Beach has experienced a tide of revitalization. Huge beach hotels, such as the recently renovated and Vegas-esque Fontainebleau and Eden Roc, are finding their niche with new international tourist markets and are attracting large convention crowds. New generations of Americans are quickly rediscovering the qualities that originally made Miami Beach so popular, and they are finding out that the sand and surf now come with a thriving international city—a technologically savvy city complete with free Wi-Fi with 95% coverage outside, which means on the sand, and 70% indoors up to the second floor of any building.

Before Miami Beach turns into Surfside, there's North Beach, where there are uncrowded beaches, some restaurants, and examples of Miami Modernism architecture. For information on North Beach and its slow renaissance, go to www.gonorthbeach.com.

Surfside, Bal Harbour, and **Sunny Isles** make up the north part of the beach (island). Hotels, motels, restaurants, and beaches line Collins Avenue and, with some outstanding exceptions, the farther north one goes, the cheaper lodging becomes. Excellent prices, location, and facilities make Surfside and Sunny Isles attractive places to stay, although, despite a slow-going renaissance, they are still a little rough around the edges. Revitalization is in the works for these areas, and, while it's highly unlikely they will ever become as chic as South Beach, there is potential for this, especially as South Beach falls prey to the inevitable spoiler: commercialism. Keep in mind that beachfront properties are at a premium, so many of the area's moderately priced hotels have been converted to condominiums, leaving fewer and fewer affordable places to stay.

In exclusive and ritzy Bal Harbour, few hotels besides the swanky Regent and expected-to-open-in-2011 St. Regis, remain amid the many beachfront condominium towers. Instead, fancy homes, tucked away on the bay, hide behind gated communities, and the Rodeo Drive of Miami (known as the Bal Harbour Shops) attracts shoppers who don't flinch at four-, five-, and six-figure price tags.

Note that **North Miami Beach,** a residential area near the Dade-Broward County line (north of 163rd St.; part of N. Dade County), is a misnomer. It is actually northwest of Miami Beach, on the mainland, and has no beaches, though it does have some of Miami's better restaurants and shops. Located within North Miami Beach is the posh residential community of **Aventura,** best known for its high-priced condos, the Fairmont Turnberry Isle Resort, and the Aventura Mall.

Note: South Beach, the historic Art Deco District, is treated as a separate neighborhood from Miami Beach.

Key Biscayne Miami's forested and secluded Key Biscayne is technically a barrier island and is not part of the Florida Keys. This island is nothing like its southern neighbors. Located south of Miami Beach, off the shores of Coconut Grove, Key Biscayne is protected from the troubles of the mainland by the long Rickenbacker Causeway and its $1.25 toll.

Largely an exclusive residential community with million-dollar homes and sweeping water views, Key Biscayne also offers visitors great public beaches, a top (read: pricey) resort hotel, world-class tennis facilities, and a few decent restaurants. Hobie Beach, adjacent to the causeway, is the city's premier spot for windsurfing, sailboarding, and jet-skiing (see "Watersports" in chapter 8). On the island's southern tip, Bill Baggs State Park has great beaches, bike paths, and dense forests for picnicking and partying.

Downtown Miami's downtown boasts one of the world's most beautiful cityscapes. Unfortunately, that's about all it offers—for now. During the day, a vibrant community of students, businesspeople, and merchants makes its way through the bustling streets, where vendors sell fresh-cut pineapples and mangoes while young consumers on shopping sprees lug bags and boxes. However, at night, downtown is mostly desolate (except for NE 11th St., where there is a burgeoning nightlife scene) and not a place where you'd want to get lost. The downtown area does have a mall (Bayside Marketplace, where many cruise passengers come to browse), some culture (Metro-Dade Cultural Center), and a few

decent restaurants, as well as the sprawling American Airlines Arena (home to the Miami Heat). A downtown revitalization project in the works promises a cultural arts center, urban-chic dwellings and lofts, and an assortment of hip boutiques, eateries, and bars, all to bring downtown back to a life it never really had. The city has even rebranded the downtown area with a new ad campaign, intentionally misspelling it as DWNTWN to inexplicably appeal to hipsters. We don't get it either. The **Downtown Miami Partnership** offers guided historic walking tours daily at 10:30am (✆ **305/379-7070**). For more information on downtown, go to www.downtown miami.com.

Design District With restaurants springing up between galleries and furniture stores galore, the Design District is, as locals say, the new South Beach, adding a touch of New York's SoHo to an area formerly known as downtown Miami's "Don't Go." The district, which is a hotbed for furniture-import companies, interior designers, architects, and more, has also become a player in Miami's ever-changing nightlife. Its bars, lounges, clubs, and restaurants—including one of Miami's best, Michael's Genuine Food and Drink—ranging from überchic and retro to progressive and indie, have helped the area become hipster central for South Beach expatriates and artsy bohemian types. In anticipation of its growing popularity, the district has also banded together to create an up-to-date website, www.designmiami.com, which includes a calendar of events, such as the internationally lauded Art Basel, which attracts the who's who of the art world. The district is loosely defined as the area bounded by NE Second Avenue, NE Fifth Avenue East and West, and NW 36th Street to the south.

Midtown/Wynwood What used to be called El Barrio is now one of Miami's hippest, still burgeoning areas. Just north of downtown and roughly divided by I-395 to the south, I-195 to the north, I-95 to the west, and Biscayne Boulevard to the east,

Wynwood actually includes the Miami Design District, but has developed an identity of its own thanks to an exploding, albeit still very rough and gritty, arts scene made popular by cheap rents and major exposure during Art Basel Miami Beach. While there are still only a very small handful of bars and restaurants, Wynwood is an edgy area for creative types with loft and gallery spaces affordable and aplenty—for now. Also within Wynwood is Midtown Miami, a mall-like town center complex of apartment buildings surrounded by shops—namely Target—and restaurants. Like its Wynwood neighbor, it's gritty and a work in progress favored by young hipster types who aren't averse to living in transitional neighborhoods.

Biscayne Corridor From downtown, near Bayside, to the 70s (affectionately known as the Upper East Side), where trendy curio shops and upscale restaurants are slowly opening, Biscayne Boulevard is aspiring to reclaim itself as a safe thoroughfare where tourists can wine, dine, and shop. Once known for sketchy, dilapidated 1950s- and 1960s-era hotels that had fallen on hard times, this boulevard is getting a boost from residents fleeing the high prices of the beaches in search of affordable housing. They're renovating Biscayne block by block, trying to make this famous boulevard worthy of a Sunday drive.

Little Havana If you've never been to Cuba, just visit this small section of Miami and you'll come pretty close. The sounds, tastes, and rhythms are very reminiscent of Cuba's capital city, and some say you don't have to speak a word of English to live an independent life here—even street signs are in Spanish and English.

Cuban coffee shops, tailor and furniture stores, and inexpensive restaurants line Calle Ocho (pronounced *Ka*-yey *O*-choh), SW Eighth Street, the region's main thoroughfare. In Little Havana, salsa and merengue beats ring loudly from old record stores while old men in *guayaberas* (loose-fitting cotton short-sleeved shirts) smoke cigars over their daily game of dominoes. The spotlight focused on the neighborhood during the Elián González situation in 2000, but the area was previously noted for the groups of artists and nocturnal types who had moved their galleries and performance spaces here, sparking culturally charged neobohemian nightlife.

Coral Gables "The City Beautiful," created by George Merrick in the early 1920s, is one of Miami's first planned developments. Houses here were built in a Mediterranean style along lush, tree-lined streets that open onto beautifully carved plazas, many with centerpiece fountains. The best architectural examples of the era have Spanish-style tiled roofs and are built from Miami oolite, native limestone commonly called "coral rock." The Gables's European-flaired shopping and commerce center is home to many thriving corporations. Coral Gables also has landmark hotels, great golfing, upscale shopping to rival Bal Harbour, and some of the city's best restaurants, headed by renowned chefs.

Coconut Grove An arty, hippie hangout in the psychedelic '60s, Coconut Grove once had residents who dressed in swirling tie-dyed garb. Nowadays, they prefer the uniform color schemes of the Gap. Chain stores, theme restaurants, a megaplex, and bars galore make Coconut Grove a commercial success, but this gentrification has pushed most alternative types out. Ritzier types have now resurfaced here, thanks, in part, to the antiboho Ritz-Carlton Coconut Grove (p. 108) and the Mayfair, which is in its umpteenth resurgence as a boutique hotel. The intersection of Grand Avenue, Main Highway, and McFarlane Road pierces the area's heart. Right in the center of it all is CocoWalk, filled with boutiques, eateries, and bars. Sidewalks here are often crowded, especially at night, when University of Miami students come out to play.

Southern Miami–Dade County To locals, South Miami is both a specific area, southwest of Coral Gables, and a general region that encompasses all of southern Dade

The Neighborhoods in Brief

County, including Kendall, Perrine, Cutler Ridge, and Homestead. For the purposes of clarity, this book has grouped all these southern suburbs under the rubric "Southern Miami–Dade County." The area is heavily residential and packed with strip malls amid a few remaining plots of farmland.

Tourists don't usually stay in these parts, unless they are on their way to the Everglades or the Keys. However, Southern Miami–Dade County contains many of the city's top attractions (see chapter 8), meaning that you're likely to spend at least some of your time in Miami here.

GETTING AROUND

Officially, Miami-Dade County has opted for a "unified, multimodal transportation network," which basically means you can get around the city by train, bus, and taxi. However, in practice, the network doesn't work very well. Things have improved somewhat thanks to the $17 billion Peoples' Transportation Plan, which has offered a full range of transportation services at several community-based centers throughout the county, but, unless you are going from downtown Miami to a not-too-distant spot, you are better off in a rental car or taxi.

With the exception of downtown Coconut Grove and South Beach, Miami is not a walker's city. Because it is so spread out, most attractions are too far apart to make walking between them feasible. In fact, most Miamians are so used to driving that they do so even when going just a few blocks.

By Public Transportation

BY RAIL Two rail lines, operated by the **Metro-Dade Transit Agency** (© 305/770-3131 for information; www.co.miami-dade.fl.us/transit), run in concert with each other.

Metrorail, the city's modern high-speed commuter train, is a 21-mile elevated line that travels north-south, between downtown Miami and the southern suburbs. Locals like to refer to this semiuseless rail system as Metro*fail*. If you are staying in Coral Gables or Coconut Grove, you can park your car at a nearby station and ride the rails downtown. However, that's about it. There are plans to extend the system to service Miami International Airport, but until those tracks are built, these trains don't go most places tourists go, with the exception of Vizcaya (p. 185) in Coconut Grove. Metrorail operates daily from about 6am to midnight. The fare is $2.

Metromover, a 4½-mile elevated line, circles the downtown area and connects with Metrorail at the Government Center stop. Riding on rubber tires, the single-car train winds past many of the area's most important attractions and its shopping and business districts. You may not go very far on the Metromover, but you will get a beautiful perspective from the towering height of the suspended rails. System hours are daily from about 6am to midnight, and the ride is free.

BY BUS Miami's suburban layout is not conducive to getting around by bus. Lines operate and maps are available, but instead of getting to know the city, you'll find that relying on bus transportation will acquaint you only with how it feels to wait at bus stops. In short, a bus ride in Miami is grueling. You can get a bus map by mail, either from the Greater Miami Convention and Visitor's Bureau (see "Visitor Information," earlier in this chapter) or by writing the Metro-Dade Transit System, 3300 NW 32nd Ave., Miami, FL 33142. In Miami, call © **305/770-3131** for public-transit information. The fare is $2. When on South Beach, however, consider the **South Beach Local,** a shuttle bus that runs every 15 to 20 minutes from First Street all the way to Collins Park at 21st Street and Park Avenue for just 25 cents a ride. Look for signs that say South Beach Local. Buses run every 12 minutes Monday through Saturday from 10am to 6pm and every 20 minutes from 7:45 to 10am and from 6pm to 1am. On Sundays, the bus will come every 12 minutes from noon to 6pm and every 20 minutes from 10am to noon and from 6pm to 1am. It makes several stops, but it's a lot cheaper than a cab.

By Car

Tales circulate about vacationers who have visited Miami without a car, but they are very few indeed. If you are counting on exploring the city, even to a modest degree, a car is essential. Miami's restaurants, hotels, and attractions are far from one another, so any other form of transportation is relatively impractical. You won't need a car, however, if you are spending your entire vacation at a resort, are traveling directly to the Port of Miami for a cruise, or are here for a short stay centered on one area of the city, such as South Beach, where everything is within walking distance and parking is a costly nightmare.

When driving across a causeway or through downtown, allow extra time to reach your destination because of frequent drawbridge openings. Some bridges open about every half-hour for large sailing vessels to make their way through the wide bays and canals that crisscross the city, stalling traffic for several minutes.

RENTALS It seems as though every car-rental company, big and small, has at least one office in Miami. Consequently, the city is one of the cheapest places in the world to rent a car. Many firms regularly advertise prices in the neighborhood of $150 per week for their economy cars. You should also check with your airline: There are often special discounts when you book a flight and reserve your rental car simultaneously. A minimum age, generally 25, is usually required of renters; some rental agencies have also set maximum ages! A national car-rental broker, **Car Rental Referral Service** (© **800/404-4482**), can often find companies willing to rent to drivers between the ages of 21 and 24 and can also get discounts from major companies as well as some regional ones.

National car-rental companies, with toll-free numbers, include **Alamo** (www. alamo.com), **Avis** (www.avis.com), **Budget** (www.budget.com), **Dollar** (www.dollar. com), **Hertz** (www.hertz.com), **National** (www.nationalcar.com), and **Thrifty** (www.thrifty.com). One excellent company that has offices in every conceivable part of town and offers extremely competitive rates is **Enterprise** (www.enterprise.com).

Comparison shop before you make any decisions—car-rental prices can fluctuate more than airfares. Many car-rental companies also offer cellular phones or electronic map rentals. It might be wise to opt for these additional safety features (the phone will definitely come in handy if you get lost), although the cost can be exorbitant.

Finally, think about splurging on a convertible. Not only are convertibles one of the best ways to see the beautiful surroundings, but they're also an ideal way to perfect a tan!

PARKING Always keep plenty of quarters on hand to feed hungry meters, most of which have been removed in favor of those pesky parking payment stations where you feed a machine and get a printed receipt to display on your dash. Or, on Miami Beach, stop by the chamber of commerce at 1920 Meridian Ave. or any Publix grocery store to buy a magnetic **parking card** in denominations of $10, $20, or $25. Parking is usually plentiful (except on South Beach and Coconut Grove), but when it's not, be careful: Fines for illegal parking can be stiff, starting at $18 for an expired meter and going way up from there.

In addition to parking garages, valet services are commonplace and often used. Because parking is such a premium in bustling South Beach as well as in Coconut Grove, prices tend to be jacked up—especially at night and when there are special events (day or night). You can expect to pay an average of $5 to $15 for parking in these areas.

LOCAL DRIVING RULES Florida law allows drivers to make a right turn on a red light after a complete stop, unless otherwise indicated. In addition, all passengers are required to wear seat belts, and children 3 and under must be securely fastened in government-approved car seats.

By Taxi

If you're not planning on traveling much within the city (and especially if you plan on spending your vacation within the confines of South Beach's Art Deco District), an occasional taxi is a good alternative to renting a car and dealing with the parking hassles that come with renting your own car. Taxi meters start at about $2.50 for the first quarter-mile and cost around $2.40 for each additional mile. You can blame the rate hikes on the gas crunch. There are standard flat-rate charges for frequently traveled routes—for example, Miami Beach's Convention Center to Coconut Grove will cost about $25. During 2008's roller coaster year of insane oil prices, many cabs instituted a fuel surcharge costing $1 extra per person. Despite the improvement in gas prices, may cabs kept the surcharge. For specifics on rate increases and surcharges, go to www.taxifarefinder.com.

Major cab companies include **Yellow Cab** (© **305/444-4444**) and, on Miami Beach, **Central** (© **305/532-5555**).

By Bike

Miami is a biker's paradise, especially on Miami Beach, where the hard-packed sand and boardwalks make it an easy and scenic route. However, unless you are a former New York City bike messenger, you won't want to use a bicycle as your main means of transportation.

For more information on bicycles, including where to rent the best ones, see "More Ways to Play, Indoors & Out," in chapter 8.

[FastFACTS] MIAMI

Airport See "Orientation," earlier in this chapter.

American Express You'll find American Express offices in Bal Harbour at 9700 Collins Ave. (© **305/865-5959;** Mon–Sat 10am–6pm); and 32 Miracle Mile, Coral Gables (© **305/446-3381;** Mon–Fri 9am–5pm

and Sat 10am–4pm). To report lost or stolen traveler's checks, call © **800/221-7282.**

Area Code The original area code for Miami and

all of Dade County is 305. That is still the code for older phone numbers, but all phone numbers assigned since July 1998 have the area code 786 (SUN). For all local calls, even if you're just calling across the street, you must dial the area code (305 or 786) first. Even though the Keys still share the Dade County area code of 305, calls to there from Miami are considered long distance and must be preceded by 1-305. (Within the Keys, simply dial the seven-digit number.) The area codes for Fort Lauderdale are 954 and 754; for Palm Beach, Boca Raton, Vero Beach, and Port St. Lucie, it's 561.

Business Hours Banking hours vary, but most banks are open weekdays from 9am to 3pm. Several stay open until 5pm or so at least 1 day during the week, and most banks feature automated teller machines (ATMs) for 24-hour banking. Most stores are open daily from 10am to 6pm; however, there are many exceptions (noted in "Shopping," in chapter 9, beginning on p. 207). As far as business offices are concerned, Miami is generally a 9-to-5 town.

Car Rentals See "Getting Around," above.

Climate See "When to Go," in chapter 3.

Curfew Although not strictly enforced, there is an alleged curfew in effect for minors after 11pm on weeknights and midnight on weekends in all of Miami-Dade County. After those hours, children younger than 17 cannot be out on the streets or driving unless accompanied by a parent or on their way to work. Somehow, however, they still manage to sneak out and congregate in popular areas such as Coconut Grove and South Beach.

Dentists A&E Dental Associates, 11400 N. Kendall Dr., Mega Bank Building (✆ **305/271-7777;** www. aedental.com), offers round-the-clock care and accepts MasterCard and Visa. If that's too out of the way, Dr. Edderai specializes in emergency dental work and features a 24/7 call dental service at (✆ **305/798-7799**).

Doctors In an emergency, call an ambulance by dialing ✆ **911** (a free call) from any phone. The Dade County Medical Association sponsors a **Physician Referral Service** (✆ **305/324-8717**), weekdays from 9am to 5pm. **Health South Doctors' Hospital,** 5000 University Dr., Coral Gables (✆ **305/666-2111**), is a 285-bed acute-care hospital with a 24-hour physician-staffed emergency department.

Driving Rules See "Getting Around," above.

Drugstores See "Pharmacies," below.

Emergencies To reach the police, an ambulance, or the fire department, dial ✆ **911** from any phone. No coins are needed. Emergency hotlines include **Crisis Intervention** (✆ **305/358-HELP** [4357]) and the **Poison Information Center** (✆ **800/222-1222**).

Eyeglasses Pearle Vision Center, 7901 Biscayne Blvd. (✆ **305/754-5144**), can usually fill prescriptions in about an hour.

Hospitals See "Doctors," above.

Information See "Visitor Information," earlier in this chapter.

Internet Access Internet access is available at **Kafka's Cyber Cafe,** 1464 Washington Ave., South Beach (✆ **305/673-9669**); the **South Beach Internet Cafe,** 1106 Collins Ave. (✆ **305/532-4331**); and, no joke, the swanky all-in-one **Mobil Station,** at 2500 NW 87th Ave., Doral (✆ **305/477-2501**).

Laundry & Dry Cleaning Clean Machine Laundry, 226 12th St., South Beach (✆ **305/534-9429**), is convenient to South Beach's Art Deco hotels and is open 24 hours a day and features wash and fold services. **Coral Gables LaSalle Cleaners,** 250 Minorca Ave., Coral Gables (✆ **305/446-6458**), offers a lifesaving same-day service (as do most Miami dry cleaners, fyi) and is open weekdays from 7am to 7pm and Saturday from 8am to 3pm.

Liquor Laws Only adults 21 or older may legally purchase or consume alcohol in the state of Florida. Minors are usually permitted in bars, as long as the bars also serve food. Liquor laws are strictly enforced; if you look young, carry identification. Beer and wine are sold in most supermarkets and convenience stores. Most of the city of Miami's liquor stores are closed on Sunday. Liquor stores in the city of Miami Beach are open daily.

Lost Property If you lost something at the airport, call the **Airport Lost and Found** office (℡ 305/876-7377). If you lost something on the bus, Metrorail, or Metromover, call **Metro-Dade Transit Agency** (℡ 305/770-3131). If you lost something anywhere else, phone the **Dade County Police Lost and Found** (℡ 305/375-3366). You may also want to fill out a police report for insurance purposes.

Luggage Storage & Lockers In addition to the baggage check at Miami International Airport, most hotels offer luggage-storage facilities. If you are taking a cruise from the Port of Miami, bags can be stored in your ship's departure terminal.

Newspapers & Magazines The *Miami Herald* is the city's only English-language daily. It is especially known for its extensive Latin American coverage and has a decent Friday "Weekend" entertainment guide. The most respected alternative weekly is the giveaway tabloid called *New Times,* which contains up-to-date listings and reviews of food, films, theater, music, and whatever else is happening in town. Also free, if you can find it, is *Ocean Drive,* an oversize glossy magazine that's limited on text (no literary value) and heavy on ads and society photos. It's what you should read if you want to know who's who and where to go for fun; it's available at a number of chic South Beach boutiques and restaurants. It is also available at newsstands. In the same vein: *Miami Magazine* and *944 Magazine,* also free and available throughout the city.

For a large selection of foreign-language newspapers and magazines, check with any of the large bookstores or try **News Cafe,** 800 Ocean Dr., South Beach (℡ 305/538-6397). Adjacent to the **Van Dyke Cafe,** 846 Lincoln Rd., South Beach (℡ 305/534-3600), is a fantastic newsstand with magazines and newspapers from all over the world. Also check out **Eddie's News,** 1096 Normandy Dr., Miami Beach

(℡ 305/866-2661), and **Worldwide News,** 1629 NE 163rd St., North Miami Beach (℡ 305/940-4090).

Pharmacies Walgreens Pharmacy has dozens of locations all over town, including 8550 Coral Way (℡ 305/221-9271), in Coral Gables; 1845 Alton Rd. (℡ 305/531-8868), in South Beach; and 6700 Collins Ave. (℡ 305/861-6742), in Miami Beach. The branch at 5731 Bird Rd., at SW 40th Street (℡ 305/666-0757), is open 24 hours, as is **CVS,** which is usually located wherever there's a Walgreens or, if you're nearby, at 6460 S. Dixie Hwy., in South Miami (℡ 305/661-0778).

Photographic Needs For those who refuse to go digital, Walgreens and CVS (see above, under "Pharmacies") will develop film for the next day for about 15¢ a print. Both will also print digital photos for less than 20¢ each, usually in under an hour. See www.walgreens.com and www.cvs.com for many locations.

Police For emergencies, dial ℡ 911 from any phone. No coins are needed for this call. For other police matters, call ℡ 305/595-6263.

Post Office The **Main Post Office,** 2200 Milam Dairy Rd., Miami, FL 33152 (℡ 800/275-8777), is located west of the Miami

International Airport. Conveniently located post offices include 1300 Washington Ave. in South Beach and 3191 Grand Ave. in Coconut Grove. There is one central number for all post offices: ℂ **800/275-8777.**

Radio On the AM dial, 610 (WIOD), 790 (WNWS), 1230 (WJNO), and 1340 (WPBR) are all talk. There is no all-news station in town, although 940 (WINZ) gives traffic updates and headline news in between its talk shows. WDBF (1420) is a good big-band station, and WPBG (1290) features golden oldies. Switching to the FM dial, the two most popular R&B stations are WEDR/99 Jams (99.1) and Hot 105 (105.1). The best rock stations on the FM dial are WPYM/93 Rock (93.1), WBGG/Big 106 (105.9), and the progressive college station WVUM (90.5). WKIS (99.9) is the top country station. Top-40 music can be heard on WHYI (100.3), and hip-hop on 103.5 The Beat (103.5). For more hip-hop and dance music, Power 96 (96.5) WPOW will help you get your groove on. WGTR (97.3) plays easy listening, WDNA (88.9) has the best Latin jazz and multiethnic sounds, and public radio can be heard either on WXEL (90.7) or WLRN (91.3).

Religious Services Miami houses of worship are as varied as the city's population and include St. Patrick Catholic Church, 3716 Garden Ave., Miami Beach (ℂ **305/531-1124**); Coral Gables Baptist Church, 5501 Granada Blvd. (ℂ **305/665-4072**); Temple Judea, 5500 Granada Blvd., Coral Gables (ℂ **305/667-5657**); Coconut Grove United Methodist, 2850 SW 27th Ave. (ℂ **305/443-0880**); Christ Episcopal Church, 3481 Hibiscus St., Coconut Grove (ℂ **305/442-8542**); Plymouth Congregational Church, 3400 Devon Rd., at Main Highway, Coconut Grove (ℂ **305/444-6521**); Masjid Al-Ansar (Muslim), 5245 NW Seventh Ave., Miami (ℂ **305/757-8741**); and Buddhist Temple of Miami, 15200 SW 240th St., Homestead (ℂ **305/245-2702**).

Restrooms Stores rarely let customers use their restrooms, and many restaurants offer their facilities only for their patrons. However, most malls have restrooms, as do many fast-food restaurants. Public beaches and large parks often provide toilets, though in some places you have to pay or tip an attendant. Most large hotels have clean restrooms in their lobbies.

Safety As always, use your common sense and be aware of your surroundings at all times. Don't walk alone at night, and be extra wary when walking or driving though downtown

Miami and surrounding areas.

Reacting to several highly publicized crimes against tourists several years ago, local and state governments alike have taken steps to help protect visitors. These measures include special highly visible police units patrolling the airport and surrounding neighborhoods, and better signs on the state's most tourist-traveled routes.

Spas & Massage There are a number of great spa packages at some of the ritzier hotels, but those without spas often have relationships with on-call massage therapists, which can be arranged by asking the concierge to make an appointment for an in-room session. Popular day spas include the **Russian Turkish Baths,** 5445 Collins Ave. at the Castle Hotel (ℂ **305/867-8313; www. russianandturkishbaths. com**), otherwise known as "The Schvitz," where the old guard meets the new in eucalyptus-scented Turkish steam rooms and aroma baths bolstered by marble columns. **Browne's Beauty Lounge,** 841 Lincoln Rd., Miami Beach (ℂ **305/532-8703; www. brownesbeauty.com**), has expanded from a small second-floor salon into a full-service, 5,250-square-foot spa, offering massages, waxing, manicures, and a sublime signature hot-rock massage.

For necessary kneading, **Massage By Design,** 959 West Ave., Miami Beach (☏ **305/532-3112; www. massagebydesign.com**), offers all sorts of treatments, from detox to hot stone massages. **Me Day Spa,** 1439B Alton Road., Miami Beach (☏ **305/534-6363; www.medayspa. com**), is one of the best day spas in the area, featuring a laundry list of facials, body treatments, laser treatment, makeup applications, waxing, manicures, pedicures and even, if you need your, uh, fill, Botox.

Taxes A 6% state sales tax (plus 1% local tax, for a total of 7% in Miami-Dade County [from Homestead to North Miami Beach]) is added on at the register for all goods and services purchased in Florida. In addition, most municipalities levy special taxes on restaurants and hotels. In Surfside, hotel taxes total 11%; in Bal Harbour, 11%; in Miami Beach (including South Beach), 13%; and in the rest of Dade County, a whopping 13%. Food and beverage tax in Miami Beach, Bal Harbour, and Surfside is 9%, in Miami-Dade restaurants not located inside hotels it's 8% and in restaurants located in hotels, 9%.

Taxis See "Getting Around," earlier in this chapter.

Television The local stations are channel 4, WFOR (CBS); channel 6, WTVJ (NBC); channel 7, WSVN (FOX); channel 10, WPLG (ABC); channel 17, WLRN (PBS); channel 23, WLTV (independent); and channel 33, WBFS (independent). Channel 39 is the CW (WBZL), and channel 33 is a MyNetworkTV affiliate (WBFS).

Time Zone Miami, like New York, is in the Eastern Standard Time (EST) zone. Between the second Sunday of March and the first Sunday of November, daylight saving time is adopted, and clocks are set 1 hour ahead. America's eastern seaboard is 5 hours behind Greenwich Mean Time. To find out what time it is, call ☏ **305/324-8811.**

Transit Information For Metrorail or Metromover schedule information, phone ☏ **305/770-3131** or surf over to www.co.miami-dade.fl.us/transit.

Weather Hurricane season in Miami runs June through November. For an up-to-date recording of current weather conditions and forecast reports, call ☏ **305/229-4522.** Also see the "When to Go" section in chapter 3 for more information on the weather.

WHERE TO STAY IN MIAMI

As much a part of the landscape as the palm trees, many of Miami's hotels are on display as if they were contestants in a beauty pageant. The city's long-lasting status on the destination A-list has given rise to an ever-increasing number of upscale hotels, and no place in Miami has seen a greater increase in construction than Miami Beach. Since the area's renaissance, which began in the late 1980s, the beach has turned what used to be a beachfront retirement community into a sand-swept hot spot for the Gucci and Prada set—even in a recession. Contrary to popular belief, however, the beach does not discriminate, and it's the juxtaposition of the chic elite and the hoi polloi that contributes to its allure.

While the increasing demand for rooms on South Beach means increasing costs, you can still find a decent room at a fair price. In fact, most hotels in the Art Deco District are less Ritz-Carlton than they are Holiday Inn, unless, of course, they've been renovated (many hotels in this area were built in the 1930s for the middle class). Unless you plan your vacation entirely in and around your hotel, most of the cheaper Deco hotels are adequate and a wise choice for those who plan to use the room only to sleep. Smart vacationers can almost name their price if they're willing to live without a few luxuries, such as an oceanfront view.

Many of the old hotels from the 1930s, 1940s, and 1950s have been totally renovated, giving way to dozens of "boutique" (small, swanky, and, for the most part, independently owned) hotels. Keep in mind that when a hotel claims that it was just renovated, it can mean that they've completely gutted the building—or just applied a coat of fresh paint or hung a new picture on the wall. Always ask what specific changes were made during a renovation, and be sure to ask if a hotel will be undergoing construction while you're there. You should also find out how near your room will be to the center of the nightlife crowd; trying to sleep directly on Ocean Drive or Collins and Washington avenues, especially during the weekend, is next to impossible, unless your lullaby of choice happens to include throbbing salsa and bass beats.

The best hotel options in each price category and those that have been fully upgraded recently are listed below. You should also know that along South Beach's Collins Avenue, there are dozens of hotels and motels—in all price categories—so there's bound to be a vacancy somewhere. If you do try the walk-in routine, don't forget to ask to see a room first. A few dollars extra could mean all the difference between fleabag and fabulous.

While South Beach may be the nucleus of all things hyped and hip, it's not the only place with hotels. The advantage to staying on South Beach as opposed to, say, Coral Gables or Coconut Grove, is that the beaches are within walking distance, the nightlife and restaurant options are aplenty, and, basically, everything you need is right there. However, staying there is definitely not for everyone. If you're wary, don't worry: South Beach is centrally located and only about a 15- to 30-minute drive from most other parts of Miami.

For a less expensive stay that's only a 10-minute cab ride from South Beach, Miami Beach proper (the area north of 23rd St. and Collins Ave. all the way up to 163rd St. and Collins Ave.) offers a slew of reasonable stays, right on the beach, that won't cost you your kids' college education fund.

What *will* cost you a small fortune are the luxury hotels in the city's financial Brickell Avenue district, the area of choice for expense-account business travelers and camera-shy celebrities trying to avoid the South Beach spotlight.

For a less frenetic, more relaxed, and more tropical experience, the ritzy resort on Key Biscayne exudes an island feel, even though, across the water, a cosmopolitan vibe beckons, thanks to the shimmering, spectacular Miami skyline.

Those who'd rather bag the beach in favor of shopping bags will enjoy North Miami Beach's proximity to the Aventura Mall. For Miami with an Old World European flair, Coral Gables and its charming hotels and exquisite restaurants provide a more prim and proper, well-heeled perspective of Miami than the trendy boutique and condo hotels on South Beach.

SEASONS & RATES South Florida's tourist season is well-defined, beginning in mid-November and lasting until Easter, though if you ask the city's most ardent spin doctors, season in So Flo now lasts year-round. It all depends on where and when you're here and what's going on at the time. Hotel prices escalate until about March, after which they begin to decline. During the off season, hotel rates are typically 30% to 50% lower than their winter highs. But timing isn't everything. Rates also depend on your hotel's proximity to the beach and how much ocean you can see from your window. Small motels a block or two from the water can be up to 40% cheaper than similar properties right on the sand.

The rates listed below are broken down into two broad categories: winter (generally, Thanksgiving through Easter) and off-season (about mid-May through Aug). The months in between, the shoulder season, should fall somewhere in between the highs and lows, while rates always go up on holidays. Remember, too, that state and city taxes can add as much as 12.5% to your bill in some parts of Miami. Some hotels, especially those in South Beach, also tack on additional service charges, and don't forget that parking is a pricey endeavor.

Greater Miami Accommodations

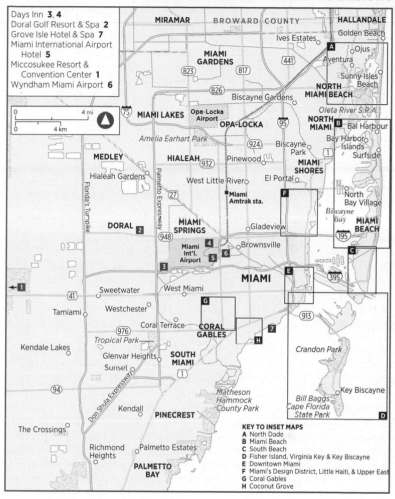

Days Inn **3**, **4**
Doral Golf Resort & Spa **2**
Grove Isle Hotel & Spa **7**
Miami International Airport
  Hotel **5**
Miccosukee Resort &
  Convention Center **1**
Wyndham Miami Airport **6**

MIRAMAR   BROWARD COUNTY   HALLANDALE
Golden Beach
Ives Estates
MIAMI GARDENS   Ojus
(823)   (817)   Aventura
(441)
(826)   Sunny Isles
Biscayne Gardens   Beach
NORTH MIAMI BEACH
Opa-Locka Airport   Oleta River S.R.A.
MIAMI LAKES   OPA-LOCKA   NORTH MIAMI   Bal Harbour
(75)
Amelia Earhart Park   (924)   Biscayne   Bay Harbor
Park   Islands
MEDLEY   HIALEAH   (932)   Pinewood   MIAMI SHORES   Surfside
Hialeah Gardens   West Little River   El Portal
North
Miami   Bay Village
Amtrak sta.
DORAL   Biscayne
MIAMI   Bay   MIAMI BEACH
SPRINGS   (948)   Gladeview
Miami   (195)
Int'l.   Brownsville
Airport
MIAMI
Sweetwater   West Miami
(41)
Tamiami   Westchester   (913)
Coral Terrace
(976)   CORAL GABLES   Crandon Park
Tropical Park
Kendale Lakes   SOUTH MIAMI
Glenvar Heights
Sunset   (1)
(94)
Matheson   Key Biscayne
Hammock
Kendall   County Park   Bill Baggs
PINECREST   Cape Florida
The Crossings   State Park
Richmond   Palmetto Estates
Heights
PALMETTO BAY

Florida's Turnpike
Palmetto Expressway
Don Shula Expressway

Biscayne Bay

0   4 mi
0   4 km

KEY TO INSET MAPS
A North Dade
B Miami Beach
C South Beach
D Fisher Island, Virginia Key & Key Biscayne
E Downtown Miami
F Miami's Design District, Little Haiti, & Upper East
G Coral Gables
H Coconut Grove

PRICE CATEGORIES   The hotels below are divided first by area and then by price (**very expensive, expensive, moderate,** or **inexpensive**). Prices are based on published rates (or rack rates) for a standard double room during the high season. You should also check with the reservations agent, since many rooms are available above and below the category ranges listed below, and ask about packages, since it's often possible to get a better deal than these "official" rates. Most important, always call the hotel to confirm rates, which may be subject to change without notice because of special events, holidays, or blackout dates.

LONG-TERM STAYS   If you plan to visit Miami for a month, a season, or more, think about renting a condominium apartment or a room in a long-term hotel. Long-term accommodations exist in every price category, from budget to deluxe, and in general are extremely reasonable, especially during the off season. Check with the reservation services below, or write a short note to the chamber of commerce in the area where you plan to stay. In addition, many local real estate agents handle short-term rentals (meaning less than a year).

RESERVATION SERVICES   **Central Reservation Service** (✆ **800/950-0232** or 305/274-6832; www.reservation-services.com) works with many of Miami's hotels and can often secure discounts of up to 40%. It also gives advice on specific locales, especially in Miami Beach and downtown. During holiday time, there may be a 3- to 5-day minimum stay required to use their services. Call for more information.

For bed-and-breakfast information throughout the state, contact **Florida Bed and Breakfast Inns** (✆ **800/524-1880;** www.florida-inns.com). For information on the ubiquitous boutique hotels, check out the **Greater Miami Convention and Visitor's Bureau**'s slick website, www.miamiboutiquehotels.com.

SOUTH BEACH

Choosing a hotel on South Beach is similar to deciding whether you'd rather pay $2 for french fries at Denny's or $15 for the same fries—but let's call them *pommes frites,* and add $5 for some fancy salt from a fancy resort town on the Mediterranean—in a pricey haute-cuisine restaurant. It's all about atmosphere. The rooms of some hotels may *look* ultrachic, but they are as comfortable as sleeping on a concrete slab. Once you decide how much atmosphere you want, the choice will be easier. Fortunately, for every chichi hotel in South Beach—and there are many—there are just as many moderately priced, more casual options.

Prices mentioned here are rack rates—that is, the price you would be quoted if you walked up to the front desk and inquired about rates. The actual price you will end up paying will usually be less than this—especially if a travel agent makes the reservations for you. Many hotels on South Beach have chosen to go with a low-to-high rate representing the hotel's complete pricing range. It pays to try to negotiate the price of a room. In some of the trendier hotels, however, negotiating is highly unfashionable and not well regarded. In other words, your attempt at negotiation will either be met with a blank stare or a snippy refusal. It never hurts to try, though.

Checking into Hotel Bars

While South Beach is known for its trendy club scene, hotel bars all over Miami are also very much a part of the nightlife—and may affect your selection of hotel. Among the hottest hotel bars are the **Lobby Bar** at The Setai, **Skybar** and the **Nobu Lounge** at The Shore Club, the **Rose Bar** at the Delano, the **Bond St. Lounge** at the Townhouse, **The Living Room** at the **W South Beach,** the **Martini Bar** at **The Raleigh,** the **M Bar** at the Mandarin Oriental, and **Bahia** at the Four Seasons. See "Swank Hotel Bars," p. 229.

South Beach Accommodations

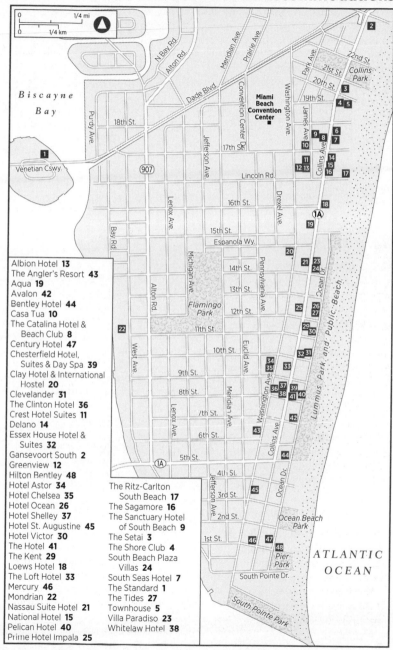

Albion Hotel **13**
The Angler's Resort **43**
Aqua **19**
Avalon **42**
Bentley Hotel **44**
Casa Tua **10**
The Catalina Hotel &
 Beach Club **8**
Century Hotel **47**
Chesterfield Hotel,
 Suites & Day Spa **39**
Clay Hotel & International
 Hostel **20**
Clevelander **31**
The Clinton Hotel **36**
Crest Hotel Suites **11**
Delano **14**
Essex House Hotel &
 Suites **32**
Gansevoort South **2**
Greenview **12**
Hilton Bentley **48**
Hotel Astor **34**
Hotel Chelsea **35**
Hotel Ocean **26**
Hotel Shelley **37**
Hotel St. Augustine **45**
Hotel Victor **30**
The Hotel **41**
The Kent **29**
Loews Hotel **18**
The Loft Hotel **33**
Mercury **46**
Mondrian **22**
Nassau Suite Hotel **21**
National Hotel **15**
Pelican Hotel **40**
Prime Hotel Impala **25**

The Ritz-Carlton
 South Beach **17**
The Sagamore **16**
The Sanctuary Hotel
 of South Beach **9**
The Setai **3**
The Shore Club **4**
South Beach Plaza
 Villas **24**
South Seas Hotel **7**
The Standard **1**
The Tides **27**
Townhouse **5**
Villa Paradiso **23**
Whitelaw Hotel **38**

If status is important to you, as it is to many South Beach visitors, then you will be quite pleased with the number of haute hotels in the area. But the times may be a-changin': **Courtyard by Marriott** (© **800/321-2211** or 305/604-8887) maintains a 90-room, moderately priced hotel on a seedy stretch of Washington Avenue, smack in the middle of Clubland, a horror to many a South Beach trend-seeker.

Meanwhile as a result of the economic downturn, two very popular South Beach hotels faced foreclosure in late 2009 and early 2010. To avoid financial disaster, the swanky Sagamore may team up with the Playboy Club. Unfortunately the Gansevoort South wasn't as lucky, hitting the auction block in 2010 after owners were forced to use hotel revenue to make debt payments on their construction debt, a task made nearly impossible due to what experts describe as the worst lodging downturn in a generation. According to the *Miami Herald,* "The Gansevoort could be the leading edge of what analysts predict will be a wave of banks seizing hotels throughout South Florida [in 2010]."

Note: Art Deco hotels, while pleasing to the eye, may be a bit run-down inside. It's par for the course on South Beach, where appearances are, at times, deceiving.

To locate the hotels in this section, see the "South Beach Accommodations" map (p. 73).

Very Expensive

The Angler's Resort ★   Set back and hidden wisely from the street, The Angler's is a welcome vision of Deco-modernity on what has become an eyesore of a stretch of seedy Washington Avenue. Ironically, however, this hotel is all about location, situated a mere 2 blocks from the beach. All together the "resort" (and we say so because it really is a small boutique hotel) is a unique collection of four very different buildings—two completely restored and two brand new buildings offering a variety of accommodations from suites and duplexes to triplex villas. All rooms feature the typical luxury comforts of Wi-Fi, flatscreen TVs, and iPod. Not so typical: One remote control works on all of these features—even the internal and external lights. An outdoor pool is surrounded by gardens. For those who'd rather do the beach than the pool, stop by the front desk to pick up a beach goodie bag complete with sunscreen, toys, water, snacks, and even the latest best-selling novel. Novel, indeed.

660 Washington Ave., South Beach, FL 33139. © **305/534-9600.** Fax 305/532-3099. www.the anglersresort.com. 46 fully furnished units, including suites and villas. Winter Studio Suites $329–$495; Duplex Suites $469–$699; off-season Studio Suites $230–$245; Duplex Suites $255–$699. AE, DISC, MC, V. Valet parking $24 per night. Pets accepted. **Amenities:** Restaurant; poolside dining cabanas; beach concession; 24-hr. concierge; pool; room service; indoor and poolside spa services; private rooftop terraces and gardens. *In room:* A/C, TV/DVD, hair dryer, minibar, MP3 docking station, Wi-Fi.

Bentley Hotel & Beach Club ★   The biggest coup the Bentley Hotel pulls off is its ability to remain immune to the throngs of pedestrians on the well-traveled Ocean Drive. A private front entrance leads, via elevator, to the main lobby. Inside this enclave of Old World luxury you will find a charming ambience and an overly accommodating, professional staff. The hotel's 40 suites are both hotel rooms and condos; some of them can be rented year-round. Rooms come complete with marble floors, well-stocked kitchens, and roomy bathrooms with steam showers. Try not to get a corner room, though, or you will learn more about your neighbors than you'd ever want to. Because it is located on South Beach's bustling strip of neon and nightlife, the Bentley, despite its efforts to stand apart from the rest of its neighbors, isn't impervious to noise. However, if you want luxe in the midst of all the action, the Bentley is a great choice.

510 Ocean Dr., South Beach, FL 33139. ✆ **800/236-8510** or 305/538-1700. Fax 305/532-4865. www. thebentleyhotel.com. 40 units. Winter $310–$1,200 double; off season $220–$900 double. AE, DC, DISC, MC, V. **Amenities:** Concierge; rooftop pool; room service. *In room:* A/C, TV/DVD, hair dryer, high-speed Internet, kitchen, minibar.

Casa Tua   This outrageous boutique offers custom-tailored amenities (from toiletries to snacks) for each of its guests, who fill out a detailed profile when booking one of Casa Tua's five suites. Styled like a glorious Mediterranean beach house, Casa Tua also has a posh restaurant with an Italian-accented menu and a second-floor lounge for afternoon tea and evening cocktails. The hotel's management is very cagey as far as hotel details are concerned, expressing a deep concern for "keeping its clientele extremely exclusive" and, essentially, by word of mouth. Enough said, I suppose. Rather than fork over the money to stay here—there's no pool anyway—I do suggest that you absolutely splurge at Casa Tua, the restaurant (p. 119), which happens to be one of South Beach's most exquisite.

1700 James Ave., Miami Beach, FL 33139. ✆ **305/673-1010.** www.casatuahotel.com.5 suites. Winter $750–$1,050; off-season $400–$600. Rates include daily breakfast. **Amenities:** Restaurant; bar. *In room:* A/C, TV/DVD, hair dryer; minibar; MP3 docking station; free Wi-Fi.

Delano ★   Though Beyoncé and Jay-Z may choose the Setai over the Delano these days, it doesn't mean South Beach's original see-and-be-seen hotel is over just yet. The stunning pool area, Rose Bar, Agua Spa, Lenny Kravitz–designed speakeasy The Florida Room, and **Blue Door** restaurant are still studded with the boldface and the beautiful; but today, the Delano, a place where smiles from staffers were as rare as snow in Miami, is somewhat kinder and gentler. But not entirely—during the worst of the recession, Delano refused to lower its room rates despite the fact that they were empty. They said they'd rather have empty rooms than budget travelers staying there. Rude or not, it certainly is still pleasantly amusing to look at—with 40-foot sheer white billowing curtains hanging outside, mirrors everywhere, Adirondack chairs, and faux fur–covered beds. Rooms that were once done up sanitarium-style, sterile yet terribly trendy, just received a revamp that boasts a splash of color and reworked bathrooms that went from spartan to spacious.

1685 Collins Ave., South Beach, FL 33139. ✆ **800/555-5001** or 305/672-2000. Fax 305/532-0099. www.delano-hotel.com. 194 units, including 1 penthouse. Winter from $495 city view, $1,250 suite, $2,200 bungalow, $4,000 penthouse; off-season from $345 city view, $950 suite, $1,000 bungalow, $3,100 penthouse. Additional person $50. AE, DC, DISC, MC, V. Valet parking $37. **Amenities:** 3 restaurants; 3 bars; children's program (seasonal); concierge; state-of-the-art gym; large outdoor pool; room service; Agua spa. *In room:* A/C, TV/DVD, CD player, hair dryer, minibar, MP3 docking station, Wi-Fi.

Fisher Island Club ★★★ 🏨   Located on an exclusive island just off Miami Beach, this hotel is a luxurious fusion of *Fantasy Island, Lifestyles of the Rich and Famous,* and *Survivor.* Just minutes from South Beach, it's still worlds away. The only way to get there is by private ferry, which shuttles guests to and from the mainland every 15 to 20 minutes. It can be a hassle, but it does run on a very regular schedule. The ferry lets residents on first, so if there's no room after all the Bentleys roll on, you'll have to wait for the next one. Don't worry if you are carless—golf carts are the island's preferred mode of transportation. Rooms vary in size and shape, and cottages come with hot tubs. There's also a world-class spa, restaurants, tennis, golf, and pretty much everything to entertain the island's offbeat millionaires—you know, the kind who tug their Gucci-clad pooches around in their Rolls Royce golf carts.

1 Fisher Island Dr., Fisher Island, FL 33190. ℭ **800/537-3708** or 305/535-6020. Fax 305/535-6003. www.fisherislandclub.com. 60 units. Winter $405–$495 double, $890–$2,040 suite or cottage; off season $325–$395 double, $450–$1,630 suite or cottage. Golf, tennis, and spa packages available seasonally. 20% gratuity added to all food and beverages. AE, DC, MC, V. **Amenities:** 3 restaurants; 3 bars; airport transportation; babysitting; concierge; P. B. Dye Golf Course; 2 marinas; limited room service; world-class spa; 18 tennis courts. *In room:* A/C, TV/DVD, hair dryer, minibar.

Gansevoort South ★   One of NYC's hippest hotels opened on South Beach in January 2008 much to the delight of hipsters, jet-setters, and the scene-obsessed. This 334-room hotel features the flagship David Barton Gym and Spa, expansive oceanview rooftop pool and bar, trendy meatery **STK,** chic Chinese restaurant **Philippe,** VIP bar and lounge by the Opium Group and, inexplicably, a shark tank with 27 types of fish and sharks that spans 50 feet of the lobby, which, compared to the rest of the hotel, is a huge, unsightly letdown. Things are much prettier up top, where a 26,000-square-foot rooftop playground (complete with a 110-ft. elevated swimming pool, Plunge bar, and lounge) offers divine views of the ocean, the bay, and downtown. On the main level is a 40,000-square-foot semicircular oceanfront pool plaza with infinity edge pool, teak decking, and cabanas. Room furniture screams hot pink, magenta, and yellow, set against charcoal-gray suede walls dotted with pictures of '40s pinup girls. Most rooms have balconies overlooking the ocean. In January 2010, the hotel went on the auction block in a foreclosure sale less than two years after it opened due to dismal sales of the hotel's adjoining condo tower.

2377 Collins Ave., South Beach, FL 33139. ℭ **305/604-1000.** Fax 305/604-6886. www.gansevoort miamibeach.com. 340 units. $250–$595 deluxe double or king; $685–$1,000 suite. AE, DC, DISC, MC, V. Valet parking $15 per night. **Amenities:** 2 restaurants; bar and lounge; beachfront lounge; concierge; fitness center; infinity-edge rooftop pool; room service; spa. *In room:* A/C, TV/DVD, CD player, hair dryer, minibar, MP3 docking stations, Wi-Fi.

Hotel Victor ★★   A victory for Ocean Drive, a street that hasn't seen such a swank stay since the Tides, Hotel Victor, managed by Hyatt, is a hyperluxe, 88-room boutique see-and-be-seen hotel designed by Parisian Jacques Garcia—this is his first hotel foray in the U.S. Best known for his design work at Paris's tragically hip Hotel Costes and the discriminating Sultan of Brunei, Garcia has lent his exquisite taste to this hotel located on notoriously tacky Ocean Drive. The hotel's cabana-dotted pool and bistro Vix have become command central for hotel hopping hipsters—especially on Thursday nights and Saturday afternoons. Directly across from the ocean, Hotel Victor stands apart from the rest of the cookie-cutter minimalist Miami hotels, breaking from bare minimalism and daring to go bold with color and rich fabrics. Deluxe rooms are just that, all with ocean views, white marble, ebony-lacquered furniture, a full—not mini—bar, flatscreen plasma TVs, and massive white-marbled bathrooms with infinity-edge bathtubs and rain showerheads. The Hotel Victor's Turkish-style spa is the hotel's hottest spot—literally, with its large unisex steam room, Turkish hammam, and heated marble slabs.

1144 Ocean Dr., South Beach, FL 33139. ℭ **305/428-1234.** Fax 305/421-6281. www.hotelvictorsouth beach.com. 88 units. Winter $470–$1,045 suite; off-season $249–$659 suite. AE, DC, DISC, MC, V. Valet parking $32. **Amenities:** 2 restaurants; 2 bars; concierge; 6,000-sq.-ft. fitness center; outdoor pool; room service; spa and Turkish hammam. *In room:* A/C, TV/DVD, stereo/CD player, hair dryer, minibar, Wi-Fi.

Loews Hotel ★ ☺   The Loews is one of the largest hotels on South Beach, consuming an unprecedented 900 feet of oceanfront. This 790-room behemoth is considered an eyesore by many, an architectural triumph by others. Rooms are a bit boxy and bland, nothing to rave about, but are clean and have new carpets and bedspreads to erase signs of wear and tear from the hotel's heavy traffic. The best rooms do not face very congested Collins Avenue, as rooms that do tend to be quite noisy. If you can steer your way past all the conventioneers in the lobby, you can escape to the equally massive pool (with an undisputedly gorgeous, landscaped entrance that's more Maui than Miami). In addition to children's fare, such as the Loews Loves Kids program, the hotel hosts fun activities for adults, such as Dive in Movies at the pool, salsa lessons, and bingo. In addition to a pretty good lobby sushi bar, Emeril Lagasse maintains his eponymous and iconic **Emeril's** restaurant here. For spa junkies, there's a sprawling Elemis Spa and Fitness Center. In 2009, the resort began a $50 million renovation which has whisked the resort from stale to stellar thanks to, among other things, the removal of the ghastly popcorn ceilings in all rooms, renovation of all bathrooms, the removal of the lobby's outdated pineapple-covered staircase in favor of a new retail area and wall-sized aquarium, and the addition of an old-fashioned ice cream parlor and water features along the hotel's driveway.

1601 Collins Ave., South Beach, FL 33139. ℂ **800/23-LOEWS** (5-6397) or 305/604-1601. www.loews hotels.com. 790 units. Winter from $499 double; off-season from $289 double. AE, DC, DISC, MC, V. Valet parking $30. Pets accepted. **Amenities:** 5 restaurants; coffee bar; ice cream parlor; 2 bars; babysitting; children's programs; concierge; health club; Jacuzzi; sprawling outdoor pool; room service; sauna; spa; watersports equipment/rentals. *In room:* A/C, TV, hair dryer, high-speed Internet, minibar.

Mondrian ★★   Much to everyone's surprise, the latest offering from the Morgans Hotel Group of Delano fame isn't just another humdrum, been-there-done-that homage to all things painfully trendy. Sure, it's painfully trendy, but it's also refreshingly different. For one, it's located on the western, residential bay side of South Beach, where its neighbors (and its former incarnation) are high-rise condos. Panoramic views of the bay and skyline are stunning. Rooms have been done up with the usual trendy trappings and are comfy enough, as they should be, considering someone's grandma used to live there. World-famous design star and *Elle Décor's* 2006 International Designer of the Year, Marcel Wanders, envisioned the property as Sleeping Beauty's castle, with whimsical adult-playground-style environs. The hotel's so-called "Modern Resort" concept features an Agua spa (of Delano fame) and Jeffrey Chodorow's **Asia de Cuba** restaurant. And while the indoor spaces are swell, it's the outdoor pool area that really must be seen, especially at sundown. Don't miss the lobby's futuristic, ridiculous vending machine in which, if you slide your credit card in, you can actually buy yourself a Bentley. Shop at your own risk.

1100 West Ave., Miami Beach, FL 33139. ℂ **305/672-2662.** Fax 305/672-3766. www.mondriansouth beach.com. 335 units. Winter $350 studio, $950 deluxe 2-bedroom suite; off-season $195 studio, $795 deluxe 2-bedroom suite. AE, DC, DISC, MC, V. Valet parking $37. **Amenities:** Restaurant; 3 bars; babysitting; concierge; fitness center; marina and boat slips; 1 pool; room service; Agua spa; watersports equipment/rentals. *In room:* A/C, TV, high-speed Internet, kitchenette.

National Hotel ★   Sceney it's not, but scenic? Absolutely. With its towering ceilings, sultry furnishings, and massive gilded mirrors, the elegant 1940s-style National is a Deco darling. At 11 stories, the main building offers grand views of the ocean. Guest rooms and suites were designed as a tranquil and elegant refuge from bustling

South Beach. Rooms are divided into two distinctive buildings: the **Historic Tower** and the **Cabana Wing,** which feature their own balconies overlooking the spectacular Infinity Pool. While all the rooms in the main hotel are comfortable and plush, the best rooms are the 32 ultramodern poolside cabana rooms. The hotel's historic Deco lobby is a rarity in a town where all vestiges of the good old days have given way to sterile minimalism. The pool, however, is the hotel's crown jewel. It's Miami's longest pool (205 ft.) and almost too sleek (rivaling even the Delano's pool) for splashing.

1677 Collins Ave., South Beach, FL 33139. © **800/327-8370** or 305/532-2311. Fax 305/534-1426. www. nationalhotel.com. 152 units. Winter $380–$480 double; off season $270–$350 double. AE, DC, DISC, MC, V. Valet parking $25. **Amenities:** Restaurant; 2 bars; concierge; exercise room; large outdoor pool; room service; watersports equipment/rentals. *In room:* A/C, TV/DVD, hair dryer, high-speed Internet, minibar, stereo.

The Ritz-Carlton, South Beach ★★ ☺   Far from ostentatious, the Ritz-Carlton South Beach moves away from gilded opulence in favor of the more soothing pastel-washed touches of Deco. Though South Beach is better known for its trendy boutique hotels, the Ritz-Carlton provides comfort to those who might prefer 100% cotton Frette sheets and goose-down pillows to high-style minimalism. The best rooms, by far, are the 72 poolside and oceanview lanai rooms. There's also a trademarked "Tanning Butler" who will spritz you with SPF and water whenever you want. With its impeccable service, an elevated pool with unobstructed views of the Atlantic and live entertainment on weekends, an impressive stretch of sand with a fabulous beach club, and a world-class 16,000-square-foot spa and wellness center, the Ritz-Carlton kicks sand in the faces of some smaller hotels that think they're doing *you* a favor by allowing you to sleep there. Parents love the Ritz Kids program for kids ages 5 through 12; and for gourmands, there's the Ritz's amazing Sunday champagne brunch.

1 Lincoln Rd., South Beach, FL 33139. © **800/241-3333** or 786/276-4000. Fax 786/276-4001. www. ritzcarlton.com. 375 units. Winter $479 standard, $769 junior suite; off-season $269 standard, $489 junior suite. AE, DISC, MC, V. Valet parking $36 (overnight), $24 (daily). **Amenities:** 2 restaurants; 2 bars; babysitting; beach service; children's program; fitness center; outdoor heated pool; room service; spa; extensive watersports equipment/rentals. *In room:* A/C, TV, hair dryer, high-speed Internet, minibar.

The Sagamore ★★   Just two doors down from the Delano Hotel is the Sagamore, fabulous in its own right, with an ultramodern lobby-cum-art-gallery-cum-restaurant that's infinitely warmer than your typical pop-art exhibit at the Museum of Modern Art. The hotel doesn't take itself too seriously and boasts a tongue-in-cheek sense of humor that was evidenced when it hosted a Lox and Botox party—no, we're not kidding. Although the lobby and its requisite restaurant, bar, and lounge areas have become command central for the international chic elite and celebrities, the Sagamore's all-suite, apartmentlike rooms are havens from the hype, with all the cushy comforts of home and then some. The sprawling outdoor lawn, dotted with cabanas with plasma TVs screening everything from Japanese anime to digital art, pool, and beachfront makes you realize you're not in Kansas anymore. A branch of Miami's coiffeur to the stars, Rik Rak, opened in one of the outdoor bungalows. And in 2009, in order to avoid the unfortunate foreclosure the hotel was facing since losing money after its restaurant closed in 2008, word was that Sagamore was in talks with Hugh Hefner to turn the hotel into the only Playboy Club outside of Las

Vegas—one without gambling, but one with the trademark bunnies, Playboy-decorated rooms, a bunny hopping nightclub, and even, if he so wishes, Hefner's very own version of, uh, art, on the walls.

1671 Collins Ave., South Beach, FL 33139. ✆ **877/SAGAMORE** (724-2667) or 305/535-8088. Fax 305/535-8185. www.sagamorehotel.com. 93 units. Winter $355–$4,500 suite; off-season $205–$3,500 suite. AE, DC, DISC, MC, V. Valet parking $37. **Amenities:** Restaurant; bar; pool bar; concierge; fitness center; pool; room service; spa. In room: A/C, TV/VCR/DVD, hair dryer, kitchenette, minibar, MP3 docking station, Wi-Fi.

The Sanctuary Hotel of South Beach ★ Set a bit off the beaten path is this modern, all-suite resident hotel (meaning people can actually rent or buy rooms and live here) that takes luxury very seriously, even if it does resemble a souped-up motel, with its ground-floor rooms only accessible from a communal outdoor courtyard area. Flying into town? Let the Sanctuary's Range Rover pick you up at the airport. Soothingly modern, all rooms have full state-of-the-art Italian kitchens, flat plasmascreen televisions, and Wi-Fi. In addition, bathrooms come with Jacuzzi tubs, and in-room fridges are stocked with everything you specify before checking into the hotel. A roof-deck "bedroom" allows you to relax in the sun or slink around in the wading pool. Star chef Douglas Rodriguez's **Ola,** a fashionable Latin eatery and hot spot, is situated smack in the middle of the very posh, albeit tiny, lobby.

1745 James Ave., South Beach, FL 33139. ✆ **305/673-5455.** Fax 305/673-3113. www.sanctuarysobe.com. 30 units. Winter $375–$1,500 suite; off-season $215–$1,050 suite. AE, DC, DISC, MC, V. Valet parking $18. **Amenities:** Restaurant; bar; pool bar; concierge; fitness center; rooftop pool; room service; spa. In room: A/C, TV/VCR/DVD, CD player, hair dryer, kitchen, minibar, Wi-Fi.

The Setai ★★★ With bank-busting room rates, dinner tabs coming in at around $200 per person (although 2009/10 saw the addition of some "recession friendly" prix-fixe menus starting at $55 per person), drinks (try the one with pork-belly-infused Jack Daniels) ranging from $14 to $20 a pop (although 2009 saw the addition of Bottleshock, a promotion in which select bottles of vino are discounted 40%. As for the original markup, well, that's another story), and a celebrity clientele who doesn't have to ask how much, the Zen-like, Asian-inspired Setai is truly for that 1% of society who can afford it. But if you want to splurge, this is where to do it. All of the suites—some are actually condos participating in the condo-hotel program—are gorgeous apartments with floor-to-ceiling windows, full kitchens, and Jacuzzi bathtubs bigger than a small swimming pool. There are 85 regular hotel rooms that are an average of 600 square feet, compared to the suites' 1,300 to 3,500 square feet. All are adorned in sleek Asian decor with over-the-top comforts, including Lavazza espresso makers, Laura Tonatto bathroom amenities, and washer/dryers. The garden area with reflecting pools is lovely, but not as cool as the pool area with a bar serving $18 chicken sandwiches to celebrity clientele. There's also **The Grill,** which features a create-your-own multicourse tapas menu, and **The Restaurant,** its proper name, which is authentically Asian, with stainless-steel tandoori ovens—but with these steep prices and small portions you may as well buy a ticket to Asia.

2001 Collins Ave., South Beach, FL 33139. ✆ **305/520-6000.** Fax 305/520-6600. www.setai.com. 130 units. Winter $1,150 studio suite, $30,000 penthouse; off-season $550 studio suite, price available on request for penthouse. AE, DC, DISC, MC, V. Valet parking $40. **Amenities:** 3 restaurants; 2 bars; concierge; fitness center; 3 pools; room service; spa. In room: A/C, TV/DVD, hair dryer, kitchen (1-, 2-, and 3-bedroom suites only), minibar, Wi-Fi.

The Shore Club ★   In the fickle world of hot hotels, the Shore Club struggles to hold on to its place at the top, but does okay thanks to Florida's only Nobu sushi restaurant and, on certain nights, a celebrity clientele that would fill up an entire issue of *Us Weekly*. Because this hotel is infinitely more cavernous than its hipster neighbors, the Delano and The Sagamore (see above), some publicity-shy celebrities such as Janet Jackson and Denzel Washington have been known to call it their home away from home—there are indeed places for them to hide. That said, this is hardly a quiet place for some silent reflection. In fact, during high seasons and spring break, it's party central. An outpost of L.A.'s celebrity-laden SkyBar reigns supreme, with a Marrakech-meets-Miami motif that stretches throughout the hotel's sprawling pool, patio, and garden areas. Beware of surly doormen if you're not a hotel guest. There's also a branch of L.A.'s—and Robert De Niro's—pricey pasta spot Ago. Rooms—80% of which have an ocean view—are loaded with state-of-the-art amenities and, frankly, have a bit more personality than those at the Delano.

1901 Collins Ave., Miami Beach, FL 33139. ⓒ **877/640-9500** or 305/695-3100. Fax 305/695-3299. www.shoreclub.com. 309 units, including 8 bungalows. Winter from $315 superior, $490 suite, $1,500 bungalow; off-season $285 superior, $490 suite, $1,500 bungalow. AE, DC, MC, V. Valet parking $42. **Amenities:** 2 restaurants; bar; concierge; 2 outdoor pools; room service; spa. *In room:* A/C, TV, CD player/stereo, high-speed Internet, minibar, MP3 docking station.

The Tides ★★★   This 10-story Art Deco masterpiece reminiscent of a gleaming ocean liner with porthole windows received a massive makeover by trendsetting designer Kelly Wearstler and is now a condo/hotel. Rooms have been newly washed in warm earth tones. Also, all rooms are at least twice the size of a typical South Beach hotel room and have a breathtaking panoramic view of the ocean. The penthouses on the 9th and 10th floors are situated at the highest point on Ocean Drive, allowing for a priceless panoramic view of the ocean, the skyline, and the beach. The hotel's restaurant, La Marea, is located in the lobby, and is good, but very pricey (although in the wake of the recession and thanks to a new chef, prices dropped about 30 percent, but we still say it's pricey). Located just off the lobby is the Coral Bar, a small and romantic spot for a cocktail or two with the help of its very own rum sommelier. A full selection of spa services is available in rooms and poolside. Best of all, the Tides has what they call "Pool Personal Assistants" who provide magazines, frozen fruits, and chilled water and will even clean and polish your sunglasses, and "Oceanfront Personal Assistants" who assist in scoring lounges, umbrellas, towels, and picnic baskets if you wish.

1220 Ocean Dr., South Beach, FL 33139. ⓒ **800/439-4095** or 305/604-5070. Fax 305/503-3275. www. tidessouthbeach.com. 45 units. Winter $595 studio suites, $1,500–$5,000 penthouse suites; off-season $395 studio suites, $1,000–$4,000 penthouse suites. Extra person $100. AE, DC, DISC, MC, V. Valet parking $35. Pets $150 1-time fee including new "Paws" program. **Amenities:** Restaurant; lounge and bar; beach lounge service; concierge; fitness room; 24-hr. Personal Assistant service; outdoor heated pool; room service. *In room:* A/C, TV/DVD, CD player, hair dryer, minibar, Wi-Fi.

The Villa by Barton G.   Just when you thought hyper luxury was so early 2000s came the announcement by the telecommunications billionaire/owner Casa Casuarina, also known as the Versace Mansion, saying he tapped party planner/restaurateur/Miami's PT Barnum Barton G. Weiss to run his 10-suite oceanfront villa as a resort. Weiss has a 10-year lease and has re-branded the manse as The Villa by Barton G., which will also be the site of special events and his third restaurant, The Dining Room (just opening as we go to print). Rooms are expected to remain unchanged from its original, ornate Versace-style, as is the manse's mosaic pool, on the bottom of which has Versace's signature Medusa icon created from a thousand mosaic tiles.

1116 Ocean Dr., South Beach, FL 33139. ✆ **305/672-6604.** Fax 305/672-5930. www.casacasuarina.com. 10 units. Prices available by request. AE, DISC, MC, V. Valet parking $36 (overnight), $24 (daily). **Amenities:** Restaurant; 3 lounges; beach service; pool; room service. *In room:* A/C, TV/DVD, hair dryer, high-speed Internet, minibar.

W South Beach ★★★   Although W stands for "whatever, whenever," this isn't just any W hotel. South Beach's newest "it" girl, the W is so stunning it has been referred to as the Starwood brand's signature property even though it's hardly the first. A work of art in itself, the property, which was completely rebuilt on a site that formerly housed a Holiday Inn, features a Bali–meets–Miami Beach sensibility, with intimate public spaces, breathtaking landscape design by conceptual design garden artist Paula Hayes and exclusive artwork by acclaimed rock-n-roll photographer Danny Clinch. W South Beach's stylish guest rooms and suites are soothing in shades of teal and white, enhanced by a fusion of white ceramic wood tiles, soft linens, and glossy acrylic accents. All rooms have a W signature bed with plush pillow-top mattress and feather-bed overlay goose-down duvet and pillows, and 350-thread count cotton-blend sheets. The most impressive aspect of each room is the expansive glass balconies with unparalleled and unobstructed views of the beach and ocean. And then there are the amenities, some more unparalleled than others, including Florida's first ever **Mr Chow** restaurant, stellar **Soleà** restaurant helmed by an El Bulli alum, three "destination" bars—The Living Room lobby bar, WETbar pool bar, and Grove, a secret garden gathering spot for cocktails—a nightclub called WALL, and a Bliss spa. Although located directly on the ocean, the pool in its rich wood teak glory is equally as picturesque and quite the see-and-be-scene spot, wet—er WET, or dry. Perhaps the most unique amenities are Swoosh and Swing, the full sized tennis and basketball courts with city views. In true W fashion, all we can say is, simply, WOW.

2201 Collins Ave., Miami Beach, FL 33139. ✆ **305/938-3000.** Fax 305/938-3005. www.whotels.com/southbeach. 312 units. Winter $569–$909 double, $799–$1699 suite; off season $369–$709 double, $599–$1,499 suite. AE, DC, DISC, MC, V. Valet parking $35. **Amenities:** 2 restaurants; 3 bars; nightclub; state-of-the-art fitness center; 2 pools; spa; tennis courts. *In room:* A/C, TV/DVD, CD player, hair dryer, Wi-Fi.

Expensive

Albion Hotel ★   An architectural masterpiece on Lincoln Road originally designed in 1939 by internationally acclaimed architect Igor Polevitzky (of Havana's legendary Hotel Nacional fame), this sleek, modern, nautical-style hotel was once the local headquarters for Abbie Hoffman and the Students for a Democratic Society during the 1972 Democratic National Convention in Miami. Though the Albion has fallen off the hipster radar somewhat and is in desperate need of a sprucing-up of its lobby and pool areas, its location 2 blocks from the beach is key. Rooms have been fully renovated—no longer are they sterile and industrial chic, but much warmer and with color, taking a little of the edge off. While there is no restaurant in the hotel, for lighter fare, the mezzanine-level Pantry provides snacks and continental breakfast items. The Albion is more of a hotel for quiet, hip, intellectual types rather than those who prefer to be on parade.

1650 James Ave. (at Lincoln Rd.), Miami Beach, FL 33139. ℰ **877/RUBELLS** (782-3557) or 305/913-1000. Fax 305/674-0507. www.rubellhotels.com. 100 units. Winter $250–$395 double; off season $175–$205 double. AE, DC, DISC, MC, V. Valet parking $30. Pets accepted. **Amenities:** Bar; airport limo service; babysitting; concierge; small exercise room; large outdoor heated pool. *In room:* A/C, TV/DVD, stereo w/CD player, hair dryer, minibar, free Wi-Fi.

The Betsy Hotel ★   Listed on the National Register of Historic Places, the Betsy is the lone surviving example of Florida Georgian architecture on the famous byway, Ocean Drive. Behind its plantation-style shutters and columned facade, the Betsy Hotel offers a tropical colonial beachside haven. Each room and suite in the ocean-front hotel is a nod to the stately colonial rooms of yesteryear blended with the modern aesthetic of South Beach. The Betsy boasts the South Florida installment of New York's **BLT Steak** restaurant by A-list chef Laurent Tourondel; a roof deck solarium with Zen garden for sunning, spa services, drinks, and light fare; a well-heeled lobby bar scene; and a private basement lounge that bills itself as the anti-celebrity bar, where guests enter by invitation only and reality stars are strictly prohibited as well they should be. While the beach is a few steps away, the hotel also offers a serene outdoor pool scene.

1440 Ocean Dr., Miami Beach, FL 33139. ℰ **866/531-8950** or 305/531-3934. Fax 305/531-9009. www.thebetsyhotel.com. 63 units. Winter $409–$879 double, $979–$4,000 suite; off-season $309–$779 double, $879–$3,500 suite. AE, DC, DISC, MC, V. Valet parking $30. **Amenities:** Restaurant; bar; babysitting; beach butlers; concierge; outdoor pool; room service; roof deck solarium with spa services. *In room:* A/C, TV/DVD, CD player, hair dryer, MP3 docking station, Wi-Fi.

Century Hotel ★★   Located in South Beach's trendy South of Fifth area, The Century was the hotel of choice for artists, celebrities, musicians, and a slew of quirky, eccentric, Warholian types—before the area became hip. Practically hidden at the southern tip of South Beach, the Century is a 1939 Hohauser masterpiece, which has been restored and fully modernized, with rooms featuring funky decor, hardwood floors, and a stellar marble bathroom with glass shower. There's no pool, but the beach is literally across the street, and the hotel is within walking distance of some of the hottest restaurants and bars in town. If you're one of those who is too cool to stay with the mainstream at W, staying at the Century is like telling people you live in the coolest apartment building in the hippest neighborhood.

140 Ocean Dr., South Beach, FL 33139. ℰ **888/982-3688** or 305/674-8855. Fax 305/538-5733. www.centurysouthbeach.com. 26 units. Year-round $95–$350. Rate includes continental breakfast. AE, DC, DISC, MC, V. Valet parking $25. **Amenities:** 24-hr. concierge. *In room:* A/C, TV/DVD, CD player/stereo, hair dryer, minibar, Wi-Fi.

Hilton Bentley ★   Reality-TV junkies may recognize the Hilton Bentley as the place where two of the Kardashian sisters stayed during their show *Kourtney and Khloe Take Miami*. Hotel fans will recognize the place as haute Hilton, sitting directly on the ocean in the swank South of Fifth neighborhood and featuring 100 suites ranging from studios to one- and two-bedroom quasi apartments with full kitchens, spacious marble bathrooms, and private balconies. Although there's a pool, a private beach club provides guests with prime sunning opportunities. Although it's located directly across from one of the busiest restaurants in town (Prime One Twelve), the hotel maintains a sense of quiet and serenity that's paramount in these parts.

Hotel Dining

Although travelers don't necessarily choose a hotel by its dining options, a number of Miami's best restaurants can be found inside hotels. Some of the city's most hailed cuisine can be had at the W's **Soleà** and **Mr Chow** (p. 121), The Setai's **Grill** and **Restaurant,** Delano's **Blue Door** (p. 118), Mondrian's **Asia de Cuba** (p. 116) **Casa Tua's** eponymous eatery (p. 119), Loews Hotel's **Emeril's Miami Beach** (p. 120), The Hotel's **Wish** (p. 125), and Mandarin Oriental's **Azul** (p. 144), Gansevoort South's **Philippe** and **STK,** The Betsy Hotel's **BLT Steak,** The Sanctuary's **Ola** (p. 122), Viceroy's **Eos** (p. 145), EPIC's **Area 31** (p. 143), Fairmont Turnberry's **Bourbon Steak** (p. 142), and the reigning king on the cuisine scene: **Nobu** (p. 122), a New York import at The Shore Club. See chapter 7 for reviews of these and other hotel restaurants.

101 Ocean Dr., Miami Beach, FL 33139. ℂ **800/236-8510** or 305/938-4600. Fax 305/938-4601. www.bentleymiamisouthbeach.hilton.com 100 units. Winter $399–$3,500 double; off-season $229–$2,500 double. AE, DC, DISC, MC, V. **Amenities:** Private beach club; concierge; exercise facilities; pool; spa. *In room:* A/C, TV/DVD, fax, hair dryer, Wi-Fi.

The Hotel ★ Kitschy fashion designer Todd Oldham whimsically restored this 1939 gem (formerly the Tiffany Hotel) as he would have restored a vintage piece of couture. He laced it with lush, cool colors, hand-cut mirrors, and glass mosaics from his ready-to-wear factory, then added artisan detailing, terrazzo floors, and porthole windows. The small, soundproof rooms are very comfortable and incredibly stylish, though the bathrooms are a bit cramped. Nevertheless, the showers are irresistible, with fantastic rain showerheads. There's no need to pay more for an oceanfront view here—go up to the rooftop, where the hip and funky Spire Bar and pool are located, and you'll have an amazing view of the Atlantic. The hotel's restaurant, **Wish** (p. 125), is one of South Beach's best and most beautiful. New to the hotel: an oceanfront addition of 20 new deluxe rooms and suites, including two new 850-square-foot oceanfront terrace suites located at 800 Ocean Dr., above News Café. Oldham-designed rooms feature warm tones of browns, grays, and orange; flatscreens; glass-enclosed showers with oversized shower heads; thick windows to block out the inevitable noise; and separate rates—$225 to $415 off season; $265 to $545 in winter. The addition shares facilities with its sister property.

801 Collins Ave., South Beach, FL 33139. ℂ **877/843-4683** or 305/531-2222. Fax 305/531-3222. www.thehotelofsouthbeach.com. 53 units. Winter $225–$545 suite; off-season $195–$415 suite. AE, DC, DISC, MC, V. Valet parking $25 per day. **Amenities:** Restaurant; bar; pool bar; concierge; gym; small pool; room service. *In room:* A/C, TV, hair dryer, MP3 docking station, free Wi-Fi.

Hotel Astor ★ This venerable Deco hotel has gone through an identity crisis over the past few years, but we think it may be over. Undergoing renovations in 2009, rooms are decorated in soothing tones of taupe with blonde oak and chrome accents, hardwood floors, and featuring large marble bathrooms. Other new additions to the hotel include a spa, and star chef Douglas Rodriguez's second Miami restaurant, **D Rodriguez Cuba,** serving progressive Latin cuisine. No pool here anymore, but it's 2 blocks from the beach.

956 Washington Ave., South Beach, FL 33139. ℂ **800/270-4981** or 305/531-8081. Fax 305/531-3193. www.hotelastor.com. 40 units. Winter $155–$220 double, $340–$700 suite; off-season $125–$170 double, $220–$500 suite. $12 daily resort fee includes beach chairs, umbrellas, newspaper. AE, DC, MC, V. Valet parking $20. **Amenities:** Restaurant; 2 bars; babysitting; 24-hr. concierge; gym; room service; spa. *In room:* A/C, TV, hair dryer, minibar, free Wi-Fi.

Hotel Ocean ★   This Mediterranean enclave, located smack in the middle of crazy Ocean Drive, remains somehow protected from the disarray, perhaps due to the lovely French-style courtyard, in which live jazz is often performed. The European-style hotel's 27 suites are great, with soundproofed windows, terraces facing the ocean, massive bathrooms with French toiletries, and original fireplaces that add to the coziness, even if you're not likely to use them. Funky and comfy furniture, wood flooring, and Spanish tile bathrooms with 20-square-foot showers are the latest additions to the hotel's rooms. Room 504 is the hotel's best-kept secret, with ocean view and private balcony. The hotel's restaurant, Hosteria Romana II, is known for its superb service, rustic decor, and big plates of Italian food. There's no pool, but since the beach is directly across the street, it really shouldn't stop you from staying at this excellent spot.

1230 Ocean Dr., Miami Beach, FL 33139. ℂ **800/783-1725** or 305/672-2579. Fax 305/672-7665. www. hotelocean.com. 27 units. Winter $230–$280 double, $330–$515 suite; $750 penthouse; off season $199–$245 double, $290–$460 suite, $555 penthouse. Rates include continental breakfast. AE, DC, DISC, MC, V. Valet parking $20. Pets accepted for $15 per day. **Amenities:** Restaurant; babysitting; concierge; half-price admission to nearby health club; limited room service. *In room:* A/C, TV/DVD, CD player, fridge, hair dryer, minibar, Wi-Fi.

Hotel St. Augustine ★★ 📖   Proving that good things do, indeed, come in small packages is this diminutive, South of Fifth boutique hotel that's part spa, part hotel, and part haven for hipsters seeking refuge from the more mainstream boutique hotel–cum–hangouts. The lobby is minute, with an equally miniature bar, but at least there is a bar, and the rooms are smallish, but designed like cosmopolitan lofts, with maple wood beds and banquettes, and outstanding, spacious bathrooms with glass-enclosed spa cabinets with steam baths and European-engineered multijet spray showers. Seriously, if you're into bathrooms, this is Nirvana. Dimmable lighting in the bathroom and a spa bar that offers aromatherapy oils, cooling eye masks, invigorating shower gels, body buffers, and protective sun products make it hard to leave the room.

347 Washington Ave., Miami Beach, FL 33139. ℂ **800/310-7717** or 305/532-0570. Fax 305/532-8493. www.hotelstaugustine.com. 24 units. Year-round $155–$175 double. Rates include continental breakfast. AE, DC, MC, V. Self-parking $15. **Amenities:** Bar; 24-hr. concierge; discounted use of nearby health club; video/CD library. *In room:* A/C, TV/DVD, CD player, hair dryer, minibar, Wi-Fi.

The Mercury South Beach ★ 📖   Another South of Fifth hot spot, The Mercury is an upscale, modern, all-suite resort that combines Mediterranean charm with trendy South Beach flair. With new ownership, the hotel has managed to iron out some kinks as reported by our readers and is now back up to speed with improved service, amenities, and housekeeping. The hotel is also attached to (but not affiliated with) two of the beach's best restaurants, Nemo and Shoji Sushi (p. 125 and 126, respectively), which also provide the hotel's room service. A small outdoor heated pool and Jacuzzi are located in a courtyard that's shared with the restaurant (yes, diners can see you swim). Accommodations are ultrastylish, with sleek light-wood furnishings, Mascioni cotton bedding, European kitchens, and spacious bathrooms with spa tubs. If you're able to splurge, the penthouse here is hypercool, with wraparound terrace and massive living and bedroom areas and kitchen. If you're looking to stay in style without the hassle of the South Beach hustle and bustle, this is the place for you.

100 Collins Ave., Miami Beach, FL 33139. © **877/786-2732** or 305/398-3000. Fax 305/398-3001. www. themercurysouthbeach.com. 44 units. Seasonal rates $159–$239. AE, DC, MC, V. Valet parking $25. **Amenities:** Concierge; access to local fitness center (Crunch); Jacuzzi; heated pool; room service. *In room:* A/C, TV/DVD, CD player/stereo, hair dryer, kitchen, minibar, Wi-Fi.

Prime Hotel Impala ★ 📷 Now owned by an Italian hotel company with properties in Rome and Milan, this charming Mediterranean hideaway is one of the area's best kept secrets, and it's just beautiful, from the Greco-Roman frescoes and friezes to an intimate garden that is perfumed with the scent of hanging lilies and gardenias. Rooms have supercushy sleigh beds, sisal rug floors, wrought-iron fixtures, imported Belgian cotton linens, wood furniture, and fabulous-looking, but also incredibly small, bathrooms done up in stainless steel and coral rock. The two smallest rooms here are nos. 102 and 206; otherwise, the rooms are pretty spacious and cushy. Adjacent to the hotel is Spiga (p. 132), an intimate, excellent Italian restaurant that is reasonably priced. Enclaves like this one are rare on South Beach. Rates include complimentary continental breakfast and access to Nikki Beach Club.

1228 Collins Ave., South Beach, FL 33139. © **800/646-7252** or 305/673-2021. Fax 305/673-5984. www.primehotels.it/eng/impalahotel.html. 17 units. Winter $195–$225 double, $325–$425 suite; off-season $145–$195 double, $250–$325 suite. Rates include continental breakfast. AE, DC, MC, V. Valet parking $20. Small pets permitted. **Amenities:** Restaurant; concierge; room service. *In room:* A/C, TV/DVD, CD player, hair dryer, high-speed Internet.

Raleigh Hotel ★★ The Raleigh is quintessential old-school Miami Beach with a modern twist. Polished wood, original terrazzo floors, and an intimate martini bar add to the fabulous atmosphere that's favored by fashion photographers, for whom the hotel's fleur-de-lis pool is the favorite subject. In fact, one look at the pool and you'll expect Esther Williams to splash up in a dramatic, aquatic plié. The entire outdoor area is a stunning oasis that elicits oohs and aahs from even the most jaded jet-setters. The cozy bar off the lobby is reminiscent of a place where Dorothy Parker and her Algonquin Round Tablers would have gathered for spirited musings. Rooms have been redone with period furnishings, iPod docking stations, gourmet minibars, and terrazzo floors (those overlooking the pool and ocean are the most peaceful). The massive penthouse is a favorite among visiting celebrities and authors. But it's the Raleigh's warm, romantic Deco atmosphere that lures people away from chillier, neighboring boutique hotels. In 2009, hip hotelier Andre Balazs sold the property to a group that insists it will maintain its current splendor. And why shouldn't they? It's a no-brainer. Expected in 2010: a big-name NYC restaurant to call the Raleigh home.

> ### Desi Was Here
>
> During the Raleigh Hotel's opening-night white-tie ball in 1940, a sick band member was replaced by a then-unknown local drummer. You may have heard of him: Desi Arnaz.

THE BEST hotel spas

- **Agua Spa at the Delano,** 1685 Collins Ave., Miami Beach (✆ **305/673-2900**), is resplendently situated on the rooftop of the hotel, overlooking the Atlantic, and features stellar treatments such as the milk-and-honey massage that make it popular with celebs and lay-women alike. Lose yourself in a tub of fragrant oils, algae, or minerals for a 20-minute revitalization, or try the collagen, mud, and hydrating masks.

- **The Ritz-Carlton, Key Biscayne Spa,** 415 Grand Bay Dr., Key Biscayne (✆ **305/648-5900**), is a sublime 20,000-square-foot West Indies–colonial style Eden in which you can treat yourself to over 60 treatments, including Shea Mango Body Buff, Seawater Therapy, Coco-Luscious Body Treatment, and Vichy Rain revitalization in which sprays of hot and cold water are said to stimulate circulation, energize the body, and bring satisfaction to your psyche.

- **The Standard,** 40 Island Ave., Miami Beach (✆ **305/673-1717**), is an updated version of an old-school, Borscht Belt–style, Miami Beach spa, featuring authentic Turkish hammam, a Wall of Sound Shower, cedar sauna room, and resplendent bayfront pool.

- **Fairmont Turnberry Isle Resort & Club,** 19999 W. Country Club Dr., Aventura (✆ **305/932-6200**), offers a sprawling 25,000-square-foot spa with a massive menu of treatments, Finnish saunas, Turkish steam rooms, turbulent whirlpools, and bracing cold-plunge tubs that are sure to give you an uplifting jolt.

- **Spa Internazionale at Fisher Island,** 1 Fisher Island Dr., Fisher Island (✆ **800/537-3708**), is the city's poshest spa, known for its picturesque setting and the Guinot Paris Hydradermie facial—a 75-minute moisturizing and cleansing facial that leaves the skin silky smooth.

- **The Spa at Mandarin Oriental,** 500 Brickell Key Dr., Miami (✆ **305/913-8288**), is a luxe, tri-level spa preferred by the likes of Jennifer Aniston and Jennifer Lopez, best known for its innovative and restorative treatments inspired by the ancient traditions of Chinese, ayurvedic, European, Balinese, and Thai cultures. The 17 private treatment rooms are done up in bamboo, rice paper,

1775 Collins Ave., Miami Beach, FL 33139. ✆ **800/848-1775** or 305/534-6300. Fax 305/538-8140. www.raleighhotel.com. 104 units. Winter $495–$925 double; $950–$2,750 suite; off-season $225–$700 double; $700–$2,000 suite. AE, DC, DISC, MC, V. Valet parking $30. **Amenities:** Restaurant; coffee bar; bar; concierge; pool; room service. *In room:* A/C, TV/DVD, CD player, fridge, hair dryer, minibar, Wi-Fi.

The Standard ★★ The quintessential spa resort, the Standard, still owned by Andre Balazs, is housed in Miami Beach's legendary Lido Spa spot, a place that was swinging back in the days when women still wore bathing caps. Today, the hotel is full of all the modern trappings of a swank spa resort, with a bayfront view and a serene location on the Venetian Causeway—walking distance to all the South Beach glass, and natural linens, and two of the spa's split-level suites include a personal multijet tub overlooking Biscayne Bay.

o **Canyon Ranch,** 6801 Collins Ave., Miami Beach (© **304/742-9000**), is a spa's spa. The largest in Miami with over 54 treatment rooms, Canyon Ranch's methods of pampering are among the most high tech in the biz, from traditional massages, scrubs, and treatments to ultimate health and wellness programs regulated by medical professionals.

o **Lapis at the Fontainebleau,** 4441 Collins Ave., Miami Beach (© **304/538-2000**), may be located in the most massive hotel in the city, but once you're inside, you'll feel like you're the only one in the universe with highlights including mineral water jet pool with red seaweed extract and heated hammam benches and a light massage that, combined with a series of electrical currents, is like a nip/tuck without the nipping.

o **ESPA at Acqualina,** 17875 Collins Ave., Miami Beach (© **304/918-6844**), the first of its kind in the United States, offers the latest facials, advanced massages, and Ayurvedic experi-

ences. The luxurious two-story spa overlooks the glistening Atlantic Ocean.

o **Sports Club/LA at the Four Seasons,** 1435 Brickell Ave., Miami (© **305/358-3535**). Although this 44,000-square-foot musclehead hangout is a cardio and weight-lifting-obsessed paradise, there's also a spa consisting of 10 treatment rooms including a couple's massage room and wet treatment room with Vichy showers.

o **The Spa at Icon Brickell at Viceroy,** 485 Brickell Ave., Miami (© **305/503-4400**), Designed by the master of minimalism Philippe Starck, the spa looks like a cozy library with bookshelves, sofa, and fireplaces. But this isn't your professor's study. Also inside: hot and cold sunken marble baths. Treatment rooms feature billowing white curtains, a Starck-ian trademark. Stunning.

o **The Spa at The Setai,** 2001 Collins Ave. (© **305/520-6500**), a stellar, Asian-style spa where the philosophy of relaxation is derived from an ancient Sanskrit legend, natural elixirs, eternal youth, and Asian treatments and ingredients such as green tea.

craziness. Remnants of the atomic age of the fabulous '50s still exist here—the lobby's white-marble walls, terrazzo floors, and stainless-steel elevators. Add to that a touch of Scandinavian retro-modernism. Whitewashed guest rooms are serviced by roaming carts offering herbal teas and aromatherapy footbaths. There's a cedar sauna; a Turkish hammam; tongue-in-cheek treatments, such as the cellulite-fighting Standard Spanking; a chlorine-free plunge pool, with a 12-foot-tall waterfall and DJ-spun music piped beneath the water; clothing-optional mud baths; and a waterfront restaurant with glorious waterfront views. Anything but standard.

40 Island Ave., Miami Beach, FL 33139. ✆ **305/673-1717.** Fax 305/673-8181. www.standardhotel.com. 105 units. $165–$1,250 suite. AE, DC, DISC, MC, V. Valet parking $25. **Amenities:** Restaurant; bar; concierge; fitness center; pool; limited room service; sauna; spa. *In room:* A/C, TV/DVD, CD player, hair dryer, minibar.

Moderate

Aqua ★ 💣   It's been described as the Jetsons meets Jaws, but the Aqua isn't all Hollywood. Animated, yes, but with little emphasis on special effects and more on a friendly staff, Aqua is a good catch for those looking to stay in style without compromising their budget. Rooms are ultramodern in an Ikea sort of way—in other words, cheap chic. There are apartment-like junior suites, suites, and a really fabulous penthouse, but the standard deluxe rooms aren't too shabby either, with decent-size bathrooms and high-tech amenities. It's a favorite among Europeans and young hipsters on a budget. This '50s-style boutique motel has definitely been spruced up and its sundeck, courtyard garden, and small pool are popular hangouts for those who prefer to stay off the nearby sand. A small yet sleek lounge inside is a good place for a quick cocktail, breakfast, or snack. Welcome complimentary cocktails are offered Thursdays through Saturdays.

1530 Collins Ave., Miami Beach, FL 33139. ✆ **305/538-4361.** Fax 305/673-8109. www.aquamiami.com. 45 units. Winter $160 double, $200–$400 suite; off season $95 double; $125–$395 suite. $7.50 nightly resort fee includes free Wi-Fi in public areas, beach towels, and continental breakfast. AE, DISC, MC, V. Valet parking $25. **Amenities:** Lounge; bar; small pool. *In room:* A/C, TV, CD player, minibar.

The Catalina Hotel & Beach Club ★★   The Catalina is something straight out of an Austin Powers movie. It's groovy, indeed! So much so that the hotel took over the space next door and added 60 more rooms, a rooftop pool, and a funky sushi restaurant. Stylish but not at all stuffy, the Catalina is perhaps the only hotel in the area that can pull off using red shag carpeting—though it tends to get a bit mangy. The mod-squad lobby decor gives way to rooms glazed in white with hints of bright colors featuring Tempur-Pedic Swedish mattresses, 300-thread-count Mascioni sheets, goose-down comforters and pillows, iPods, and, of course, flatscreen TVs. The three-building hotel has a happening bar and lounge scene and features a 24-hour restaurant, Maxine's Bistro& Bar, with a decidedly European jet-set vibe and a splashy beach club where you can get poolside manicures and pedicures. Want the newest and freshest? Request a room in the recently upgraded Maxine building featuring marble bathrooms and espresso wood floors. Free passes to nightclubs and free transportation to and from Miami International are among the many perks here. If Catalina is sold out, check out its sister hotel, the **Metropole South Beach,** 635 Collins Ave. (✆ **305/672-0009;** www.metropolesouthbeach.com). An all-suite hotel with one- and two-bedroom suites is another favorite for hipsters and recording artists. Rates there start at $195 in season and $125 off-season.

1732 Collins Ave., South Beach, FL 33139. ✆ **877/SOBEGRP** [762-3477] or 305/674-1160. Fax 305/672-8216. www.catalinahotel.com. 136 units. Winter $225–$300 double; off-season $125–$250 double. Rates include continental breakfast bar and unlimited happy-hour cocktails daily from 7–8pm. AE, DC, MC, V. Valet parking $30. **Amenities:** 2 restaurants; 3 bars; beach club access; free bike cruisers; 2 pools. *In room:* A/C, TV/VCR, CD player, hair dryer, minibar, Wi-Fi ($15 a day).

Chesterfield Hotel, Suites & Day Spa ★   This charismatic sliver of a property has won the loyalty of fashion industrialists and romantics alike. Unfortunately, not everyone loves it. Some have complained of the constant construction, apathetic

Two Good-Value South Beach Hotels

For a taste of South Beach action without breaking the bank, check out the **South Seas Hotel** (1751 Collins Ave.; ℰ 800/345-2678 or 305/538-1411; www.southseashotel.com) or the **Avalon** (700 Ocean Dr.; ℰ 800/933-3306 or 305/538-0133; www.avalonhotel.com). Both offer good deals on their websites for clean, functional rooms. The South Seas common areas may be bland, but the hotel sits on a stretch of Collins between the Delano and Raleigh—a great location if you want to hang at either hotel's happening poolside bar. The Avalon is smack in the middle of Ocean Drive's *Girls Gone Wild* scene; thumping bass and wet T-shirt contests might rage around you, but the hotel maintains an aura of Art Deco calm—as does its excellent restaurant, **A Fish Called Avalon.**

—*Kelly Regan*

service, and run-down or complete lack of amenities. But if you're in a partying mood, this place is for you. The very central location (1 block from the ocean) is a plus, especially because the hotel lacks a pool. Most of the rooms are immaculate and reminiscent of a loft apartment; large bathrooms with big, deep tubs are especially enticing. However, some rooms are dark and have not had such upgrades (we have gotten complaints), and are to be avoided; do not hesitate to ask for a room change. We've also gotten complaints about the music coming from the hotel next door, but you have to realize that if you're staying on Collins or Washington avenues, you're going to hear noise: South Beach isn't known for its quiet, peaceful demeanor. For R&R, try the hotel's day spa, and for good and fast sushi, try the hotel's new sushi bar, I Love Sushi, for a quick combo of sushi and sake.

841 Collins Ave., South Beach, FL 33139. ℰ **305/673-3767.** Fax 305/535-9665. www.thechesterfield hotel.com. 90 units. Winter $175–$245 suite, $395 penthouse; off-season $125–$195 suite, $335 penthouse. Additional person $20. AE, DC, MC, V. Valet parking $30. Well-behaved pets accepted. **Amenities:** Restaurant; 2 bars; concierge; reduced rates at local gym; spa. *In room:* A/C, TV, CD player, hair dryer, high-speed Internet, minibar.

The Clinton Hotel ★ The former president has nothing to do with this chic boutique hotel, but once he gets a gander of the model types who hang here, he may want to endorse it as his own. The Clinton Hotel brings a space-age meets South Beach vibe to the area thanks to funky furniture, a somewhat sedate lobby bar, and a restaurant that has changed hands several times. Freebies including drinks every night from 8 to 9pm, Wi-Fi, and nightclub passes make up for what the hotel lacks. Although boutique hotels are becoming as dime-a-dozen as, say, Holiday Inns, this one manages to stand out from the rest thanks to its inner sanctum of serenity that includes a sleek (but tiny) pool, private sunning deck, and rooftop spa.

825 Washington Ave., South Beach, FL 33139. ℰ **305/938-4040.** Fax 305/538-1472. www.clinton southbeach.com. 88 units. Winter $215–$450 suite; off season $69–$189 suite. AE, DC, DISC, MC, V. Valet parking $22. **Amenities:** Restaurant; coffee and sandwich bar; bar; pool bar; concierge; fitness center and spa; pool; room service. *In room:* A/C, TV, hair dryer, minibar.

Crest Hotel Suites ★ 🛄 One of South Beach's best-kept secrets, the Crest Hotel has a quietly fashionable, contemporary, relaxed atmosphere with friendly service. Built in 1939, the Crest was restored to preserve its Art Deco architecture, but the interior of the hotel is thoroughly modern, with rooms resembling cosmo-politan apartments. All suites have a living room/dining room area, kitchenette, and executive work space. An indoor/outdoor cafe with terrace and poolside dining isn't besieged with trendy locals, but does attract a younger crowd. Around the corner from the hotel is Lincoln Road, with its sidewalk cafes, gourmet restaurants, the-aters, and galleries. In an effort to expand its quiet trendiness, the Crest opened its second hotel, the **South Beach Hotel,** at 236 21st St., in an area that presently isn't so great (though it's on its way up). Until the neighborhood goes through more of a renaissance, this second hotel should be a last resort if you can't get a room elsewhere.

1670 James Ave., Miami Beach, FL 33139. © **800/531-3880** or 305/531-0321. Fax 305/531-8180. www.crestgrouphotels.com/cresthotelsuites.htm. 64 units. Winter $120–$165 double, $211 suite; off-season $115 double, $175 suite. Packages available and 10% discount offered if booked on website. AE, MC, V. **Amenities:** Restaurant; cafe; pool. In room: A/C, TV, kitchenette.

Essex House Hotel and Suites ★ The Essex House Hotel was created by Deco pioneer Henry Hohauser in 1938 and has received numerous awards for its authen-tic restoration. The hotel's whimsically created shiplike architecture rises from the shore with decks that are designed to take in succulent ocean breezes. The sleek Bauhaus interiors add to the distinct charm of the place. All suites feature solid-oak furnishings and have a fridge, wet bar, and Jacuzzi. Although the hotel is right on the pulse of South Beach's constant activity, the new double-glazed, sound-absorbing windows provide an acoustical barrier to the street noise. A spa pool graces the south patio and gardens. In an area where the infamous Al Capone used to play cards, there is now an intimate dining area where complimentary breakfast is served and evening cocktails can be enjoyed.

1001 Collins Ave., Miami Beach, FL 33139. © **800/553-7739** or 305/534-2700. Fax 305/532-3827. www.essexhotel.com. Year-round $99–$299. Rates include breakfast. AE, DC, DISC, MC, V. **Amenities:** Bar; concierge; outdoor pool. In room: A/C, TV, fridge, hair dryer, Wi-Fi.

Greenview The Greenview is located just 2 blocks from the ocean on a quiet corner that's close enough to the action, but far enough away that you'll actually feel secluded from the nearby hyperactivity. A jewel-box, living-room-like lobby opens to a serene courtyard. Rooms feature handcrafted furnishings, original Modernist art-work, hardwood floors, and Sisal area rugs, although some are rather tawdry and hostel-like. Hallways are a bit dingy, too, and a far cry from the inviting lobby.

1671 Washington Ave. (at Lincoln Rd.), Miami Beach, FL 33139. © **305/531-6588.** Fax 305/531-4580. www.greenviewhotel.com. 42 units. Winter $199–$219 double; off season $89–$129 double. Rates include continental breakfast. AE, DC, DISC, MC, V. In room: A/C, TV, hair dryer upon request.

Hotel Chelsea ★ This funky Art Deco property is a boutique hotel with a bit of a twist, with accents and decor based on the principles of feng shui. Soft amber lighting, bamboo floors, full-slate bathrooms, and Japanese-style furniture arranged in a way that's meant to refresh and relax you are what separate the Chelsea from just about any other so-called boutique hotel on South Beach. Chelsea also serves free drinks at happy hour, and, in case you've had enough relaxation, free passes to South Beach's hottest nightclubs are added bonuses.

944 Washington Ave. (at 9th St.), Miami Beach, FL 33139. ℂ **305/534-4069.** Fax 305/672-6712. www. thehotelchelsea.com. 42 units. Winter $95–$225 double, $125–$245 king, $165–$300 minisuite; off-season $75–$125 double, $95–$145 king, $115–$165 minisuite excluding special event and holiday time periods; rates are subject to change. Rates include cocktails 7–8pm daily. AE, MC, DC, V. Valet parking $20. **Amenities:** Bar; free shuttle to and from MIA; concierge; discounted pass to local gym. *In room:* A/C, TV, CD player, hair dryer, minibar, free Wi-Fi.

The Kent ★ 🔥   For a funky boutique hotel in the heart of South Beach, The Kent is quite a deal. All rooms feature blond wood floors and ultramodern steel furnishings and accessories, which surprisingly aren't cold, but rather inviting and whimsical. The staff is eager to please and the clientele comes largely from the fashion industry. The decor is high on the kitsch factor, heavy on multicolored Lucite with toys and other assorted articles of whimsy, and even if you can't afford to stay in it, the very James Bond–esque Lucite Suite is a must-see. There's no pool or sundeck, but you're only 1 block from the beach here.

1131 Collins Ave., South Beach, FL 33139. ℂ **866/826-KENT** (5368) or 305/604-5068. Fax 305/531-0720. www.thekenthotel.com. 54 units. Winter $145–$250 double; off season $79–$250 double. Additional person $15. Rates include continental breakfast bar. AE, DC, DISC, MC, V. Valet parking $16; self-parking $6. **Amenities:** Bar; garden. *In room:* A/C, TV/DVD, CD player, hair dryer, minibar, free Wi-Fi.

Nassau Suite Hotel ★★   Stylish and reasonably priced, this 1937 hotel feels more like a modern apartment building with its 22 suites (studios or one-bedrooms) featuring wood floors, rattan furniture, and fully equipped open kitchens. Beds are all king-size and rather plush, but the bed isn't the room's only place to rest. Each room also has a sitting area that's quite comfortable. Registered as a National Historic Landmark, the Nassau Suite Hotel may exist in an old building, but both rooms and lobby are fully modernized. The Nassau Suite caters to a young, hip crowd of both gay and straight guests. Continental breakfast is available for $5 per person.

1414 Collins Ave., South Beach, FL 33139. ℂ **866/859-4177** or 305/532-0043. Fax 305/534-3133. www. nassausuite.com. 22 units. Winter $150 studio, $190 1-bedroom; off season $120 studio, $160 1-bedroom. AE, DC, DISC, MC, V. Parking $12. **Amenities:** Bike rental; concierge; access to nearby health club. *In room:* A/C, TV, fax, hair dryer, high-speed Internet.

Pelican Hotel ★★   Owned by the same creative folks behind the Diesel Jeans company, the fashionable Pelican is South Beach's only self-professed "toy-hotel," in which each of its 30 rooms and suites is decorated as outrageously as some of the area's more colorful drag queens. Each room has been designed daringly and rather wittily by Swedish interior decorator Magnus Ehrland. Countless trips to antiques markets, combined with his wild imagination, have turned room no. 309, for instance, into the "Psychedelic(ate) Girl"; room no. 201 into the "Executive Fifties" suite; and no. 209 into the "Love, Peace, and Leafforest" room. But the most popular room is the tough-to-score no. 215, or the "Best Whorehouse," which is said to have made even former Hollywood madam Heidi Fleiss red with envy. The Ocean Drive location and the hotel's cafe make the Pelican a very popular people-watching spot.

826 Ocean Dr., Miami Beach, FL 33139. ℂ **800/7-PELICAN** (773-5422) or 305/673-3373. Fax 305/673-3255. www.pelicanhotel.com. 30 units. Winter $280–$450 double, $480–$800 oceanfront suite; off-season $165–$220 double, $330–$540 oceanfront suite. AE, DC, MC, V. Valet parking $22. **Amenities:** Restaurant; bar; concierge; access to area gyms; room service; Wi-Fi. *In room:* A/C, TV, stereo/CD player, fridge with complimentary water, hair dryer.

South Beach Plaza Villas ★   This charming place and all its lush gardens, villas, suites, rooms, and bungalows stands apart from the rest of South Beach for one reason—it's the first and only entirely nonsmoking hotel in the area. The renovated Spanish Mediterranean–style 1930s villas feature wood-planked vaulted ceilings, fireplaces (just what we need here, though it does add to the cozy ambience), modern stainless-steel kitchens, and great lighting. The villas look down upon the spruced-up so-called Exotic Hawaiian Gardens and waterfalls. Standard king-sized hotel rooms are nearly the same but without the kitchens. All rooms, of course, have flatscreen TVs, but strangely enough, not all have full-length mirrors. If you plan to stay 4 or more nights, check out and check into one of the private bungalows featuring stainless-steel kitchens, bedroom, office, den, and pullout sofa. The bar is a great place for martinis, and the restaurant in the garden serves breakfast, lunch, and dinner.

1411 Collins Ave., South Beach, FL 33139. ✆ **305/531-1331.** Fax 305/538-9898. www.brighamgardens. com. 23 units. Winter $100–$199 1-bedroom; off season $70–$110 1-bedroom. Resort fee $8.95 per day. 10% discount on stays of 7 days or longer. AE, MC, V. Pets accepted for $6 a night. **Amenities:** Restaurant; bar; concierge. *In room:* A/C, TV, fridge, microwave, Wi-Fi.

Townhouse ★★   New York hipster Jonathan Morr felt that Miami Beach had lost touch with the bons vivants who gave the city its original cachet, so he decided to take matters into his own hands. His solution: this 67-room, five-story so-called shabby-chic hotel. The charm of this hotel is in its clean and simple yet chic design with quirky details: exercise equipment that stands alone in the hallways, free laundry machines in the lobby, and a water bed–lined rooftop. Comfortable, shabby-chic rooms boast L-shaped couches for extra guests (for whom you aren't charged). Though the rooms are all pretty much the same, consider the ones with the partial ocean view. The hotel also offers beach access, with chair and umbrella rentals available. The hotel's basement features the hot sushi spot, Bond St. Lounge (p. 128).

150 20th St., South Beach, FL 33139. ✆ **877/534-3800** or 305/534-3800. Fax 305/534-3811. www. townhousehotel.com. 69 units. Winter $195–$395 double, $395–$450 penthouse; off-season $105–$215 double, $295–$390 penthouse. Rates include Parisian-style (coffee and pastry) breakfast. AE, MC, V. Valet parking $25. **Amenities:** Restaurant; bar; bike rental; workout stations; free Wi-Fi. *In room:* A/C, TV/VCR, CD player, fridge, hair dryer.

Whitelaw Hotel ★   With a slogan that reads "Clean sheets, hot water, and stiff drinks," the Whitelaw Hotel stands apart from other boutique hotels with its fierce sense of humor. Only half a block from Ocean Drive, this hotel, like its clientele, is full of distinct personalities, pairing such disparate elements as luxurious Belgian sheets with shag carpeting to create an innovative setting. All-white rooms manage to be homey and plush, and not at all antiseptic, with white wood floors, a much needed improvement from the old linoleum. Bathrooms are pretty small and not that well stocked, and towels are sometimes in short supply, but those who stay here aren't really looking for luxury—they just want to party. Complimentary cocktails in the lobby every night from 7 to 8pm contribute to a very social atmosphere. In 2008, the owners of the Whitelaw opened a new stay, the **Riviera** (✆ **877/762-3477**), tucked away at 2000 Liberty Ave., on South Beach, featuring imaginatively designed one-bedroom apartmentlike accommodations with full gourmet kitchens; a courtyard pool complete with an outdoor bar, grill, and private cabanas; a lobby lounge; a state-of-the-art spa and yoga room; and a sundeck with sweeping views of the city and ocean. Rates start at $215 in the winter and $145 off-season.

808 Collins Ave., Miami Beach, FL 33139. ☎ **305/398-7000**. Fax 305/398-7010. www.whitelawhotel. com. 49 units. Winter $145–$195 double/king; off-season $95–$145 double/king. Rates subject to change during special events. Rates include continental breakfast and cocktails in the lobby (7–8pm daily). AE, DC, MC, V. Parking $30. **Amenities:** Lounge; free airport pickup (to and from MIA); concierge; free passes to area nightclubs. *In room:* A/C, TV, CD player, hair dryer, Wi-Fi ($15/day).

Inexpensive

Clay Hotel & International Hostel ★ ✦

A member of the International Youth Hostel Federation (IYHF), the Clay occupies a beautiful 1920s-style Spanish Mediterranean building at the corner of historic Española Way. Like other IYHF members, this hostel is open to all ages and is a great place to meet people. The usual smattering of Australians, Europeans, and other budget travelers makes it Miami's best clearinghouse of "insider" travel information. Although a thorough renovation in 1996 made this hostel an incredible value and a step above any others in town, don't expect nightly turndown service or chocolates. But, for a hostel, it's full of extras. Ninety rooms have private bathrooms and 12 VIP rooms have balconies overlooking quaint Española Way. There are also male and female dorm rooms with four to six beds and private bathrooms. You will find occasional movie nights, an outdoor weekend market, and a tour desk with car rental available. Reservations for private rooms are essential in season and recommended year-round.

> **Impressions**
>
> *I think South Beach targets vacationers who, if not affluent, would like to feel that way for a little while.*
> —Rachel Ponce on PBS's *Going Places*

1438 Washington Ave. (at Española Way), South Beach, FL 33139. ☎ **800/379-2529** or 305/534-2988. Fax 305/673-0346. www.clayhotel.com. 120 units. $42–$88 double; $16–$20 dorm beds. During the off season, pay for 6 nights in advance and get 7th night free. MC, V. Parking $10. **Amenities:** Cafe; bike rental; concierge; access to nearby health club; kitchen. *In room:* A/C, TV, fridge, hair dryer.

Clevelander ★

A South Beach institution favored by the beer-swilling set, the Clevelander is best known for its neon- and glass-blocked poolside and bar used in countless photo shoots and Budweiser commercials. As far as its reputation as a hotel, it has improved thanks to a major face-lift in the form of new lobby and guest rooms with Wi-Fi, 300-thread-count Egyptian cotton bedding, high-definition plasma TVs, blackout curtains, noise-reducing systems, and flatscreens, and, of course, more bars and a rooftop lounge. Despite the noise-reducing systems, the makeover hasn't really changed the noise level, which on Ocean Drive can be deafening. Party animals don't mind at all. But if your idea of a party doesn't involve drinking challenges and wet-T-shirt contests, visit the Clevelander for a cocktail and stay elsewhere.

1020 Ocean Dr., Miami Beach, FL 33139. ☎ **877/532-4006** or 305/532-4006. Fax 305/534-4707. www. clevelander.com. 60 units. Winter $189–$269 double; off season $129–$209 double. AE, DC, MC, V. Valet parking $20. **Amenities:** Restaurant; 5 bars; concierge; gym; outdoor pool; rooftop decks. *In room:* A/C, TV, Wi-Fi.

Hotel Shelley ★

The renovated Hotel Shelley has a laid-back beach atmosphere, yet cutting-edge style. The architecturally sound boutique hotel built in 1931 in the heart of the Art Deco District of Miami Beach has reinvented itself with a complete $1.5-million renovation of its 49 guest rooms. Complete with Mascioni

300-thread-count linens, goose-down pillows and comforters, LCD plasma TVs, and custom-built cabinetry, the guest rooms at the Shelley allow you to chill out after a long day at the beach or rock out before a big night of partying. The subtle purple hues in the rooms and public areas are in true Art Deco style. The bar in the lobby offers free drinks from 7 to 8pm every night and VIP passes to area nightclubs.

844 Collins Ave., Miami Beach, FL 33139. © **305/531-3341.** Fax 305/535-9665. www.hotelshelley.com. 49 units. Winter $145–$225 double, $165–$245 king, $165–$300 minisuite; off-season $75–$125 double, $95–$145 king, $115–$165 minisuite. Rates are subject to change for special events and holidays. Rates include cocktails in the lobby. AE, DC, MC, V. Parking $30. **Amenities:** Lounge; free airport pickup (to and from MIA); concierge; free passes to area nightclubs. *In room:* A/C, TV, CD player, hair dryer, mini-bar.

The Loft Hotel   A boutique hotel along the lines of the Aqua (p. 88)—though less whimsical, enticing, and airy-feeling—this renovated apartment building (which really gives you the feeling of staying in an apartment rather than a hotel) offers 20 suites, all surrounding a tidy, tropically landscaped garden. Rooms are especially spacious, with queen-size beds, breakfast room, conversation area, and hardwood or tile floors. Bathrooms are brand new and, for an old Art Deco building, pretty spacious. This hotel is popular with young, hip, European types, just as the Aqua is, but there isn't that much difference between the two hotels other than the fact that the Loft's rooms have fully equipped kitchens while Aqua's rooms don't, and Aqua has a bar/restaurant while the Loft does not. Prices at the Loft are very reasonable and the owners, who also own Villa Paradiso (see below), are extremely accommodating.

952 Collins Ave., Miami Beach, FL 33139. © **305/534-2244.** Fax 305/538-1509. www.thelofthotel.com. 57 units. Winter $139–$179 double; off season $89–$129 double. AE, DC, MC, V. Valet parking $20. **Amenities:** VIP passes to local nightclubs. *In room:* A/C, TV/DVD, hair dryer, kitchen, free Wi-Fi.

Villa Paradiso ★★ 🛍   This guesthouse, like South Beach Villas (see above), is more like a cozy apartment house than a hotel. There's no elegant lobby or restaurant, but the amicable staff is happy to give you a room key and advice on what to do. The recently renovated spacious apartments are simple but elegant—hardwood floors, French doors, and stylish wrought-iron furniture—and are remarkably quiet considering their location, a few blocks from Lincoln Road and all of South Beach's best clubs. All have full kitchens, and guests have a choice of either a queen or two double beds or foldout couches for extra friends. All rooms overlook the hotel's pretty courtyard garden.

1415 Collins Ave., Miami Beach, FL 33139. © **305/532-0616.** Fax 305/673-5874. www.villaparadisohotel.com. 17 units. Winter $100–$165 apartment; off season $75–$129 apartment. Weekly rates are 10% cheaper. Additional person $10. AE, DC, MC, V. Parking nearby $15. Pets (including small "nonbarking" dogs) accepted for $10 with a $100 deposit. *In room:* A/C, TV, kitchen, free Wi-Fi.

MIAMI BEACH: SURFSIDE, BAL HARBOUR & SUNNY ISLES

The area just north of South Beach, known as Miami Beach, encompasses Surfside, Bal Harbour, and Sunny Isles. Unrestricted by zoning codes throughout the 1950s, 1960s, and especially the 1970s, area developers went crazy, building ever-bigger and more brazen structures, especially north of 41st Street, which is now known as Condo Canyon. Consequently, there's now a glut of medium-quality condos, with a few scattered holdouts of older hotels and motels casting shadows over the newer, swankier stays emerging on the beachfront.

The western section of the neighborhood used to be inundated with Brooklyn's elderly Jewish population during the season. Though the area still maintains a religious preference, visiting tourists from Argentina to Germany, replete with Speedos and thong bikinis, are clearly taking over.

Miami Beach, as described here, runs from 24th Street to 192nd Street, a long strip that varies slightly from end to end. Staying in the southern section, from 24th to 42nd streets, can be a good deal—it's still close to the South Beach scene, but the rates are more affordable. The North Beach area begins at 63rd Street and extends north to the city limit at 87th Terrace and west to Biscayne Bay (at Bay Dr. W.). Bal Harbour and Bay Harbor are at the center of Miami Beach and retain their exclusivity and character. The neighborhoods north and south of here, such as Surfside and Sunny Isles, have nice beaches and some shops, but are a little worn around the edges.

Very Expensive

Canyon Ranch Miami Beach ★   Opened in late 2008 in the former Carillon Hotel on an unseemly stretch of Collins Avenue, the Miami version of the famous Arizona and Lenox, Massachusetts, spa and wellness hotel is located directly on the beach. If you're looking to drop in excess of, say, $330 for a Japanese bathing ritual, or $350 for an insomnia consultation with a doctor, then this place is for you. The main draw isn't a trendy bar, restaurant, or nightclub, but a 70,000-square-foot health club that includes a two-story rock-climbing wall as well as equipment for testing oxygen saturation and bone density. There's even a $125,000 body scanner that, according to the property's medical director, is the best in the world. The hotel has a full-time medical staff of 11, including a Chinese medicine specialist/acupuncturist, nutritionist, and physical therapist. Because the place operates as a condo as well, every suite has fine furnishings, top electronics, and a designer kitchen. All have balconies. The oceanfront Canyon Ranch Grill features all healthy fare. In addition to 750 feet of beach, there are four pools, a reading garden, and water therapy programs. To preserve the tranquil vibe here, cellphone use is prohibited in many of the hotel's public areas.

6900 Collins Ave., Miami Beach, FL 33140. *©* **800/742-9000** or 305/514-7000. Fax 305/864-2744. www.canyonranch.com. 150 units. Winter suites from $650; off-season suites from $450. AE, DISC, MC, V. Valet parking $35. **Amenities:** 3 restaurants; juice and smoothie bar; babysitting; fitness center; 4 outdoor pools; rock-climbing arena; room service; spa. *In room:* A/C, TV, high-speed Internet, kitchen.

Expensive

Alexander All-Suite Luxury Hotel ★   Just a few miles from happening South Beach or ritzy Bal Harbour, the Alexander is pricey, but worth it for the size of the suites and the doting attention. Like staying at a rich grandparent's condo, suites are spacious one- and two-bedroom mini-apartments with private balconies overlooking the Atlantic Ocean and Miami's Intracoastal Waterway. Each contains a living room, a fully equipped kitchen, *two* bathrooms (one with just a shower and the other with a shower/tub combo), and a balcony. The hotel itself is well decorated, with sculptures, paintings, antiques, and tapestries, most of which were garnered from the Cornelius Vanderbilt mansion. Two oceanfront pools are surrounded by lush

Miami Beach

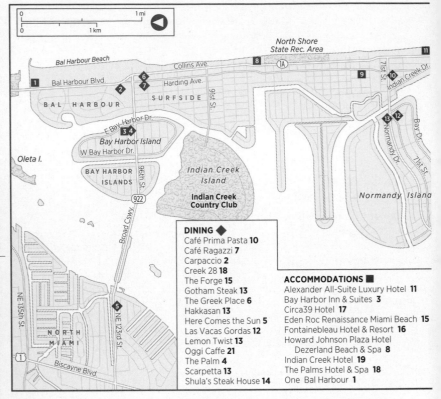

DINING ◆
Café Prima Pasta **10**
Café Ragazzi **7**
Carpaccio **2**
Creek 28 **18**
The Forge **15**
Gotham Steak **13**
The Greek Place **6**
Hakkasan **13**
Here Comes the Sun **5**
Las Vacas Gordas **12**
Lemon Twist **13**
Oggi Caffe **21**
The Palm **4**
Scarpetta **13**
Shula's Steak House **14**

ACCOMMODATIONS ■
Alexander All-Suite Luxury Hotel **11**
Bay Harbor Inn & Suites **3**
Circa39 Hotel **17**
Eden Roc Renaissance Miami Beach **15**
Fontainebleau Hotel & Resort **16**
Howard Johnson Plaza Hotel
  Dezerland Beach & Spa **8**
Indian Creek Hotel **19**
The Palms Hotel & Spa **18**
One Bal Harbour **1**

vegetation; one of these "lagoons" is fed by a cascading waterfall. Shula's Steak House, owned by former Dolphins football coach Don Shula, is open for lunch and dinner daily.

5225 Collins Ave., Miami Beach, FL 33140. ☎ **800/327-6121** or 305/865-6500. Fax 305/341-6553. www.alexanderhotel.com. 150 units. Winter: 1-bedroom suite $399, 2-bedroom suite $599; Summer: 1-bedroom suite $239, 2-bedroom suite $399 and up. Packages available. AE, MC, V. Parking $25. Very small pets accepted for a $250 nonrefundable deposit for cleaning the suite. **Amenities:** 3 restaurants; 2 bars; concierge; small fitness center; Jacuzzis; 2 large outdoor pools; limited room service; sauna; spa; watersports equipment/rentals. *In room:* A/C, TV, hair dryer, kitchen, Wi-Fi.

Eden Roc Renaissance Miami Beach ★★ Just next door to the mammoth Fontainebleau, this Morris Lapidus–designed flamboyant hotel, which opened in 1956, in 2008 received a $200-million face-lift, doubling its size from 349 to 631 rooms and complete with a new 283-room oceanfront tower, 17 bungalow suites, four pools, two restaurants, and a spa. The focal point is now an oasis of pools, water features, and gardens, threaded with walkways and intimate seating areas. If we had a choice between Eden Roc and Fontainebleau, we'd choose the Eden Roc, hands

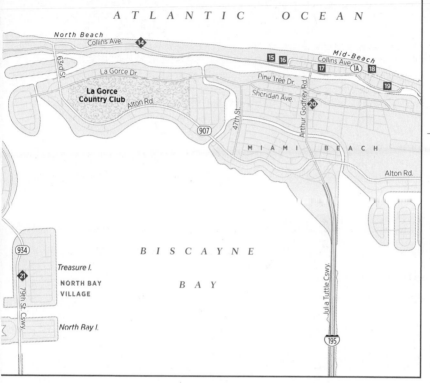

down, for the seamless service and for a more relaxed, much less Las Vegasy vibe than its neighbor.

4525 Collins Ave., Miami Beach, FL 33140. © **800/327-8337** or 305/531-0000. Fax 305/674-5555. www.renaissancehotels.com. 631 units. Winter $339–$425 double, $394–$450 suite, $750–$1,500 bungalow suites, $2,500–$3,500 penthouse; off-season $199–$274 double, $239–$409 suite, $450–$750 bungalows, $1,500 penthouse. Additional person $15. Packages available. AE, DC, DISC, MC, V. Valet parking $24. Pets accepted for a fee. **Amenities:** 2 restaurants; lounge; bar; babysitting; concierge; health club; 4 outdoor pools; room service; spa; watersports equipment/rentals. *In room:* A/C, TV, hair dryer, high-speed Internet, kitchenettes (in suites and penthouse), minibar.

Fontainebleau Hotel and Resort ★ Big changes—$1 *billion* worth—are afoot at Miami Beach's legendary hotel. Designed by the late Morris Lapidus, this grand monolith symbolized Old Miami decadence. This is where all the greats performed in their prime; but now it's all just nostalgia, as the hotel readies itself for the 21st century with a massive renovation. Reopened in 2008 as a modern Vegas-style hotel, entertainment, and dining complex, the Fontainebleau features all the trappings of a luxury hotel—flatscreen TVs, plush bedding, and, well, you get the idea. Choose from the main property or the modern, brand-new all-suite hotel tower, where rooms are plush and posh. A 40,000-square-foot spa, with mineral-rich water therapies and co-ed swimming pools; a dramatic oceanfront poolscape, featuring "walls of water," intermingled with a free-form, Lapidus-influenced pool; and a sexy, intimate enclave surrounded by cabanas and sun loungers are among the many highlights. The hotel has brought celebrity chefs as well—with Alfred Portale's Gotham Steak, Scott Conant's hot New York Italian outpost Scarpetta, and London's highly rated Chinese restaurant Hakkasan all among the 11 (yes 11) restaurants and lounges. In addition, there's one hotter-than-hot nightclub, two lounges, big-name musical headliners, and other Vegas-style entertainment options. Bottom line here: It's huge. And in some ways, it resembles an airport, only airports have the hustle, bustle, and crowd factor. This place is so spread out you may feel like you're in a closed terminal. But some people like that frenetic, airport vibe, especially when boldface chefs and celebrities pass through. In its infancy in early 2009, we received many complaints about the service, the emptiness—1,500 plus rooms are hard to fill at these prices and during this economy—and the lack of any sort of vibe (unless you consider our airport analogy), but if you're looking for a one-stop hot spot that you won't likely want to leave, this is the place to be.

4441 Collins Ave., Miami Beach, FL 33140. ☎ **800/548-8886** or 305/538-2000. Fax 305/535-3286. www.fontainebleau.com. 1,504 units. Winter from $399 double, from $509 suite; off-season from $229 double, from $299 suite. AE, DISC, MC, V. Valet parking $32. Pets accepted. **Amenities:** 11 restaurants and lounges; concierge; fitness center; 11 pools with cabanas; room service; spa. *In room:* A/C, TV/DVD, fax, hair dryer, iMac with high-speed Internet, kitchenette (in suites), minibar.

Moderate

Circa39 Hotel ★ 🎁 Some folks like to get away, take a holiday from the neighborhood, which is why Circa39 had the wisdom to open up where it did—close enough to the South Beach action for those who want to play, but far enough away to actually get some sleep when you want it. The 100-room boutique hotel known as the Copley Plaza circa 1939, hence the name, has been redone and spruced up with modern amenities such as Wi-Fi, bistro for light snacks, lounge for cocktails, pool deck, tropical courtyard with laid-back day beds, and a fitness room. If you're looking to stay in a hip hotel but don't want to deal with the frenzy of South Beach, this is a great option. Otherwise, consider staying in one of the countless boutiques on South Beach, where you'll get a lot more scene for your buck.

3900 Collins Ave., South Beach, FL 33139. ☎ **877/824-7223** or 305/538-4900. Fax 305/538-4998. www.circa39.com. 82 units. Winter $139–$289 double; off season $99–$189 double. Additional person $25. AE, MC, V. Self-parking $15. Pet friendly. **Amenities:** Bistro; lounge; beach chairs and umbrellas; concierge; tropical courtyard; fitness room; outdoor pool. *In room:* A/C, TV, hair dryer, Wi-Fi.

Indian Creek Hotel ★ 🎁 Located off the beaten path, the Indian Creek Hotel is a meticulously restored 1936 building with one of the first operating elevators in Miami Beach. Because of its location, which faces the Indian Creek waterway, and its lush landscaping, this place feels like an old-fashioned Key West bed-and-breakfast. The revamped rooms are outfitted in Art Deco furnishings, such as antique writing desks, pretty tropical prints, and small but spotless bathrooms. Just 1 block from a good stretch of sand, the hotel also has a landscaped pool area in the back garden. Although one reader who stayed there complained that the staff was surly, the room was dirty, the lush courtyard was overgrown, and he wasn't informed that he needed a parking pass—obtainable at the hotel—the good news is that there is new ownership and things seem to be running smoother. The hotel's restaurant, Creek 28, is one of Miami's best-kept secrets.

2727 Indian Creek Dr. (1 block west of Collins Ave. and the ocean), Miami Beach, FL 33140. ℭ **800/491-2772** or 305/531-2727. Fax 305/531-5651. www.indiancreekhotel.com. 61 units. Winter $149–$199 double, $269–$289 suite; off-season $69–$199 double, $179–$249 suite. Additional person $25. Group packages and summer specials available. AE, DC, DISC, MC, V. **Amenities:** Restaurant; bar; concierge; pool; limited room service. *In room:* A/C, TV/VCR, CD player (in suites), fridge (in suites), hair dryer, Wi-Fi.

The New Hotel ★ ❦   If you drive too fast on Harding Avenue, you will miss this charming, funky boutique hotel located amidst North Beach's ramshackle, Art Deco motel-like apartment buildings. But don't be dismayed by its neighbors because inside is a secret oasis of all things eco-conscious, stylish, and economically savvy too. The tiny, 10-room New Hotel is located a block from the beach and features comfortably modern rooms with wood floors, Ikea-chic furniture, spacious, colorful bathrooms, and in-room recycling systems. Out back is a nice pool and bar called Lou's Beer Garden, which attracts local hipsters as well as visitors. Hungry? The Beach Market Bistro serves Mediterranean fare poolside. Staff is extremely friendly and accommodating. If you don't mind being off the beaten path and close to the beach and can snag a room here, do so.

7337 Harding Ave., Miami Beach, FL 33140. ℭ **305/704-7879** Fax 305/647-0636. www.thenewhotel miami.com. 10 units. Winter $150–$200 double; off-season $99–$129 double. AE, DC, MC, V. Public parking nearby $10 a day. **Amenities:** Restaurant; poolside bar; lounge; bike rental; concierge; pool; room service; spa; free Wi-Fi. *In room:* A/C, TV, hair dryer, free high-speed Internet, kitchenette, minibar, MP3 docking station.

The Palms Hotel & Spa ★   Just a stone's throw away from Miami Beach's entertainment district, the Palms Hotel & Spa is ideally located on the beach on the northern, more tranquil side of South Beach. As a sophisticated yet genuine oceanfront resort, it features lush gardens landscaped with palms and other tropical plants and a large freshwater pool as its centerpiece. Luxurious accommodations—recently redone and featuring fabulous spa-inspired bathrooms—as well as warm and caring service are also signature features of this property. The hotel boasts the Palms Spa, South Florida's only Aveda destination spa, offering a highly personalized experience through Aveda's holistic treatments in five multipurpose treatment rooms and four outdoor treatment cabanas, as well as hair, nail, and makeup services. In its quest to provide a natural and wholesome experience for every guest, the hotel also features a new restaurant and lounge—Essensia, the pure essence of taste—featuring a worldly menu of organic, seasonal, and locally sourced ingredients.

3025 Collins Ave., Miami Beach, FL 33140. ℭ **800/550-0505** or 305/534-0505. Fax 305/534-0515. www.thepalmshotel.com. 243 units. Winter $229–$629 double, $799 suite; off-season $169–$599 double, $649 suite. AE, DC, MC, V. Valet parking around $27. **Amenities:** Restaurant; poolside bar; lounge; bike rental; concierge; heated pool; room service; spa. *In room:* A/C, plasma TV, hair dryer, minibar, MP3 docking station, Wi-Fi.

KEY BISCAYNE

Locals call it the Key, and technically, Key Biscayne, a barrier island, isn't even part of the Florida Keys. A relatively unknown area until Richard Nixon bought a home here in the 1970s, Key Biscayne, at 1¼ square miles, is an affluent but hardly lively residential and recreational island known for its pricey homes, excellent beaches, and actor Andy Garcia, who makes his home here. The island is far enough from the mainland to make it feel semiprivate, yet close enough to downtown for guests to take advantage of everything Miami has to offer.

For a map of this listing, see p. 157.

Very Expensive

The Ritz-Carlton, Key Biscayne ★★★ ☺   The Ritz-Carlton takes Key Biscayne to the height of luxury with 44 acres of tropical gardens, a 20,000-square-foot destination spa, and a world-class tennis center under the direction of tennis pro Cliff Drysdale. Decorated in British colonial style, the Ritz-Carlton is straight out of Bermuda, with its impressive flower-laden landscaping. The Ritz Kids programs provide children ages 5 to 12 with fantastic activities, including quality time with the resort's affectionate blue and gold macaw mascot, and the 1,200-foot beachfront, named among the Top 10 Beaches in the U.S. by Dr. Stephen "Beach" Leatherman, offers everything from pure relaxation to fishing, boating, or windsurfing. Spacious and luxuriously appointed rooms feature new decor that embodies the resort's island-destination feel and large balconies that overlook the ocean or lush gardens. The oceanview Italian restaurant **Cioppino** is excellent for formal dining, or, if you prefer casual dining, the oceanfront **Cantina Beach** serves great authentic Mexican food and even has a "tequlier"—a sommelier for tequila. The St. Tropez–inspired **Dune Oceanfront Burger Lounge** is ideal for lazy afternoons on the sand with one of their gourmet burgers and a glass of champagne, while the resort's nighttime spot RUMBAR hearkens back to Old Havana with an impressive rum selection and light Cuban-inspired fare. The hotel's remote location—just a 10-minute drive from the hustle and bustle—makes it a favorite for those (John Travolta, among others) who want to avoid the hubbub.

455 Grand Bay Dr., Key Biscayne, FL 33149. ☎ **800/241-3333** or 305/365-4500. Fax 305/365-4501. www.ritzcarlton.com. 402 units. Winter $629 double, $1,100 suite; off-season $269 double, $525 suite. AE, DC, DISC, MC, V. Valet parking (call for fees). **Amenities:** 4 restaurants; 3 bars; children's programs; concierge; fitness center; 2 outdoor heated pools; room service; spa; tennis center with lessons available; watersports equipment/rentals. *In room:* A/C, TV, hair dryer, high-speed Internet, minibar.

DOWNTOWN

If you've ever read Tom Wolfe's *Bonfire of the Vanities,* you may understand what downtown Miami is all about. If not, it's this simple: Take a wrong turn and you could find yourself in some serious trouble. Desolate and dangerous at night, downtown is trying to change its image, but it's been a long, tedious process. Recently, however, part of the area has experienced a renaissance in terms of nightlife, with several popular dance clubs and bars opening up in the environs of NE 11th Street, off Biscayne Boulevard. If you're the kind of person who digs an urban setting, you may enjoy downtown, but if you're looking for shiny, happy Miami, you're in the wrong place (for now). As posh, pricey lofts keep going up faster than the nation's deficit, downtown is about to experience the renaissance it has been waiting for. Keep your eye on this area, and remember that you read it here first: Like orange—or pink, or white, or blue—being the new black, downtown Miami will be the new South Beach.

Most downtown hotels cater primarily to business travelers and cruise passengers, although with the slower-than-slow downtown renaissance in progress a few higher-end luxury hotels are set to open in the area, including a **JW Marriott Marquis** (up

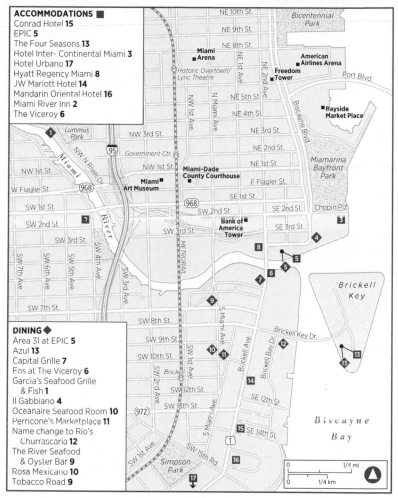

ACCOMMODATIONS ■
Conrad Hotel **15**
EPIC **5**
The Four Seasons **13**
Hotel Inter- Continental Miami **3**
Hotel Urbano **17**
Hyatt Regency Miami **8**
JW Mariott Hotel **14**
Mandarin Oriental Hotel **16**
Miami River Inn **2**
The Viceroy **6**

DINING ◆
Area 31 at EPIC **5**
Azul **13**
Capital Grille **7**
Fos at The Viceroy **6**
Garcia's Seafood Grille & Fish **1**
Il Gabbiano **4**
Oceanaire Seafood Room **10**
Perricone's Marketplace **11**
Name change to Rio's Churrascaria **12**
The River Seafood & Oyster Bar **9**
Rosa Mexicano **10**
Tobacco Road **9**

the road from the already existent **JW Marriott** at 1109 Brickell Ave. ✆ **305/329-3500;** www.marriott.com), at 345 Avenue of the Americas (✆ **305/350-0750**) and **Tempo Miami, A Rock Resort,** 1100 Biscayne Blvd. (✆ **305/396-4082;** www.rockresorts.com), scheduled to open in the summer of 2010, attached to one of downtown Miami's vacant condos, and featuring 56 luxurious guest rooms and suites with floor-to-ceiling windows, a gourmet restaurant, 8,000-square-foot RockResorts Spa, an infinity-edge sunrise swim spa, and lagoon-style sunset swimming pool.

Although business hotels can be expensive, quality and service are of a high standard. Look for discounts and packages on weekends, when offices are closed and rooms often go empty.

Very Expensive

Conrad Miami ★★★ Although you won't find ubiquitous Hilton heiresses Paris and Nicky at this business-oriented hotel (they hang out on South Beach), you will find luxury-lovers who have no interest in minimalism or celebrity spottings. In this 203-room, 36-floor skyscraper located in the heart of Miami's financial district, you may feel as if you're in an office building, but once you walk over the bridge across a sparkling pool, visions of cramped cubicles and bad lighting will immediately disappear. Located on the 25th floor, the lobby is illuminated by a magnificent atrium that shares the attention with a restaurant, lounge, and private event room—it splits the difference between the 203 guest rooms and the 116 fully serviced luxury apartments. All rooms feature hyper–high-tech amenities and, best of all, INNCOM, a bedside remote that controls all lights and thermostat. There's a superbly equipped gym, spa, and two tennis courts.

1395 Brickell Ave., Miami, FL 33131. ℂ **305/503-6500.** Fax 305/533-7177. www.conradmiami.com. 203 units. Winter $269–$319 double; off season $159–$239 double. AE, DC, DISC, MC, V. Valet parking $32. **Amenities:** 2 restaurants; 2 bars; babysitting; concierge; fitness center; outdoor Jacuzzi; rooftop pool; full-service spa. *In room:* A/C, TV/DVD, hair dryer, high-speed Internet, minibar.

EPIC ★★★ Although it's yet another hotel with adjacent condo (with not nearly as many empty hotel rooms as condos), the new in 2009 EPIC, a Kimpton Hotel, has its own separate entry and therefore doesn't make you feel like you're intruding on someone's privacy. In fact, it feels as if you are a resident as well in a posh, plush high rise with stunning views of the Miami skyline and Biscayne Bay. The dramatic lobby—separate from the resident lobby—features vaulted ceilings, glass walls, and shimmering pools, not to mention a buzzing two-story lounge and London, Hong Kong, and Dubai-based **Zuma** restaurant, the brainchild of German chef Rainer Becker offering informal Japanese dining known as *Izakaya*. The guest rooms and suites are full of open space and light, offering breathtaking views, exceptional bathroom amenities, and a huge bathroom with open cutout into the bedroom area. Luxury services include an on-site hotel spa by exhale (lower case), an expansive outdoor deck and lounge with private cabanas and two infinity pools up on the 16th floor, and an excellent seafood restaurant/lounge, **Area 31,** also on the 16th floor. The hotel is extremely pet friendly, offering beds, bones, and bottled water for your furry friend. Another perk: a daily wine hour in the lobby, featuring free pours of reds, whites, and bubbly along with some tasty snacks courtesy of Area 31.

270 Biscayne Blvd. Way, Miami, FL 33131. ℂ **305/424-5226.** Fax 305/424-5232. www.epichotel.com. 411 units. Winter $279–$409 double, $429–$609 suite; off-season $229–$409 double, $304–$609 suite. Rates include morning coffee and tea and evening wine reception. AE, DC, DISC, MC, V. Valet parking $32. **Amenities:** 2 restaurants; waterfront lounge; concierge; concierge-level rooms; fitness center; 2 outdoor pools; room service; spa. *In room:* A/C, TV, desktop computer, hair dryer, MP3 docking station, Wi-Fi.

The Four Seasons ★★★ ☺ Deciding between the hyperluxe Mandarin Oriental and the equally luxe, albeit somewhat museumlike, Four Seasons is almost like trying to tell the difference between Ava and Zsa Zsa Gabor. There are some obvious differences and some similarities, but they're kind of subtle. While the architecturally striking Mandarin is located on the semiprivate Brickell Key, the 70-story Four Seasons resembles an office building and is smack in the middle of the business district, making it more of a business hotel than a resort, per se. The rooms and suites are plush, and, like the Mandarin, service is paramount. Most rooms overlook Biscayne Bay, and while all rooms are cushy, thanks to the hotel's signature "untucked" beds, the bland decor leaves a lot to be desired, really. The best rooms are the corner suites with views facing both south and east over the water. There are three gorgeous pools spread out on more than 2 acres. Poolside amenities include fully loaded Kindles for poolside reading and minispa treatments. Guests at the hotel all have access to and free classes at the Sports Club/LA, a gym popular with visiting celebs.

1435 Brickell Ave., Miami, FL 33131. ℂ **305/358-3535.** Fax 305/358-7758. www.fourseasons.com/miami. 260 units. Winter $365–$500 double, $600 suite; off-season $250–$355 double, $455 suite. AE, DC, DISC, MC, V. Valet parking $34. **Amenities:** 2 restaurants; 2 bars; concierge; the Sports Club/LA fitness center; outdoor Jacuzzi; 3 outdoor pools; full-service spa. *In room:* A/C, TV, hair dryer, minibar, Wi-Fi.

Hotel Inter-Continental Miami ★ This hotel presents a serious catch-22: It's got a front-row view of all of Miami Beach, Biscayne Bay, the Miami River, and the Atlantic Ocean, but it is also located in downtown Miami. If it's a view that you want, stay here; but if it's location you want, reconsider. With the decidedly threatening presence of the brand-new EPIC around the corner and the hyperluxurious Mandarin Oriental and Viceroy just over the Brickell Bridge, the Inter-Continental had no choice but to keep up with the competition. A $34-million renovation brought it up to speed with the rest, but it's still a bit old fashioned. It boasts more marble than the Liberace Museum, but it is warmed by bold colors and a fancified Florida flavor. Rooms are a tad nicer than those in a typical chain hotel, with marble bathrooms and sit-in windowsills. Ten treatment rooms and a Vichy shower are among the amenities at the excellent mySPA. *Note:* Construction on several new condominiums/hotels adjacent to the Inter-Continental may disturb the deafening silence common to downtown Miami.

100 Chopin Plaza, Miami, FL 33131. ℂ **800/327-3005** or 305/577-1000. Fax 305/577-0384. www.icmiamihotel.com. 641 units. Winter $179–$389 double; off season $139–$339 double; year-round $550–$3,000 suite. Additional person $30. Weekend and other packages available. AE, DC, DISC, MC, V. Valet parking $20. **Amenities:** 3 restaurants; 2 lounges; concierge; access to nearby golf course; Olympic-size outdoor heated pool; room service; spa. *In room:* A/C, TV/DVD, CD player, hair dryer, minibar.

Mandarin Oriental, Miami ★★★ Corporate big shots and celebrities not in the mood for the South Beach spotlight have a high-end luxury hotel to stay in while wheeling and dealing their way through Miami. Catering to business travelers, big-time celebrities (Jennifer Aniston, J-Lo, the late, great Jacko, Will Smith, and so on), and the leisure traveler who doesn't mind spending big bucks, the swank Mandarin Oriental features a waterfront location, residential-style rooms with Asian touches (all with balconies), upscale dining, and bathrooms equipped with Aromatherapy Associates products. The waterfront view of the city is the hotel's best asset. The hotel's two restaurants, the high-end Azul (p. 144) and the more casual Café Sambal, are two of Miami's best, as is the 15,000-square-foot spa, the only official five-star spa in the state, in which traditional Thai massages and ayurvedic treatments are the norm. The hotel is also home to a 20,000-foot white-sand beach club complete with beach butlers and beachside cabana treatments, which is nice, considering that the hotel is 15 minutes from the beach. For those who want to venture out, the Mandarin offers the city's only official "nightlife guide" to lead you to the hot spots.

500 Brickell Key Dr., Miami, FL 33131. ☎ **305/913-8383.** Fax 305/913-8300. www.mandarinoriental. com. 326 units. $435–$900 double; $1,300–$6,500 suite. AE, DC, DISC, MC, V. Valet parking $34. Pets welcome. **Amenities:** 2 restaurants; 3 bars; beach club; children's club; concierge; nearby golf; state-of-the-art fitness center; outdoor Jacuzzi; outdoor jogging trail; infinity pool; full-service holistic spa; nearby tennis. *In room:* A/C, TV, hair dryer, minibar, Wi-Fi.

The Viceroy ★   One of the few condo-hotel combos to open before the bust, the trendy Kelly Wearstler–designed Viceroy is located on prime real estate on Biscayne Bay between downtown Miami and trendy Brickell Avenue. The hotel itself occupies its own tower within a three-tower structure and is the only facility to house a 162-room hotel in conjunction with residences. All rooms are full of the modern trappings—Wii and PlayStation gaming systems, DVD players, portable printers, 42-inch flatscreen televisions, and hair- and body-care products by Aromapothecary. Residents and guests alike share exclusive access to the 15th-floor outdoor podium's sweeping recreation area—lounge and deck space, sundeck with cabanas, and a 310-foot infinity pool overlooking the bay. In late 2009, it was announced that new Miami Dolphins "owners" Jennifer Lopez and Marc Anthony bought a crash pad at the Icon at Viceroy, so don't be surprised if you run into them or their, uh, new teammates. As with any new hotel, there's a chic restaurant, Eos, overlooking the 15th-floor pool, with alfresco dining, fireplace, and waterfront views. Even better is Club Fifty, the upscale rooftop lounge/restaurant right next to the pool on the 50th floor, not to mention a magnificently modern, full-service 28,000-square-foot spa at Icon Brickell with treatment rooms that overlook the bay.

> ### Wanna Be Signin' Something
>
> Celebrity tidbit: The late Michael Jackson stayed at the **Mandarin Oriental Miami** and felt the need to sign his name to a painting in his suite—despite the fact that he didn't paint it. Amused, the hotel decided to keep it. Imagine what it's worth now?

485 Brickell Ave., Miami, Florida 33131. ☎ **866/720-1991.** www.viceroymiami.com. 162 units. Winter $400–$500 double; off-season $300 double. AE, DC, DISC, MC, V. Valet parking $35. **Amenities:** Restaurant; lounge; 500-sq.-ft. state-of-the-art fitness facility; 2 outdoor pools; room service; full-service spa. *In room:* A/C, TV, table GPS device, hair dryer, kitchen or kitchenette, Wi-Fi.

Expensive

Hyatt Regency Miami   The Hyatt Regency is located just off the Miami River in the heart of downtown Miami. It shares space with the Miami Convention Center, the James L. Knight Convention Center Theater, an exhibition hall, and a 5,000-seat auditorium and concert hall. This hotel is perfect for large groups, business travelers, or basketball fanatics in town to see the Miami Heat play at the nearby American Airlines Arena. The People Mover and Metrorail are just blocks away, and water taxis are available at the front steps. Most of the spacious, recently renovated guest rooms have great bathrooms, products, and a balcony with a view of either the city or the bay.

400 SE 2nd Ave., Miami, FL 33131. ☎ **800/233-1234** or 305/358-1234. Fax 305/374-1728. www.miami. hyatt.com. 612 units. Winter $329–$369 double, suite $379–$409; off season $159–$189 double, $199–$269 suite. AE, DC, DISC, MC, V. Valet parking $29. **Amenities:** Restaurant; health club; outdoor pool. *In room:* A/C, TV, hair dryer, high-speed Internet.

Moderate

Hotel Urbano A new boutique hotel on the southern, more residential end of Brickell Ave., Hotel Urbano is a welcome addition to all the haughty high rises with just three stories and such style and personality you'd never know you were in a former Hampton Inn. The 65-room Urbano features contemporary decor and a gorgeous, free-form pool with poolside lounge surrounded by private cabanas with a fire pit. Rooms feature city or pool views with big walk-in showers. Artwork displayed throughout the hotel has been selected by William Braemer, curator of Art Fusion Galleries in Miami's Design District. Curious about the art? Tune into the hotel's art channel to get an education on what's displayed. A restaurant offers alfresco dining and Florida cuisine with Cuban accents. Although geared to business travelers, its location just feet away from Key Biscayne's Rickenbacker Causeway and Vizcaya Museum and Gardens, to downtown Miami and Brickell nightlife and to all parts south make this urbane oasis an excellent—and surprisingly affordable place to be.

2500 Brickell Ave., Miami, FL 33129. © **866/384-2997** or 305/854-2070. Fax 305/856-5055. www. hotelurbano.com. 65 units. Winter $159–$289 double; off-season $109–$169 double. AE, DC, DISC, MC, V. Free parking. **Amenities:** Restaurant; bar; babysitting; access to nearby gym facilities; pool. *In room:* A/C, TV/DVD, fridge on request, hair dryer, Wi-Fi.

Miami River Inn ★★★ 🏠 The Miami River Inn, listed on the National Register of Historic Places, is a quaint, country-style hideaway (Miami's *only* bed-and-breakfast!), consisting of four cottages smack in the middle of downtown Miami. In fact, it's so hidden that most locals don't even know it exists, which only adds to its panache. Every room has hardwood floors and is uniquely furnished with antiques dating from 1908. In one room, you might find a hand-painted bathtub, a Singer sewing machine, and an armoire from the turn of the 20th century, restored to perfection. Thirty-eight rooms have private bathrooms—four have showers only, six have tubs only, and 28 have splendid tub/shower combinations. One- and two-bedroom apartments are available as well. In the foyer, you can peruse a library filled with books about Old Miami. It's close to public transportation, restaurants, and museums, and only 5 minutes from the business district.

118 SW South River Dr., Miami, FL 33130. © **800/468-3589** or 305/325-0045. Fax 305/325-9227. www. miamiriverinn.com. 38 units. Winter $149–$299 double; off-season $89–$149 double. Rates include continental breakfast. Extra person $15. AE, DC, DISC, MC, V. Free parking. Pets accepted for $25 per night. **Amenities:** Babysitting; access to nearby gym facilities; Jacuzzi; small pool. *In room:* A/C, TV, hair dryer (upon request).

CORAL GABLES

Translated appropriately as "City Beautiful," the Gables, as it's affectionately known, was one of Miami's original planned communities and is still among the city's prettiest, most pedestrian-friendly, albeit preservation-obsessed neighborhoods. Pristine with a European flair, Coral Gables is best known for its wide array of excellent upscale restaurants of various ethnicities, as well as a hotly contested (the quiet city didn't want to welcome new traffic) shopping megacomplex, with upscale stores such as Nordstrom.

If you're looking for luxury, Coral Gables has a number of wonderful hotels, but if you're on a tight budget, you may be better off elsewhere. One well-priced chain in the area is the **Holiday Inn,** 1350 S. Dixie Hwy. (© **800/HOLIDAY** [465-4329] or 305/667-5611), with rates between $105 and $209. It's directly across the street from the University of Miami and is popular with families and friends of students.

For a map of these listings, see p. 161.

Very Expensive

Biltmore Hotel ★★★ A romantic sense of Old World glamour combined with a rich history permeates the Biltmore as much as the pricey perfume of the guests who stay here. Built in 1926, it's the oldest Coral Gables hotel and is a National Historic Landmark—one of only two operating hotels in Florida to receive that designation. Rising above the Spanish-style estate is a majestic 300-foot copper-clad tower, modeled after the Giralda bell tower in Seville and visible throughout the city. Large Moorish-style rooms are decorated with tasteful decor, European feather beds, Egyptian cotton duvets, writing desks, and some high-tech amenities. The landmark 23,000-square-foot winding pool now has the requisite hipster accessories—the private cabana, alfresco bar, and restaurant.

> ### The Biltmore's Oldest Guests
>
> Rumor has it that Al Capone, for whom the Biltmore's Everglades Suite is nick-named, roams the halls here, as do wounded soldiers from the days when this was a post WWII hospital. Even if you don't stay at the Biltmore, a tour of the property is worth taking (call ℭ **305/445-1926** for more information; see p. 192).

Always a popular destination for golfers, including former President Clinton (who stays in the Al Capone suite), the Biltmore is situated on a lush, rolling, 18-hole Donald Ross course that is as challenging as it is beautiful. Sunday brunch is an equal feat—book early.

1200 Anastasia Ave., Coral Gables, FL 33134. ℭ **800/727-1926** or 305/445-1926. Fax 305/442-9496. www.biltmorehotel.com. 276 units. Winter $395–$895 double; off-season $229–$499 double; year-round $659–$6,500 specialty suites. Additional person $20. Special packages available. AE, DC, DISC, MC, V. Valet parking $25; self-parking free. **Amenities:** 4 restaurants; 4 bars; concierge; 18-hole golf course; state-of-the-art health club; outdoor pool; room service; sauna; full-service spa; 10 lit tennis courts. *In room:* A/C, TV, fax, hair dryer, high-speed Internet, kitchenette (in tower suites), minibar, VCR (upon request).

Hyatt Regency Coral Gables ★★ High on style, comfort, and price, this Hyatt is part of Coral Gables' Alhambra, an office-hotel complex with a Mediterranean motif. The building itself is gorgeous, designed with pink stone, arched entrances, grand courtyards, and tile roofs. Most recently, the pool and lobby were beautifully renovated. Inside you'll find overstuffed chairs on marble floors surrounded by opulent antiques and chandeliers. The large guest rooms are comfortable, if uninspired. A few rooms have balconies. The hotel underwent a $10-million renovation that added a little more pizzazz to the rooms, which all feature Mediterranean-inspired decor, comfy beds, and a marble bath with great amenities. Though the hotel fails to authentically mimic something much older and much farther away, it is attractive in its newness and is an excellent place from which to admire the more historic properties in the neighborhood.

50 Alhambra Plaza, Coral Gables, FL 33134. ℂ **800/233-1234** or 305/441-1234. Fax 305/441-0520. www.coralgables.hyatt.com. 250 units. Winter $339–$399 double, $409–$629 suite; off season $159–$199 double, $200–$250 suite. Additional person $25. Packages and senior discounts available. AE, MC, V. Valet parking $21; self-parking $16 Mon–Thurs, $13 Fri–Sun. **Amenities:** Restaurant; bar; babysitting; concierge; nearby golf course; health club; Jacuzzi; large outdoor heated pool; limited room service; 2 saunas. *In room:* A/C, TV, hair dryer, high-speed Internet access, minibar.

Expensive

Hotel St. Michel ★★   This European-style hotel, in the heart of Coral Gables, is one of the city's most romantic options. The accommodations and hospitality are straight out of Old World Europe, complete with dark-wood-paneled walls, cozy beds, beautiful antiques, and a quiet elegance that seems startlingly out of place in trendy Miami. Everything here is charming—from the brass elevator and parquet floors to the paddle fans. One-of-a-kind furnishings make each room special. Of course, the antiquity is countered with modernity in the form of flatscreens in all rooms. Bathrooms are on the smaller side, but are hardly cramped. All have tub/shower combinations except for two, which have one or the other. If you're picky, request your preference. Guests are treated to fresh fruit upon arrival and enjoy seamless service throughout their stay. A new restaurant, **GaetanoRistorante,** opened in 2010, replacing the beloved Restaurant St. Michel, serving, strangely, rustic Italian cuisine.

162 Alcazar Ave., Coral Gables, FL 33134. ℂ **800/848-HOTEL** (4683) or 305/444-1666. Fax 305/529-0074. www.hotelstmichel.com. 28 units. Winter $169 double, $199 suite; off-season $119 double, $149 suite. Additional person $10. Rates include continental breakfast and fresh fruit daily. AE, DC, MC, V. Self-parking $9. **Amenities:** Bar; lounge; concierge; access to nearby health club; room service; free Wi-Fi in all public areas. *In room:* A/C, TV, hair dryer.

COCONUT GROVE

This waterfront village hugs the shores of Biscayne Bay, just south of U.S. 1 and about 10 minutes from the beaches. Once a haven for hippies, head shops, and artsy bohemian characters, the Grove succumbed to the inevitable temptations of commercialism and has become a Gap nation, featuring a host of theme restaurants, bars, a megaplex, and lots of stores. Outside the main shopping area, however, you'll find the beautiful remnants of Old Miami in the form of flora, fauna, and, of course, water.

For a map of these listings, see p. 159.

Very Expensive

Grove Isle Hotel and Spa ★   Hidden away in the bougainvillea and lushness of the Grove, the Grove Isle Hotel and Spa is off the beaten path on its own lushly landscaped 20-acre island, just outside the heart of Coconut Grove. The isolated exclusivity of this resort contributes to a country-club vibe, though for the most part, the people here aren't snooty, but just value their privacy and precious relaxation time. Everyone dresses in white and pastels, and if they're not on their way to a set of tennis, they're not in a rush to get anywhere. You'll step into suites that are elegantly furnished, with mosquito-netted canopy beds and a patio overlooking the bay. You'll need to reserve early here—rooms go very fast. Introduced in early 2010, **Gibraltar,** a haute-cuisine restaurant whose executive chef used to cook for Donald

Trump, serves fresh seafood and other regional specialties in a spectacular, elegant dining room, or, better yet, outside on the water. The 6,000-square-foot, Indonesian-inspired Spaterre is, er, terre-ific.

4 Grove Isle Dr., Coconut Grove, FL 33133. ℂ **800/884-7683** or 305/858-8300. Fax 305/854-6702. www.groveisle.com. 50 units. Winter $689–$849 double, $839–$949 suite; off-season $379–$549 double, $589–$675 suite. Packages available. AE, DC, MC, V. Valet parking $17. **Amenities:** Restaurant; babysitting; concierge; large outdoor heated pool; room service; full-service spa; 12 tennis courts. *In room:* A/C, TV/VCR, CD player, hair dryer, high-speed Internet, minibar.

Mayfair Hotel and Spa ★★ Coconut Grove's alternative to cookie-cutter hotel brands, the Mayfair Hotel and Spa is an eclectic, Art Deco/Nouveau retreat. Complimentary Wi-Fi, terry robes, 300-thread-count sheets, and plasma TVs are in every room of this newly renovated gem. Located on the rooftop is the Cabana One Rooftop Pool & Lounge featuring a floating cabana roof and planks of teakwood, a serpentine bench built into the parapet which winds around a fire feature, and billowing white curtains surrounding eight private cabanas with L-shaped sofas, flatscreen TVs, Nintendo Wiis, and private safes. The famed New York steakhouse **Angelo and Maxie's** is also here, as is the Jurlique Spa, which exclusively utilizes its own line of organic products and follows a holistic approach to outer beauty and inner health.

3000 Florida Ave., Coconut Grove, FL 33133. ℂ **800/433-4555** or 305/441-0000. Fax 305/447-9173. www.mayfairhotelandspa.com. 179 units. Winter $279–$679 suite; off-season $149–$579 suite; year-round $3,000 penthouse. Packages available. AE, DC, DISC, MC, V. Valet parking $26. Pets accepted. **Amenities:** Restaurant; rooftop snack bar; concierge; Jacuzzi; outdoor pool; room service. *In room:* A/C, TV/DVD, CD player, fax, hair dryer, minibar, Wi-Fi.

Mutiny Hotel ★ En route to the center of the Grove, docked along Sailboat Bay and the marina, lies this revamped hotel best known as the hangout for the *Miami Vice* set—drug kingpins, undercover cops, and other shady characters—during the mid-'80s. Now it caters to a much more legitimate clientele. Service and style are bountiful at the Mutiny, which somehow has avoided the Nouveau-hotel hype and managed to stand on its own quiet merits without becoming part of the scene. The newly converted condos are among the best-kept secret in the Grove, voted by the *Miami Herald* as "the second best kept secret among hotels" in South Florida (1st was Kona Kai). The suites' British Colonial motif is warmed up with soft drapes, comfortable mattresses, and regal Old English furnishings. Each suite comes with a large bathroom (executive and two-bedroom suites have two bathrooms), full kitchen complete with china and complimentary coffee, and all the usual amenities associated with this class of hotel.

2951 S. Bayshore Dr., Miami, FL 33133. ℂ **888/868-8469** or 305/441-2100. Fax 305/441-2822. www. mutinyhotel.com. 120 suites. Winter $239–$799 1- and 2-bedroom suites; off season $119–$599 1- and 2-bedroom suites. AE, DC, DISC, MC, V. Valet parking $21. **Amenities:** Restaurant; babysitting; concierge; health club; small outdoor heated pool with whirlpool; limited room service; spa. *In room:* A/C, TV/DVD, hair dryer, kitchen, Wi-Fi.

The Ritz-Carlton Coconut Grove, Miami The third and smallest of Miami's Ritz-Carlton hotels is, hands down, the most intimate of its properties, surrounded by 2 acres of tropical gardens and overlooking Biscayne Bay and the Miami skyline. Decorated in the likeness of an Italian villa, the hotel's understated luxury is a welcome addition to an area known for its gaudiness. A room renovation in 2008 saw the addition of Italian damask patterns, Carrara marble bathrooms and dark

Emperador marble-topped dressers that create the feeling of being in a luxurious, private villa. That said, this is more of a business hotel than a vacation or resort property. In addition to the usual Ritz-Carlton standard of service and comfort, the hotel has an excellent, extremely elegant Italian trattoria (with footstools for women to put their purses on—how classy!), Bizcaya, and a sophisticated wine-tasting scene at the chic lobby lounge, the Villa Living Room.

3300 SW 27th Ave., Coconut Grove, FL 33133. © **800/241-3333** or 305/644-4680. Fax 305/644-4681. www.ritzcarlton.com. 115 units. Winter $469 double, $569 suite; off-season $249 double, $359 suite. AE, DC, DISC, MC, V. Valet parking $25. **Amenities:** Restaurant; pool grill; 2 bars; babysitting; concierge; fitness center; outdoor heated pool; room service; spa. *In room:* A/C, TV, hair dryer, high-speed Internet, minibar.

Moderate

Hampton Inn This very standard chain hotel is a welcome reprieve in an area otherwise known for very pricey accommodations. The rooms are nothing exciting, but the freebies, like local phone calls, parking, in-room movies, breakfast buffet, and hot drinks around the clock, make this a real steal. Although there is no restaurant or bar, it is close to lots of both—only about half a mile to the heart of the Grove's shopping and retail area and about as far from Coral Gables. Rooms are brand new, sparkling clean, and larger than that of a typical motel. Located at the residential end of Brickell Avenue, it's a quiet, convenient location 15 minutes from South Beach and 5 minutes from Coconut Grove. If you'd rather save your money for dining and entertainment, this is a good bet.

2800 SW 28th Terrace (at U.S. 1 and SW 27th Ave.), Coconut Grove, FL 33133. © **305/448-2800.** Fax 305/442-8655. www.hampton-inn.com. 137 units. Winter $159–$209 double; off season $134–$179 double. Rates include continental breakfast buffet and local calls. AE, DC, DISC, MC, V. Free parking. **Amenities:** Exercise room; Jacuzzi; large outdoor pool. *In room:* A/C, TV, fridge and microwave (on request).

Sonesta Bayfront Hotel Coconut Grove ★ With a great location offering panoramic views of Biscayne Bay, the marina and the Miami skyline, the Sonesta is more than just a chain hotel—it's a condo too! And because of that, it's meticulously maintained and features 225 contemporary styled guest rooms, all with flatscreens and balconies and many with ocean views. The fantastic eighth-floor pool and Sky Lounge, which received a $500,000 renovation, overlooks the water and the hustle and bustle down below in the Grove, while the restaurant, Panorama, serves delicious Peruvian cuisine.

2889 McFarlane Road., Coconut Grove, FL 33133. © **305/529-2828.** Fax 305/529-2008. www.sonesta. com/coconutgrove. 205 units. Winter $139–$399 double, $209–$659 suite; off season $140–$189 double, $209–$340 suite. AE, DC, DISC, MC, V. Valet parking $23. **Amenities:** Restaurant; sky bar; concierge; state-of-the-art fitness center; business center; pool; spa; squash courts. *In room:* A/C, TV/ DVD, CD player, hair dryer, Wi-Fi.

WEST MIAMI/AIRPORT AREA

As Miami continues to grow at a rapid pace, expansion has begun westward, where land is plentiful. Several resorts have taken advantage of the space to build world-class tennis courts and golf courses. Although there's no sea to swim in, a plethora of facilities makes up for the lack of an ocean view.

For a map of these listings, see p. 71.

Expensive

Doral Golf Resort and Spa ★ ☺

This sprawling 650-acre resort in a suburban West Miami enclave is all about golf. Doral is where world-class tournaments and the excruciating Blue Monster course have seen even Tiger frustrated. There's also the Great White Course—the Southeast's first desertscape course, designed by The Shark himself, Greg Norman. Repeat guests usually book the season well in advance. Rooms are spacious, all with private balconies, many overlooking a golf course or garden. Rooms reveal a plantation-style decor with lots of wicker and wood and large marble bathrooms. Enhancements to the golf courses, spa suites, and driving range have also brought the resort up to speed with its competition. There's a phenomenal kids program and The Blue Lagoon water park featuring two 80,000-gallon pools with cascading waterfalls, a rock facade, and a 125-foot water slide. For a spa or golf vacation, the Doral is an ideal choice. Otherwise, consider investing your money in a hotel that's better located.

4400 NW 87th Ave., Miami, FL 33178. ℂ **800/71-DORAL** (713-6725) or 305/592-2000. Fax 305/594-4682. www.doralresort.com. 693 units. Winter $269 double, $370 suite, $420 1-bedroom suite, $500 2-bedroom suite; off season $119 double, $280 suite, $400 1-bedroom suite, $480 2-bedroom suite. Additional person $35. Golf and spa packages available. AE, DC, DISC, MC, V. Valet parking $17. **Amenities:** 5 restaurants; babysitting; concierge; driving range; 5 golf courses; health club; 6 pools, 1 with a 125-ft. water slide; room service; world-class spa; 10 tennis courts. *In room:* A/C, TV, hair dryer, minibar.

Miccosukee Resort and Convention Center ★

Located on the edge of the Everglades, about 30 to 40 minutes west of the airport, the Miccosukee Resort is the closest thing South Florida's got to Las Vegas, but accommodations really are just a step above a Holiday Inn. The Miccosukee tribe was originally part of the lower Creek Nation, which lived in areas now known as Alabama and Georgia. After the final Seminole War in 1858, the last of the Miccosukees settled in the Everglades. Following the lead set recently by many other Native American tribes, they built the resort to accumulate gambling revenue. Although many tourists go out to the resort solely to gamble, it also has expansive meeting and banquet facilities, spa services, great children's programs, entertainment, and excursions to the Florida Everglades. Guest rooms are standard, furnished with custom pieces made exclusively for the resort, but if you're here, you're not likely to spend that much time in your room.

500 SW 177th Ave. (at intersection with SW 8th St.), Miami, FL 33194. ℂ **877/242-6464** or 305/221-8623. Fax 305/925-2556. www.miccosukee.com. 309 units. Year-round $149 double; $189 suite. All rooms sleep up to 3 people; suites sleep 4–6 people. AE, DC, DISC, MC, V. Free parking. **Amenities:** 5 restaurants; 24-hr. deli; state-of-the-art health club and spa; indoor heated pool; room service. *In room:* A/C, TV, in-room movies, hair dryer, minibar, Wi-Fi, some suites have whirlpool and wet bar.

Moderate

Miami International Airport Hotel ★

I don't know of a nicer airport hotel, and you can't beat the convenience—it's actually in the airport at Concourse E. Every amenity of a first-class tourist hotel is here. The rooms are modern, clean, and spacious, with newly renovated furnishings, mattresses, fixtures, and carpeting. You might think you'd be deafened by the roar of the planes, but all of the rooms have been soundproofed and actually allow in very little noise. In addition, the hotel has modern security systems and is extremely safe. Renovations were made in 2009 including the Top of the Port Restaurant located on the seventh floor with panoramic views of the runways and city skyline.

Airport Terminal Concourse E (at the intersection of NW 20th St. and Le Jeune Rd.; P.O. Box 997510), Miami, FL 33299-7510. © **800/327-1276** or 305/871-4100. Fax 305/871-0800. http://miahotel.miami-airport.com. 260 units. Winter $169–$219 double; off season $129–$259 double. Additional person $10. AE, DC, MC, V. Parking $15. **Amenities:** Restaurant; cocktail lounge; concierge; limited room service. *In room:* A/C, TV, hair dryer, Wi-Fi.

Bargain Chains

If you must stay near the airport, consider any of the dozens of moderately priced chain hotels. You'll find one of the cheapest and most recommendable options at either of the **Days Inn** locations at 7250 NW 11th St. and 4767 NW 36th St. (© **800/329-7466** for both, or 305/888-3661 or 305/261-4230, respectively), each about 2 miles from the airport. The larger property on 36th Street offers slightly cheaper rates, with singles starting as low as $69. The 11th Street locale may charge more on weekends, but prices usually start at $70. Prices include free transportation from the airport.

A more luxurious option is the **Wyndham Miami Airport,** at 3900 NW 21st St. (© **305/871-3800**), with rates from about $125 to $225.

NORTH DADE COUNTY

For a map of these listings, see p. 141.

Very Expensive

Acqualina ★★★   Some people are still scratching their heads as to why this luxurious resort opened across the street from a Denny's and T-shirt shops, but once you step inside, you forget that you're even in Miami and feel as if you're on the Italian Riviera. On 4½ beachfront acres, with more than 400 feet of Atlantic coastline, Acqualina is a Mediterranean-style resort towering over all the others, with its baroque fountains, 97 impeccably appointed suites, and a branch of NYC's acclaimed Il Mulino restaurant. The ESPA is one of Miami's priciest and poshest spas, and while there are three pools just steps away from the beach, the outdoor area is uninspiring. The hotel's AcquaMarine Program has a splashy array of marine-biology activities for kids and adults. Best of all, the chance of some teenybopper tabloid figure partying here is unlikely. In fact, there's really no scene here at all, which for some is just blissful.

17875 Collins Ave., Sunny Isles Beach, FL 33160. © **305/918-8000.** Fax 305/918-8100. www.acqualina. com. 97 units. Winter $850–$1,050 double, $1,600–$3,350 suite; off-season $475–$675 double, $1,025–$2,000 suite. AE, DC, DISC, MC, V. Valet parking $30. **Amenities:** 2 restaurants; bar; babysitting; 24-hr. concierge; 3 outdoor pools; room service; state-of-the-art spa. *In room:* A/C, TV, CD player, fax, hair dryer, minibar, Wi-Fi.

Fairmont Turnberry Isle Resort & Club ★★★   One of Miami's classiest—and priciest—resorts (along the lines of the Mandarin Oriental), this gorgeous 300-acre retreat has every possible facility for relaxation seekers and active guests, particularly golfers. You'll pay a lot to stay here thanks to a $150-million makeover of all guest rooms and suites, golf courses, restaurants, the spa and fitness center, pool, tennis center, and beach club. The main attractions are two Raymond Floyd championship courses, available only to members and guests of the hotel; a Laguna Pool with a waterslide, lazy river, and private cabanas; and Bourbon Steak, a restaurant by star chef Michael Mina. The Willow Stream Spa offers an unabridged menu of treatments. A location in the well-manicured residential and shopping area of Aventura appeals to those who want peace, quiet, and a great mall. A complimentary shuttle bus takes guests to and from the Ocean Club and Aventura Mall.

19999 W. Country Club Dr., Aventura, FL 33180. ✆ **866/612-7739** or 786/279-6770. Fax 305/933-6560. www.fairmont.com/turnberryisle. 392 units. Winter $399–$899 double, $919–$5,500 suite; off-season $199–$299 double, $499–$2,700 suite. AE, DC, DISC, MC, V. Valet parking $30. **Amenities:** 4 restaurants; 5 bars and lounges; concierge; 2 golf courses; state-of-the-art fitness center and spa; 3 outdoor pools; room service; 4 clay hydro tennis courts; watersports equipment/rentals. *In room:* A/C, TV/VCR, CD player, fax, fridge (upon request), hair dryer, minibar.

Marenas Resort ★ This all-suite beachfront resort, formerly a Le Meridien, brings a nice touch of European-style glitz and glamour to the area and, sorry Donald, it trumps the nearby Trump resort in many ways. All rooms—there are 130 one-bedroom suites and 80 two-bedroom suites—feature king-size beds with Egyptian cotton linens, and the latest in technology, not to mention full-size Italian kitchens, washer/dryers, and spa-quality bathrooms. Service throughout the hotel is impeccable. The hotel's 6,000-square-foot spa is also a hot spot for those seeking pampering, but I prefer the pool area, where an infinity-edged beachfront pool stands out like a supermodel in a crowd of circus clowns.

18683 Collins Ave., Sunny Isles Beach, FL 33160 ✆ **877/858-2305** or 305-503-6000. Fax 305-503-6001. www.marenasresortmiami.com. Winter rates from $289 doubles and suites; off-season from $229 doubles and suites. AE, MC, V. **Amenities:** Restaurant; pool and beach bar; beach club; concierge; health club; pool; spa. *In room:* A/C, TV, MP3 docking station, Wi-Fi.

One Bal Harbour ★★★ Formerly a Regent Hotel, which ironically couldn't make it here or on South Beach, this resort may have no big-name affiliation, but it's still big-time luxe. Until the St. Regis finishes completion in the former Sheraton Bal Harbour, this is the only oceanfront resort in the area, and despite that, there's no competition. The penultimate in luxury, suites are resplendent in mahogany floors, with leather walls, panoramic views of the ocean, and bathrooms with 10-foot floor-to-ceiling windows and, my favorite, a free-standing tub overlooking the ocean. Elevators take you directly into your suite, like a luxury apartment building. A Guerlain spa, butler service, spectacular pool and 750 feet of beachfront, and restaurant that seems to be in constant transition will cost you a pretty penny; but if you're looking to be doted on hand and foot without lifting a finger—except to pay your bill at the end—this is the place.

10295 Collins Ave., Bal Harbour, FL 33154. ✆ **877/545-5410** or 305/455-5400. Fax 305/866-2419. www.oneluxuryhotels.com. 124 units. Winter from $700 doubles; off-season from $375 doubles; presidential suite $8,000. AE, MC, V. Valet parking $32. **Amenities:** Restaurant; bar; butler service; 24-hr. concierge; private jet/yacht charter; outdoor pool; room service; spa. *In room:* A/C, 42-in flatscreen TV/DVD/CD player, hair dryer, minibar, Wi-Fi.

Trump International Beach Resort ✋ Donald, Donald, Donald, what were you thinking when you opened this uninspiring 32-story, 390-room beach resort? Yes, the Trump International sits on a prime piece of beachfront property, but I've seen rooms in Holiday Inns that have more personality than these. Completely bland with no style whatsoever, the Trump International is a folly of massive proportions despite a recent renovation that added a pool and increased the beachfront. With a cavernous, blasé lobby in which you can hear a pin drop, a restaurant that looks like a common room ripped out of an old Catskills resort (and not updated), and views of T-shirt shops and Denny's, this hotel is a travesty. That's really all I can say. *Maybe*, with an emphasis on the *maybe*, if there were a casino in here, it would justify a stay. Otherwise, it's just more vanity fare for the egomaniacal developer who seems to think that bigger is always better.

18001 Collins Ave., Sunny Isles Beach, FL 33160. (C) **800/SONESTA** (766-3782) or 305/692-5600. Fax 305/692-5601. www.trumpmiami.com. 390 units. Winter $296–$445 double, $445–$1,100 suite; off season $299–$350 double, $420–$1,080 suite. AE, DC, DISC, MC, V. Valet parking $18. **Amenities:** 2 restaurants; 2 bars and lounges; babysitting; air-conditioned cabanas on pool and beach; children's program (ages 5–12); concierge; 2 outdoor pools; room service; full-service spa; watersports equipment/rentals. *In room:* A/C, TV, CD player, hair dryer, high-speed Internet, microwave, minibar, radio, washer/dryer (suites only).

WHERE TO DINE IN MIAMI

Don't be fooled by the plethora of superlean model types you're likely to see posing throughout Miami. Contrary to popular belief, dining in this city is as much a sport as plastic surgery and in-line skating on Ocean Drive. With more than 6,000 restaurants to choose from, dining out in Miami has become a passionate pastime for locals and visitors alike. Our star chefs have fused Californian-Asian with Caribbean and Latin elements to create a world-class flavor all its own: Floribbean. Think mango chutney splashed over fresh swordfish or a spicy sushi sauce served alongside Peruvian ceviche.

Formerly synonymous with early-bird specials, Miami's new-wave cuisine now rivals that of San Francisco—or even New York. Nouveau Cuban chef Douglas Rodriguez returned to his roots with a fabulous South Beach nouveau Latino eatery. In addition, other stellar chefs—such as Michael Schwartz, Michelle Bernstein, Allen Susser, Norman Van Aken, and Clay Conley—remain firmly planted in the city's culinary scene, fusing local ingredients into edible masterpieces. Florida foodies are still bracing themselves for the arrival of Alain Ducasse—sometime when the construction ends on Biscayne Boulevard—just as they did for Alfred Portale at the swanky new Fontainebleau, and Laurent Tourondel at The Betsy on Ocean Drive. Now that Masaharu Morimoto's restaurant has finally opened (in the Boca Raton Resort & Club), foodies fixate on which mega-chef plans to open in Miami next. This New World cuisine is not only high in calories, it's high in price. But if you can manage to splurge at least once, it'll be worth it.

Thanks to a thriving cafe society in both South Beach and Coconut Grove, you can also enjoy a moderately priced meal and linger for hours without having a waiter hover over you. In Little Havana, you can chow down on a meal that serves about six for less than $10. Because seafood is plentiful, it doesn't have to cost you an arm and a leg to enjoy the appendages of a crab or lobster. Don't be put off by the looks of our recommended seafood shacks in places such as Key Biscayne—often, these spots get the best and freshest catches.

Whatever you're craving, Miami's got it—with the exception of decent Chinese food and a New York–style slice of pizza. If you're craving a scene with your steak, then South Beach is the place to be. Like many cities in Europe and Latin America, it is fashionable to dine late in South Beach, preferably after 9pm, sometimes as late as midnight. Service on South Beach is notoriously slow and arrogant, but it comes with the turf. (Of course, it is possible to find restaurants that defy the notoriety and actually pride themselves on friendly service.) On the mainland—especially in Coral Gables and, more recently, downtown and on Brickell Avenue—you can also experience fine dining without the pretense.

The biggest complaint when it comes to Miami dining isn't the haughtiness, but rather the dearth of truly moderately priced restaurants, especially in South Beach and Coral Gables. It's either really cheap or really expensive; the in-between somehow gets lost in the culinary shuffle. Quick-service diners don't exist here as they do in other cosmopolitan areas. I've tried to cover a range of cuisine in a range of prices. But with new restaurants opening on a weekly basis, you're bound to find an array of savory dining choices for every budget.

Many restaurants keep extended hours in high season (roughly Dec–Apr) and may close for lunch and/or dinner on Monday, when the traffic is slower. Always call ahead, as schedules do change. During the month of August, many Miami restaurants participate in Miami Spice, where three-course lunches and dinners are served at affordable prices. Check out www.miamirestaurantmonth.com. Also, always look carefully at your bill—many Miami restaurants add a 15% to 18% gratuity to your total due to the enormous influx of European tourists who are not accustomed to tipping. Keep in mind that this amount is the *suggested* amount and can be adjusted, either higher or lower, depending on your assessment of the service provided. Because of this tipping-included policy, South Beach waitstaff are best known for their lax or inattentive service. *Feel free to adjust it* if you feel your server deserves more or less.

SOUTH BEACH

The renaissance of South Beach started in the early '90s and is still continuing as classic cuisine gives in to modern temptation by inevitably fusing with more chic, nouveau developments created by faithful followers and devotees of the Food Network school of cooking. The ultimate result has spawned dozens of first-rate restaurants. In fact, big-name restaurants from across the country have capitalized on South Beach's international appeal and have continued to open branches here with great success. A few old standbys remain from the *Miami Vice* days, but the flock of newcomers dominates the scene, with places going in and out of style as quickly as the tides.

On South Beach, new restaurants are opening and closing as frequently as Emeril says "Bam!" Even in an economic downturn. And, ironically, most are upscale. As it's impossible to list them all, I recommend strolling and browsing. Most restaurants post a copy of their menu outside. With very few exceptions, the places on Ocean Drive are crowded with tourists and priced accordingly. You'll do better to venture a little farther onto the pedestrian-friendly streets just west of Ocean Drive.

Very Expensive

Asia de Cuba ★ ASIAN/LATIN   Located within the remarkably stunning lobby of the Mondrian hotel, this stylish fusion import from NYC and L.A. is the latest Miami offering from the China Grill empire. A blend of Latin and Asian cuisines, the menu features some familiar favorites tweaked from other China Grill eateries and served as new here, including the calamari salad Asia de Cuba, featuring the same crispy calamari as China Grill, only this time with more of a tropical twist with ingredients such as chayote, hearts of palm, and banana. Main courses include the best chicken I've had in a long time—Cuban BBQ chicken with Thai coconut sticky rice, avocado cilantro fruit salsa, and tamarind sauce; and a coconut mustard seed sustainable Chilean sea bass with crab and corn flan, cilantro chimichurri, and jalapeño plum coulis. Definitely not your corner takeout or bodega, nor are the prices, which are steep. But you are paying for prime real estate. Now if only you could just move in.

In the Mondrian, 1100 West Ave., South Beach. (© **305/673-1010.** www.chinagrillmgt.com. Reservations required. Main courses $35–$76. AE, DC, MC, V. Daily 7am–10:45pm.

Barton G. The Restaurant ★ AMERICAN   For those who are jaded by pan-fusion, pan-everything cuisine these days, Barton G. The Restaurant is the culinary antithesis, an homage to gourmet kitsch. Set on a residential block on the west side of South Beach, Barton G., named after its owner, who happens to be one of Miami's best-known, most over-the-top event planners, is a place that looks like a trendy restaurant, but eats like a show. Here, presentation is paramount. Take, for instance, the popcorn shrimp appetizer. This is not your average Red Lobster popcorn shrimp. Served on a plateful of, yes, popcorn, with field greens and the plump, crispy rock shrimp stuffed into an actual popcorn box, this dish is one of many awe-inspiring—and tasty—items you'll find in this unique restaurant in Miami. A grilled sea bass that is light and flavorful is served in a brown paper bag with laundry clips keeping the steam in until your server unclips them and releases the flavor within. Desserts are equally outrageous, including the $89 Chocolate Fun-Do, a mini chocolate fountain overflowing with 4 pounds of Belgian chocolate and tons of dipping delicacies from cake to fruit. A giant plume of cotton candy reminiscent of drag diva Dame Edna's hair is surrounded by three white-, dark-, and milk-chocolate-covered popcorn balls that, when cracked, reveal a sinful chocolate truffle inside. There's nothing ordinary about this seemingly ordinary restaurant, which is why people such as Tom Cruise and Will Smith are regulars. An elegant, well-lit indoor dining room is popular with members of the socialite set, for whom Barton G. has done many an affair, while the bar area and outdoor courtyard is the place to be for younger trend-seekers who appreciate what's on their plates as much as they do who's sitting next to them. Another show stopping production of Barton G.'s, **Prelude by Barton G.,** 1300 Biscayne Blvd. ((© **305/576-8888**), opened within the Adrienne Arsht Center and features a supper clubby vibe and choose-your-own three-course (you can do all desserts if you have a sweet tooth!) prix-fixe pre- and post-theater dinners. They don't load on the drama as much, saving it for the actual show, but it's a swell place to go if not for dinner, for dessert and drinks before or after curtain call.

1427 West Ave., South Beach. (© **305/672-8881.** www.bartong.com. Reservations suggested. Main courses $21–$50. AE, DC, DISC, MC, V. Daily 6pm–midnight.

A La Folie **26**
Asia de Cuba **37**
Balan's **5**
Barton G. The
 Restaurant **24**
Big Pink **50**
Blue Door **21**
Bond St. Lounge **18**
The Café at
 Books & Books **7**
Casa Tua **20**
China Grill **44**
Clarke's **48**
David's Café II **10**
DeVito South Beach **51**
11th Street Diner **36**
El Rancho Grande **14**
Emeril's Miami Beach **23**
Escopazzo **33**
Front Porch Café **31**
Grillfish **29**
Icebox Café **6**
Jerry's Famous Deli **28**
Joe Allen **2**
Joe's Stone Crab
 Restaurant **55**
La Sandwicherie **32**
Larios on the Beach **39**
Macaluso's **3**
Mark's South Beach **35**
Monty's Raw Bar **46**
Mr Chow **16**
Nemo **49**
News Café **40**
Nexxt Café **12**
Nobu **17**
Ola **19**
Osteria del Teatro **27**
Paninoteca **11**
Piola **4**
Pizza Rustica **38**
Philippe **16**
Prime One Twelve **52**
Puerto Sagua **42**
Quattro **5**
Red, the Steakhouse **47**
San Loco Tacos **32**
Sardinia **1**
Shoji Sushi **49**
Smith & Wollensky **56**

Solea **16**
Spiga **34**
STK Miami **16**
Sushi Samba
 Dromo **13**
Table 8 **30**
Talula **15**
Tantra **25**
Tap Tap **43**
Taverna Opa **54**
Touch **8**
Tuscan Steak **45**
Van Dyke Café **9**
Vivi **53**
Wish **41**

BLT Steak ★★★ STEAKHOUSE Despite a weak economy, for some reason, steakhouses in Miami seem to multiply faster than the Octomom's embryos. And just when we thought we'd had enough meat, BLT Steak opened its doors in the colonial chic Betsy Hotel and, without sounding like a James Bond rip-off, we changed our minds—too much meat is never enough if it comes from the hands of Laurent Tourondel and his protégé and chef de cuisine, 25-year-old Samuel Gorenstein. Unlike other steakhouses, this one is unpretentious and unstuffy with superb service and a serene setting composed of comfy lobby seating or the preferred outdoor verandah seating which, at the northern end of Ocean Drive, is actually quite relaxing. But enough about the ambience. The food, simply put, is outstanding, from the minute they put down the complimentary plate of puffy, fluffy cheesy popovers and chicken liver pâté to your last lingering moment before forcing yourself to leave. Skip the tuna tartare and head straight for a selection of fresh and briny East and West Coast oysters, or, if you don't do mollusks, consider the fantastic *hamachi* with avocado, hearts of palm, and *yuzu* vinaigrette. As for the steaks: exceptional, no matter which cut you order. The rib-eye is huge and seasoned perfectly, with marbling so perfect it would have made Liberace cry. Side dishes are delicious too, but thanks to the meat, they're almost an unnecessary afterthought, though the creamed spinach jalapeño mashed potatoes are rather irresistible. For mushroom fans like myself, a side order of hard to find in these parts hen-of-the-woods mushrooms are a must, too.

1440 Ocean Dr. (in the Betsy Hotel)., South Beach. ✆ **305/673-0044.** Reservations required. Main courses $26–$85. AE, DC, MC, V. Daily 6–11pm.

Blue Door ★ FRENCH This really is quintessential South Beach dining—expensive, gorgeous backdrop, spotty service, and inconsistent food that keeps masochists coming back for more. Dubious qualities aside and ignoring the fact that the eye candy may often be tastier than the cuisine, Blue Door is an excellent place for a business meal or if you want to impress someone who cares more about aesthetics than food. It's a shame award-winning chef Claude Troisgros (rhymes with foie gras)—a star in his own right—isn't here more often, because when he is, you taste the difference. As for the menu, it frowns upon the ubiquitous fusion moniker in favor of a more classic French approach to tropical spices and ingredients. Roasted Maine lobster with raisins, onions, lime, and cilantro with caramelized banana and bok choy; roasted lacquered duck breast with bananas, apple, pineapple, raisins, mango, star fruit, yogurt, and a madras curry sauce; or caramelized rack of lamb and toasted Moroccan couscous with raisins, almonds, pearl onions, and passion-fruit mint glaze are just a few of the Blue Door's tempting offerings, but the menu changes frequently. Service fluctuates between snippy, slow, and, at times, downright rude, although some say it has improved dramatically, which is scary. In an effort to appeal to late night diners and those on a quasi budget, Blue Door introduced a Plat Bleu menu which is so far from Blue Plate it may as well be red—besides the $18 *croque monsieur* and $18 macaroni and cheese, this menu offers soggy flatbreads for up to $25, duck foie gras for $27, a Cobb salad for $29, and, well, you get the pricey picture. Better dining option in the Delano—Blue Sea, the lobby sushi bar, where it's not cheap with tasty rolls ranging from $14 to $24, but if you're hungry and want to stay here, it's your best bet.

In the Delano Hotel, 1685 Collins Ave., South Beach. ☏ **305/674-6400.** www.chinagrillmgt.com. Reservations recommended for dinner. Main courses $31–$46. AE, DC, MC, V. Daily 7am–4pm and 7pm–midnight (bar until 3am); Plat Bleu menu offered 11pm–2am Mon–Wed and 11pm–4am Fri–Sat; Sun brunch 10:30am–2:30pm.

Casa Tua ★★ 🗏 ITALIAN   The stunning Casa Tua is a sleek and chic, country Italian–style establishment set in a refurbished 1925 Mediterranean-style house-cum-hotel. It has several dining areas, including a resplendent outdoor garden, comfy Ralph Lauren–esque living room, and a communal eat-in kitchen whose conviviality does not translate to some of the staff who have been known to turn a nose up at customers. The roasted rack of lamb is stratospheric in price—upwards of $50—but sublime in taste, and a bargain compared to the whole branzino served for two at twice that price. Risottos are also highly recommended. Service is, as always with South Beach eateries, inconsistent, ranging from ultraprofessional to absurdly lackadaisical. For these prices, they should be wiping our mouths for us. What used to be a fabulous lounge upstairs is now a members-only club, so don't even try to get in.

1700 James Ave., South Beach. ☏ **305/673-1010.** Reservations required. Main courses $20–$100. AE, DC, MC, V. Mon–Sat 7pm–midnight.

China Grill ★ PAN-ASIAN   If ever a restaurant could be as cavernous as, say, the Asian continent, this would be it. Formerly a hub of hype and pompous circumstance, China Grill has calmed on the coolness meter despite the infrequent appearance of the likes of J-Lo and Enrique Iglesias, but its cuisine is still sizzling, if not better than ever. With an incomparable and dizzying array of amply portioned dishes (such as the outrageous crispy spinach, wasabi mashed potatoes, seared rare tuna in spicy Japanese pepper, broccoli rabe dumplings, lobster pancakes, and a sinfully delicious dessert sampler complete with sparklers), this epicurean journey into the world of near-perfect Pan-Asian cuisine is well worth a stop on any foodie's itinerary. Keep in mind that China Grill is a family-style restaurant and dishes are for sharing. For those who can't stay away from sushi, China Grill also has Dragon, a 40-seat "sushi den" in a private back room with such one-of-a-kind rolls as the Havana Roll—yellowtail snapper, rum, coconut, avocado, and red *tobiko*   and cocktails such as the Lemongrass Saketini. Located right next door in what used to be China Grill's private room is the South Beach branch of the ultrapricey **Kobe Club** (☏ **305/673-5370**), a 52-seat restaurant devoted to all things meaty, where a "flight" of beef—Kobe, Wagyu, American—costs upwards of $350. You really better love meat to spend that money. Because it's not something people can afford to eat every night, Kobe Club is open on weekends only, Friday and Saturday from 7 to 11pm. For those in Fort Lauderdale, there's a China Grill up there now, with water views, at 881 SE 17th St. (☏ **954/759-9950**).

404 Washington Ave., South Beach. ☏ **305/534-2211.** www.chinagrillmgt.com. Reservations strongly recommended. Main courses $27–$59. AE, DC, MC, V. Mon–Thurs 11:45am–midnight; Fri 11:45am–1am; Sat 6pm–1am; Sun 6pm–midnight.

DeVito South Beach ★ ITALIAN CHOPHOUSE   The latest production from actor Danny DeVito (and a few bona fide restaurant professionals), this sexy Italian-style chophouse is a stunning homage to decor—and, although he's not exactly someone you'd equate with the word *sexy*, DeVito delivers. Brick walls and rich, textured bordello-style paneling are adorned with flatscreen TVs playing DeVito's greatest hits, although one weekend night they switched it up with James Bond. An elegant, warm interior is matched by an even more elegant price tag—dinner for two can cost upwards of $200 thanks to a heavily sauced, heavily priced menu of steaks and assorted family-style dishes including Dover sole, Maine lobster risotto, an excellent calamari appetizer, and a gargantuan veal parmigiana that is enough to serve the entire restaurant. Clearly DeVito's sense of humor never translated to the menu, which is seriously pricey. The $275 (!) Global Steak Flight is the restaurant's signature dish, with three different kinds of Kobe beef—authentic Japanese Kobe Beef, Australian Wagyu Rollatini, and American Kobe Flat Iron. Order wisely here, and take advantage of the freebies you get when you sit down—homemade popovers and a selection of salumi, cheese, and veggies.

150 Ocean Dr., South Beach. (C) **305/531-0911.** www.devitosouthbeach.com. Reservations strongly recommended. Main courses $18–$300. AE, DC, MC, V. Daily noon–3pm; Sun–Thurs 5pm–midnight; Fri–Sat 5pm–1am.

Emeril's Miami Beach ★★★ CREOLE   This is the real deal. In a city where restaurants pride themselves on celebrity sightings and snooty service, Emeril's is a spicy breath of fresh air. If you've never dined at Emeril's original restaurant(s) in New Orleans and you're craving gourmet Creole cuisine, dine here ASAP. Elaborately designed by David Rockwell, the 8,000-square-foot restaurant is reminiscent of a bustling and cavernous New York City hot spot with chandeliers, massive wine cellars, and a very inviting open kitchen in which Emeril himself sometimes stars. Call the restaurant ahead to find out when he's in town, and book your reservations immediately. Portions are massive, and signature dishes include New Orleans barbecue shrimp with a petite rosemary biscuit; Niman Ranch double-cut pork chop with tamarind glaze, caramelized sweet potatoes, and green chili mole sauce; and banana cream pie with banana crust, caramel sauce, and chocolate shavings. Service is stellar and should serve as an example to other area restaurants. A 3-hour Sunday Jazz Brunch is worth breaking the diet for, too.

In the Loews Hotel, 1601 Collins Ave., South Beach. (C) **305/695-4550.** www.emerils.com. Reservations required. Main courses $18–$50. AE, MC, V. Sun–Thurs 11:30am–2pm and 5:30–10pm; Fri–Sat 11:30am–2pm and 5:30–11pm.

Escopazzo ★★★ ITALIAN   *Escopazzo* means "I'm going crazy" in Italian, but the only sign of insanity in this externally unassuming Northern Italian eatery is the fact that it seats only 90 and it's one of the best restaurants in town. The wine bottles have it better—the restaurant's cellar holds 1,000 bottles of various vintages. Escopazzo now bills itself as an "Organic Italian Restaurant," a redundant moniker considering the ingredients here have always been of the freshest, but newish is a menu of raw vegan and vegetarian appetizers and entrees including vegan raw lasagna of organic marinated tomatoes, zucchini, eggplant, cashew "ricotta," sundried tomatoes, and basil pesto. Should you be so lucky to score a table at this romantic local favorite (choose one in the back dining room that's reminiscent of an Italian courtyard, complete with fountain and faux windows; it's not cheesy at all), you'll have trouble deciding between dishes that will have you swearing off the Olive Garden with your first bite. Standouts are milk and basil dough pasta with baby calamari, chickpeas, tomatoes, and arugula, or grass-fed hanger steak with roasted baby organic veggies in a truffle sauce. The hand-rolled pastas and risotto are near perfection. Eating here is like dining with a big Italian family—it's never boring (the menu changes five or six times a year), the service is excellent, and nobody's happy until you are blissfully full.

1311 Washington Ave., South Beach. © **305/674-9450.** www.escopazzo.com. Reservations required. Main courses $17–$36. AE, MC, V. Mon-Fri 6pm-midnight; Sat 6pm-1am; Sun 6-11pm.

Joe's Stone Crab Restaurant ★ SEAFOOD   Unless you grease the palms of one of the stone-faced maitre d's with some stone-cold cash, you'll be waiting for those famous claws for up to 2 hours—if not more. As much a Miami landmark as the beaches themselves, Joe's is a microcosm of the city, attracting everyone from T-shirted locals to a bejeweled Ivana Trump. Whatever you wear, however, will be eclipsed by a kitschy, unglamorous plastic bib that your waiter will tie on you unless you say otherwise. Open only during stone-crab season (Oct–May), Joe's reels in the crowds with the freshest (though some disagree and consider Joe's stash subpar to less-assuming area restaurants), meatiest stone crabs and their essential accoutrements: creamed spinach and excellent sweet-potato fries. The claws come in medium, large, and jumbo. Some say size doesn't matter; others swear by the jumbo (and more expensive) ones. Whatever you choose, pair them with a savory mustard sauce (a perfect mix of mayo and mustard) or hot butter. Not feeling crabby? The fried chicken and liver and onions on the regular menu are actually considered by many as far superior—they're definitely far cheaper—to the crabs. Oh yes, and save room for dessert. The Key lime pie here is the best in town. If you don't feel like waiting, try Joe's Takeaway, which is next door to the restaurant—it's a lot quicker and just as tasty.

11 Washington Ave. (at Biscayne St., just south of 1st St.), South Beach. © **305/673-0365** or 673-4611 for takeout. www.joesstonecrab.com. Reservations not accepted. Market price varies but averages $45–$65. AE, DC, DISC, MC, V. Sun 11:30am-2pm and 4-10pm; Mon-Thurs 11:30am-2pm and 5-10pm; Fri-Sat 11:30am-2pm and 5-11pm. Closed mid-May to mid-Oct.

Meat Market ★★★ STEAKHOUSE   As unoriginal yet as telling as its name is, this bustling Lincoln Road steakhouse is one of the city's best—for many things. Thanks to its sexy, loungey vibe it's a great bar scene and, at times, a bona fide pickup joint or, rather, a meat market. And thanks to a talented chef/co-owner, Sean Brasel, it's also a serious eating place too. Raw bar selections such as oysters on the half shell with delicious dipping sauces (habanero cocktail sauce is a favorite) or mahimahi with lime, jalapeño, cilantro, and tequila will prepare your taste buds for an epicurean journey that differentiates this meat market from the rest, almost rendering its name a misnomer of sorts. Seafood appetizers such as crispy crab tail bathed in egg batter and pan fried with passion-fruit butter sauce and sesame-and-aji-panca oil make you wonder why they didn't call it Fish Market. That said, the steaks are indeed delicious too, but we especially love almost each and every one of the 21 side dishes offered—especially the Gouda-filled tater tots. Meat, what?

915 Lincoln Rd., South Beach. © **305/532-0088.** www.meatmarketmiami.com. Reservations required. Main courses $20–$84. AE, MC, V. Daily 6pm--midnight.

Mr Chow ★ ♨ CHINESE   For whatever reason, celebrities love Michael Chow's exorbitantly priced Chinese cuisine. And I may have liked it as well if it didn't have less flavor than PF Chang's and if my bill for two wasn't pushing $400. Yes, $400 for Chinese food. If Confucius were alive, he'd say it was outrageous. That said, you're paying for location, scene, and reputation, which, whether you like it or not, is somewhat stellar. Food critics disagree, but the A-listers of the world don't care. In fact, without celebrities, Mr Chow would be, well, lonely. Pushy, tuxedoed waiters trained to up-sell offer you customized prix fixe menus upwards of $60 a person as they try to snatch the actual menu out of your hand. Don't fall for it. Order what you want, but order wisely. And maybe eat beforehand; portions are tiny. Skip the signature green shrimp—they have no taste. Crispy beef is mushy, and the white rice should have gold flecks in it at $12 a bowl for two. Don't be fooled by the champagne pushcarts with prices turned in a way that only a Cirque de Soleil acrobat could see them. If you do indulge, watch your glass. Refills come fast and furious—at a price. Nothing is free here. After all, they have to pay for that magnificent Swarovski crystal chandelier and plush royal blue carpeting. As for our one-star rating? It's for those celebrities who continue to confound us by calling Mr Chow their favorite restaurant.

At the W South Beach, 2201 Collins Ave., South Beach. ℂ **305/695-1695.** Reservations required. Main courses $28–$45 and above. AE, MC, V. Sun–Wed 6–11:30pm; Thurs–Sat 6pm–12:30am.

Nobu ★★ SUSHI   When Madonna ate here, no one really noticed. The same thing happened when Jay-Z and Beyoncé canoodled here. Okay, well they noticed, but not for long. It's not because people were purposely trying not to notice, but because the real star at Nobu is the sushi. The raw facts: Nobu has been hailed as one of the best sushi restaurants in the world, with always-packed eateries in New York, London, and Los Angeles. The *Omakase,* or Chef's Choice—a multicourse menu entirely up to the chef for $70 per person and up—gets consistent raves. Some people, however, say Nobu is overpriced and mediocre. Not being a sushi fan, I can only agree on the fact that it's very expensive. When you do go here, expect to spend at least what Beyoncé pays for a pair of shoes. Enjoy the scenery and have fun pretending not to notice, because although you won't wait long for your food to be cooked, you will wait forever to score a table here even if you have a reservation.

At The Shore Club Hotel, 1901 Collins Ave., South Beach. ℂ **305/695-3232.** Reservations suggested. Main courses $26 and above. AE, MC, V. Sun 7–11pm; Mon–Thurs 7pm–midnight; Fri–Sat 7pm–1am.

Ola ★★ NUEVO LATINO   Star chef Douglas Rodriguez single-handedly created the nouveau Latino and Cubano cuisine in Miami when he founded Lincoln Road's Yuca restaurant in 1989. From there, he skyrocketed to fame (and left Yuca to rot in mediocrity) and became co-owner and executive chef at New York City's lauded Patria (leaving Miami restaurant-goers to wallow in their sorrows). But now Rodriguez is back in full force with Ola, serving Spanish tapas and ceviches as well as Rodriguez's very own inimitable culinary concoctions including a sensational Mar Y Tierra—NY Strip with smoked chocolate rub served with lobster-stuffed ancho chili relleno. In late 2009, Rodriguez opened a new restaurant, **D Rodriguez Cuba,** at the Hotel Astor, 956 Washington Ave. (ℂ **305/673-3763;** www.drodriguezcuba.com) serving progressive Latin cuisine (think: Cuban pizza with yucca crust).

In the Sanctuary Hotel, 1745 James Ave., Miami Beach. ℂ **305/673-5455.** www.olamiami.com. Reservations recommended. Main courses $20–$50. AE, DC, MC, V. Mon–Thurs 5:30–11pm; Fri–Sat 5:30pm–midnight.

Osteria del Teatro ★★★ ITALIAN   Located in an unassuming storefront beneath the flashy Cameo nightclub, it's hard to believe that Osteria del Teatro is the best Italian bistro on the beach. What it might be lacking in decor is certainly not absent in the elaborate cuisine. Regulars who swear by this place won't even bother looking at the menu; instead they concentrate on the enormous changing list of specials on the blackboard. You will definitely be faced with some tough choices: plump chicken breast sautéed with shallots and sun-dried tomatoes in champagne cream sauce; seafood baked with linguine, garlic, fresh tomatoes, and olive oil in parchment paper; or homemade ravioli stuffed with scallops and crab in lobster sauce. The regulars here are on a first-name basis with the waiters, who always seem to know what you're in the mood for.

1443 Washington Ave. (at Española Way), South Beach. ✆ **305/538-7850.** www.osteriadelteatro miami.com. Reservations recommended. Main courses $17–$31. AE, DC, MC, V. Mon–Sat 6pm–midnight. Closed Sept.

Philippe ★ CHINESE   Located a block away from its arch nemesis Mr Chow (with whom they are embroiled in a crazy lawsuit brought on by Chow, who claims his former employee Philippe Chow stole all his secrets), Philippe was the first on the block with pricey Chinese, with an upscale white against black motif and a noodle-master/showman who wows the crowds with his noodle-making skills with the enthusiasm of a Vegas magician. Gimmicks aside, Philippe's food is fickle, from good to bland. Signature neon orange chicken satay skewers are dyed in carrot juice and *look* as if they may boast the flavor of a zesty Buffalo wing, but no such luck. As for the rest of the menu, you'll find all the classics—duck, prawns, beef in all sorts of sauces, dumplings—albeit gussied up—price wise, not flavor wise. Stick with noodle dishes if you can. Heck, stick with PF Chang's if you can. Chinese food shouldn't be this expensive. As for the Chinese Hatfields vs. McCoys—that is, Philippe vs. Mr Chow? They both lose in our book. If you're going to drop a second mortgage on Chinese, head to Hakkasan, a place where even Mr Chow has been known to frequent from time to time.

In the Gansevoort South, 2305 Collins Ave., South Beach. ✆ **305/674-0250.** www.philippechow.com. Reservations required. Main courses $29–$60. AE, DC, MC, V. Mon–Sat noon–4pm; Sun 1:30–4pm; Sun–Wed 6pm–midnight; Thurs–Sat 6pm–1am.

Prime One Twelve ★★★ STEAKHOUSE   Part of the ever-expanding culinary empire of Nemo, Big Pink, and Shoji Sushi, Prime One Twelve is the media darling of the exclusive group of restaurants in the hot South of Fifth Street area of South Beach, ranking near the top of the list of highest-grossing restaurants in the entire country in 2007 and proving recession proof in 2009, reporting an unheard-of *increase* in business and profits. A frenzied, celebrity-saturated sleek steakhouse ambience and bustling bar (complete with dried strips of bacon in lieu of nuts) play second fiddle to the beef, which is arguably the best in the entire city, although some carnivores say it's all flash and no flesh (of the edible kind) and prefer BLT Steak, Bourbon Steak, and stalwarts like Capital Grille. The 12-ounce filet mignon is seared to perfection and can be enhanced with optional dipping sauces (for a price)—truffle, garlic herb, foie gras, and chipotle. The 22-ounce bone-in rib-eye is a good choice if you can afford it, as is the gigantic 48-ounce porterhouse. Prime One Twelve also features a $20 Kobe-beef hot dog, Kobe-beef sliders—think White Castle on an expense account ($20)—and a Kobe burger, a $30 version of sheer ecstasy. Fries are extra at $10, as are all the sauces ($2 each, but don't bother) and side dishes (the broccoli rabe sautéed in garlic is outstanding, as are the scalloped potatoes)—typical in a steakhouse, but the prices here are hefty. A powerhouse crowd gathers here for lunch and dinner, and reservations are rarer than the yellow-fin tuna tartare appetizer, but should you be lucky enough to score such a "prime" reservation, take it without hesitation. If not, consider Prime's sister restaurant across the street, **Prime Italian,** 101 Ocean Dr. (📞 **305/695-8484**), a pricey red-sauce spot that's not nearly as much of a scene, but features swift service, outdoor seating with a view of the Prime One Twelve parade across the street and, yes, an easier reservation to snag.

In the Browns Hotel, 112 Ocean Dr., South Beach. 📞 **305/532-8112.** www.prime112.com. Reservations recommended. Main courses $20–$88. AE, DISC, MC, V. Mon–Fri 11:30am–3pm; daily 6:30pm–midnight.

Red, the Steakhouse ★★ STEAKHOUSE   When this high-styled, black, red, and stone-walled, clubby-contemporary meatery from Cleveland opened two blocks away from Prime One Twelve, people laughed. But it was no joke. Red proved itself and has held its own in the glitzy shadows of its neighbor thanks to spectacularly seasoned steaks that don't taste like those found anywhere else. Purists may sneer at it, but those looking for mad flavor revel in this magical seasoning that is composed of oil, kosher salt, and black peppercorns. Must be a Midwestern thing, some say, but whatever it is, it works. Don't fill up too much on the delicious bread and hearty starters like the savory trio of green peppers stuffed with sweet Italian sausage, but don't pass on them either. And if it's good enough for one of its most repeat customers, Michael Jordan, who is usually holed up in the glass-enclosed private room complete with flatscreens to watch games on, it's good enough for us.

119 Washington Ave., South Beach. 📞 **305/534-3688.** www.redthesteakhouse.com. Reservations required. Main courses $28–$89. AE, DC, MC, V. Sun–Fri 5:30pm–midnight; Sat 5:30pm–2am.

Smith & Wollensky ★ STEAKHOUSE   Although it's a chain steakhouse, Miami Beach's Smith & Wollensky has a waterfront view that separates it from the rest. Inside seating is typical steakhouse—dark woods, and so on—but make sure to request a table by the window so you can watch the cruise ships pass by as they leave the port. Outdoor seating, weather permitting, is resplendent, with a bar that doubles as command central for the happy-hour set on Friday nights. The menu here is a lot more basic than the priceless views, almost austere, with a few chicken and fish choices and beef served about a dozen ways. The classic is the sirloin, seared lightly and served naked. The veal chop is of Flintstonian proportion. Mediocre side dishes such as asparagus, baked potato, onion rings, creamed spinach, and hash browns are sold a la carte. Service is erratic, from highly professional to rudely aloof. You'll find much tastier steaks (at comparable prices) at BLT Steak and Capital Grille (p. 118 and 144).

1 Washington Ave. (in South Pointe Park), South Beach. 📞 **305/673-2800.** www.smithandwollensky.com. Reservations recommended. Main courses $20–$50. AE, DC, DISC, MC, V. Mon–Sat noon–2am; Sun 11:30am–2am.

Soleá ★★★ SPANISH   The antithesis of its neighbor Mr Chow, Soleá is a lively yet low-key spot for stellar modern Spanish cuisine. Excellent lighting, cozy banquettes, outdoor poolside patio, and even a *jamón y queso* and brick oven station make for a relaxed night of exceptional cuisine thanks to chef Marc Vidal, best known for his tutelage under the revered Ferran Adrià, who some call the best chef in the world. Vidal does a bang-up job himself, starting with tapas featuring renowned Ibérico ham, cured meats and cheeses from Spain as well as flatbreads and a focus on seafood. Main courses further tango with the sea, from seared imported sea bass to elaborately prepared paella-style rice and pasta. Carnivores aren't ignored either, with classic grill cuts and brick-oven-roasted meats. Don't miss the Arroces section of the menu where dishes, served piping hot in a cast-iron pot, can be enjoyed as a side or a main, and include *arroz de montaña* (mountain rice), which is a delicious combo of Calasparra rice with squab, artichokes, and porcini mushrooms.

In the W South Beach, 2201 Collins Ave., South Beach. ✆ **305/938-3111.** Reservations required. Main courses $21–$34. AE, DC, MC, V. Sun–Wed 6–11pm; Thurs–Sat 6pm–midnight.

STK ★ STEAKHOUSE   After opening delays that lasted several years, STK, the see-and-be-seen meatery that's "not your daddy's steakhouse" finally opened off the lackluster lobby of the Gansevoort South. Sexy it is, featuring sleek decor, second-floor catwalk perfect for being seen, and a glazed screen spanning the restaurant's two stories depicting an abstract shape of a woman's body reflecting off the glass. Because that's just what you want to see when stuffing your face with meat, right? To answer that question is the menu's not so tongue-in-cheeky "female friendly portions." Located next to the restaurant is a 2,000-square-foot lounge, Coco DeVille, featuring DJ booth and requisite celebrity clientele. By the looks of things, you understand why it took so long to open. As for the food, some Miami-inspired selections include seared big eye tuna, with roasted pineapple, habanero chili pepper, and *congri* basmati rice, and pork *mojo cazuela,* with citrus chili *maduros* and yuca. Fans of the steakhouse in L.A. and NYC will be happy to see favorites from those parts, shrimp rice krispies (tiger prawns, shrimp bisque, and cilantro), foie gras French toast, and Lil' Big Macs (the Mack Daddy of Big Macs—Japanese Wagyu, "special sauce on a sesame seed bun" at $20 a pop). And then there are the steaks, signature cuts of meat in small, medium, and large. As for whether to choose this place over the four hundred other sceney steakhouses in Miami, the jury's still out. Too new to tell, which means the place will be packed for a long while.

In the Gansevoort South, 2377 Collins Ave., South Beach. ✆ **305/604-6988.** Reservations required. Main courses $24–$65. AE, DC, MC, V. Mon–Sun 5:30pm–2am.

Wish ★★★ MEDITERRANEAN   Located in the stylish Todd Oldham–designed The Hotel, this is one of the most beautiful, romantic outdoor garden restaurants in South Beach which was recently spruced up and looks better than ever. Chef Marco Ferraro, who has worked under the toque of Jean-Georges Vongerichten, has taken the restaurant to a new level of taste with a menu he describes as "fresh, seasonal, light, and vibrant." He's putting it mildly. Think New American with Latin and Mediterranean accents. The Cuban coffee–braised osso buco is exquisite, as is the grilled pork tenderloin with cream cheese–fingerling potato salad, watercress, and guava-habanero reduction. And then there are the "electric cocktails," such as the glowing green-apple martini served with psychedelic ice cubes. The only thing you'll wish for after you leave here is to go back!

801 Collins Ave., South Beach. ✆ **305/531-2222.** Reservations recommended. Main courses $26–$37. AE, DC, MC, V. Mon 11:30am–3pm; Tues–Sun 11:30am–3pm and 6–11pm (Fri–Sat to midnight).

Expensive

Nemo ★ PAN-ASIAN   A pioneer in the chic South Beach area known as SoFi ("South of Fifth St."), Nemo is now the neighborhood's stalwart funky, high-style eatery with an open kitchen and an outdoor courtyard canopied by trees and lined with an eclectic mix of model types and foodies (although not as see-and-be-sceney as it used to be since its younger, more fabulous sibling Prime One Twelve stole its thunder a few years ago). Among the reasons to still eat in this restaurant (whose name is actually *omen* spelled backward): grilled Indian-spiced pork chop; grilled local mahimahi with citrus and grilled sweet-onion salad, kimchi glaze, basil, and crispy potatoes; and an inspired dessert menu that's not for the faint of calories. Seating inside is comfy-cozy, but borders on cramped. On Sunday mornings, the open kitchen is converted into a buffet counter for the restaurant's unparalleled brunch.

100 Collins Ave., South Beach. © **305/532-4550.** www.mylesrestaurantgroup.com. Reservations recommended. Main courses $26–$75; Sun brunch $34. AE, MC, V. Mon–Sat noon–3pm and 6:30pm–midnight; Sun 11am–3pm and 6pm–midnight. Valet parking $10–$20.

Quattro ★★ ITALIAN   Not just another Italian restaurant on Lincoln Road, Quattro is a Northern Italian standout thanks to its chefs—30-something-year-old twin brothers hailing from the Piedmont region of Italy who barely speak English, but speak pasta fluently. Signature dishes on the menu include homemade fontina ravioli with white truffle oil and veal wraps with melted Parmesan cheese and bread crumbs. The wine list is all Italian and reasonably priced. The room is gorgeous, with dramatic lighting, chandeliers, and an all-glass bar that buzzes with *la dolce vita*. Try the cheese plate if you're not too hungry—it's a meal in itself and features that salami you wished you had smuggled back home the last time you returned from Italy. And not to miss a calling, located across the road from Quattro is its sister restaurant, **Sosta Pizzeria,** 1025 Lincoln Rd. (© **305/722-5454**), serving pretty good thin-crust brick oven pizzas.

1014 Lincoln Rd., South Beach. © **305/531-4833.** www.quattromiami.com. Reservations recommended. Main courses $31–$50. AE, MC, V. Sun–Thurs noon–4pm and 6pm–midnight; Fri–Sat noon–4pm and 6pm–1am.

Sardinia ★★ ITALIAN   A quiet sensation in South Beach terms, Sardinia doesn't need celebrity sightings and publicists to boost their business. And it's not your typical caprese salad and fusilli pasta factory, either. For starters, the cheese and salumi plates will transport you—or at least your palate—to Italy, as will the rest of the innovative menu, consisting of orecchiette with wild boar; crunchy fried sweetbreads with Brussels sprouts; and rabbit with Brussels sprouts and beets. Sure, the food's a bit heavy, but it's worth it. As for scene here, it's all about the food, although the bar is always bustling with people waiting for highly coveted tables. For seafood lovers, don't miss the branzino baked in salt crust. If you're craving pizza, around the corner, Sardinia opened **Casale Pizzeria and Mozzarella Bar,** 1800 Bay Road (© **305/763-8088**), featuring great eats, drinks, and a cool rooftop lounge.

1801 Purdy Ave., South Beach. © **305/531-2228.** www.sardinia-ristorante.com. Reservations highly suggested. Main courses $8–$36. AE, DC, MC, V. Daily noon–midnight.

Shoji Sushi ★ SUSHI   Despite a sushi saturation on South Beach, Shoji stands apart from the typical sashimi-and-California-roll routine with expertly prepared, exquisitely fresh, and innovative top-notch rolls. The diminutive sister to its next-door neighbor Nemo, Shoji is known for its authentic Japanese box sushi technique, in which the sushi, rice, and ingredients are packed into a tidy, tasty cake that won't crumble into your lap. Among the rolls I can't seem to get enough of here are the *hamachi* jalapeño—cilantro, daikon sprout, asparagus, avocado, and jalapeños—and the spicy lobster roll, which consists of mango, avocado, scallion, *shiso,* salmon egg, and huge chunks of lobster. Wash it all down with a "saketini," or my personal fave, the "gingertini," which is made with ginger, vodka, triple sec, ginger ale, and pickled ginger juice.

100 Collins Ave., South Beach. ✆ **305/532-4245.** www.mylesrestaurantgroup.com. Reservations recommended. Sushi $3–$13; main courses $20–$36. AE, MC, V. Sun–Thurs noon–midnight; Fri–Sat noon–1am.

Sushi Samba Dromo ★ SUSHI/CEVICHE   It's Brazilian, it's Peruvian, it's Japanese, it's . . . super sushi! This multinational New York City import is definitely scene-worthy: It's a hipster's paradise. This stylish, sexy restaurant charges a pretty penny for some exotic sushi rolls such as the soft-shell crab roll, a tasty combo of chives, jalapeño, and crab, and the South Asian roll with shrimp, tomato, cucumber, chives, cilantro, and onions. And while the sushi is top notch, the sashimi ceviches are even better. An assortment—your choice of four from either lobster, salmon, yellowtail, tuna, *kanpachi,* and shrimp—is somewhat of a deal at $33, considering the fact that separately each can run you from $13 to $17. For main plates, try the *churrasco à Rio Grande,* a divine assortment of meats served with rice, beans, collard greens, and chimichurri sauce. In 2010, Sushi Samba opened **Sugarcane Raw Bar Grill,** 3250 NE First St. in Midtown Miami (✆ **786/369-0353**), a 4,000-plus-square-foot space with three kitchens including one with a Japanese charcoal grill, raw bar, and lounge.

600 Lincoln Rd., South Beach. ✆ **305/673-5337.** www.sushisamba.com. Reservations recommended. Main courses $19–$44; sushi rolls $10–$15. AE, MC, V. Mon–Wed noon–midnight; Thurs 11:30am–1am; Fri–Sat noon–2am; Sun brunch 11:30am–3:30pm, dinner 3:30pm–1am.

Talula ★★★ 👶 NEW AMERICAN   Owned by husband-and-wife team Andrea Curto-Randazzo and Frank Randazzo, Talula is a blissful marriage of many flavors, as seen in such signature dishes as grilled Hudson Valley foie gras, with caramelized fruit, blue-corn pancakes, chili syrup, and candied walnuts; and sausage-and-Vidalia-onion-stuffed grilled center pork chop, with garlic-sautéed broccoli rabe, apple smoke bacon, bean ragout, caramelized Granny Smith apple, and whole-grain mustard sauce. Chef Frank's chophouse specials are also hot-ticket items, including the 14-ounce, 21-day dry-aged rib-eye. Daily specials always include a chopped salad, soup, risotto, and a meat or fish dish. The wine list is well-balanced, featuring 85 vintages from California, Italy, France, Australia, and South America. Wines by the glass are a reasonable, un–South Beach $9 to $20. As to be expected with any restaurant in South Beach, Talula is cool looking, with an unpretentious, warm decor and outdoor garden patio that is a popular spot for the fantastic buffet-style Sunday brunches. An exhibition kitchen is a tempting seating option, with five seats that offer a view of the culinary action. A seven-course tasting menu is also available for $78 and an excellent way to taste a little of everything.

210 23rd St., South Beach. ✆ **305/672-0778.** www.talulaonline.com. Reservations recommended. Main courses $27–$42. AE, MC, V. Tues–Thurs noon–2:30pm and 6:30–11pm; Fri noon–2:30pm and 6:30–11:30pm; Sat 6:30–11:30pm; Sun 6–10pm. Happy hour Tues–Sun 5–7pm.

Moderate

Balan's ★ MEDITERRANEAN   Balan's provides undeniable evidence that the Brits actually do know a thing or two about cuisine. A direct import from London's Soho, Balan's draws inspiration from various Mediterranean and Asian influences, labeling its cuisine "Mediterrasian." With a brightly colored interior straight out of a mod '60s flick, Balan's is a favorite among the gay and arty crowds, especially on weekends during brunch hours. The moderately priced food is rather good here—especially the double-baked cheese soufflé; citrus-tossed mixed greens; Thai red curry; and the pan-fried tilapia with Indian garbanzo bean curry and mint yogurt. When in doubt, the restaurant's signature US1 Burger is always a good choice. Adding to the ambience is the restaurant's people-watching vantage point on Lincoln Road. In 2009, Balan's expanded over the causeway and opened a second location at 901 S. Miami Ave., in the bustling Brickell area. In early 2010, they opened a *third* at Biscayne Boulevard and 67th Street in the Upper East Side neighborhood.

1022 Lincoln Rd. (btw. Lenox and Michigan), South Beach. ✆ 305/534-9191. www.balans.co.uk. Reservations accepted, except for weekend brunch. Main courses $8–$37 (breakfast and dinner specials Mon–Fri). AE, DISC, MC, V. Sun–Thurs 8am–midnight; Fri–Sat 8am–1am; Sat–Sun brunch noon–3:30pm.

Big Pink ★ ☺ AMERICAN "Real Food for Real People" is the motto to which this restaurant strictly adheres. Set on what used to be a gritty corner of Collins Avenue, Big Pink—owned by the folks at the higher-end Nemo—is quickly identified by a whimsical Pippi Longstocking–type mascot on a sign outside. Scooters and motorcycles line the streets surrounding the place, which is a favorite among beach bums, club kids, and those craving Big Pink's comforting and hugely portioned pizzas, sandwiches, salads, and hamburgers. The fare is above average, at best, and the menu is massive, but it comes with a good dose of kitsch, such as the "gourmet" spin on the classic TV dinner, which is done perfectly, right down to the compartmentalized dessert. Televisions line the bar area, and the family-style table arrangement (there are several booths, too) promotes camaraderie among diners. Outdoor tables are available. Even picky kids will like the food here, and parents can enjoy the family-friendly atmosphere (not the norm for South Beach) without worrying whether their kids are making too much noise.

157 Collins Ave., Miami Beach. ✆ **305/532-4700.** www.mylesrestaurantgroup.com. Salads, sandwiches, burgers, pizzas, main courses $6–$22. AE, DC, MC, V. Sun–Wed 8am–midnight; Thurs 8am–2am; Fri–Sat 8am–5am.

Bond St. Lounge ★ SUSHI A New York City import, the sceney, subterranean Bond St. Lounge is in the basement of the shabby-chic Townhouse Hotel and is packing in hipsters as tightly as the crabmeat in a California roll. Despite its tiny size, Bond St. Lounge's superfresh *nigiri* and sashimi, and funky sushi rolls such as the sun-dried tomato and avocado or the arugula crispy potato, are worth cramming in here for. As the evening progresses, however, Bond St. becomes more of a bar scene than a restaurant, but sushi is always available at the bar to accompany your sake Bloody Mary.

Townhouse Hotel, 150 20th St., South Beach. ✆ **305/398-1806.** Reservations recommended. Sushi $6–$20. AE, MC, V. Daily 6pm–2am.

Burger & Beer Joint AMERICAN A refreshing alternative to the throngs of high end eateries that opened in the area over the past year, B&B, as it's known, is a down home, family-friendly, well, burger and beer joint with no attitude, just great, thick, juicy burgers, fabulously salted skinny fries, beer, cocktails, and, if you're so inclined, ice cream sundaes or sodas. Hip without trying too hard, B&B offers all sorts of burgers, from the plain and classic (all perfectly cooked at medium rare unless otherwise specified) to the rock-'n'-roll inspired: a $39 "Stairway to Heaven," 10 ounces of Wagyu beef, 3 ounces Hudson Valley foie gras, and black truffle demi on a brioche bun; $9 "buck naked" with 10 ounces of prime Angus beef wrapped in lettuce with tomato, grilled red onion, and pickle; or the $12 "Fly Like an Eagle," two turkey patties with homemade stuffing, brown gravy, and cranberry sauce. You can also create your own burgers, with an intimidating list of cheeses, buns, veggies, sauces, bells, and whistles. Before you start with burgers, you may want to try the sassy tempura fried pickles or braised Buffalo wings, which are unlike the ones found in your typical sports bar with meat marinated in a spicy, zippy sauce and falling off the bone. For the insane, try the Mother Burger, a 10-pound patty the size of a manhole, which, if finished within 2 hours, is free. After dinner, check out the back sports bar which tends to be a bit smoky or the upstairs lounge with comfy couches and local DJs.

1766 Bay Rd., South Beach. © **305/672-3287.** www.burgernbeerjoint.com. No reservations. Burgers $9–$39. AE, MC, DC, V. Daily noon–5pm; Sun–Thurs 5pm–1am; Fri–Sat 5pm–2am.

The Café at Books & Books ★ AMERICAN   Not only does this sidewalk cafe offer some of the best, freshest breakfasts and lunches in town—the egg-and-tuna-salad combo is my favorite, as are the amazing yucca and leek homemade hash browns—but gourmet dinners as well. This is not your chain bookstore's prefab tuna sandwich. Sadly, in 2009, the bookstore became a Diesel store, but the cafe stayed. Chef Bernie Matz gave star chef Douglas Rodriguez his start—enough said. Sandwiches, salads, and burgers are good, but after 5pm the real gourmand comes out in Matz with specials that change often and include things like a juicy flank steak marinated in espresso and brown sugar, seared, sliced, and served with a pineapple and onion salsa and a pair of plantain nests smothered in garlicky mojo. The menu also features an impressive selection of vegetarian and vegan options. If you're still inspired to buy a cookbook after your meal, Books & Books set up a small annex in the back of the courtyard.

933 Lincoln Rd., South Beach. © **305/695-8898.** Main courses $5–$25. AE, MC, V. Daily 9am–11pm.

Clarke's ★ IRISH   There's more to this neighborhood pub than pints of Guinness. With a warm, inviting ambience and a gorgeously rich wood bar as the focal point, Clarke's is the only true gastropub in Miami, with excellent fare that goes beyond bangers and mash and delicious burgers, and delves into the gourmet. Highlights include poached snapper with mushroom confit, tomato marmalade, and frisée salad; Sazerac House crab cakes (the secret recipe hails from owner Laura Cullen's father's New York City landmark, the Sazerac House); and Mom's Montauk-style scallops. If you're not in the mood for full fare, my favorite is the New York–style pretzel, served on a spike with mustard on the side. The vibe here is very friendly, which is why everyone from Miami Heat basketball players to South Beach celebrity types choose Clarke's when they want a low-key night with delicious fare—and even more delicious "dish."

840 1st St., South Beach. © **305/538-9885.** www.clarkesmiamibeach.com. Main courses $6–$27. AE, MC, V. Mon–Fri 5pm–midnight; Sat 11:30am–midnight; Sun 11am–3pm (brunch) and 4pm–midnight.

El Rancho Grande ★★ MEXICAN   Hidden on a side street off of Lincoln Road, El Rancho Grande is a favorite local cantina that has attracted the likes of Cher and Matt Damon, thanks to its ultrafresh fare and unassuming ambience. With a "Pottery Barn meets Acapulco" decor, El Rancho Grande doesn't hold anything back when it comes to the cuisine. The Aztec soup, a hot-and-spicy blend of chicken and tortilla strips, is one of the best I've had. The salsa here is not at all watery and is freshly made—a tongue-tickling blend of spices, cilantro, tomatoes, onions, and peppers—and the Mexican favorites of burritos, enchiladas, and fajitas are all very well represented. All portions are huge and can be shared or taken home for extra meal mileage. Margaritas are a little weak when frozen and better ordered on the rocks. Expect a wait at the small bar for your table, especially on weekends. Limited outdoor seating is also available.

1626 Pennsylvania Ave., South Beach. ☎ **305/673-0480.** Main courses $10–$20. AE, DC, MC, V. Daily 11am–11pm.

Grillfish ★ SEAFOOD The Cher of South Beach seafood spots, Grillfish is one of the city's longest lasting, and, frankly, most well preserved. From the beautiful Byzantine-style mural and the gleaming oak bar, you'd think you were eating in a much more expensive restaurant, but Grillfish manages to pay the exorbitant South Beach rent with the help of a loyal following of locals who come for fresh, simple seafood in a relaxed but upscale atmosphere. The servers are friendly and know the menu well, as well they should. It's a simple one with a selection of mostly seafood starters—have the mussels or the blackened Grillfish cakes, and main courses of seafood over pasta, grilled or sautéed seafood with a side of corn on the cob, choice of sweet onion or creamy garlic tomato sauce and side of pasta, or three meat dishes—filet mignon, New York strip, or surf and turf. Stick to the fish, especially because, at these prices, it's worth a visit to try some local fare, including mako shark, swordfish, tuna, marlin, and wahoo.

1444 Collins Ave. (corner of Española Way), South Beach. ☎ **305/538-9908.** www.grillfish.com. Reservations accepted for parties of 6 or more only. Main courses $13–$28. AE, DC, DISC, MC, V. Daily 11:30am–4pm and 5:30pm–midnight.

Jerry's Famous Deli ★ DELI Answering the cries for a real, New York–style deli on South Beach is Jerry's Famous Deli, actually a Los Angeles import, which occupies the cavernous space that used to house the very decadent gay disco, the Warsaw Ballroom. In a way, Jerry's still channels that same decadence, albeit with a menu that features over 700 monstrously portioned items, from your typical corned beef on rye to your atypical brisket burrito. While the quality of the food is excellent, the service pales in comparison: This 24-hour deli is not a place to go if you're in a rush. The modern cafeteria, complete with full bar, is dimly lit with a disco soundtrack that is somewhat reminiscent of its predecessor. People come here to linger over sandwiches that can feed at least two people, if not more, and should you be craving a Reuben sandwich after a night of clubbing at 5am, Jerry's is command central for that set as well as the original early birders who are first waking at 5am and will have their dinner at 5pm. One thing, though: This is *not* your grandfather's deli, where sandwiches were only a few bucks. Prepare to shell out at least $10 and up for one of Jerry's. What do you expect? It's 21st-century South Beach.

1450 Collins Ave., South Beach. ☎ **305/532-8030.** www.jerrysfamousdeli.com. Main courses $10–$30. AE, DC, DISC, MC, V. Daily 24 hr.

Joe Allen ★ 🍴 AMERICAN It's hard to compete in a city with haute spots everywhere you look, but Joe Allen, a restaurant that has proven itself in both New York and London, has stood up to the challenge by establishing itself off the beaten path in possibly the only area of South Beach that has remained impervious to trendiness and overdevelopment. Located on the bay side of the beach, Joe Allen is conspicuously devoid of neon lights, valet parkers, and fashionable pedestrians. Inside, however, one discovers a hidden jewel: a stark yet elegant interior and no-nonsense, fairly priced, ample-portioned dishes such as meatloaf, pizza, fresh fish, and salads. The scene has a homey feel favored by locals looking to escape the hype without compromising quality.

1787 Purdy Ave./Sunset Harbor Dr. (3 blocks west of Alton Rd.), South Beach. (*) **305/531-7007.** Reservations recommended, especially Sat–Sun. Main courses $15–$25. MC, V. Daily 11:30am–11:30pm.

Larios on the Beach ★ ♨ CUBAN If you're a fan of singer Gloria Estefan, you will definitely want to check out this restaurant, which she and her husband Emilio own; if not, you may want to reconsider, as the place is an absolute mob scene, especially on weekends. The classic Cuban dishes get a so-so rating from the Cubans, but a better one from those who aren't as well versed in the cuisine. The portions here are larger than life, as are some of the restaurant's patrons, who come here for the sidewalk scenery and the well-prepared black beans and rice. Inside, the restaurant turns into a makeshift salsa club, with music blaring over the animated conversations and the sounds of English clashing with Spanish. Because of its locale on Ocean Drive, at the Seminole Hard Rock Hotel & Casino in Hollywood, and in downtown Miami at the American Airlines Arena, plus its affiliate Bongos Cuban Café's locations in Orlando, this place is positioned for visitors who have never experienced the Cuban culture or tasted its cuisine.

820 Ocean Dr., South Beach. (*) **305/532-9577.** www.bongoscubancafe.com. Reservations recommended. Main courses $10–$37. AE, MC, V. Sun–Thurs 11:30am–midnight; Fri–Sat 11:30am–1am.

Macaluso's ★★ ITALIAN This restaurant epitomizes the Italians' love for—and mastery of—savory, plentiful, down-home Staten Island–style food. While the storefront restaurant is intimate and demure in nature, there's nothing delicate about the bold mix of flavors in every meat and pasta dish here. Catch the fantastic clam pie when in season—the portions are huge. Pricier items vary throughout the season but will likely feature fresh fish handpicked by Chef (and owner) Michael, the don of the kitchen, who is so accommodating that he'll take special requests or even bring to your table a complimentary signature meatball. If he doesn't, don't hesitate to ask your waiter for one; he should be glad to bring it to you. Everyone will recommend favorites such as the rigatoni and broccoli rabe. There are also delicious desserts ranging from homemade anisette cookies to gooey pastries. The wine list is also good. Keep your eyes peeled, as this is a major celeb hot spot, where everyone from Lindsay Lohan to Roger Federer and Billy Joel have been known to eat here and kibitz with the chef in the kitchen.

1747 Alton Rd., Miami Beach. (*) **305/604-1811.** Main courses $15–$40; pizza $10–$20. MC, V. Tues–Sat 6pm–midnight; Sun 6–11pm. After 10:30pm, only pies are served.

Monty's Raw Bar ★ ♦ SEAFOOD This restaurant is the antithesis of South Beach trendiness, with scrappy wood floors and a very casual raw bar set outside around a large swimming pool. Enjoy the incredible views but don't expect much in the way of cuisine. With happy hour Monday through Friday from 4 to 8pm featuring half-priced drinks, your best bet is to have a few drinks and stick with snacks— peel-and-eat shrimp, smoked-fish dip, and Buffalo wings go really well with beer or rum runners. Beware of Friday nights, when the happy-hour crowds convene around (and sometimes in) the pool for post-work revelry.

300 Alton Rd., South Beach. ✆ **305/673-3444.** www.montyssouthbeach.com. Reservations recommended. Main courses $20–$40. AE, DC, MC, V. Sun–Thurs 5:30–11pm; Fri–Sat 5:30pm–midnight.

Nexxt Café AMERICAN   Locals joke that this lively, always-packed outdoor cafe should be called Nexxt Year to reflect the awfully slow service that has become its unfortunate trademark. In fact, since the last book was written, I'm still waiting for my Southwestern chicken salad. Service aside, however, Nexxt has made quite a splash on South Beach, attracting an evening crowd looking for nighttime revelry and a morning crowd on the weekends for a standing-room-only brunch sensation. The fresh food comes in lavish portions that could easily feed two; the salads are an especially good bargain and are big enough for more than one person or more than one meal. The burgers and sandwiches are similarly big. They have coffees in tall, grande, and "maxxi." There are also plenty of coffee cocktails, mixed drinks, frozen beverages, and wines, giving this place a nice bar life, too, but buyer beware: drink prices, like much of the menu, are on the outrageous-for-a-cafe side.

700 Lincoln Rd. (off Euclid Ave.), South Beach. ✆ **305/532-6643.** Main courses $10–$30. AE, MC, V. Daily 9am–1am.

Spiga ★★ 🍴 ITALIAN   If you want a side scene with your spaghetti, don't even think of dining at Spiga, a place that's so cozy and so low-key that many of South Beach's most ostentatious hipsters have never even heard of it. The simple gnocchi with tomato and basil is a garlicky sensation, not to mention a most filling entree. The fresh asparagus baked in Parmesan cheese is so fresh that gourmands insist that Alice Waters, the queen of organic cooking, had something to do with it; and the red snapper with kalamata olives, fresh tomatoes, capers, and onions is a refreshingly simple departure from the fusion variety that can be found in almost any area restaurant. The place is extremely romantic and vaguely reminiscent of a Florentine trattoria.

Prime Hotel Impala, 1228 Collins Ave., South Beach. ✆ **305/534-0079.** www.spigarestaurant.com. Reservations accepted. Main courses $14–$25. AE, DC, MC, V. Daily 6pm–midnight.

Tap Tap ★ HAITIAN   The whole place looks like an overgrown *tap tap*, a brightly painted jitney common in Haiti before the devastating 2010 earthquake. But pre-quake Haiti is alive and well in this restaurant that pays homage to the recovering island nation. Every inch is painted in vibrant neon hues (blue, pink, purple, and so on), and the atmosphere is always fun. It's where the Haiti-philes and Haitians, from journalists to politicians, hang out. There's often live music or other cultural programs happening here. The *lanbi nan citron,* a tart, marinated conch salad, is perfect with a tall tropical drink and maybe some lightly grilled goat tidbits, which are served in a savory brown sauce and are less stringy than typical goat dishes. Another super-satisfying choice is the pumpkin soup, a rich brick-colored purée of subtly seasoned pumpkin with a dash of pepper. Shrimp in Creole sauce is another standout. An excellent salad of avocado, mango, and watercress is a great finish. Soda junkies should definitely try the watermelon soda. For the ethnophobic, there's a rather tasty vegetable stew, but I strongly recommend the goat—it tastes just like chicken.

819 5th St. (between Jefferson and Meridian aves., next to the Shell Station), South Beach. ✆ **305/672-2898.** Reservations accepted. Main courses $15–$20. AE, DC, DISC, MC, V. Mon–Thurs 5–11pm; Fri–Sat 5pm–midnight; Sun 5–10pm. Closed in July.

Van Dyke Cafe ★ AMERICAN   News Cafe's younger, less harried sibling, Van Dyke, which now has a new corporate parent (which also owns several Lincoln Road eateries including a trio of Italian spots: Segafredo, Tiramesu, and Spris), is a locals' favorite, at which people-watching is also premium, but attitude is practically non-existent. The menu here spans a variety of cuisines—sandwiches, panini, burgers, Middle Eastern specialties, pasta, seafood, salads, eggs, and so on—but the Van Dyke's warm, wood-floored interior, upstairs jazz bar, accessible parking, and intense chocolate soufflé make it a less taxing alternative. Also, unlike News, Van Dyke turns into a sizzling nightspot featuring live jazz nearly every night of the week. Outside there's a vast tree-lined seating area that's ideal for people-watching. Those allergic to or afraid of dogs might reconsider eating here, as Van Dyke is also a canine hot spot.

846 Lincoln Rd., South Beach. ⓒ **305/534-3600.** www.thevandykecafe.com. Main courses $8–$24. AE, DC, MC, V. Daily 8am–2am.

Inexpensive

Don't miss the South Beach branch of the Gold Coast's fun and tasty **Taverna Opa** (36–40 Ocean Dr., 1 block south of 1st St.; ⓒ **305/673-6730**) in South Beach. For a review of the restaurant, see p. 229.

A La Folie ★★ FRENCH   The Left Bank took a wrong turn and ended up on the quiet(er) end of Española Way in the form of A La Folie. Reflecting the *positive* things about our erstwhile allies, A La Folie is an authentic French cafe in which wooden booths and walls full of foreign newspapers and magazines make you have to take a second look at your plane ticket to make sure you're still in Miami. In addition to the affected, über-French waitstaff (not snotty, but aloof), A La Folie features some of the best cafe fare in Miami including delicious, hugely portioned sandwiches such as the French fave *croque monsieur,* salads, crepes, and, of course, cafe au lait and plenty of wine. Indoor and outdoor seating are equally conducive to whiling away many hours sipping coffee, reading a magazine, and reflecting on that whole Freedom Fry controversy of last decade. A tiny outpost opened at 1701 Sunset Harbor Dr. (ⓒ **305/672-9336**), but stick with the original, it's much more *charmant.*

516 Española Way, South Beach. ⓒ **305/538-4484.** Main courses $5–$15. MC, V. Daily 9am–midnight.

David's Café II ★ CUBAN   The furthest thing from a trendy spot, David's Cafe's Cuban food is good, cheap, and available 24 hours a day in case you need a jolt of Cuban coffee at, say, 4am. Enjoy supercheap breakfasts (two eggs, home fries or grits, coffee, and toast is $4.75), Cuban sandwiches (ham, pork, Swiss, pickles, and mustard), midnight *arroz con pollo,* fantastic cheeseburgers, a wonderful grilled-cheese sandwich, *ropa vieja* habanera (shredded sirloin and sauce), and pretty much anything you can think of—even, oddly enough, brown rice. Hey, this is South Beach, what can you expect? David's also has a recently renovated second location at 1058 Collins Ave. (ⓒ **305/534-8736**), also open 24 hours.

1654 Meridian Ave., South Beach. ⓒ **305/672-8707.** www.davidscafe.com. Main courses $4–$20. AE, MC, V. Daily 24 hr.

11th Street Diner AMERICAN   The only real diner on the beach, the 11th Street Diner is the antidote to a late-night run to Denny's. Some of Miami's most colorful characters, especially the drunk ones, convene here at odd hours, and your greasy-spoon experience can quickly turn into a three-ring circus. Uprooted from its 1948 Wilkes-Barre, Pennsylvania, foundation, the actual structure was dismantled and rebuilt on a busy—and colorful (a gay bar is right next door, so be on the lookout for flamboyant drag queens) corner of Washington Avenue. Although it can use a good window cleaning, it remains a popular round-the-clock spot that attracts all walks of life. If you're craving french fries, order them smothered in mozzarella with a side of gravy—a tasty concoction that I call disco fries because of its popularity among starving clubbers.

1065 Washington Ave., South Beach. ℂ 305/534-6373. Items $8–$15. AE, MC. Daily 24 hr.

Front Porch Café ★ AMERICAN   Located in an unassuming, rather dreary-looking Art Deco hotel, the Front Porch Café is a relaxed local hangout known for cheap breakfasts. Some of the servers tend to be a bit attitudinal and lackadaisical (many are bartenders or club kids by night), so this isn't the place to be if you're in a hurry, especially on the weekends, when the place is packed all day long and lines are the norm. Enjoy home-style French toast with bananas and walnuts, omelets, fresh fruit salads, pizzas, and classic breakfast pancakes that put IHOP to shame. If you're looking to avoid the tourists and prefer to dine with the locals, Front Porch is where it's at for breakfast, lunch, and even dinner.

In the Penguin Hotel, 1418 Ocean Dr., South Beach. ℂ 305/531-8300. Main courses $5–$18. AE, DC, DISC, MC, V. Daily 8am–10:30pm.

Icebox Café ★ AMERICAN   Locals love this place for its homey comfort food—tuna melts, potpies, and eggs for breakfast, lunch, and dinner. Oprah Winfrey singled it out for its desserts, which is really why people raid the Icebox whenever that sweet tooth calls. In the Icebox, you'll discover the best chocolate cake, pound cake, and banana cream pies outside of your grandma's kitchen.

1657 Michigan Ave., South Beach. ℂ 305/538-8448. Main courses and desserts $3–$10. AE, MC, V. Daily 8am–10:30pm.

La Sandwicherie ★ SANDWICHES   You can get mustard, mayo, or oil and vinegar on sandwiches elsewhere in town, but you'd be missing out on all the local flavor. This gourmet sandwich bar, open until the crack of dawn, caters to ravenous club kids, biker types, and the body artists who work in the tattoo parlor next door. For many people, in fact, no night of clubbing is complete without capping it off with a turkey sub from La Sandwicherie.

229 14th St. (behind the Amoco station), South Beach. ℂ 305/532-8934. Sandwiches and salads $6–$12. AE, MC, V. Daily 9am–5am. Delivery 9:30am–11pm.

News Cafe ★ AMERICAN   This South Beach cafe-cum-landmark hasn't fallen off the radar, it's just on a different one, this time as an iconic South Beach figure rather than a currently hip one. The quintessential South Beach experience, News is still au courant, albeit swarming with mostly tourists. Unless it's appallingly hot or rainy out, you should wait for an outside table, where you must be to fully appreciate the experience. Service is abysmal and often arrogant (perhaps because the tip is included), but the menu is reliable, running the gamut from sandwiches and salads to pasta dishes and omelets. My favorite here is the Middle Eastern platter, a dip lover's paradise, with hummus, tahini, tabbouleh, baba ghanouj, and fresh pita bread. If it's not too busy, feel free to order just a cappuccino—your server may snarl, but that's what News is all about; creative types like to bring their laptops and sit here all day (or all night—this place is open 24 hr. a day). If you're alone and need something to read, there's an extensive collection of national and international newspapers and magazines at the in-house newsstand. **The News Lounge,** at the 55th Street Station off Biscayne Blvd., 5582 NE Fourth Court (✆ **305/758-9932**), has a 100-seat interior video bar, limited bar menu, and 100-seat outdoor space that's open daily from 5pm until 1am, sometimes later.

800 Ocean Dr., South Beach. ✆ **305/538-6397.** www.newscafe.com. Items $5–$30. AE, DC, MC, V. Daily 24 hr.

Piola ★ PIZZA   This hip Italian import miraculously transforms pizza from an eat-out-of-the-box-stuff-a-slice-into-your-mouth experience into a fun, sit-down meal that's hard to beat for the price, quality, and quantity. An unabridged menu of nearly 80 different kinds of pizzas-for-one that are really enough to share between two people is mind numbing and mouthwatering. I suggest that you order several pizzas, depending on how many people you are dining with (two is more than enough for two, for example). Start with the *quattro formaggio* pizza—brie, Gorgonzola, Parmesan and mozzarella—and then consider a funkier version, say, smoked salmon and caviar. All pizzas are thin crusted and full of flavor. Waitstaff is extremely friendly, too, but be prepared for a lengthy wait, especially on weekend nights when the movie-going crowds next door spill over for a snack. Capitalizing on its South Beach success, Piola is now a minichain, with locations all over the country, and another in Miami, in the Brickell area at 1250 S. Miami Ave. (✆ **305/374-0031**).

1625 Alton Rd., South Beach. ✆ **305/674-1660.** www.piola.it. Reservations accepted. Main courses $10–$16. AE, DC, MC, V. Daily 6pm–1am.

Puerto Sagua ★ CUBAN/SPANISH   This brown-walled diner is one of the only old holdouts on South Beach. Its steady stream of regulars ranges from *abuelitos* (little old grandfathers) and local politicos who meet here every Tuesday morning to hipsters who stop in after clubbing. It has endured because the food is good, if a little greasy. Some of the less heavy dishes are a superchunky fish soup with pieces of whole flaky grouper, chicken, and seafood paella, or marinated kingfish. Also good are most of the shrimp dishes, especially the shrimp in garlic sauce, which is served with white rice and salad. This is one of the most reasonably priced places left on the beach for simple, hearty fare. Don't be intimidated by the hunched, older waiters in their white button-down shirts and black pants. If you don't speak Spanish, they're usually willing to do charades. Anyway, the extensive menu, which ranges from BLTs to grilled lobsters to yummy fried plantains, is translated into English. Hurry, before another boutique goes up in its place.

700 Collins Ave., South Beach. ✆ **305/673-1115.** Main courses $6–$24; sandwiches and salads $5–$10. AE, DC, MC, V. Daily 7:30am–2am.

MIAMI BEACH TO NORTH MIAMI

The area north of the Art Deco District—from about 21st Street to 163rd Street—had its heyday in the 1950s when huge hotels and gambling halls blocked the view of the ocean. Now, many of the old hotels have been converted into condos or budget lodgings, and the bayfront mansions have been renovated by and for wealthy entrepreneurs, families, and speculators. The area has many more residents, albeit seasonal, than visitors. On the culinary front, the result is a handful of superexpensive, traditional restaurants as well as a number of value-oriented spots.

For a map of these listings (covering Miami Beach, North Beach, Surfside, Bal Harbour, Sunny Isles, and North Miami), see p. 96.

Very Expensive

The Forge ★★★ ORGANIC/STEAK   Like many of its most loyal, uh, seasoned customers, The Forge underwent a major nip/tuck and traded its dark roots for a lighter, blonder look and a menu that focuses on organic, locally sourced foods. The bar is stunning in a refreshingly rich, not stark, way, and its electronic dispensing wine system turns oenophiles into kids on a video-game bender at the Chuck E. Cheese's, only with booze. Good booze, of course. Thankfully the old-school wine cellar, one of the country's best, still remains just that. Menu by Chef Dewey LoSasso offers a modern, largely organic twist on everything, from seafood and salads to pastas and steaks. Yes, the classic Forge Super Steak is still on the menu to the delight of many. This re-imagined Forge is nothing like its previous incarnation as a bacchanalian den of decadence, so no more raucous parties or weekly see-and-be-scene fests. Sure, it's decadent, but it's much more subtly so, just like its customers.

432 Arthur Godfrey Rd. (41st St.), Miami Beach. ℂ **305/538-8533.** Reservations recommended. Main courses $25–$60. AE, DC, MC, V. Sun–Thurs 6pm–midnight; Fri–Sat 6pm–1am.

Gotham Steak ★ STEAKHOUSE   NYC's Gotham Bar & Grill chef/owner Alfred Portale's Miami offering is this, a stunning, yet somewhat disappointing steakhouse that fits right into its environs as something with all style yet hardly any substance. The bi-level restaurant is photo-worthy with a chandelier of hand-blown glass and glass-enclosed wine tower, but as for the food? Uninspired. Steaks, pricey and often overcooked, include a gigantic 20-ounce Brandt Farms rib-eye grilled over hardwood charcoal and finished on a 1,200-degree broiler ($52); 8-ounce American Wagyu filet mignon that you can get pretty much anywhere these days ($50), and the bargain $28 skirt steak that a no-name bodega in Little Havana makes better for less than half. Yawn. If you're going to the Fontainebleau, have a drink here, take a few pictures, but save your appetite for one of the other two highly lauded eateries.

In the Fontainebleau, 4441 Collins Ave., Miami Beach. ℂ **305/674-4780.** Reservations required. Main courses $28–$52. AE, DC, MC, V. Daily 6–10:30pm.

Hakkasan ★★★ CHINESE   A flashy bastion of the luxe life, this higher-than-high-end haute Chineserie owned by Michelin-starred Chef Alan Yau of London's Hakkasan fame, is a sight to be seen and tasted. Tucked away on the fourth floor of the labyrinthine Fontainebleau, Hakkasan exudes a nightclubby, Vegas vibe with thumping music, scantily clad diners who think they're in Vegas, and screened-off nooks of semi-private dining areas. There is and has never been a recession in this place, that's for sure. Although I am of the PF Chang's school of Chinese, I can't deny the fact that this is some seriously good, gourmet food. Signature dishes include a fabulous fillet of roasted silver cod over tender stalks of *gai lan* (Chinese broccoli) in honey and champagne, roasted duck served in bite-size slices with crisped skin with a savory soy sauce, and red snapper with a spicy scallion soy sauce. Service is professional with the exception of one or two aloof types who slipped through the screens. Your best bet is to go with a group of people if you can so you can share dishes. Just watch the drinks—that's where they always get you. New in 2010: dim sum lunch on Saturdays and Sundays from noon to 3pm.

In the Fontainebleau, 4441 Collins Ave., Miami Beach. ☎ **786/276-1388.** Reservations required. Main courses $18-$195. AE, DC, MC, V. Sun, Tues, Wed 6-11pm; Thurs-Sat 6pm-12:30am.

The Palm ★★ STEAKHOUSE   As sturdy as the tree that shares its name, the Palm is one of the country's most heralded steakhouses, known for its Jurassic portions and no-nonsense service. Everything here is a la carte, and the prices add up quicker than the cholesterol courses through your veins. Both fish and meat are praiseworthy; the blackened swordfish steak is as hearty and massive as the filet mignon. Prime rib and New York strip are full of flavor as well and cooked to perfection. To complicate matters further, the veal and lamb chops are absolutely divine. For those who like a little surf with their turf, the lobsters here are truly freaks of nature, weighing in at 4 pounds and up. The food is prepared simply, but needs no enhancement. Sharing is encouraged unless you're a linebacker, and even they've been known to split a steak. Side dishes include salads, potatoes, and vegetables; be sure to try the superb creamed spinach.

9650 E. Bay Harbor Dr., Bay Harbor Island. ☎ **305/868-7256.** Reservations highly recommended. Main courses $20-$50. AE, DC, MC, V. Daily 5-11pm. From Collins Ave., turn west onto 96th St.; at Bal Harbour Shops, go over a small bridge, and turn right onto East Bay Harbor Dr. The restaurant is half a block down on the left.

Scarpetta ★★★ ITALIAN   Miami Beach's very own version of the wildly popular NYC Italian restaurant of the same name, Scarpetta has consistently been one of the city's hottest reservations since it opened in late 2008. Chef Scott Conant is a talent and, unlike many star chefs too busy to cook in their own kitchens, he is often found massaging his homemade pasta right here, in his Miami Beach kitchen. And while that kitchen is indeed high tech, the dining room is a showpiece, with ambient lighting, beautiful chandeliers, banquettes, and an aura that's reminiscent of the first class dining room in an Old World ocean liner that sailed into the 21st century. Once you are seduced by the room, you may not notice that you're paying $23 for a bowl of chef's signature spaghetti *pomodoro*—you know, the pasta he was in the kitchen kneading and massaging at 5am? Skip the spaghetti. We've had it twice and it doesn't compare to dishes on the rest of the menu. But first the bread basket, a selection of ciabatta, focaccia, and a stromboli-like round stuffed with salami, mozzarella, and basil is tempting to polish off, but pace yourself. The pappardelle with short rib and chestnut ragu and the agnolotti *dal plin* with melted fontina and mushrooms and the polenta served in a silver ramekin alongside a fricassee of mushrooms with a hint of truffle oil will have you wishing you could sail away on this gastronomical vessel and massage pasta as you sail into the sunset. Scarpetta also has a great Sunday Bellini brunch at $50 for adults, $25 for kids under 10.

In the Fontainebleau, 4441 Collins Ave., Miami Beach. ☎ **305/672-4660.** Reservations required. Main courses $23-$38. AE, DC, MC, V. Sun-Thurs 6-11pm; Fri-Sat 6pm-midnight.

Expensive

Carpaccio ★ ITALIAN   A favored spot for the ladies who lunch, Carpaccio's location in the ritzy Bal Harbour Shops is its tastiest aspect: It's definitely a place to see and be seen. Ask for specials rather than ordering off the regular menu; they're much more interesting—linguine lobster, snapper piccata, and veal chop any style—though they may be a bit pricier. Wear sunglasses to block the blinding glare of all the diamonds.

9700 Collins Ave. (97th St., in Bal Harbour Shops), Bal Harbour. © **305/867-7777**. www.carpaccioat balharbour.com. Reservations recommended. Main courses $12–$33; pastas $13–$26; pizzas $12–$14. AE, MC, V. Daily 11:30am–11pm.

Timo ★★★ ITALIAN/MEDITERRANEAN This hip, haute restaurant is in Sunny Isles, where, not so long ago, Tony Roma's was the hottest eatery. Timo is a stylish Italian/Mediterranean restaurant catering to mostly North Miami Beach locals who have been yearning for something else besides the fabulous Chef Allen's. Among the specialties, try the handcrafted pastas, including foie gras ravioli with wild mushrooms, asparagus, and black truffle jus; sea bass with truffled polenta and roasted wild mushrooms; and a phenomenal veal scaloppini. Less pricey, less heavy items are also available, such as a delicious ricotta-and-fontina wood-fired pizza with white truffle oil—perfect for lunch or a happy-hour snack. At Timo, a cool bistro-meets-lounge atmosphere gives way to a decidedly cool vibe, something that was always conspicuously lacking at Tony Roma's.

17624 Collins Ave., Sunny Isles. © **305/936-1008**. www.timorestaurant.com. Reservations required. Main courses $9–$32. AE, DC, MC, V. Sun–Thurs 11:30am–3pm and 6–10:30pm; Fri–Sat 11:30am–3pm and 6–11pm.

Moderate

Cafe Prima Pasta ★ ITALIAN Once a small, unknown trattoria on a very traf-ficky, tacky street, Cafe Prima Pasta has expanded into a place to be for excellent Italian food and quite a bit of fanfare, especially when regular customer Matt Damon comes in. Because a massive waiting line always spilled out onto the street, the cafe expanded to include ample outdoor seating that is set back from the street noise and traffic, thanks to some creative landscaping. The pasta here is homemade and the kitchen's choice ingredients include ripe, juicy tomatoes; imported olive oil that would cost you a boatload if you bought it in the store; fresh, drippy mozzarella; and fish that tastes as if it has just been caught right out back. The zesty, spicy garlic and oil that is brought out as dip for the bread should be kept with you during your meal, for it doubles as extra seasoning for your food—not that it's necessary. Though tables are packed in, the atmosphere still manages to be romantic. Due to the chef's fancy for garlic, this is a three-Altoid restaurant, so be prepared to pop a few or request that they go light on the garlic.

414 71st St. (half a block east of the Byron movie theater), Miami Beach. © **305/867-0106**. Reserva-tions accepted for parties of 6 or more. Main courses $10–$28; pastas $12–$20. MC, V. Mon–Thurs noon–midnight; Fri noon–1am; Sat 1pm–1am; Sun 5pm–midnight.

Cafe Ragazzi ★★ ITALIAN This diminutive Italian cafe, with its rustic decor and a swift, knowledgeable waitstaff, enjoys great success for its tasty, simple pastas. The spicy *puttanesca* sauce with a subtle hint of fish is perfectly prepared. Also recommended is the salmon with radicchio. You can choose from many decent sal-ads and carpaccio, too. Ragazzi has a faithful following of regulars, so be prepared for the crowd spill on the street—especially on weekend nights.

9500 Harding Ave. (on the corner of 95th St.), Surfside. © **305/866-4495**. Reservations accepted for parties of 3 or more. Main courses $10–$25. MC, V. Mon–Fri 11:30am–3pm; daily 5–11:30pm.

Creek 28 ★★ 🍴 MEDITERRANEAN Tucked away inside the Indian Creek Hotel, this hidden gem of a restaurant is one of Miami Beach's best-kept secrets. Chef Kira Volz has woven flavors from Spain, Greece, and Morocco into an elegant, yet affordable dining experience. If weather permits, sit in the lovely outdoor garden. Among the signature entrees, grilled sea scallops with tomato saffron sauce, currants, chorizo and grilled bread; or a Mexican pozole with braised chicken in a hearty veggie and hominy stew. Menu changes often, but make sure they're still serving the signature warm baklava with poached dried apricots and honeyed homemade yogurt.

In the Indian Creek Hotel, 2727 Indian Creek Dr., Miami Beach. ✆ **305/672-7825.** www.creek28.com. Reservations recommended. Main courses $19–$25. AE, DISC, MC, V. Mon–Fri 6–11pm; Sat–Sun 11:30am–11pm.

Las Vacas Gordas ★★ ARGENTINE STEAKHOUSE Got meat? Or, rather, how do you say it in Spanish, because you may need a translator at this popular Argentine steakhouse, where service doesn't dilly-dally, nor do they typically speak understandable English. But don't worry, the culture shock wears off once they start bringing out your meat. And meat. And more meat, which explains why the name of the restaurant translates to The Fat Cows. It's quite a fun experience, actually, as long as you hold off on your food coma—if one of the surly staff catches you snoozing, you're out of there. Specialties are the marinated and grilled steaks, but order carefully. I made the mistake of pointing, like one does in a foreign country when they can't read the menu, and I ended up with blood sausage, which is as nasty as it sounds though a delicacy to some. All meats are served with a divine chimichurri sauce, but sauces aren't really needed. Neither are sides and salads, but sometimes you'll need something more than red wine to wash your meat down with.

933 Normandy Dr., Miami Beach. ✆ **305/867-1717.** Reservations highly suggested. Main courses $15–$25. MC, V. Daily 6pm–midnight.

Lemon Twist ★ FRENCH When you're at Lemon Twist, you are not on 71st Street, but, rather the 71st Arrondissement, an honorary offshoot of Paris's 20 neighborhoods. Or, you may be somewhere in Provence, depending on your inner GPS. Wherever you feel you may be, when you're here in this resurrected North Beach bistro, you are amongst friends. And family. Albeit mostly French speaking, but, *mon Dieu,* what a welcome departure from the usual. Owned and operated by a husband-and-wife team, the cozy, chic Lemon Twist features a simple Mediterranean bistro fare with French accents featuring familiar faves such as French onion soup, escargot, and pâtés. Main courses include poached salmon, mussels in white wine marinade (which some already say are the best in town and judging by the smell and sounds emanating from the table next to us, we believe 'em), sea bass in parchment Provençal, steak tartare, pot-roasted chicken, chicken paillard, and crispy duck with oranges and glazed turnips. Desserts include crème brûlée, bananas flambé, sorbets, and a divine Fondant au Chocolat.

908 71st St., Miami Beach ✆ **305/865-6465.** www.lemontwist-miami.com. Reservations suggested. Main courses $14–$24. MC, V. Mon–Thurs 6–11pm; Fri–Sat 6pm–midnight.

Oggi Caffe ★ ITALIAN Tucked away in a tiny strip mall on the 79th Street Causeway, this neighborhood favorite makes fresh pastas daily. Each one, from the agnolotti stuffed with fresh spinach and ricotta to the wire-thin spaghettini, is tender and tasty. Though you could fill up on the starters, the entrees, especially the grilled dishes, are superb. The place is small and a bit rushed, but it's worth the slight discomfort for this authentic, moderately priced food.

1666 79th St. Causeway, North Bay Village. ✆ **305/866-1238.** Reservations recommended. Main courses $14–$30; pastas $10–$15. AE, DC, MC, V. Mon–Fri 11:30am–2:30pm; daily 6–11pm.

Inexpensive

The Greek Place GREEK   This little hole-in-the-wall diner with sparkling white walls and about 10 wooden stools serves fantastic Greek and American diner-style food. Daily specials like *pastitsio,* chicken *alcyone,* and roast turkey with all the fixings are big lunchtime draws for locals working in the area. Typical Greek dishes like shish kabob, souvlakia, and gyros are cooked to perfection as you wait. Even the hamburger, prime ground beef delicately spiced and freshly grilled, is wonderful. If you're not in the mood for heavy entrees, appetizers and salads are big enough and make for hearty meals, too.

233 95th St. (between Collins and Harding aves.), Surfside. © **305/866-9628.** Main courses $15–$25; appetizers $5–$12. No credit cards. Mon–Fri 10am–5pm; Sat 11am–3pm.

Here Comes the Sun ★ AMERICAN/HEALTH FOOD   One of Miami's first health-food spots (and it still looks like it did when it opened in 1970, yikes), this bustling grocery-store-turned-diner serves hundreds of plates a night, mostly to blue-haired locals. It's noisy and hectic but worth it. Fresh grilled fish and chicken entrees are reliable and served with a nice array of vegetables. The miso burgers with "sun sauce" are a vegetarian's dream.

2188 NE 123rd St. (west of the Broad Causeway), North Miami. © **305/893-5711.** Reservations recommended in season. Main courses $8–$18; sandwiches and salads $5–$15 AE, DC, DISC, MC, V. Mon–Sat 11am–8:30pm.

NORTH MIAMI BEACH

Although there aren't many hotels in North Dade, the population in the winter months explodes due to the onslaught of seasonal residents from the Northeast. A number of exclusive condominiums and country clubs (including William's Island and Turnberry) breed a demanding clientele, many of whom dine out nightly. That's good news for visitors, who can find superior service and cuisine at value prices.

Very Expensive

Chef Allen's ★★★ NEW WORLD   If anyone deserves to have a restaurant named after him, it's Chef Allen Susser, winner of the esteemed James Beard Award for Best American Chef in the Southeast—the Academy Award of cuisine—and practically every other form of praise and honor awarded by the most discriminating palates. Chef Allen, the man, is royalty around here. Chef Allen's, the restaurant, is his province, and foodies are his disciples. His platform? New World cuisine and the harmony of exotic tropical fruits, spices, and vegetables. In 2009, Susser introduced a new bistro concept, focusing on the best locally caught sustainable fish, seafood, and regional produce. It is under Chef Allen's magic that ordinary Key limes and mangoes reappear in the forms of succulent salsas

> ### Impressions
>
> *What's really exciting about Miami is its growth as an international destination. We don't have many restrictions as to what our neighborhoods should look like, and that's reflected in our food . . . It's very open and exciting.*
> —Chef Allen Susser

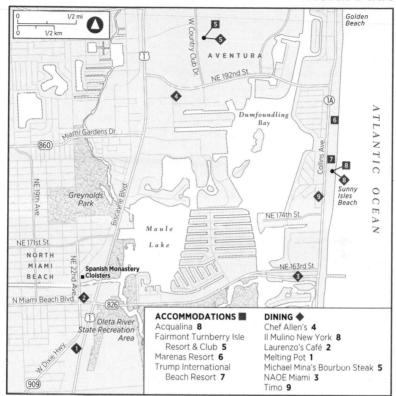

ACCOMMODATIONS ■
Acqualina **8**
Fairmont Turnberry Isle
  Resort & Club **5**
Marenas Resort **6**
Trump International
  Beach Resort **7**

DINING ◆
Chef Allen's **4**
Il Mulino New York **8**
Laurenzo's Café **2**
Melting Pot **1**
Michael Mina's Bourbon Steak **5**
NAOE Miami **3**
Timo **9**

and sauces. Main courses include a surf-and-turf combo of garlicky guava shrimp and Niman Ranch skirt steak served with crisp yuca fries; blackened red snapper with *platanos maduros* and a cool orange *raita;* meaty swordfish with wood-grilled pineapple, Thai stir-fry, and tomato salsa; grouper with rock shrimp, leeks, mango, and coconut rum; mahimahi in a savory *sofrito* with Peruvian lima beans; wild Florida shrimp scampi, with zucchini and ricotta ravioli, shallots, lemon, and caviar. Save room for dessert, because they rock, too. Try the milk chocolate hazelnut "Kit Kat" or the peanut butter mousse bombe. Unlike other restaurants where location is key, the recently renovated 100-seat Chef Allen's, located at the rear of a strip mall, could be in the desert and hordes of people would still make the trek.

19088 NE 29th Ave. (at Biscayne Blvd.), North Miami Beach. ☎ **305/935-2900.** www.chefallens.com. Reservations recommended. Main courses $15–$32. AE, DC, MC, V. Sun–Thurs 6–10pm; Fri–Sat 6–11pm.

Christine Lee's ★ CHINESE   This Cantonese restaurant is a 35-year-old Miami staple that serves excellent but overpriced Chinese-style dishes featuring steak, shrimp, and lobster sauce, as well as a good rendition of steak *kew,* a Cantonese dish with oyster sauce and hot bean paste. Considering the dearth of good Chinese restaurants in Miami, this is a fine choice if you absolutely *must* satisfy your cravings for Chinese, but it will definitely cost you more than it should, especially since it moved to its swank new location at the Gulfstream Racing and Casino.

Gulfstream Racing and Casino, 901 S. Federal Hwy., Hallandale. © **954/457-6255.** www.christinelees. com. Reservations recommended. Main courses $11–$40. AE, DISC, MC, V. Daily 11:30am–3pm and 4-10:30pm (not open for lunch May–Sept).

Il Mulino New York ★ ITALIAN   New York's veritable Greenwich Village Italian hot spot opened in Sunny Isles to mixed reviews. An ornate restaurant located in the even more ornate Acqualina Resort, Il Mulino is a saucy affair with signature dishes such as spaghettini Bolognese, a cartoon-size rack of lamb, veal chop, and more. Service ranges from spotty to spectacular, but there's something about the tuxedoed waiters that makes it all so elegant and romantic. But again, there's that sauce issue. When I ate here, my dish was so covered in sauce I forgot what I had ordered. This restaurant is hit or miss, but when it does hit, it's a fancy Italian pleasure.

In Acqualina, 17875 Collins Ave., Sunny Isles. © **305/466-9191.** Reservations recommended. Main courses $25–$60. AE, MC, V. Mon–Thurs 5-10:30pm; Fri–Sat 5-11:30pm.

Michael Mina's Bourbon Steak ★★ STEAKHOUSE   Although there's no shortage of steakhouses in Miami, there's nothing like this one. Reminiscent of something out of Las Vegas, everything here is massive—from the stunning all-glass wine cellar that takes up an entire wall, to the sheer size of the place at 7,600 square feet. And then there are the prices. But if you don't mind splurging, a meal at the star chef's first and only South Florida location is worth it. Start off with some oysters on the half shell—East Coast or West Coast, your choice—and then continue with the all-natural farm-raised Angus beef, American Kobe beef, or actual Japanese Kobe beef—where a 6-ounce rib-eye will set you back $190! Side dishes are delicious—jalapeño creamed corn ($9), truffled mac and cheese ($12), and a Bourbon Steak trio of duck fat fries comes complimentary to every table (additional orders are $8 a pop), along with a potato focaccia bread with truffle butter and chives. Not in the mood for steak? Some say the burger, a Kobe version with duck fat fries, fennel slaw, and watercress pickled veggies, is the best in town. A scene of well-heeled Aventura residents—including actor James Caan and perma-tanned man George Hamilton—and elegantly dressed hotel guests compose the equally rich crowd.

In the Fairmont Turnberry Isle Resort & Club, 19999 West Country Club Dr., Aventura. © **786/279-6600.** Reservations recommended. Main courses $22–$190. AE, DC, DISC, MC, V. Mon–Thurs 6-10pm; Fri–Sat 6-11pm.

NAOE Miami ★★★ SUSHI   Simply put NAOE is Japanese for "OMG *omakase*." Well, not really, but chef Kevin Cory sure makes you think that with his exquisitely prepared, hyperfresh sushi, possibly the best in the city. Its motto is very blunt: "It's not fresh, it's alive." Open only Wednesday through Sunday, Chef Cory serves his chef choice's menu ($26) every night. All menus are prepared daily and if you have special requests, you need to make it at least a week in advance. Be careful about what you ask for, though, as extras can add up quickly. They even charge for fresh grated wasabi. That's fresh stuff, not the tubed stuff, but still. Another translation for NAOE: "Nobu, what?"

175 Sunny Isles Blvd. (across from St. Tropez Condominium), Sunny Isles. © **305/947-6263.** www. naoemiami.com. Reservations recommended. Tasting menus $26. AE, MC, V. Wed–Sun seatings 8pm, 9pm, and midnight.

Moderate

Melting Pot FONDUE   Traditional fondue is supplemented by combination meat-and-fish dinners, which are served with one of almost a dozen different sauces. With its lace curtains and cozy booths, the Melting Pot can be quite romantic. To satisfy health-conscious diners, the owners have introduced a more wholesome version of fondue, in which you cook vegetables and meats in a low-fat broth. It tastes good, although this version is less fun than watching drippy cheese flow from the hot pot. Best of all is dessert: chunks of fruit that you dip into a creamy chocolate fondue. No liquor is served here, but the wine list is extensive, and beer is available. For those über-conscious of smelling like your last meal, bring along some perfume, because the eau de fondue scent will stay with you for hours after. A second Melting Pot is located at 11520 SW 72nd St. (Sunset Dr.) in Kendall (*©* **305/279-8816**).

15700 Biscayne Blvd., North Miami Beach. *©* **305/947-2228.** www.meltingpot.com. Reservations recommended on weekends. Fondues $16–$25. AE, DC, DISC, MC, V. Sun–Thurs 5:30–11pm; Fri–Sat 5:30pm–midnight.

Inexpensive

Laurenzo's Café ITALIAN   This Italian restaurant in the middle of a chaotic grocery store used to be among the city's best, but now, thanks to a mediocre, somewhat dirty-looking buffet and abysmal service, we lament the old Laurenzo's. Stick to buying your own stuff at the grocery and you'll be much better off.

16385 W. Dixie Hwy. (south of the corner of 163rd St.), North Miami Beach. *©* **305/945-6381.** www. laurenzosmarket.com. Main courses $4–$10; salads $3–$10. No credit cards. Mon–Fri 8:30am–7:30pm; Sat 8am–7pm; Sun 8am–5pm.

DOWNTOWN MIAMI

Downtown Miami is a large sprawling area divided by the Brickell Bridge into two distinct areas: Brickell Avenue and the bayfront area near Biscayne Boulevard. You shouldn't walk from one to the other—it's quite a distance and unsafe at night. Convenient Metromover stops do adjoin the areas, so for a quarter, it's better to hop on the scenic sky tram (closed after midnight). Thanks to the urban renaissance taking place in downtown, a lot more hip, chichi, and bona fide foodie-caliber restaurants are starting to pop up. **The Shops at Midtown Miami,** 3401 N. Miami Ave. (*©* **305/573-3371;** www.shopmidtownmiami.com), for instance, is the quintessence of urban revival, featuring anchor stores like Target and Marshall's and some really good restaurants including a branch of NYC's mod Mexican spot **Mercadito** and Sushi Samba's hipper sister, the tapas-oriented **Sugarcane Raw Bar Grill.** That said, while it's safe(ish) to walk the Shops at Midtown, surrounding areas not so much. Perhaps one day soon, it'll be safe to walk through the city at night from one hot spot to the next. Wishful thinking, perhaps, but then again, South Beach used to be unsafe as well.

For maps of these listings, see p. 101 and p. 145.

Very Expensive

Area 31 ★★★ SEAFOOD   Miami's very first sustainable seafood restaurant, Area 31 is named after a U.N.-designated, ecologically sustainable area of Western Central Atlantic Ocean encompassing the coastal waters of Florida, Central

America, and northern South America. In addition to being eco-conscious, Area 31 is a gorgeous, 65-seat restaurant on the 16th floor of the EPIC hotel featuring a spectacular outdoor terrace with views of the water and skyline. Up-and-coming star-chef John Critchley takes his seafood seriously, with seamless, simple, and locally inspired preparations including yellowfin tuna with green apple and yellow pepper juice; Key West pink shrimp with olive oil, Key lime juice, and chili; fresh shucked oysters; and an assortment of grilled, fresh catches of the day served with mix-and-match sauces. If you dig seafood but care for the environment, Area 31 is your conscientiously sanctioned culinary hot spot.

At the EPIC, 270 Biscayne Blvd., Miami. 🄒 **305/424-5234.** Reservations strongly recommended. Main courses $20–$30. AE, DC, DISC, MC, V. Mon–Sat 5–11pm; Sun 5–10pm.

Azul ★★★ GLOBAL FUSION Azul is one of the most upscale, prettiest—and priciest—waterfront restaurants in town. The views of the city skyline are stunning and rival the food—well, almost. Executive Chef Clay Conley, who honed his skills with star chef Todd English, creates a tour de force of international cuisine, inspired by Asian and Mediterranean flavors. Like a stunning designer gown, the restaurant's decor, with its waterfront view, high ceilings, walls burnished in copper, and silk-covered chairs, is complemented by sparkling jewels—in this case, the food. Among the standouts: Moroccan-inspired lamb; a miso-marinated duck breast; and, my favorite, "A Study in Tuna": raw tuna, tempura avocado, and Asian sauces with osetra caviar. Downstairs is the Mandarin's more casual, less expensive **Café Sambal,** an Asian eatery serving breakfast, lunch, and dinner with the same priceless views and a sushi bar.

> **Impressions**
>
> *Miami's cuisine is fearless; there are no boundaries.*
> —Chef Michelle Bernstein, Michy's/Sra. Martinez

At the Mandarin Oriental, 500 Brickell Key Dr., Miami. 🄒 **305/913-8538.** Reservations strongly recommended. Main courses $24–$55. AE, DC, DISC, MC, V. Mon–Sat 7–11pm.

Capital Grille ★★ STEAKHOUSE The best of all the chain steakhouses, Capital Grille is a serious power spot. Wine cellars are filled with high-end classics, and the dark-wood paneling, pristine white tablecloths, chandeliers, and marble floors all contribute to the clubby atmosphere. For an appetizer, start with the lobster and crab cakes. If you're not in the mood for beef or lobster, try the pan-seared red snapper and asparagus covered with hollandaise. You're surrounded by wine cellars filled with about 5,000 bottles of wine—too extensive and rare to list. While some people prefer the more stalwart style and service of Morton's up the block, others find Capital to be a bit livelier. The food's pretty much the same between the two, though I find the steaks at Morton's to be a notch better; however, the atmosphere at the Capital Grille is *much* more inviting. Complimentary valet parking here (as opposed to Morton's, which charges a fee) is another reason to visit this carnivorous capital.

444 Brickell Ave., Miami. 🄒 **305/374-4500.** www.thecapitalgrille.com. Reservations recommended. Main courses $25–$39. AE, DC, DISC, MC, V. Mon–Thurs 11:30am–3pm and 5–10:30pm; Fri 11:30am–3pm and 5–11pm; Sat 6–11pm; Sun 5–10pm.

Brickell, Miami's Design District, Wynwood & Upper East Side

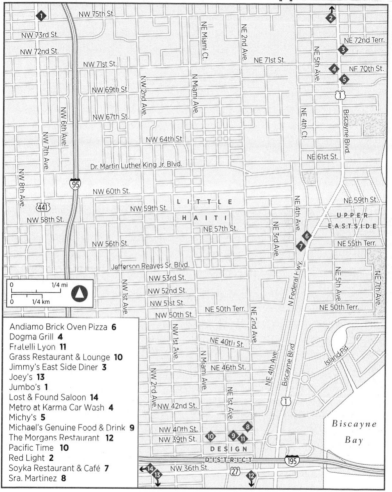

Andiamo Brick Oven Pizza **6**
Dogma Grill **4**
Fratelli Lyon **11**
Grass Restaurant & Lounge **10**
Jimmy's East Side Diner **3**
Joey's **13**
Jumbo's **1**
Lost & Found Saloon **14**
Metro at Karma Car Wash **4**
Michy's **5**
Michael's Genuine Food & Drink **9**
The Morgans Restaurant **12**
Pacific Time **10**
Red Light **2**
Soyka Restaurant & Café **7**
Sra. Martinez **8**

Eos ★★★ MEDITERRANEAN   New York chef Michael Psilakis and restaurateur Donatella Arpaia begrudgingly came to Miami to open this gorgeous Mediterranean hot spot in the Viceroy Hotel. Elegant and richly designed by Kelly Wearstler, the dining room boasts impressive 15th-floor views which can be a nice distraction from what is often an unfortunately empty dining room. No wonder the chef and owner were reluctant to come down here. The emptiness has everything to do with prices and nothing to do with the excellent tapas-style fare—grouper and oyster ceviches, a superb selection of cheeses and crostini, pastas including a spicy Greek "paella" of prawns, *merguez,* shellfish and orzo, fish dishes including a stellar smoked octopus and smoked escolar, and meat dishes including smoked pork ribs and crispy rabbit. Much more crowded than at dinner is Sunday brunch, where any reasonably priced egg dish comes with all you can drink Mimosas or Bloody Marys and free admission to Club 50's Sunday afternoon pool party—chic or not, Miamians and its visitors like a good deal. Can you blame us?

At the Viceroy, 485 Brickell Ave., Miami. © **305/503-4400.** Reservations strongly recommended. Tapas $14–$48. AE, DC, DISC, MC, V. Mon–Wed 6–10pm; Thurs–Sat 6–11pm; Sun brunch 7am–noon.

Il Gabbiano ★★ ITALIAN   Located in the back of a newish high-rise condo on Biscayne Bay, this high end Italian restaurant is not necessarily all about location. Owned by the same folks who own the actual Il Mulino in NYC, the similarities are striking, from the fresh shaved Parmesan and fried zucchini brought to the table with your bread, to the serious demeanors of what seems to be a mostly Italian waitstaff. The menu is intimidating—written mostly in Italian to describe a slew of pasta, meat, and fish dishes—and should come with a translator if you don't have the iPhone app for that. But the menu is secondary to the specials, lots of them, recited verbally by your charming waiter with the thick accent. Listen carefully unless you expect to spend the entire night there, which isn't such a bad thing considering the water views. While the bustling, buzzy dining room has water views, you can't beat the alfresco seating. Food is high quality with a heavy emphasis on pastas such as fettuccine Alfredo or *pollo alla Valdostano* with prosciutto, foie gras, fontina cheese, and wild mushrooms. However, I sent my orecchiette with spicy sausage and sautéed broccoli rabe back because it was drowning in oil. They took it graciously, asked if I wanted something else, and took it off the bill without hassle. Order the double veal chop at your own risk—while the presentation is impressive and the meat tender, I'm not necessarily sure it was worth $65.

335 S. Biscayne Blvd., Miami. © **305/373-0063.** Reservations necessary. AE, DC, MC, V. Daily noon–11:30pm.

Rio's Churrascaria ★ BRAZILIAN   The beloved Porcao was taken over by Rio's, and while the name isn't as fun, it's still an excellent Brazilian *churrascaria* (a Brazilian-style restaurant devoted mostly to meat—it's the Portuguese translation of "steakhouse"). For about $40, you can feast on salads and meat *after* you sample the unlimited gourmet buffet, which includes such fillers as pickled quail eggs, marinated onions, and an entire pig. Do not stuff yourself here, as the next step is the meaty part: Choose as much lamb, filet mignon, chicken hearts, and steak as you like, grilled, skewered, and sliced right at your table. Side dishes also come with the meal, ranging from beans and rice to fried yucca.

801 Brickell Bay Dr., Miami. © **305/373-2777.** www.lvitale.com/riosus. Reservations accepted. Prix-fixe $40 per adult, $20 per child 6 and up, all you can eat. AE, DC, MC, V. Daily noon–midnight.

Expensive

Grass Restaurant and Lounge ★★ 🏆 GLOBAL   What once used to be a snooty, haughtier-than-thou lounge/restaurant is now a welcoming restaurant/lounge, where the priority is excellent, fresh cuisine, not fresh doormen (who have thankfully been weeded out). Chef Micah Edelstein, a former *Top Chef* contestant, describes her cuisine as global comfort food and it shows in dishes such as bison carpaccio with pan-roasted focaccia croutons, *Dukkah*—an Egyptian blend of toasted nuts, seeds, and herbs pounded into a coarse powder of toasted peanuts, pumpkin seeds, coriander seeds, sesame seeds, fresh mint, and thyme—with a Rooibos tea-smoked tomato oil; a caramelized shallot foccacio with hibiscus rosemary mascarpone and black lava sea salt; and Tuscan sushi—Italian prosciutto wrapped around mascarpone and Gorgonzola cheeses with fresh and dried figs. The Tiki-chic eatery—surrounded by vines, bamboo, and cozy banquettes—is all outdoors, so it's weather-permitting, but when it's nice out, it's a stunning departure from the rest of Miami's ultramodern restaurants. A soon-to-open indoor dining area and lounge will make this an all-season restaurant—but most importantly, the food's always fresh. After dinner, check out the latest to sprout up on the expanding Grass—the **King Is Dead**—a strangely named, fabulously hip cocktail lounge.

28 NE 40th St. ℂ **305/573-3355.** www.grasslounge.com. Reservations recommended. Main courses $16–$40. AE, DC, MC, V. Wed–Sat 6–11pm; late-night bar menu 11pm–2am.

Michy's ★★ 🍴 LATIN   Star chef Michelle Bernstein left the fancy confines of the Mandarin Oriental Miami's Azul to open her own, homey 50-seat eatery on Miami's burgeoning Upper East Side. If you drive too fast, you'll miss the small storefront restaurant, a deceiving facade for a whimsical retro orange-and-blue interior where stellar small plates such as ham-and-blue-cheese croquettes are consumed in massive quantities because they're that good. There's also a zingy ceviche that changes daily; sautéed black cod with sunchoke purée, carrot ginger emulsion; sautéed sweetbreads in a cassoulet of duck sauterne sausage, root vegetables, and cranberry beans; and on Wednesday nights, all-you-can-eat fried chicken. Fabulous fried chicken. There's nothing ordinary about Michy's, except for the fact that a reservation here is nearly impossible to score if not made weeks in advance.

6927 Biscayne Blvd. ℂ **305/759-2001.** Reservations recommended. Main courses $15–$30. AE, DC, MC, V. Tues–Thurs noon–3pm and 6–10:30pm; Fri noon–3pm and 6–11pm; Sat 6–11pm; Sun 6–10:30pm.

Oceanaire Seafood Room ★★ SEAFOOD   The first restaurant to open in the Mary Brickell Village, Oceanaire is a pricey ocean liner–inspired chain seafooder known for fresh-caught fare. The elegant streamlined dining room is always abuzz with power types and foodies looking for the freshest fish dishes in town. This is not always the case, but it's not everywhere in Miami where you can indulge in *guajillo* barbecue salmon with spicy crispy red onions, or order Nairagi marlin for that matter. Chef Sean Bernal is a rare talent, so much so that the folks behind Discovery Channel's hit reality show *The Deadliest Catch* invited him on board one of the crab vessels in the Bering Sea to exercise his fishing skills. So if you're in the downtown area and in the mood for serious fish dishes, this is the place. If you want stone crabs or something simpler, save your money and check out Garcia's (reviewed below) instead.

900 S. Miami Ave. ℂ **305/372-8862.** Reservations recommended. Main courses $15–$30. AE, DC, MC, V. Sun–Thurs 5–10pm; Fri–Sat 5–11pm.

Pacific Time ★★ NEW AMERICAN   This former Lincoln Road pioneer moved off the beach and into the up-and-coming Design District and while it wasn't the first restaurant there (Michael's Genuine Food & Drink has the honors) it is one of the few that have experienced wild success in its new uncharted territory. Although he changed addresses and moved into some ultramodern new digs, chef/owner Jonathan Eismann's main focus is the food—Asian-inspired fare, including standouts such as Indochine beef salad with seared Angus beef, Chinese cabbage, Boston lettuce, and a spicy satay vinaigrette; Szechuan grilled local mahimahi with sweet shallots, Hawaiian ginger, and tempura sweet potatoes; and grilled Colorado lamb chops with field greens, truffled hash browns, and green herb vinaigrette. Carried over from the old Lincoln Road days is PT's made-to-order chocolate bomb, which, as some of the restaurant's famous hip-hop clientele would agree is, indeed, the bomb, just like the restaurant in general. Up the block is Eismann's **Pizza Volante,** 3918 N. Miami Ave. (© **305/573-5325**), featuring dollar beers and thin-crust pizza. Debuting around the corner in 2010 are Eismann's two new restaurant concepts, **Q,** a down-home barbecue joint and **Fin,** a sustainable seafood spot.

35 NE 40th St., Miami. © **305/722-7369.** Reservations recommended Sat–Sun. Main courses $25–$29. AE, MC, V. Mon–Thurs 11:30am–11pm; Fri–Sat 11:30am–midnight; Sun 5–11pm.

Rosa Mexicano ★★ MEXICAN   Also in the Mary Brickell Village, this upscale chain Mexican is always lively and not just because the frozen pomegranate margaritas pack a major punch. A stunning decor with 15-foot waterfall and a great bar scene are two assets, but Rosa's use of serious spices and tableside guacamole preparation, served in a lava rock bowl with homemade tortillas (they make them right there in the middle of the dining room) make this one of Miami's most talked about in a long time. Among the dishes: Mole de Xico, a Veracruz mole made with mulatto, ancho, and pasilla chilies; and Chamorro, a crispy pork shank, slow-roasted for 6 hours, dipped in the deep-fryer, and served with mushroom-chipotle cream sauce and red bean–chorizo chili. And did we mention the margaritas and the guacamole? *Ole!*

900 S. Miami Ave. © **786/425-1001.** www.rosamexicano.com. Reservations recommended. Main courses $13–$30. AE, DC, MC, V. Mon–Fri 11am–3pm; Sun–Thurs 5–10pm; Fri–Sat 5–11pm.

Sra. Martinez ★★ TAPAS   Housed in a historic post office, this upscale tapas joint, whose name is short for Senora Martinez, features traditional items and several others with Chef Michelle Bernstein's creative flair. Speaking of flair, the menus come folded up inside envelopes in tribute to the venue's original function. Be careful ordering—if you go nuts, your bill could end up costing $40 to $50 a head excluding tax, tip, and booze. That said, some of the standouts include the pork belly—crispy outside and supertender within—topped with a smear of a not-too-sweet fennel-orange marmalade and accompanied with a small salad; sweetbreads are crispy outside and tender and fluffy inside, served with a pestolike paste of dried red peppers, almonds and garlic, a caper berry, and a lemon wedge; massive head-on Madagascar prawns grilled and served with cloves of confit garlic and a schmear of a smooth chimichurri; and a sea urchin sandwich pressed and grilled with some soy-ginger butter. To wash it all down, try one of the amazingly updated takes on old-school cocktail classics, including the sazerac, pisco sour, and Bloody Mary.

4000 NE 2nd Ave. © **305/573-5474.** Reservations recommended. Tapas $10–$20. AE, DC, MC, V. Mon–Thurs 6–11pm; Fri–Sat 6pm–2am.

Moderate

Fratelli Lyon ★ 🏠 ITALIAN   We've heard of restaurants housed in markets and even department stores, but this Design District standout appropriately resides in a fabulously industrial modern furniture showroom. And while the not-so-comfy but cool-looking chairs you'll be sitting on may be for sale at an astronomical price, when it comes to the wine and cheese, well, they're bargain-basement in comparison. Owned by a former caterer, Fratelli, as it's known by locals, offers everything from a multitiered platter of antipasti to pizzas, bruschettas, salads, and main courses that include delicious saffron risotto served with boneless osso buco. A popular spot for appetizers and wine, Fratelli's also a top spot for lunches among the arty set who live, work, and play in the Design District. In late 2009, owner/chef Ken Lyon crossed the causeway and opened his second restaurant, **The Cape Cod Room,** 5937 Collins Ave. (© **305/864-1262**), a Nantucket-style seafooder in the swanky Bath Club condo.

4141 NE 2nd Ave., Miami. © **305/572-2901.** Reservations recommended. Main courses $8–$25. AE, DC, DISC, MC, V. Mon–Sat 11:30am–2pm; Mon–Thurs 6–10pm; Fri–Sat 6pm–midnight.

Garcia's Seafood Grille & Fish ★ 🎁 SEAFOOD

A good catch on the banks of the Miami River, Garcia's has a great waterfront setting and a fairly simple yet tasty menu of fresh fish cooked in a number of ways—grilled, broiled, fried, or, the best in my opinion, in garlic or green sauce. Meals are quite the deal here, all served with green salad or grouper soup, and yellow rice or french fries. The complimentary fish-spread appetizer is also a nice touch. Because of this, not to mention the great, gritty ambience that takes you away from neon, neo-Miami in favor of the old seafaring days, there's usually a wait for a table. If so, hang out at the bar and order an appetizer of inexpensive stone crabs or famous conch fritters. They also recently opened an upstairs bar and lounge overlooking the river.

398 NW North River Dr., Miami. © **305/375-0765.** Reservations recommended. Main courses $14–$23. AE, DC, DISC, MC, V. Sun–Thurs 11am–10pm; Fri–Sat 11am–11pm.

Joey's ★★ 🎁 ITALIAN

Sometimes you have to go out of your way for good pizza in Florida, even if that means driving into the still dodgy, yet arty, Wynwood area for it. Owned by the son of South Beach pioneer Tony Goldman, Joey's is carving out yet another ahead-of-its-time visionary type of niche with this cozy, minimalistic, industrial-style concrete-floored eatery with open kitchen, a few tables inside, and an outdoor patio. A full-blown menu of pastas and meat and seafood entrees include dishes like baked cod with eggplant and tomato *gremolata* or lamb chips with juniper berry reduction, but we personally go there for the pizza. As close to NY-style as you can get, from classic Margherita to a fashionable pie dotted with figs, Gorgonzola, honey, and hot pepper. There are also some nice, reasonably priced Italian wines by the glass. As for the neighborhood, Joey's insists it's on its way. We say take a cab or car straight there, hand the keys to the valet, and enter an oasis of urban evolution.

2506 NW 2nd Ave., Miami. © **305/438-0488.** www.joeyswynwood.com. Reservations recommended. Main courses and pizzas $7–$24. AE, DC, DISC, MC, V. Mon–Wed 11:30am–9:30pm; Thurs 11:30am–10:30pm; Fri–Sat 11:30am–11:30pm.

Michael's Genuine Food and Drink ★★★ NEW AMERICAN

The sleek, yet unassuming dining room and serene courtyard seating are constantly abuzz with Design District hipsters, foodies, and celebrities (Jennifer Aniston had her first public date with John Mayer here in '08) thanks to Chef/Owner Michael Schwartz's fresh vision for fabulous food. The food is stellar, a fresh mix of all organic products, some from Schwartz's own stash, including eggs from his own hens. With an emphasis on products sourced from local growers and farmers, the menu, which changes daily, is divided into small, medium, large, and extra large plates, all rather reasonably priced and extremely hard to choose from. There are also excellent pizzas, such as the exotic mushroom pizza with cave-aged Gruyère, caramelized onion, fresh thyme, and truffle oil; an astoundingly good Fudge Farms pork chop with Anson Mills cheese grits, pickled onion, and parsley sauce; and my personal favorite, the $4 to $6 bar menu, featuring crispy hominy with chili and lime, deviled eggs, kimchi, and chicken liver crostini. For a sweet tooth, nobody satisfies it better than pastry genius Hedy Goldsmith, whose candied Granny Smith apple and walnut streusel panini is beyond description. There's something for everyone here—that is except a reservation. Book early for Michael's, as it's always crowded. Genuinely. New in 2009, Sunday brunch featuring spectacular Bloody Marys and cocktails as well as a fantastic assortment of farm fresh egg dishes, main courses and Goldsmith's sublime Red Velvet Cupcakes, homemade Pop-Tarts, doughnuts, and more.

> ## Impressions
>
> *Bliss is a locally grown ingredient.*
> —Hedy Goldsmith, pastry chef at
> Michael's Genuine Food & Drink

130 NE 40th St., Miami. ℂ 305/573-5550. www.michaelsgenuine.com. Reservations recommended. Main courses $14–$46. AE, DC, DISC, MC, V. Mon–Fri 11:30am–3pm; Mon–Thurs 5:30–11pm; Fri 5:30pm–midnight; Sat 6pm–midnight; Sun 5:30–10pm.

The Morgans ★★ 💼 ITALIAN   Smack in the middle of the dodgy, yet up-and-coming Wynwood Arts District is this diamond in the rough, a modern, organic comfort-food restaurant with a fantastic outdoor patio. Although the dining room is Ikea-chic, very Scandinavian, grab a seat outside where the only real view that matters is of your plate. Serving breakfast, lunch, and dinner daily except Mondays, Morgans menu offerings range from meatloaf with smoky mash and braised beef short ribs with horseradish mashed potatoes to dare we say lighter fare including a delicious hamburger, "Voluptuous Grilled Cheese" (three kinds of cheese on perfectly grilled brioche), and a fresh house club with oven-roasted, free-range Bell & Evans chicken breast with fresh basil and basil mayo. Do not miss the perfectly salted, skinny fries. Desserts include a daily changing bread pudding, which is not to be missed, whatever the flavor. Service is sassy, swift, and friendly and best of all, there's a parking lot, which is, indeed, a novelty in these parts. Beer and wine only.

28 NE 29th St., Miami. ℂ 305/573-9678. www.themorgansrestaurant.com. Reservations not necessary. Main courses $8–$32. AE, DC, DISC, MC, V. Tues–Thurs 8am–10pm; Fri–Sat 8am–11pm; Sun 8am–5pm. Closed Mondays.

Perricone's Marketplace ★ ITALIAN   A large selection of groceries and wine, plus an outdoor porch and patio for dining, makes this one of the most welcoming spots downtown. Its rustic setting in the midst of downtown is a fantastic respite from city life. Sunday offers buffet brunches and all-you-can-eat dinners, too. But the place is most popular on weekdays at noon, when the "suits" show up for delectable sandwiches, quick and delicious pastas, and hearty salads.

15 SE 10th St. (corner of S. Miami Ave.), Miami. ℂ 305/374-9693. Sandwiches $6 and up; pastas $14 and up. AE, MC, V. Sun–Mon 7am–10pm; Tues–Sat 7am–11pm.

Red Light ★★ 💼 CAJUN/CREOLE   This one takes the award for the most offbeat location in town, as the on-site restaurant for one of Biscayne Boulevard's grittier motels (which since the restaurant opened is in the process of its own revitalization). If you can ignore the location, not to mention some of the motel's more, uh, colorful clientele, consider Chef Kris Wessell's daring menu instead. Although the place looks like a greasy spoon with vinyl booths and an old diner vibe, this is gourmet fare on the Boulevard at its finest, with Southern accents. The BBQ shrimp are outstanding, typically themselves sautéed and served in a pan sauce made by sautéing the shrimp heads with butter, lemon, Worcestershire, and Tabasco—served with bread for dipping in the sauce. For an entree, don't miss the quail. A full order features two birds, deboned except for wings and legs, perfectly roasted, stuffed with cubed brioche and sauced with mushrooms and roasted cherries with a sweet reduction. After dinner, head downstairs and have a cocktail on the shore of the very pungent Little Miami River. It's just par for the offbeat course.

In the Motel Blu, 7700 Biscayne Blvd., Miami. © **305/757-7773.** Reservations recommended on weekends. Main courses $8–$18. AE, DC, MC, V. Tues–Sat 6pm–2am.

The River Seafood & Oyster Bar ★★ SEAFOOD   A small, yet always packed seafood hot spot next door to Tobacco Road, The River is a buzzy and unpretentious spot for some of the best oysters in town—shipped fresh from all over the world daily—as well as some delicious dishes, including pan-fried Alaskan halibut with roasted garlic chive and pickled asparagus; monkfish paella with chorizo, roasted peppers, and pigeon peas; and for the land lubber, outstanding braised short ribs with creamy mac and cheese. A great spot for happy hour, River Oyster's bar is a lively one, where you can suck down some oysters with some seriously stiff drinks or excellent wines.

15 SE 10th St. (corner of S. Miami Ave.), Miami. © **305/374-9693.** www.therivermiami.com. Oysters $1–$10; main courses $15–$28. AE, MC, V. Mon–Fri 11:30am–5pm; Mon–Thurs 6–10:30pm; Fri 6pm–midnight; Sat 5:30pm–midnight.

Soyka Restaurant & Café ★ AMERICAN   Brought to us by the same man who owned the News and Van Dyke cafes in South Beach, Soyka, like its former siblings, was catalyst to the Biscayne Corridor revival. The motif inside is industrial chic, reminiscent of a souped-up warehouse you might find in New York. Lunches focus on burgers, sandwiches, and wood-fired-oven pizzas. Dinners include simple fare, such as an excellent, massive Cobb salad, or more elaborate dishes such as the delicious turkey Salisbury steak. The bar area provides a few comfy couches and bar stools and tables at which to dine, if you prefer not to sit in the open dining room. A children's menu is available for both lunch and dinner. A lively crowd of bohemian Design District types, professionals, and singles gather here for a taste of urban life. On weekends, the place is packed and very loud. Do not expect an after-dinner stroll around the neighborhood—it's still too dangerous for pedestrian traffic. Head over the causeway to South Beach and stroll there.

5556 NE 4th Court (Design District, off Biscayne Blvd. and 55th St.), Miami. © **305/759-3117.** Reservations recommended for parties of 8 or more. Main courses $8–$26. AE, MC, V. Sun–Thurs 11am–11pm (bar open until midnight); Fri–Sat 11am–midnight (bar open until 1am). Happy hour Mon–Fri 4–7pm.

Inexpensive

Andiamo Brick Oven Pizza ★ PIZZA   Leave it to visionary Mark Soyka (News Cafe, Van Dyke Cafe, Soyka) to turn a retro-style 1960s carwash into one of the city's best pizza places. The brick-oven pizzas are to die for, whether you choose the simple Andiamo pie (tomato sauce, mozzarella, and basil) or the designer combos of pancetta and caramelized onions; hot and sweet sausage with broccoli rabe; or portobello mushrooms with truffle oil and goat cheese. Pizzas come in three sizes—10, 13, and 16 inch. Though the pizza is undeniably delicious here, the most talked-about aspect of Andiamo is the fact that while you're washing down slice after slice, you can get your car washed and detailed at Leo's, the space's original and still-existing occupant out back.

5600 Biscayne Blvd., Miami. © **305/762-5751.** Main courses $3–$15. MC, V. Sun–Thurs 11am–11pm; Fri–Sat 11am–midnight.

Dogma Grill ★★ HOT DOGS   A little bit of L.A. comes to a gritty stretch of Biscayne Boulevard in the form of this very tongue-and-cheeky hot-dog stand whose motto is "A Frank Philosophy." The brainchild of a former MTV executive, Dogma will change the way you view hot dogs, offering a plethora of choices, from your typical chili dog to Chicago style, with celery salt, hot peppers, onions, and relish. The tropical version with pineapple is a bit funky but fitting for this stand, which attracts a very colorful, arty crowd from the nearby Design District. The buns here are softer than feather pillows, and the hot dogs are grilled to perfection. Try the garlic fries and the lemonade, too. Two new locations of Dogma opened, one across the street from the Museum of Contemporary Art at 899 NE 125th St., in North Miami.

7030 Biscayne Blvd., Miami. © **305/759-3433.** www.dogmagrill.com. Main courses $3–$4. No credit cards. Daily 11am–9pm.

Jimmy's East Side Diner ★ DINER   The only thing wrong with this quintessential, consummate greasy-spoon diner is that it's not open 24 hours. Other than that, for the cheapest breakfasts in town, not to mention lunches and early dinners, Jimmy's is a dream come true. Try the banana pancakes, corned-beef hash, roasted chicken, or Philly cheesesteak. Located on the newly hip Upper East Side of Biscayne Boulevard, Jimmy's is a very neighborhoody place, where late Bee Gee Maurice Gibb used to dine every Sunday. Adding to the aging regulars is a new, eclectic contingency of hung-over hipsters for whom Jimmy's is a sweet—and cheap—morning-after salvation.

7201 Biscayne Blvd., Miami. © **305/759-3433.** Main courses $3–$11. No credit cards. Daily 7am–4pm.

Jumbo's ★★★ 🍴 SOUL FOOD   Open 24 hours daily, this Miami institution is the kind of place where you'll see everyone from Rastafarian musicians and cabdrivers to Lenny Kravitz. It's in a shady neighborhood—Carol City—so if you go there, you're going for only one reason—Jumbo's. Family owned for more than 50 years, Jumbo's is known for its world-famous fried shrimp, fried chicken, catfish fingers, and collard greens. Their motto—["]Life is to be enjoyed, not to be endured . . . Making friends is our business"—is spot on. The service is friendly and fun, and there's history here, too. Jumbo's was the first restaurant in Miami to integrate in 1966, and the first to hire African-American employees in 1967.

7501 NW 7th Ave., Miami. © **305/751-1127.** Main courses $5–$15. AE, DC, MC, V. Daily 24 hr.

Lost & Found Saloon ★ 🍴 SOUTHWESTERN   Located in the heart of Wynwood, this rough-and-tumble cowboy-style eatery is the OK Corral for area artists, hipsters, and fans of Tex-Mex and Southwestern fare not really found anywhere else in town, with a nice nod to vegetarians in the form of dishes such as tofu sampler with pine nuts and sun-dried tomatoes and grilled and marinated portobello mushrooms. But we'll stick with the meat and seafood dishes including a chipotle-seared mahimahi with grilled asparagus and fresh-made pico de gallo. Tacos and sandwiches are good, too, especially during the Giddy Up Happy Hours from 4 to 7pm weeknights and 5 to 10pm on Sundays, when food, wine, and beer are all discounted and a taco will set you back about $3.

185 NW 36th St., Miami. ✆ **305/576-1008.** www.thelostandfoundsaloon-miami.com. Tacos, burritos, sandwiches $4.75–$8.50, main courses $9.25–$17. AE, MC, V. Sun–Thurs 11am–10pm; Fri–Sat 11am–midnight.

Metro at Karma Car Wash ★ 🎁 BISTRO   The funkiest thing to hit Biscayne Boulevard since Dogma, this carwash-cum-bistro is a big hit with the locals who love their SUVs as much as their hot spots. Put your car in for a wash and relax on the outdoor patio, reminiscent of your best friend's backyard, where you can sip from an impressive number of micro beers, wines, and coffees, and snack on delicious fare including sandwiches, salads, and a very good burger made with grass-fed, organic filet mignon. DJs and cocktail parties make it a happening spot from Thursday on, and while we don't encourage you to drink and drive, of course, there's never been a better excuse to shine your car (it's pricey, but they do a spotless job!) while waxing social at the same time.

7010 Biscayne Blvd., Miami. ✆ **305/759-1392.** www.metrobistromiami.com. Sandwiches $11–$13; entrees $14–$20. AE, DC, MC, V. Tapas bar/cafe Wed–Sat 8am–1am. Car wash daily 8am–8pm.

Tobacco Road AMERICAN   Miami's oldest bar is a bluesy, Route 66–inspired institution favored by barflies, professionals, and anyone else who wishes to indulge in good and greasy bar fare—chicken wings, nachos, and so on—at reasonable prices in a down-home, gritty-but-charming atmosphere. The burgers are also good—particularly the Death Burger, a deliciously unhealthful combo of choice sirloin topped with grilled onions, jalapeños, and pepper-jack cheese (bring on the Tums!). Also a live-music venue, the Road, as it's known by locals, is well traveled, especially during Friday's happy hour and Tuesday's Lobster Night, when 100 1¼-pound lobsters go for only $12 apiece.

626 S. Miami Ave. ✆ **305/374-1198.** www.tobacco-road.com. Main courses $7–$10; nightly specials $12–$15. AE, DC, MC, V. Mon–Sat 11:30am–5am; Sun noon–5am. Cover $5–$6 Fri–Sat nights.

LITTLE HAVANA

The main artery of Little Havana is a busy commercial strip called SW Eighth Street, or Calle Ocho. Auto-body shops, cigar factories, and furniture stores line this street, and on every corner there seems to be a pass-through window serving super-strong Cuban coffee and snacks. In addition, many of the Cuban, Dominican, Nicaraguan, Peruvian, and other Latin American immigrants have opened full-scale restaurants ranging from intimate candlelit establishments to bustling stand-up lunch counters.

Expensive

Casa Juancho ★ SPANISH   A generous taste of Spain comes to Miami in the form of the cavernous Casa Juancho, which looks like it escaped from a production of *Don Quixote*. The numerous dining rooms are decorated with traditional Spanish furnishings and enlivened nightly by strolling Spanish musicians who tend to be annoying and expect tips—do not encourage them to play at your table; you'll hear them loud and clear from other tables, trust me. Try not to be frustrated with the older staff members who don't speak English or respond quickly to your subtle glance—the food is worth the frustration. Your best bet is to order lots of tapas, small dishes of Spanish finger food. Some of the best include mixed seafood vinaigrette, fresh shrimp in hot garlic sauce, and fried calamari rings. A few entrees stand out, such as roast suckling pig, baby eels in garlic and olive oil, and Iberian-style snapper.

2436 SW 8th St. (just east of SW 27th Ave.), Little Havana. © **305/642-2452.** www.casajuancho.com. Reservations recommended but not accepted Fri–Sat after 8pm. Main courses $25–$42; tapas $6–$38. AE, DC, DISC, MC, V. Sun–Thurs noon–midnight; Fri–Sat noon–1am.

Moderate

Hy-Vong ★★ VIETNAMESE   This place is a must in Little Havana, so expect to wait hours for a table and don't even think of mumbling a complaint. This Vietnamese cuisine combines the best of Asian and French cooking with spectacular results. Food at Hy-Vong is elegantly simple and superspicy. Appetizers include small, tightly packed Vietnamese spring rolls, and kimchi, a spicy, fermented cabbage (they ran out of it on my last visit, because I got there too late—so get there early!). Star entrees include pastry-enclosed chicken with watercress cream-cheese sauce and fish in tangy mango sauce. Unfortunately, service here is not at all friendly or stellar—in fact, it borders on abysmal, but once you finally get your food, all will be forgotten.

Enjoy the wait with a traditional Vietnamese beer and lots of company. Outside this tiny storefront restaurant, you'll meet interesting students, musicians, and foodies who come for the large, delicious portions.

3458 SW 8th St. (btw. 34th and 35th aves.), Little Havana. © **305/446-3674.** Reservations accepted for parties of 5 or more. Main courses $7–$20. AE, DISC, MC, V. Sun–Thurs 6–11pm; Fri–Sat 6–11:30pm. Closed 2 weeks in Aug.

CUBAN coffee

Despite the more than a dozen Starbucks that dot the Miami landscape, locals still rely on the many Cuban cafeterias for their daily caffeine fix. Beware of the many establishments throughout Miami that serve espresso masked as Cuban coffee. For the real deal, go to the most popular—and most animated—Cuban cafeterias: **La Carreta** and **Versailles** (see below).

Cuban coffee is a longstanding tradition in Miami. You'll find it served from the takeout windows of hundreds of cafeterías or loncherías around town, especially in Little Havana, Downtown, Hialeah, and the beaches. Depending on where you are and what you want, you'll spend between 40¢ and $1.50 per cup.

The best café cubano has a rich layer of foam on top formed when the hot espresso shoots from the machine into the sugar below. The result is the caramelly, sweet, potent concoction that's a favorite of locals of all nationalities.

To partake, you've just got to learn how to ask for it en español.

FROM CEVICHE TO PICADILLO: latin cuisine AT A GLANCE

In Little Havana for dinner? Many restaurants list menu items in English for the benefit of *norteamericano* diners. In case they don't, though, here are translations and suggestions for filling and delicious meals:

Arroz con pollo: Roast chicken served with saffron-seasoned yellow rice and diced vegetables.

Café cubano: Very strong black coffee, served in thimble-size cups with lots of sugar. It's a real eye-opener.

Camarones: Shrimp.

Ceviche: Raw fish seasoned with spice and vegetables and marinated in vinegar and citrus to "cook" it.

Croquetas: Golden-fried croquettes of ham, chicken, or fish.

Paella: A Spanish dish of chicken, sausage, seafood, and pork mixed with saffron rice and peas.

Palomilla: Thinly sliced beef, similar to American minute steak, usually served with onions, parsley, and a mountain of french fries.

Pan cubano: Long, white, crusty Cuban bread. Ask for it *tostado* — toasted and flattened on a grill with lots of butter.

Picadillo: A rich stew of ground meat, brown gravy, peas, pimientos, raisins, and olives.

Plátano: A deep-fried, soft, mildly sweet banana.

Pollo asado: Roasted chicken with onions and a crispy skin.

Ropa vieja: A shredded beef stew whose name literally means "old clothes."

Sopa de pollo: Chicken soup, usually with noodles or rice.

Tapas: A general name for Spanish-style hors d'oeuvres, served in grazing-size portions.

Inexpensive

El Palacio de los Jugos ★★★ CUBAN   Although the original is on West Flagler Street, this Little Havana outpost of the Cuban culinary landmark is just as good, if not better, serving fresh squeezed juices (guava, papaya, sugar cane, mango), tropical shakes and some of the most authentic Cuban fare this side of Havana at prices that go back to the days when Havana was a bustling hot spot. Here, you'll find everything from oxtail to roasted chicken, pork ribs, roast pork, and pretty much anything that comes dished from a steam table with a heaping helping of either *arroz con pollo* or red beans and rice. You also get a generous hunk of boiled yuca with its traditional accompaniment of garlic and citrus mojo sauce. They also serve a fantastically cheap breakfast. It's loud, it's frenzied, it's almost 100% in Spanish, and it's one of the most delicious Miami experiences you will have for around five bucks.

14300 SW 8th St., Little Havana. ℂ **305/221-1615.** Juices and main courses $2–$5. Cash only. Mon–Sat 7am–9pm; Sun 7am–8pm.

La Carreta ★ CUBAN   This cavernous family-style restaurant is filled with relics of an old farm and college kids eating *medianoches* (midnight sandwiches with ham, cheese, and pickles) after partying all night. Waitresses are brusque but efficient and will help Anglos along who may not know the lingo. The menu is vast and very authentic, but is known for its sandwiches and smaller items. Try the *sopa de pollo*, a rich golden stock loaded with chunks of chicken and fresh vegetables, or the *ropa vieja*, a shredded beef stew in thick brown sauce. Because of its immense popularity and low prices, La Carreta has opened seven branches throughout Miami, including a counter in the Miami airport. Check the White Pages for other locations.

3632 SW 8th St., Little Havana. ℂ **305/444-7501.** www.lacarreta.com. Main courses $5–$25. AE, DC, DISC, MC, V. Daily 24 hr.

Latin American Cafeteria ★★ CUBAN   The name may sound a bit generic, but this no-frills indoor-outdoor cafeteria has the best Cuban sandwiches in the entire city. They're big enough for lunch and a doggie-bagged dinner, too. Service is fast, prices are cheap, but be forewarned: English is truly a second language at this chain, so have patience—it's worth it.

6820 SW 40th St., Miami. ℂ **305/663-2600.** Main courses $5–$10. AE, MC, V. Daily 7:30am–11pm.

Versailles ★ CUBAN   Versailles is the meeting place of Miami's Cuban power brokers, who meet daily over *café con leche* to discuss the future of the Cuban exiles' fate. A glorified diner, the place sparkles with glass, chandeliers, murals, and mirrors meant to evoke the French palace. There's nothing fancy here—nothing French, either—just straightforward food from the home country. The menu is a veritable survey of Cuban cooking and includes specialties such as Moors and Christians (flavorful black beans with white rice), *ropa vieja* (shredded beef stew), and fried whole fish. Versailles is the place to come for *mucho* helpings of Cuban kitsch. With its late hours, it's also the perfect place to come after spending your night in Little Havana.

3555 SW 8th St., Little Havana. ℂ **305/444-0240.** Main courses $5–$20; soup and salad $2–$10. DC, DISC, MC, V. Mon–Thurs 8am–2am; Fri 8am–3am; Sat 8am–4:30am; Sun 9am–1am.

KEY BISCAYNE

Key Biscayne has some of the world's nicest beaches, hotels, and parks, yet it is not known for great food. Locals, or "Key rats" as they're known, tend to go off-island for meals or takeout, but here are some of the best on-the-island choices.

Expensive

Rusty Pelican ★ SEAFOOD   The Pelican's private tropical walkway leads over a lush waterfall into one of the most romantic dining rooms in the city, located right on beautiful blue-green Biscayne Bay. The restaurant's windows look out over the water onto the sparkling stalagmites of Miami's magnificent downtown. Inside, quiet wicker paddle fans whirl overhead and saltwater fish swim in pretty tableside aquariums. The restaurant's surf-and-turf menu features conservatively prepared prime steaks, veal, shrimp, and lobster. The food is good, but the atmosphere—the reason why you're here—is even better, especially at sunset, when the view over the city is magical.

3201 Rickenbacker Causeway, Key Biscayne. ℂ **305/361-3818.** http://miami.therustypelican.com. Reservations recommended. Main courses $16–$30. AE, DC, MC, V. Sun–Thurs 11:30am–4pm and 5–11pm; Fri–Sat 11:30am–4pm and 5pm–midnight.

Key Biscayne, Virginia Key & Fisher Island

ATLANTIC OCEAN

Biscayne Bay

Brickell Key

Fisher I. **1**

Virginia Key

Hobie Beach

Rickenbacker Cswy.

Virginia Key Beach Park

Miami Seaquarium

Marjory Stoneman Douglas Biscayne Nature Center

Crandon Park

Crandon Blvd.

Crandon Beach

Harbor Dr.

Key Biscayne **6**

W. Wood Dr.

Bill Baggs Cape Florida State Park

C. Florida

0   1 mi
0   1 km

ACCOMMODATIONS ■
Fisher Island Club **1**
The Ritz-Carlton Key Biscayne **6**

DINING ◆
Bayside Seafood Hut **3**
Jimbo's **4**
Oasis **5**
Rusty Pelican **2**

Inexpensive

Bayside Seafood Hut ★ 🍴 SEAFOOD   Known by locals as "the Hut," this ramshackle restaurant and bar is a laid-back outdoor Tiki hut and terrace that serves pretty good sandwiches and fish platters on paper plates. A blackboard lists the latest catches, which can be prepared blackened, fried, broiled, or in a garlic sauce. The fish dip is wonderfully smoky and moist, if a little heavy on mayonnaise. Local fishers and yachties share this rustic outpost with equal enthusiasm and loyalty. A completely new, air-conditioned area for those who can't stand the heat is a welcome addition, as is the new deck and the spruced-up decor. But behind it all, it's nothing fancier than a hut—if it were anything else, it wouldn't be nearly as appealing.

3501 Rickenbacker Causeway, Key Biscayne. ✆ **305/361-0808.** Reservations accepted for parties of 15 or more. Appetizers, salads, and sandwiches $5–$15; platters $7–$15. AE, MC, V. Daily 10am until closing (which varies).

Jimbo's 🎁 SEAFOOD   Locals like to keep quiet about Jimbo's, a ramshackle seafood shack that started as a gathering spot for fishermen and has since become the quintessential South Florida watering hole, snack bar, and hangout for those in the know. If ever Miami had a backwoods, this is it, right down to the smoldering garbage can, stray dogs, and chickens. Do *not* get dressed up to come here—you will get dirty. Go to the bathroom before you get here, too, because the porta-potties are absolutely rancid. Grab yourself a dollar can of beer (there's only beer, water, and soda, but you are allowed to bring your own choice of drink if you want) from the cooler and take in the view of the tropical lagoon where they shot *Flipper.* You may even see a manatee or two. Vacant shacks that served as backdrops for films such as *True Lies* surround this hidden enclave, which attracts everyone from shrimpers and politicians to well-oiled beach bums. Oddly enough, there's even a bocce court here, and the owner, Jimbo, may challenge you to a game. Play if you must, but word has it he never loses. Jimbo's smoked fish—marlin or salmon—is the best in town, but be forewarned: There are no utensils or napkins. When I asked for some, the woman said, "Lady, this is a place where you eat with your hands." I couldn't have said it better.

Off the Rickenbacker Causeway at Sewerline Rd., Virginia Key. ✆ **305/361-7026.** Smoked fish about $8 a pound. No credit cards. Mon–Fri 6am–6:30pm; Sat–Sun 6am–7:30pm. Head south on the main road toward Key Biscayne, make a left just after the MAST Academy (there will be a sign that says VIRGINIA KEY); tell the person in the tollbooth you're going to Jimbo's, and he'll point you in the right direction.

Oasis 🍴 CUBAN   Everyone, from the city's mayor to the local handymen, meet for delicious paella and Cuban sandwiches at this little shack. They gather outside, around the little takeout window, or inside at the few tables for superpowerful *cafecitos* and rich *croquetas.* It's slightly dingy, but the food is good and cheap.

19 Harbor Dr. (on corner of Crandon), Key Biscayne. ✆ **305/361-5709.** Main courses $4–$15; sandwiches $5–$10. No credit cards. Daily 6am–9pm.

COCONUT GROVE

Coconut Grove was long known as the artists' haven of Miami, but the rush of developers trying to cash in on the laid-back charm of this old settlement has turned it into something of an overgrown mall. Still, there are several great dining spots both in and out of the confines of Mayfair or CocoWalk.

Expensive

George's in the Grove ★★ FRENCH   When the former owner of Le Bouchon du Grove opened his own bistro around the corner, shouts of *"mon Dieu!"* were heard loud and clear. But there's really no comparison. Whereas Le Bouchon is a traditional French bistro, George's is a modern version, with sleek decor and a sleeker champagne-sipping clientele. Entrees range from such classics as ratatouille and steak

Coconut Grove

ACCOMMODATIONS ■
Hampton Inn **7**
Mayfair Hotel & Spa **4**
Mutiny Hotel **5**
Ritz-Carlton Coconut Grove **6**
Sonesta Bayfront Hotel
  Coconut Grove **3**
◆
DINING
George's in the Grove **1**
Le Bouchon du Grove **2**

Getting Back Into the Grove

Aging hippies may recall **Coconut Grove** as a hub of all things peace and love. When the '60s ended, the beatniks made The Grove a retro-fab kind of town. Then came the '80s, and the Grove was as dead as Joplin and Hendrix. The '90s saw a resurgence with **CocoWalk,** whose sole purpose was to attract tourists, locals, and college students to its open-air debauchery, which went bankrupt in 2009 but still continues with **Fat Tuesday's** (📞 **305/534-1328**) and **Hooters** (📞 **305/442-7283**).

Cafe Tu Tu Tango changed things a bit with its then-unique tapas-only menu and excellent sangria, but it closed in 2008. So did Dan Marino's, a sports pub and grill owned by the former Miami Dolphin. Unbelievably, so did the Cheesecake Factory. Today, Hooters is alive and well, as is Fat Tuesday's and Cheesecake Factory. Joining the group is a **Chili's** (📞 **305/772-5472**). It's nothing innovative or spectacular, but it may suit this town well, like an old Crosby, Stills & Nash song.

frites to a very Miami mango tarte tatin. Food is good, but the ambience is better. As the night goes on, music gets louder and a party scene ensues. If you want romance, go to Le Bouchon; if you want a *Sex and the City* scene, George's is *le place*.

3145 Commodore Plaza, Coconut Grove. ✆ **305/444-7878.** Main courses $13–$40. AE, DC, MC, V. Sun and Tues-Wed 6–11pm; Thurs-Sat 6pm–1am.

Le Bouchon du Grove ★ FRENCH This very authentic bistro is French right down to the waitstaff, who may speak only French to you, forgetting they're in the heart of Coconut Grove, U.S.A. But it matters not. The food, prepared by an animated French (what else?) chef, is good. It used to be superb, but it has fallen off a bit. Still, a delicious starter that's always reliable is the *gratinée Lyonnaise* (traditional French onion soup). Fish is brought in fresh daily; try the Chilean sea bass (*filet de loup poele*) when it's in season. Though slightly heavy on the oil, it is delivered with succulent artichokes, tomato confit, and seasoned roasted garlic and it is a gastronomic triumph. The *carre d'agneau roti* (roasted rack of lamb with Provence herbs) is served warm and tender, with a perfect amount of seasoning. There's also an excellent selection of pricey, but drinkable, French and American red and white wines.

3430 Main Hwy., Coconut Grove. ✆ **305/448-6060.** Reservations recommended. Main courses $18–$26. AE, MC, V. Mon-Thurs 10am–3pm and 5–11pm; Fri 10am–3pm and 5pm–midnight; Sat 8am–3pm and 5pm–midnight; Sun 8am–3pm and 5–11pm.

CORAL GABLES

Coral Gables is a foodie's paradise—a city in which you certainly won't go hungry. What Starbucks is to most major cities, excellent gourmet and ethnic restaurants are to Coral Gables, where there's a restaurant on every corner, and everywhere in between.

Very Expensive

Christy's ★★ STEAK/AMERICAN Power is palpable at this old-school English-style Miami steakhouse where a rock star can be sitting at one table, an ex-president at another. When we say rock star, we mean aging rock star à la Rod Stewart, though. This isn't your flashy South Beach scenery. But Christy's is the kind of place where conversations are at a hush and no one seems to care whom they're sitting next to. The selling point here, rather, is the broiled lamb chops, prime rib of beef with horseradish sauce, teriyaki-marinated filet mignon, herb-crusted sea bass, crab cakes, and perfectly tossed Caesar salad. Baked sweet potatoes and a sublime blackout cake are also yours for the taking. For a little drama, order the baked Alaska. It livens things up. Just like a fine wine or the typical Christy's customer, the meat here is aged a long time. A landmark since 1978, Christy's has thrived amid the comings and goings of neighboring nouveau Coral Gables restaurants. It's located on a nondescript corner, and you'll know you've arrived at the right place if you can count the Rolls-Royces parked out front.

> **Impressions**
>
> *Miami is the same place that New Orleans was a hundred years ago in the emergence of different cultures. It's fascinating because in the same way North Americans have come to understand the difference between Northern Italian and Southern Italian, we're coming to understand the difference between Peruvian, Venezuelan, and Brazilian cuisine.*
> —Chef Norman Van Aken

Coral Gables

ACCOMMODATIONS
Biltmore Hotel 1
Hotel St. Michel 7
Hyatt Regency Coral Gables 10
DINING
Caffe Abbracci 4
Christy's 12
Daily Bread Marketplace 2
John Martin's 6
Mint Leaf 9
Miss Saigon Bistro 8
Ortanique on the Mile 5
Palme d'Or 1
Pascal's on Ponce 11
Randazzo's Little Italy 3
SW 14th St.
SW 15th St.
Hernando St.
Mendoza Ave.
Salzedo St.
Ponce de Leon Blvd.
Galiano St.
S Douglas Rd.
Casilla St.
Segovia St.
Zamora Ave.
Madeira Ave.
S Le Jeune Rd.
Majorca Ave.
Navarre Ave.
Minorca Ave.
Alhambra Cir.
953
Alcazar Ave.
Alhambra Plaza
Merrick Wy.
Giralda Ave.
Aragon Ave.
N Greenway Dr.
Coral Way
972
Miracle Mile
Andalusia Ave.
Valencia Ave.
Almeria Ave.
Cardena St.
Cordova St.
Columbus Blvd.
De Soto Blvd.
Venetian Pool
Sevilla Ave.
Palermo Ave.
Catalonia Ave.
Anderson Rd.
Granada Blvd.
Toledo St.
Coconut Grove Dr.
University Dr.
San Sebastian Ave.
Malaga Ave.
Santander Ave.
Romano Ave.
Anastasia Ave.
Sarto Ave.
Riviera Dr.
University Park
Camilo Ave.
Biltmore Golf Course
Durango St.
Aledo Ave.
Cadima Ave.
Escobar Ave.
0
1/4 mi
1/4 km

3101 Ponce de León Blvd., Coral Gables. ✆ **305/446-1400.** www.christysrestaurant.com. Reservations recommended. Main courses $23–$46. AE, DC, MC, V. Mon–Thurs 11:30am–10pm, Fri 11:30am–11pm, Sat 5–11pm; Sun 5–10pm.

Palme d'Or ★★★ FRENCH Don't be fooled by the ornate setting—yes, it's rich, yes it's fancy, oozing with Old World elegance, but the cuisine and the service is far from stuffy. Hailed by many as the city's top restaurant, Palme d'Or's New French cuisine is made utterly delicious and accessible via a unique tasting menu showcasing innovative interpretations of classic Continental cuisine, featuring exceptional local ingredients with specialties flown in directly from France and elsewhere. You can order a la carte, but we suggest you go with the prix-fixe menus—three plates at $42, four plates at $54, or five plates at $70. And choosing is tough with Chef Philippe Ruiz's genius in the form of dishes such as pan-seared Hudson Valley foie gras with caramelized mango and Badiane spice sauce; grilled buffalo tenderloin with potato *boulangere* and wild mushroom sauce; roasted white sturgeon filet with carrot coulis, Masala spice and Sevruga caviar; braised short ribs with farro risotto, shallots, and carrot confit in a red wine reduction; and grilled rack of lamb with Caribbean-style sweet potato mousseline, chayote, and aged rum sauce. Service is equally exceptional, almost seamless, making this one of Miami's best, if not the best, upscale dining experiences which, in light of other city restaurants of lesser quality and higher prices, is a deal in comparison.

At the Biltmore Hotel, 1200 Anastasia Ave., Coral Gables. ✆ **305/913-3201.** Reservations recommended. Tasting menus $42–$70; a la carte $14–$20. AE, DC, MC, V. Tues–Sat 6–10:30pm.

Pascal's on Ponce ★★★ FRENCH Straight from the tutelage of world-renowned chef Alain Ducasse, chef Pascal Oudin has established himself as a star student at his very own restaurant that takes French food to another level. Diver sea scallops topped with beef short rib, young fennel, carrot Vichy, and fava beans; and filet mignon with escargot Provençal are just a few outstanding examples of how Oudin combines classical French techniques with the ingredients of the Americas.

2611 Ponce de León Blvd., Coral Gables. ✆ **305/444-2024.** www.pascalmiami.com. Reservations recommended. Main courses $20–$38. AE, DISC, MC, V. Sun–Thurs 6–10pm; Fri–Sat 6–11pm; Mon–Thurs 11:30am–3pm.

Expensive

Caffe Abbracci ★★ ITALIAN You'll understand why this restaurant's name means "hugs" in Italian the moment you enter the dark, romantic enclave: Your appetite will be embraced by the savory scents of fantastic Italian cuisine wafting through the restaurant. The homemade black-and-red ravioli filled with lobster in pink sauce, risotto with porcini and portobello mushrooms, and the house specialty—grilled veal chop topped with tricolor salad—are irresistible and perhaps the culinary equivalent of a warm, embracing hug. A cozy bar and lounge were added recently to further encourage the warm and fuzzy feelings.

318 Aragon Ave. (1 block north of Miracle Mile, btw. Salzedo St. and Le Jeune Rd.), Coral Gables. ✆ **305/441-0700.** www.caffeabbracci.com. Reservations recommended for dinner. Main courses $23–$37; pastas $17–$25. AE, DC, MC, V. Sun 6–11:30pm; Mon–Thurs 11:30am–3pm and 6–11:30pm; Fri 11:30am–3pm and 6pm–12:30am; Sat 6pm–12:30am.

Ortanique on the Mile ★★★ NEW WORLD CARIBBEAN Chef Cindy Hutson has truly perfected tantalizing New World Caribbean cuisine. For starters, ask if the pumpkin bisque with a hint of pepper sherry is on the menu. If not, a spicy fried calamari salad is exceptional. Afterward, move on to the tropical mango salad with fresh marinated sable hearts of palm, julienne mango, baby field greens, toasted Caribbean candied pecans, and passion-fruit vinaigrette. For an entree, I recommend the pan-sautéed Bahamian black grouper marinated in teriyaki and sesame oil. It's served with an *ortanique* (an orangelike fruit) orange liqueur sauce and topped with steamed seasoned chayote, zucchini, and carrots on a lemon-orange *boniato*–sweet plantain mash. For dessert, try the chocolate mango tower—layers of brownie, chocolate mango mousse, meringue, and sponge cake, accompanied by mango sorbet and tropical-fruit salsa. Entrees may not be cheap, but they're a lot less than airfare to the islands, which is where most, if not all, of the ingredients hail from.

278 Miracle Mile (next to Actor's Playhouse), Coral Gables. ✆ **305/446-7710.** Reservations requested. Main courses $21–$44. AE, DC, MC, V. Mon–Tues 6–10pm; Wed–Sat 6–11pm; Sun 5:30–9:30pm.

Moderate

John Martin's ★ IRISH PUB Forest-green and dark-wood walls provide a very intimate, publike atmosphere in which local businesspeople and barflies alike come to hoist a pint or two. The menu offers some tasty British specialties (not necessarily an oxymoron!), such as bangers and mash and shepherd's pie, as well as Irish lamb stew and corned beef and cabbage. Of course, to wash it down, you'll want to try one of the ales on tap or one of the more than 20 single-malt scotches. The crowd is upscale and chatty, as is the young waitstaff. Check out happy hour on weeknights, plus the Sunday brunch with loads of hand-carved meats and seafood.

253 Miracle Mile, Coral Gables. ☎ **305/445-3777.** Reservations recommended on weekends. Main courses $9–$20; sandwiches and salads $5–$16. AE, DC, DISC, MC, V. Sun–Thurs 11:30am–midnight; Fri–Sat 11:30am–2am.

Mint Leaf ★ INDIAN   Straight from London is this cozy (read: tiny) modern Indian eatery where Bollywood films play on the flatscreen and the congenial owner runs around making sure everyone's happy. And you will be happy as long as you score a table here—there are only about 15 inside and a miniature bar with two stools. Cuisine is authentic if not particularly spicy (I asked for extra hot sauce on the side but was given a watery concoction instead), with all traditional tandoori favorites, samosas, naans, and *dosas*.

276 Alhambra Circle, Coral Gables. ☎ **305/443-3739.** Reservations strongly recommended. Main courses $16–$20. AE, DC, DISC, MC, V. Daily noon–3pm and 6–10:30pm.

Randazzo's Little Italy ★★★ ITALIAN   This old-school, *Godfather*-influenced, *Goodfellas*-inspired, *Sopranos*-style Italian restaurant is a guaranteed knockout and not just because the owner is a former professional boxer, either. Come hungry and leave with your pants unbuttoned as this bustling, fun, and phenomenally garlicky restaurant has a way of making Little Italy seem mammoth thanks to huge portions of traditional favorites—sausage and peppers, meatballs and spaghetti, and rigatoni with vodka sauce which one critic said was so good it could "bring any homesick Italian-American to tears." House specialty is spaghetti with Sunday gravy—al dente strands of pasta studded with meatballs the size of wrecking balls (appropriately enough they will wreck your appetite) and large chunks of sweet and hot sausage. Although there are many distractions here, from the cacophonous crowd and gregarious former-boxer owner to the TVs showing the aforementioned Italian-themed classics, the focus here is fully on the plate—which if you finish, will earn you, too, major heavyweight status.

385 Miracle Mile, Coral Gables. ☎ **305/448-7002.** Reservations strongly recommended. Main courses $22–$32. AE, DC, DISC, MC, V. Mon–Fri 11:30am–2:30pm; Mon–Thurs 6–10pm; Fri–Sat 6–11pm.

Red Fish Grill ★ SEAFOOD   Hidden away at the edge of the saltwater lagoon in lush and tropical Matheson Hammock Park, Red Fish Grill is a decent seafood restaurant, but people don't come here for the food. Judging by the ambience alone, the restaurant deserves four stars, but because the food is just okay (fish is either greasy or dry), it only gets one. But that's okay. A new owner (Christy's steakhouse) promises better things to come. In the meantime, romantic, hard to find, and truly reminiscent of Old Miami, Red Fish Grill makes up for its lack of flavor with its hard-to-beat, majestic setting.

In Matheson Hammock Park, 9610 Old Cutler Rd., Coral Gables. ☎ **305/668-8788.** www.redfishgrill. net. Reservations accepted. Main courses $26–$35. AE, DC, DISC, MC, V. Tues–Thurs 6–10pm; Fri–Sun 5–10pm. Enter Matheson Hammock Park; stay on the main road until you see the restaurant's parking lot.

Inexpensive

Daily Bread Marketplace GREEK This place is great for takeout food and homemade breads. The falafel and gyro sandwiches are large, fresh, and filling. The spinach pie for less than $1 is also recommended, though it's short on spinach and heavy on pastry. Salads and spreads, including luscious tabbouleh, hummus, and eggplant, are also worth a go. To eat in or take out, the Middle Eastern fare here is a real treat, especially in an area so filled with fancy French and Cuban fare. Plus, you can pick up groceries such as grape leaves, fresh olives, couscous, fresh nuts, and pita bread.

2400 SW 27th St. (off U.S. 1 under the monorail), Coral Gables. (✆ **305/856-0363** or 856-0366. Sandwiches and salads $4-$10. MC, V. Mon–Sat 9am–8pm; Sun 11am–5pm.

Miss Saigon Bistro ★★ VIETNAMESE Unlike Alain Boublil and Claude-Michel Schönberg's bombastic Broadway show, this Miss Saigon is small, quiet, and not at all flashy. Servers at this family-run restaurant will graciously recommend dishes or even have something custom-made for you. The menu is varied and reasonably priced, and the portions are huge—large enough to share. Noodle dishes and soup bowls are hearty and flavorful; caramelized prawns are fantastic, as is the whole snapper with lemongrass and ginger sauce. Despite the fact that there are few tables inside and a hungry crowd usually gathers outside in the street, you won't be rushed through your meal, which is worth savoring. There is also a much larger location at 9503 S. Dixie Hwy., in South Miami's Pinecrest (✆ **305/661-2911**).

148 Giralda Ave. (at Ponce de León and 37th Ave.), Coral Gables. (✆ **305/446-8006.** Main courses $10–$22. AE, DC, DISC, MC, V. Mon and Wed–Thurs 11:30am–3pm and 5:30–10pm; Tues 11:30am–3pm and 6:30–10pm; Fri 11:30am–3pm and 5:30–11pm; Sat 5:30–11pm; Sun 5:30–10pm.

SOUTH MIAMI & WEST MIAMI

Though mostly residential, these areas nonetheless have several eating establishments worth the drive.

Expensive

Tropical Chinese ★★ CHINESE This strip-mall restaurant, way out in West Miami–Dade, is hailed as the best Chinese restaurant in the city. While the food is indeed very good—certainly more interesting than at your typical beef-and-broccoli place—it still seems overpriced. Garlic spinach and prawns in a clay pot are delicious, with the perfect mix of garlic cloves, mushrooms, and fresh spinach. But this isn't your typical Chinese takeout. It's not cheap. Unlike most Chinese restaurants, the dishes here are not large enough to share. Sunday-afternoon dim sum is extremely popular, and lines often snake around the shopping center.

7991 Bird Rd., West Miami. (✆ **305/262-7576.** Reservations highly recommended on weekends. Main courses $15–$30. AE, DC, MC, V. Mon–Fri 11:30am–10:30pm; Sat 11am–11:30pm; Sun 10:30am–10pm. Take U.S. 1 to Bird Rd. and go west on Bird, all the way down to 78th Ave. The restaurant is btw. 78th and 79th on the north side of Bird Rd.

Inexpensive

Crepe Maker Café ★ ☺ CREPES/FRENCH Create your own delicious crepes at this little French cafe. You can choose from ham, tuna, black olives, red peppers,

Greater Miami Dining

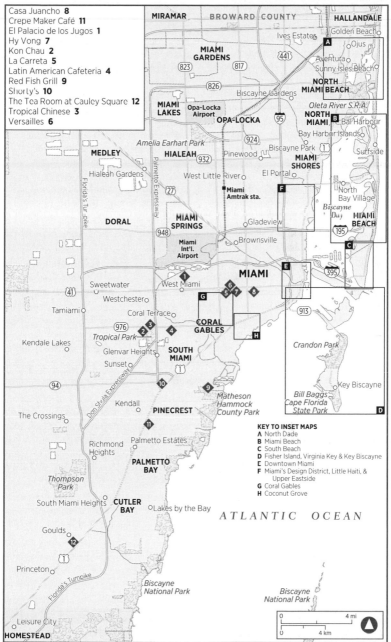

Casa Juancho **8**
Crepe Maker Café **11**
El Palacio de los Jugos **1**
Hy Vong **7**
Kon Chau **2**
La Carreta **5**
Latin American Cafeteria **4**
Red Fish Grill **9**
Shorty's **10**
The Tea Room at Cauley Square **12**
Tropical Chinese **3**
Versailles **6**

KEY TO INSET MAPS
A North Dade
B Miami Beach
C South Beach
D Fisher Island, Virginia Key & Key Biscayne
E Downtown Miami
F Miami's Design District, Little Haiti, &
   Upper Eastside
G Coral Gables
H Coconut Grove

ATLANTIC   OCEAN

Miami's Best Food Trucks

Perhaps because of our location at the bottom of the map, Miami is often last in receiving trends that have already swept the nation several times over. In 2009, we saw a welcome, albeit minor, congestion of food trucks clogging our arteries both literally and figuratively. The first is **gastroPod Mobile Gourmet** (www.twitter.com/gastropodmiami), a customized, vintage 1962 Airstream with ultra-modern kitchen serving up some serious street food—triple-decker sliders stuffed with shaved pork belly on a potato bun, and short rib hot dogs. Joining this retro-fab, nomadic kitchen on wheels on the streets of Miami is Food Network star Ingrid Hoffmann's **Latin Burger and Taco** (www.twitter.com/latinburger) and the more bare-bones greasy spoon on wheels **A Chef's Burger** (330 NW 29th St.; ℂ 786/344-5825). And, racking up mileage, albeit in a Scion instead of a truck, is **Feverish Ice Cream** (www.twitter.com/feverishmiami), a hipster's version of the old-school ice cream truck serving gourmet frozen treats. Look for these trucks everywhere from downtown and the beaches to Coral Gables and Coconut Grove.

capers, artichoke hearts, and pine nuts. Some of the best include a Philly cheesesteak with mushrooms, and a classic chicken *cordon bleu*. Delicious dessert crepes include ice cream, strawberries, peaches, walnuts, and pineapples. Enjoy your crepe fresh off the griddle at the counter or from a bar stool. The soups are delicious. Kids can run around in a small play area.

8269 SW 124th St., South Miami. ℂ **305/233-4458** or 233-1113. Crepes $1.50–$8.50. AE, DC, MC, V. Sun–Thurs 11:30am–9:30pm; Fri–Sat 11:30am–10:30pm. Take U.S. 1 south to 124th St. and make a left. The restaurant is on the north side of the street, across from the park.

El Toro Taco Family Restaurant ★★★ 🍴 MEXICAN   I've put major mileage on my car since I first stumbled upon this 96-seat family-run restaurant a few years ago, when I was lost and very hungry. Fabulous (and I mean fabulous) Mexican fare—tacos, enchiladas, and burritos drenched with the freshest and zestiest salsa this side of Baja—is what you'll find here in abundance, although other Mexican fans disagree. It may sound odd to travel from a big city with tons of restaurants to farm country for Mexican food, but trust me: It's so cheap and delicious, it's worth the trip.

1 S. Krome Ave., Homestead. ℂ **305/245-8182.** Main courses $1.75–$12. DISC, MC, V. Tues–Sun 10am–9pm; Fri–Sat 10am–10pm. Take 836 W. (Dolphin Expwy.) toward Miami International Airport. Take Florida Turnpike S. ramp toward Florida City/Key West. Take U.S. 41/SW 8th St. exit (exit 25) and turn left onto SW 8th St. Take SW 8th St. to Krome Ave. (¼ mile) and turn left.

Kon Chau ★ CHINESE/DIM SUM   Don't be put off by the rather unappealing shopping center in which this cheap dim-sum place is located. If you want fancy plastic chopsticks and fancy prices, go up the block to Tropical Chinese (see above). If you want delicious dim sum at ridiculously low prices, Kon Chau is where you'll find it. A simple checklist allows you to choose as many items as you want, from savory steamed shrimp dumplings to airy pork buns, for as little as $1 apiece, all day long. There are also regular dishes if you don't want dim sum.

8376 Bird Rd., West Miami. ℂ **305/553-7799.** Items $1 and up. MC, V. Mon–Sat 11am–9:45pm; Sun 10am–9:30pm. Take Bird Rd. west to 83rd St. The restaurant is btw. 83rd and 84th sts., on the south side of the road, in a Dunkin' Donuts shopping center.

Shorty's ★ BARBECUE   A Miami tradition since 1951, this honky-tonk of a log cabin still serves some of the best ribs and chicken in South Florida. People line up for the smoke-flavored, slow-cooked meat that's so tender it seems to fall off the bone. The secret, however, is to ask for your order with sweet sauce. The regular stuff tastes bland and bottled. All of the side dishes, including the coleslaw, corn on the cob, and baked beans, look commercial but complete the experience. This is a jeans-and-T-shirt kind of place, but you may want to wear jeans with an elastic waistband, as overeating is not uncommon.

9200 S. Dixie Hwy. (btw. U.S. 1 and Dadeland Blvd.), South Miami. ℂ **305/670-7732.** Main courses $5–$15. DISC, MC, V. Sun–Thurs 11am–10pm; Fri–Sat 11am–11pm.

The Tea Room at Cauley Square ★ ENGLISH TEA   Do stop in for a spot of tea at this cozy tearoom in historic Cauley Square, off U.S. 1. The little lace-curtained room is an unusual sight in this heavily industrial area better known for its warehouses than its doilies. Try one of the simple sandwiches, such as the turkey club with potato salad and a small lettuce garnish, or onion soup—rich brown broth and stringy cheese. The ambrosia with finger sandwiches or banana nut bread is an interesting choice, served with a blend of pineapple, mandarin oranges, miniature marshmallows, and sour cream. Daily specials (such as spinach-and-mushroom quiche) and delectable desserts are musts before you begin your explorations of the old antiques and art shops in this little enclave of civility down south. Oh, and remember to put your pinky up while sipping your tea.

12310 SW 224th St. (at Cauley Sq.), South Miami. ℂ **305/258-0044.** Sandwiches and salads $7–$12; soups $3–$6. AE, DISC, MC, V. Daily 11am–4pm. Take 836 W. (Dolphin Expwy.) toward Miami International Airport. Take Palmetto Expwy. S. ramp toward Coral Way. Merge onto 826 S. Follow signs to Florida Tpk. toward Homestead. Take the tpk. south and exit at Caribbean Blvd. (exit 12). Go about 1 mile on Caribbean Blvd. and turn left on S. Dixie Hwy. and then right at SW 224th St. Then turn left onto Old Dixie Hwy. and take a slight right onto SW 224th St. The restaurant is at Cauley Square Center.

White Lion Cafe ★ AMERICAN   The quintessence of a quaint off-the-beaten-path eatery in not-so-quaint Miami, the White Lion Cafe is a hidden gem serving Southern-style blue-plate specials, including delicious meatloaf and fried chicken. There's also an extensive entertainment calendar here, with everything from live jazz to karaoke. If you're in the Homestead area en route to or coming from the Keys, it's definitely worth a stop here, where time seems to stand still, at least until the band starts playing.

146 NW 7th St., Homestead. ℂ **305/248-1076.** www.whitelioncafe.com. Main courses $10–$22. AE, DISC, MC, V. Daily 5pm until "the fat lady sings." Take the 836 E. to the 826 S., at exit 6 make a left and head west on 8th St. (Campbell Dr.), after crossing Krome Ave. take a left at 1st Ave. (the very next light) and turn right on 7th St. The cafe is on the left.

WHAT TO SEE & DO IN MIAMI

8

f there's one thing Miami doesn't have, it's an identity crisis. Multiple personalities, maybe, but hardly a crisis. In fact, it's the city's vibrant, multifaceted personality that attracts millions each year from all over the world. South Beach may be on the top of many Miami to-do lists, but the rest of the city, a fascinating assemblage of multicultural neighborhoods, some on the verge of a popularity explosion, should not be overlooked. Once considered "God's Waiting Room," the Magic City now attracts an eclectic mix of old and young, celebs and plebes, American and international, and geek and chic with an equally varied roster of activities.

For starters, Miami boasts some of the world's most natural beauty, with dazzling blue waters, fine sandy beaches, and lush tropical parks. The city's man-made brilliance, in the form of crayon-colored architecture, never seems to fade in Miami's unique Art Deco district. For cultural variation, you can experience the tastes, sounds, and rhythms of Cuba in Little Havana.

As in any metropolis, though, some areas aren't as great as others. Downtown Miami, for instance, is still in the throes of a major, albeit slow, renaissance, in which the sketchier warehouse sections of the city are being transformed into hubs of all things hip. In contrast to this development, however, are the still poverty-stricken areas of downtown such as Overtown, Liberty City, and Little Haiti (though Overtown is striving to transform itself into the Overtown Historic Village, showcasing its landmarks such as the famous Lyric Theater and the home of DA Dorsey, Miami's first African-American millionaire). While I obviously advise you to exercise caution when exploring the less-traveled parts of the city, I would also be remiss in telling you to bypass them completely.

Lose yourself in the city's nature and its neighborhoods and, best of all, its people—a sassy collection of artists and intellectuals, beach bums and international transplants, dolled-up drag queens and bodies beautiful. No wonder celebrities love to vacation here—the spotlight is on the city and its residents. Also, unlike most stars, Miami is always ready for its close-up. With so much to do and see, Miami is a virtual amusement park that's bound to entertain all those who pass through its palm-lined gates.

In this chapter, you'll find a "Miami Area Attractions" map on p. 175 and a "South Beach Attractions" map on p. 173.

MIAMI'S BEACHES

Perhaps Miami's most popular attraction is its incredible 35-mile stretch of beach-front, which runs from the tip of South Beach north to Sunny Isles, then circles Key Biscayne and numerous other pristine islands dotting the Atlantic. The characteristics of Miami's many beaches are as varied as the city's population: There are beaches for swimming, socializing, or serenity; for family, seniors, or gay singles; some to make you forget you're in the city, others darkened by huge condominiums. Whatever type of beach vacation you're looking for, you'll find it in one of Miami's two distinct beach areas: Miami Beach and Key Biscayne. And in keeping up with technology, Miami Beach is now officially a hot spot—as in a wireless hot spot, offering 95 percent coverage outdoors (70 percent indoors) of free Wi-Fi throughout the entire city and yes, even on the sand.

MIAMI BEACH'S BEACHES Collins Avenue fronts more than a dozen miles of white-sand beach and blue-green waters from 1st to 192nd streets. Although most of this stretch is lined with a solid wall of hotels and condos, beach access is plentiful. There are lots of public beaches here, wide and well maintained, complete with lifeguards, bathroom facilities, concession stands, and metered parking (bring lots of quarters). Except for a thin strip close to the water, most of the sand is hard-packed—the result of a $10-million Army Corps of Engineers Beach Rebuilding Project meant to protect buildings from the effects of eroding sand.

In general, the beaches on this barrier island (all on the eastern, ocean side of the island) become less crowded the farther north you go. A wooden boardwalk runs along the hotel side of the beach from 21st to 46th streets—about 1½ miles—offering a terrific sun-and-surf experience without getting sand in your shoes. Miami's lifeguard-protected public beaches include 21st Street, at the beginning of the boardwalk; 35th Street, popular with an older crowd; 46th Street, next to the Fontainebleau Hilton; 53rd Street, a narrower, more sedate beach; 64th Street, one of the quietest strips around; and 72nd Street, a local old-timers' spot.

From Desert Island to Fantasy Island

Miami Beach wasn't always a beach-front playground. In fact, it was a deserted island until the late 1800s, when a developer started a coconut farm there. That action sparked an interest in many other developers, including John Collins (for whom Collins Ave. is named), who began growing avocados. Other visionaries admired Collins's success and eventually joined him, establishing a ferry service and dredging parts of the bay to make the island more accessible. In 1921, Collins built a 2½-mile bridge linking downtown Miami to Miami Beach, creating excellent accessibility *and* the longest wooden bridge in the world. Today Miami Beach has six links to the mainland.

KEY BISCAYNE'S BEACHES If Miami Beach doesn't provide the privacy you're looking for, try Virginia Key and Key Biscayne. Crossing the Rickenbacker Causeway ($1.50 toll), however, can be a lengthy process, especially on weekends, when beach bums and tan-o-rexics flock to the Key. The 5 miles of public beach there, however, are blessed with softer sand and are less developed and more laid-back than the hotel-laden strips to the north. In 2008, Key Biscayne reopened the historic **Virginia Key Beach Park,** 4020 Virginia Beach Dr. (© **305/960-4600;** www.virginiakeybeachpark.net), the former "colored only" beach that opened in 1945 and closed in 1982 because of high maintenance costs. After an $11-million renovation, the 83-acre historic site features picnic tables and grills, shoreline renourishment, a new playground for children with special needs, and a miniature railroad. The beach eventually plans to open a civil rights museum as well. Open from sunrise to sunset daily, with free admission.

The Best Beaches

o **Best Party Beach:** In Key Biscayne, **Crandon Park Beach,** on Crandon Boulevard, is National Lampoon's *Vacation* on the sand. It's got a diverse crowd consisting of dedicated beach bums and lots of leisure-seeking families, set to a soundtrack of salsa, disco, and reggae music blaring from a number of competing stereos. With 3 miles of oceanfront beach, bathrooms, changing facilities, 493 acres of park, 75 grills, three parking lots, several soccer and softball fields, and a public 18-hole championship golf course, Crandon is like a theme park on the sand. The beach also offers Eco-Adventure Tours, including kayaking and snorkeling. For more information, call © **305/365-3018.** It's open daily from 8am to sunset.

o **Best Beach for People-Watching: Lummus Park Beach,** also known as South Beach, runs along Ocean Drive from about 6th to 14th streets on South Beach. It's the best place to go if you're seeking entertainment as well as a great tan. On any day of the week, you might spy models primping for a photo shoot, nearly naked (topless is legal here) sun-worshippers avoiding tan lines, and an assembly line of washboard abs off of which you could (but shouldn't) bounce your bottle of sunscreen. Bathrooms and changing facilities are available on the beach, but don't expect to have a Cindy Crawford encounter in one of these. Most people tend to prefer using the somewhat drier, cleaner bathrooms of the restaurants on Ocean Drive.

o **Best Beach for Communing with Nature: Bill Baggs Cape Florida State Park** is the pot of gold at the end of Key Biscayne, with over a mile of unfettered beach, a historic lighthouse, and nature trails that take you back to the days when South Florida was a tropical wilderness.

o **Best Swimming Beach:** The **85th Street Beach,** along Collins Avenue, is the best place to swim away from the maddening crowds. It's one of Miami's only stretches of sand with no condos or hotels looming over sunbathers. Lifeguards patrol the area throughout the day and bathrooms are available, though they are not exactly the benchmark of cleanliness.

o **Best Windsurfing Beach: Hobie Beach,** on the side of the causeway leading to Key Biscayne, is not really a beach, but an inlet with predictable winds and a number of places where you can rent windsurf boards. Bathrooms are available but not exactly the cleanest.

Miami's Best Beaches

Bal Harbour Beach **2**
Bill Baggs Cape Florida State Park **9**
Crandon Park Beach **8**
85th Street Beach **3**
Haulover Beach **1**
Hobie Beach **6**
Lummus Park Beach **4**
Matheson Hammock Park Beach **10**
12th Street Beach **5**
Virginia Key **7**

- **Best Shell-Hunting Beach:** You'll find plenty of colorful shells at **Bal Harbour Beach,** Collins Avenue at 96th Street. There's also an exercise course and good shade—but no lifeguards, bathrooms, or changing facilities.

- **Best (Ahem) All-Around Tanning Beach:** For that all-over tan, head to **Haulover Beach,** just north of the Bal Harbour border, and join nudists from around the world in a top-to-bottom tanning session. Should you choose to keep your swimsuit on, however, there are changing rooms and bathrooms.

- **Best Surfing Beach: Haulover Beach,** just over the causeway from Bal Harbour, seems to get Miami's biggest swells. Go early to avoid getting mauled by the aggressive young locals prepping for Maui. Formerly rancid bathrooms were fixed up, though some homeless people do tend to use the bathrooms to wash up, so use at your own risk. Surfers also like the southern tip of South Beach, not necessarily for the waves, but for the surfers themselves.

- **Best Scenic Beach: Matheson Hammock Park Beach,** at 9610 Old Cutler Rd. in South Miami (✆ **305/665-5475**), is the epitome of tranquillity. And while it's scenic, it's not too much of a scene. It's a great beach for those seeking "alone time." Bathrooms and changing facilities are available.

- **Best Family Beach:** Because of its man-made lagoon, which is fed naturally by the tidal movement of the adjacent Biscayne Bay, the waters of **Matheson Hammock Park Beach** are extremely calm, not to mention safe and secluded enough for families to keep an eye on the kids. Clean bathrooms are a plus.
- **Best Beach for Seclusion: Virginia Key** on Key Biscayne is where people go when they don't want to be found. It's also incredibly picturesque. Bathrooms are decent.
- **Best for Gay Beachgoers:** South Beach's **12th Street Beach** is *the* place to be for Miami's best gay beach scene. Here you'll see strutting, kibitzing, and gossiping among some of Miami's most beautiful gay population. You might even find yourself lucky enough to happen upon a feisty South Beach party while you're soaking up some rays here. If you can hold it, skip the public bathroom and head over to the Palace on Ocean Drive to use their bathroom.

THE ART DECO DISTRICT (SOUTH BEACH)

"You know what they used to say? 'Who's Art?'" recalls Art Deco revivalist Dona Zemo. "You'd say, 'This is an Art Deco building,' and they'd say, 'Really, who is Art?' These people thought 'Art Deco' was some guy's name."

How things have changed. This guy Art has become one of the most popular Florida attractions since, well, that mouse named Mickey. The district is roughly bounded by the Atlantic Ocean on the east, Alton Road on the west, Sixth Street to the south, and Dade Boulevard (along the Collins Canal) to the north.

 Walking by Design

The Miami Design Preservation League offers several tours of Miami Beach's historic architecture, all of which leave from the Art Deco Welcome Center at 1001 Ocean Dr., in Miami Beach. A self-guided audio tour (available 7 days a week, 10am–4pm) turns the streets into a virtual outdoor museum, taking you through Miami Beach's Art Deco District at your own leisure, with tours in several languages for just $15 for adults, $10 for seniors. Guided tours conducted by local historians and architects offer an in-depth look at the structures and their history. The 90-minute Ocean Drive and Beyond tour (offered every Wed and Sat at 10:30am) takes you through the district, pointing out the differences between Mediterranean Revival and Art Deco for $20 for adults, $15 for seniors. If you're not blinded by neon, the Thursday night Art Deco District Up-to-Date Tour (leaving at 6:30pm) will whisk you around for a 90-minute walk, making note of how certain local hot spots were architecturally famous way before the likes of Madonna and Co. entered the scene. The cost is $20 for adults, $15 for seniors. For those who have no time or patience for group tours, there are self-guided ones and even a cellphone tour for that person who can't keep the phone off his or her ears. For more information on tours or reservations, call ✆ **305/672-2014** or try www.mdpl.org.

South Beach Attractions

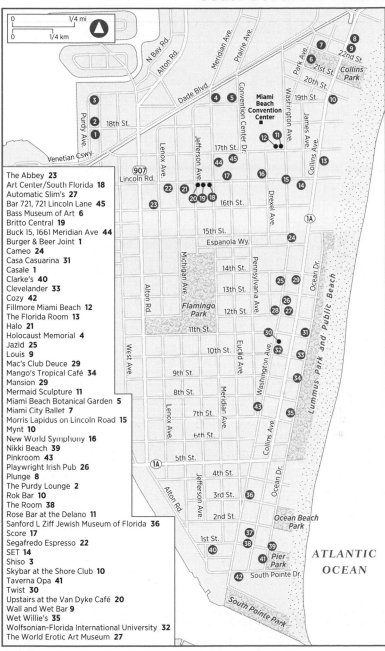

The Abbey **23**
Art Center/South Florida **18**
Automatic Slim's **27**
Bar 721, 721 Lincoln Lane **45**
Bass Museum of Art **6**
Britto Central **19**
Buck 15, 1661 Meridian Ave **44**
Burger & Beer Joint **1**
Cameo **24**
Casa Casuarina **31**
Casale **1**
Clarke's **40**
Clevelander **33**
Cozy **42**
Fillmore Miami Beach **12**
The Florida Room **13**
Halo **21**
Holocaust Memorial **4**
Jazid **25**
Louis **9**
Mac's Club Deuce **29**
Mango's Tropical Café **34**
Mansion **29**
Mermaid Sculpture **11**
Miami Beach Botanical Garden **5**
Miami City Ballet **7**
Morris Lapidus on Lincoln Road **15**
Mynt **10**
New World Symphony **16**
Nikki Beach **39**
Pinkroom **43**
Playwright Irish Pub **26**
Plunge **8**
The Purdy Lounge **2**
Rok Bar **10**
The Room **38**
Rose Bar at the Delano **11**
Sanford L Ziff Jewish Museum of Florida **36**
Score **17**
Segafredo Espresso **22**
SET **14**
Shiso **3**
Skybar at the Shore Club **10**
Taverna Opa **41**
Twist **30**
Upstairs at the Van Dyke Café **20**
Wall and Wet Bar **9**
Wet Willie's **35**
Wolfsonian-Florida International University **32**
The World Erotic Art Museum **27**

Miami or Madrid?

On a tiny street in South Beach, there's a piece of Spain that's so vibrant, you almost feel as if you're in Madonna's "La Isla Bonita" video. In 1925, Miami Beach developer NBT Roney hired architect Robert Taylor to design a Spanish village on the property he just purchased on a street called Española Way. Today, the historic Mediterranean-Revival-style Spanish Village—or Plaza De España—envisioned by Roney and complete with fountain, stretches from Washington Avenue to Drexel Avenue and features charming boutiques, cafes, and a weekend market.

Simply put, Art Deco is a style of architecture that, in its heyday of the 1920s and 1930s, used to be considered ultramodern. Today, fans of the style consider it retro fabulous. But while some people may not consider the style fabulous, it's undoubtedly retro. According to the experts, Art Deco made its debut in 1925 at an exposition in Paris in which it set a stylistic tone, with buildings based on early neoclassical styles with the application of exotic motifs such as flora, fauna, and fountains based on geometric patterns. In Miami, Art Deco is marked by the pastel-hued buildings that line South Beach and Miami Beach. But it's a lot more than just color. If you look carefully, you will see the intricacies and impressive craftsmanship that went into each building back in Miami in the '20s, '30s, '40s, and today, thanks to intensive restoration.

Most of the finest examples of the whimsical Art Deco style are concentrated along three parallel streets—Ocean Drive, Collins Avenue, and Washington Avenue—from about 6th to 23rd streets.

After years of neglect and calls for the wholesale demolition of its buildings, South Beach got a new lease on life in 1979. Under the leadership of Barbara Baer Capitman, a dedicated crusader for the Art Deco region, and the Miami Design Preservation League, founded by Baer Capitman and five friends, an area made up of an estimated 800 buildings was granted a listing on the National Register of Historic Places. Designers then began highlighting long-lost architectural details with soft sherbet shades of peach, periwinkle, turquoise, and purple. Developers soon moved in, and the full-scale refurbishment of the area's hotels was underway.

Not everyone was pleased, though. Former Miami Beach Commissioner Abe Resnick said, "I love old buildings. But these Art Deco buildings are 40, 50 years old. They aren't historic. They aren't special. We shouldn't be forced to keep them." But Miami Beach kept those buildings, and Resnick lost his seat on the commission.

Today hundreds of new establishments—hotels, restaurants, and nightclubs—have renovated these older, historic buildings, putting South Beach on the cutting edge of Miami's cultural and nightlife scene.

Exploring the Area

If you're touring this unique neighborhood on your own, start at the **Art Deco Welcome Center,** 1001 Ocean Dr. (© **305/531-3484**), which is run by the Miami Design Preservation League. The only beachside building across from the Clevelander Hotel and bar, the center gives away lots of informational material, including

Miami Area Attractions

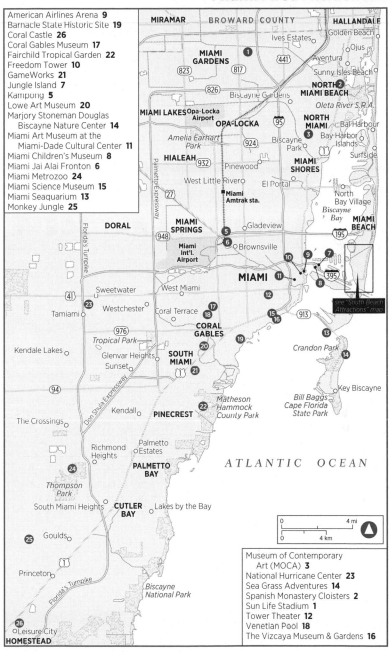

maps and pamphlets, and runs guided tours around the neighborhood. Art Deco books (including *The Art Deco Guide,* an informative compendium of all the buildings here), T-shirts, postcards, mugs, and other paraphernalia are for sale. It's open daily from 10am to 7:30pm.

Take a stroll along **Ocean Drive** for the best view of sidewalk cafes, bars, colorful hotels, and even more colorful people. Another great place for a walk is **Lincoln Road,** which is lined with boutiques, large chain stores, cafes, and funky art and antiques stores. The Community Church, at the corner of Lincoln Road and Drexel Avenue, was the neighborhood's first church and is one of its oldest surviving buildings, dating from 1921.

Or, if you prefer to cruise South Beach in a tiny yellow buggy—part scooter, part golf cart—consider **GoCar,** 1661 James Ave. (© **888/462-2755;** www.gocartours. com), a three-wheeled vehicle for two that comes with a GPS device that not only tracks and tells you where to go, but prompts a recorded tour that kicks on with every site you cruise by. Cost is $49 for the first hour, $39 for the second hour, and $29 for the third hour, or $150 for the entire day. A 3-hour tour is $99. Prices include gas.

MIAMI'S MUSEUM & ART SCENE

The Design District is, as locals say, the new South Beach, adding a touch of New York's SoHo to an area formerly known as downtown Miami's "Don't Go." The district is a hotbed for furniture-import companies, interior designers, architects, and artists and is loosely defined as the area bounded by NE 2nd Avenue, NE 5th Avenue East and West, and NW 36th Street to the south. Just south of the Design District is yet another burgeoning arts district, a sketchy strip of Miami bounded by NE 2nd Avenue to the east and NE 36th Street to the north, known as Wynwood. While most of the galleries are open during regular business hours, some are open during gallery nights and by appointment. Call ahead to make sure. For a complete listing of galleries, showrooms and studios as well as information on events and openings in the Design District, go to www.miamidesigndistrict.net.

Bernice Steinbaum Gallery   Check out the modern multimedia exhibits here by contemporary artists including Hung Liu, Glexis Novoa, and Maria Gonzalez. 3550 N. Miami Ave. © **305/573-2700.** www.bernicesteinbaumgallery.com. Mon–Sat 10am–6pm.

CIFO   An outstanding nonprofit gallery established by Ella Fontanals Cisneros and her family to foster cultural exchange among the visual arts, CIFO is dedicated to the support of emerging and mid-career contemporary multidisciplinary artists from Latin America. 1018 N. Miami Ave. at NW 10th St. © **305/445-3880.** www.cifo.org. Mon–Thurs 10am–4pm during exhibitions or by appointment.

Diana Lowenstein Fine Arts   One of Miami's preeminent modern art collectors, Lowenstein's gallery in the burgeoning Wynwood area of downtown Miami is a hot spot for serious collectors and admirers. 2043 N. Miami Ave. © **305/576-1804.** www.dlfinearts.com. Tues–Sat 10:30am–6pm.

Dorsch Gallery   An expansive gallery known for hosting some fabulous parties for the who's who in the art world, Dorsch is known for some seriously funky exhibitions. 151 NW 24th St. at N. Miami Ave. © **305/576-1278.** www.dorschgallery.com. Thurs–Sat 1–5pm.

ROADSIDE attractions

The following examples of public art and prized architecture are great photo opportunities and worth visiting if you're in the area.

o **Casa Casaurina, also known as Versace Mansion (Amsterdam Palace):** Morbid curiosity has led hordes of people—tourists and locals—to this, once the only private home (now a country club) on Ocean Drive. If you can get past the fact that the late designer was murdered on the steps of this palatial estate, you should definitely observe the intricate Italian architecture that makes this house stand out from its streamlined Deco neighbors. Built in the 1930s as a replica of Christopher Columbus's son's palace in Santo Domingo, the house was originally called Casa Casaurina (House of the Pine), but was rechristened the Amsterdam Palace in 1935 when George Amsterdam purchased it. After several stints as a private country club and hotel, it's now a hotel, **Villas by Barton G.,** open to the public and run by restaurateur and events planner Barton G. Weiss. Located at the northwest corner of Ocean Drive and 11th Street, South Beach.

o **Mermaid Sculpture:** A pop-art masterpiece designed by Roy Lichtenstein, this sculpture captures the buoyant spirit of Miami Beach and its environs. It's in front of the Jackie Gleason Theater of the Performing Arts, at 1700 Washington Ave., Miami Beach.

o **Morris Lapidus on Lincoln Road:** Famed designer/architect, the late Morris Lapidus—the "high priest of high kitsch"—who is best known for the Fontainebleau Hotel, created a series of sculptures that are angular, whimsical, and quirky, competing with the equally amusing mix of pedestrians who flock to Lincoln Road. In addition to the sculptures on Lincoln Road (at Washington Ave.), which you can't miss, Lapidus also created the Colony Theater, 1040 Lincoln Rd., which was built by Paramount in 1943; the 1928 Sterling Building, 927 Lincoln Rd., whose glass blocks and blue neon are required evening viewing; and the Lincoln Theater, 555 Lincoln Rd., which features a remarkable tropical bas-relief.

Fredric Snitzer Gallery The catalyst to the explosion of the Wynwood arts scene, this warehouse pays homage to works by local stars and New World School of the Arts grads as well as artists from Cuba's legendary 80s Generation. 2247 NW 1st Place at N. Miami Ave. ✆ **305/448-8976.** www.snitzer.com. Tues–Sat 11am–5pm.

Gary Nader Fine Art If you're into Latin American art by the likes of Botero, Matta, and Lam, this is the place for you. In addition there are monthly exhibits of emerging artists. 62 NE 27th St. at N. Miami Ave. ✆ **305/576-0256.** www.garynader.com. Mon–Sat 10am–6pm.

Kevin Bruk Gallery   Up-and-coming sculptors, photographers, and painters from around the world aspire to be featured in this excellent gallery of international art. 2249 NW 1st Place at N. Miami Ave. ✆ **305/576-2000.** www.kevinbrukgallery.com. Tues–Fri 10am–6pm; Sat noon–5pm.

Margulies Collection 🎁   This massive, 45,000-square-foot Wynwood warehouse is the city's crown jewel, showcasing contemporary and vintage photography, video, sculpture, and installations in various genres including pop art, minimalism, and expressionism. 591 NW 27th St. at 6th Ave. ✆ **305/576-1051.** www.margulies warehouse.com. Wed–Sat 11am–4pm.

Rubell Family Collection 🎁   This impressive collection, owned by the Miami hotelier family the Rubells, is housed in a two-story, 40,000-square-foot, former Drug Enforcement Agency warehouse in a sketchy area north of downtown Miami. The building looks like a fortress, which is fitting: Inside is a priceless collection of more than 1,000 works of contemporary art by the likes of Keith Haring, Damien Hirst, Julian Schnabel, Jean-Michel Basquiat, Paul McCarthy, Charles Ray, and Cindy Sherman. 95 NW 29th St. at NW 1st Ave. ✆ **305/573-6090.** www.rubellfamily collection.com. 10am–10pm second Saturday of every month.

Miami has never been known as a cultural mecca as far as museums are concerned, though its reputation is improving thanks to the international attention brought to the scene by such esteemed fairs as Switzerland's Art Basel, which comes to Miami for a few days every December. Though several exhibition spaces have made forays into collecting nationally acclaimed work, limited support, political infighting, and, of course, the dreaded recession have made it a difficult proposition. Recently, however, things have changed slowly but surely as museums such as the Wolfsonian, the Museum of Contemporary Art, the Bass Museum of Art, and the Miami Art Museum have gotten on the bandwagon, boasting collections and exhibitions high on the list of art aficionados. It's now safe to say that world-class exhibitions start here. Listed below are the most lauded museums that have become a part of the city's cultural heritage and are as diverse as the city itself. Art lovers should check local listings for periodic gallery walks. Please note that many art museums and galleries are closed in the summer; call ahead so you won't be disappointed.

> ### Impressions
>
> *You don't find inspiration in Miami; it finds you.*
> —Pepe Mar, sculptor

The focal point of December's enormously popular Art Basel is **Collins Park Cultural Center** (www.collinspark.us), which comprises a trio of arts buildings on Collins Park and Park Avenue (off Collins Ave.), bounded by 21st to 23rd streets—the expanded Bass Museum of Art (see below), the new Arquitectonica-designed home of the Miami City Ballet, and the Miami Beach Regional Library, an ultramodern building designed by architect Robert A. M. Stern, with a special focus on the arts. Collins Park, the former site of the Miami Beach Library, returned to its original incarnation as an open space extending to the Atlantic, but it is also now the site of large sculpture installations and cultural activities planned jointly by the organizations that share the space. In 2009, the park was completely ripped out for renovations that are said to continue into early 2011. Other cultural institutions that are

---

The Last Holdout

As all the galleries move to the Design District and Wynwood, one original South Beach holdout exists and it may seem very familiar to you. **Britto Central**, 818 Lincoln Rd., South Beach (*(C)* **305/531-8821; www.britto.com),** featuring the works of Brazilian artist Romero Britto, is the only one that can afford the rent considering he is con- stantly commissioned by the city for various public works of art. Some people liken Britto to Andy Warhol because of his colorful, whimsical paintings of young children and animals, among other things. Serious art lovers, however, consider Britto's cartoonish works more along the lines of a second-rate Walt Disney. You decide.

---

part of the emerging Collins Park neighborhood are: local arts organization SoBe Arts at the Carl Fisher complex, the Miami Beach Botanical Garden, and The Holocaust Memorial. For updates on construction progress and a brochure of all Collins Park venues, check out the neighborhood's comprehensive website.

ArtCenter/South Florida ★   Not exactly a museum in the classic sense of the word, ArtCenter/South Florida is a multichambered space, where local artists display their works in all media—from photography and sculpture to video and just about anything else that might exemplify their artistic nature. Admission is free, and it's quite fun to mosey through the space viewing the various artists at work in their studios. Of course, all the art is for sale, but there's no pressure to buy. If you call ahead, you can schedule a guided tour of all the studios, which will give you extra insight into the exhibits. Otherwise, just wander and enjoy.

800-924 Lincoln Rd. (at Meridian Ave.), South Beach. *(C)* **305/674-8278.** www.artcentersf.org. Free admission. Daily 11am–10pm.

Bass Museum of Art ★★★   The Bass Museum of Art has expanded and received a dramatically new look, rendering it Miami's most progressive art museum. World-renowned Japanese architect Arata Isozaki designed the magnificent new facility, which has triple the former exhibition space, and added an outdoor sculpture terrace, a museum cafe and courtyard, and a museum shop, among other improvements. In addition to providing space in which to show the permanent collection, exhibitions of a scale and quality not previously seen in Miami will now be featured at the Bass. The museum's permanent collection includes European paintings from the 15th through the early 20th centuries, with special emphasis on northern European art of the Renaissance and baroque periods, including Dutch and Flemish masters. Among the artists in the museum's permanent collection: Jacob Jordaens, Peter Paul Rubens, Gerard Seghers, Ferdinand Bol, and Giovanni Barbagelata. Past exhibitions have included the works of Picasso, Frida Kahlo, and Francois-Marie Banier. The museum also has a lab, the New Information Workshop, making it possible for all aspiring artists to create their own masterpieces on computers for free or a nominal charge.

2121 Park Ave. (1 block west of Collins Ave.), South Beach. *(C)* **305/673-7530.** www.bassmuseum.org. Admission $8 adults, $6 students and seniors, free for children 6 and under. Free 2nd Thurs of the month 6–9pm. Tues–Wed and Fri–Sat 10am–5pm; Thurs 10am–9pm; Sun 11am–5pm.

Eyeing the Storm

For Weather Channel fanatics and those who are just curious, the **National Hurricane Center** offers free tours before and after hurricane season, from January 15 through May 15, explaining everything from keeping track of storms to the history of some of the nation's most notorious and devastating hurricanes. Reservations required. Florida International University. 11691 SW 17th St., Miami. ℭ **305/229-4470.** Free admission.

Coral Gables Museum   Expected to open on October 10, 2010, this museum, housed in a restored version of the city's original 1930 coral rock police and fire station, will pay homage to the City Beautiful with a 3,000-square-foot gallery, 5,000-square-foot public plaza, and a permanent, evolving exhibit examining Coral Gables's history. Exhibits and programming will have a heavy focus on architecture, urban design and sustainable development.

285 Aragon Ave., Coral Gables. ℭ **305/910-3996.** www.coralgablesmuseum.org. No hours or admission information yet available.

Holocaust Memorial ★★★   This heart-wrenching memorial is hard to miss and would be a shame to overlook. The powerful centerpiece, Kenneth Treister's *A Sculpture of Love and Anguish,* depicts victims of the concentration camps crawling up a giant yearning hand stretching up to the sky, marked with an Auschwitz number tattoo. Along the reflecting pool is the story of the Holocaust, told in cut marble slabs. Inside the center of the memorial is a tableau that is one of the most solemn and moving tributes to the millions of Jews who lost their lives in the Holocaust I've seen. You can walk through an open hallway lined with photographs and the names of concentration camps and their victims. From the street, you'll see the outstretched arm, but do stop and tour the sculpture at ground level.

1933 Meridian Ave. (at Dade Blvd.), South Beach. ℭ **305/538-1663.** www.holocaustmmb.org. Free admission. Daily 9am–9pm.

Lowe Art Museum ★★   Located on the University of Miami campus, the Lowe Art Museum has a dazzling collection of 8,000 works that include American paintings, Latin American art, Navajo and Pueblo Indian textiles, and Renaissance and baroque art. Traveling exhibits, such as *Wine Spectator* magazine's classic posters of the Belle Epoque, also stop here. For the most part, the Lowe is known for its collection of Greek and Roman antiquities, and, as compared to the more modern MOCA, Bass, and Miami Art Museum, features mostly European and international art hailing back to ancient times.

University of Miami, 1301 Stanford Dr. (at Ponce de León Blvd.), Coral Gables. ℭ **305/284-3603.** www.lowemuseum.org. Admission $10 adults, $5 seniors and students with ID. Donation day is 1st Tues of the month. Tues–Wed and Fri–Sat 10am–5pm; Thurs noon–7pm; Sun noon–5pm.

Miami Art Museum ★★★   The Miami Art Museum (MAM) features an eclectic mix of modern and contemporary works by such artists as Eric Fischl, Max Beckmann, Jim Dine, Robert Rauschenberg, Chuck Close, James Rosenquist, Jose Bedia, Marcel Duchamp and Stuart Davis. Rotating exhibitions span ages and styles, and often focus on Latin American or Caribbean artists. JAM at MAM is the museum's popular happy hour, which takes place on the third Thursday of the month and is tied in to a particular exhibit. Almost as artistic as the works inside the museum is the composite sketch of the people—young and old—who attend these events.

The Miami-Dade Cultural Center, where the museum is housed, is a fortresslike complex designed by Philip Johnson. In addition to the acclaimed Miami Art Museum, the center houses the main branch of the Miami-Dade Public Library, which sometimes features art and cultural exhibits, and the Historical Museum of Southern Florida, which highlights the fascinating history of the area. Unfortunately, the plaza onto which the complex opens is home to many of those in downtown Miami's homeless population, which makes it a bit off-putting but not dangerous. Work has yet to begin on Museum Park, a $200-million-plus project on an under-used 29-acre property on the bay in downtown Miami that will become MAM's new home. The 125,000-square-foot Museum Park will include a sculpture garden and spacious galleries as well as the new Miami Science Museum. Estimated comple-tion is sometime in 2013. To check on its status—or lack thereof—go to www.miamiartmuseum.org/museum_park.asp.

101 W. Flagler St., Miami. © **305/375-3000.** www.miamiartmuseum.org. Admission $8 adults, $4 seniors, free for children 11 and under. Tues–Fri 10am–5pm; 3rd Thurs of each month 10am–9pm; Sat-Sun noon–5pm. Closed major holidays. From I-95 south, exit at Orange Bowl–NW 8th St. and continue south to NW 2nd St.; turn left at NW 2nd St. and go 1½ blocks to NW 2nd Ave.; turn right.

Miami Children's Museum ★★ ☺ The Children's Museum, located on the MacArthur Causeway, across from Jungle Island, is a modern, albeit odd-looking, 56,500-square-foot facility that includes 14 galleries, classrooms, a parent/teacher resource center, a Kid Smart educational gift shop, a 200-seat auditorium, a Subway restaurant, and an outdoor, interactive play area. The museum offers hundreds of bilingual, interactive exhibits as well as programs, classes, and learning materials related to arts, culture, community, and communication. Even as an adult, I have to say I was tempted to participate in some kids-only activities and exhibitions, such as the miniature Bank of America and Publix Supermarket, and a re-creation of the NBC 6 television studio. There's also a re-creation of a Carnival cruise ship and a gallery of teddy bears from around the world. Perhaps the coolest thing of all is the World Music Studio, in which aspiring rock stars can lay down a few tracks and play instruments.

980 MacArthur Causeway, Miami. © **305/373-5437.** www.miamichildrensmuseum.org. Admission $15 adults and children 13 months and over. Daily 10am–6pm.

Miami Science Museum ★★ ☺ The Miami Science Museum features more than 140 hands-on exhibits that explore the mysteries of the universe. Live demon-strations and collections of rare natural history specimens make a visit here fun and informative. Many of the demos involve audience participation, which can be lots of fun for willing and able kids and adults alike. There is also the Wildlife Center, with more than 175 live reptiles and birds of prey. The adjacent Space Transit Planetar-ium projects astronomy and laser shows as well as interactive demonstrations of upcoming computer technology and cyberspace features. Call or visit the website for a list of upcoming exhibits and laser shows. In late 2010, construction was expected to begin on the museum's new $275-million home at Museum Park (see above), a tri-level natural-light and solar-powered homage to high-tech science and technology including a cone-shaped aquarium tank and egg-shaped planetarium with views of Biscayne Bay.

3280 S. Miami Ave. (just south of the Rickenbacker Causeway), Coconut Grove. ✆ **305/646-4200.** www.miamisci.org. Admission $15 adults; $11 seniors, students, and children 3–12; free for children 2 and under. Daily 10am–6pm; 1st Fri of every month 10am–10pm; call for show times (last show is at 4pm Mon–Fri and 5pm Sat–Sun). Closed Thanksgiving and Christmas.

Museum of Contemporary Art (MOCA) ★★★   MOCA boasts an impressive collection of internationally acclaimed art with a local flavor. It is also known for its forward thinking and ability to discover and highlight new artists. A high-tech screening facility allows for film presentations to complement the exhibitions. Permanent collection includes works by John Baldessari, Dan Flavin, Dennis Oppenheim, Alex Katz, Louise Nevelson, Edward Ruscha, Gabriel Orozco, Julian Schnabel, Zoe Leonard, Nam June Paik, Uta Barth, Teresita Fernandez, Garry Simmons, Jose Bedia, Anna Gaskel, Thomas Hirschhorn, Mariko Mori, John Bock, Pierre Huyghe, Philippe Parreno, Edward Kienholz, Raymond Pettibon, and Matthew Ritchie, plus there are often special exhibitions by such artists as Yoko Ono, Sigmar Polke, and Goya. Guided tours are offered in English, Spanish, French, Creole, Portuguese, German, and Italian. Construction on a 4,000-square-foot expansion of the museum is expected to begin in late 2010 and will include an education wing, new art storage facility, and enhanced public areas.

770 NE 125th St., North Miami. ✆ **305/893-6211.** Fax 305/891-1472. www.mocanomi.org. Admission $5 adults, $3 seniors and students with ID, free for children 12 and under. Tues by donation. Tues–Sat 11am–5pm; Sun noon–5pm. Closed major holidays.

Patricia and Phillip Frost Art Museum ★★   Housed in a $16-million building designed by architect Yann Weymouth, the Patricia and Phillip Frost Art Museum, located on the campus of Florida International University, was closed to the public until 2009. Today, it is the only art museum in Florida to attempt to exhibit paintings in natural light. The museum has recently begun to present exhibitions in Latin America and is working on future collaborations and partnerships with leading art institutions in these regions. Among the permanent collections is the General Collection, which holds a strong representation of American printmaking from the 1960s and 1970s, photography, pre-Columbian objects dating from A.D. 200 to 500, and a growing number of works by contemporary Caribbean and Latin American artists.

Florida International University, 10975 SW 17th St., Miami. ✆ **305/348-2890.** http://thefrost.fiu.edu. Free admission. Tues–Sat 10am–5pm; Sun noon–5pm.

Sanford L. Ziff Jewish Museum of Florida ★   Chronicling over 230 years of Jewish heritage and experiences in Florida, the Jewish Museum presents a fascinating look at religion and culture through films, lectures, and exhibits such as Mosaic: Jewish Life in Florida, which features over 500 photos and artifacts documenting the Jewish experience in Florida since 1763. Housed in a former synagogue, the museum also delves into the Jewish roots of Latin America.

301 Washington Ave., South Beach. ✆ **305/672-5044.** www.jewishmuseum.com. Admission $6 adults, $5 seniors and students, $12 families. Free admission Sat. Tues–Sun 10am–5pm. Closed Jewish holidays.

Wolfsonian—Florida International University ★★★ 🏛   Mitchell Wolfson, Jr., heir to a family fortune built on movie theaters, was known as an eccentric, but I'd call him a pack rat. A premier collector of propaganda and advertising art,

Wolfson was spending so much money storing his booty that he decided to buy the warehouse that was housing it. It ultimately held more than 70,000 of his items, from controversial Nazi propaganda to King Farouk of Egypt's match collection. Thrown in the eclectic mix are also zany works from great modernists such as Charles Eames and Marcel Duchamp. He then gave this incredibly diverse collection to Florida International University. The former 1927 storage facility has been transformed into a museum that is the envy of curators around the world. The museum is unquestionably fascinating and hosts lectures and rather swinging events surrounding particular exhibits. The Dynamo, the museum's cafe and shop, is a fun and funky spot serving coffee, wine, beer, and nibbles, whose focal point is a large library shelving system from the late 19th century, donated by Samson Management, designed by Bernard R. Green, and crafted of iron by the Snead & Company Iron Works. The design represents the first modular book-stacking system ever created. Leave it to the Wolfsonian to make even its restaurant a piece of work!

1001 Washington Ave., South Beach. © **305/531-1001.** www.wolfsonian.org. Admission $7 adults; $5 seniors, students with ID, and children 6–12. Free Fri after 6pm. Sat–Tues noon–6pm; Thurs–Fri noon–9pm.

The World Erotic Art Museum ★   The Hustler store across the street has nothing on this wacky, X-rated museum. Opened in 2005 by then 70-year-old grandmother Naomi Wilzig, the museum features Wilzig's collection of more than 4,000 pieces of erotic art, including Kama Sutra temple carvings from India, peek-a-boo Victorian figurines that flash their booties, and a prop from the sexual thriller *A Clockwork Orange*. The 12,000-square-foot museum is located above Mansion, a club that's no stranger to erotic art—that is, performance art. This is a great place to spend an hour or two on a rainy day, and more than anything, the stuff is more amusing than sexy or racy.

1205 Washington Ave., South Beach. © **305/532-9336.** www.weam.com. Admission $15; under 18 not admitted. Mon and Wed–Thurs 11am–10pm; Fri–Sun 11am–midnight.

HISTORIC HOMES & SITES

South Beach's well-touted Art Deco District is but one of many colorful neighborhoods that can boast dazzling architecture. The rediscovery of the entire Biscayne Corridor (from downtown to about 80th St. and Biscayne Blvd.) has given light to a host of ancillary neighborhoods on either side, which are filled with Mediterranean-style homes and Frank Lloyd Wright gems. Coral Gables is home to many large and beautiful homes, mansions, and churches that reflect architecture from the 1920s, 1930s, and 1940s. Some of the homes, or portions of their structures, have been created from coral rock and shells. The Biltmore Hotel is also filled with history; see p. 106 for information on touring it.

Barnacle State Historic Site ★★   The former home of naval architect and early settler Ralph Middleton Munroe is now a museum in the heart of Coconut Grove. It's the oldest house in Miami and it rests on its original foundation, which sits on 5 acres of natural hardwood forest and landscaped lawns. The house's quiet surroundings, wide porches, and period furnishings illustrate how Miami's first snowbird lived in the days before condomania and luxury hotels. Enthusiastic and knowledgeable state park employees provide a wealth of historical information to

FREEDOM tower

Driving north on Biscayne Boulevard in downtown Miami, some may be distracted by the traffic, the neon lights coming from the Bayside Marketplace, or the behemoth cruise ships docked at the port. But perhaps the most dramatic presence on this heavily trafficked stretch of downtown is the Freedom Tower, 600 Biscayne Blvd. at NE Sixth Street, built in 1925 and modeled after the Giralda Tower in Spain. Once home to the now-defunct *Miami Daily News* and *Metropolis* newspapers, the Freedom Tower was sold in 1957 to the U.S. General Services Administration, which used the building to process over 500,000 Cubans fleeing the island once Castro took over.

Considered the Ellis Island of the Cuban Exile community, Miami's Freedom Tower has remained largely vacant over the years (the government left the building in 1974) despite hopes and unfulfilled plans to turn it into a museum reflecting its historical significance. In 2004, developers donated the tower to Miami Dade College, which has since used the space for hosting various exhibitions and cultural programs. In 2008, the tower was designated a U.S. National Historic Landmark.

those interested in quiet, low-tech attractions such as this one. On Wednesdays from 6 to 7:30pm they have sunset yoga by the sea. Call for details on the fabulous monthly moonlight concerts during which folk, blues, or classical music is presented and picnicking is encouraged.

3485 Main Hwy. (1 block south of Commodore Plaza), Coconut Grove. © **305/448-9445.** Fax 305/448-7484. Admission $2. Tours $3 adults, $1 children 6–12. Concerts $7 adults, $3 children 6–9, free for children 5 and under. Fri–Mon 9am–4pm. Tours Fri–Mon at 10am, 11:30am, 1pm, and 2:30pm. From downtown Miami, take U.S. 1 south to 27th Ave., make a left, and continue to S. Bayshore Dr.; then make a right, follow to the intersection of Main Hwy., and turn left.

Coral Castle ★ ▮▮ There's plenty of competition, but Coral Castle is probably the strangest attraction in Florida. In 1923, the story goes, a 26-year-old crazed Latvian, suffering from the unrequited love of a 16-year-old who left him at the altar, immigrated to South Miami and spent the next 25 years of his life carving huge boulders into a prehistoric-looking roofless "castle." It seems impossible that one rather short man could have done all this, but there are scores of affidavits on display from neighbors who swear it happened. Apparently, experts have studied this phenomenon to help figure out how the great pyramids and Stonehenge were built. Rocker Billy Idol was said to have been inspired by this place to write his song "Sweet 16." An interesting 25-minute audio tour guides you through the spot, now on the National Register of Historic Places. Although Coral Castle is overpriced and undermaintained, it's worth a visit when you're in the area, which is about 37 miles from Miami.

28655 S. Dixie Hwy., Homestead. © **305/248-6345.** www.coralcastle.com. Admission $9.75 adults, $6.50 seniors, $5 children 7–12. Group rates available. Sun–Thurs 8am–6pm; Fri–Sat 8am–8pm. Take 836 W (Dolphin Expwy.) toward Miami International Airport. Merge onto 826 S (Palmetto Expwy.) and take it to the Florida Tpk. toward Homestead. Take the 288th St. exit (no. 5) and then take a right on S. Dixie Hwy., a left on SW 157th Ave., and then a sharp left back onto S. Dixie Hwy. Coral Castle is on the left side of the street.

Spanish Monastery Cloisters ★★★ 🎁   Did you know that the alleged oldest building in the Western Hemisphere dates from 1133 and is located in Miami? The Spanish Monastery Cloisters were first erected in Segovia, Spain. Centuries later, newspaper magnate William Randolph Hearst purchased and brought them to America in pieces. The carefully numbered stones were quarantined for years until they were finally reassembled on the present site in 1954. It has often been used as a backdrop for weddings, movies, and commercials, and is a very popular tourist attraction.

16711 W. Dixie Hwy. (at NE 167th St.), North Miami Beach. © **305/945-1461.** www.spanishmonastery. com. Admission $5 adults, $2.50 seniors and students with ID, $1 children 3–12. Mon–Fri 10am–4:30 pm; Sun 1–5pm. Call ahead because the monastery closes for special events without notice.

Venetian Pool ★★★ ☺   Miami's most beautiful and unusual swimming pool, dating from 1924, is hidden behind pastel stucco walls and is honored with a listing in the National Register of Historic Places. Underground artesian wells feed the free-form lagoon, which is shaded by three-story Spanish porticos and has both fountains and waterfalls. It can be cold in the winter months. During summer, the pool's 800,000 gallons of water are drained and refilled nightly, thanks to an underground aquifer, ensuring a cool, *clean* swim. Visitors are free to swim and sunbathe here, just as Esther Williams and Johnny Weissmuller did decades ago. For a modest fee, you or your children can learn to swim during special summer programs. At the time of this writing, the pool was closed for renovations and was expected to reopen in mid-2010.

2701 DeSoto Blvd. (at Toledo St.), Coral Gables. © **305/460-5356.** www.venetianpool.com. Admission Nov–Mar $5 for those 13 and older, $3 for children 12 and under; May–Sept $10 for those 13 and older, $6 for children 12 and under. Children must be at least 3 years old and provide proof of age with birth certificate, or 38 in. tall to enter. Daily hours are at least 11am–4:30pm but are often longer. Call for more information.

The Vizcaya Museum and Gardens ★★★   Sometimes referred to as the "Hearst Castle of the East," this magnificent villa is more Gatsby-esque than anything else you'll find in Miami. It was built in 1916 as a winter retreat for James Deering, cofounder and former vice president of International Harvester. The industrialist was fascinated by 16th-century art and architecture, and his ornate mansion, which took 1,000 artisans 5 years to build, became a celebration of that period. If you love antiques, this place is a dream come true, packed with European relics and works of art from the 16th to the 19th centuries. Most of the original furnishings, including dishes and paintings, are still intact. You will see very early versions of a

A Glimpse into the Past

Coconut Grove's link to the Bahamas dates from before the turn of the 20th century, when islanders came to the area to work in a newly opened hotel called the Peacock Inn. Bahamian-style wooden homes built by these early settlers still stand on Charles Street.

Goombay, the lively annual Bahamian festival, celebrates the Grove's Caribbean link and has become one of the largest black-heritage street festivals in America.

digging MIAMI

Until the controversial discovery of the archaeological site known as the Miami River Circle, the oldest existing artifacts in the city were presumed to have existed in the closets of Miami's retirement homes. In September 1998, during a routine archeological investigation on the mouth of the Miami River, several unusual and unique features were discovered cut into the bedrock: a prehistoric circular structure, 38 feet in diameter, with intentional markings of the cardinal directions as well as a 5-foot-long shark and two stone axes, suggesting the circle had ceremonial significance to Miami's earliest inhabitants—the Tequesta Indians. Radiocarbon tests confirm that the circle is about 2,000 years old.

While some have theorized that the circle is a calendar or Miami's own version of Stonehenge, most scholars believe that the discovery represents the foundation of a circular structure, perhaps a council house or a chief's house. Expert scientists, archeologists, and scholars who have made visits to the site indicate that the circle is of local, regional, and national significance. Local preservationists formed an organization, Save the Miami Circle, to ensure that developers didn't raze the circle to make way for condominiums. As a result, the circle remains put, albeit surrounded by the EPIC and Viceroy/Icon hotels and condos, and the mystery continues. See www.miamicircle.org for more information.

telephone switchboard, central vacuum-cleaning system, elevators, and fire sprinklers. A free guided tour of the 34 furnished rooms on the first floor takes about 45 minutes. The second floor, which consists mostly of bedrooms, is open to tour on your own. The spectacularly opulent villa wraps itself around a central courtyard. Outside, lush formal gardens, accented with statuary, balustrades, and decorative urns, front an enormous swath of Biscayne Bay. Definitely take the tour of the rooms, but immediately thereafter, you will want to wander and get lost in the resplendent gardens.

3251 S. Miami Ave. (just south of Rickenbacker Causeway), North Coconut Grove. © **305/250-9133.** www.vizcayamuseum.com. Admission $15 adults, $10 seniors, $6 children 6–12, free for children 5 and under. Villa daily 9:30am–5pm (ticket booth closes at 4:30pm); gardens daily 9:30am–5:30pm.

NATURE PRESERVES, PARKS & GARDENS

The Miami area is a great place for outdoor types, with beaches, parks, nature preserves, and gardens galore. For information on South Florida's two national parks, the Everglades and Biscayne National Park, see chapter 11.

Although South Beach is more known for its sand than its greenery, **South Pointe Park,** 1 Washington Ave. (© **305/673-7730**), reopened after a $22.4-million renovation that transformed the formerly shabby spot into 17.5 waterfront acres of green space, walkways, playground and observation deck. It is also home to **Smith and Wollensky** (© **305/673-2800**), which is one of the best spots from which to view the departing cruise ships in Government Cut.

The **Amelia Earhart Park,** 401 E. 65th St., Hialeah (© **305/685-8389**), is the only real reason to travel to industrial, traffic-riddled Hialeah. The park has five lakes stocked with bass and bream for fishing, playgrounds, picnic facilities, a skate park, and a big red barn that houses cows, sheep, and goats for petting and ponies for riding. There's also the Bill Graham Farm Village, a re-created Miami–Dade County homestead housing a country store and dozens of old-time farm activities such as horseshoeing, sugar-cane processing, and more. Parking is free on weekdays and $4 per car on weekends. The park is open daily from 9am to sunset, but all the attractions close at about 4pm. To drive here, take I-95 north to the NW 103rd Street exit, go west to East 4th Avenue, and then turn right. Parking is 1½ miles down the street. Depending on traffic, Hialeah is about a half-hour from downtown Miami.

Newly reopened in 2009 is the historic **Hialeah Park ★,** 2200 E. Fourth Ave. (© **305/885-8000;** www.hialeahparkracing.com), primarily known for horse racing but also for its legendary flock of neon-pink flamingos, which still roam the property and are definitely worth a photo op. After decades of decay, the park is back and spruced up for the most part although experts say the restoration of the National Historic Landmark to its former glory will take years and $100 million to complete. Open only for races for now, admission is free.

At the historic **Bill Baggs Cape Florida State Park ★,** 1200 Crandon Blvd. (© **305/361-5811**), at the southern tip of Key Biscayne about 20 minutes from downtown Miami, you can explore the unfettered wilds and enjoy some of the most secluded beaches in Miami. There's also a historic lighthouse that was built in 1825, which is the oldest lighthouse in South Florida. The lighthouse was damaged during the Second Seminole War (1836) and again in 1861 during the Civil War. Out of commission for a while, it was restored to working lighthouse condition in 1978 by the U.S. Coast Guard. A rental shack leases bikes, hydrobikes, kayaks, and many more water toys. It's a great place to picnic, but there are also two restaurants on-site: the Lighthouse Café, which serves homemade Latin food, including great fish soups and sandwiches, and the Boater's Grill offering casual waterfront dining. Just be careful that the raccoons don't get your lunch—the furry black-eyed beasts are everywhere. Wildlife aside, however, Bill Baggs has been consistently rated as one of the top 10 beaches in the U.S. for its 1¼ miles of wide, sandy beaches and its secluded, serene atmosphere. Admission is $8 per car with up to eight people (or $4 for a car with only one person; $2 to enter by foot or bicycle). Open daily from 8am to sunset. Tours of the lighthouse are available every Thursday through Monday at 10am and 1pm. Arrive at least half an hour early to sign up—there is room for only 10 people on each tour. Take I-95 to the Rickenbacker Causeway and take that all the way to the end.

Fairchild Tropical Garden ★★★, at 10901 Old Cutler Rd., in Coral Gables (© **305/667-1651;** www.ftg.org), is the largest of its kind in the continental United States. A veritable rainforest of both rare and exotic plants, as well as 11 lakes and countless meadows, are spread across 83 acres. Palmettos, vine pergola, palm glades, and other unique species create a scenic, lush environment. More than 100 species of birds have been spotted at the garden (ask for a checklist at the front gate), and it's home to a variety of animals. You should not miss the 30-minute narrated tram tour (tours leave on the hour 10am–3pm weekdays and 10am–4pm on weekends) to learn about the various flowers and trees on the grounds. There is also a museum, a cafe, a picnic area, and a gift shop with edible gifts and fantastic books on gardening and cooking. Fairchild often hosts major art exhibits by the likes of Dale Chihuly and Roy Lichtenstein. The 2-acre rainforest exhibit, Windows to the Tropics, will save you a trip to the Amazon. Expect to spend a minimum of 2 hours here.

Admission is $20 for adults, $15 for seniors, $10 for children ages 6 to 17, and free for children 5 and under. Open daily, except Christmas, from 9:30am to 4:30pm. Take I-95 south to U.S. 1, turn left onto Le Jeune Road, and follow it straight to the traffic circle; from there, take Old Cutler Road 2 miles to the park.

On Biscayne Bay in Coconut Grove (4013 Douglas Rd.; www.ntbg.org/gardens/kampong.php), the **Kampong** ★★ is a 7-acre botanical garden with a stunning array of flowering trees and tropical fruit trees, including mango, avocado, and pomelos. In the early 1900s, noted plant explorer David Fairchild traveled the world seeking rare plants of economic and aesthetic value that might be cultivated in the United States. In 1928, Fairchild and his wife, Marian—the daughter of Alexander Graham Bell—decided to build a residence here (now listed on the National Register of Historic Places) surrounded by some of his findings, and named it after the Malaysian word *kampong,* meaning "home in a garden." In the 1960s, the Fairchilds sold the Kampong to Catherine Hauberg Sweeney, who donated it to the National Tropical Botanical Garden to promote and preserve this South Florida treasure. It's a must-see for those interested in horticulture. Admission and tours are by appointment only, from Monday to Friday. For tour and price information, call ℭ **305/442-7169** from 9am to 5pm Monday through Friday. Take U.S. 1 to Douglas Road (SW 37th Ave.). Go east on Douglas Road for about a mile. The Kampong will be on your left.

Named after the late champion of the Everglades, the **Marjory Stoneman Douglas Biscayne Nature Center** ★, 6767 Crandon Blvd., Key Biscayne (ℭ **305/361-6767;** www.biscaynenaturecenter.org), is housed in a $4-million facility and offers hands-on marine exploration, hikes through coastal hammocks, bike trips, and beach walks. Local environmentalists and historians lead intriguing trips through the local habitat. Call to reserve a spot on a regularly scheduled weekend tour or program. Be sure to wear comfortable, closed-toe shoes for hikes through wet or rocky terrain. Open daily 10am to 4pm. Admission to the park is $5 per person; admission to the nature center is free. Special programs and tours cost $10 per person. Call for weekend programs. To get there, take I-95 to the Rickenbacker Causeway exit (no. 1) and take the causeway all the way until it becomes Crandon Boulevard. The center is on the east side of the street (the Atlantic Ocean side) and about 25 minutes from downtown Miami.

Because so many people are focused on the beach itself, the **Miami Beach Botanical Garden,** 2000 Convention Center Dr., Miami Beach (ℭ **305/673-7256**), remains a secret garden. The lush, tropical 4½-acre garden is a fabulous natural retreat from the hustle and bustle of the silicone-enhanced city. Open Tuesday through Sunday from 9am to 5pm; admission is free.

The **Oleta River State Recreation Area** ★★, 3400 NE 163rd St., North Miami (ℭ **305/919-1846**), consists of 993 acres—the largest urban park in the state—on Biscayne Bay. The beauty of the Oleta River, combined with the fact that you're essentially in the middle of a city, makes this park especially worth visiting. With miles of bicycle and canoe trails, a sandy swimming beach, kayak and mountain bike rental shop, Blue Marlin Fish House Restaurant, shaded picnic pavilions, and a fishing pier, Oleta River State Recreation Area allows for an outstanding outdoor recreational experience cloistered from the confines of the big city. There are

14 air-conditioned cabins on the premises that sleep four people. The cost is $55 per night, and guests are required to bring their own linens. Bathrooms and showers are outside, as is a fire circle with a grill for cooking. For reservations, call © **800/326-3521.** It's open daily from 8am to sunset. Admission for pedestrians and cyclists is $2 per person. By car: Driver plus car costs $4; driver plus one to seven passengers and car costs $6. Take 1-95 to exit 17 (S.R. 826 E.) and go all the way east until just before the causeway. The park entrance is on your right. Driving time from downtown Miami is about a half-hour.

A testament to Miami's unusual climate, the **Preston B. Bird and Mary Heinlein Fruit and Spice Park** ★, 24801 SW 187th Ave., Homestead (© **305/247-5727;** www.fruitandspicepark.org), harbors rare fruit trees that cannot survive elsewhere in the country. If a volunteer is available, you'll learn some fascinating things about this 30-acre living plant museum, where the most exotic varieties of fruits and spices—ackee, mango, Ugli fruits, carambola, and breadfruit—grow on strange-looking trees with unpronounceable names. There are also original coral rock buildings dating back to 1912. The Strawberry Folk Festival in February and an art festival here in January are among the park's most popular—and populated—events. The best part? You're free to take anything that has *naturally* fallen to the ground (no picking here). If the ground is bare, don't worry. The Mango Café in the park's historic Bauer-Mitchell-Neill House features indoor and outdoor garden seating and is open for lunch and late afternoon dining and serves "Florida Tropical" cuisine—fruit salads, lots of dishes with mango, smoothies, shakes, and, our fave, Florida lobster roll. You'll also find samples of interesting fruits and jellies made from the park's bounty, as well as exotic ingredients and cookbooks in the gift store.

Admission to the spice park is $8 for adults and $1.50 for children 12 and under. It's open daily from 9am to 5pm; closed on Christmas. Tours are included in the price of admission and are offered at 11am, 1:30pm, and 3pm. Take U.S. 1 south, turn right on SW 248th Street, and go straight for 5 miles to SW 187th Avenue. The drive from Miami should take 45 minutes to an hour.

Tropical Park, 7900 SW 40th St. (© **305/226-8315**), is remotely located out in West Miami, but it has lots to offer, especially if it's during the holiday season when the place is all decked out in millions of holiday lights, with attractions such as Santa's Enchanted Forest. Enjoy a game of tennis or racquetball for a minimal fee, swim and sun yourself on the secluded little lake, rent bikes, or try horseback riding. You can use the fishing pond for free, and they'll even supply you with the rods and bait. If you catch anything, however, you're on your own. Open daily from 7am to 10pm; admission is free. To get there, go west on Bird Road until you reach the overpass for the Palmetto Expressway (826). The park is on the left side immediately after the overpass.

SIGHTSEEING CRUISES & ORGANIZED TOURS
Boat & Cruise-Ship Tours

You don't need a boating license or a zillion-dollar yacht to explore Miami by boat. Thanks to several enterprising companies, boat tours are easy to find, affordable, and an excellent way to see the city from a more liquid perspective.

Celebration Cruising ★ Dinner cruises, sunset sails, and a 2-hour air-conditioned cruise will take you past Millionaires' Row and the Venetian Islands (see "Venice in Miami," above). There's a food stand and cash bar. Tours are bilingual. There are also powerboat tours and various lunch and dinner cruise packages.

Bayside Marketplace Marina, 401 Biscayne Blvd., Downtown. ✆ **305/373-7001.** www.celebration cruising.com. $18–$40, free for children 12 and under. Millionaires' Row tour daily 11am and 1, 3, 5, and 7pm. Evening party cruise (music and cash bar) Fri-Sat 9-11pm.

Heritage Miami II Topsail Schooner This relaxing ride aboard Miami's only tall ship is a fun way to see the city, since it's on a schooner (as opposed to the other tour company's cruising boats), which gives you more of a feel of the water. The 2-hour cruise passes by Villa Vizcaya, Coconut Grove, and Key Biscayne, and puts you in sight of Miami's spectacular skyline and island homes. Call ahead to confirm the ship's schedule.

Bayside Marketplace Marina, 401 Biscayne Blvd., Downtown. ✆ **305/442-9697.** www.heritage schooner.com. Tickets for day tours $23 adults, $15 children 12 and under. Sept-May only. Tours leave Mon-Fri at 1:30, 3:30, and 7:30pm; Sat-Sun at 11:30am, 1:30, 3:30, 5:30, and 7:30pm.

Miami Beach Architecture Cruise ★★★ Fantastic for design fanatics or for those who just want to take a nice little boat ride, this 30-minute cruise through the waterways of Miami Beach takes you past roaring '20s Mediterranean Revival estates, Art Deco and magnificent MiMo landmarks such as the Fontainebleau and Eden Roc hotels, and, finally past some cutting-edge contemporary new architecture housing some of the city's still-available-for-purchase condos. Departs Friday afternoons starting at 5:30pm in the summer and 4pm in winter.

6500 Indian Creek Dr. ✆ **305/865-4147.** Tour $30. Tours depart Fri at 5:30pm in summer (May-Oct) and 4pm in winter (Nov-Apr).

Miami Duck Tours Hands down, this is the corniest, kookiest tour in the entire city. In fact, the company prefers to call these tours the "Quackiest" way to visit Miami and the beaches. Whatever you call it, it's weird. The *Watson Willy* is the first of several Miami Duck Tours "vesicles," not a body part, but a hybrid name that means part vessel, part vehicle (technical name: Hydra Terra Amphibious Vehicle). Each "vesicle" seats 49 guests, plus a captain and tour guide, and leaves from

Venice in Miami

You don't have to endure jet lag and time-zone differences to enjoy the beauty of Italy. Located just off Miami Beach, Florida's own Venetian Islands (NE 15th St. and Dade Blvd.) were joined together in 1926 by a bascule bridge known as the **Venetian Causeway.** A series of 12 bridges connecting the Venetian Islands and stretching between Miami and Miami Beach feature octagonal concrete entrance towers, which give you a great view of the water. The oldest causeway in metropolitan Miami, the Venetian is rickety in a charming way, with fantastic views of the city and the mammoth cruise ships docked at the port, not to mention glimpses of some of Miami's most beautiful waterfront homes. Bikers and joggers especially love the Venetian Causeway, thanks to its limited traffic and beautiful scenery.

vintage MIAMI

Although it's hardly Napa Valley, Miami does have an actual winery: Schnebly Redland's Winery, 30205 SW 217th Ave., Homestead (© **888/717-WINE** [9463]; www.schneblywinery.com), which recently debuted its $1.5-million tasting room in which you can sample from various vintages. I've tried some and while they're too fruity for my taste, it's still worth a trip down just to see the press deck where fruit becomes juice and eventually wine. There's live music and extended hours on Saturday and Sunday, and if you like what you taste, you can buy any four bottles of wine for $65. Open 10am to 5pm Monday to Friday, 10am to 8pm Saturday, and noon to 7pm Sunday.

Watson Island behind Jungle Island, traveling through downtown Miami and South Beach. If you're image conscious, you may want to reconsider traveling down Ocean Drive in a duck. That's right, a duck, which is what the "vesicle" looks like. After driving the streets in the duck, you'll end up cruising Biscayne Bay, past all the swank houses. Embarrassing or downright hilarious, Miami Duck Tours is definitely unique.

1665 Washington Ave., South Beach. © **877/DUCK-TIX** (382-5849). www.ducktoursmiami.com. Tickets $32 adults, $26 seniors and military, $18 children 12 and under.

Tropicalboat Charters   Private boat trips on 22-foot powerboats are a fantastic way to explore the bays and waterways of Miami, if you can afford it. There are also beautiful yachts and catamarans for rent. Tour Biscayne Bay or even go as far as Bimini in the Bahamas. Among the best tours: "Islands of the Rich and Famous," in which you cruise past Star Island, Hibiscus Island, Fisher Island, and Palm Island. Keep your eyes open—Star Island resident Rosie O'Donnell always goes jet-skiing out by these boats. A sunset cruise of Miami is also highly recommended. We hear that Tropicalboat Charters are a popular activity among visiting celebrities who relish their privacy—even on the high seas.

© **786/218-3030.** www.tropicalboat.com. Trips $145–$1,400.

Sightseeing Tours

Miami Nice Excursion Travel and Service ★   Pick your destination and the Miami Nice tours will take you by bus to the Everglades, Fort Lauderdale, South Beach, the Seaquarium, Key West, Cape Canaveral, or wherever else you desire. The best trip for first-timers is the City Tour, a comprehensive tour of the entire city and its various neighborhoods. If you've got the time, you will definitely want to add on a side trip to the Everglades and/or Key West (though I suggest exploring the Everglades on your own). Included in most Miami trips is a fairly comprehensive city tour narrated by a knowledgeable guide. A tour of Miami by helicopter will help you understand why locals have such a lofty opinion of their city. The company is one of the oldest in town.

18801 Collins Ave., Miami Beach. © **305/949-9180.** www.miaminicetours.com. Tours $29–$279 adults, $25–$140 children 3–9. Mon–Sat 7am–10pm. Call ahead for directions to various pickup areas.

Specialized Tours

In addition to tours listed below, a great option for seeing the city is a tour led by **Dr. Paul George.** Dr. George is a history teacher at Miami-Dade Community College and a historian at the Historical Museum of Southern Florida. He also happens to be "Mr. Miami." There's a variety of tours (including the "Mystery, Mayhem and Vice Crime Bus Tour," detailed below), all fascinating to South Florida buffs. Tours focus on such neighborhoods as Little Havana, Brickell Avenue, or Key Biscayne, and on themes such as Miami cemeteries, the Miami River, and Stiltsville, the "neighborhood" of houses on stilts in the middle of Biscayne Bay. There are also eco-history coach, walking, and bike tours. The often-long-winded discussions can be a bit much for those who just want a quick look around, but Dr. George certainly knows his stuff. The cost is $5 to $44, and reservations are required (📞 **305/375-1621;** www.hmsf.org/programs-adult.htm). Tours leave from the Historical Museum at 101 W. Flagler St., downtown. Call for a schedule.

Biltmore Hotel Tour ★★★ 🔥 Take advantage of these free, 55-minute Sunday walking tours to enjoy the hotel's history and beautiful grounds. Starting in the upstairs lobby, the tour will even take you to Everglades Suite, when available, home to dignitaries, heads of state, and a sanctuary for celebrities. Call ahead to confirm.

1200 Anastasia Ave., Coral Gables. 📞 **305/445-1926.** www.biltmorehotel.com. Free admission. Tours depart Sun at 1:30, 2:30, and 3:30pm.

Eco-Adventure Tours ★★★ For the eco-conscious traveler, the Miami-Dade Parks and Recreation Department offers guided nature, adventure, and historic tours involving biking, canoeing, snorkeling, hiking, and bird-watching all over the city. Contact them for more information.

📞 **305/365-3018.** www.miamidade.gov/ecoadventures.

Hispanic Heritage Tour This is offered during October only (Hispanic Heritage Month): For those looking to immerse themselves in Miami's rich Latin American culture, the Herencia Hispana Tour is the ideal way to explore it all. Hop on a bus and zoom past such hotbeds of Latin activity as downtown's Flagler Street, the unavoidable Elián González house, and Little Havana's Domino Park and Tower

---

Now Playing en Espanol

A cultural gem in Little Havana, **The Tower Theatre,** 1508 SW Eighth St. (📞 **305/237-6180**) is one of Miami's oldest cultural landmarks, opening in 1926 as the finest state-of-the-art theater in the south. After the Cuban influx in the 1960s, the theater started showing English-language programming with Spanish subtitles, eventually switching to all Spanish. After years of closings and changing hands, the theater was purchased by the City of Miami and in 1993 added to the National Register as a historic site. After a complete renovation in 1997, the Tower Theatre was back to its Deco-glory and is currently managed by Miami-Dade College, who continues the theater's history with various cultural and arts programming including films and exhibitions of Cuban art by highly regarded artists such as Carlos Navarro among others.

Theatre, among others. Not just a sightseeing tour, this one includes two very knowledgeable, albeit corny, guides who know just when to infuse a necessary dose of humor into the Elián saga, a segment of history that some people may not consider so amusing.

Tours depart from the Steven P. Clark Government Center, 111 NW 1st St. *C* **305/770-3131.** www.miamidade.gov/transit/news_tours.asp. Tours (in Spanish or English, but you must specify which one you require) are free, but advanced reservations are required. Tours depart at 9, 9:30, and 10am every Sat in Oct.

Little Havana Walking Tour ★★★

Dr. Paul George will guide you through Little Havana, pointing out the significance of South Florida bungalow architecture, the Tower Theater, old-fashioned hand rollers at a cigar factory, and more. Visit Cuban Memorial Boulevard and observe the monuments that speak to the exile presence in Miami. See the home of Miami's first mayor. The tour ends with an optional lunch at the iconic Versailles.

C **305/375-1621.** www.hmsf.org. Tour $25.

Miami Design Preservation League ★★

On Thursday evenings and Saturday mornings, the Design Preservation League sponsors walking tours that provide a fascinating inside look at the city's historic Art Deco District. Tourgoers meet for a 1½-hour walk through some of America's most exuberantly "architectured" buildings. The league led the fight to designate this area a National Historic District and is proud to share the splendid locale with visitors. Also see p. 172 for more information.

Art Deco Welcome Center, 1001 Ocean Dr., South Beach. *C* **305/672-2014.** www.mdpl.org. Walking tours $20 per person. Tours leave Wed and Sat at 10:30am and Thurs at 6:30pm. Self-guided audio tours also available daily for $15. No reservations necessary, but arrive 15 min. early. Call ahead for updated schedules.

Mystery, Mayhem and Vice Crime Bus Tour ★★★

Visit the past by video and bus to Miami-Dade's most celebrated crimes and criminals from the 1800s to the present, including some sites where the '80s TV series *Miami Vice* was filmed. From the murder spree of the Ashley Gang to the most notorious murders and crimes of the last century, including the murder of designer Gianni Versace, historian Paul George conducts a most fascinating 3-hour tour of scandalous proportions.

Leaves from the Dade Cultural Center, 101 W. Flagler St., Miami. *C* **305/375-1621.** Tickets $44. Advance reservations required. Held twice a year, usually in Apr and Oct.

Redland Tropical Trail Tours ★★★

Check out South Florida farmlands—yes, they do exist in an area near Homestead called the Redlands—on this tour featuring a circuit of stops, tastings, and sightseeing that will take you from gardens and jungles to an orchid farm, an actual working winery (see above), fruit stand, and more. There's no cost to follow the trail with a map (available on the website) on your own, but call for pricing information for certain attractions found on the trail.

C **305/245-9180.** www.redlandtrail.com.

WATERSPORTS

There are many ways to get well acquainted with Miami's wet look. Choose your own adventure from the suggestions listed below.

Boating

Private rental outfits include **Boat Rental Plus,** 2400 Collins Ave., Miami Beach (☎ **305/534-4307**), where 50-horsepower, 18-foot powerboats rent for some of the best prices on the beach. There's a 2-hour minimum, and rates go from $100 to $500, including taxes and gas. They also have great specials on Sunday. Cruising is permitted only in and around Biscayne Bay (ocean access is prohibited), and renters must be 21 or older to rent a boat. The rental office is at 23rd Street, on the inland waterway in Miami Beach. It's open daily from 10am to sunset. If you want a specific type of boat, call ahead to reserve. Otherwise, show up and take what's available.

    Club Nautico, of Coconut Grove, 2560 S. Bayshore Dr. (☎ **305/858-6258;** www.clubnauticousa.com), rents high-quality powerboats for fishing, water-skiing, diving, and cruising in the bay or ocean. All boats are Coast Guard–equipped, with VHF radios and safety gear. Rates start at $359 for 4 hours and $469 for 8 hours; prices go up as the boats get larger. You can also rent by the hour at $125. Club Nautico is open daily from 8am to 6pm (weather permitting). Other locations include the Crandon Park Marina, 4000 Crandon Blvd., Key Biscayne (☎ **305/361-9217**), with the same rates and hours as the Coconut Grove location; and the Miami Beach Marina, Pier E, 300 Alton Rd., South Beach (☎ **305/673-2502**). Nautico, on Miami Beach, is open daily from 9am to 5pm.

Jet Skis/WaveRunners

Don't miss a chance to tour the islands on the back of your own powerful watercraft. Bravery is, however, a prerequisite, as Miami's waterways are full of speeding jet skiers and boaters who think they're in the Indy 500. Many beachfront concessionaires rent a variety of these popular (and loud) water scooters. The latest models are fast and smooth. **American Watersports,** at the Miami Beach Marina, 300 Alton Rd. (☎ **305/538-7549;** www.jetskiz.com), is the area's most popular spot for jet-ski rental. Rates begin at $60 for a half-hour and $109 for an hour. They also offer fun jet-ski tours past celebrity homes for $119 for the first hour and $60 for the second.

Kayaking

The **Blue Moon Outdoor Center** rents kayaks at 3400 NE 163rd St., in Oleta River Park (☎ **305/957-3040;** www.bluemoonmiami.com). The outfitters here give explorers a map to take with them and quick instructions on how to work the paddles and boats. They also operate very scenic 4-hour guided tours through rivers with

---

A Whole New World

Every Columbus Day, Biscayne Bay becomes a veritable mob scene of boaters celebrating the discovery of another day off of work. The unofficial Columbus Day Regatta has become a tradition in which people take to the water for a day of boating, sunning, and, literally, the bare necessities, as they often strip down to their birthday suits in an eye-opening display of their appreciation for Columbus's discovery of the nude, er, new world.

mangroves and islands—fewer than 10 people on the tour costs $45 per person; more than 10 people costs $35 per person. Their signature tour, a 3-hour kayak and mountain bike tour exploring the park and trails costs $75 for two to four partici- pants, and $65 for five or more. Without the bike tour it's $20 less. These must be booked in advance. There are also separate bike and kayak tours that last 2½ to 3 hours and cost $55 per person. Hourly and half-day rentals are available for single, tandem, and canoe. Prices range from $18 to $45. Guided eco-tours are also avail- able with advance reservation for $45 to $55 per person. A full-moon kayak tour includes a bonfire on the beach. While you are on the paddling route, make sure to stop at the Blue Marlin Fish House for some smoked fish. They also rent mountain bikes. Open daily from 9am to sunset. Special event tours at night are also available.

Sailing

You can rent sailboats and catamarans through the beachfront concessions desks of several top resorts, such as the Doral Golf Resort and Spa (p. 110).

Aquatic Rental Center, at northern Biscayne Bay in the Pelican Harbor Marina, 1275 NE 79th St. (✆ **305/751-7514** days, 279-7424 evenings; www.arcmiami.com), can also get you out on the water. A 22-foot sailboat rents for $85 for 2 hours, $125 for 3 hours, $150 for a half-day, and $225 for a full day. A Sunfish sailboat for two people rents at $35 per hour. If you've always had a dream to win the America's Cup but can't sail, the able teachers here will get you started. They offer a 10-hour course over 5 days for $400 for one person, or $500 for two.

Scuba Diving & Snorkeling

In 1981, the U.S. government began a wide-scale project designed to increase the number of habitats available to marine organisms. One of the program's major accomplishments has been the creation of nearby artificial reefs, which have attracted all kinds of tropical plants, fish, and animals. In addition, Biscayne National Park (see the park's section in chapter 11, beginning on p. 257) offers a protected marine environment just south of downtown.

Several dive shops around the city offer organized weekend outings, either to the reefs or to one of more than a dozen old shipwrecks around Miami's shores. Check "Divers" in the Yellow Pages for rental equipment and for a full list of undersea tour operators.

Diver's Paradise, of Key Biscayne, 4000 Crandon Blvd. (✆ **305/361-3483;** www.keydivers.com), offers one dive expedition per day during the week and two per day on the weekends to the more than 30 wrecks and artificial reefs off the coast of Miami Beach and Key Biscayne. You can take a 3-day certification course for $499, which includes all the dives and gear. If you already have your C-card, a dive trip costs about $100 if you need equipment and $60 if you bring your own gear. It's open Tuesday through Friday from 10am to 6pm and Saturday and Sunday from 8am to 6pm. Call ahead for times and locations of dives. For snorkeling, they will set you up with equipment and maps on where to see the best underwater sights. Rental for mask, fins, and snorkel is $60.

South Beach Divers, 850 Washington Ave., Miami Beach (✆ **305/531-6110;** www.southbeachdivers.com), will also be happy to tell you where to go under the sea and will provide you with scuba rental equipment as well for $65. You can rent snorkel gear for about $20. They also do dive trips to Key Largo three times a week and do dives off Miami on Sunday at $120 for a two-tank dive or $85 if you have your own equipment.

The most amusing and apropos South Beach diving spot has to be the **Jose Cuervo Underwater Bar,** located 150 yards southeast of the Second Street life-guard station—a 22-ton concrete margarita bar that was sunk on May 5, 2000. Nicknamed "Sinko De Mayo," the site is designed with a dive flag roof, six bar stools, and a protective wall of tetrahedrons.

Windsurfing

Many hotels rent windsurfers to their guests, but if yours doesn't have a watersports concession stand, head for Key Biscayne. **Sailboards Miami,** Rickenbacker Causeway, Key Biscayne (© 305/361-SAIL [7245]; www.sailboardsmiami.com), operates out of two big yellow trucks on Windsurfer Beach, the most popular (though our pick for best is Hobie Beach) windsurfing spot in the city. For those who've never ridden a board but want to try it, they offer a 2-hour lesson for $79 that's guaranteed to turn you into a wave warrior, or you get your money back. After that, you can rent a board for $25 to $30 an hour. If you want to make a day of it, a 10-hour prepaid card costs $240 to $290. These cards reduce the price by about $70 for the day. You can use the card year-round, until the time on it runs out. Open Tuesday through Sunday from 10am to 5:30pm. Make your first right after the tollbooth (at the beginning of the causeway—you can't miss it) to find the outfitters. They also rent kayaks.

MORE WAYS TO PLAY, INDOORS & OUT

BIKING   The cement promenade on the southern tip of South Beach is a great place to ride. Biking up the beach (either on the beach or along the beach on a cement pathway—which is a lot easier!) is great for surf, sun, sand, exercise, and people-watching—just be sure to keep your eyes on the road, as the scenery can be most distracting. Most of the big beach hotels rent bicycles, as does the **Miami Beach Bicycle Center,** 601 Fifth St., South Beach (© 305/674-0150; www.bikemiamibeach.com), which charges $8 per hour, $24 for up to 24 hours and $80 weekly. It's open Monday through Saturday from 10am to 7pm, Sunday from 10am to 5pm.

Bikers can also enjoy more than 130 miles of paved paths throughout Miami. The beautiful and quiet streets of Coral Gables and Coconut Grove (several bike trails are spread throughout these neighborhoods) are great for bicyclists, where old trees form canopies over wide, flat roads lined with grand homes and quaint street markers.

The terrain in Key Biscayne is perfect for biking, especially along the park and beach roads. If you don't mind the sound of cars whooshing by your bike lane, **Rickenbacker Causeway** is also fantastic, as it is one of the only bike-able inclines in Miami from which you get fantastic elevated views of the city and waterways. However, be warned that this is a grueling ride, especially going up the causeway. **Key Cycling,** 61 Harbor Dr., Key Biscayne (© 305/361-0061; www.keycycling.com),

A berry GOOD TIME

South Florida's farming region has been steadily shrinking in the face of industrial expansion, but you'll still find several spots where you can get back to nature while indulging in a local gastronomic delight—picking your own produce at the "U-Pic-'Em" farms that dot South Dade's landscape. Depending on what's in season, you can get everything from fresh herbs and vegetables to a mélange of citrus fruits and berries. During berry season—January through April—it's not uncommon to see hardy pickers leaving the groves with hands and faces that are stained a tale-telling crimson and garnished with happy smiles. On your way through South Dade, keep an eye out for the bright red U-Pic signs.

There are also a number of fantastic fruit stands in the region. **Burr's Berry Farms,** 12741 SW 216th St. (© **305/251-0145**), located in the township of Goulds, about an hour from downtown Miami, has created a sensation with its fabulous strawberry milkshakes. To get there, go south on U.S. 1 and turn right on SW 216th St. The fruit stand is about 1 mile west. It's open daily from 9am to 5:30pm.

For fresh fruit in a tasty pastry or tart, head over to **Knaus Berry Farm,** at 15980 SW 248th St. (© **305/247-0668**), in an area known as the Redlands. Some people erroneously call this farm an Amish farm, but in actuality, it's run by a sect of German Baptists. The stand offers items ranging from fresh flowers to homemade ice cream, but be sure to indulge in one of their famous homemade cinnamon buns. Be prepared to wait in a long line to stock up—people flock here from as far away as Palm Beach. Head south on U.S. 1 and turn right on 248th St. The stand is 2½ miles farther on the left side. Open Monday through Saturday from 8am to 5:30pm.

rents mountain bikes for $15 for 2 hours, $24 a day, or $80 a week. It's open Tuesday through Friday from 10am to 7pm, Monday and Saturday from 10am to 6pm, and Sunday from 10am to 3pm.

If you want to avoid the traffic altogether, head out to **Shark Valley** in the Everglades National Park—one of South Florida's most scenic bicycle trails and a favorite haunt of city-weary locals. For more information on Shark Valley and the Everglades, see chapter 11.

For a decent list of trail suggestions throughout South Florida, visit http://www.trails.com/activity.aspx?area=10227. *Biking note:* Children 15 and under are required by Florida law to wear a helmet, which can be purchased at any bike store or retail outlet selling biking supplies.

FISHING Fishing licenses are required in Florida. If you go out with one of the fishing charter boats listed below, you are automatically accredited because the companies are. If you go out on your own, however, you must have a Florida fishing license, which costs $17 for 3 days and $30 for a week. Call © **888/FISH-FLO** (347-4356) or visit www.wildlifelicense.com for more information.

Some of the best surf-casting in the city can be had at **Haulover Beach Park** at Collins Avenue and 105th Street, where there's a bait-and-tackle shop right on the pier. **South Pointe Park,** at the southern tip of Miami Beach, is another popular

A Fisherman's Friend

The Biscayne Bay area is prime tarpon fishing country and a pretty good spot for a lot of other trophy sportfish: snook, bonefish, dolphin fish, swordfish, and sailfish. For a fee, local guides are happy to show you the hot spots and make sure you reel one in. One such guide is **Captain David Parsons** (✆ 305/968-9603; www.fishingmiami florida.com), who owns a great 36-foot boat, *Hakuna Matada*. He knows where the fish are biting and will take you from Biscayne Bay to the Atlantic Ocean in search of the best catch of the day for $700 for four people (swordfish can be caught at nighttime only; those trips are also $700), including rods, gear, and bait. All you bring is food/drink. Captain Parsons also leads trips to Bimini for those who want to explore the fishing in the Bahamas.

fishing spot and features a long pier, comfortable benches, and a great view of the ships passing through Government Cut, the deep channel made when the port of Miami was dug.

You can also do some deep-sea fishing in the Miami area. One bargain outfitter, the **Kelley Fishing Fleet,** at the Haulover Marina, 10800 Collins Ave. (at 108th St.), Miami Beach (✆ **305/945-3801;** www.miamibeachfishing.com), has half-day, full-day, and night fishing aboard diesel-powered "party boats." The fleet's emphasis on drifting is geared toward trolling and bottom fishing for snapper, sailfish, and mackerel. Half-day and night-fishing trips are $40 for adults and $30 for children up to 10 years old, and full-day trips are $60 for adults and $50 for children. Daily departures are scheduled at 9am and 1:45 and 8pm; reservations are recommended.

Also at the Haulover Marina is the charter boat **Helen C** (10800 Collins Ave.; ✆ **305/947-4081;** www.fishmiamibeach.com). Although there's no shortage of private charter boats here, Captain Dawn Mergelsberg is a good pick, because she puts individuals together to get a full boat. The *Helen C* is a twin-engine 55-footer, equipped for big-game fish such as marlin, tuna, mahimahi, shark, and sailfish. The cost is $160 per person. Private, full-day trips are available for groups of six people per vessel and cost $1,350; half-days are $750. Group rates and specials are also available. Trips are scheduled for 8am to noon and 1 to 5pm daily; call for reservations. Beginners and children are always welcomed.

For a serious fishing charter, Captain Charlie Hotchkiss's **Sea Dancer** (✆ **305/775-5534;** www.seadancercharter.com) offers a first-class experience on a 38-foot Luhrs boat complete with tuna tower and air-conditioned cabin. If you're all about big game—marlin, dolphin, tuna, wahoo, swordfish, and sailfish—this is the charter for you. Catch and release or fillet your catch to take home. The *Sea Dancer* also offers two fun water adventures, including a 6-hour Bar Cruz, covering the finest watering holes in Miami and Fort Lauderdale, or a Sandbar Cruz, where the boat drops anchor out by Biscayne Bay's historic Stiltsville where you'll swim, bounce on a water trampoline, and play sports—all in the middle of the bay. Auto transportation is available to wherever the boat may be docked. Rates are $700 for a half-day and $1,100 for a full day and $500 for the specialty tours. Tours are also available to Bimini. Call for pricing.

Key Biscayne offers deep-sea fishing to those willing to get their hands dirty and pay a bundle. The competition among the boats is fierce, but the prices are basically the same, no matter which you choose. The going rate is about $400 to $500 for a half-day and $600 to $900 for a full day of fishing. These rates are usually for a party of up to six, and the boats supply you with rods and bait as well as instruction for first-timers. Some will also take you out to the Upper Keys if the fish aren't biting in Miami.

You might also consider the following boats, all of which sail out of the Key Biscayne marina and are in relatively good shape and nicer than most out there: **Sonny Boy** (© 305/361-2217; www.sonnyboysportfishing.com), **Top Hatt** (© 305/361-2528), and **L & H** (© 305/361-9318; www.landhsportfishing.com). Call for reservations.

Bridge fishing in Biscayne Bay is also popular in Miami; you'll see people with poles over almost every waterway. But look carefully for signs telling you whether it's legal to do so wherever you are: Some bridges forbid fishing.

GAMBLING Although gambling is technically illegal in Miami, there are plenty of loopholes that allow all kinds of wagering. Gamblers can try their luck at offshore casinos or on shore at bingo, jai alai, card rooms, horse tracks, dog races, and Native American reservations. The newly reopened **Hialeah Park Racing** (www.hialeah parkracing.com) has thoroughbred and quarter horse racing and sometime in the near future, because no racetrack in Florida is complete without it, poker and slot machines. For slots and poker, you can check out the **Magic City Casino,** five minutes from the airport and downtown Miami at 450 NW 37th Ave (© 888/56-MAGIC [566-2442]; www.magiccitycasino.com), but we recommend you stick with the brand new casino at **Calder Casino & Race Course,** located by Sun Life Stadium at 21001 NW 27th Ave. in Miami Gardens (© 305/625-1311; www.calderracecourse.com), featuring 1,200 slot machines, poker, and horse racing. You can also drive up to Broward County, where the **Seminole Hard Rock Hotel and Casino** (www.seminolehardrock.com), **Seminole Casino Coconut Creek** (www.seminolecoconutcreekcasino.com), **Mardi Gras Racetrack and Gaming** (www.playmardigras.com), **Isle Casino & Racing** (www.pompano-park.isleofcapri casinos.com), and the new and still expanding **Gulfstream Park Casino and Racing** (www.gulfstreampark.com) in Hallandale offer slots, poker, and in the cases of Hard Rock and Gulfstream, blackjack too.

Despite the Hard Rock in Hollywood's behemoth presence on the gambling circuit (and its many imitators), some people prefer the less flashy **Miccosukee Indian Gaming,** 500 SW 177th Ave. (off S.R. 41, in West Miami, on the outskirts of the Everglades; © 800/741-4600 or 305/222-4600), where a touch of Vegas meets west Miami. This tacky casino isn't Caesar's Palace, but you can play tab slots, high-speed bingo (watch out for the serious blue-haired players who will scoff if you make too much noise or if you win before they do), and even poker (with more tables added now that they're competing with Seminole Hard Rock; see above). With more than 85,000 square feet of playing space, the complex even provides overnight accommodations for those who can't get enough of the thrill and don't want to make the approximately 1-hour trip back to downtown Miami. Take the Florida Turnpike south toward Florida City/Key West. Take the SW Eighth Street exit (no. 25) and turn left onto SW Eighth Street. Drive for about 3½ miles and then turn left onto Krome Avenue, and left again at 177th Street; you can't miss it.

GOLF There are more than 50 private and public golf courses in the Miami area. Contact the **Greater Miami Convention and Visitor's Bureau** (© 800/933-8448; www.miamiandbeaches.com) for a list of courses and costs.

The best hotel courses in Miami are found at the **Doral Golf Resort and Spa** (p. 110), home of the legendary Blue Monster course, as well as the Gold Course, designed by Raymond Floyd; the Great White Shark Course; and the newest course, the former Silver Course, refinished by Jim McLean and known as the Jim McLean Signature course which, according to experts, has one of the toughest starting holes in the entire state.

Other hotels with excellent golf courses include the **Fairmont Turnberry Isle Resort & Club** (p. 111), with two Robert Trent Jones, Sr.–designed courses for guests and members, and the **Biltmore Hotel** ★★ (p. 106), which is my pick for best public golf course because of its modest greens fees and an 18-hole par-71 course located on the hotel's spectacular grounds. It must be good: Despite his penchant for privacy, former President Bill Clinton prefers teeing off at this course more than any other in Miami!

Otherwise, the following represent some of the area's best public courses. **Crandon Park Golf Course,** formerly known as the Links, 6700 Crandon Blvd., Key Biscayne (© 305/361-9129; www.crandongolfclub.com), is the number-one-ranked municipal course in the state and one of the top five in the country. The park is situated on 200 bayfront acres and offers a pro shop, rentals, lessons, carts, and a lighted driving range. The course is open daily from dawn to dusk; greens fees (including cart) range from $64–$160 depending on season for nonresidents. Special twilight rates are also available.

One of the most popular courses among real enthusiasts is the **Doral Park Golf and Country Club,** 5001 NW 104th Ave., West Miami (© 305/591-8800); it's not related to the Doral Hotel or spa. Call to book in advance, as this challenging, semiprivate 18-holer is extremely popular with locals. The course is open from 6:30am to 6pm during the winter and until 7pm during the summer. Cart and greens fees vary, so call © 305/592-2000, ext. 2104, for information.

Known as one of the best in the city, the **Country Club of Miami,** 6801 Miami Gardens Dr., at NW 68th Avenue, North Miami (© 305/829-8456; www.golfmiamicc.com), has three 18-hole courses of varying degrees of difficulty. You'll encounter lush fairways, rolling greens, and some history, to boot. The west course, designed in 1961 by Robert Trent Jones, Sr., and updated in the 1990s by the PGA, was where Jack Nicklaus played his first professional tournament and Lee Trevino won his first professional championship. The course is open daily from 7am to sunset. Cart and greens fees are $29 to $56 depending on season and tee times. Special twilight rates are available.

The recently renovated **Miami Beach Golf Club,** 2301 Alton Rd., South Beach (© 305/532-3350; www.miamibeachgolfclub.com), is a gorgeous, 79-year-old course that, par for the, er, course in Miami Beach, received a $10-million face-lift. Miami Heat players and Matt Damon have been known to tee off here. Greens fees range from $100 to $200 depending on the season.

Golfers looking for some cheap practice time will appreciate **Haulover Beach Park,** 10800 Collins Ave., Miami Beach (© 305/940-6719), in a pretty bayside location. The longest hole on this par-27 course is 125 yards. It's open daily from

7:30am to 6pm during the winter, and until 7:30pm during the summer. Greens fees range from $6 to $10 per person depending on day and season.

IN-LINE SKATING   Miami's consistently flat terrain makes in-line skating a breeze. Lincoln Road, for example, is a virtual skating rink, as bladers compete with bikers and walkers for a slab of slate. But the city's heavy traffic and construction do make it tough to find long routes suitable for blading.

Because of the popularity of blading and skateboarding, the city passed a law prohibiting skating on the west side (the cafe-lined strip) of Ocean Drive in the evenings, as well as a law that all bladers must skate slowly and safely. Also, if you're going to partake of the sport, remember to keep a pair of sandals or sneakers with you, as many area shops won't allow you inside with skates on.

Despite all the rules, you can still have fun, and the following rental outfit can help chart an interesting course for you and supply you with all the necessary gear. In South Beach, **Fritz's Skate Shop,** 1620 Washington Ave. (© **305/532-1954;** www.fritzsmiamibeach.com), rents top-quality skates, including safety pads, for $10 per hour, $24 per day, and $69 per week. They provide free lessons at 10:30am on Sunday when you rent equipment, or they can hook you up with an instructor for private lessons. The shop also stocks lots of gear and clothing and rents surfboards and assorted surf-related items as well.

SWIMMING   There is no shortage of water in the Miami area. See the Venetian Pool listing (p. 185) and the "Miami's Beaches" section on p. 169 for descriptions of good swimming options.

TENNIS   Hundreds of tennis courts in South Florida are open to the public for a minimal fee. Most courts operate on a first-come, first-served basis and are open from sunrise to sunset. For information and directions, call the **City of Miami Beach Recreation, Culture, and Parks Department** (© 305/673-7730) or the **City of Miami Parks and Recreation Department** (© 305/575-5256). Of the 590 public tennis courts throughout Miami, the three hard courts and seven clay courts at the **Crandon Tennis Center,** 6702 Crandon Blvd. (© **305/361-5263**), are the best and most beautiful. Because of this, they often get crowded on weekends. You'll play on the same courts as Lendl, Graf, Evert, McEnroe, Federer, the Williams sisters, and other greats; this is also the venue for one of the world's biggest annual tennis events, the Sony Ericsson Open. There's a pleasant, if limited, pro shop, plus many good pros. Only four courts are lit at night, but if you reserve at least 24 to 48 hours in advance, you can usually take your pick. Hard courts cost $4 person per hour during the day, $6 per person per hour at night. Clay courts cost $7 per person per hour during the day. There are no night hours on the clay courts. The courts are open Monday through Friday from 8am to 9pm, Saturday and Sunday until 6pm.

Other courts are pretty run-of-the-mill and can be found in most neighborhoods. I do, however, recommend the **Miami Beach public courts at Flamingo Park,** 1001 12th St., in South Beach (© **305/673-7761**), where there are 19 clay courts that cost $4 per person an hour for Miami Beach residents and $8 per person an hour for nonresidents. It's first-come, first-served. Open 8am to 9pm Monday through Friday, 8am to 8pm Saturday and Sunday.

Hotels with the best tennis facilities are the Biltmore, Fairmont Turnberry Isle Resort and Spa, Doral Resort and Spa, and Inn and Spa at Fisher Island.

Health Clubs

Being situated in a very body-conscious city, many of Miami's hotels have state-of-the-art gyms. **Sports Club/LA** at the Four Seasons, among others. Guests of hotels with health clubs can usually use the equipment for free. Although many of Miami's full-service hotels have fitness centers and may be convenient, you can't always count on them in less-upscale establishments or in the small Art Deco District hotels. Instead, you may want to turn to the several health clubs around the city that will take in nonmembers on a daily basis. For **Bally's Total Fitness,** dial ℭ **800/777-1117** to find the clubs closest to where you'll be staying. (There are no outlets on the beaches; most are in South Miami.) A popular club that welcomes walk-in guests is **Crunch,** which has two locations: 1253 Washington Ave., South Beach (ℭ **305/674-8222**) and 1676 Alton Road (ℭ **305/531-4783**), where you might work out on the top-of-the-line equipment next to one of the city's most famous drag queens or, perhaps, a celebrity or two. Use of the facility is $35 daily or $130 weekly. It keeps late hours, especially in season, when it's often open until midnight. The newest member of the fitness club in Miami is **Equinox Fitness Club & Spa,** which has two locations, one at 520 Collins Ave. (ℭ **305/673-1172;** www.equinoxfitness.com), a huge space complete with every piece of fitness equipment you can imagine or haven't yet imagined and a stellar A-list celebrity clientele including Matt Damon, who trains here for his movies; and the other in the Village of Merrick Park in Coral Gables, 358 San Lorenzo Ave. (ℭ **786/497-8200**) where Yankee slugger Alex Rodriguez pumps iron. Fees vary for out-of-town guests so call and inquire.

on location IN MIAMI

With its warm weather, picturesque skylines, and gorgeous sunsets, Miami is the perfect setting for making movies.

Since the earliest days of the film industry, Miami has had a starring role in some of America's most celebrated celluloid classics, from the Marx Brothers' first feature, *The Cocoanuts* (1929), to the 1941 classic, *Citizen Kane,* which used the spectacular South Florida coastline as the setting for Kane's own Hearst Castle, Xanadu. As the film industry evolved and productions became more elaborate, Miami was thrice seized by a suave international man of intrigue known as Bond, James Bond, in *Dr. No, Live and Let Die,* and *Goldfinger.* In the past 5 years, there were over 60 major motion pictures filmed in Miami–Dade County, from action flicks like the hideous *Miami Vice* remake, *True Lies, Bad Boys II* and *Transporter II,* and *Any Given Sunday* to comedies such as *There's Something About Mary* and dramas such as *Random Hearts, Marley & Me,* and *Up in the Air.*

At any given time of day—or night—actors, directors, and film crews can be spotted on the sands and streets of Miami working on what may be the next blockbuster to hit the big screen. Watching a film being shot is fun, free entertainment. Unfortunately, filming schedules are not publicized, so keep an eye out for CREW signs posted throughout the city and check with hotel personnel, who are usually up-to-date on who's in town shooting what. Who knows? You could be discovered!

ANIMAL PARKS

For a tropical climate, Miami's got a lot of nontropical animals to see, and we're not talking about the motorists on I-95. Everything from dolphins and alligators to lions, tigers, and bears call Miami home (most in parks, some in nature). Call the parks to inquire about discount packages or coupons, which may be offered at area retail stores or in local papers.

Jungle Island ★ ☺ Not exactly an island and not quite a jungle, Jungle Island is an excellent diversion for the kids and for animal lovers. While the island doubles as a protected bird sanctuary, the very pricey 19-acre park features an Everglades exhibit, a petting zoo, and several theaters, jungle trails, and aviaries. Watch your heads because flying above are hundreds of parrots, macaws, peacocks, cockatoos, and flamingos. Continuous shows star bicycle-riding cockatoos, high-flying macaws, and numerous stunt-happy parrots. One of the most entertaining shows is *Tale of the Tiger*, featuring awesome animals. Jungle Island also features the only African penguins in South Florida as well as a liger—part lion, part tiger—and endangered baby lemurs. There are also tortoises, iguanas, and a rare albino alligator on exhibit. The park's website sometimes offers downloadable discount coupons, so take a look before you visit because you definitely won't want to pay full price for this park, which has nerve to charge for parking. If you do get your money's worth and see all the shows and exhibits, expect to spend upward of 4 hours here. **Note:** The former South Miami site of (Parrot) Jungle Island is now known as **Pinecrest Gardens,** 11000 Red Rd. (✆ **305/669-6942**), which features a petting zoo, mini water park, lake, natural hammocks, and banyan caves. Open daily from 8am until sunset; admission is free.

1111 Parrot Jungle Trail, Watson Island (on the north side of MacArthur Causeway/I-395). ✆ **305/372-3822.** www.jungleisland.com. Admission $30 adults, $28 seniors, $24 children 3–10, free for military personnel with valid ID. Parking $7 per vehicle. Mon–Fri 10am–5pm; Sat–Sun 10am–6pm. From I-95, take I-395 E. (MacArthur Causeway); make a right on Parrot Jungle Trail, which is the 1st exit after the bridge. Follow the road around and under the causeway to the parking garage on the left side.

Miami Metrozoo ★★ ☺ This 290-acre complex is quite a distance from Miami proper and the beaches—about 45 minutes—but worth the trip. Isolated and never really crowded, it's also completely cageless—animals are kept at bay by cleverly designed moats. This is a fantastic spot to take younger kids; there are wonderful play areas, safari cycles for rent, and the zoo offers several daily programs designed to educate and entertain like The Wildlife Show and Diego's Discovery Den Show. Mufasa and Simba (of Disney fame) were modeled on a couple of Metrozoo's lions. Other residents include one rare white Bengal tiger, Komodo dragons, koalas, kangaroos, and African meerkats. The air-conditioned monorail and tram tours offer visitors a nice overview of the park. The zoo is always upgrading its facilities, including the impressive aviary, Wings of Asia. Cool activities include the Samburu Giraffe Feeding Station, where, for $2, you get to feed the giraffes veggies, and Humpy's Camel Rides where you can hop on a camel for $5. Opened in December 2008, Amazon & Beyond features jaguars, anacondas, giant river otters, harpy eagles, a stingray touch tank, two interactive water features, the Flooded Forest building with a unique display of a forest before and during flood times, and an indoor Cloud Forest building that houses reptiles. At 27 acres and a cost of $50 million, the exhibit

A Japanese Garden

If you ask someone what Japanese influences can be found in Miami, they'll likely point to Nobu, Sushi Siam, Sushi Rock Café, and even Benihana. But back in the '50s, well before sushi became trendy, Kiyoshi Ichimura became obsessed with Miami and started sending people and objects from Tokyo, including carpenters, gardeners, and a landscape architect, to design and construct the San-Ai-An

Japanese Garden. Originally located in the Jungle Island space, the garden was dismantled during construction and re-created adjacent to the park. The completed 1-acre garden was renamed Ichimura Miami Japan Garden in honor of its original benefactor, and its sculptures and Japanese artifacts are managed by a coalition of city organizations. Japanese holidays and festivals are celebrated here.

is massive and makes Metrozoo the third zoo in the country to have giant river otters, one of its keystone species. Private tours and overnights are also available for those who really want to commune with nature. *Note:* The distance between animal habitats can be great, so you'll do *a lot* of walking here. There are benches, shaded gazebos, cool misters, a water-shooting mushroom and two water-play areas strategically positioned throughout the zoo so you can escape the heat when you need to. Also, because the zoo can be miserably hot during summer months, plan these visits in the early morning or late afternoon. Expect to spend all day here if you want to see it all.

12400 SW 152nd St., Miami. © **305/251-0400.** www.miamimetrozoo.com. Admission $16 adults, $12 children 3–12. Free parking. Daily 9:30am–5:30pm (ticket booth closes at 4pm). From U.S. 1 south, turn right on SW 52nd St., and follow signs about 3 miles to the entrance. From Florida Tpk. South, take exit 16 west to the entrance.

Miami Seaquarium ★ ☺ ✋ If you've been to Orlando's SeaWorld, you may be disappointed with Miami's version, which is considerably smaller and not as well maintained. It's hardly a sprawling Seaquarium, but you will want to arrive early to enjoy the effects of its mild splash. You'll need at least 3 hours to tour the 35-acre oceanarium and see all four daily shows, starring a number of showy ocean mammals. You can cut your visit to 2 hours if you limit your shows to the better, albeit corny, Flipper Show and Killer Whale Show. The highly regarded Dolphin Encounter allows visitors to touch and swim with dolphins in the Flipper Lagoon. The program costs $139 per person participating, $45 per adult observer, $36 per child observer ages 3 to 9, and is offered daily at 12:15 and 3:15pm. Children must be at least 52 inches tall to participate. Reservations are necessary for this program. Call © 305/365-2501 in advance for reservations. The Seaquarium also debuted a new sea lion show.

4400 Rickenbacker Causeway (south side), en route to Key Biscayne. © **305/361-5705.** www.miami seaquarium.com. Admission $36 adults, $27 children 3–9, free for children 2 and under. Parking $8. Daily 9am–6pm (ticket booth closes at 4pm).

Monkey Jungle ★ Personally, I think this place is nasty. It reeks, the monkeys are either sleeping or in heat, and it's really far from the city, even farther than the zoo. But if primates are your thing and you'd rather pass on the zoo, you'll be in paradise.

You'll see rare Brazilian golden lion tamarins and Asian macaques. There are no cages to restrain the antics of the monkeys as they swing, chatter, and play their way into your heart. Screened-in trails wind through acres of "jungle," and daily shows feature the talents of the park's most progressive pupils. People who come here are not monkeying around—many of the park's frequent visitors are scientists and anthropologists. In fact, an interesting archaeological exhibition excavated from a Monkey Jungle sinkhole displays 10,000-year-old artifacts, including human teeth and animal bones. A somewhat amusing attraction here, if you can call it that, is the Wild Monkey Swimming Pool, a show in which you get to watch monkeys diving for food. If you can stand the humidity, the smell, and the bugs (flies, mosquitoes, and so on), expect to spend about 2 hours here. The park's website sometimes offers downloadable discount coupons, so if you have Internet access, take a look before you visit.

14805 SW 216th St., South Miami. ℂ **305/235-1611.** www.monkeyjungle.com. Admission $30 adults, $28 seniors and active-duty military, $24 children 4–12. Daily 9:30am–5pm (tickets sold until 4pm). Take U.S. 1 south to SW 216th St., or from Florida Tpk., take exit 11 and follow the signs.

Sea Grass Adventures ★ 🐟 ☺ Even better than the Seaquarium is Sea Grass Adventures, in which a naturalist from the Marjory Stoneman Douglas Biscayne Nature Center introduces ($10 per person) kids and adults to an amazing variety of creatures that live in the sea grass beds of the Bear Cut Nature Preserve near Crandon Beach on Key Biscayne. You will be able to wade in the water with your guide and catch an assortment of sea life in nets provided by the guides. At the end of the program, participants gather on the beach while the guide explains what everyone has just caught, passing the creatures around in miniature viewing tanks. Call for available dates, times, and reservations.

Marjory Stoneman Douglas Biscayne Nature Center, 6767 Crandon Blvd., Key Biscayne. ℂ **305/361-6767.** Free admission to the center. Daily 10am–4pm.

VIDEO ARCADES & ENTERTAINMENT CENTERS

GameWorks ☺ At Steven Spielberg's GameWorks in the Shops at Sunset Place, you'll see people fighting off dinosaurs from *Jurassic Park,* racing in the Indy 500, swooshing down a snowy ski trail, throwing darts, and shooting pool in this multilevel playground. The young and the young at heart will find a good combination of vintage arcade games, high-tech videos, virtual-reality arenas, pool tables, food, and cocktails in this playground occupying more than 33,000 square feet. Bring lots—and we mean lots—of change.

5701 Sunset Dr., South Miami. ℂ **305/667-4263.** www.gameworks.com. Sun–Mon 11am–11pm; Tues–Thurs noon–11pm; Fri–Sat 11am–2am.

Lucky Strike Lanes ☺ South Beach's only bowling alley is a pricey blast for adults and children, with 14 lanes, 2 pool tables, free Wi-Fi (to cheat on bowling?), a pulsating nightclub-esque soundtrack, full bar, TVs, and restaurant. Kids are only allowed up until 9pm, after which time Lucky Strike turns into a 21 and over scene.

1691 Michigan Ave. ℂ **305/532-0307.** www.bowlluckystrike.com. Mon–Thurs 11:30am–1am; Fri 11:30am–2am; Sat 11am–2am; Sun 11am–1am. $45–$55 per hour depending on day and time including shoe rental.

Splitsville Luxury Lanes & Dinner Lounge ☺ Located at Sunset Place, Splitsville is South Miami's Lucky Strike, with 12 lanes, six pool tables, full-service restaurant, TVs, and multiple bars. Like Lucky Strike, no kids or under 21 after 8pm, when the place turns into a thumping club scene until 5am. Unlike Lucky Strike, Splitsville is affordable and because of that, there's usually a wait list for a lane. Luckily there are plenty other distractions to keep you busy while you wait.

5701 Sunset Dr. ℂ **305/665-5263.** www.splitsvillelanes.com. Mon–Thurs 4pm–2am; Fri–Sat 11am–5am; Sun 11am–2am. $6 per person per game, $4 for shoe rental.

Strike Miami ☺ Located at the Dolphin Mall, this one is Miami's biggest bowling alley, with 34 lanes and, like the others, a nightclub setting. This one, owned by NYC's famed Bowlmor, even has glow-in-the-dark bowling. Food, bars, TVs, you get the picture. It's 18 and over after 9pm.

In the Dolphin Mall, 11401 NW 12th St. ℂ **305/594-0200.** www.bowlmor.com. Mon–Thurs 4pm–1am; Fri noon–3am; Sat 11am–3am; Sun 11am–1am. $30–$40 per hour depending on day and time including shoe rental.

Video Arcades & Entertainment Centers

WHAT TO SEE & DO IN MIAMI

MIAMI SHOPPING

M iami is one of the world's premier shopping cities; more than 12 million visitors come every year and typically spend, well, billions. People come to Miami from all over—from Latin America to Hong Kong—in search of some products that are all-American (in other words, Levi's, Nike, and such).

9

So if you're not into sunbathing and outdoor activities, or you just can't take the heat, you'll be in good company in one of Miami's many malls—and you are not likely to emerge empty-handed. In addition to the strip malls, Miami offers a choice of megamalls, from the upscale Village of Merrick Park and the mammoth Aventura Mall to the ritzy Bal Harbour Shops and touristy, yet scenic, Bayside Marketplace (just to name a few).

Miami also offers more unique shopping spots, such as the up-and-coming area near downtown known as the Biscayne Corridor, where funky boutiques dare to defy the Gap, and Little Havana, where you can buy hand-rolled cigars and *guayabera* shirts (loose-fitting cotton or gauzy shirts).

You may want to order the Greater Miami Convention and Visitors Bureau's "Shop Miami: A Guide to a Tropical Shopping Adventure." Although it is limited to details on the bureau's paying members, it provides some good advice and otherwise unpublished discount offers. The glossy little pamphlet is printed in English, Spanish, and Portuguese and provides information about transportation from hotels, translation services, and shipping. Call © **888/76-MIAMI** (766-4264) or 305/447-7777 for more information.

THE SHOPPING SCENE

Below you'll find descriptions of some of the more popular retail areas, where many stores are conveniently clustered together to make browsing easier.

As a general rule, shop hours are Monday through Saturday from 10am to 6pm, and Sunday from noon to 5pm. Many stores stay open late (until 9pm or so) 1 night of the week, usually Thursday. Shops in Coconut Grove are open until 9pm Sunday through Thursday, and even later on Friday and Saturday. South Beach's stores also stay open later—as late as midnight. Department stores and shopping malls keep longer hours as well, with most staying open from 10am to 9 or 10pm Monday through Saturday, noon to 6pm on Sunday. With all these variations, you may want to call specific stores to find out their hours.

The 7% state and local sales tax is added to the price of all nonfood purchases. In Surfside, hotel taxes total 11%; in Bal Harbour, 11%; in Miami Beach (including South Beach), 13%; and in the rest of Dade County, a whopping 13%. Food and beverage tax in Miami Beach, Bal Harbour, and Surfside is 9%; in Miami-Dade restaurants not located inside hotels it's 8%; and in restaurants located in hotels, 9%.

Most Miami stores can wrap your purchase and ship it anywhere in the world via United Parcel Service (UPS). If they can't, you can send it yourself, either through FedEx (𝒞 **800/463-3339**), UPS (𝒞 **800/742-5877**), or through the U.S. Mail (see "Fast Facts: South Florida" on p. 387).

Shopping Areas

Most of Miami's shopping happens at the many megamalls scattered from one end of the county to the other; however, there is also some excellent boutique shopping and browsing to be done in the following areas (see "The Neighborhoods in Brief" on p. 59 for more information):

AVENTURA   On Biscayne Boulevard between Miami Gardens Drive and the county line at Hallandale Beach Boulevard is a 2-mile stretch of major retail stores including Target, Best Buy, Borders, DSW, Bed Bath & Beyond, Loehmann's, Marshall's, Ross Dress For Less, Filene's Basement, Old Navy, Sports Authority, and more. Also here is the mammoth Aventura Mall, housing a fabulous collection of shops and restaurants. Nearby in Hallandale Beach you'll find The Village at Gulfstream Park, a new outdoor dining, shopping, and entertainment complex at the ever-expanding racetrack.

BISCAYNE CORRIDOR ★   Amid the ramshackle old motels of yesteryear exist several funky, kitschy, and arty boutiques along the stretch of Biscayne Boulevard from 50th Street to about 79th Street known as the Biscayne Corridor. Everything from hand-painted tank tops to expensive Juicy Couture sweat suits can be found here, but it's not just about fashion: Several furniture stores selling antiques and modern pieces exist along here as well, so look carefully, as you may find something here that would cause the appraisers on *Antiques Road Show* to lose their wigs.

> ### Impressions
>
> *Someday . . . Miami will become the great center of South American trade.*
> —Julia Tuttle, Miami's founder, 1896

For more mainstream creature comforts—Target, PetSmart, Loehmann's, Marshall's, and West Elm—a new complex called The Shops at Midtown Miami has opened on a gritty, yet, developing street at North Miami Avenue and NE 36th Street.

CALLE OCHO   For a taste of Little Havana, take a walk down 8th Street between SW 27th Avenue and SW 12th Avenue, where you'll find some lively streetlife and many shops selling cigars, baked goods, shoes, furniture, and record stores specializing in Latin music. For help, take your Spanish dictionary.

COCONUT GROVE   Downtown Coconut Grove, centered on Main Highway and Grand Avenue, and branching onto the adjoining streets, is one of Miami's most pedestrian-friendly zones. The Grove's wide sidewalks, lined with cafes and boutiques, can provide hours of browsing pleasure. Coconut Grove is best known for its chain stores (Gap, Victoria's Secret, Bath & Body Works, and so on) and some funky holdovers from the days when the Grove was a bit more bohemian, plus some good sidewalk cafes and lively bars.

DESIGN DISTRICT   Although it's still primarily an interior design, art, and furniture hub, Design District is slowly adding retail to its roster with a few funky and fabulous boutiques catering to those who don't necessarily have to ask "how much?"

DOWNTOWN MIAMI   If you're looking for discounts on all types of goods—especially watches, fabric, buttons, lace, shoes, luggage, and leather—Flagler Street, just west of Biscayne Boulevard, is the best place to start. I wouldn't necessarily recommend buying expensive items here, as many stores seem to be on the shady side and do not understand the word *warranty.* However, you can still have fun here as long as you are a savvy shopper and don't mind haggling. Most signs are printed in English, Spanish, and Portuguese, however, many shopkeepers may not be entirely fluent in English. Mary Brickell Village, a 192,000-square-foot urban entertainment center west of Brickell Avenue and straddling South Miami Avenue between 9th and 10th streets downtown, hasn't been so quick to emerge as a major shopping destination as much as it is a dining and nightlife one with a slew of trendy restaurants, bars, a few boutiques, and the requisite Starbucks—a sure sign that a neighborhood has been revitalized.

MIRACLE MILE (CORAL GABLES)   Actually only a half-mile long, this central shopping street was an integral part of George Merrick's original city plan. Today the strip still enjoys popularity, especially for its bridal stores, ladies' shops, haberdashers, and gift shops. Recently, newer chain stores, such as Barnes & Noble, Old Navy, and Starbucks, have been appearing on the Mile. The hyperupscale **Village of Merrick Park,** a mammoth, 850,000-square-foot outdoor shopping complex between Ponce de León Boulevard and Le Jeune Road, just off the Mile, houses Nordstrom, Neiman Marcus, Armani, Gucci, Jimmy Choo, and Yves St. Laurent, to name a few.

SOUTH BEACH ★   South Beach has come into its own as far as trendy shopping is concerned. While the requisite stores such as the Gap and Banana Republic have anchored here, several higher-end stores have also opened on the southern blocks of Collins Avenue, which has become the Madison Avenue of Miami. For the hippest clothing boutiques (including Armani Exchange, Ralph Lauren, Intermix, Benetton, Levi's, Barneys Co-Op, Diesel, Guess, Club Monaco, Kenneth Cole, and Nicole Miller, among others), stroll along this pretty strip of the Art Deco District.

For those who are interested in a little more fun with their shopping, consider South Beach's legendary Lincoln Road. This pedestrian mall, originally designed in 1957 by Morris Lapidus, has expanded with a multimillion-dollar renovation, transforming a formerly shabby bank building into yet another block of swank shopportunities and dining (coming soon: a branch of NYC's hailed burger joint, Shake Shack, a Nespresso store, Taschen book store, and more) adding to the menagerie of sidewalk cafes flanked on one end by a multiplex movie theater and, at the other, by the Atlantic Ocean.

SHOPPING A TO Z
Antiques & Collectibles

Miami's antiques shops are scattered in small pockets around the city. Many that feature lower-priced furniture can be found in North Miami, in the 1600 block of NE 123rd Street, near West Dixie Highway. About a dozen shops sell china, silver, glass, furniture, and paintings. But you'll find the bulk of the better antiques in Coral Gables and in Southwest Miami along Bird Road between 64th and 66th avenues and between 72nd and 74th avenues. For international collections from Bali to France, check out the burgeoning scene in the Design District centered on NE 40th Street west of 1st Avenue. Miami also hosts several large antiques shows each year. In October and November, the most prestigious one—the **Original Miami Beach Antique Show**—hits the Miami Beach Convention Center (✆ **305/673-7311;** www.originalmiamibeachantiqueshow.com). Exhibitors from all over come to display their wares, including jewelry. Miami's huge concentration of Art Deco buildings from the '20s and '30s makes this the place to find the best selections of Deco furnishings and decorations. A word to the serious collectors: Dania Beach, up in Broward County (see chapter 13), about half an hour from downtown Miami, is the best place for antiques (it's known as the antiques capital of South Florida), so you may want to consider browsing in Miami and shopping up there.

Alhambra Antiques   This fabulous store specializes in 18th- and 19th-century European antiques, accessories, lighting, and art. Exhibits open to the public—and for sale—include post-Impressionist female artists from the early 20th century. The store prides itself on the fact that they do not use outsourced buyers or wholesalers. Every piece in the store has been purchased by the owners on their quarterly trips to Europe. Every Saturday they offer free wine and cheese while you peruse. 2850 Salzedo St., Coral Gables. ✆ **305/446-1688.** www.alhambraantiques.com.

Architectural Antiques   A great place to browse—if you don't mind a little dust—this huge warehouse has an impressive stash of ironwork, bronzes, paintings, lamps, furniture, and sculptures which have been salvaged from estates worldwide. Don't be surprised to find odd items, too, like an old British phone booth or a pair of gargoyles off an ancient church. 2520 SW 28th Lane (just west of U.S. 1), Miami. ✆ **305/285-1330.** www.miamiantique.com.

Industrian   What's a retro-fabulous Charles Eames chair doing sitting next to an ultramodern 21st-century, Jetsonian piece of furniture? The answer is Industrian, where vintage and new furniture live in harmony. 5580 NE 4th Court, Miami. ✆ **305/754-6070.**

Miami Twice   While they are not technically antiques yet, the Old Florida furniture and decorations from the '30s, '40s, and '50s are great fun (and collectible). In addition to loads of Deco memorabilia, there are also vintage clothes, shoes, and jewelry. 6562 Bird Rd., South Miami. ✆ **305/666-0127.** www.miami-twice.com.

Modernism Gallery   Specializing in 20th-century furnishings from Gilbert Rohde, Noguchi, and Heywood Wakefield, this shop has some of the most beautiful examples of Deco goods from France and the United States. If they don't have what you're looking for, ask. They possess the amazing ability to find the rarest items. 1500 Ponce de León Blvd., Coral Gables. ✆ **305/442-8743.** www.modernism.com.

Senzatempo 🎁 If the names Charles Eames, George Nelson, or Gio Ponti mean anything to you, this is where you'll want to visit. There's retro, Euro-fabulous designer furniture and decorative arts from 1930 to 1960 here, as well as collectible watches, timepieces, and clocks. 1655 Meridian Ave., 2nd floor (at Lincoln Rd.), South Beach. © **305/534-5588.** www.senzatempo.com.

Stone Age Antiques 🎁 Movie posters, military memorabilia, tribal masks, cowboy hats—you name it, they probably have it, but nautical antiques are their specialty. Looking for a certain ship's wheel? Stone Age most likely has it. 3236 NW S. River Dr. at NW 32nd St. N. Miami. © **305/633-5114.** www.stoneage-antiques.com.

Art Galleries

See p. 176 for a list of some of the art galleries in the greater Miami area.

Books

You can find local branches of **Barnes & Noble** at 152 Miracle Mile (© 305/446-4152), 5701 Sunset Dr. (© 305/662-4770), 18711 NE Biscayne Blvd. (© 305/935-9770), 7710 N. Kendall Dr. (© 305/598-7292), and 12405 N. Kendall Dr. (© 305/598-7727). **Borders** can be found at 9205 S. Dixie Hwy. (© 305/665-8800), 11401 NW 12th St. (© 305/597-8866), and 19925 Biscayne Blvd. (© 305/935-0027).

Books & Books A dedicated following turns out to browse at this warm and wonderful little independent shop. Enjoy the upstairs antiquarian room, which specializes in art books and first editions. If that's not enough intellectual stimulation for you, the shop hosts free lectures from noted authors, experts, and personalities almost nightly, from Monica Lewinsky to Martin Amis. At another location (933 Lincoln Rd., South Beach; © **305/532-3222**), you'll rub elbows with tanned and buffed South Beach bookworms sipping cappuccinos at the Russian Bear Cafe inside the store. This branch stocks a large selection of gay literature and also features lectures. And if you happen to be at the ritzy Bal Harbour Shops and not in the mood to do the Gucci thing, there's another Books & Books here, too (© **305/864-4241**). 265 Aragon Ave., Coral Gables. © **305/442-4408.** www.booksandbooks.com.

Kafka's Cyberkafe Check your e-mail and surf the Web while you sip a latte or snack on a sandwich or pastry with friendly neighborhood regulars. This popular used bookstore also stocks a wide range of foreign and domestic magazines and caters to an international-youth-hostel-type crowd. 1464 Washington Ave., South Beach. © **786/348-0901.** www.kafkas-cafe.com.

Cigars

Although it is illegal to bring Cuban cigars into the United States, somehow, forbidden *Cohibas* show up at every dinner party and nightclub in town. Not that I condone it, but if you hang around the cigar smokers in town, no doubt one will be able to tell you where you can get some of the highly prized contraband. Be careful, however, of counterfeits, which are typically Dominican cigars posing as Cubans. Cuban cigars are illegal and unless you go down a sketchy alley to buy one from a dealer (think of it as shady as a drug deal), you are going to be smoking Dominican ones.

The stores listed below sell excellent hand-rolled cigars made with domestic- and foreign-grown tobacco. Many of the *viejitos* (old men) got their training in Cuba working for the government-owned factories in the heyday of Cuban cigars.

El Credito Cigars   This tiny storefront shop employs about 45 veteran Cuban rollers who sit all day rolling the very popular torpedoes and other critically acclaimed blends. They're usually back-ordered, but it's worth stopping in: They will sell you a box and show you around. 1106 SW 8th St., Little Havana. © **305/858-4162.** www.elcreditocigars.com.

Mike's Cigars 🎁   Mike's may have abandoned its old digs for a bigger, newer location, but it's one of the oldest and best smoke shops in town. Since 1950, Mike's has been selling the best from Honduras, the Dominican Republic, and Jamaica, as well as the very hot local brand, La Gloria Cubana. Many say it has the best prices, too. Mike's has the biggest selection of cigars in town and the employees speak English. 1030 Kane Concourse (at 96th St.), Bay Harbor Island. © **305/866-2277.** www. mikescigars.com.

Cosmetics, Fragrances, Beauty Products & a Salon

Brownes & Co. Apothecary 🎁   Designed to look like an old-fashioned apothecary, this recently expanded beauty emporium combines the best selection of makeup and hair products—MAC, Shu Uemura, Kiehl's, Stila, Molton Brown, Francois Nars, and Dr. Hauschka, just to name a few—with lots of delicious-smelling bath and body stuff, plus a full-service beauty salon. Feel free to browse and sample here, as perfume-spritzing salespeople won't bother you. If you do need help, the staff is a collection of experts when it comes to beauty and hair products. Upstairs is the Browne's Beauty Lounge, in which you can get fabulously coiffed, colored, buffed, and waxed by the experts at the store's renowned salon, Some Like It Hot. For those of you looking for that J-Lo glow, she shops here, so ask one of the staff to point you in the right direction. A second, smaller location opened in the Design District at 87 NE 40th St. 841 Lincoln Rd., South Beach. © **305/532-8703.** www.brownesbeauty.com.

MAC   Viva glam! The innovative brand of makeup is all here, and if you're lucky you may get a free makeover. 650 Collins Ave., South Beach. © **305/604-9040.** www. maccosmetics.com.

Sephora   The Disney World of makeup, Sephora offers a dizzying array of cosmetics, perfumes, and styling products. Unlike Brownes & Co., however, personal service and attentiveness is at a minimum. Because there are so many products, shopping here can be a harrowing experience. Three locations: 721 Collins Ave., South Beach (© **305/532-0904**); 19575 Biscayne Blvd., Aventura (© **305/931-9579**); or in the Dadeland Mall, 7535 SW 88th St., Miami (© **305/740-3445**). www.sephora.com.

Fashion: Clothing & Accessories

Miami didn't become a fashion capital until—believe it or not—the pastel-hued, Armani-clad cops on *Miami Vice* had their close-ups on the tube. Before that, Miami was all about old men in white patent leather shoes and well tanned women in bikinis. How things have changed! Miami is now a fashion mecca in its own right, with some of the same high-end stores you'd find on Rue de Fauborg St. Honore in Paris or Bond Street in London. You'll find all the chichi labels, including Prada and Gucci, right here at the posh Bal Harbour Shops. For funkier frocks, South Beach is the place, where designers such as Nicole Miller, Ralph Lauren and Giorgio Armani compete for window shoppers with local up-and-coming designers, some of whom design for drag queens and club kids only. Miami's edgy Upper East Side and Design District neighborhoods also slowly but surely are developing as a hot spot for hip-wear. The strip on Collins Avenue between 7th and 10th streets has become quite upscale, including such shops as Armani Exchange and Intermix, along with the inescapable Gap and Banana Republic. Of course, there's also more mainstream (and affordable) shopping in the plethora of malls and outdoor shopping and entertainment complexes that are sprinkled throughout the city (see "Malls," below).

UNISEX

Atrium   Young Hollywood always makes Atrium a stop on their South Beach shopping list. With designer brands at designer prices, don't be surprised if you see that $200 white T-shirt on an Olsen twin in the latest issue of *Us Weekly.* 1925 Collins Ave., South Beach. ✆ **305/695-0757.**

Barneys Co-Op   An outpost of Barneys New York, only this time, it's more "affordable." Hooey. If you think a T-shirt for $150 is affordable, then this store is for you. Otherwise, Barneys Co-Op is always great for browsing and marveling over the fashion victims who actually do pay such absurd prices for a cotton T-shirt. 832 Collins Ave., South Beach. ✆ **305/421-2010.**

Base USA   A hipster hangout, featuring clothing that's fashionable, and, of course, pricey. Base is also known for its cool and funky CD collection (all for sale, of course), coffee table books, and nice smelling candles. 939 Lincoln Rd., South Beach. ✆ **305/531-4982.**

En Avance   If you couldn't get into LIV or SET last night, consider plunking down some major pocket change for the au courant labels that En Avance is known for. One outfit bought here and the doormen have no ground to stand on when it comes to high-fashion dress codes. 734 Lincoln Rd., South Beach. ✆ **305/534-0337.**

> ## Impressions
>
> *We're the only city that has big-butt mannequins.*
> —Anna Maria Diaz-Balart, Miami-based fashion designer

Original Penguin Store   Remember the Izod alligator? Forget it for a second and consider this, the hippest, retro men's line since, well, Izod, featuring sweaters, polo shirts, T's, and more sporting a, well, penguin logo. 925 Lincoln Rd., South Beach. ✆ **305/673-0722.** www.originalpenguin.com.

Style Lab   Urban hipster-wear outpost selling unisex clothing and accessories at often affordable prices. Check out the 70%-off rack up front. 5580 NE 4th Court, Biscayne Corridor. ✆ **305/756-1010.** www.stylelabmiami.com.

Urban Outfitters   It took a while for this urban outpost to hit Miami, but once it did, it became a favorite for the young hipster set who favor T-shirts that say "Princess" instead of Prada. Cheapish, utilitarian, and funky, Urban Outfitters is an excellent place to pick up a pair of used jeans or some funky tchotchkes for your apartment. Two locations: 653 Collins Ave., South Beach (✆ **305/535-9726**); or Shops at Sunset, 5701 SW 72nd St., South Miami (✆ **305/663-1536**).

The Webster A Parisian-style couture emporium straight out of *Women's Wear Daily*, Webster features runway-ready *prêt a porter* for men and women by all those boldface names you read in the fashion magazines. It's so swanky, there's even a champagne and caviar bar, Caviar Kaspia, inside. Recession, what? 1220 Collins Ave., South Beach. ℂ 305/674-7899. www.thewebstermiami.com.

Y-3 A collaboration between couture designer Yohji Yamamoto and Adidas, Y-3 chose Miami's Design District as its first freestanding store ever, but bigger news than that is that it's the district's first-ever clothing store, featuring a full range of funky men's and women's apparel, shoes, and accessories. The two-story store prides itself on fusing style and sport and often hosts very fabulous art and culture events. Two locations: 150 NE 40th St., Design District (ℂ 305/535-9726 or 305/573-1603); 1111 1111 Lincoln Road. ℂ 305/538-9302. www.adidas.com.

WOMEN'S

Belinda's Designs This German designer makes some of the most beautiful and intricate teddies, nightgowns, and wedding dresses. The styles are a little too Stevie Nicks for me, but the creations are absolutely worth admiring. The prices are appropriately high. 917 Washington Ave., South Beach. ℂ 305/532-0068. www.belindasdesigns.net.

Christian Louboutin What the Beatles are to music, Christian Louboutin may be to women's shoes. The French shoe god, immortalized on the feet of every well-heeled celebrity and socialite and in a Jennifer Lopez song, chose the Miami Design District as the place for his very first Miami outpost. As gorgeous as the shoes, so is the store, so if it's not in the budget to buy, just go browse. If you can handle it. 155 NE 40th St., Design District. ℂ 305/576-6820.

HiHo Batik Hand-painted tank tops, adorable accessories, and funky jewelry is what you'll discover in this colorful North Miami boutique, which also hosts make-your-own batik parties. Although they also sell boy's clothing, it's much more of a girlie thing. 2174 NE 123rd St., North Miami. ℂ 305/754-8890. www.hihobatik.com.

Intermix Pretty young things can get all dolled up thanks to Intermix's fun assortment of hip women's fashions, from Stella McCartney's pricey rhinestone T-shirts to the latest jeans worn by everyone at the MTV Awards. 634 Collins Ave., South Beach. ℂ 305/531-5950. www.intermixonline.com.

Kore Boutique A high-fashion Biscayne Corridor boutique with dressy and chic-casual wear as well as shoes, jewelry, and bags. 7226 Biscayne Blvd., Biscayne Corridor. ℂ 305/573-8211.

La Perla The only store in Florida that specializes in superluxurious Italian intimate apparel. Of course, you could fly to Milan for the price of a few bras and a nightgown, but you can't find better quality. 342 San Lorenzo Ave., Coral Gables. ℂ 305/864-2070.

Marni Looking for the Miami fashionista set? Look no further than this gorgeous flagship store that, like The Webster, looks as if it jumped out of a *Women's Wear Daily* photo shoot, with prices to boot. 3930 NE 2nd Ave., Design District. ℂ 305/764-3357. www.marni.com.

> ### Impressions
>
> *Miami's culture inspires my couture. Fashion without a foundation is just posing.*
>
> —Rene Ruiz, Miami-based fashion designer

Morgan Miller A dream come true for shoe lovers, Morgan Miller is a design-your-own shoe boutique where you pick everything from heel to toe—Swarovski crystals, gold chains, bamboo rings—and the experts put it all together for you. Prices range from $150 to $500. 618 Lincoln Road. ✆ **305/672-8700.** www.morgan millershoes.com.

Place Vendome This shop is for cheap and funky club clothes from zebra-print pants to bright, shiny tops. Two locations: 934 Lincoln Rd., South Beach (✆ **305/673-4005**); and Aventura Mall, North Miami Beach (✆ **305/932-8931**).

Rebel Fashionable and funky clothing for mom and daughter is what you'll find in this fabulous Biscayne Corridor boutique that carries labels not found anywhere else. Super-friendly help is a bonus, too. 6669 Biscayne Blvd., Biscayne Corridor. ✆ **305/758-2369.**

Savvy Girl A small South Miami boutique sandwiched between a tire center and a supermarket with not a whole lot of merchandise, but a nice selection of jeans, dresses, and what I like to call "disco tops," or, nightclub wear. 5781 SW 40th St., South Miami. ✆ **305/665-9833.** www.shopsavvygirl.com.

Scoop Here's the real scoop: The Shore Club hotel boutique hails from New York City and is the shop of choice for visiting celebs who just walk in and don't have to ask the price of the latest from Diane Von Furstenberg, Helmut Lang, Marc Jacobs, Paul Smith, Malo, and Jimmy Choo. The Shore Club, 1901 Collins Ave. ✆ **305/532-5929.**

MEN'S

Bertini European Men's Clothing Coral Gables men's store featuring a complete selection of Canali and Zanella as well as custom-made shirts. 315 Miracle Mile, Coral Gables. ✆ **305/461-3374.** www.pepibertini.com.

Culture Kings Catering to the "limited edition lifestyle," this urban hip boutique is a favorite among the boldface and the beautiful, with a big rapper clientele. 4300 NE 2nd Ave., Design District. ✆ **305/573-2399.** www.culturekings.com.

La Casa de las Guayaberas 🎁 Miami's premier purveyor of the traditional yet retro-hip Cuban shirt known as the *guayabera*—a loose-fitting, pleated, button-down shirt—was founded by Ramon Puig, who emigrated to Miami over 40 years ago. He still uses the same scissors he did back then, only now he's joined by a team of seamstresses who hand-sew 20 shirts a day in all colors and styles. Prices range from $15 to $375. 5840 SW 8th St., Little Havana. ✆ **305/266-9683.**

CHILDREN'S

Most department stores have extensive children's sections. But if you can't find what you are looking for, consider one of the many Baby Gaps or Gap Kids outlets around town or try one of the specialty boutiques listed here.

Benini Bug Starting early, this boutique trains kids from newborns to 6-year-olds the fine art of being trendy with apparel, gifts, accessories, and bedding. 5881 Sunset Drive, South Miami. ✆ **305/662-1755.** www.beninibug.com.

Genius Jones In addition to the requisite, adorable and pricey kids' threads, Genius Jones has high-end kids' furniture by the likes of Agatha Ruiz de la Prada, David Netto, and other brands that will set you back some serious bucks. Three locations: 1661 Michigan Ave., South Beach (✆ **305/534-7622**); 49 NE 30th St., Design District (✆ **305/571-2000**); Mizner Park, 417 Plaza Real, Boca Raton (✆ **561/300-4004**). www.geniusjones.com.

ACCESSORIES

Me & Ro Jewelry   This store carries fun and funky baubles (not cheap) as seen on Sarah Jessica Parker and Julia Roberts. The Shore Club, 1901 Collins Ave., South Beach. ℭ **305/672-3566.**

SEE   This fantastic eyewear store features an enormous selection of stylish specs at decent prices. The staff is patient and knowledgeable. 921 Lincoln Rd., South Beach. ℭ **305/672-6622.**

Simons and Green   Fantastic sterling silver jewelry, leather goods, and other assorted high-end tchotchkes and gift items are what you'll find in this quaint mainstay on South Miami's Sunset Drive. 5843 Sunset Dr., South Miami. ℭ **305/667-1692.**

Turchin Love and Light Collections   Besides the fact that we saw Jennifer Aniston shopping here, we love this tiny Design District jewel box for its collection designed using unique artifacts made in Tibet, Nepal, Africa, India, Bhutan, and Pakistan. 130 NE 40th St., Design District. ℭ **305/573-7117.** www.turchinjewelry.com.

Food

There are dozens of ethnic markets in Miami, from Cuban bodegas (little grocery stores) to Jamaican import shops and Guyanese produce stands. Check the phone book under grocers for listings. I've listed a few of the biggest and best markets in town that sell prepared foods as well as staple items. On Saturday mornings, vendors set up stands loaded with papayas, melons, tomatoes, and citrus, as well as cookies, ice creams, and sandwiches on South Beach's Lincoln Road.

Epicure Market   This is the closest thing Miami Beach has to the famed Balducci's or Dean & DeLuca. Here, you'll find not only fine wines, cheeses, meats, fish, and juices, but some of the best produce, such as portobello mushrooms the size of a yarmulke. This neighborhood landmark is best known for supplying the Jewish residents of the beach with all their Jewish favorites, such as matzo ball soup, gefilte fish, and deli items. Prices are steep, but generally worth it. A much larger, newer Epicure Market opened in the old Rascal House space at 17190 Collins Ave. in Sunny Isles Beach (ℭ **305/936-7703**), featuring an expansive outdoor cafe (in a former parking lot) and bar which often hosts wine tastings. 1656 Alton Rd., Miami Beach. ℭ **305/672-1861.**

Gardner's Market   Anything a gourmet or novice cook could desire can be found here. One of the oldest and best grocery stores in Miami, Gardner's now has three locations, all of which offer great takeout and the freshest produce. 7301 Red Rd., South Miami (ℭ **305/667-9953**); 8287 SW 124th St., Pinecrest (ℭ **305/255-2468**); 3117 Bird Ave., Miami (ℭ **305/476-9900**).

Joe's Takeaway   If you don't want to wait 2 hours to get your paws on Joe's Stone Crab's meaty claws, let Joe's, Miami's stone-crab institution (p. 121), ship you stone crabs anywhere in the country, but only during the season, which runs from mid-October through mid-May. 11 Washington Ave., South Beach. ℭ **800/780-CRAB** (2722) or 305/673-0365.

La Brioche Doree   This tiny storefront off 41st Street is packed most mornings with French expatriates and visitors who crave the real thing. There are luscious pastries and breads, plus soup and sandwiches at lunch. No one makes a better croissant. 4017 Prairie Ave., Miami Beach. ℭ **305/695-3477.**

La Estancia Argentina   The best of edible Buenos Aires is found at this small, but comprehensive gourmet Argentine and Latin market. There are two locations. 17870 Biscayne Blvd., North Miami Beach (© **305/932-6477**); 4425 Ponce de León Blvd., Coral Gables (© **305/445-3933**). www.laestanciaweb.com.

Laurenzo's Italian Supermarket and Farmer's Market   Anything Italian you want—homemade ravioli, hand-cut imported Romano cheese, plus fresh fish and meats—can be found here. Laurenzo's also offers one of the most comprehensive wine selections in the city. Be sure to see the neighboring store full of just-picked herbs, salad greens, and vegetables from around the world. A daily Farmer's Market is open from 7am to 6pm. Incredible daily specials lure thrifty shoppers from all over the city. 16385 and 16445 W. Dixie Hwy., North Miami Beach. © **305/945-6381** or 305/944-5052. www.laurenzosmarket.com.

Marky's   Shopping here is sort of like shopping at the deli owned by the Sopranos, only in Russian. Here, you'll find the finest caviar, cheeses and pretty much anything else you can't get in Miami that's edible—but make sure to ask about the secret back room. 687 NE 79th St., Biscayne Corridor. © **305/758-9288**. www.markys.com.

Morning Call Bakery   You'll be happy to pay a pretty penny for a loaf when you sink your teeth into these inimitable Old World–style breads. Also, most of the locations have a to-die-for prepared-food counter serving up everything from chicken curry salad to hummus and potpies. Pastries and cakes are as gorgeous as they are delicious. 5868 Sunset Dr., South Miami. © **305/667-9333**.

Jewelry

For name designers like Gucci and Tiffany & Co., go to the Bal Harbour Shops (see "Malls," below).

The International Jewelry Exchange   At least 50 reputable jewelers hustle their wares from individual counters at one of the city's most active jewelry centers. Haggle your brains out for excellent prices on timeless antiques from Tiffany's, Cartier, or Bulgari, or on unique designs you can create yourself. Stop by Dahlia's Unique booth and ask for Dorie. She'll give you a good deal. 19275 Biscayne Blvd. (in the Fashion Island), North Miami Beach. © **305/931-3383**.

Seybold Buchwald's Jewelers   Jewelers who specialize in an assortment of goods (diamonds, gems, watches, rings, and such) gather here daily to sell diamonds and gold. With 300 jewelry stores located inside this independently owned and operated multilevel treasure chest, the glare is blinding as you enter. You'll be sure to see handsome and up-to-date designs, but not too many bargains. 36 NE 1st St., Downtown. © **305/374-7922**.

Malls

There are so many malls in Miami and more being built all the time that it would be impossible to mention them all. What follows is a list of the biggest and most popular.

You can find any number of nationally known department stores including Saks Fifth Avenue, Macy's, Bloomingdale's, Sears, and JCPenney in the Miami malls listed below. Miami's own, Burdines, is now a Macy's, too, located at 22 E. Flagler St., Downtown, and 1675 Meridian Ave. (just off Lincoln Rd.) in South Beach.

9

MIAMI SHOPPING

Shopping A to Z

Aventura Mall ☺   A multimillion-dollar makeover has made this spot one of the premier places to shop in South Florida. With more than 2.3 million square feet of space, this airy, Mediterranean-style mall has a 24-screen movie theater and more than 280 stores, including megastores Nordstrom, Macy's, Macy's Men's and Home Furniture, JCPenney, and Sears. Specialty stores are impressive and high end, including Calvin Klein, M Missoni, Ted Baker, Lily Pulitzer, Apple, Betsey Johnson, Hugo Boss, Coach, Diesel, Miss Sixty, Henri Bendel, Herve Leger by Max Azria, 7 For All Mankind, True Religion, and more. A large indoor playground, Adventurer's Cove, is a great spot for kids, and the mall frequently offers activities and entertainment for children. There are numerous restaurants, including Cheesecake Factory, Grand Lux Café, Ocean Prime, Paul Maison de Qualite, The Grill on the Alley, and Sushi Siam, and a food court that eschews the usual suspects in favor of local operations. 19501 Biscayne Blvd. (at 197th St. near the Dade–Broward County line), Aventura. ✆ **305/935-1110.** www.shopaventuramall.com.

Bal Harbour Shops   One of the most prestigious fashion meccas in the country, Bal Harbour offers the best-quality goods from the finest names. Giorgio Armani, Dolce & Gabbana, Christian Dior, Fendi, Joan & David, Harry Winston, Pucci, Krizia, Rodier, Gucci, Agent Provocateur, Carolina Herrera, Celine, Chanel, Chloe, Diane Von Furstenberg, Brooks Brothers, Waterford, Cartier, H. Stern, Tourneau, and many others are sandwiched between Neiman Marcus and a newly expanded Saks Fifth Avenue. Well-dressed shoppers stroll in a pleasant open-air emporium featuring several good cafes, covered walkways, and lush greenery. Parking costs $1 an hour with a validated ticket. ***Tip:*** You can stamp your own at the entrance to Saks Fifth Avenue, even if you don't make a purchase. 9700 Collins Ave. (on 97th St., opposite the Sheraton Bal Harbour Hotel), Bal Harbour. ✆ **305/866-0311.** www.balharbourshops.com.

Bayside Marketplace   A popular stop for cruise-ship passengers, this touristy waterfront marketplace is filled with the usual suspects of chain stores as well as a slew of tacky gift shops and carts hawking assorted junk in the heart of downtown Miami. The second-floor food court is stocked with dozens of fast-food choices and bars. Most of the restaurants and bars stay open later than the stores. There's Bubba Gump Shrimp Co., Hooters, Hard Rock Cafe, Fat Tuesday, and Let's Make a Daiquiri. Parking is $1 per hour. While we wouldn't recommend you necessarily drop big money at Bayside, you should go by just for the view (of Biscayne Bay and the Miami skyline) alone. Beware of the adjacent amphitheater known as Bayfront Park, which usually hosts large-scale concerts and festivals, causing major pedestrian and vehicle traffic jams. 401 Biscayne Blvd., Downtown. ✆ **305/577-3344.** www.baysidemarketplace.com.

CocoWalk   CocoWalk is a lovely outdoor Mediterranean-style mall with the usual fare of Americana: Gap, Victoria's Secret, and so on. Its open air architecture is inviting not only for shoppers but also for friends or spouses of shoppers who'd prefer to sit at an outdoor cafe while said shopper is busy in the fitting room. In 2010, the shopping center went bankrupt after the movie theater closed and is currently in the throes of coming up with its own stimulus plan which is said to include a Muvico Premium Theater. 3015 Grand Ave., Coconut Grove. ✆ **305/444-0777.** www.cocowalk.net.

Dadeland Mall   One of the county's first malls, Dadeland features more than 185 specialty shops, anchored by four large department stores: Macy's, JCPenney, Nordstrom, and Saks Fifth Avenue. The mall also boasts the country's largest Limited/ Express store. Sixteen restaurants serve from the adjacent food court. New retail stores are constantly springing up around this centerpiece of South Miami suburbia. If you're not in the area, however, the mall is not worth the trek. Additionally, many non-Spanish-speaking people are put off by Dadeland because of the predominance of Spanish-speaking store employees. 7535 N. Kendall Dr. (intersection of U.S. 1 and SW 88th St., 15 min. south of Downtown), Kendall. ℂ **305/665-6226.**

Dolphin Mall As if Miami needed another mall, this $250-million megamall is similar to Broward County's monstrous Sawgrass Mills outlet, albeit without the luxury stores. The 1.4-million-square-foot outlet mall features outlets such as Off Fifth (Saks Fifth Avenue), plus several discount shops, a 28-screen movie theater, and bowling alley. Florida Tpk. at S.R. 836, West Miami. ℂ **305/365-7446.** www.shopdolphinmall.com.

The Falls Traffic to this mall borders on brutal, but once you get there, you'll feel a slight sense of serenity. Tropical waterfalls are the setting for this outdoor shopping center with dozens of moderately priced and slightly upscale shops. Miami's first Bloomingdale's is here, as are Polo, Ralph Lauren, Caswell-Massey, and more than 95 other specialty shops. Also there: Macy's, Crate & Barrel, Brooks Brothers, and Pottery Barn, among others. If you are planning to visit any of the nearby attractions, which include Metrozoo and Monkey Jungle, check with customer service for information on discount packages. 8888 Howard Dr. (at the intersection of U.S. 1 and 136th St., about 3 miles south of Dadeland Mall), Kendall. ℂ **305/255-4570.** www.shopthefalls.com.

Sawgrass Mills Just as some people need to take a tranquilizer to fly, others need one to traipse through this mammoth mall—the largest outlet mall in the country. Depending on what type of shopper you are, this experience can either be blissful or overwhelming. If you've got the patience, it is worth setting aside a day to do the entire place. Though it's located in Broward County, it is a phenomenon that attracts thousands of tourists and locals sniffing out bargains. In 2006, the mall debuted its swank new luxe section, the Colonnade Outlets, featuring outlet versions of Coach, Miss Sixty USA, Salvatore Ferragamo and other luxury outlets offering savings of up to 70%. When driving, take I-95 north to 595 west to Flamingo Road. Exit and turn right, driving 2 miles to Sunrise Boulevard. You can't miss this monster on the left. Parking is free, but don't forget where you parked your car or you might spend a day looking for it. 12001 W. Sunrise Blvd., Sunrise (west of Fort Lauderdale). ℂ **954/846-2300.** www.millscorp.com.

Shops at Sunset Place This sprawling outdoor shopping complex offers more than just shopping. Visitors experience high-tech special effects, such as daily tropical storms (minus the rain) and the electronic chatter of birds and crickets. In addition to a 24-screen movie complex and an IMAX theater, there's a GameWorks (Steven Spielberg's Disney-esque playground for kids and adults), and a Niketown as well as mall standards such as Victoria's Secret, Gap, Hollister, American Eagle Outfitters, Urban Outfitters, bebe, and so on. 5701 Sunset Dr. (at 57th Ave. and U.S. 1, near Red Rd.), South Miami. ℂ **305/663-0482.**

Shoppes at Mayfair in The Grove This sleepy, desolate, labyrinthine shopping area conceals a movie theater, several shops (Ann Taylor Loft and Bath & Body Works are the two most recognizable), a bookstore, and the Improv Comedy Club. It was meant to compete with the CocoWalk shopping complex (just across the street), but its structure is very mazelike. Though it is open air, it is not wide open like CocoWalk and pales in comparison to that more populated neighbor. 2911 Grand Ave. (just east of Commodore Plaza), Coconut Grove. ℂ **305/448-1700.**

The Shops at Midtown Miami   Located just off Biscayne Boulevard in a gritty, yet transitional neighborhood near the Design District and Wynwood, The Shops at Midtown Miami is more of a locals' spot, with Target, West Elm, Loehmann's, Marshall's, and PetSmart. There are also some great dining options here, including Five Guys Burgers and Fries, The Cheese Course, Lime Fresh Mexican Grill, and Sugarcane Raw Bar, the new hotspot from the owners of Sushi Samba on South Beach. Go here at your own risk, as the area is still a bit sketchy. 3401 N. Miami Ave, Midtown Miami. ✆ **305/573-3371.** www.shopmidtownmiami.com.

The Village at Gulfstream Park   New in 2010, Gulfstream Park's outdoor dining and entertainment venue on the border of Miami–Dade and Broward counties near Aventura in Hallandale Beach, featuring an expanding list of stores—Crate & Barrel, Pottery Barn, Williams-Sonoma, West Elm among other clothing and accessories boutiques; restaurants including Ola Cuba by Douglas Rodriguez, BRIO Tuscan Grill, and American Pie Brick Oven Pizza; and bars including a branch of South Beach's popular Playwright Irish Pub, Cadillac Ranch, Yard House, and more. 501 S. Federal Highway, Hallandale Beach. ✆ **954/458-0145.** www.thevillageatgulfstreampark.com.

Village of Merrick Park   Giving Bal Harbour Shops a literal run for its money is this Coral Gables Mediterranean-style outdoor mall consisting of extremely high-end stores such as Jimmy Choo, Sonia Rykiel, Neiman Marcus, Miami's very first Nordstrom, and upscale eateries such as The Palm. In fact, the owner of Bal Harbour Shops was so paranoid he'd lose his business to Merrick Park that he shoveled a ton of cash in an ad campaign making sure people wouldn't forget that Bal Harbour was here first. People who can afford it won't be forgetting about either anytime soon. 4425 Ponce de León Blvd., Coral Gables. ✆ **305/529-0200.**

Music Stores

Casino Records Inc.   The young, hip salespeople here speak English and tend to be music buffs. This store has the largest selection of Latin music in Miami. Their slogan translates to: "If we don't have it, forget it." Believe me, they've got it. 2290 SW 8th St., Little Havana. ✆ **786/394-8899.**

Yesterday and Today Records 🎁   This is Miami's most unique and well-stocked store for vinyl—you know, the audio dinosaur that went out with the Victrola? Y & T, as it's known, is a collector's heaven, featuring every genre of music imaginable on every format. Chances are, you could find some eight-track tapes, too. 9274 SW 40th St., Miami. ✆ **305/554-1020.** http://vintagerecords.com.

Sports Equipment

People-watching seems to be the number-one sport in South Florida, but for the more athletic pursuits, consider the shops listed below. One of the area's largest sports-equipment chains is the **Sports Authority,** with at least six locations throughout the county. Check the White Pages for details.

Alf's Golf Shop   This is the best pro shop around. The knowledgeable staff can help you with equipment for golfers of every level, and the neighboring golf course offers discounts to Alf's clients. There are three locations. 524 Arthur Godfrey Rd., Miami Beach (✆ **305/673-6568**); 15369 S. Dixie Hwy., Miami (✆ **305/378-6086**); and 2600 NW 87th Ave., in Doral near the Miami International Airport (✆ **305/470-0032**). www.alfsgolf.com.

Bass Pro Shops Outdoor World Fishing and sports enthusiasts must head north to Broward County to see this huge retail complex, which offers demonstrations in such sports as fly-fishing and archery, classes in marine safety, and every conceivable gadget you could ask for. 200 Gulf Stream Way (west side of I-95), Dania Beach. (C) **954/929-7710.**

Edwin Watts Golf Shops One of 30 Edwin Watts shops throughout the Southeast, this full-service golf retail shop is one of the most popular in Miami. You can find it all here, including clothing, pro-line equipment, gloves, bags, balls, videos, and books. Plus, you can get coupons for discounted greens fees on many courses. There are two locations. 15100 N. Biscayne Blvd., North Miami Beach ((C) **305/944-2925**); 8484 NW 36th St., in Doral ((C) **305/591-1220**). www.edwinwattsgolf.com.

Island Water Sports You'll find everything from booties to gloves to baggies and tanks. Check in here before you rent that WaveRunner or windsurfer. 16231 Biscayne Blvd., North Miami. (C) **305/944-0104.** www.iwsmiami.com.

South Beach Dive and Surf Shop Prices are slightly higher at this beach location, but you'll find the hottest styles and equipment. They also offer surfboard rental. Free surf report at (C) **305/534-7873.** 850 Washington Ave., South Beach. (C) **305/673-5900.**

Thrift Stores/Resale Shops

C. Madeleine's The best vintage store in town, brands from Gucci, Pucci, Fiorucci, and even Chanel and Balenciaga are usually snatched up by the likes of Jessica Simpson, Lenny Kravitz, or their stylists, who call this fashion emporium home. 13702 Biscayne Blvd., North Miami. (C) **305/945-0010.** www.cmadeleines.com.

The Children's Exchange ☺ Selling everything from layettes to overalls, this pleasant little shop is chock-full of good Florida-style stuff for kids to wear to the beach and in the heat. 1415 Sunset Dr., Coral Gables. (C) **305/666-6235.** http://the childrenexchange.com.

Douglas Gardens Jewish Home and Hospital Thrift Shop Prices here are no longer the major bargain they once were, but for housewares and books, you can do all right. Call to see if they are offering any specials for seniors or students. 5713 NW 27th Ave., North Miami Beach. (C) **305/638-1900.**

Out of the Closet The chain of thrift stores from Northern and Southern California owned and operated by AIDS Healthcare Foundation has finally opened in Miami and Wilton Manors in Fort Lauderdale. 2900 N. Biscayne Blvd., Biscayne Corridor ((C) **305/764-3773**); 2097 Wilton Drive, Wilton Manors ((C) **954/358-5590**). www.outofthecloset.org.

Rags to Riches This is an old-time consignment shop where you might find some decent rags, and maybe even some riches. Though not as upscale as it used to be, this place is still a good spot for costume jewelry and shoes. 12577 Biscayne Blvd., North Miami. (C) **305/891-8981.** www.ragstoriches-sale.com.

Red White & Blue Thrift Store 💼 Miami's best-kept secret is this mammoth thrift store that is meticulously organized and well stocked. You've got to search for great stuff, but it is there. There are especially good deals on children's clothes and housewares. 12640 NE 6th Ave., North Miami. (C) **305/893-1104.** www.redwhiteand bluethriftstore.com.

MIAMI AFTER DARK

With all the hype, you'd expect Miami to have long outlived its 15 minutes of fame by now. But you'd be wrong. Miami's nightlife, in South Beach *and,* slowly but surely, downtown and its urban environs, is hotter than ever before—and getting cooler with the opening of each funky, fabulous watering hole, lounge, and club. Not always cool, however, is the presence of ubiquitous, closely guarded velvet ropes used to often erroneously create an air of exclusivity. Don't be fooled or intimidated by them—*anyone* can go clubbing in the Magic City, and throughout this section, I've provided tips to ensure that you gain entry to your desired venue.

10

South Beach is certainly Miami's uncontested nocturnal nucleus, but more and more diverse areas, such as the Design District, Wynwood, Brickell, South Miami, and even Little Havana, are increasingly providing fun alternatives without the ludicrous cover charges, "fashionably late" hours of operation (things don't typically get started on South Beach until after 11pm), lack of sufficient self-parking, and outrageous drink prices that are standard in South Beach.

While South Beach dances to a more electronic beat, other parts of Miami dance to a Latin beat—from salsa and merengue to tango and cha-cha. However, if you're looking for a less frenetic good time, Miami's bar scene has something for everyone, from haute hotel bars to sleek, loungey watering holes.

Parts of downtown, such as the Biscayne Corridor, the Miami River, and the Design District, are undergoing a trendy makeover à la New York City's Meatpacking District. Cool lounges, bars, and clubs are popping up and providing the "in" crowds with a newer, more urban-chic nocturnal pasture.

But if the possibility of a celebrity sighting in one of the city's lounges, bars, or clubs doesn't fulfill your cultural needs, Miami also provides a variety of first-rate diversions in theater, music, and dance, including a world-class ballet (under the aegis of Edward Villella), a recognized symphony, and a talented opera company. The new Cesar Pelli–designed,

$446-million Adrienne Arsht Center for the Performing Arts is the focal point for the arts, created to prove to the world that Miami isn't as shallow and devoid of culture as people once thought.

For up-to-date listing information, and to make sure the club of the moment hasn't expired, check the *Miami Herald*'s "Weekend" section, which runs on Friday, or the more comprehensive listings in *New Times,* Miami's free alternative weekly, available each Wednesday; or visit www.miami.com online.

BARS & LOUNGES

There are countless bars and lounges in and around Miami (most require proof that you are 21 or older to enter), with the highest concentration on trendy South Beach. The selection here is a mere sample. Keep in mind that many of the popular bars—and the easiest to get into—are in hotels (with a few notable exceptions—see below). For a clubbier scene, if you don't mind making your way through hordes of inebriated club kids, a stroll on Washington Avenue will provide you with ample insight into what's hot and what's not. Just hold on to your bags. It's not dangerous, but, occasionally, a few shady types manage to slip into the crowd. Another very important tip when in a club: *Never put your drink down out of your sight*—there have been unfortunate incidents in which drinks have been spiked with illegal chemical substances. For a less hard-core, more collegiate nightlife, head to Coconut Grove. Oh, yes, and when going out in South Beach, make sure to take a so-called disco nap, as things don't get going until at least 11pm. If you go earlier, be prepared to face an empty bar or club. Off of South Beach and in hotel bars in general, the hours are fashionably earlier, with the action starting as early as, say, 7pm.

> **Impressions**
>
> *Miami is where neon goes to die.*
> —Lenny Bruce

The Abbey   Dark, dank, and hard to find, this local microbrewery is a favorite for locals looking to escape the $20 candy-flavored martini scene. Best of all, there's never a cover and it's always open until 5am, perfect for those pesky and insatiable hops cravings that pop up at 3 or 4am. 1115 16th St., South Beach. ℂ **305/538-8110.**

Automatic Slim's   This is *the* bar where Ozzie and Harriet types become more like Ozzy and Sharon. Automatic Slim's is indeed a slim space of bar, but it packs people in, thanks to an exhaustive list of cheap(er) drinks, lack of attitude, great rock music, and a decor that can only be described as white trash–chic. 1216 Washington Ave., South Beach. ℂ **305/695-0795.**

Bar 721   Hidden behind bustling Lincoln Road is this bar that looks as if the 1970s took a time machine to the 21st century, and got off for a bathroom break in the 1950s. Whatever decade you may be in mentally or otherwise, the bar is great fun, something guys would want as their man rooms and women wouldn't mind visiting for a drink or two. 721 N. Lincoln Lane, South Beach. ℂ **305/532-1342.**

Bardot 🎁   Modeled after the basement of a rock star circa 1972, Bardot is Miami proper's hottest new scene despite the fact that it prides itself on being the antithesis of being sceney. A mixed crowd of young and old, gay and straight, and everything in between is what you'll find at this off-the-beaten-path lounge-cum-speakeasy located in the back of a Midtown furniture store. Shag carpeting, comfy couches, and decor straight out of *That 70s Show* make for a very comfy backdrop for cocktailing, listening to live music and watching what may be, at the time of this writing, Miami's most colorful hipster crowd. 3456 N. Miami Ave., Miami. ② **305/576-5570.** bardotmiami.com.

Buck 15 Located above a Chinese restaurant, this hipster hangout may be high above Lincoln Road but it feels more like you are hanging out in someone's basement, with cabinets of Japanese anime collectibles as decor. Kitschy to say the least, Buck 15 has that cozy, comfy vibe, but when the DJ starts spinning it's rare to see anyone slouching in the couches. 1661 Meridian Ave., South Beach. ② **305/534-5488.**

Burger & Beer Joint Although downstairs at this bustling, well, burger and beer joint, is more about food, in back is a sports bar complete with flatscreen TVs to catch the latest game. Not in the mood for athletics, consider the lounge upstairs where a chilled-out scene attracts everyone from barflies and models to overly full diners from downstairs looking to veg out on the couches. 1766 Bay Rd., South Beach. ② **305/672-3287.** www.burgernbeerjoint.com.

Casale Although it's a nice pizza restaurant, upstairs at Casale is a fantastic rooftop bar and lounge where you can relax with a glass of wine, enjoy a cocktail or have a meal to the tune of a Euro-accented soundtrack of lounge music. 1800 Bay Rd., South Beach. ② **305/763-8088.**

Clarke's This classy, brassy, and sassy Irish pub and restaurant in the chichi South of Fifth Street area of South Beach has become command central for everyone from *Burn Notice* star Jeffrey Donovan, Miami Heat players, and the Miami Beach police chief to local moguls and club kids looking for cold beer and, surprisingly, a gourmet menu consisting of shepherd's pie, seared scallops, and the best burger in the 'hood. My personal favorite, however, is the New York–style pretzel served on a spike with a side of mustard. 840 1st St., South Beach. ② **305/538-9885.** www.clarkesmiamibeach.com.

Clevelander If wet-T-shirt contests and a fraternity-party atmosphere are your thing, then this Ocean Drive mainstay is your kind of place. Popular with tourists and locals who like to pretend they're tourists, the Clevelander, which was the recent recipient of much needed renovations, attracts a lively, sporty crowd of only adults (the burly bouncers *will* confiscate fake IDs) who have no interest in being part of a scene, but, rather, like to take in the very revealing scenery. A great time to check out the Clevelander is on a weekend afternoon, when beach Barbies and Kens line the bar for a post-tanning beer or frozen cocktail. 1020 Ocean Dr., South Beach. ② **305/531-3485.** www.clevelander.com.

Club 50 at The Viceroy If you're afraid of heights, you may want to bypass this stunning, swanky lounge located 50 stories above Brickell Avenue. But you may want to conquer your fear as Club 50 is entirely worth it if you're looking for a sophisticated swilling spot that caters to Miami's elite. Indoors is reminiscent of a lounge in

South Beach After Dark

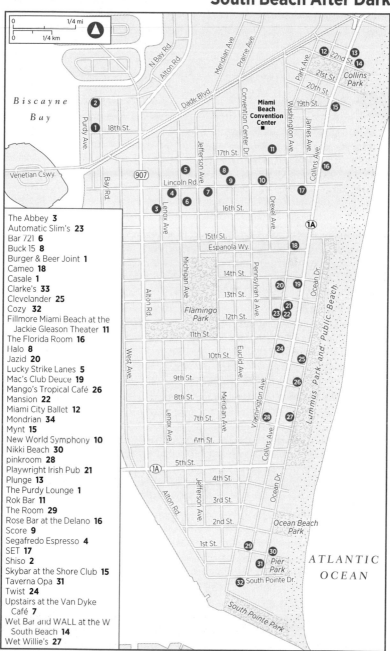

The Abbey **3**
Automatic Slim's **23**
Bar 721 **6**
Buck 15 **8**
Burger & Beer Joint **1**
Cameo **18**
Casale **1**
Clarke's **33**
Clevelander **25**
Cozy **32**
Fillmore Miami Beach at the
  Jackie Gleason Theater **11**
The Florida Room **16**
Halo **8**
Jazid **20**
Lucky Strike Lanes **5**
Mac's Club Deuce **19**
Mango's Tropical Café **26**
Mansion **22**
Miami City Ballet **12**
Mondrian **34**
Mynt **15**
New World Symphony **10**
Nikki Beach **30**
pinkroom **28**
Playwright Irish Pub **21**
Plunge **13**
The Purdy Lounge **1**
Rok Bar **11**
The Room **29**
Rose Bar at the Delano **16**
Score **9**
Segafredo Espresso **4**
SET **17**
Shiso **2**
Skybar at the Shore Club **15**
Taverna Opa **31**
Twist **24**
Upstairs at the Van Dyke
  Café **7**
Wet Bar and WALL at the W
  South Beach **14**
Wet Willie's **27**

an old-school, first-class ocean liner, while outside is more L.A. with lap pool, bar and panoramic views of the downtown skyline. 485 Brickell Ave., Miami. © **305/503-4400.** www.viceroymiami.com.

Cozy A very French, very expensive piano bar in the South of Fifth neighborhood right next door to the zillion-dollar Apogee condo, where the likes of actor Michael Caine and basketball's Pat Riley call home, Cozy lives up to its name in ambience with blood-red walls and chandeliers; but when it comes to the check, there's nothing cozy about it, with a cheese plate coming in at a whopping $50 and glasses of wine starting at $20. But if you're in the mood for a nightcap—and we mean just one—and some great live piano and surprise celebrity musicians (the Gypsy Kings love dropping in and jamming out here when in town), Cozy, or Sarkozy as we like to call it, is entirely worth the splurge. 500 South Pointe Dr., South Beach. © **305/532-2699.** www.thecozybar.com.

DRB Miami A tiny spot across the street from the performing arts center, DRB—Democratic Republic of Beer—is where Miami meets Williamsburg, Brooklyn, with an unabridged list of microbrews from all over the world, a better-than-average bar menu, and a crowd of hops-loving hipsters sporting ironic facial hair and quoting Kafka. 255 NE 14th St., Miami. © **305/372-4565.** www.drbmiami.com.

Electric Pickle 🎁 A tiny bar with upstairs lounge and a parking lot out back that doubles as its outdoor area, Electric Pickle is the unofficial clubhouse of Miami's indie music scene, where the long-running Brit-pop, hipster-happy, one-nighter Pop Life takes up residence every Saturday. We completely recommend the place if that's your scene, but go at your own risk, as its host neighborhood is still very dodgy. 2826 N. Miami Ave., Wynwood. © **305/456-5613.**

The Florida Room The Florida Room is a dimly chandelier-lit den of old-school Florida decor meets swanky cruise-ship lounge—a place of 200 maximum capacity—where everyone from young hipsters and swanky sophisticates to the Golden Girls would go for a fancy night out, where Rue McClanahan's feisty, randy Blanche would climb atop the Lucite piano channeling Michelle Pfeiffer in *The Fabulous Baker Boys.* Designed by rocker Lenny Kravitz, the interior of this subterranean speakeasy is the antithesis of the sleek, stark hotel in which it resides, and for that, we love it. 1685 Collins Ave. (in the Delano), South Beach. © **305/672-2000.** www.delano-hotel.com.

Fox's Sherron Inn 🎁 The spirit of Frank Sinatra is alive and well at this dark and smoky watering hole that dates back to 1946. Everything down to the vinyl booths and the red lights make Fox's a retro-fabulous dive bar. Cheap drinks, couples cozily huddling in booths, and a seasoned staff of bartenders and barflies make Fox's the perfect place to retreat from the trenches of trendiness. Oh, and the food's actually good here, too. 6030 S. Dixie Hwy. (at 62nd Ave.), South Miami. © **305/661-9201.**

Louis 🎁 Another product of the Opium Group, Louis is, if you will, the French foreign exchange student where Louis XVI meets South Beach's reigning royalty on the nightlife circuit. Boasting (and we do mean boasting) a French sensibility—and attitude—Louis, located on the street level at the Gansevoort South—has been known to host everyone from Lindsay Lohan to Marilyn Manson with a few unsuspecting, low-key folks thrown in to throw you off. 2325 Collins Ave. www.louismiami. com. Cover $30 and up.

Mac's Club Deuce Standing amid an oasis of trendiness, Mac's Club Deuce is the quintessential dive bar, with cheap drinks and a cast of characters ranging from your typical barfly to your atypical drag queen. It's got a well-stocked jukebox, friendly bartenders, and a pool table. Best of all, it's an insomniac's dream, open daily from 8am to 5am. 222 14th St., South Beach. ℂ **305/673-9537.**

Mondrian If you can only stop at one South Beach bar for a beverage, we say this one should be it thanks to its jaw-dropping views of Biscayne Bay and an equally impressive interior surrealist decor (even more so after a few) in which Alice in Wonderland Spring Breaks on South Beach. Drinks are delicious and you'll pay a pretty price for it, but save some money for either a bottle in the lobby's tiny, couchy, VIP Sunset Lounge, a snack at Asia de Cuba, or for the automated vending machines hawking Bentleys and assorted luxuries. 1100 West Ave., South Beach. ℂ **305/514-1500.** www.mondrian-miami.com.

Mynt A massive 6,000-square-foot place, Mynt is nothing more than a huge living room in which models, celebrities, and assorted hangers-on bask in the green glow to the beat of very loud lounge and dance music. If you want to dance—or move, for that matter—this is not the place in which to do so. It's all about striking a pose in here. Unless you know the person at the door, be prepared to be ridiculed, emasculated, and socially shattered, as you may be forced to wait outside upward of an hour. If that's the case, forget it; it's not worth it. Wait next door at the Greek place for a celebrity sighting, as you'll have a better chance of seeing people from there instead of just waiting in the melee at the door. 1921 Collins Ave., South Beach. ℂ **786/276-6132.** www.myntlounge.com. Cover $10–$20.

pinkroom South Beach's very first "eco and female friendly" nightlife destination featuring 4,000 square feet of pink-hued fabulousness, pinkroom was inspired by the color pink—drinks are pink, the decor is pink and, after a while you may be pink too. Pinkroom also features a special Female Concierge—a hot male beefcake who will be available to help remove, uh, stains from your clothing or to run out and get you a new pair of panty hose if need be. But it's not for women only. Sort of the ladies' night of lounges, pinkroom is the ideal place for male suitors to find a date. And giving you more reasons to imbibe: A portion of the lounge's profits will go to breast cancer charities. 737 Washington Ave., South Beach. No phone.

Stargazing

The most popular places for celebrity sightings include Louis, Mansion, LIV, WALL, Mondrian, The Florida Room, Skybar, The Rose Bar at Delano, and, when it comes to stars gazing at other stars, Miami Heat basketball games. That, or when it comes to the edgier, under-the-radar celebs, Mac's Club Deuce around 5 in the morning.

Playwright Irish Pub Bono came here once when U2 was in town, not because it's such an authentic Irish pub, but because the bar was showing some European soccer match—and serves pints of Guinness. A great pre- or postclub spot, Playwright is one of the few places in town that also features live music from time to time. 1265 Washington Ave., South Beach. © **305/534-0667.** www.playwrightirishpub.com.

Plunge Possibly the best thing about the Gansevoort South, Plunge is the hotel's rockin' rooftop pool lounge, where on any given day or night, scantily clad scene- (and bikini-) chasers can be found either in or out of the water, sipping colorful cocktails to the tune of DJ-spun music. 2399 Collins Ave., South Beach. © **305/604-1000.**

The Purdy Lounge With the exception of a wall of lava lamps, Purdy is not unlike your best friend's basement, featuring a pool table and a slew of board games such as Operation to keep the attention-deficit-disordered from getting bored. It even has a bingo and spelling-bee night! Because it's a no-nonsense bar with relatively cheap cocktails (by South Beach standards), Purdy gets away with not having a star DJ or fancy bass-heavy Bose sound system. A CD player somehow does the trick. With no cover and no attitude, a line is inevitable (it gets crowded inside), so be prepared to wait. Saturday night has become the preferred night for locals, while Friday night's happy hour draws a young professional crowd on the prowl. 1811 Purdy Ave. at Sunset Harbor, South Beach. © **305/531-4622.** www.purdylounge.com.

River Lounge A lobby-level lounge in the EPIC hotel featuring beautiful views of the Miami River and a pretty packed Friday- and Saturday-night scene of local lounge lizards sipping and spinning to the tune of popular local DJs. 270 Biscayne Blvd. Way, Miami. © **305/424-5226.**

Rok Bar Larger-than-life rocker Tommy Lee has assembled a motley Miami crew at this paradox of a bar that combines down-'n'-dirty rock 'n' roll with the swank comforts of a chic lounge. The place is claustrophobic, with limited seating (unless you're Pamela Anderson, forget about scoring a table), high-priced drinks, and an oxymoronic soundtrack of Lynyrd Skynyrd, Michael Jackson, and Kid Rock. 1905 Collins Ave., South Beach. © **305/538-7171.** www.rokbarmiami.com.

The Room It's beer and wine only at this South of Fifth hideaway, where locals and NY expats (there are a few Rooms in NYC) come to get away from the insanity just a few blocks away. The beer selection is comprehensive with brews from almost everywhere in the world. The wine is not so great, but there's no whining here at this tiny, industrial-style, candlelit spot that doesn't have a DJ—just a CD player spinning indie tunes—or those pesky Paris Hilton sightings. 100 Collins Ave., South Beach. © **305/531-6061.** www.theotheroom.com.

Rose Bar at the Delano If every rose has its thorn, the thorn at this painfully chic hotel bar is the excruciatingly high price of cocktails. Otherwise, the crowd here is full of the so-called glitterati and other assorted poseurs who view life through (Italian-made) rose-colored glasses. 1685 Collins Ave., South Beach. © **305/672-2000.** www.delano-hotel.com.

Segafredo Espresso Although Segafredo is technically a cafe, it has become an integral part of Miami's nightlife as command central for Euros who miss that very special brand of European cafe society. Not in the mood for a club or bar, but want to hear great music, sip a few cocktails, snack on delicious sandwiches and pizza, and sit outside and people-watch? This is the place. European lounge music, tons of outdoor tables on a prime corner of Lincoln Road, and always a mob scene make 'Fredo one of my—and many other Miamians'—favorite nocturnal diversions. Although South Beach boasts the original, another Segafredo, with different owners,

SWANK hotel bars

Long gone are the days of the old-school Holiday Inn lounges. In fact, some hotels seem to spend more money on their bars than they do on their bedding. That aside, hotel bar-hopping is very popular in Miami. The newest hotel in town, the fabulous **W South Beach,** has several watering holes, from the Living Room lobby bar and poolside Wet Bar to the bars in their star studded Mr Chow and Soleà restaurants. Here's my list of the rest of the best:

Rose Bar at the Delano (p. 229): For seeing and being seen.

Skybar at The Shore Club (p. 230): Also for seeing and being seen.

Sunset Lounge at Mondrian (p. 228): Picture Alice in Wonderland going through the wrong mouse hole and ending up in South Beach. Trippy.

Bond St. Lounge at the Townhouse Hotel (p. 128): A tiny bar/lounge that also serves food. A New York import, it's known for excellent sushi and a hip, chic, jet-set crowd.

Martini Bar at the Raleigh Hotel (p. 85): A true throwback to the days of deco set to the tunes of Edith Piaf, Tony Bennett, Sinatra, and more.

Club 50 at The Viceroy (p. 226): There are lofty spots in Miami and then there's this, located high above the city on the 50th floor with some of the best views—and people watching in Miami.

The Setai (p. 79): The Champagne and Crustacean Bar may be a thing of more liquid economic times, but the bars at The Setai still offer pricey drinks in stunning settings. This time, however, cocktails look like drinks but eat like meals. Huh? Try the one with the bacon-infused bourbon and see what we mean.

a larger food menu, and separate nightclub is open in the Brickell Area, at 1421 S. Miami Ave., and another cafe opened on Española Way on South Beach. At the time of this writing, yet another was in the works for South Miami. 1040 Lincoln Rd., South Beach. (C) **305/673-0047,**

Skybar at The Shore Club Skybar lives up to its name in terms of loftiness, something this place has perfected better than anyone else, whether at its original L.A. location or the sprawling South Beach location at the Shore Club. If you're not a hotel guest, not Beyoncé, or not on the "list," or if you're a guy with several other guys and no girls, forget about it. For those of you who can't get in, the Skybar is basically the entire backyard area of the Shore Club, consisting of several areas, including the Moroccan-themed garden area, the hip-hop-themed indoor Red Room, the Sand Bar by the beach, and the Rum Bar by the pool. Sunday afternoon pool parties are a magnet for celebs and locals alike. Popular on any given night, Skybar is yet another brilliant example of how hotelier Ian Schrager has managed to control the hipsters in a most Pavlovian way. At The Shore Club, 1901 Collins Ave., South Beach. (C) **305/695-3100.** www.shoreclub.com.

Taverna Opa Although this Greek taverna (also located in Hollywood and Fort Lauderdale) calls itself a restaurant, I consider it more of a raucous dance club that just happens to serve excellent Greek food. How many restaurants do you know of that allow patrons to dance suggestively with waiters on tables, throw napkins in the air as if they were confetti, and guzzle ouzo straight from the bottle, all to the tune of some very loud, jazzed-up Greek dance music? Get here early, as the place is always packed—and I mean *packed* as in standing room only. Although there is an outdoor bar, the real fun and scenery are indoors in the dining room, where the tables double as dance floors and some very animated characters channel their best Zorbas. Be prepared for a big, fat Greek hangover the next day. 36 Ocean Dr., South Beach. ℂ **305/673-6730.** www.tavernaoparestaurant.com.

Transit Lounge   It's hard to locate, but once you do find Transit Lounge, you'll be happy you did. Reminiscent of what locals describe as "a real big-city lounge," Transit is cavernous, featuring a huge bar, tons of cozy couches and tables, board games, a funky crowd, and, hallelujah, live music. 1729 SW 1st Ave., Miami. ℂ **305/377-4628.** www.transitlounge.us.

Wet Bar at the W South Beach   As wholly unoriginal as the name is, the poolside Wet Bar, along with the secret-garden Grove and lobby level Living Room at the fabulous new W South Beach, are among the city's most stylish, creative and buzzworthy thanks to a stellar combo of master mixologists who shake and stir up some of the most creative—and pricey—cocktails you'll ever drink, celebrities and locals who drink them, and resplendent settings and backdrops worthy of Facebook photo ops. 2201 Collins Ave., South Beach. ℂ **305/938-3000.**

Wet Willie's   With such telling drinks as Call a Cab, this beachfront oasis is not the place to go if you have a long drive ahead of you. A well-liked pre- and postbeach hangout, Wet Willie's inspires serious drinking. Popular with the Harley-Davidson set, tourists, and beachcombers, this bar is best known for its rooftop patio (get there early if you plan to get a seat) and its half-nude bikini beauties. 760 Ocean Dr., South Beach. ℂ **305/532-5650.**

CLUBS, LIVE MUSIC & OTHER PARTY SPOTS

Dance Clubs

Clubs are as much a cottage industry in Miami as is, say, cheese in Wisconsin. Clubland, as it is known, is a way of life for some. On any given night in Miami, there's something going on—no excuses are needed to throw a party here. Short of throwing a glamorous event for the grand opening of a new gas station, Miami is very party hearty, celebrating everything from the fact that it's Tuesday night to the debut of a hot new DJ. Within this very bizarre after-dark community, a colorful assortment of characters emerges, from (a)typical 9-to-5ers to shady characters who have reinvented themselves as hot shots on the club circuit. While this see-and-be-seen scene may not be your cup of Absolut, it's certainly never boring.

The club music played on Miami's ever-evolving social circuit is good enough to get even the most rhythmically challenged wallflowers dancing. For aspiring DJs, a branch of the renowned **Scratch DJ Academy,** 2 NE 40th St. (ℂ **305/535-2599**), opened; for $300 a session, you, too, can become a master of the turntables.

To keep things fresh in Clubland, local promoters throw one-nighters, which are essentially parties with various themes or motifs, from funk to fashion. Because these change so often, we can't possibly list them here. Word of mouth, local advertising,

GROUND RULES: stepping out IN MIAMI

- Nightlife on South Beach doesn't really get going until after 11pm. As a result, you may want to consider taking what is known as a disco nap so that you'll be fully charged until the wee hours.

- If you're unsure of what to wear out on South Beach, your safest bet is anything black.

- Do *not* try to tip the doormen manning the velvet ropes. That will only make you look desperate, and you'll find yourself standing outside for what will seem like an ungodly amount of time. Instead, try to land your name on the ever-present guest list by calling the club early in the day yourself or, better yet, having the concierge at your hotel do it for you. If you don't have connections and you find

yourself without a concierge, then act assertive, not surly, at the velvet rope, and your patience will usually be rewarded with admittance. If all else fails—for men, especially—surround yourself with a few leggy model types and you'll be noticed quicker.

- If you are a man going out with a group of men, unless you're going to a gay bar, you will most likely not get into any South Beach hot spot unless you are with women.

- Finally, have fun. It may look like serious business when you're on the outside, but once you're in, it's another story. Attacking Clubland with a sense of humor is the best approach to a successful, memorable evening out.

Clubs, Live Music & Other Party Spots

and listings in the free weekly *New Times*, www.miami.citysearch.com, or the "Weekend" section of the *Miami Herald* are the best ways to find out about these ever-changing events.

Before you get all decked out to hit the town as soon as the sun sets, consider the fact that Miami is a very late town. Things generally don't get started here before 11pm. The Catch-22 is that if you don't arrive on South Beach early enough, you may find yourself driving around aimlessly for parking, as it is very limited outside of absurd $20+ valet charges. Municipal lots fill up quickly, so your best bet is to arrive on South Beach somewhat early and kill time by strolling around, having something to eat, or sipping a cocktail in a hotel bar. Another advantage of arriving a bit earlier than the crowds is that some clubs don't charge a cover before 11pm or midnight, which could save you a wad of cash over time. Most clubs are open every night of the week, though some are open only Thursday to Sunday and others are open only Monday through Saturday. Call ahead to get the most up-to-date information possible: Things change very quickly around here, and a call in advance can help you make sure that the dance club you're planning to go to hasn't become a video arcade. Cover charges are very haphazard, too. If you're not on the ubiquitous guest list (ask your concierge to put you on the list—he or she usually has the ability to do so, which won't help you with the wait to get in, but will eliminate the cover charge), you may have to fork over a ridiculous $20 to walk past the ropes. Don't fret, though.

WINTER music CONFERENCE

Every March, Miami is besieged by the most unconventional conventioneers the city has ever seen. These fiercely dedicated souls descend upon the city in a very audible way, with dark circles under their eyes and bleeps, blips, and scratches that can wake the dead. No, we're not talking about a Star Trek convention, but, rather, the Winter Music Conference (WMC), the world's biggest and most important gathering of DJs, remixers, agents, artists, and pretty much anyone who makes a dime off of the booming electronic music industry hailing from more than 60 countries from all over the world. But unlike most conventions, this one is completely interactive and open to the paying public as South Beach and Miami's hottest clubs transform into showcases for the various audio wares. For 5 consecutive days and nights, DJs, artists, and software producers play for audiences comprised of A&R reps, talent scouts, and locals just along for the ride. Parties take place everywhere, from hotel pools to street corners. There's always something going on every hour on the hour, and most people who really get into the throes of the WMC get little or no sleep. Energy drinks become more important than water, and, for the most part, if you see people popping pills, they're not likely to be vitamins.

At any rate, the WMC is worth checking out if you get ecstatic over names such as Peter Rauhoffer, Roger Sanchez, Frankie Knuckles, Hex Hector, Paul Oakenfold, Armand Van Helden, Deep Dish, among many, many others. For more information on WMC events, go to www.wmcon.com.

There are many clubs and bars that have no cover charge—they just make up for it by charging $20 for a martini!

Bongos Cuban Café   Gloria Estefan's latest hit in the restaurant business pays homage to the sights, sounds, and cuisine of pre-Castro Cuba. Bongos is a mammoth restaurant attached to the American Airlines Arena in downtown Miami. On Friday after 11pm and Saturday after 11:30pm, it's transformed from a friendly family restaurant into the city's hottest 21-and-over salsa nightclub. Cover charges can be hefty, but consider it your ticket to an astounding show of some of the best salsa dancers in the city. Prepare yourself for standing room only. Salsa lessons are also available for those with two left feet. At the American Airlines Arena, 601 Biscayne Blvd., Downtown Miami. © **786/777-2100.** www.bongoscubancafe.com. Cover Fri-Sat; women free until 11pm, $20 after 11pm; men $20.

Cameo ★   Still haunted by the ghost of clubs past, the space formerly known as crobar has undergone much-needed renovations and reopened as Cameo, its original incarnation, albeit under the ever-expanding umbrella of the Opium Group—the Microsoft of Miami nightclubs. Under Opium's direction, Cameo, which boasts a supersonic sound system, star DJs, and plenty of VIP seating, once again another must stop on the nocturnal itineraries of any die hard or erstwhile clubber. Open Thursday through Monday from 10pm to 5am. 1445 Washington Ave., South Beach. © **305/531-8225.** www.cameomiami.com. Cover Thurs, Sun, Mon $20–$40; Fri-Sat $25–$50.

Club Space ★   Clubland hits the mainland with this cavernous downtown warehouse of a club. With more than 30,000 square feet of dance space, you can spin around à la Stevie Nicks (albeit to a techno beat) without having to worry about banging into someone. On Saturday and Sunday nights, the party usually extends to the next morning, sometimes as late as 10am. It's quite a sight to see club kids rushing off to work straight from Space on a Monday morning. Known as the venue of choice for world-renowned DJs, Club Space sometimes charges ludicrous admission fees to cover its hefty price tags. **Note:** Club Space doesn't really get going until around 3am. Call for more information, as it doesn't have a concrete schedule. 34 NE 11th St., Miami. ☎ **305/372-9378.** www.clubspace.com. Cover up to $50.

LIV and Blade The latest in Miami's celebrity saturated nightlife, LIV (as in, "celebrities live for LIV") and Blade are the recently revamped Fontainebleau's dance club and subterranean lounge/pool bar, respectively. Because they're new, they're at the top of the A-list and among the hardest to get into. Go early even if it means lining up in the lobby. In the cavernous LIV, expect to see celebs ensconced in visible VIP areas. At Blade, which also doubles as a sushi restaurant, you'll see the stars wolfing down sashimi along with shots of tequila before moving back upstairs to LIV. Two separate entrances, two totally different vibes, two times the fun. 4441 Collins Ave., South Beach. ☎ **305/538-2000.** www.livnightclub.com. Cover $10–$50.

Mansion A product of the same team behind the utterly addictive Opium Group (see above) this place is a massive multilevel lounge that, according to the owners and promoters, is entirely "VIP," meaning you'd best know someone to get in or else you'll be among the masses outside and not even close to the manse. Live DJs, models, and celebrities galore—ubiquitous Paris Hilton, Britney Spears, Lindsay Lohan, Justin Timberlake, Beyoncé, Jay Z, and more—not to mention high ceilings, wood floors, brick walls, and a decidedly nonsmoky interior—make this Mansion, despite its cheesy name, a *must* on the list of see-and-be-scenesters. Open Tuesday through Sunday from 11pm to 5am. 1235 Washington Ave., South Beach. ☎ **305/531-5535.** www.theopiumgroup.com. Cover $10–$40.

Nikki Beach What the Playboy Mansion is to L.A., the Nikki Beach is to South Beach—but if you want a locals scene, you won't find it here. The allure is mostly for visiting tourists who love to gawk at their fellow half-naked ladies and men actually venturing into the daylight on Sunday (around 4pm, which is ungodly in this town) to see, be seen, and, at times, be obscene. At night, it's very "Brady Bunch goes to Hawaii," with a sexy Tiki hut/Polynesian theme style, albeit rated R. Also located within this bastion of hedonism is the second-floor nightclub for those who want to dance on an actual dance floor and not sand. The club recently debuted a new spruced-up dining room serving very massive portions of "global cuisine," but we'd stick with cocktails. 101 Ocean Dr., South Beach. ☎ **305/538-1111.** www.nikkibeach.com. Cover $10–$20.

> ### Impressions
>
> *Working the door teaches you a lot about human nature.*
> —A former South Beach doorman

Parkwest Nightclub A 6,000-foot dance and lounge palace, Parkwest features the usual top-of-the-line sound system and an unusual LED wall, the only one of its size in South Florida. With five bars—two of the most popular are Stereo and Rehab, the club's indie-rock-inspired dance lounge featuring antique gas pumps, celebrity mug shots, three bars, two levels, and 2,500 square feet—VIP areas and lounge seating throughout the space, Parkwest is for the hard-core clubgoer. 30 NE 11th St., Downtown. ✆ **305/350-7444.** www.stereomiami.com. Cover $20.

SET   The Opium Group's undisputed "it" child, SET is *the* place to be, at least at the time of this writing. A luxurious lounge with chandeliers and design-mag-worthy decor is always full of trendsetters, celebs, and wannabes. Where you really want to be, however, is upstairs, in the private VIP room, where Britney Spears was seen downing Purple Hooter shots. A classy place that doesn't designate the behavior of its patrons, SET is also known for a ruthless door policy. Ask your hotel concierge to get you in or else you may find yourself standing on the wrong side of the velvet ropes wasting precious vacation time. 320 Lincoln Rd., South Beach. ✆ **305/531-2800.** www.setmiami.com. Cover $20.

WALL   The W South Beach's requisite velvety-roped-off hipster nightclub run by—who else—the Opium Group in collaboration with some other heavy hitters in the Miami club scene, WALL is a place you definitely want to bang up against if you're into that very VIP scene complete with couches reserved for only those dropping thousands on booze even in a recession. With its mirrored walls and flashy ambience, a night in WALL is not unlike what we think it would feel like to spin around inside a disco ball. 2201 Collins Ave., South Beach. ✆ **305/938-3000.**

Live Music

Unfortunately, Miami's live music scene is not thriving. Instead of local bands garnering devoted fans, local DJs are more admired, skyrocketing much more easily to fame—thanks to the city's lauded dance-club scene. However, there are still several places that strive to bring Miami up to speed as far as live music is concerned. You just have to look—and listen—for it a bit more carefully. The following is a list of places where you can, from time to time, catch some live acts.

Churchill's Hideaway 🍴   British expatriate Dave Daniels couldn't live in Miami without a true English-style pub, so he opened Churchill's Hideaway, the city's premier space for live rock music. Filthy and located in a rather unsavory neighborhood, Churchill's is committed to promoting and extending the lifeline of the lagging local music scene. A fun no-frills crowd hangs out here. Bring earplugs with you, as it is deafening once the music starts. Monday is open-mic night, while Wednesday is reserved for ladies' wrestling. 5501 NE 2nd Ave., Little Haiti. ✆ **305/757-1807.** www. churchillspub.com. Cover up to $6.

Jazid 🍴   Smoky, sultry, and illuminated by flickering candelabras, Jazid is the kind of place where you'd expect to hear Sade's "Smooth Operator" on constant rotation. Instead, however, you'll hear live jazz (sometimes acid jazz), soul, and funk. An eclectic mix of mellow folk convenes here for a much-needed respite from the surrounding Washington Avenue mayhem. 1342 Washington Ave., South Beach. ✆ **305/673-9372.** www.jazid.net. Cover up to $10.

Tobacco Road   Al Capone used to hang out here when it was a speakeasy. Now locals flock here to see local bands perform, as well as national acts such as George Clinton and the P-Funk All-Stars, Koko Taylor, and the Radiators. Tobacco Road (the proud owner of Miami's very first liquor license) is small and gritty, and meant to be that way. Escape the smoke and sweat in the backyard patio, where air is a welcome commodity. The downright cheap nightly specials, such as the $11 lobster on Tuesday, are quite good and served until 2am; the bar is open until 5am. 626 S. Miami Ave. (over the Miami Ave. Bridge, near Brickell Ave.), Downtown. (*) **305/374-1198.** www.tobacco-road.com. Cover Thurs–Sat $5–$10.

Upstairs at the Van Dyke Cafe 🏠 The cafe's jazz bar, located on the second floor, resembles a classy speakeasy in which local jazz performers play to an intimate, enthusiastic crowd of mostly adults and sophisticated young things, who often huddle at the small tables until the wee hours. 846 Lincoln Rd., South Beach. (*) **305/534-3600.** www.thevandykecafe.com. Cover Sun–Thurs $5, Fri–Sat $10 for a seat; no cover at the bar.

The Gay & Lesbian Scene

Miami and the beaches have long been host to what is called a "first-tier" gay community. Similar to the Big Apple, the Bay Area, or LaLa land, Miami has had a large alternative community since the days when Anita Bryant used her citrus power to boycott the rise in political activism in the early 1970s. Well, things have changed and Miami-Dade now has a gay-rights ordinance.

Newcomers intending to party in any bar, whether downtown or certainly on the beach, will want to check ahead for the schedule, as all clubs must have a gay or lesbian night to pay their rent. Miami Beach, in fact, is a capital of the gay circuit party scene, rivaling San Francisco, Palm Springs, and even the mighty Sydney, Australia, for tourist dollars. However, ever since South Beach got bit by the hip-hop bug, many of Miami's gays have been crossing county lines into Fort Lauderdale, where there are, surprisingly, many more gay establishments.

MOVA Just off Lincoln Road, MOVA (formerly Halo) is the beach's boutiquey gay lounge. Smoke free and überstylish, Halo is open nightly until 3am and features DJs and daily buy-one-get-one-free happy hour from 3 until 6pm. 1625 Michigan Ave., South Beach. No phone. www.movalounge.com.

Score There's a reason this Lincoln Road hotbed of gay activity is called Score. In addition to the huge pickup scene, Score offers a multitude of bars, dance floors, lounge areas, and outdoor tables, in case you need to come up for air. Sunday afternoon tea dances are legendary. 727 Lincoln Rd., South Beach. (*) **305/535-1111.** www.scorebar.net.

Twist One of the most popular bars (and hideaways) on South Beach, this recently expanded bar (which is literally right across the street from the police station) has a casual yet lively atmosphere. 1057 Washington Ave., South Beach. (*) **305/538-9478.** www.twistsobe.com.

Latin Clubs

Considering that Hispanics make up a large part of Miami's population and that there's a huge influx of Spanish-speaking visitors, it's no surprise that there are some great Latin nightclubs in the city. Plus, with the meteoric rise of the international music scene based in Miami, many international stars come through the offices of MTV Latino, SONY International, and a multitude of Latin TV studios based in Miami—and they're all looking for a good club scene on weekends. Most of the Anglo clubs also reserve at least 1 night a week for Latin rhythms.

Casa Panza 🏠 This *casa* is one of Little Havana's liveliest and most popular nightspots. Every Tuesday, Thursday, and Saturday night, Casa Panza, in the heart

Clubs, Live Music & Other Party Spots

of Little Havana, becomes the House of Flamenco, with shows at 8 and 11pm. You can either enjoy a flamenco show or strap on your own dancing shoes and participate in the celebration. Enjoy a fantastic Spanish meal before the show, or just a glass of sangria before you start stomping. Open until 4am, Casa Panza is a hot spot for young Latin club kids and, occasionally, a few older folks who are so taken by the music and the scene that they've failed to realize it's well past their bedtime. 1620 SW 8th St. (Calle Ocho), Little Havana. © **305/643-5343.**

Hoy Como Ayer　Formerly known as Cafe Nostalgia, the Little Havana hangout dedicated to reminiscing about Old Cuba, Hoy Como Ayer is like the Brady Bunch of Latin hangouts—while it was extremely popular with old-timers in its Cafe Nostalgia incarnation, it is now experiencing a resurgence among the younger generation seeking its own brand of nostalgia. Its Thursday night party, Fuacata (slang for "Pow!"), is a magnet for Latin hipsters, featuring classic Cuban music mixed in with modern DJ-spun sound effects. Open Thursday to Sunday from 9pm to 4am. 2212 SW 8th St. (Calle Ocho), Little Havana. © **305/541-2631.** Cover Thurs–Sun $10.

La Covacha 🎁　This hut, located virtually in the middle of nowhere (West Miami), is the hottest Latin joint in the entire city. Sunday features the best in Latin rock, with local and international acts. But the shack is really jumping on weekend nights, when the place is open until 5am. Friday is *the* night here, so much so that the owners had to place a red velvet rope out front to maintain some semblance of order. It's an amusing sight—a velvet rope guarding a shack—but once you get in, you'll understand the need for it. Do not wear silk here, as you *will* sweat. 10730 NW 25th St. (at NW 107th Ave.), West Miami. © **305/594-3717.** www.lacovacha.com. Cover up to $10.

Mango's Tropical Café　Claustrophobic types do not want to go near Mango's—ever. One of the most popular spots on Ocean Drive, this outdoor enclave of Latin liveliness shakes with the intensity of a Richter-busting earthquake. Mango's is *Cabaret,* Latin style. Nightly live Brazilian and other Latin music, not to mention scantily clad male and female dancers, draws huge gawking crowds in from the sidewalk. But pay attention to the music, if you can: Incognito international musicians often lose their anonymity and jam with the house band on stage. Open daily from 11am to 5am. 900 Ocean Dr., South Beach. © **305/673-4422.** www.mangostropical cafe.com. Cover $5–$15.

Bowling Alleys

Think of it as the Big Lebowski meets Studio 54, because in Miami, this is not your Sunday afternoon ESPN bowling tournament. As much a fun rainy-day activity as it is with the kids, bowling in Miami gives new meaning to partying in the gutter.

Lucky Strike Lanes ☺　South Beach's only bowling alley is a pricey blast for adults and children, with 14 lanes, 2 pool tables, free Wi-Fi (to cheat on bowling?), a pulsating nightclub-esque soundtrack, full bar, TVs, and restaurant. Kids are only allowed up until 9pm, after which time Lucky Strike turns into a 21-and-over scene (until 1am Sunday through Thursday; open until 2am Friday and Saturday). 1691 Michigan Ave. © **305/532-0307.** www.bowlluckystrike.com. $45–$55 per hour depending on day and time including shoe rental.

THE rhythm IS GONNA GET YOU

Are you feeling shy about hitting a Latin club because you fear your two left feet will stand out? Then take a few lessons from one of the following dance companies or dance teachers. They offer individual and group lessons to dancers of any origin who are willing to learn. These folks have made it their mission to teach merengue and flamenco to non-Latinos and Latino left-foots, and are among the most reliable, consistent, and popular ones in Miami. So what are you waiting for?

Thursday and Friday nights at **Bongos Cuban Café** (American Airlines Arena, 601 Biscayne Blvd., Downtown, ℂ **786/777-2100**) are amazing showcases for some of the city's best salsa dancers, but amateurs need not be intimidated, thanks to the instructors from Latin Groove Dance Studios, who are on hand to help you with your two left feet. Lessons are free.

At **Ballet Flamenco La Rosa** (in the Performing Arts Network [PAN] building, 13126 W. Dixie Hwy., North Miami; ℂ **305/899-7730**), you can learn to flamenco, salsa, or merengue. This is the only professional flamenco company in the area. They charge $15 per class.

Nobody teaches salsa like **Luz Pinto** (ℂ **305/868-9418; www.latin-heat. com**). She teaches 7 days a week and, trust me, with her, you'll learn cool turns easily. She charges $50 for a private lesson for up to four people, and $10 per person for a group lesson. She also teaches group classes at PAN on Miami Beach. Although she teaches everything from classic to hip wedding dances to ballroom and merengue, her specialty is Casino-style salsa, popularized in the 1950s in Cuba, Luz's homeland. You will be impressed with how well and quickly Luz can teach you to have fun and feel great dancing. Call her for more information.

Angel Arroyo has been teaching salsa to the clueless out of his home (at 16467 NE 27th Ave., North Miami Beach; ℂ **305/949-7799**) for the past 10 years. Just $10 will buy you an hour's time. He traditionally teaches Monday and Wednesday nights, but call ahead to check for any schedule and rate changes.

Splitsville Luxury Lanes & Dinner Lounge ☺ Located at Sunset Place, Splitsville is South Miami's Lucky Strike, with 12 lanes, six pool tables, full-service restaurant, TVs, and multiple bars. Like Lucky Strike, no kids or under 21 after 8pm, when the place turns into a thumping club scene until 5am. Unlike Lucky Strike, Splitsville is affordable and because of that, there's usually a wait list for a lane. Luckily there are plenty other distractions to keep you busy while you wait. Open until 2am Sunday through Thursday, and until 5am Friday and Saturday. 5701 Sunset Dr. ℂ **305/665-5263.** www.splitsvillelanes.com. $6 per person per game, $4 for shoe rental.

Strike Miami ☺ Located at the Dolphin Mall, this one is Miami's biggest bowling alley, with 34 lanes and, like the others, a nightclub setting. This one, owned by NYC's famed Bowlmor, even has glow-in-the-dark bowling. Food, bars, TVs, you get the picture. It's 18 and over after 9pm (open until 1am Sunday through Thursday and 3am Friday and Saturday). In the Dolphin Mall, 11401 NW 12th St. ℂ **305/594-0200.** www.bowlmor.com. $30–$40 per hour depending on day and time including shoe rental.

THE PERFORMING ARTS

Highbrows and culture vultures complain that there is a dearth of decent cultural offerings in Miami. What do locals tell them? Go back to New York! In all seriousness, however, in recent years, Miami's performing arts scene has improved greatly. The city's Broadway Series features Tony Award–winning shows (the touring versions, of course), which aren't always Broadway caliber, but usually pretty good and not nearly as pricey. Local arts groups such as the Miami Light Project, a not-for-profit cultural organization that presents live performances by innovative dance, music, and theater artists, have had huge success in attracting big-name artists such as Nina Simone and Philip Glass to Miami. Also, a burgeoning bohemian movement in Little Havana has given way to performance spaces that are nightclubs in their own right.

Theater

The **Actors' Playhouse,** a musical theater at the newly restored Miracle Theater at 280 Miracle Mile, Coral Gables (© **305/444-9293;** www.actorsplayhouse.org), is a grand 1948 Art Deco movie palace with a 600-seat main theater and a smaller theater/rehearsal hall that hosts a number of excellent musicals for children throughout the year. In addition to these two theaters, the Playhouse recently added a 300-seat children's balcony theater. Tickets run from $27 to $40.

The **GableStage,** at the Biltmore Hotel (p. 106), Anastasia Avenue, Coral Gables (© **305/445-1119**), stages at least one Shakespearean play, one classic, and one contemporary piece a year. This well-regarded theater usually tries to secure the rights to a national or local premiere as well. Tickets cost $35 for adults, and $15 and $32, respectively, for students and seniors. GableStage announced in 2009 that it would take over the abandoned, landmark Coconut Grove Playhouse using $20 million in designated county improvement funds to create a larger, 600-seat theater. Construction was expected to start in 2012 and end in 2014.

The **Jerry Herman Ring Theatre** is on the main campus of the University of Miami in Coral Gables (© **305/284-3355**). The University's Department of Theater Arts uses this stage for advanced-student productions of comedies, dramas, and musicals. Faculty and guest actors are regularly featured, as are contemporary works by local playwrights. Performances are usually scheduled Tuesday through Saturday during the academic year. In the summer, don't miss "Summer Shorts," a selection of superb one acts. Tickets sell for $14 to $16.

The **New Theatre,** 4120 Laguna St., Coral Gables (© **305/443-5909;** www.new-theatre.org), prides itself on showing renowned works from America and Europe. As the name implies, you'll find mostly contemporary plays, with a few classics thrown in. Performances are staged Thursday through Sunday year-round. Tickets are $35 on Thursday, $40 on Friday and Saturday, and $35 to $40 on Sunday. If tickets are available on the day of the performance—and they usually are—students pay half-price.

Classical Music

In addition to a number of local orchestras and operas (see below), which regularly offer quality music and world-renowned guest artists, each year brings a slew of classical-music special events and touring artists to Miami. The **Concert Association of Florida** (**CAF;** © **877/433-3200**) produces one of the most important and longest-running series. Known for more than a quarter of a century for its high-caliber, star-packed schedules, CAF regularly arranges the best "serious" music concerts for the city. Season after season, the schedules are punctuated by world-renowned dance companies and seasoned virtuosi such as Itzhak Perlman, Andre Watts, and Kathleen Battle. Because CAF does not have its own space, performances are usually scheduled in the Miami–Dade County Auditorium or the Jackie Gleason Theater of the Performing Arts (see the "Major Venues" section below). The season lasts October through April, and ticket prices range from $20 to $70.

Miami Chamber Symphony   This professional orchestra is a small, subscription-series orchestra that's not affiliated with any major arts organizations and is therefore an inexpensive alternative to the high-priced classical venues. Renowned international soloists perform regularly here. The season runs October to May, and most concerts are held in the Gusman Concert Hall, on the University of Miami campus. 5690 N. Kendall Dr., Kendall. ✆ **305/284-6477.** Tickets $15–$30.

New World Symphony   This organization, led by artistic director Michael Tilson Thomas, is a stepping stone for gifted young musicians seeking professional careers. The orchestra specializes in innovative, energetic performances, and often features renowned guest soloists and conductors. The season lasts from October to May, during which time there are many free concerts. 541 Lincoln Rd., South Beach. ✆ **305/673-3331.** www.nws.org. Tickets free–$60. Rush tickets (remaining tickets sold 1 hr. before performance) $20. Students $10 (1 hr. before concerts; limited seating).

Opera

Florida Grand Opera   Around for more than 60 years, this company regularly features singers from top houses in both America and Europe. All productions are sung in their original language and staged with projected English supertitles. Tickets become scarce when Placido Domingo comes to town. The season runs roughly from November to April, with five performances each week. In 2007, the opera moved into more upscale headquarters in the Sanford and Dolores Ziff Ballet Opera House at the Arsht (formerly Carnival Center) Center for the Performing Arts. Box office: 1300 Biscayne Blvd. Miami. ✆ **305/949-6722.** www.fgo.org. Tickets $24–$125. Student discounts available.

Dance

Several local dance companies train and perform in the Greater Miami area. In addition, top traveling troupes regularly stop at the venues listed below. Keep your eyes open for special events and guest artists.

Ballet Flamenco La Rosa   For a taste of local Latin flavor, see this lively troupe perform impressive flamenco and other styles of Latin dance on Miami stages. (They also teach Latin dancing—see the "The Rhythm Is Gonna Get You" box above.) 13126 W. Dixie Hwy., North Miami. ✆ **305/899-7729.** www.balletflamencolarosa.com. Tickets $20 at door, $15 in advance, $8 for students and seniors.

Miami City Ballet   This artistically acclaimed and innovative company, directed by Edward Villella, features a repertoire of more than 60 ballets, many by George Balanchine, and has had more than 20 world premieres. The company's three-story center features eight rehearsal rooms, a ballet school, a boutique, and ticket offices.

The City Ballet season runs from September to April. Ophelia and Juan Jr. Roca Center, Collins Ave. and 22nd St., South Beach. © **305/929-7000,** or 929-7010 for box office. Tickets $17–$50.

Major Venues

The **Colony Theater,** 1040 Lincoln Rd. in South Beach (© **305/674-1040**), which has become an architectural showpiece of the Art Deco District, opened in 2006 after a $4.3-million renovation that added wing and fly space, improved access for those with disabilities, and restored the lobby to its original Art Deco look.

At the **Miami–Dade County Auditorium,** West Flagler Street at 29th Avenue, Southwest Miami (© **305/547-5414**), performers gripe about the lack of space, and for patrons, this 2,430-seat auditorium was once the only Miami space in which you could hear the opera (not any more; see the Arsht Center below). The Auditorium is home to the city's Florida Grand Opera, and it also stages productions by the Concert Association of Florida, many programs in Spanish, and a variety of other shows.

At the 1,700-seat **Gusman Center for the Performing Arts,** 174 E. Flagler St., downtown Miami (© **305/372-0925**), seating is tight, and so is funding, but the sound is superb. In addition to hosting the Miami Film Festival, the elegant Gusman Center features pop concerts, plays, film screenings, and special events. The auditorium was built as the Olympia Theater in 1926, and its ornate palace interior is typical of that era, complete with fancy columns, a huge pipe organ, and twinkling "stars" on the ceiling.

Not to be confused with the Gusman Center (above), the **Gusman Concert Hall,** 1314 Miller Dr., at 14th Street, Coral Gables (© **305/284-6477**), is a roomy 600-seat hall that gives a stage to the Miami Chamber Symphony and a varied program of university recitals.

The newly revamped **Fillmore Miami Beach at the Jackie Gleason Theater,** located in South Beach at Washington Avenue and 17th Street (© **305/673-7300**), may be a mouthful, but when it comes to live music, it truly rocks. In addition to its very modern Hard Rock–meets–Miami Beach decor, complete with requisite bars, chandeliers, and an homage to the original legendary Fillmore in San Francisco, Fillmore, which was taken over by Live Nation, brings major talent to the beach, from Kid Rock and Fall Out Boy to comediennes Sarah Silverman and Lisa Lampanelli. Fillmore also hosts various awards shows, from the Food Network Awards to the Fox Sports Awards.

Last, but definitely not least, the **Adrienne Arsht Center for the Performing Arts,** 1300 Biscayne Blvd. (© **786/468-2000**), opened in late 2006 after a whopping $446-million tab. In 2008, philanthropist Adrienne Arsht donated $30 million to the financially troubled center, renaming it the Adrienne Arsht Center for the Performing Arts of Miami–Dade County (or the Arsht Center, for short). Included: The 2,400-seat **Sanford and Dolores Ziff Ballet Opera House** and the 2,200-seat **Knight Concert Hall** are Miami venues for the **Concert Association of Florida, Florida Grand Opera, Miami City Ballet,** and **New World Symphony,** as well as premier venues for a wide array of local, national, and international performances, ranging from Broadway musicals and visiting classical artists to world and urban music, Latin concerts, and popular entertainment from many cultures.

MIAMI AFTER DARK   The Performing Arts

The **Studio Theater,** a flexible black-box space designed for up to 200 seats, hosts intimate performances of contemporary theater, dance, music, cabaret, and other entertainment. The **Peacock Education Center** acts as a catalyst for arts education and enrichment programs for children and adults. Finally, the **Plaza for the Arts** is a magnificent setting for outdoor entertainment, social celebrations, and informal community gatherings.

Designed by world-renowned architect Cesar Pelli, the Carnival Center is the focal point of a planned Arts, Media, and Entertainment District in mid-Miami. The complex is wrapped in limestone, slate, decorative stone, stainless steel, glass curtain walls, and tropical landscaping, and was completed in mid-2006. Newly opened within the complex is a bona fide restaurant, **Prelude by Barton G.** (© 305/357-7900; www.preludebybartong.com), an old-school yet modern supper club featuring prix-fixe pre- and post-theater menus. The biggest joke in town, however, is that after spending all that money, the planners forgot to include parking facilities. As a result, valet parking is available for $10 to $20 or you can park at the Marriott nearby, but it's truly a pain, so to make things easy, just take a cab. It'll cost you the same and you won't have to deal with traipsing across Biscayne Boulevard in your fine theater threads. For more information, check out the website at www.arshtcenter.org.

LATE-NIGHT BITES

Although some dining spots in Miami stop serving at 10pm, many are open very late or even around the clock—especially on weekends. So, if it's 4am and you need a quick bite after clubbing, don't fret. There are a vast number of pizza places lining Washington Avenue in South Beach that are open past 6am. Especially good are **La Sandwicherie,** 229 14th St. (behind the Amoco station; © 305/532-8934), which serves up a great late-night sandwich until 5am. Nearby is the new in 2010 **BK Whopper Bar,** 1101 Washington Ave. (no tel. yet), Burger King's spin on a hip burger joint, open 24 hours a day, serving beer and as gourmet a burger as BK can make. Another place of note for night owls is the **News Café,** 800 Ocean Dr. (© 305/538-6397), a trendy and well-priced cafe that has an enormous menu offering great all day breakfasts, Middle Eastern platters, fruit bowls, or steak and potatoes—and everything is served 24 hours a day. If you're craving a corned beef on rye at 5am, **Jerry's Famous Deli,** 1450 Collins Ave. (© 305/534-3244), is open 24/7. If your night out was at one of the Latin clubs around town, stop in at **Versailles,** 3555 SW Eighth St. (© 305/444-0240), in Little Havana. What else but a Cuban *medianoche* (midnight sandwich) will do? It's not open all night, but its hours extend well past midnight—usually until 3 or 4am on weekends—to cater to gangs of revelers, young and old.

For a more thorough listing of Miami's most notable restaurants, see chapter 7.

11

THE EVERGLADES & BISCAYNE NATIONAL PARK

President Harry S Truman once declared the Everglades "an irreplaceable primitive area." While those words don't exactly do justice to the Everglades and the surrounding Biscayne National Park, he clarified what he said: "Here are no lofty peaks seeking the sky, no mighty glaciers or rushing streams wearing away the uplifted land. Here is land, tranquil in its quiet beauty, serving not as the source of water, but as the last receiver of it. To its natural abundance, we owe the spectacular plant and animal life that distinguishes this place from all others in our country."

There's no better reality show than the one that exists in the Everglades. Up-close-and-personal views of alligators, crocodiles, and bona fide wildlife—not the kind you'd find on, say, South Beach after midnight—make for an interesting, photo-opportunistic experience that's worthy of a show on Animal Planet.

Tourists in South Florida shouldn't leave the area without taking time to see some of the wild plant and animal life in the swampy Everglades and the underwater treasures of Biscayne National Park.

A GLIMPSE OF EVERGLADES NATIONAL PARK ★★

35 miles SW of Miami

Before visiting it, my conception of the Everglades was that it was one big swamp swarming with ominous creatures, like something from the programming geeks at the Sci-Fi Channel. For someone who'd rather endure an endless series of root canals than audition for a role on *Survivor* (the closest I'd ever been to nature was sleep-away camp), the Everglades might as well have been the *Never*glades—that is, until I finally decided to venture there. To my surprise, and contrary to popular belief, the Everglades isn't really a swamp at all, but one of the country's most fascinating natural resources.

For first-timers or those with dubious athletic skills, the best way to see the 'Glades is probably via airboats, which aren't actually allowed in the park proper, but cut through the saw grass on the park's outskirts, taking you past countless birds, alligators, crocodiles, deer, and raccoons. A walk on one of the park's many trails will provide you with a different vantage point: up-close interaction with an assortment of tame wildlife. But the absolute best way to see the 'Glades is via canoe, which allows you to get incredibly close to nature. Whichever method you choose, I guarantee that you will marvel at the sheer beauty of the Everglades. Despite the multitude of mosquito bites (the bugs seem to be immune to repellent—wear long pants and cover your arms), an Everglades experience will definitely contribute to a newfound appreciation for Florida's natural (and beautiful) wonderland.

Lazy River

It takes a month for 1 gallon of water to move through Everglades National Park.

This vast and unusual ecosystem is actually a shallow, 40-mile-wide, slow-moving river. Rarely more than knee-deep, the water is the lifeblood of this wilderness, and the subtle shifts in water level dictate the life cycles of the native plants and animals. In 1947, 1.5 million acres—less than 20% of the Everglades' wilderness—were established as Everglades National Park. At that time, few lawmakers understood how neighboring ecosystems relate to each other. Consequently, the park is heavily affected by surrounding territories and is at the butt end of every environmental insult that occurs upstream in Miami.

While there has been a marked decrease in the indigenous wildlife here, Everglades National Park nevertheless remains one of the few places where you can see dozens of endangered species in their natural habitat, including the swallowtail butterfly, American crocodile, leatherback turtle, southern bald eagle, West Indian manatee, and Florida panther.

Take your time on the trails, and a hypnotic beauty begins to unfold. Follow the rustling of a bush, and you might see a small green tree frog or tiny brown anole lizard, with its bright-red spotted throat. Crane your neck to see around a bend, and discover a delicate, brightly painted mule-ear orchid.

The slow and subtle splendor of this exotic land may not be immediately appealing to kids raised on video games and rapid-fire commercials, but they'll certainly remember the experience and thank you for it later. Your kids will find plenty of dramatic fun around the park, such as airboat rides, hiking, and biking, to keep them satisfied for at least a day.

Just the Facts

GETTING THERE & ACCESS POINTS Although the Everglades may seem overwhelmingly large and unapproachable, it's easy to get to the park's two main

The Everglades

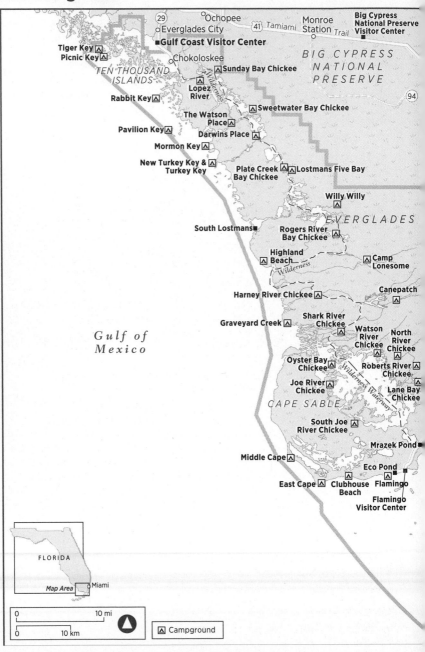

Ochopee
Everglades City
29
41 Tamiami
Monroe Station Trail
Big Cypress National Preserve Visitor Center
■Gulf Coast Visitor Center

BIG CYPRESS NATIONAL PRESERVE

Tiger Key
Picnic Key
Chokoloskee
Sunday Bay Chickee

TEN THOUSAND ISLANDS
Lopez River

94

Rabbit Key
Sweetwater Bay Chickee

The Watson Place
Pavilion Key
Darwins Place

Mormon Key
New Turkey Key & Turkey Key
Plate Creek Bay Chickee
Lostmans Five Bay

Willy Willy

EVERGLADES

South Lostmans■
Rogers River Bay Chickee

Highland Beach
Camp Lonesome
Wilderness

Harney River Chickee
Canepatch

Graveyard Creek
Shark River Chickee
Watson River Chickee
North River Chickee

Gulf of Mexico
Oyster Bay Chickee
Roberts River Chickee

Joe River Chickee
Wilderness Waterway
Lane Bay Chickee

CAPE SABLE

South Joe River Chickee

Mrazek Pond ■

Middle Cape
Eco Pond

East Cape
Clubhouse Beach
Flamingo

Flamingo Visitor Center

FLORIDA

Map Area
○ Miami

0   10 mi
0   10 km

▲ Campground

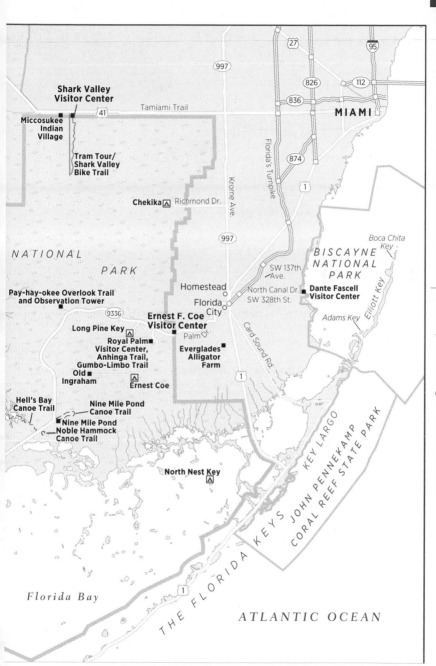

areas—the northern section, accessible via Shark Valley and Everglades City, and the southern section, accessible through the Ernest F. Coe Visitor Center, near Homestead and Florida City.

NORTHERN ENTRANCES A popular day trip for Miamians, **Shark Valley,** a 15-mile paved loop road (with an observation tower in the middle of the loop) over-looking the pulsating heart of the Everglades, is the easiest and most scenic way to explore the national park. Just 25 miles west of the Florida Turnpike, Shark Valley is best reached via the Tamiami Trail, South Florida's preturnpike, two-lane road, which cuts across the southern part of the state along the park's northern border. Roadside attractions (boat rides and alligator farms, for example) along the Tamiami Trail are operated by the Miccosukee Indian Village and are worth a quick, fun stop. An excellent tram tour (leaving from the Shark Valley Visitor Center) goes deep into the park along a trail that's also terrific for biking. Shark Valley is about an hour's drive from Miami.

A little less than 10 miles west along the Tamiami Trail from Shark Valley, you'll discover **Big Cypress National Preserve,** in which stretches of vibrant green cypress and pine trees make for a fabulous Kodak moment. If you pick up S.R. 29 and head south from the Tamiami Trail, you'll hit a modified version of civilization in the form of Everglades City (where the Everglades meet the Gulf of Mexico), where there's another entrance to the park and the **Gulf Coast Visitor Center.** From Miami to Shark Valley: Go west on I-395 to S.R. 821 S. (the Florida Tpk.). Take the U.S. 41/SW Eighth Street (Tamiami Trail) exit. The Shark Valley entrance is just 25 miles west. To get to Everglades City, continue west on the Tamiami Trail and head south on S.R. 29. Everglades City is approximately a 2½-hour drive from Miami, but because it is scenic, it may take longer if you stop or slow down to view your surroundings.

SOUTHERN ENTRANCE (VIA HOMESTEAD & FLORIDA CITY) If you're in a rush to hit the 'Glades and don't care about the scenic route, this is your best bet. Just southeast of Homestead and Florida City, off S.R. 9336, the southern access to the park will bring you directly to the Ernest F. Coe Visitor Center. Right inside the park, 4 miles beyond the Ernest F. Coe Visitor Center, is the Royal Palm Visitor Center, which is the starting point for the two most popular walking trails, Gumbo Limbo and Anhinga, where you'll witness a plethora of birds and wildlife roaming freely, unperturbed by human voyeurs. Thirteen miles west of the Ernest F. Coe Visitor Center, you'll hit Pa-hay-okee Overlook Trail, which is worth a trek across the boardwalk to reach the observation tower, over which vultures and hawks hover protectively amid a resplendent, picturesque, bird's-eye view of the Ever-glades. From Miami to the southern entrance: Go west on I-395 to S.R. 821 S. (Florida Tpk.), which will end in Florida City. Take the first right through the center of town (you can't miss it) and follow signs to the park entrance on S.R. 9336. The Ernest F. Coe Visitor Center is about 1½ hours from Miami.

VISITOR CENTERS & INFORMATION General inquiries and specific ques-tions should be directed to **Everglades National Park Headquarters,** 40001 S.R. 9336, Homestead, FL 33034 (© **305/242-7700**). Ask for a copy of *Parks and Preserves,* a free newspaper that's filled with up-to-date information about goings-on in the Everglades. Headquarters is staffed by helpful phone operators daily from 8:30am to 4:30pm. You can also try www.nps.gov/ever.

'Glades in the Spotlight

ABC's canceled television series Invasion may have been shot mostly on a set in Los Angeles, but its creator, Shaun Cassidy, a Florida resident and, yes, that Shaun Cassidy, has been to the Everglades and is as intrigued as the rest of us. "It's a very primordial place," Cassidy said in a magazine interview. "There are a lot of species that have existed there that have not existed anywhere else. It's a place that was cut off from the rest of the world for a very long time."

Note that all hours listed are for the high season, generally November through May. During the slow summer months, many offices and outfitters keep abbreviated hours. Always call ahead to confirm hours of operation.

The **Ernest F. Coe Visitor Center,** located at the Park Headquarters entrance, west of Homestead and Florida City, is the best place to gather information for your trip. In addition to details on tours and boat rentals, and free brochures outlining trails, wildlife, and activities, you will find state-of-the-art educational displays, films, and interactive exhibits. A gift shop sells postcards, film, an impressive selection of books about the Everglades, unusual gift items, and a supply of your most important gear: insect repellent. The shop is open daily from 8am to 5pm.

The **Royal Palm Visitor Center,** a small nature museum located 3 miles past the park's main entrance, is a smaller information center. The museum is not great (its displays are equipped with recordings about the park's ecosystem), but the center is the departure point for the popular Anhinga and Gumbo Limbo trails. The center is open daily from 8am to 4pm.

Knowledgeable rangers, who provide brochures and personal insight into the park's activities, also staff the **Flamingo Visitor Center,** 38 miles from the main entrance, at the park's southern access, with natural-history exhibits and information on visitor services, and the **Shark Valley Visitor Center,** at the park's northern entrance. Both are open daily from 8:30am to 5pm.

ENTRANCE FEES, PERMITS & REGULATIONS   Permits and passes can be purchased only at the main park or Shark Valley entrance station. Even if you are just visiting the park for an afternoon, you'll need to buy a 7-day permit, which costs $10 per vehicle. Pedestrians and cyclists are charged $5 each. An Everglades Park Pass, valid for a year's worth of unlimited admissions, is available for $25. You may also purchase a 12-month America the Beautiful National Parks and Federal Recreation Lands Pass–Annual Pass for $50, which is valid for entrance into any U.S. national park. U.S. citizens ages 62 and older pay only $10 for an America the Beautiful National Parks and Federal Recreation Lands Pass–Senior Pass that's valid for life. An America the Beautiful National Parks and Federal Recreation Lands Pass–Access Pass is available free to U.S. citizens with disabilities.

Permits are required for campers to stay overnight either in the backcountry or at the primitive campsites. See "Camping in the Everglades," on p. 256.

Those who want to fish without a charter captain must obtain a standard State of Florida saltwater fishing license. These are available in the park, at any tackle shop or sporting goods store nearby, or online at www2.fl.wildlifelicense.com/start.php.

Would You Like Some More Mercury with Your Bass?

Warning: High levels of mercury have been found in Everglades' bass and in some fish species in northern Florida Bay. Do not eat bass caught north of the Main Park Road. Do not eat bass caught south of the Main Park Road more than once a week. Children and pregnant women should not eat any bass. The following saltwater species caught in northern Florida Bay should not be consumed more than once per week by adults or once per month by women of child-bearing age and children: spotted sea trout, gaff-topsail, catfish, bluefish, jack crevalle, or lady-fish.

Nonresidents pay $30 for a 7-day license or $17 for a 3-day license. Florida residents pay $17 for an annual fishing license. Snook and crawfish licenses must be purchased separately at a cost of $2 each.

Charter captains carry vessel licenses that cover all paying passengers, but ask to be sure. Freshwater fishing licenses are available at various bait-and-tackle stores outside the park at the same rates as those offered inside the park. A good one nearby is **Don's Bait & Tackle,** 30710 S. Federal Hwy., right on U.S. 1 in Homestead (© **305/247-6616**). *Note:* Most of the area's freshwater fishing, limited to murky canals and artificial lakes near housing developments, is hardly worth the trouble when so much good saltwater fishing is available.

SEASONS There are two distinct seasons in the Everglades: high season and mosquito season. High season is also dry season and lasts from late November to May. Most winters here are warm, sunny, and breezy—a good combination for keeping the bugs away. This is the best time to visit because low water levels attract the largest variety of wading birds and their predators. As the dry season wanes, wildlife follows the receding water; by the end of May, the only living things you are sure to spot will make you itch. The worst, called "no-see-ums," are not even swattable. If you choose to visit during the buggy season, be vigilant in applying bug spray. Also, realize that many establishments and operators either close or curtail offerings in summer, so always call ahead to check schedules.

RANGER PROGRAMS More than 50 ranger programs, free with entry, are offered each month during high season and give visitors an opportunity to gain an expert's perspective. Ranger-led walks and talks are offered year-round from Royal Palm Visitor Center, and at the Flamingo and Gulf Coast visitor centers, as well as Shark Valley Visitor Center during winter months. Park rangers tend to be helpful, well informed, and good humored. Some programs occur regularly, such as Royal Palm Visitor Center's Glade Glimpses, a walking tour on which rangers point out flora and fauna, and discuss issues affecting the Everglades' survival. Tours are scheduled at 1:30pm daily. The Anhinga Amble, a similar program that takes place on the Anhinga Trail, starts at 10:30am daily. Because times, programs, and locations vary from month to month, check the schedule, available at any of the visitor centers.

SAFETY There are many dangers inherent in this vast wilderness area. *Always* let someone know your itinerary before you set out on an extended hike. It's mandatory that you file an itinerary when camping overnight in the backcountry (which you can do when you apply for your overnight permit at either the Flamingo Visitor Center or the Gulf Coast Visitor Center). When you're on the water, watch for weather changes; severe thunderstorms and high winds often develop rapidly. Swimming is not recommended because of the presence of alligators, sharks, and barracudas. Watch out for the region's four indigenous poisonous snakes: diamondback and pygmy rattlesnakes, coral snakes (identifiable by their colorful rings), and water moccasins (which swim on the surface of the water). Bring insect repellent to ward off mosquitoes and biting flies. First aid is available from park rangers. The nearest hospital is in Homestead, 10 miles from the park's main entrance.

Seeing the Highlights

Shark Valley, a 15-mile paved road (ideal for biking) through the Everglades, provides a fine introduction to the wonders of the park, but don't plan on spending more than a few hours here. Bicycling and taking a guided tram tour (p. 252) are fantastic ways to cover the highlights.

If you want to see a greater array of plant and animal life, make sure that you venture into the park through the main entrance, pick up a trail map, and dedicate at least a day to exploring from there.

Stop first along the Anhinga and Gumbo Limbo trails, which start right next to each other, 3 miles from the park's main entrance. These trails provide a thorough introduction to Everglades' flora and fauna and are highly recommended to first-time visitors. Each is a .5-mile round-trip. **Gumbo Limbo Trail** (my pick for best walking trail in the Everglades) meanders through a gorgeous, shaded, junglelike hammock of gumbo-limbo trees, royal palms, ferns, orchids, air plants, and a general blanket of vegetation, though it doesn't put you in close contact with much wildlife. **Anhinga Trail** is one of the most popular trails in the park because of its abundance of wildlife: There's more water and wildlife in this area than in most parts of the Everglades, especially during dry season. Alligators, lizards, turtles, river otters, herons, egrets, and other animals abound, making this one of the best trails for seeing wildlife. Arrive early to spot the widest selection of exotic birds, such as the Anhinga bird, the trail's namesake, a large black fishing bird so accustomed to humans that many of them build their nests in plain view. Take your time—at least an hour is recommended for each trail. Both are wheelchair accessible. If you treat the trails and modern boardwalk as pathways to get through quickly, rather than destinations to experience and savor, you'll miss out on the still beauty and hidden treasures that await you.

To get closer to nature, a few hours in a canoe along any of the trails allows paddlers the chance to sense the park's fluid motion and to become a part of the ecosphere. Visitors who choose this option end up feeling more like explorers than observers. (See "Sports & Outdoor Activities," below.)

No matter which option you choose (and there are many), I strongly recommend staying for the 7pm program, available during high season at the Long Pine Key Amphitheater. This ranger-led talk and slide show will give you a detailed overview of the park's history, natural resources, wildlife, and threats to its survival.

And while the nature tours and talks are undoubtedly fascinating, so are the tours of the newly opened to the public in 2009 **Nike Hercules Missile Base HM-69.** This brainchild of President John F. Kennedy and his advisors (that arose out of very real Cold War fears) was turned back over to the park in 1979 and hasn't been open until now. Free ranger-led tours take visitors from January 1 to March 28 on a

90-minute driving and walking tour of the missile assembly building, three barns where 12 missiles were stored, the guardhouse, and underground control room. Tours depart from the Ernest Coe Visitor Center at 2pm Saturday and Sunday and at 10am and 2pm Tuesday. Tour is free but $10 park admission still applies. Reservations are highly suggested by calling © **305/242-7700.**

Sports & Outdoor Activities

BIKING The relatively flat, 38-mile paved **Main Park Road** is great for biking because of the multitude of hardwood hammocks (treelike islands or dense stands of hardwood trees that grow only a few inches above land) and a dwarf cypress forest (stunted and thinly distributed cypress trees, which grow in poor soil on drier land).

Shark Valley, however, is the best biking trail by far. If the park isn't flooded from excess rain (which it often is, especially in spring), this is South Florida's most scenic bicycle trail. Many locals haul their bikes out to the 'Glades for a relaxing day of wilderness-trail riding. You'll share the flat, paved road only with other bikers, trams, and a menagerie of wildlife. (Don't be surprised to see a gator lounging in the sun or a deer munching on some grass. Otters, turtles, alligators, and snakes are common companions in the Shark Valley area.) There are no shortcuts, so if you become tired or are unable to complete the entire 15-mile trip, turn around and return on the same road. Allow 2 to 3 hours to bike the entire loop.

Those who love to mountain-bike and who prefer solitude might check out the **Southern Glades Trail,** a 14-mile unpaved trail lined with native trees and teeming with wildlife, such as deer, alligators, and the occasional snake. The remote trail runs along the C-111 canal, off S.R. 9336 and SW 217th Street.

Bicycles are available from **Shark Valley Tram Tours,** at the park's Shark Valley entrance (© **305/221-8455;** www.sharkvalleytramtours.com), for $7.25 per hour; rentals can be picked up anytime between 8:30am and 3pm and must be returned by 4pm.

BIRD-WATCHING More than 350 species of birds make their home in the Everglades. Tropical birds from the Caribbean and temperate species from North America can be found here, along with exotics that have flown in from more distant regions. Eco and Mrazek ponds, located near Flamingo, are two of the best places for birding, especially in early morning or late afternoon in the dry winter months. Pick up a free birding checklist from one of the visitor centers (p. 248) and inquire about what's been spotted in recent days. In late 2009, a survey revealed that there were over 77,000 nests in the Everglades. In fact, the endangered woo stork increased its nesting activity 1,776 percent from the previous year. For a guided birding tour, consider **Everglades Area Tours** (© **239/695-9107;** www.everglades areatours.com) **National Park and Grand Heritage Birding Tour,** a comprehensive, 6- to 7-hour naturalist-led tour with multiple forms of transportation—power boats, kayaks, and even a beach walk, so you don't miss any of the spectacular feathered (among others) species who call the park home. Tour is $179 per person and limited to six per tour.

CANOEING Canoeing through the Everglades may be one of the most serene, surprisingly diverse adventures you'll ever have. From a canoe (where you're incredibly close to the water level), your vantage point is priceless. Canoers in the 'Glades can coexist with the gators and birds in a way no one else can; the creatures behave as if you're part of the ecosystem—something that won't happen on an airboat. A ranger-guided boat tour is your best bet and oftentimes they are either free or very inexpensive at around $7 to $12 per person. As always, a ranger will help you understand the surroundings and what you're seeing. They don't take reservations, but for more information on the various boat tours, call ℂ **239/695-3311.**

Everglades National Park's longest "trails" are designed for boat and canoe travel, and many are marked as clearly as walking trails. The **Noble Hammock Canoe Trail,** a 2-mile loop, takes 1 to 2 hours and is recommended for beginners. The **Hell's Bay Canoe Trail,** a 3- to 6-mile course for hardier paddlers, takes 2 to 6 hours, depending on how far you choose to go. Fans of this trail like to say, "It's hell to get in and hell to get out." Park rangers can recommend other trails that best suit your abilities, time limitations, and interests.

You can rent a canoe at the **Ivey House B&B** (ℂ 877/577-0679; www.everglades adventures.com; p. 257) for $50 for 24 hours, $35 per full day (any 8-hr. period), or for $25 per half-day (1–5pm only). Kayaks and tandem kayaks are also available. The rental agent will shuttle your party to the trail head of your choice and pick you up afterward. Rental facilities are open daily from 8am to 5pm.

Overnight canoe rentals are available for $50 to $60. During ideal weather conditions (stay away during bug season!), you can paddle right out to the Gulf and camp on the beach. However, Gulf waters at beach sites can be extremely rough, and people in small watercraft such as a canoe should exercise caution.

You can also take a canoe tour from the Parks Docks on Chokoloskee Causeway on S.R. 29, ½ mile south of the traffic circle at the ranger station in Everglades City. Call **Everglades National Park Boat Tours** (ℂ 800/445-7724) for information. And for an eco-tour of the 'Glades, **Everglades Area Tours** (ℂ 239/695-9107; www.evergladesareatours.com) not only offers guided kayak fishing, but also guided half-day kayak eco-tours, customized bird-watching expeditions, full-moon paddling, as well as bicycle and aerial tours of the Everglades. Captain Charles Wright can put six kayaks and six passengers into the Yak Attack shuttle motorboat for the trip out to the Wilderness Waterway, deep within Everglades National Park's Ten Thousand Islands, where you will paddle in the absolute wilderness, spotting birds, dolphins, manatees, sea turtles, and perhaps even the elusive American crocodile. The shuttle then brings you back to Everglades City. The trip costs $169 per angler and includes transportation, guide services, outfitted kayaks, and all safety equipment.

FISHING   About a third of Everglades National Park is open water. Freshwater fishing is popular in brackish **Nine-Mile Pond** (25 miles from the main entrance) and other spots along the Main Park Road, but because of the high mercury levels found in the Everglades, freshwater fishers are warned not to eat their catch (see "Would You Like Some Mercury with Your Bass," above). Before casting, check in at a visitor center, as many of the park's lakes are preserved for observation only. Fishing licenses are required; see p. 249 for more information.

Saltwater anglers will find snapper and sea trout plentiful. For an expertly guided fishing trip through the backcountry, **Adventures in Backwater Fishing** (ℂ **239/643-1261**), will send you out with Captain Dave Harding and Captain George LeClair who promise unique fishing—fly fishing, spin casting, among other things—without breaking the bank. Six-hour trips will set you back around $385. A great list of charters and guides can be found at the Flamingo Marina (see above).

MOTORBOATING Motorboating around the Everglades seems like a great way to see plants and animals in remote habitats, and, indeed, it's an interesting and fulfilling experience as you throttle into nature. However, environmentalists are taking stock of the damage inflicted by motorboats (especially airboats) on the delicate ecosystem. If you choose to motor, remember that most of the areas near land are "no wake" zones and that, for the protection of nesting birds, landing is prohibited on most of the little mangrove islands. Motorboating is allowed in certain areas, such as Florida Bay, the backcountry toward Everglades City, and the Ten Thousand Islands area. In all the freshwater lakes, however, motorboats are prohibited if they're above 5 horsepower. There's a long list of restrictions and restricted areas, so get a copy of the park's boating rules from Park Headquarters before setting out.

The Everglades' only marina—accommodating about 50 boats with electric and water hookups—is **Flamingo Marina,** 1 Flamingo Lodge Hwy., Everglades City (✆ **239/695-3101**). The marina is the only remnant of the now demolished Flamingo Lodge, which suffered terrible damage from Hurricanes Katrina and Wilma in 2005. Word is that if enough funds can be rounded up, it'll be replaced with a hurricane-resistant lodging complex featuring a small hotel, cottages, and eco-tents. As of this writing, the marina was still renting boats, but only from May through October. The well-marked channel to the Flamingo is accessible to boats with a maximum 4-foot draft and is open year-round. Reservations can be made through the marina store (✆ **239/695-3101**). 17-foot skiffs with 15-horsepower motors are available for rent. These low-power boats cost $80 for 2 hours, $150 for 4 hours, and $190 for an entire day. A $100 deposit is required.

Organized Tours

AIRBOAT TOURS Shallow-draft, fan-powered airboats were invented in the Everglades by frog hunters who were tired of poling through the brushes. Airboats cut through the saw grass and are sort of like hydraulic boats; at high-enough speeds, a boat actually rises above the saw grass and into the air. Even though airboats are the most efficient (not to mention fast and fun!) way to get around, they are not permitted in the park—these shallow-bottom runabouts tend to inflict severe damage on animals and plants. Just outside the boundaries of the Everglades, however, you'll find a number of outfitters offering rides. *Tip:* Consider bringing earplugs, as these high-speed boats are loud. Sometimes they give you plugs, but bring a pair just in case.

One of the best airboat outfitters is **Gator Park,** 12 miles west of the Florida Turnpike at 24050 SW Eighth St. (✆ **305/559-2255;** www.gatorpark.com), which, despite its touristy name, happens to be one of the most informative and entertaining airboat-tour operators around, not to mention the only one to give out free earplugs. Some of the guides deserve a medal for getting into the water and poking around a massive alligator, even though they're not really supposed to. After the boat ride, there's a free interactive wildlife show that features alligator wrestling and several other frightening acts involving scorpions. Take note of the gorgeous peacocks that live in the trees here. Admission for the boat ride and show is $21 for adults, $11 for children 6 to 11; prices are cheaper if you purchase tickets online. Airboats depart every 20 minutes. Gator Park is open daily from 9am to 5pm.

Another outfitter I recommend is **Coopertown Airboat Tours** (✆ **305/226-6048;** www.coopertownairboats.com), located about 11 miles west of the Florida Turnpike on the Tamiami Trail (U.S. 41), in a town that boasts a total population of eight humans! The super friendly staff has helped the company garner the title of "Florida's Best" by the *Miami Herald* for 40 years in a row. You never know what you're going to see, but with great guides, you're sure to see *something* of interest on the 40-minute, 8-mile round-trip tours. There's also a restaurant and a small gator farm on the premises. Airboat rides cost $22 for adults, $11 for children 7 to 11. Private airboat tours are $50 per hour, per person. The company is open daily from 8am to 6pm; tours leave frequently.

Thirty-minute airboat rides are also offered at the **Miccosukee Indian Village,** just west of the Shark Valley entrance on U.S. 41/Tamiami Trail and MM 70 (© **305/223-8380;** www.miccosukeetours.com). The price is $10 per person, with cheaper rates online. However, *be warned and advised*: I am not recommending this particular outfit over others—it's merely the one closest to the Shark Valley entrance. As always, the quality of your tour is only as good as the quality of your tour guide, and, unfortunately, I've gotten some complaints about the Miccosukee tours.

The **Everglades Alligator Farm,** 4 miles south of Palm Drive on SW 192nd Avenue (© **305/247-2628;** www.everglades.com), offers half-hour guided airboat tours daily from 9am until 6pm. The price, which includes admission to the park, is $23 for adults and $16 for children 4 to 11.

Another reputable company is **Captain Doug's,** located 35 miles south of Naples and 1 mile past the bridge in Everglades City (© **800/282-9194**).

CANOE TOURS   A fabulous way to explore the Everglades backcountry is via canoe. Slink through the mangroves, slide across saw-grass prairies, and even walk the sands of the unfettered Ten Thousand Islands. Expert guides will lead you in the right direction. Contact **Everglades Adventures** (© **877/567-0679;** www.evergladesadventures.com) at the Ivey House B&B (p. 257).

ECO-TOURS   Although it's fascinating to explore on your own, it would be a shame for you to tour the Everglades without a clue about what you're seeing. It's a lot more than saw grass and alligators in the backcountry, which is why **Everglades Adventures** (© **877/567-0679;** www.evergladesadventures.com), located within the Ivey House B&B (p. 257), is there to guide and entertain you, as well as explain such key issues as the differences between alligators and crocodiles, or between swamps and the Everglades.

MOTORBOAT TOURS   Both Florida Bay and backcountry tours are offered Thursday to Monday at the **Flamingo Marina** (see "Motorboating" above). Florida Bay tours cruise nearby estuaries and sandbars, while six-passenger backcountry boats visit smaller sloughs. Passengers can expect to see birds and a variety of other animals (I once saw a raccoon and some wild pigs). Both cost $27 for adults, $13 for children 5 to 12. Tours depart throughout the day; reservations are recommended. Charter-fishing and sightseeing boats can also be booked through the resort's main reservation number (© **239/695-3101**). If you're on the Gulf Coast side of things, the naturalist-guided Gulf Coast boat tour of the Ten Thousand Islands departs from the **Gulf Coast Marina** (located in the **Gulf Coast Visitor Center,** 5 miles south of U.S. 41 [Tamiami Trail] on S.R. 29, in Everglades City; © **239/695-2591**) area and lasts an hour and a half. There's also a mangrove wilderness tour through the swampier part of the park. Tour prices are the same as the tours at the Flamingo Marina.

TRAM TOURS   At the park's Shark Valley entrance, open-air tram buses take visitors on 2-hour naturalist-led tours that delve 7½ miles into the wilderness and are the best quick introduction you can get to the Everglades. At the trail's midsection, passengers can disembark and climb a 65-foot observation tower with good views of the 'Glades (though the tower on the Pa-hay-okee Trail is better). Visitors will see plenty of wildlife and endless acres of saw grass. Tours run December through April, daily on the hour between 9am and 4pm, and May through November at 9:30am, 11am, 1pm, and 3pm. They're sometimes stalled by flooding or particularly heavy mosquito infestation. Reservations are recommended from December to March. The cost is $17 for adults and seniors, and $11 for children 12 and under. For further information, contact **Shark Valley Tram Tours** (© 305/221-8455; www.sharkvalleytramtours.com).

Where to Stay

With the destruction of the Flamingo Lodge, there is no lodging within Everglades National Park proper unless you count your tent as lodging. However, there are a few accommodations just outside the park that are clean and reasonably priced. A $45-million casino hotel, **Miccosukee Resort** (© 877/242-6464; www.miccosukee. com), is adjacent to the Miccosukee bingo and gaming hall on the northern edge of the park. Although bugs can be a major nuisance, especially in the warm months, camping (the best way to fully experience South Florida's wilderness) is really the way to go in this very primitive environment.

CAMPING IN THE EVERGLADES

Campgrounds are available year-round in Flamingo and Long Pine Key. Both have drinking water, picnic tables, charcoal grills, restrooms, and tent and trailer pads, and welcome RVs (Flamingo allows up to 40-ft. vehicles, while Long Pine Key accepts up to 60-footers), though there are no electrical hookups. Flamingo has cold-water showers; Long Pine Key does not have showers or hookups for showers. Private ground fires are not permitted, but supervised campfire programs are conducted during winter months. Long Pine Key and Flamingo are popular and require reservations in advance, which can be made through the National Park Reservations Service (© 800/365-CAMP [2267]; www.nps.gov). Campsites are $16 per night, and during winter season (Nov–Apr), there's a 14-day consecutive-stay limit, and a maximum of 30 days a year.

Camping is also available year-round in the **backcountry** (those remote areas accessible only by boat, foot, or canoe—basically most of the park), on a first-come, first-served basis. Campers must register with park rangers and get a permit in person or by phone no less than 24 hours before the start of their trip. Permits cost $10 plus $2 per camper per night. For more information, contact the **Gulf Coast Visitor Center** (© 239/695-3311) or the **Flamingo Visitor Center** (© 239/695-2945), which are the only two places that give out these permits. Once you have one, camping sites cost $16 (with a maximum of eight people per site), or $30 for a group site (maximum of 15 people). Campers can use only designated campsites, which are plentiful and well marked on visitor maps.

Many backcountry sites are *chickee huts*—covered wooden platforms (with toilets) on stilts. They're accessible only by canoe and can accommodate freestanding tents (without stakes). Ground sites are located along interior bays and rivers, and beach camping is also popular. In summer especially, mosquito repellent is necessary gear.

LODGING IN EVERGLADES CITY

As Everglades City is 35 miles southeast of Naples and 83 miles west of Miami, many visitors choose to explore this western entrance to Everglades National Park, located off the Tamiami Trail, on S.R. 29. An annual seafood festival held the first weekend in February is a major event that draws hordes of people. Everglades City (the gateway to the Ten Thousand Islands), where the 'Glades meet the Gulf of Mexico, is the closest thing you'll get to civilization in South Florida's swampy frontier, with a few tourist traps—er, shops—a restaurant, and one bed-and-breakfast.

Ivey House B&B ★★ 🎁 The first certified Green Lodging in Collier County, the Ivey House offers a variety of accommodations: the Ivey House Inn, featuring spacious rooms with private bathrooms, TVs, phones, and a view of the courtyard pool and waterfall; the Ivey House Lodge, housed in what used to be a recreational center for the men who built the Tamiami Trail, featuring 10 small rooms with communal bathrooms (one each for women and men), no TVs or phones; and the Ivey House Cottage, with two bedrooms, a full kitchen, a private bathroom, and a screened-in porch. Owners Sandee and David Harraden are extremely knowledgeable about the Everglades and assist guests providing a variety of daily excursions. Rates include a continental breakfast, served from 6:30 to 10am. A full hot breakfast is provided during peak season. Box lunches are available year-round for $11. **Note:** There is no smoking in any of the buildings.

107 Camellia St., Everglades City, FL 34139. ✆ **877/567-0679** or 239/695-3299. Fax 239/695-4155. www.iveyhouse.com. 28 units. Winter $100–$200 in Inn, $60–$105 in Lodge, $175–$235 in Cottage; off-season $75–$85 in Inn, $60–$65 in Lodge, $135 in Cottage. 2-night minimum in all facilities during Everglades Seafood Festival in Feb. MC, V. **Amenities:** Restaurant; pool; Wi-Fi. *In room:* A/C, TV, fridge (in Inn), kitchen (in Cottage).

Rod & Gun Lodge ★ Set on the banks of the sleepy Baron River, this rustic, old, white-clapboard house has plenty of history and all kinds of activities for sports enthusiasts, including a pool, bike rentals, a tennis center, and nearby boat rentals and private fishing guides. Hoover vacationed here after his 1928 election victory, and Truman flew in to sign Everglades National Park into existence in 1947 and stayed over as well. Other guests have included Richard Nixon, Burt Reynolds, and Mick Jagger. The public rooms are beautifully paneled and hung with tarpon, wild boar, deer antlers, and other trophies. Guest rooms in this single-story building are unfussy but perfectly comfortable. All have porches looking out on the river. Out by the pool, a screened verandah with ceiling fans is a pleasant place for a libation. The excellent seafood restaurant serves breakfast, lunch, and dinner. The entire property is nonsmoking.

Riverside Dr. and Broadway (P.O. Box 190), Everglades City, FL 34139. ✆ **239/695-2101.** www.everglades rodandgun.com. 17 units. Winter $110–$140 double; off-season $95 double. No credit cards. Closed after July 4 for the summer. **Amenities:** Restaurant; bike rental; pool; tennis courts. *In room:* A/C, TV.

LODGING IN HOMESTEAD & FLORIDA CITY

Homestead and Florida City, two adjacent towns that were almost blown off the map by Hurricane Andrew in 1992, have come back better than before. About 10 miles from the park's main entrance, along U.S. 1, 35 miles south of Miami, these somewhat rural towns offer several budget options, including chain hotels. There is a **Days Inn** (✆ **305/245-1260**) in Homestead and a **Ramada Inn** (✆ **800/272-6232** or 305/247-8833) right off the turnpike in Florida City. The best options are listed below.

Best Western Gateway to the Keys   This standard two-story newly renovated motel provides contemporary style and comfort about 10 miles from the park's main entrance. A decent-size pool and a small spa make it attractive to some. Each standard room has bright, tropical bedspreads and oversize picture windows. The suites have convenient extras such as microwaves, coffeemakers, extra sinks, and small fridges. Clean and conveniently located, the only drawback is that, in season, there is often a 3-day minimum-stay requirement. You would do best to call the local reservation line instead of the toll-free number—on several occasions, the hotel has made an exception to the rule, while the central reservation line could not.

411 S. Krome Ave. (U.S. 1), Florida City, FL 33034. (✆ **800/528-1234** or 305/246-5100. Fax 305/242-0056. www.bestwestern.com. 114 units. $89–$150 double. Rates include continental breakfast. During races and the very high season, there may be a 3-night minimum stay. AE, DC, DISC, MC, V. **Amenities:** Pool; spa. *In room:* A/C, TV, fridge, hair dryer, Internet access.

Everglades International Hostel ★   This is what a hostel *should* be. Sure, I've seen cleaner, more modern ones, but the feeling of camaraderie here is what hostels are all about. Located in a 1930s boardinghouse, this hostel has dorm rooms as well as doubles (all with shared bathrooms), a great kitchen, a washer/dryer, high-speed Internet access, bike rentals, and a garden (with tents, forts, and an outdoor chess board). The friendly, amazingly accommodating staff here provides tons of helpful information and runs sightseeing/canoe trips to the Everglades. *Note:* Some rooms here are cheaper than the rates listed below, but do not have air-conditioning.

20 SW 2nd Ave., Florida City, FL 33034. (✆ **800/372-3874** or 305/248-1122. www.evergladeshostel.com. $25–$28 dorm bed; $75 private double; $55 semiprivate room; $18 per person garden camping. MC, V. **Amenities:** Bike rental; Internet access; kitchen. *In room:* A/C (in some).

Where to Dine In & Around the Park

You won't find fancy nouvelle cuisine in this suburbanized farm country, but there are plenty of fast-food chains along U.S. 1 and a few old favorites worth a taste.

Here for nearly a quarter of a century, **El Toro Taco Family Restaurant,** 1 S. Krome Ave., near Mowry and Campbell drives, Homestead (✆ 305/245-8182), opens daily at 9:30am and stays crowded until at least 9pm most days. The fresh grilled meats, tacos, burritos, salsas, guacamole, and stews are all mild and delicious. No matter how big your appetite, it's hard to spend more than $15 per person at this Mexican outpost. Bring your own beer or wine.

Housed in a one-story, windowless building that looks something like a medieval fort, the **Capri Restaurant,** 935 N. Krome Ave., Florida City (✆ 305/247-1542), has been serving hearty Italian-American fare since 1958. Great pastas and salads complement a menu of meat and fish dishes; portions are big. Lunch and dinner are served Monday through Friday until 9:30pm and Saturday until 10:30pm. The **White Lion Café,** 146 NW Seventh St., Homestead (✆ 305/248-1076), is a quaint home-and-gardens-cum-cafe with live blues, jazz, and swing music at night, and a menu with Blue Plate specials and cheekily named appetizers and entrees such as Dirty Little Shrimp and Garlic Romanian, which is actually delicious skirt steak sliced thin and served with fresh mushrooms, spinach, and garlic over real mashed potatoes and gravy. Entree prices range from $10 to $22. Dinner is served Tuesday through Saturday from 5pm until "the fat lady sings."

The **Miccosukee Restaurant,** just west of the Shark Valley entrance on the Tamiami Trail/U.S. 41 (© **305/223-8380**), serves authentic pumpkin bread, fry bread, and fish, and not-so-authentic Native American interpretations of tacos and fried chicken. It's worth a stop for brunch, lunch, or dinner.

Near the Miccosukee reservation is the **Pit Bar-B-Q,** 16400 SW Eighth St. (© **305/226-2272**), a total pit of a place known for some of the best smoked ribs, barbecued chicken, and corn bread this side of the Deep South. It's open daily from 11am to 8pm.

In Everglades City, the **Oyster House,** on Chokoloskee Causeway, S.R. (the locals call it Hwy.) 29 S. (© **239/695-2073**), is a large but homey seafood restaurant with modest prices, excellent service, and a fantastic view of the Ten Thousand Islands. Try the hush puppies. For more authentic local flavor, try the **Camellia Street Grill,** 208 Camellia St. (© **239/695-2003**), an off-the-beaten-path, rust waterfront fish joint fusing Southern hospitality with outstanding seafood served with a gourmet twist. An on-site herb and veggie garden provides the freshest ingredients and stellar salads. Some say the oysters here are among the best they've ever had. Everything is homemade, including the Key lime pie, and there's live music on Fridays and Saturdays.

BISCAYNE NATIONAL PARK ★

35 miles S of Miami; 21 miles E of Everglades National Park

With only about 500,000 visitors each year (mostly boaters and divers), the unusual Biscayne National Park is one of the least-crowded parks in the country. Perhaps that's because the park is a little more difficult than most to access—more than 95% of its 181,500 acres is underwater.

The park's significance was first formally acknowledged in 1968 when, in an unprecedented move (and despite intense pressure from developers), President Lyndon B. Johnson signed a bill to conserve the barrier islands off South Florida's east coast as a national monument—a protected status just a rung below national park. After being twice enlarged, once in 1974 and again in 1980, the waters and land surrounding the northernmost coral reef in North America became a full-fledged national park—the largest of its kind in the country.

To be fully appreciated, Biscayne National Park should be thought of as more preserve than destination. Use your time here to explore underwater life, but also to relax. The park's small mainland mangrove shoreline and keys are best explored by boat. Its extensive reef system is renowned by divers and snorkelers worldwide.

The park consists of 44 islands, but only a few of them are open to visitors. The most popular is **Elliott Key,** which has campsites and a visitor center, plus freshwater showers (cold water only), restrooms, trails, and a buoyed swim area. It's about 9 miles from **Convoy Point,** the park's official headquarters on land. During Columbus Day weekend, there is a very popular regatta for which a lively crowd of party people gathers—sometimes in the nude—to celebrate the long weekend. If you'd prefer to rough it a little more, the 29-acre island known as **Boca Chita Key,** once an exclusive haven for yachters, has now become a popular spot for all manner of boaters. Visitors can camp and tour the island's restored historic buildings, including the county's second-largest lighthouse and a tiny chapel.

Just the Facts

GETTING THERE & ACCESS POINTS   Convoy Point, the park's mainland entrance, is 9 miles east of Homestead. To reach the park from Miami, take the Florida Turnpike to the Tallahassee Road (SW 137th Ave.) exit. Turn left, then left again at North Canal Drive (SW 328th St.), and follow signs to the park. Another option is to rent a speedboat in Miami and cruise south for about 1½ hours. If you're coming from U.S. 1, whether you're heading north or south, turn east at North Canal Drive (SW 328th St.). The entrance is approximately 9 miles away. The rest of the park is accessible only by boat.

Because most of Biscayne National Park is accessible only to boaters, mooring buoys abound, as it is illegal to anchor on coral. When no buoys are available, boaters must anchor on sand or on the docks surrounding the small harbor off Boca Chita. Boats can also dock here overnight for $20. Even the most experienced boaters should carry updated nautical charts of the area, which are available at Convoy Point's Dante Fascell Visitor Center. The waters are often murky, making the abundant reefs and sandbars difficult to detect—and there are more interesting ways to spend a day than waiting for the tide to rise. There's a boat launch at adjacent Homestead Bayfront Park and 66 slips on Elliott Key, available free on a first-come, first-served basis.

Round-trip transportation to and from the visitor center to Elliott Key costs $50 (plus tax) round-trip per person and takes about an hour. This is a convenient option, ensuring that you don't get lost on some deserted island by boating there yourself. Call ✆ **305/230-1100** for the seasonal schedule.

VISITOR CENTERS & INFORMATION   Dante Fascell Visitor Center, often referred to by its older name, **Convoy Point Visitor Center,** 9700 SW 328th St., Homestead, FL 33033-5634, at the park's main entrance (✆ **305/230-7275;** fax 305/230-1190; www.nps.gov/bisc), is the natural starting point for any venture into the park without a boat. It provides comprehensive information about the park; on request, rangers will show you a short video on the park, its natural surroundings, and what you may see. The center is open daily from 9am to 5pm.

For information on transportation, glass-bottom boat tours, and snorkeling and scuba-diving expeditions, contact the park concessionaire, **Biscayne National Underwater Park, Inc.,** P.O. Box 1270, Homestead, FL 33030 (✆ **305/230-1100;** fax 305/230-1120; www.nps.gov/bisc). It's open daily from 8:30am to 5pm.

ENTRANCE FEES & PERMITS   Entering Biscayne National Park is free. There is a $20 overnight docking fee at both Boca Chita Key Harbor and Elliott Key Harbor, which includes a campsite. Campsites are $15 for those staying without a boat. Group camping costs $30 a day and covers up to six tents and 25 people. See p. 249 for information on fishing permits. Backcountry camping permits are free and can be picked up from the Dante Fascell Visitor Center. For more information on fees and permits, call the park ranger at ✆ **305/230-1144.**

Seeing the Highlights

Because the park is primarily underwater, the only way to truly experience it is with snorkel or scuba gear. Beneath the surface of Biscayne National Park, the aquatic universe pulses with multicolored life: abounding bright parrotfish and angelfish, gently rocking sea fans, and coral labyrinths. (See the "Snorkeling & Scuba Diving" section below for more information.) Afterward, take a picnic out to Elliott Key and taste the crisp salt air blowing off the Atlantic. Or head to Boca Chita, an intriguing island that was once the private playground of wealthy yachters.

Sports & Outdoor Activities

CANOEING & KAYAKING Biscayne National Park affords excellent canoeing, both along the coast and across the open water to nearby mangroves and artificial islands dotting the longest uninterrupted shoreline in the state of Florida. Because tides can be strong, only experienced canoeists should attempt to paddle far from shore. If you do plan to go far, first obtain a tide table from the visitor center and paddle with the current. Free ranger-led canoe tours are scheduled from 9am to noon on the second and fourth Saturdays of the month between January 10 and April 24; phone for information. You can rent a canoe at the park's concession stand for $12 an hour. Two-person kayaks go for $16 an hour. Call ✆ **305/230-1100** for reservations, information, ranger tours, and boat rentals. You can also view information on the website of the park's concession, www.biscayneunderwater.com.

FISHING Ocean fishing is excellent year-round at Biscayne National Park; many people cast their lines from the breakwater jetty at Convoy Point. A fishing license is required. (See p. 249 for more information.) Bait is not available in Biscayne National Park, but it is sold in adjacent Homestead Bayfront Park. Stone crabs and Florida lobsters can be found here, but you're allowed to catch these only on the ocean side when they're in season. There are strict limits on size, season, number, and method of take (including spearfishing) for both freshwater and saltwater fishing. The latest regulations are available at most marinas, bait-and-tackle shops, and the park's visitor centers; or you can contact the **Florida Fish and Wildlife Conservation Commission,** Bryant Building, 620 S. Meridian St., Tallahassee, FL 32399-1600 (✆ **850/488-0331**). For those looking to learn a little about fishing, Biscayne National Park offers a free class, The Fisheries Awareness Class, given on the third Wednesday of every month (during even-numbered months, classes are in Spanish) from 6 to 9:30pm at Suniland Park, 12855 S. Dixie Hwy (✆ **305/230-1144,** ext. 3089), in Miami.

HIKING & EXPLORING As the majority of this park is underwater, hiking is not the main attraction here, but there are some interesting sights and trails nonetheless. At Convoy Point, you can walk along the 370-foot boardwalk and along the half-mile jetty that serves as a breakwater for the park's harbor. From here, you can usually see brown pelicans, little blue herons, snowy egrets, and a few exotic fish.

Elliott Key is accessible only by boat, but once you're there, you have two good trail options. True to its name, the Loop Trail makes a 1.5-mile circle from the bayside visitor center, through a hardwood hammock and mangroves, to an elevated oceanside boardwalk. You'll likely see land crabs scurrying around the mangrove roots.

Reopened in 1998, Boca Chita Key was once a playground for wealthy tycoons, and it still has the peaceful beauty that attracted elite anglers from cold climates. Many of the historic buildings are still intact, including an ornamental lighthouse that was never put to use. Take advantage of the tours, usually led by a park ranger and available every Sunday in winter only at 1:30pm. The tour, including the boat trip, takes about 3 hours. The price is $35 for adults, $25 for seniors, and $20 for children 11 and under. However, call in advance to see if the sea is calm enough for the trip—the boats won't run in rough waters. See "Glass-Bottom Boat Tours," below, for information about the daily 10am excursions.

SNORKELING & SCUBA DIVING The clear, warm waters of Biscayne National Park are packed with colorful tropical fish that swim in the offshore reefs. If you don't have your own gear, or if you don't want to lug it to the park, you can rent or buy snorkeling and scuba gear at the full-service dive shop at Convoy Point. Rates are in line with those at mainland dive shops.

The best way to see the park from underwater is to take a snorkeling or diving tour operated by **Biscayne National Underwater Park, Inc.** (© **305/230-1100;** www.nps.gov/bisc). Snorkeling tours depart at 1:30pm daily, last about 3 hours, and cost $38 per adult and $30 per child, including equipment. There are also weekend two-tank dives for certified divers; the price is $75, including two tanks and weights. Make your reservations in advance. The shop is open daily from 9am to 5pm.

Before entering the water, be sure to apply waterproof sunblock—once you begin to explore, it's easy to lose track of time, and the Florida sun is brutal, even during winter.

SWIMMING You can swim off the protected beaches of Elliott Key, Boca Chita Key, and adjacent Homestead Bayfront Park, but none of these match the width or softness of other South Florida beaches. Check the water conditions before heading into the sea: The strong currents that make this a popular destination for windsurfers and sailors can be dangerous, even for strong swimmers. Homestead Bayfront Park is really just a marina next to Biscayne National Park, but it does have a beach and picnic facilities, as well as fishing areas and a playground. It's located at Convoy Point, 9698 SW 328th St., Homestead (© **305/230-3034**).

Glass-Bottom Boat Tours

If you prefer not to dive, the best way to see the sights is on a glass-bottom boat. **Biscayne National Underwater Park, Inc.** (© **305/230-1100;** www.nps.gov/bisc), has daily trips to view some of the country's most beautiful coral reefs and tropical fish. Boats depart year-round from Convoy Point at 10am and stay out for about 3 hours. At $45 for adults, $35 for seniors, and $30 for children 12 and under, the scenic and informative tours are pricey but if you don't enjoy the trip, they promise a full refund. Boats carry fewer than 50 passengers; reservations are almost always necessary.

Where to Stay

Besides campsites, there are no facilities available for overnight guests to this watery park. Most noncamping visitors come for an afternoon, on their way to the Keys, and stay overnight in nearby Homestead, where there are many national chain hotels and other affordable lodgings; see p. 258 for more information.

Although you won't find hotels or lodges in Biscayne National Park, it does have some of the state's most pristine campsites. Because they are inaccessible by motor vehicle, you'll be sure to avoid the mass of RVs so prevalent in many of the state's other campgrounds. The sites on Elliott Key and Boca Chita can be reached only by boat. If you don't have your own boat, call © **305/230-1100** to arrange a drop-off. Transportation to Elliott Key from the visitor center costs $50 (plus tax). They do not provide transportation to Boca Chita, so you'll have to rent a boat. Boca Chita has only saltwater toilets (no showers or sinks); Elliot Key has freshwater, cold-water showers and toilets, but is otherwise no less primitive. If you didn't pay for the overnight docking fee, campsites are $15.

stiltsville, **USA**

Miami's boat enthusiasts have an affinity for it because of its kitschy, offbeat nature, but what most of them don't know is that **Stiltsville** isn't their forbidden watery playground but a part of **Biscayne National Park.** So what is it, exactly? Floating above Biscayne Bay are seven cottage-like buildings built on, yes, stilts. And as funky as it looks, its history is even funkier, dating back to the 1930s. Because it's accessible only by water, Stiltsville was *the* place to see and be seen back in the day—especially if you were involved in illegal gambling, rum running, or assorted forbidden activities. In fact, police raids were common back then, when the Stiltsville structures had titillating names such as the Bikini Club. At it's peak, no pun intended, Stiltsville boasted 27 structures. Unfortunately today that's not the case. But in 2003, a nonprofit organization called the Stiltsville Trust was created to preserve and rehabilitate the ramshackle buildings, which the public is prohibited from touching. But despite the NO TRESPASSING signs and true to its original reputation as haven for all things forbidden, boaters to this day throw illegal parties here. If you see one in the works, however, don't even think about it, just take a picture and keep boating.

With a backcountry permit, available free from the visitor center, you can pitch your tent somewhere even more private. Ask for a map and be sure to bring plenty of bug spray. Sites cost $15 a night for up to six persons staying in one or two tents. Backcountry camping is allowed only on Elliott Key, which is a very popular spot (accessible only by boat) for boaters and campers. It is approximately 9 miles from the Dante Fascell Visitor Center and offers hiking trails, fresh water, boat slips, showers, and restrooms. While there, don't miss the Old Road, a 7-mile tropical hammock trail that runs the length of Elliott Key. This trail is one of the few places left in the world to see the highly endangered Schaus swallowtail butterfly, recognizable by its black wings with diagonal yellow bands. These butterflies are usually out from late April to July.

THE KEYS & THE DRY TORTUGAS

The drive from Miami to the Keys is a slow descent into an unusual but breathtaking American ecosystem: On either side of you, for miles ahead, lies nothing but emerald waters. (On weekends, however, you will also see plenty of traffic.) Strung out across the Atlantic Ocean like loose strands of cultured pearls, more than 400 islands make up this 150-mile-long necklace.

Despite the usually calm landscape, these rocky islands can be treacherous, as tropical storms, hurricanes, and tornadoes are always possibilities. The exposed coast poses dangers to those on land as well as at sea.

When Spanish explorers Juan Ponce de León and Antonio de Herrera sailed amid these craggy, dangerous rocks in 1513, they and their men dubbed the string of islands "Los Martires" (The Martyrs) because they thought the rocks looked like men suffering in the surf. It wasn't until the early 1800s that rugged and ambitious pioneers, who amassed great wealth by salvaging cargo from ships sunk nearby, settled the larger islands (legend has it that these shipwrecks were sometimes caused by "wreckers," who removed navigational markers from the shallows to lure unwitting captains aground). At the height of the salvaging mania (in the 1830s), Key West boasted the highest per-capita income in the country.

However, wars, fires, hurricanes, mosquitoes, and the Depression took their toll on these resilient islands in the early part of the 20th century, causing wild swings between fortune and poverty. In 1938, the spectacular Overseas Highway (U.S. 1) was finally completed atop the ruins of Henry Flagler's railroad (which was destroyed by a hurricane in 1935, leaving only bits and pieces still found today), opening the region to tourists, who had never before been able to drive to this sea-bound destination. These days, the highway connects more than 30 of the populated islands in the Keys. The hundreds of small, undeveloped islands that surround these "mainline" keys are known locally as the "backcountry" and are home to dozens of exotic animals and plants. Therein lie some of the most renowned outdoor sporting opportunities, from bonefishing to spearfishing and—at appropriate times of the year—diving for lobsters and stone crabs. To get to the backcountry, you must take to the water—a vital part of any trip to the Keys. Whether you fish, snorkel, dive, or cruise, include some time on a boat in your itinerary; otherwise, you haven't truly seen the Keys.

Of course, people go to the Keys for the peaceful waters and year-round warmth, but the sea and the teeming life beneath and around it are the main attractions here: Countless species of brilliantly colored fish can be found swimming above the ocean's floor, and you'll discover a stunning abundance of tropical and exotic plants, birds, and reptiles.

The warm, shallow waters (deeper and rougher on the eastern/Atlantic side of the Keys) nurture living coral that supports a complex, delicate ecosystem of plants and animals—sponges, anemones, jellyfish, crabs, rays, sharks, turtles, snails, lobsters, and thousands of types of fish. This vibrant underwater habitat thrives on one of the only living tropical reefs on the entire North American continent. As a result, anglers, divers, snorkelers, and watersports enthusiasts of all kinds come to explore.

Heavy traffic has taken its toll on this fragile eco-scape, but conservation efforts are under way (traffic laws are strictly enforced on Deer Key, for example, due to deer crossings that have been contained, thanks to newly installed fences). In fact, environmental efforts in the Keys exceed those in many other high-traffic visitor destinations.

Although the atmosphere throughout the Keys is that of a laid-back beach town, don't expect many impressive beaches here, especially after the damaging effects of recent hurricane seasons. Nice beaches are mostly found in a few private resorts, though there are some small, sandy strips in John Pennekamp Coral Reef State Park, Bahia Honda State Park, and Key West. One great exception is Sombrero Beach, in Marathon (p. 267), which is well maintained by Monroe County and is larger and considerably nicer than other beaches in the Keys. Sombrero Beach has a beach-front park, picnic facilities, a playground, and a protected cove for children.

The Keys are divided into three sections, both geographically and in this chapter. The Upper and Middle Keys are closest to the Florida mainland, so they are popular with weekend warriors who come by boat or car to fish or relax in such towns as Key Largo, Islamorada, and Marathon. Farther on, just beyond the impressive Seven-Mile Bridge (which actually measures 6½ miles), are the Lower Keys, a small, unspoiled swath of islands teeming with wildlife. Here, in the protected regions of the Lower Keys, is where you're most likely to catch sight of the area's many endangered animals—with patience, you may spot the rare eagle, egret, or Key deer. You should also keep an eye out for alligators, turtles, rabbits, and a huge variety of birds.

Key West, the most renowned—and last—island in the Lower Keys, is literally at the end of the road. The southernmost point in the continental United States (made famous by Ernest Hemingway), this tiny island is the most popular destination in the Florida Keys, overrun with cruise-ship passengers and day-trippers, as well as franchises and T-shirt shops. More than 1.6 million visitors pass through it each year. Still, this "Conch Republic" has a tightly knit community of permanent residents who cling fiercely to their live-and-let-live attitude—an atmosphere that has made Key West famously popular with painters, writers, and free spirits, despite the recent influx of money-hungry developers who want to turn Key West into Palm Beach south.

The last section in this chapter is devoted to the Dry Tortugas, a national park located 68 nautical miles from Key West.

The Florida Keys

GULF OF MEXICO

Marquesas Keys

Great White Heron National Wildlife Refuge

Snipe Keys

Cudjoe Key Knockemdown Key

Big Torch Key

Howe Key

Annette Key

Key West

Stock Island

Big Coppitt Key

Key West

Boca Chica Key

Sugarloaf Key

Summerland Key

Saddlebunch Keys

Ramrod Key

Little Torch Key

Cudjoe Key Big Pine Key

National Key Deer Refuge

Little Pine Key

Big Pine Key Bahia Honda State Park

No Name Key

Seven-Mile Bridge

Bahia Honda Key

Boot Key

Marathon

Key Vaca Key Colony Beach

Straits of Florida

0   10 mi
0   10 km

12

THE KEYS & THE DRY TORTUGAS | Exploring the Keys by Car

EXPLORING THE KEYS BY CAR

After you've left the Florida Turnpike and landed on U.S. 1, which is also known as the Overseas Highway (see "Getting There" under "Essentials," below), you'll have no trouble negotiating these narrow islands, as only one main road connects the Keys. The scenic, lazy drive from Miami can be very enjoyable if you have the patience to linger and explore the diverse towns and islands along the way. If you have the time, I recommend allowing at least 2 days to work your way down to Key West, and 3 or more days once there.

Don't Be Fooled

Avoid the many "tourist information centers" that dot the main highway. Most are private companies hired to lure visitors to specific lodgings or outfitters (anything that says FREE DISNEY TICKETS or something like that is probably a scam or timeshare racket). You're better off sticking with the official, not-for-profit centers (the legit ones usually don't advertise on the turnpike) that are extremely well located and staffed.

Encouraging you to slow down is the new $21-million, 106-mile Florida Keys Overseas Heritage Trail, a work in progress that is creating a scenic, multi-use paved trail for bikers, hikers, runners, fishermen, and sightseers running parallel to the Overseas Highway and extending from Key Largo all the way down to Key West. With 66 of the 106 miles already completed and 11.5 miles of trail and five bridges under construction, the rest of the trail is still under design and scheduled for completion by 2013.

Most of U.S. 1 is a narrow two-lane highway, with some wider passing

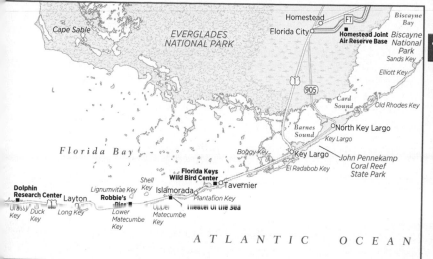

zones along the way. The speed limit is usually 55 mph (35–45 mph on Big Pine Key and in some commercial areas). Despite the protests of island residents, there has been talk of expanding the highway, but plans have not been finalized. Even on the narrow road, you can usually get from downtown Miami to Key Largo in just over an hour. If you're determined to drive straight through to Key West, allow at least 3½ hours. Weekend travel is another matter entirely: When the roads are jammed with travelers from the mainland, the trip can take upward of 5 to 6 hours (when there's an accident, traffic is at an absolute standstill). If at all possible, I strongly urge you to avoid driving anywhere in the Keys on Friday afternoon or Sunday evening.

To find an address in the Keys, don't bother looking for building numbers; most addresses (except in Key West and parts of Marathon) are delineated by mile markers (MM), small green signs on the roadside that announce the distance from Key West. The markers start at no. 127, just south of the Florida mainland. The zero marker is in Key West, at the corner of Whitehead and Fleming streets. Addresses in this chapter are accompanied by a mile marker (MM) designation when appropriate.

THE UPPER & MIDDLE KEYS

58 miles SW of Miami

The Upper Keys, from Key Largo to Marathon, are a popular year-round refuge for South Floridians, who take advantage of the islands' proximity to the mainland. This is the fishing and diving capital of America, and the swarms of outfitters and billboards never let you forget it.

Key Largo, once called Rock Harbor but renamed to capitalize on the success of the 1948 Humphrey Bogart film (which wasn't actually filmed here), is the largest

Sweet Home Alabama (Jack's)

On its own, there's not much to the waterfront shack that is **Alabama Jack's,** 5800 Card Sound Rd., Card Sound (© 305/248-8741). The bar serves beer and wine only, and the restaurant specializes in delicious, albeit greasy, bar fare. But this quintessential Old Floridian dive, located in a historic fishing village called Card Sound between Homestead and Key Largo, is a colorful must on the drive south, especially on Sunday, when bikers mix with barflies, anglers, line dancers, and Southern belles who look as if they just got off the *Hee Haw* set in all their fabulous frills. Live country music resurrects the legendary Johnny Cash and Co. Pull up a bar stool, order a cold one, and take in the sights—in the bay and at the bar. The views of the mangroves are spectacular. To get here, pick up Card Sound Road (the old Rte. 1) a few miles after you pass Homestead, heading toward Key Largo. Alabama Jack's is on the right side and can't be missed.

key and is more developed than its neighbors to the south. Dozens of chain hotels, restaurants, and tourist information centers service the water enthusiasts who come to explore the nation's first underwater state park, **John Pennekamp Coral Reef State Park,** and its adjacent marine sanctuary. **Islamorada,** the unofficial capital of the Upper Keys, has the area's best atmosphere, food, fishing, entertainment, and lodging. It's an unofficial "party capital" for mainlanders seeking a quick tropical excursion. Here (Islamorada is actually composed of four islands) nature lovers can enjoy walking trails, historic exploration, and big-purse fishing tournaments. For a more tranquil, less party-hearty Keys experience, all other keys besides Key West and Islamorada are better choices. **Marathon,** smack in the middle of the Florida Keys, is known as the heart of the Keys and is one of the most populated. It is part fishing village, part tourist center, and part nature preserve. This area's highly developed infrastructure includes resort hotels, a commercial airport, and a highway that expands to four lanes.

Essentials

GETTING THERE From Miami International Airport (there is also an airport in Marathon), take Le Jeune Road (NW 42nd Ave.) to Rte. 836 W. Follow signs to the Florida Turnpike South, about 7 miles. The turnpike extension connects with U.S. 1 in Florida City. Continue south on U.S. 1. For a scenic option, take Card Sound Road, south of Florida City, a backcountry drive that reconnects with U.S. 1 in upper Key Largo. The view from Card Sound Bridge is spectacular and well worth the $1 toll.

If you're coming from Florida's west coast, take Alligator Alley to the Miami exit and then turn south onto the turnpike extension. The turnpike ends in Florida City, at which time you will be dumped directly onto the two-lane U.S. 1, which leads to the Keys. Have around $15 for the tolls. If you take U.S. 1 straight down and bypass the Turnpike, it's free, but a lot longer.

Greyhound (© 800/231-2222; www.greyhound.com) has three buses leaving Miami for Key West every day, with stops in Key Largo, Tavernier, Islamorada,

Marathon, Big Pine Key, Cudjoe Key, Sugarloaf, and Big Coppit on the way south. Prices range from $16 to $48 one-way and $32 to $93 round-trip; the trip takes from 1 hour and 40 minutes to 4 hours and 40 minutes, depending on how far south you're going. Seats fill quickly in season, so come early. It's first-come, first-served.

Once you've arrived in the Keys, let **Scenic Helicopters** (© 866/596-7006) take you on 10- to 20-minute helicopter tours of the Middle Keys and Marathon areas, departing from Florida Keys Marathon Airport, MM (mile marker) 52.2 bay side. Up to three passengers can be accommodated on each tour, depending on weight. Cost is $100 to $250 for two, $195 to $350 for three.

VISITOR INFORMATION   Make sure you get your information from an official not-for-profit center. The **Key Largo Chamber of Commerce,** U.S. 1 at MM 106, Key Largo, FL 33037 (© 800/822-1088 or 305/451-1414; fax 305/451-4726; www. keylargo.org), runs an excellent facility, with free direct-dial phones and plenty of brochures. Headquartered in a handsome clapboard house, the chamber operates as an information clearinghouse for all of the Keys and is open daily from 9am to 6pm.

The **Islamorada Chamber of Commerce,** housed in a little red caboose, U.S. 1 at MM 82.5, P.O. Box 915, Islamorada, FL 33036 (© 800/322-5397 or 305/664-4503; fax 305/664-4289; www.islamoradachamber.com), offers maps and literature on the Upper Keys.

You can't miss the big, blue visitor center at MM 53.5, **Greater Marathon Chamber of Commerce,** 12222 Overseas Hwy., Marathon, FL 33050 (© 800/262-7284 or 305/743 5417; fax 305/289-0183; www.floridakeysmarathon. com). Here you can receive free information on local events, festivals, attractions, dining, and lodging.

Outdoor Sights & Activities

Anne's Beach (MM 73.5, on Lower Matecumbe Key, at the southwest end of Islamorada) is really more picnic spot than full-fledged beach, but die-hard tanners still congregate on this lovely but tiny strip of coarse sand that was damaged beyond recognition during the series of storms in 1998. The place has been spruced up a bit, even the bathrooms, which are (for now) clean and useable.

A better choice for real beaching is **Sombrero Beach** ★★, in Marathon, at the end of Sombrero Beach Road (near MM 50). This wide swath of uncluttered beachfront actually benefited from Hurricane George in 1998, with generous deposits of extra sand and a face-lift courtesy of the Monroe County Tourist Development Council. More than 90 feet of sand is dotted with palms, Australian pines, and royal poincianas, as well as with grills, clean restrooms, and Tiki huts for relaxing in the shade. It's also a popular nesting spot for turtles that lay their eggs at night.

If you're interested in seeing the Keys in their natural, pre–modern development state, you must venture off the highway and take to the water. Two backcountry islands that offer a glimpse of the "real" Keys are **Indian Key** and **Lignumvitae Key** ★★★. Visitors come here to relax and enjoy the islands' colorful birds and lush hammocks (elevated pieces of land above a marsh).

Named for the lignum vitae ("wood of life") trees found there, Lignumvitae Key supports a virgin tropical forest, the kind that once thrived on most of the Upper Keys. Over the years, human settlers imported "exotic" plants and animals to the Keys, irrevocably changing the botanical makeup of many backcountry islands and threatening much of the indigenous wildlife. Over the past 25 years, however, the Florida Department of Natural Resources has successfully removed most of the exotic vegetation from this key, leaving the 280-acre site much as it existed in the 18th century. The island also holds the Matheson House, a historic structure built in 1919 that has survived numerous hurricanes. You can go inside, but it's interesting only if you appreciate the coral rock of which the house is made. It's now a museum dedicated to the history, nature, and topography of the area. More interesting are the Botanical Gardens, which surround the house and are a state preserve. Lignumvitae Key has a visitor center at MM 88.5 (© **305/664-2540**).

Indian Key, a much smaller island on the Atlantic side of Islamorada, was occupied by Native Americans for thousands of years before European settlers arrived. The 10-acre historic site was also the original seat of Dade County before the Civil War. Interestingly, from an archaeological standpoint, you can see the ruins of the previous settlement and tour the lush grounds on well-marked trails (off Indian Key Fill, Overseas Hwy., MM 79). For more information on Indian Key, call the Florida Park Service (© **305/664-4815**) or check out www.abfla.com/parks/indiankey/indiankey.html.

If you want to see both islands, plan to spend at least half a day. You can rent your own powerboat from **Robbie's Rent-A-Boat,** U.S. 1 at MM 77.5 (on the bay side), on Islamorada. It's then a $1 admission fee to each island, which includes an informative hour-long guided tour by park rangers. This is a good option if you're a confident boater. I also recommend Robbie's **ferry service.** A visit to Lignumvitae Key costs $20 for adults and $15 for kids 12 and under, which includes the $1 park admission. For a ride to Indian Key, take the 2½-hour Florida Bay Eco-Nature Tour which costs $35 for adults and $20 for children 12 and under, The ferry is a more economical, easier way to enjoy the beauty of the islands when you aren't negotiating the shallow reefs along the way. The runabouts, which carry up to six people, depart from Robbie's Pier (p. 270) Thursday through Monday at 10am and 2pm for Lignumvitae Key. In high season, you may need to book 2 days before departure. Robbie's also does eco-tours, 2-hour trips through passages among the sea-grass beds that rim the many protected shallow bays. You'll get to cruise among the hundreds of small, uninhabited mangrove and hardwood hammock islands, which host an amazing variety of wildlife and create the island network of the Florida Bay. Call © **305/664-4815** for information from the park service; or call © **305/664-9814,** or visit www.robbies.com for Robbie's.

Crane Point Hammock ★★ 🏛😊 Crane Point Hammock is a little-known but worthwhile stop, especially for those interested in the rich botanical and archaeological history of the Keys. This privately owned, 64-acre nature area is considered one of the most important historic sites in the Keys. It contains what is probably the last virgin thatch-palm hammock in North America, as well as a rainforest exhibit and an archaeological site with prehistoric Indian and Bahamian artifacts.

Also headquarters for the Florida Keys Land and Sea Trust, the hammock's impressive nature museum has simple, informative displays of the Keys' wildlife, including a walk-through replica of a coral-reef cave and life-size dioramas with tropical birds and Key deer. Kids can participate in art projects, see 6-foot-long iguanas, climb through a scaled-down pirate ship, and touch a variety of indigenous aquatic and landlubber creatures.

5550 Overseas Hwy. (MM 50), Marathon. © **305/743-9100.** www.cranepoint.net. Admission $11 adults, $9 seniors 66 and over, $7 students, free for children 5 and under. Mon–Sat 9am–5pm; Sun noon–5pm.

Bridge Mix

The Seven-Mile Bridge is the longest fragmented (unconnected pieces) bridge in the world. Completed in 1985, it was constructed parallel to the original bridge, part of Henry Flagler's Florida East Coast Railroad, which served as the original link to the Lower Keys. Some people may recognize the remnants of the old bridge from the Arnold Schwarzenegger movie *True Lies.* Others fearfully contemplate a wrong turn leading them to the old bridge instead of the new one. Not to worry: The old bridge is closed to cars and has been transformed into the world's longest fishing pier.

Pigeon Key ★★   At the curve of the old bridge on Pigeon Key is an intriguing historic site that has been under renovation since late 1993. This 5-acre island once had the camp for the crew that built the old railway in the early 20th century, which later served as housing for the bridge builders. From here, the vista includes the vestiges of Henry Flagler's old Seven-Mile Bridge and the one on which traffic presently soars, as well as many old wooden cottages and a truly tranquil stretch of lush foliage and sea. If you miss the shuttle tour from the Pigeon Key visitor center or would rather walk or bike to the site, it's about 2½ miles. Either way, you may want to bring a picnic to enjoy after a brief self-guided walking tour of the Key and a museum visit to what has become an homage to Flagler's railroad, featuring artifacts and photographs of the old bridge. An informative 28-minute video of the island's history is shown every hour starting at 10am. Parking is available at the Knight's Key end of the bridge, at MM 48, or at the visitor center at MM 47, on the ocean side.

East end of the Seven-Mile Bridge near MM 47, Marathon. ℂ **305/743-5999.** www.pigeonkey.net. Admission $11 adults, $8.50 children 12 and under. Prices include shuttle transportation from the visitor center. Daily 10am–3pm; shuttle tours run hourly 10am–4pm.

Seven-Mile Bridge ★★★   A stop at the Seven-Mile Bridge is a rewarding and relaxing break on the drive south. Built alongside the ruins of oil magnate Henry Flagler's incredible Overseas Railroad, the "new" bridge (btw. MMs 40 and 47) is considered an architectural feat. The apex of the wide-arched span, completed in 1985 at a cost of more than $45 million, is the highest point in the Keys. The new bridge and its now-defunct neighbor provide excellent vantage points from which to view the stunning waters of the Keys. In the daytime, you may want to walk, jog, or bike along the scenic 4-mile stretch of old bridge. Or you may join local anglers, who catch barracuda, yellowtail, and dolphin (the fish, not the mammal) on what is known as "the longest fishing pier in the world." Parking is available on both sides of the bridge.

Btw. MMs 40 and 47 on U.S. 1. ℂ **305/289-0025.**

Visiting with the Animals

Dolphin Research Center ★★★ ☺   If you've always wanted to touch, swim, or play with dolphins, this is the place to do it. Of the several such centers in the continental United States (all located in the Keys), the Dolphin Research Center is a nonprofit facility and one of the most organized and informative. Although some people argue that training dolphins is cruel and selfish, this is one of the most respected of the institutions that study and protect the mammals. Knowledgeable trainers at the center will also tell you that the dolphins need stimulation and enjoy human contact. They certainly seem to. They nuzzle and seem to smile and kiss the lucky people who get to interact with them in daily interactive programs. The "family" of 19 dolphins swims in a 90,000-square-foot natural saltwater pool carved out of the shoreline. If you can't get into an interactive program, you can watch the frequent sessions that cover a variety of topics from fun facts about dolphins, to therapeutic qualities of dolphins, to research projects in progress. Because the Dolphin Encounter swimming program is the most popular, advanced reservations are required and can be made up to 6 months in advance. The cost is $189 per person. If you're not brave enough to swim with the dolphins or if you have a child under 5 (not permitted to swim with dolphins), try the Dolphin Dip program, in which participants stand on a submerged platform from which they can "meet and greet" the critters. A participating adult must hold children younger than 5. Cost for this program is $104 per person (free for children 4 and under).

Note: Swimming with dolphins has both its critics and its supporters. (See the "Dol-Fans Beware" box below.)

U.S. 1 at MM 59 (on the bay side), Marathon. ☏ **305/289-1121.** www.dolphins.org. Admission $20 adults, $17 seniors, $14 children 4-12. Daily 9am–4:30pm. Narrated behavior sessions with Atlantic bottlenose dolphins and California sea lions as well as educational presentations roughly every half-hour throughout the day.

Florida Keys Wild Bird Center ★   Wander through lush canopies of mangroves on wooden walkways to see some of the Keys' most famous residents—the large variety of native birds, including broad-wing hawks, great blue and white herons, roseate spoonbills, cattle egrets, and pelicans. This not-for-profit center operates as a hospital for the many birds that have been injured by accident or disease. In 2002, the World Parrot Mission was established here, focusing on caring for parrots and educating the public about the birds. Visit at feeding time, usually about 3:30pm, when you can watch the dedicated staff feed the hundreds of hungry birds.

U.S. 1 at MM 93.6 (bay side), Tavernier. ☏ **305/852-4486.** www.fkwbc.org. Donations suggested. Daily 8:30am–6pm.

Robbie's Pier ★★★ 🎣   One of the best and definitely one of the cheapest attractions in the Upper Keys is the famed Robbie's Pier. Here the fierce steely tarpons, a prized catch for backcountry anglers, have been gathering for the past 20 years. You may recognize these prehistoric-looking giants that grow up to 200 pounds; many are displayed as trophies and mounted on local restaurant walls. To see them live, head to Robbie's Pier, where tens and sometimes hundreds of these behemoths circle the shallow waters waiting for you to feed them. Robbie's Pier also offers ranger-led boat tours and guided kayak tours to Indian Key, where you can go snorkeling or just bask in the glory of your surroundings.

U.S. 1 at MM 77.5, Islamorada. ☏ **305/664-9814.** www.robbies.com. Admission to see the tarpon $1. Bucket of fish to feed them $3. Daily 8am–5pm. Make a hard right U-turn off the highway, then it's a short drive before you'll see a HUNGRY TARPON restaurant sign. Robbie's driveway is just before the restaurant.

Theater of the Sea ★ ☺   Established in 1946, the Theater of the Sea is one of the world's oldest marine zoos. Recently refurbished, the park's dolphin and sea-lion shows are entertaining and informative, especially for children. If you want to swim with dolphins and haven't booked well in advance, you may be able to get into this place with just a few hours' notice, as opposed to the more rigid Dolphin Research Center in Marathon (see above). While the Dolphin Research Center is a legitimate, scientific establishment, Theater of the Sea is more like a theme-park attraction. That's not to say the dolphins are mistreated, but it's not as educational and professional as the Dolphin Research Center. Theater of the Sea also permits you to swim with sea lions. (Children 4 and under cannot participate.) There are twice-daily 4-hour adventure and snorkel cruises that cost $69 for adults and $45 for children ages 3 to 12, during which you can learn about the history and ecology of the marine environment.

U.S. 1 at MM 84.5, Islamorada. © **305/664-2431.** www.theaterofthesea.com. Admission $26 adults, $19 children 3-12. Dolphin swim $175; sea-lion swim $135. Reservations are a must. Daily 10am–5pm (ticket office closes at 4pm).

Two Exceptional State Parks

One of the best places to discover the diverse ecosystem of the Upper Keys is its most famous park, **John Pennekamp Coral Reef State Park ★★★**, located on U.S. 1 at MM 102.5, in Key Largo (© **305/451-6300;** www.pennekamppark.com). Named for a former *Miami Herald* editor and conservationist, the 188-square-mile park is the nation's first undersea preserve: It's a sanctuary for part of the only living coral reef in the continental United States. The original plans for Everglades National Park included this part of the reef within its boundaries, but opposition from local homeowners made its inclusion politically impossible.

Because the water is extremely shallow, the 40 species of coral and more than 650 species of fish here are accessible to divers, snorkelers, and glass-bottom boat passengers. To experience this park, visitors must get in the water—you can't see the reef from the shore. Your first stop should be the visitor center, which has a mammoth 30,000 gallon saltwater aquarium that re-creates a reef ecosystem. At the adjacent dive shop, you can rent snorkeling and diving equipment and join one of the boat trips that depart for the reef throughout the day. Visitors can also rent motorboats, sailboats, sailboards, and canoes. The 2½-hour glass-bottom boat tour is the best way to see the coral reefs if you don't want to get wet. Watch for the lobsters and other sea life residing in the fairly shallow ridge walls beneath the coastal waters. **Remember:** These are protected waters, so you can't remove anything from them.

Canoeing around the park's narrow mangrove channels and tidal creeks is also popular. You can go on your own in a rented canoe or, in winter, sign up for a tour led by a local naturalist. Hikers have two short trails from which to choose: a boardwalk through the mangroves, and a dirt trail through a tropical hardwood hammock. Ranger-led walks are usually scheduled daily from the end of November to April. Call © **305/451-1202** for schedule information and reservations.

Park admission is $8 per vehicle of two to eight passengers, $4 for single driver, $2 for pedestrians and bicyclists, plus a 50¢ Monroe County surcharge per person. On busy weekends, there's often a line of cars waiting to get into the park. On your way in, ask the ranger for a map. Glass-bottom boat tours cost $24 for adults and $17 for children 11 and under. Tours depart three times daily, at 9:15am, 12:15pm, and 3pm. Snorkeling tours are $23 for adults and $25 for children 17 and under; masks, fins, and snorkels cost $7 and the snorkel is yours to keep. Canoes rent for

THE 10 "keymandments"

The Keys have always attracted independent spirits, from Ernest Hemingway and Tennessee Williams to Jimmy Buffett, Zane Grey, and local hero Mel Fisher. Writers, artists, and freethinkers have long drifted down here to escape.

Although you'll generally find a very laid-back and tolerant code of behavior in the Keys, some rules do exist. Be sure to respect the 10 "Keymandments" while you're here, or suffer the consequences.

1. Don't anchor on a reef. (Reefs are alive.)
2. Don't feed the animals. (They'll want to follow you home.)
3. Don't trash our place (or we'll send Bubba to trash yours).
4. Don't touch the coral. (After all, you don't even know them. Some pose a mild risk of injury to you as well.)
5. Don't speed (especially on Big Pine Key, where deer reside and tar-and-feathering is still practiced).
6. Don't catch more fish than you can eat. (Better yet, let them go. Some of them support schools.)
7. Don't collect conch. (This species is protected by Bubba.)
8. Don't disturb the birds' nests. (They find it very annoying.)
9. Don't damage the sea grass (and don't even think about making a skirt out of it).
10. Don't drink and drive on land or sea. (There's nothing funny about it.)

$12 per hour; kayaks are $12 per hour for a single, $17 per hour for a double. For experienced boaters only, four different sizes of reef boats (powerboats) rent for $160 to $210 for 4 hours, and $259 to $359 for a full day; call ✆ **305/451-6325** for information. A minimum $400 deposit (or more, depending on boat size) is required. The park's boat-rental office is open daily from 8am to 5pm (last boat rented at 3pm); phone for tour and dive times. Reservations are recommended for all of the above. Also see below for more options on diving, fishing, and snorkeling off these reefs.

Long Key State Recreation Area ★★★, U.S. 1 at MM 68, Long Key (✆ **305/664-4815;** www.abfla.com/parks/longkey/longkey.html), is one of the best places in the Middle Keys for hiking, camping, snorkeling, and canoeing. This 965-acre site is situated atop the remains of an ancient coral reef. At the entrance gate, ask for a free flyer describing the local trails and wildlife.

Three nature trails can be explored via foot or canoe. The Golden Orb Trail is a 40-minute walk through mostly plants; the Layton Trail is a 15-minute walk along the bay; and the Long Key Canoe Trail glides along a shallow-water lagoon. The excellent 1.5-mile canoe trail is short and sweet, allowing visitors to loop around the mangroves in about an hour. Long Key is also a great spot to stop for a picnic if you get hungry on your way to Key West. Campsites are available along the Atlantic Ocean. The swimming and saltwater fishing (license required) are top-notch here, as is the snorkeling, which is shallow and on the shoreline of the Atlantic. For novices, educational programs on the aforementioned are available, too.

Railroad builder Henry Flagler created the Long Key Fishing Club here in 1906, and the waters surrounding the park are still popular with game fishers. In summer, sea turtles lumber onto the protected coast to lay their eggs. Educational programs are available to view this phenomenon.

Admission is $5 per car of two to eight people, $4 single-occupant vehicle, $2 pedestrian or bicyclist, plus 50¢ per person Monroe County Surcharge (except for the Layton Trail, which is free). The recreation area is open daily from 8am to sunset. You can rent canoes at the trail head for about $5 per hour or $10 a day. The nearest place to rent snorkel equipment is **Holiday Isle,** 84001 U.S. 1, Islamorada (© **800/327-7070**).

Watersports from A to Z

There are literally hundreds of outfitters in the Keys who will arrange all kinds of water activities, from cave dives to parasailing. If those recommended below are booked up or unreachable, ask the local chamber of commerce for a list of qualified members.

BOATING In addition to the rental shops in the state parks, you'll find dozens of outfitters along U.S. 1 offering a range of runabouts and skiffs for boaters of any experience level. **Captain Pip's,** U.S. 1 at MM 47.5, Marathon (© **800/707-1692** or 305/743-4403; www.captainpips.com), charges $145 to $300 per day. Overnight accommodations are available and include a free boat rental: 2-night minimum $250 to $450 in season and $225 to $415 off-season; weekly $1,185 to $2,595. Rooms are Key West comfortable and charming, with ceiling fans, tile floors, and pine paneling. But the best part is that every room comes with an 18- to 21-foot boat for your use during your stay. **Robbie's Rent-a-Boat,** U.S. 1 at MM 77.5, Islamorada (© **305/664-9814;** www.robbies.com), rents 18- to 26 foot motorboats with engines ranging from 60 to 130 horsepower. Boat rentals are $135 to $185 for a half-day and $185 to $235 for a full day.

CANOEING & KAYAKING I can think of no better way to explore the uninhabited backcountry on the Gulf side of the Keys than by kayak or canoe, as you can reach places that big boats just can't get to because of their large draft. Manatees will sometimes cuddle up to the boats, thinking them to be another friendly species.

Many area hotels rent kayaks and canoes to guests, as do the outfitters listed here. **Florida Bay Outfitters,** U.S. 1 at MM 104, Key Largo (© **305/451-3018;** www.kayakfloridakeys.com), rents canoes and sea kayaks for use in and around John Pennekamp Coral Reef State Park for $35 to $75 for a half-day, $45 to $90 for a full day. **Florida Keys Kayak and Sail,** U.S. 1 at MM 75.5, Islamorada (© **305/664-4878;** www.robbies.com), at Robbie's Pier, offers backcountry tours, botanical-preserve tours of Lignumvitae Key, historic-site tours of Indian Key, and sunset tours through the mangrove tunnels and saltwater flats. Tour rates are from $39 to $49; rental rates range from $15 per hour to $45 per day for a single kayak, and $20 per hour to $60 per day for a double kayak. **Reflections Nature Tours** (© **305/872-4668;** www.floridakeyskayaktours.com) is a small mobile company that specializes in kayak tours through the Lower Keys. Guided kayak excursions cost $50 per person for a 3-hour tour, $40 per person for a 2-hour full-moon tour. The 3-hour custom tours start at $125 for one person and $195 for two people. All tours are by appointment only. Kayak rentals are $45 for single kayak all day and $60 for full-day tandem. Nature lovers can slip through the silent backcountry waters off Key West and the Lower Keys in a kayak, discovering the flora and fauna that make up the unique Keys ecosystem, on **Blue Planet Kayak Tours'** (✆ **305/294-8087;** www.blue-planet-kayak.com) starlight tour. All excursions are led by an environmental scientist. The starlight tours last between 2½ and 3 hours. No previous kayaking experience is necessary. Cost for the guided kayak adventure is $50 per person.

DIVING & SNORKELING Just 6 miles off Key Largo is a U.S. Navy Landing Ship Dock, the latest artificial wreck site to hit the Keys—or, rather, to be submerged 130 feet *below* the Keys.

The **Florida Keys Dive Center,** U.S. 1 at MM 90.5, Tavernier (✆ **305/852-4599;** www.floridakeysdivectr.com), takes snorkelers and divers to the reefs of John Pennekamp Coral Reef State Park and environs every day. PADI (Professional Association of Diving Instructors) training courses are available for the uninitiated. While some people have complained that employees are rude here, others disagree; I suggest you decide for yourself. Tours leave at 8am and 12:30pm; the cost is $35 per person to snorkel (plus $10 rental fee for mask, snorkel, and fins), and $50 per person to dive (plus an extra $24 if you need to rent all the gear).

> ## Dol-Fans Beware
>
> Swimming with dolphins has both its critics and its supporters. You may want to visit the Whale and Dolphin Conservation Society's website at www.wdcs.org. For more information about responsible travel in general, check out www.treadlightly.org and www.ecotourism.org.

At **Hall's Dive Center & Career Institute,** U.S. 1 at MM 48.5, Marathon (✆ **305/743-5929;** www.hallsdiving.com), snorkelers and divers can dive at Looe Key, Sombrero Reef, Delta Shoal, Content Key, or Coffins Patch. Tours are scheduled daily at 9am and 1pm. You'll spend 1 hour at each of two sites per tour. It's $40 per person to snorkel (gear included), $35 for children, and $55 to $65 per person to dive (tanks $7.50–$15 each).

FISHING **Robbie's Partyboats & Charters,** U.S. 1 at MM 77.5, Islamorada (✆ **305/664-8070** or 664-8498; www.robbies.com), located at Robbie's Marina on Lower Matecumbe Key, offers day and night deep-sea and reef-fishing trips aboard a 65-foot party boat. Big-game fishing charters are also available, and "splits" are arranged for solo fishers. Party-boat fishing costs about $35 for a half-day morning tour ($3 for rod and reel rental); it's $20 extra if you want to go back out on an afternoon tour. Charters run about $700 for a half-day, $900 for a full day; splits begin at $120 per person. Phone for information and reservations.

Bud n' Mary's Fishing Marina, U.S. 1 at MM 79.8, Islamorada (✆ **800/742-7945** or 305/664-2461; www.budnmarys.com), one of the largest marinas between Miami and Key West, is packed with sailors offering backcountry fishing charters. This is the place to go if you want to stalk tarpon, bonefish, and snapper. If the seas are not too rough, deep-sea and coral fishing trips can also be arranged. Charters cost $375 for a half-day, $550 for a full day; splits begin at $75 per person.

Where to Stay

U.S. 1 is lined with chain hotels in all price ranges. In the Upper Keys, the best moderately priced option is the **Key Largo Ramada,** off U.S. 1 at MM 100, Key Largo (✆ **800/THE-KEYS** [843-5397] or 305/451-3939), which has three pools and a casino boat, and is just 3 miles from John Pennekamp Coral Reef State Park. Another good Upper Keys option is **Days Inn Oceanfront Resort,** U.S. 1 at MM 82.5 (© **800/DAYS-INN** [329-7466] or 305/664-3681). In the Middle Keys, the **Siesta Motel,** 7425 Overseas Hwy., MM 54 in Marathon (© **305/743-5671;** www.siestamotel.net), offers reasonably priced, very clean ocean-side rooms.

Because the real beauty of the Keys lies mostly beyond the highways, there is no better way to see this area than by boat. So why not stay in a floating hotel? Especially if you're traveling with a group, houseboats can be economical. To rent a houseboat, contact **Houseboat Vacations,** 85944 Overseas Hwy., Islamorada (© **305/664-4009;** www.floridakeys.com/houseboats). Rates are from $1,112 to $1,350 for 3 nights. Boats accommodate up to six people.

If you'd rather stay on land and do so for an extended period of time with a bunch of friends or family, consider the **Getaway Cedar Chalet** (© **586/909-4553**), a 3-bedroom, 3-bathroom home located on a cul-de-sac right across from the ocean in Islamorada. The home features panoramic ocean views, a big gourmet kitchen, tropical landscaping, lofted wood ceilings made of Dade County Pine, lower level rec room and private cabana suite with kitchenette and full bathroom. Rates range from $2,500 to $2,800 a week.

For other options, consider the recommendations below.

VERY EXPENSIVE

Cheeca Lodge & Spa ★★★ ☺ Located on 27 lush acres of beachfront, this rambling resort, which was closed for nearly a year after suffering serious fire damage, sports one of the only golf courses in the Upper Keys and a whole lot more. Rooms have the amenities of a world-class resort in a very laid-back setting. Post-fire upgrades include new Premier Suites, enormous 840-square-foot rooms with huge balconies, floor-to-ceiling glass walls opening to ocean or island views, open-air round spa tubs for two, and glass rain showers. Also revamped, the lobby, which includes a new bar, 2,400 square feet of retail shops, and the restaurants—Nikai Sushi Bar serving the raw goods along with Asian-inspired fare and a revamped signature restaurant, **Atlantic's Edge,** which is now under the creative direction of James Beard-approved Chef Dean Max of 3030 Ocean fame in Fort Lauderdale. Standard guest rooms still feature luxurious West Indies–style decor, marble baths, fine linens, plasma TVs, and wireless DSL. The Spa at Cheeca offers a variety of massage therapies, skin care, signature body treatments, fitness room, fitness classes, and butler-serviced poolside cabanas. For recreation, Cheeca offers tennis, a 9-hole Jack Nicklaus–designed golf course, eco-tours, sunset cruises, snorkel excursions, on-property flats boats with seasoned guides for backcountry fishing, Camp Cheeca children's environmental program, and much more. The $39 daily resort fee may seem steep at first, but it's worth it, including unlimited tennis, golf, fishing rods, bicycles, beach shade cabanas, sea kayaks, valet parking, wireless Internet access, exercise classes, in-room Starbucks coffee service and bottled water, housekeeping gratuity, local calls, daily newspaper, and fax services.

U.S. 1 at MM 82 (P.O. Box 527), Islamorada, FL 33036. © **305/664-4651.** Fax 305/664-2893. www.cheeca.com. 212 units. Season $599–$1,099 for Superior, $599–$1,399 for Luxury, $899–$999 for Premier; off-season $199–$599 for Superior, $249–$549 for Luxury, $399–$499 for Premier. AE, DC, DISC, MC, V. **Amenities:** Restaurant; sushi bar; 2 lounges (1 poolside); babysitting; bike rental; children's nature programs; concierge; 9-hole golf course; 5 Jacuzzis; saltwater lagoon; 2 outdoor heated pools; limited room service; full-service spa; 6 lighted hard tennis courts; watersports equipment/rentals. *In room:* A/C, TV/DVD, CD player, hair dryer, kitchenette (in suites), minibar, Wi-Fi.

Hawks Cay Resort ★★★ ☺ Set on its own 60-acre island in the Middle Keys, when it comes to activities, this resort is far superior to Cheeca Lodge. In addition to sailing, fishing, snorkeling, and water-skiing, guests have the unique opportunity to interact directly with dolphins in the resort's natural saltwater lagoon. (You'll need to reserve a spot well in advance for this.) Guest rooms are large, with spacious bathrooms, island-style furniture, and private balconies with ocean or tropical views. There are also 225 hyperposh villas modeled after the kitschy 1950s concept of the "boatel," the recipients of a sophisticated redesign. The 7,000-square-foot Calm Waters Spa provides stellar treatments. Organized children's activities include marine- and ecology-inspired programs. A $35-million renovation in 2008 included a verandah and a new lobby incorporating direct water views, a bar and lounge, as well as a vastly expanded main resort pool featuring new landscaping, multitiered sun terrace, and private butlered cabanas. Fine dining options include a Nuevo-Latino restaurant and bar featuring hard-to-find rums.

61 Hawks Cay Blvd., at MM 61, Duck Key, FL 33050. ☎ **888/432-2242** or 305/743-7000. Fax 305/743-5215. www.hawkscay.com. 402 units, including 225 2- and 3-bedroom villas. Winter $329–$539 double, $549–$1,300 suite, $519–$1,400 villa; off-season $279–$459 double, $479–$900 suite, $449–$1,000 villa. Packages available. AE, DC, DISC, MC, V. **Amenities:** 5 restaurants; lounge; bike rental; children's programs ($48–$75 per child); concierge; nearby golf course (transportation available); exercise room; Jacuzzi; full-service marina; 5 outdoor heated pools; room service; full-service spa; 8 tennis courts (6 hard, 2 clay, 2 lighted); watersports equipment/rentals. In room: A/C, TV, fridge, hair dryer, Internet access.

EXPENSIVE

Casa Morada ★★ 🏨 The closest thing to a boutique hotel in the Florida Keys, Casa Morada is the brainchild of a trio of New York women who used to work for hip hotelier Ian Schrager. This 16-suite property is a hipster haven tucked away off a sleepy street and radiates serenity and style in an area where serenity is aplenty, but style is elusive. Sitting on 1¾ acres of prime bayfront, the hotel features a limestone grotto, freshwater pool, and poolside beverage service. Each of the cool rooms has either a private garden or a terrace—request the one with the open-air Jacuzzi that faces the bay. While the decor is decidedly island, think St. Barts rather than, say, Gilligan's. There's no on-site restaurant, a complimentary breakfast is served daily, and there's free yoga Wednesday to Sunday at 8:30am. Enjoy free use of bikes, bocce balls, and board games. Despite the games, this place is not recommended for kids.

136 Madeira Rd., Islamorada, FL 33036. ☎ **888/881-3030** or 305/664-0044. Fax 305/664-0674. www.casamorada.com. 16 units. Winter $329–$659 double; off-season $249–$509 double. Rates include continental breakfast. AE, DISC, MC, V. From U.S. 1 S., at MM 82.2, turn right onto Madeira Rd. and continue to the end of the street. The hotel is on the right. Friendly pets are welcome. **Amenities:** Free bike use; bocce ball; freshwater pool. In room: A/C, TV/DVD, CD player, hair dryer, minibar.

Jules' Undersea Lodge ★★★ 🏨 Staying here is certainly an experience of a lifetime—if you're brave enough to take the plunge. Originally built as a research lab, this small underwater compartment, which rests on pillars on the ocean floor, now operates as a two-room hotel. As expensive as it is unusual, Jules' is most popular with diving honeymooners. To get inside, guests swim 21 feet under the structure and pop up into the unit through a 4×6-foot "moon pool" that gurgles soothingly all night long. The 30-foot-deep underwater suite consists of two separate bedrooms that share a common living area. Room service will deliver your meals, daily newspapers, and even a late-night pizza in waterproof containers, at no extra charge. If you don't have time or a desire to spend the night, you can hang out and explore the lodge for 3 hours for $125 to $165 per person.

51 Shoreland Dr., Key Largo, FL 33037. ℂ **305/451-2353.** Fax 305/451-4789. www.jul.com. 2 units. $375–$475 per person. Rates include breakfast and dinner, as well as all equipment and unlimited scuba diving in the lagoon for certified divers. Packages available. AE, DISC, MC, V. From U.S. 1 S., at MM 103.2, turn left onto Transylvania Ave., across from the Central Plaza shopping mall. **Amenities:** Entertainment center; dining area. *In room:* A/C, kitchenette.

Kona Kai Resort & Gallery ★★★ 🏨   This little haven is an exquisite, adults-only waterfront property right on Florida Bay—a choice location that offers a stunning sunset view overlooking Everglades National Park. Highly stylized, modern rooms and suites dot the lush 2-acre property, brimming with native vegetation and fruit-bearing trees from which you're free to sample. An orchid house has more than 350 flowers. Lounge chairs, hammocks, a beachfront freshwater pool (heated in winter and cooled in summer), complimentary bottled water and fresh fruit poolside, a Jacuzzi, and one of the largest private beaches on the island make Kona Kai perfect for relaxation. For the more adventurous, Kona Kai's complimentary concierge services will organize excursions to the Everglades and the backcountry as well as fishing, snorkeling, diving, and more. Kayaks, paddleboats, tennis, Wi-Fi, and CD/DVD libraries are included at no extra charge. In-room massage and private yoga are available. For meals, three restaurants are within walking distance and the exceptional staff will give you insider tips—and discounts—to their favorite local eateries and watering holes. A fine art gallery doubles as the lobby.

97802 Overseas Hwy. (U.S. 1 at MM 97.8), Key Largo, FL 33037. ℂ **800/365-7829** or 305/852-7200. Fax 305/852-4629. www.konakairesort.com. 11 units. Winter $308–$561 double and 1-bedroom suite, $736–$940 2-bedroom suite; off-season $211–$454 double and 1-bedroom suite, $552–$656 2-bedroom suite. AE, DISC, MC, V. Closed Sept. Children 15 and under not permitted. **Amenities:** Boat dockage; concierge; Jacuzzi; beachside Ping-Pong; beachfront heated/cooled pool; shuffleboard; lighted tennis court; watersports equipment/rentals; Wi-Fi. *In room:* A/C, TV/DVD, CD player, fridge, hair dryer, full kitchen (suites only), no phone.

The Moorings ★★★ 🏨   You'll never see another soul on this 18-acre resort, a former coconut plantation, if you choose not to. There isn't even maid service unless you request it. The romantic whitewashed units, from cozy cottages to three-bedroom houses, are spacious with fully equipped kitchens and rustic, yet modern, decor. Most have washers and dryers, and all have CD players and DVD players; ask when you book. The real reason to come to this resort is to relax on the 1,000-plus-foot beach (one of the only real beaches around). You'll also find a great pool, hard tennis court, and a few kayaks and sailboards, but no motorized water vehicles in the waters surrounding the hotel, making it completely tranquil. There's no room service or restaurant, but Morada Bay and Pierres across the street are excellent. This is a place for people who like each other a lot. Leave the kids at home unless they're extremely well-behaved and not easily bored.

123 Beach Rd., near MM 81.5, on the ocean side, Islamorada, FL 33036. ℂ **305/664-4708.** Fax 305/664-4242. www.mooringsvillage.com. 18 units. Winter $325 small cottage, $650 1-bedroom house, $5,775–$10,500 weekly oceanfront house; off-season $250 small cottage, $450 1-bedroom house, $4,200–$7,700 weekly oceanfront house. 2-night minimum for smaller cottages; 1-week minimum for larger cottages and oceanfront house. AE, MC, V. **Amenities:** Large outdoor heated pool; spa; tennis court; watersports equipment. *In room:* A/C, TV/DVD, CD player, hair dryer, kitchen, microwave, washer/dryer.

Tranquility Bay Beach House Resort ★★★ ☺ The newest luxury resort in the Middle Keys, Tranquility Bay sits on a tropically landscaped 12 acres on the Gulf of Mexico. You'll feel like you're in your own beach house—literally, with gorgeous two- and three-bedroom homes all with water views. All of the subtly decorated beach houses come equipped with everything a techno-savvy beach bum needs— even washers and dryers. Best of all, every beach house has spacious porches with French doors, wooden deck chairs, and 180-degree views of the water. The restaurant, Butterfly Café, is just as fine, with seasonal seafood menus. A private spa, Island Spice, helps you relax, but, really, this is one of the most relaxing resorts in all the Keys. Grounds sport lagoon pools, gazebos, a great lawn, and a beachfront Tiki bar. There are also activities, from adventure fishing and snorkeling to an adventure kids' program. *Note:* This is a nonsmoking resort. Smoking isn't even permitted on porches, only in designated areas.

2600 Overseas Hwy., Marathon, FL 33036.℡ **305/289-0888.** Fax 305/289-0667. www.tranquilitybay. com. 87 units. Winter $399–$539 doubles; off-season $279–$509 doubles. AE, DC, MC, V. **Amenities:** Fitness center; large outdoor heated pool; spa; watersports equipment/rentals. *In room:* A/C, TV/DVD, CD player, hair dryer, kitchen, microwave, Wi-Fi.

MODERATE

Banana Bay Resort & Marina ★★ 🏨 It doesn't look like much from the sign-cluttered Overseas Highway, but once you enter the lush, 10-acre grounds of Banana Bay, you'll realize you're in one of the most bucolic and best-run properties in the Upper Keys. The resort is a beachfront maze of two-story buildings hidden among banyans and palms, with moderately sized rooms, many with private balconies. A recreational activity area has horseshoe pits, a bocce court, barbecue grills, and a giant lawn chessboard. The pool is one of the largest freshwater pools in the Keys. The kitschy restaurant serves three meals a day, indoors and poolside. The hotel also rents bikes, boats, WaveRunners, kayaks, day-sailing dinghies, and bait and tackle. Another surprising amenity is Pretty Joe Rock, the hotel's private island, available for long weekends and weekly rentals. On it is a two-bedroom, two-bathroom cottage that's ideal for romantic escapes. Banana Bay is family friendly, but for an adults-only resort, there's **Banana Bay Resort,** at 2319 N. Roosevelt Blvd., in Key West (℡ **305/296-6925**), which doesn't allow children.

U.S. 1 at MM 49.5, Marathon, FL 33050.℡ **800/BANANA-1** (226-2621) or 305/743-3500. Fax 305/743-2670. www.bananabay.com. 60 units. Winter $185–$245 double; off-season $105–$225 double. Rates include continental breakfast. 3- and 7-night honeymoon and wedding packages available. AE, DC, DISC, MC, V. **Amenities:** Restaurant; bar; barbecue pit; bicycle rentals; Jacuzzi; marina; pool; snorkeling area; tennis courts; watersports equipment/rentals. *In room:* A/C, TV, fridge, hair dryer.

Coconut Palm Inn ★★★ 🏨 This former 1940s fishing camp is Key Largo's best kept secret, located on a private, white-sand beach in the middle of a coconut grove. All 20 rooms feature Bali-style decor and gorgeous bay views, but it's truly the outdoor space that makes this place so special. Sure, there's Wi-Fi on the beach, but you'll want to chuck that BlackBerry, iPod or laptop when you see the 400 feet of sunning beach, heated freshwater pool, two 200-foot private docks, Tikis, BBQs, boat ramp, paddle boats, and kayaks. Alfresco breakfasts and Adirondack chairs reinforce why you need to be outdoors here.

198 Harborview Dr., Key Largo FL 33037.℡ **800/765-5397** or 305/852-3017. Fax 305/852-3880. www. coconutpalminn.com. 20 units. Winter $129–$239 double, $339–$399 suite; off-season $159–$199 double, $279–$319 suite. AE, DISC, MC, V. **Amenities:** Beach; kayaks and paddleboats; heated freshwater pool; Wi-Fi. *In room:* A/C, TV, minifridge, hair dryer.

Conch Key Cottages ★★ 🎁   Here's your chance to play castaway in the Keys. Occupying its own private micro-island just off U.S. 1, Conch Key Cottages is a comfortable hideaway, a place to get away from it all. The cottages exude a sense of bohemian luxury (not an oxymoron) and old-Florida architecture with tin roofs and Dade County Pine. Located miles from neon-hued tourist traps and towering hotels, the cottages offer solitude. The romantic, beachfront cottages are situated on a small natural sandy beach just steps from the ocean The two-bedroom oceanview stilt cottages, the garden-view cottage, and the marina/sunset cottage are the most spacious, well designed and tailor-made for families. On the other side of the pool is an adorable studio cottage for two with a private Jacuzzi in a tropical garden. At the entrance to the compound are a total of four very comfy island rooms and apartments with garden views. On the other side of the pool is a handful of efficiency apartments that are similarly outfitted but don't enjoy beach frontage. All units feature full size kitchens plus a microwave, coffee maker, toaster, juicer and blender, utensils, dishes, pots and pans, and outside individual barbecue grills with charcoal and lighter fluid. The cottages are impeccably clean and well appointed with luxury linens and daily housekeeping service. Other fantastic amenities include free use of kayaks, check-in gift of chocolates, a delicious complimentary continental breakfast of fresh muffins, bagels and croissants, coffee and tea delivered to your door, and an unlimited supply of fresh Florida oranges that you can juice right in your own cottage. A heated pool is surrounded by lush foliage and, for those who break out in hives with no connection to the real world, free Wi-Fi.

Private Island off U.S. 1 at MM 62.3, Marathon, FL 33050. © **800/330-1577** or 305/289-1377. Fax 305/743-8661. www.conchkeycottages.com. 13 cottages. $110–$499 depending on occupancy and time of year. Rates include continental breakfast daily. AE, DISC, MC, V. **Amenities:** Private beach; concierge; dockage; complimentary kayaks; heated pool; free Wi-Fi. *In room:* A/C, TV, hair dryer, kitchen, no phone.

Holiday Isle Beach Resort & Marina   Holiday Isle attracts a Spring Break kind of crowd year-round, a crowd that tends not to care about the rooms themselves—and has no qualms cramming an entire fraternity into a single unit for budget reasons. The famous Tiki Bar claims to have invented the Rum Runner drink (151-proof rum, blackberry brandy, banana liqueur, grenadine, and lime juice), and there's no reason to doubt it. It's the Tiki Bar that brings the people, really. Hordes of partiers are attracted to the resort's nonstop merrymaking, live music, and beachfront bars. As a result, some of the accommodations can be noisy. Rooms are bare-bones; despite the ocean views, they're pretty awful and need a good scrub down—especially the units that lead to the filthy, sandy Tiki Bar. But, really, isn't that why you're here in the first place?

U.S. 1 at MM 84, Islamorada, FL 33036. © **800/327-7070** or 305/664-2321. Fax 305/664-2703. www.holidayisle.com. 178 units. Winter $144–$294 double, $274–$450 suite; off-season $119–$199 double, $245–$425 suite. AE, DISC, MC, V. **Amenities:** 5 restaurants; 12 bars; children's programs; Jacuzzi; 3 outdoor heated pools; kids' pool; watersports equipment/rentals. *In room:* A/C, TV, fridge, hair dryer.

Key Largo Grande ★   A short drive from Miami, this Hilton-run property is an ideal escape for a weekend or longer, situated on 13 acres of forest and the Gulf and featuring recently revamped rooms, most with water views. Forget the pools—there are two, a kids' and an adult pool, located in the middle of the parking lot, and although it is hidden by trees and a waterfall, you will want to spend your time on the private, white-sand beach where you can partake in watersports activities, walk on nature trails, lounge on chairs, or hang out at the Tiki bar. It's very peaceful and beautiful here and you'd never know it from it's motel-esque façade. There's a restaurant on site and it's okay—stick to area restaurants if you can or, better yet, bring some snacks and stick them in the in-room fridge. Once you see the beach here you may never want to leave for a food run.

97000 South Overseas Hwy., Key Largo FL 33037. ℂ **888/871-3437** or 305/852-5553. Fax 305/852-8669. www.keylargoresort.com. 200 units. Winter $144–$294 double, $274–$450 suite; off-season $119–$199 double, $245–$425 suite. AE, DISC, MC, V. **Amenities:** Restaurant; 3 bars; beach; children's activities; Jacuzzi; 2 outdoor pools; 2 tennis courts; watersports equipment/rentals. *In room:* A/C, TV, fridge, hair dryer, Internet access.

Lime Tree Bay Resort Motel The only place to stay in the tiny town of Layton (pop. 183), Lime Tree is midway between Islamorada and Marathon and is situated on a pretty piece of waterfront graced with hundreds of mature palm trees and tropical foliage. It prides itself on its promise of no hustle, no valets, and, most amusingly, no bartenders in Hawaiian shirts! Motel rooms and efficiencies have tiny bathrooms with showers, but are clean and well maintained. The best deal is the two-bedroom bay-view suite: A spacious living area with new furnishings leads to a large private deck overlooking the Gulf. There's also a full kitchen and two full bathrooms. Fifteen efficiencies and suites have kitchenettes. Pretty cool in its own right is the Zane Grey Suite (named after the famous author and screenwriter, who lived right around the corner), a two-bedroom, one-bathroom unit with the best views and a second-story location with private stairs.

U.S. 1 at MM 68.5, Layton, Long Key, FL 33001. ℂ **800/723-4519** or 305/664-4740. Fax 305/664-0750. www.limetreebayresort.com. 36 units. Winter $117–$375 double; summer $100–$320 double; off-season $89–$290 double. AE, DC, DISC, MC, V. **Amenities:** Restaurant; Jacuzzi; small outdoor pool; tennis court; Wi-Fi in business center. *In room:* A/C, TV, fridge, kitchenette (in some).

Pines and Palms ★★★ 🧳 Looking for a beachfront cottage or, better yet, an oceanfront villa, but don't want to spend your (future) child's college fund? This is the place. Cheery, one- to three-bedroom cozy cottages, Atlantic views, and a private beachfront with hammocks and a pool give way to a relaxed, tropical paradise. Service is friendly and accommodating. All rooms and cottages have full kitchens and balconies, and are ideal for extended stays. Although there's no restaurant on-site, the staff will be happy to bring a Weber barbecue to your patio so you can grill out by the beach. Because of its popularity, Pines and Palms usually has a 2-night minimum.

MM 80.4 (ocean side), Islamorada, FL 33036. ℂ **800/624-0964** or 305/664-4343. www.pinesand-palms.com. 25 units. $89–$219 double; $129–$299 suite; $159–$459 cottage; $399–$579 villa. AE, MC, V. **Amenities:** Bike rental; oceanfront heated freshwater pool; watersports equipment/rentals. *In room:* A/C, fridge, kitchen (in most).

INEXPENSIVE

Ragged Edge Resort ★★ This small oceanfront property's Tahitian-style units are spread along more than half a dozen gorgeous, grassy waterfront acres. All are immaculately clean and comfortable, and most are outfitted with full kitchens and tasteful furnishings. There's no bar, restaurant, or staff to speak of, but the retreat's affable owner is happy to lend bicycles and give advice on the area's offerings. A large dock attracts boaters and a variety of local and migratory birds. An outdoor heated freshwater pool is a bonus for those months when the temperature gets a bit chilly.

243 Treasure Harbor Rd. (near MM 86.5), Islamorada, FL 33036. © **800/436-2023** or 305/852-5389. www.ragged-edge.com. 11 units. $69–$99 double; $109–$259 suite. AE, MC, V. **Amenities:** Free bike use; outdoor pool. *In room:* A/C, fridge, kitchen (in most).

CAMPING

John Pennekamp Coral Reef State Park ★★   One of Florida's best parks (p. 271), Pennekamp has 47 well-separated campsites, half of which are available by advance reservation. The tent sites are small but equipped with restrooms, hot water, and showers. Note that the local environment provides fertile breeding grounds for insects, particularly in late summer, so bring repellent. Two man-made beaches and a small lagoon nearby attract many large wading birds. Reservations are held until 5pm; the park must be notified of late arrival by phone on the check-in date. Pennekamp opens at 8am and closes around sundown.

U.S. 1 at MM 102.5 (P.O. Box 487), Key Largo, FL 33037. © **305/451-1202.** www.pennekamppark.com. Reservations can be made in advance by calling Reserve America (© 800/326-3521). 47 campsites. $36 (with electricity) per site, 8 people maximum. Park entry $8 per vehicle with driver (plus 50¢ per person Monroe County surcharge). Yearly permits and passes available. AE, DISC, MC, V. No pets.

Long Key State Park ★   The Upper Keys' other main state park is more secluded than its northern neighbor—and more popular. All sites are located ocean side and surrounded by narrow rows of trees and nearby restroom facilities. Reserve well in advance, especially in winter.

U.S. 1 at MM 67.5 (P.O. Box 776), Long Key, FL 33001. © **305/664-4815.** www.abfla.com/parks/long-key/longkey.html. 60 sites. $36 per site for 1–8 people; $5 per vehicle. (plus 50¢ per person Monroe County surcharge) AE, DISC, MC, V. No pets.

Where to Dine

Although not known as a culinary hot spot (though always improving), the Upper and Middle Keys do have some excellent restaurants, most of which specialize in seafood. The landmark **Green Turtle Inn** (below) is alive and well, featuring classic and contemporary Florida cuisine by star chef Andy Niedenthal, a full bar and tasting station, custom catering, gourmet to go, and a Green Turtle product line, all in a beautiful, laid-back rustic environment. The restaurant is flanked by an art gallery and sport-fishing outfitter, making it a one-stop shop for locals and fun-loving tourists who have put Islamorada on the map.

Often, visitors (especially those who fish) take advantage of accommodations that have kitchen facilities and cook their own meals. Some restaurants will even clean and cook your catch, for a fee.

VERY EXPENSIVE

Atlantic's Edge ★★★ SEAFOOD   Continuing its award-winning culinary tradition albeit with a modern twist, the 21st-century version of Atlantic's Edge under the culinary direction of Chef Dean Max of 3030 Ocean in Fort Lauderdale, is a welcome addition to the impressive Upper Keys dining scene. Max has packed his modern American seafood and taken it with him on the road trip down to the Keys. Signature dishes include grilled Florida cobia with organic squash tortellini, local marinated eggplant, grilled *tardivo*, green onions, and red pepper cumin sauce; and deepwater Keys barrel fish with Parmesan risotto, maitake mushrooms, Asian greens, and lemon thyme sauce. With an emphasis on farm-to-table ingredients and, of course, the freshest seafood possible, Atlantic's Edge takes things to the, uh, max, and puts on an impressive show. Speaking of shows, the revamped restaurant itself is stunning, with views of its namesake and a gorgeous glassed-in wine cellar featuring over 150 wines selected by the chef.

Cheeca Lodge, U.S. 1 at MM 82 (P.O. Box 527), Islamorada, FL 33036. ✆ **305/664-4651.** Reservations recommended. Main courses $27–$52. AE, DC, MC, V. Daily 7am–5pm and 6–10pm.

Kaiyo ★★★ JAPANESE/SUSHI   This funky, colorful restaurant looks out of place in an area where most eateries are housed in shanty shacks, and its exquisite, modern sushi is a first for Islamorada—but the food is so good, people from all over South Florida plan trips around a meal at Kaiyo. It's not your typical sushi restaurant, but rather one that fuses Florida's fine ingredients with some of the freshest raw fish this side of Tokyo. Signature sushi items, such as the spicy volcano conch roll and the Key lime lobster roll, are outstanding, as are the farm-raised raw oysters and farmed baby-conch tempura. A hip, modern interior is an amusing contrast to the casually dressed, Key-ed up diners, and service here is of five-star caliber—something not typically found in the laid-back Keys. Before you say that you came to the Keys not for trendy sushi, but for fresh fish and conch fritters, do have a meal at Kaiyo. It may change the way you view Keys cuisine.

81701 Old Hwy., U.S. 1 at MM 82, Islamorada. ✆ **305/664-5556.** www.kaiyokeys.com. Reservations recommended. Main courses $22–$32; sushi $7.50–$16. AE, DC, MC, V. Mon–Sat noon–10pm.

Pierre's ★★★ FRENCH   The two-story British West Indies–style plantation home that houses this exquisite French restaurant is only part of the dramatic effect of a memorable dinner at Pierre's. Inside, you'll find more design drama—in a good way, of course—in the form of an eclectic mix of Moroccan, Indian, and African artifacts. Lighting is dim, with candlelight and Tiki torches outside, and it's completely romantic—especially outdoors on the second-floor verandah overlooking the water. The food challenges the setting, with amazing flavors and gorgeous presentation. The tempura lobster tail with hearts of palm hash, soy glaze, and wasabi crème fraîche, and the Florida Keys Hogfish Meunière with roasted creamer potatoes, pattypan squash, and baby zucchini are to die for. Desserts are equally divine, and if you can't decide what to have, order the Valrhona Chocolate Fondue with biscotti, *pâté a choux*, lemon sugar cookies, strawberries, and mandarin oranges. After dinner, head downstairs to the Green Flash Lounge, where you'll find a laid-back cocktail scene, with locals and visitors marveling at the exquisite, priceless setting. Pierre's also hosts a fabulous, monthly Full Moon Party with its casual dining sister, Morada Bay Beach Café.

U.S. 1 at MM 81.6 (bay side), Islamorada. ✆ **305/664-3225.** www.pierres-restaurant.com. Main courses $35–$40. AE, MC, V. Sun–Thurs 6–10pm; Fri–Sat 6–11pm. Lounge open at 5pm daily. Restaurant closed on Tues during summer.

EXPENSIVE

Barracuda Grill ★ SEAFOOD   This small, casual spot serves really good seafood, steaks, and chops, although lately we've heard some complaints that the food is mediocre and not worthy of the hefty prices. Some favorites here are the Caicos gold conch, braised pork shank, and mangrove snapper and mango. Try the appetizer of tipsy olives, marinated in gin or vodka, to kick-start your meal. For fans of spicy food, go for the red-hot calamari. Decorated with barracuda-themed art, the restaurant also features a well-priced American wine list with lots of California vintages.

U.S. 1 at MM 49.5 (bay side), Marathon. © **305/743-3314.** Main courses $15–$30. AE, MC, V. Wed–Sat 6–10pm.

Butterfly Café ★★★ SEAFOOD Housed in the stunning Tranquility Bay resort, Butterfly Café is the newest gourmet hot spot in the Middle Keys, with water views and a stellar menu of fresh local seafood. Among the dishes not to miss: grouper encrusted with panko and horseradish, served with mashed potatoes, fresh vegetables, tropical coulis, and crispy shallots; and Cuban-spiced, grilled double-cut pork chops with mango-lime mojo and spiced macadamia basmati rice. Service is very friendly and knowledgeable, and desserts are to die for. Save room for the sticky toffee pudding and nutty-crust Key lime pie with white chocolate mousse. Open for breakfast, lunch, and dinner, but Sunday brunch is especially spectacular. Don't miss the tropical French toast.

2600 Overseas Hwy., in the Tranquility Bay Resort, Marathon. © **305/289-0888.** www.tranquilitybay. com. Main courses $18–$37. AE, MC, V. Daily 7–10am and 11:30am–10pm; Sun brunch 10:30am–2:30pm.

Green Turtle Inn ★★★ SEAFOOD The legend is back, but this time with a gourmet market and cuisine cooked with locally farmed vegetables and microgreens. While it may not be a throwback to the old Florida Keys, Green Turtle, reopened by Dawn Sieber, who subsequently left "for a change of scenery," and now helmed by star chef Andy Niedenthal, remains a must stop for anyone looking for a fabulous dining experience. Some old menu items remain—the famous turtle chowder with pepper sherry, and luscious conch chowder. But the new menu items are nothing to sneer at either. Small plates, including pan-seared scallops with goat cheese–whipped potatoes, sherry vinegar brown butter, white truffle oil, and sizzled leeks make for satisfying main courses, but don't miss entrees such as pan-fried, butter-flied yellowtail with sautéed spinach, whipped potatoes, Key-lime brown butter, and crispy phyllo dough. And whatever you do, do not pass up the chocolate decadence mousse cake. After dinner, check out the art gallery and gourmet shop. Green Turtle also serves excellent breakfast (try the coconut French toast) and lunch (I love the fried green tomato BLT).

81219 Overseas Hwy., at MM 81.2, Islamorada. © **305/664-2006.** www.greenturtlekeys.com. Main courses $20–$38. AE, MC, V. Daily 7–10am and 11:30am–10pm.

Marker 88 ★★★ SEAFOOD An institution in the Upper Keys, Marker 88 has been pleasing locals and visitors since it opened in the 1970s. New chefs and owners have infused a new life into the place and the menu, which still utilizes fresh fruits, local ingredients, and fish caught in the Keys' waters. Among the menu highlights are the yellowtail Rangoon, sautéed and topped with black currant gelée and cinnamon, and served with fresh tropical fruits; and yellowtail Martinique, sautéed and topped with sweet basil, grilled bananas, and garlic butter. The waitresses, who are pleasant enough, require a bit of patience, but the food—not to mention the spectacular Gulf views—is worth it.

U.S. 1 at MM 88 (bay side), Islamorada. © **305/852-9315.** www.marker88.info. Reservations suggested. Main courses $20–$39. AE, DC, DISC, MC, V. Tues–Sun 5–11pm. Closed Sept.

Ziggie and Mad Dog's ★★★ STEAKHOUSE   When former Miami Dolphins player Jim Mandich, also known as Mad Dog, bought Ziggie's Crab Shack from Sigmund "Ziggie" Stockie, he decided to keep the ex-owner's name up there with his own. And despite the wacky name, people are mad for this fine Florida Keys steak and chophouse. Casually elegant, Ziggie and Mad Dog's is quite the Upper Keys scene, attracting everyone from colorful locals and tourists to hungry day trippers looking for something more than a ramshackle fish shack. If you're starving, we dare you to order the 28-ounce Czonka porterhouse named after Mandich's fellow 'Fins teammate Larry Csonka. People also rave about the bone-in rib-eye and the mac and cheese. Service is friendly and the vibe is fun. Sports fans love it here not because of the games on in the bar, but because many of Mandich's famous athlete friends come here often.

83000 Overseas Hwy., Islamorada. ✆ 305/664-3391. www.ziggieandmaddogs.com. Reservations suggested. Main courses $20–$42. AE, DC, DISC, MC, V. Daily 5:30–10pm.

MODERATE

Lazy Days ★ SEAFOOD/BAR FARE   Making good on its name, this laid-back oceanfront eatery is the quintessence of Keys lifestyle. One good thing, however: Chef/owner Lupe is far from lazy, preparing excellent fresh seafood, seafood pastas, vegetarian pastas, sandwiches, steaks and chicken. He'll even cook your own catch for you. A popular daily happy hour at the bar from 4 to 6pm features 3-for-$1 appetizers. Lazy Days is so popular that Lupe and co-owner Michelle Ledesma have opened **Lazy Days South,** featuring an identical menu and waterfront seating at the Marathon Marina (✆ **305/289-0839**).

79867 Overseas Highway, Islamorada. ✆ **305/664-5256.** www.lazydaysrestaurant.com. Reservations not usually required. Main courses $15–$28, lighter fare and appetizers $7–$18. AE, DC, DISC, MC, V. Sun–Thurs 11am–9:30pm, Fri–Sat 11am–10pm.

Lorelei Restaurant and Cabana Bar ★ SEAFOOD/BAR FARE   Don't resist the siren call of the enormous roadside mermaid—you won't be dashed onto the rocks. This big old fish house and bar, with excellent views of the bay, is a great place for a snack, a meal, or a beer. A good-value menu focuses mainly on seafood; in season, lobster is the way to go. Other fare includes the standard clam chowder, fried shrimp, and doughy conch fritters. For those tired of fish, the menu offers a few beef options, but we say the simpler the better. Food is definitely trumped by ambience. The outside bar has live music every evening, and you can order snacks and light meals from a limited menu.

U.S. 1 at MM 82, Islamorada. ✆ **305/664-4656.** www.loreleifloridakeys.com. Reservations not usually required. Main courses $10–$22. AE, DC, DISC, MC, V. Daily 7am–10:30pm. Outside bar serves breakfast 7–11am; lunch/appetizer menu 11am–9pm. Bar closes at midnight.

INEXPENSIVE

Calypso's Seafood Grill ★★ 🍴 SEAFOOD   With a motto proudly declaring "Yes, we know the music is loud and the food is spicy. That's the way we like it!" you know you're in a typical Keys eatery. Thankfully the food is anything but, with inventive seafood dishes in a casual and rustic waterside setting. Among the house specialties is cracked conch and superb steamed clams; but if you're not too hot out there, try the She-Crab soup. It's exceptional. If it's offered, try the deep fried corn and the hog snapper however they prepare it. Outstanding. The prices are surprisingly reasonable, but the service may be a bit more laid-back than you're used to.

1 Seagate Blvd. (near MM 99.5), Key Largo. © **305/451-0600.** Main courses $10–$20. No credit cards. Wed–Thurs and Sun–Mon 11:30am–10pm; Fri–Sat 11:30am–11pm. From the south, turn right at the blinking yellow lights near MM 99.5 to Ocean Bay Dr. and then turn right. Look for the blue vinyl-sided building on the left.

Harriette's Restaurant ★ BREAKFAST/BRUNCH   This little yellow shack packs in a major crowd for breakfast, thanks to friendly service, old school greasy spoon–style fare, and colossal homemade biscuits and muffins. Despite the grease factor, Harriette's realizes some people want to eat healthy—you're in the Keys, though, go nuts—and offers South Beach Diet and Atkins menu items as well.

MM 95.7, Key Largo. © **305/852-8689.** Breakfast $5–$7. No credit cards. Daily 6am–2pm.

Islamorada Fish Company ★★ SEAFOOD   Pick up a cooler of stone crab claws in season (mid-Oct to Apr), or try the great fried-fish sandwiches. A few hundred yards up the road (at MM 81.6) is Islamorada Fish Company Restaurant & Bakery, the newer establishment, which looks like an average diner but has fantastic seafood, pastas, and breakfasts. Locals gather here for politics and gossip as well as delicious grits, oatmeal, omelets, and pastries. Keep your eyes open while dining outside—the last time I was here, baby manatees were floating around, waiting for their close-ups.

U.S. 1 at MM 81.5 (up the street from Cheeca Lodge), Islamorada. © **800/258-2559** or 305/664-9271. www.islamoradafishco.com. Reservations not accepted. Main courses $11–$22. DISC, MC, V. Sun–Thurs 11am–9pm; Fri–Sat 11am–10pm.

Island Grill ★ SEAFOOD   If you drive too fast over Snake Creek Bridge, you may miss one of the best Keys dining experiences around. Located just under the bridge and on the bay, Island Grill is a locals' favorite, with an expansive outdoor deck and bar and cozy waterfront dining room serving some fresh fare, including their famous tuna nachos, guava barbecued shrimp, and graham cracker–dusted calamari. There are also salads, sandwiches—try the lobster roll—and entrees, including a whole yellowtail snapper with Thai sweet chili sauce that's out of this world. Bring your own catch, and they'll cook and prepare it for you—served family style with veggies and rice for only $12. Live entertainment almost every night brings in a great, colorful Keys crowd. Although they serve breakfast, too, we say skip the food and just stick to the Bloody Marys.

MM 88.5 (ocean side at Snake Creek Bridge), Islamorada. © **305/664-8400.** www.keysislandgrill.com. Reservations not necessary. Main courses $8–$25. Sun–Thurs 11am–10pm; Fri–Sat 11am–11pm.

Key Largo Conch House Restaurant & Coffee Bar ★★ AMERICAN   A funky, cozy, and off-the-beaten-path hot spot for breakfast, lunch, and dinner, Key Largo Conch House is exactly that—a house set amid lush foliage, complete with resident dog, parrot, wraparound verandah for outdoor dining, and a warm and inviting indoor dining room reminiscent of your grandma's. Food is fresh and fabulously priced—from the heaping $13 plate of Mom's Lasagna, to $8-to–$13 twists on the usual eggs Benedict, including my favorite, the crab cakes Benedict. Featured on the Food Network, Conch House should be a feature on everyone's trip down to the

Keys, if not just for a cup of excellent coffee and a slice of homemade Key lime pie. It's also one of the few pet-friendly restaurants in the area.

U.S. 1 at MM 100, Key Largo. ✆ **305/453-4844.** www.keylargocoffeehouse.com. Reservations recommended. Main courses $8–$21. AE, DC, DISC, MC, V. Daily 7am–10pm.

Snapper's ★ SEAFOOD A locals' waterfront favorite, Snapper's serves fresh seafood caught by local fishermen—or by you, if you dare! The blackened mahimahi is exceptional and a bargain, complete with salad, vegetable, and choice of starch. There's also live music nightly and a lively, colorful—and deliciously casual—crowd. A popular Sunday brunch features live jazz from the barge out back and a make-your-own Bloody Mary bar. Kids love feeding the tarpon off the docks, and for those who just can't stay away from work, there's free Wi-Fi throughout the property, indoors and out. If you were lucky on the water and caught the big one, clean it and they will cook it for you at $14 for 8 ounces a person.

139 Seaside Ave., at MM 94.5, Key Largo. ✆ **305/852-5956.** www.snapperskeylargo.com. Main courses $10–$26. DISC, MC, V. Sun–Thurs 11am–9pm; Fri–Sat 11am–10pm.

The Upper & Middle Keys After Dark

Nightlife in the Upper Keys tends to start before the sun goes down, often at noon, as most people—visitors and locals alike—are on vacation. Also, many anglers and sports-minded folk go to bed early.

Hog Heaven, MM 85.3, just off the main road on the ocean side, Islamorada (✆ **305/664-9669**), opened in the early 1990s, the joint venture of young locals tired of tourist traps. This whitewashed biker bar is a welcome respite from the neon-colored cocktail circuit. It has a waterside view and diversions such as big-screen TVs and video games. The food isn't bad, either. The atmosphere is cliquish because most patrons are regulars, so start up a game of pool to break the ice. Open daily from 11am to 4am.

No trip to the Keys is complete without a stop at the **Tiki Bar at the Holiday Isle Resort** (p. 279), U.S. 1 at MM 84, Islamorada (✆ **305/664-2321**). Hundreds of revelers visit this ocean-side spot for drinks and dancing at any time of day, but the live rock starts at 8:30pm. The thatched-roof Tiki Bar draws a mix of thirsty people, all in pursuit of a good time. In the afternoon and early evening (when everyone is either sunburned, drunk, or just happy to be dancing to live reggae), head for **Kokomo's,** next door. It often closes at 7:30pm on weekends (5:30pm on weekdays), so arrive early. For information, call the Holiday Isle Resort. Rumor has it that greedy developers are going to raze the Tiki Bar to make way for million-dollar condos, but loyal boozehounds are raising hell over it, and some are even trying to have the Tiki Bar declared a Florida landmark! Stay tuned.

Locals and tourists mingle at the outdoor cabana bar at **Lorelei** (see "Where to Dine," above). Most evenings after 5pm, you'll find local bands playing on a thatched-roof stage—mainly rock or reggae, and sometimes blues.

Woody's Saloon and Restaurant, U.S. 1 at MM 82, Islamorada (✆ **305/664-4335**), is a lively, wacky, loud, raunchy, local legend of a place serving up mediocre pizzas, buck-naked strippers, and live bands almost every night. The house band, Big Dick and the Extenders, showcases a 300-pound Native American who does a lewd, rude, and crude routine of politically incorrect jokes and songs starting at 9pm Tuesday through Sunday. He is a legend. By the way, don't think you're lucky if you're offered the front table: It's the target seat for Big Dick's haranguing. Avoid the lame karaoke performance on Sunday and Monday evenings. There's a small cover on most nights. Drink specials, contests, and the legendary Big Dick keep this place packed until 4am almost every night. **Note:** This place is not for the faint of heart, but more for those from the Howard Stern school of nightlife.

For a more subdued atmosphere, try the handsome stained-glass and mahogany-wood bar and club at **Zane Grey's,** on the second floor of World Wide Sportsman, MM 81.5 (© 305/664-4244). Outside, enjoy a view of the calm waters of the bay; inside, soak up the history of real longtime anglers. It's open from 11am to at least 11pm (later on weekends). Call to find out who's playing on Friday and Saturday nights, when there's live entertainment and no cover.

THE LOWER KEYS: BIG PINE KEY TO COPPITT KEY

128 miles SW of Miami

Unlike their neighbors to the north and south, the Lower Keys (including Big Pine, Sugarloaf, and Summerland) are devoid of rowdy Spring Break crowds, boast few T-shirt and trinket shops, and have almost no late-night bars. What they do offer are the very best opportunities to enjoy the vast natural resources on land and water that make the area so rich. Stay overnight in the Lower Keys, rent a boat, and explore the reefs—it might be the most memorable part of your trip.

Essentials

GETTING THERE See "Essentials" for the Upper and Middle Keys (p. 266) and continue south on U.S. 1. The Lower Keys start at the end of the Seven-Mile Bridge. There are also airports in Marathon and Key West.

VISITOR INFORMATION **Big Pine and Lower Keys Chamber of Commerce,** ocean side of U.S. 1 at MM 31 (P.O. Box 430511), Big Pine Key, FL 33043 (© **800/872-3722** or 305/872-2411; fax 305/872-0752; www.lowerkeyschamber. com), is open Monday through Friday from 9am to 5pm, and Saturday from 9am to 3pm. The pleasant staff will help with anything a traveler may need. Call, write, or stop in for a comprehensive, detailed information packet.

What to See & Do

Once the centerpiece (these days, it's Big Pine Key) of the Lower Keys and still a great asset is **Bahia Honda State Park ★**, U.S. 1 at MM 37.5, Big Pine Key (© **305/872-2353;** www.bahiahondapark.com), which, even after the violent storms of 2005, has one of the most beautiful coastlines in South Florida. Bahia (pronounced *Bah*-ya) Honda is a great place for hiking, bird-watching, swimming, snorkeling, and fishing. The 524-acre park encompasses a wide variety of ecosystems, including coastal mangroves, beach dunes, and tropical hammocks. There are miles of trails packed with unusual plants and animals, plus a small white-sand beach. Shaded seaside picnic areas are fitted with tables and grills. Although the beach is never wider than 5 feet, even at low tide, this is the Lower Keys' best beach area.

True to its name (Spanish for "deep bay"), the park has relatively deep waters close to shore—perfect for snorkeling and diving. Easy offshore snorkeling here gives even novices a chance to lie suspended in warm water and simply observe diverse marine life passing by. Or else head to the stunning reefs at Looe Key, where the coral and fish are more vibrant than anywhere else in the United States. Snorkeling trips go from the Bahia Honda concessions to Looe Key National Marine Sanctuary (4 miles offshore). They depart twice daily (9:30am and 1:30pm) March through September and cost $30 for adults, $25 for children 6 to 17, and $8 for equipment rental. Call ✆ **305/872-3210** for a schedule.

Entry to the park is $8 per vehicle of two to eight passengers, $4 for solo passenger, $2 per pedestrian or bicyclist, free for children 5 and under, and a 50¢ per person Monroe County surcharge. Open daily from 8am to sunset.

The most famous residents of the Lower Keys are the tiny Key deer. Of the estimated 300 existing in the world, two-thirds live on Big Pine Key's **National Key Deer Refuge** ★. To get your bearings, stop by the rangers' office at the Winn-Dixie Shopping Plaza, near MM 30.5 off U.S. 1. They'll give you an informative brochure and map of the area. The refuge is open Monday through Friday from 8am to 5pm.

If the office is closed, head out to the **Blue Hole,** a former rock quarry now filled with the fresh water that's vital to the deer's survival. To get there, turn right at Big Pine Key's only traffic light at Key Deer Boulevard (take the left fork immediately after the turn) and continue 1½ miles to the observation-site parking lot, on your left. The .5-mile **Watson Hammock Trail,** about one-third mile past the Blue Hole, is the refuge's only marked footpath. The deer are more active in cool hours, so try coming out to the path in the early morning or late evening to catch a glimpse of these gentle dog-size creatures. There is an observation deck from which you can watch and photograph the protected species. Refuge lands are open daily from a half-hour before sunrise to a half-hour after sunset. Don't be surprised to see a lazy alligator warming itself in the sun, particularly in outlying areas around the Blue Hole. If you do see a gator, do not go near it, do not touch it, and do not provoke it. Keep your distance; if you must get a photo, use a zoom lens. Also, whatever you do, do not feed the deer—it will threaten their survival. Call the **park office** (✆ **305/872-2239**) to find out about the infrequent free tours of the refuge, scheduled throughout the year.

Outdoor Activities

BIKING   The Lower Keys are a great place to get off busy U.S. 1 to explore the beautiful back roads. On Big Pine Key, cruise along Key Deer Boulevard (at MM 30). Those with fat tires can ride into the National Key Deer Refuge. Many lodgings offer bike rentals.

BIRD-WATCHING   A stopping point for migratory birds on the Eastern Flyway, the Lower Keys are populated with many West Indian bird species, especially in spring and fall. The small, vegetated islands of the Keys are the only nesting sites in the U.S. for the white-crowned pigeon. They're also some of the few breeding places for the reddish egret, roseate spoonbill, mangrove cuckoo, and black-whiskered vireo. Look for them on Bahia Honda Key and the many uninhabited islands nearby.

BOATING   Dozens of shops rent powerboats for fishing and reef exploring. Most also rent tackle, sell bait, and have charter captains available. For instance, **Florida**

Keys Boat Rental (© **305/664-2003**; www.keysboat.com) offers an impressive selection of boats from $125 to $450 for a half-day and $105 to $650 for a full day. They also offer kayaks and paddle boats for eco-tours.

CANOEING & KAYAKING The Overseas Highway (U.S. 1) touches on only a few dozen of the many hundreds of islands that make up the Keys. To really see the Lower Keys, rent a kayak or canoe—perfect for these shallow waters. **Reflections Kayak Nature Tours,** operating out of the Old Wooden Bridge Fishing Camp, 1791 Bogie Dr., MM 30, Big Pine Key (© **305/872-4668**; www.floridakeyskayak tours.com), offers fully outfitted backcountry wildlife tours, either on your own or with an expert. The expert, U.S.C.G.-licensed Captain Bill Keogh, literally wrote the book on the subject. *The Florida Keys Paddling Guide* (Countryman Press), written by Bill in 2004, covers all the unique ecosystems and inhabitants as well as launches and favorite routes from Key Biscayne to the Dry Tortugas National Park. The 3-hour kayak tours cost $50 per person. An extended 4-hour backcountry tour for two to six people costs $125 per person and uses a mother ship to ferry kayaks and paddlers to the remote reaches of the refuge. Reservations required.

FISHING A day spent fishing, either in the shallow backcountry or in the deep sea, is a great way to ensure a fresh-fish dinner, or you can release your catch and just appreciate the challenge. Whichever you choose, **Strike Zone Charters,** U.S. 1 at MM 29.5, Big Pine Key (© **305/872-9863**; www.strikezonecharter.com), is the charter service to call. Prices for fishing boats start at $650 for a half-day and $850 for a full day with the possibility of a $50 fuel surcharge added to the cost. If you have enough anglers to share the price (they take up to six people), it isn't too steep. The outfitter may also be able to match you with other interested visitors. Strike Zone also offers daily trips to Looe Key National Marine Sanctuary on a glass-bottom boat. The 2-hour trip costs $25 for viewing, $35 for snorkeling, and $45 for scuba diving, all with a $3 per person fuel charge. Strike Zone's 5-hour **Eco Island** excursion offers a vivid history of the Keys from the glass-bottom boat. The tour stops for snorkeling and light tackle fishing and eventually docks at an island for their famous island fish cookout. Cost is $55 per person plus an additional $3 surcharge for fuel, including mask, snorkel, fins, vests, rods, reel, bait, fishing licenses, food, and all soft drinks.

HIKING You can hike throughout the flat, marshy Keys on both marked trails and meandering coastlines. The best places to trek through nature are **Bahia Honda State Park,** at MM 29.5, and **National Key Deer Refuge,** at MM 30 (for more information on both, see "What to See & Do," above). Bahia Honda Park has a free brochure describing an excellent self-guided tour along the Silver Palm Nature Trail. You'll traverse hammocks, mangroves, and sand dunes, and cross a lagoon. The walk (less than a mile) explores a great cross section of the natural habitat in the Lower Keys and can be done in less than half an hour.

SNORKELING & SCUBA DIVING Snorkelers and divers should not miss the Keys' most dramatic reefs at the **Looe Key National Marine Sanctuary.** Here you'll see more than 150 varieties of hard and soft coral—some centuries old—as well as every type of tropical fish, including gold and blue parrotfish, moray eels, barracudas, French angels, and tarpon. **Looe Key Dive Center,** U.S. 1 at MM 27.5, Ramrod Key (© **305/872-2215**; www.diveflakeys.com), offers a mind-blowing 5-hour tour aboard a 45-foot catamaran with two shallow 1-hour dives for snorkelers and scuba divers. Snorkelers pay $44, children 6 and under pay $34; divers pay $84 for three dives, $69 for two. Equipment is available for rental for $10. On Wednesday and Saturday, you can do a fascinating dive to the *Adolphus Busch, Sr.,* a shipwreck off Looe Key in 100 feet of water, for $50 with $30 per additional diver. (See "What to See & Do," above, for other diving options.)

Where to Stay

There are a number of cheap, fairly unappealing fish shacks along the highway for those who want bare-bones accommodations. So far, there are no national hotel chains in the Lower Keys. For information on lodging in cabins or trailers at local campgrounds, see "Camping," below.

VERY EXPENSIVE

Little Palm Island Resort & Spa ★★★   This exclusive island escape—host to presidents, royalty, and even Howard Stern—is not just a place to stay while in the Lower Keys; it is a destination all its own. Built on a private 5½-acre island, it's accessible only by boat or seaplane. Guests stay in thatched-roof duplexes amid lush foliage and flowering tropical plants—and gentle Key deer, which are to this island what cats are to Key West. Many villas have ocean views and private decks with hammocks. Inside, the romantic suites have all the comforts of a swank beach cottage, but without phones, TVs, or alarm clocks. Mosquitoes can be a problem, even in winter. (Bring spray and lightweight, long-sleeved clothing.) Known for a stellar spa and innovative and pricey food, Little Palm also hosts visitors just for dinner, brunch, or lunch. If you're staying on the island, opt for the full American plan, which includes three meals a day.

Launch is on the ocean side of U.S. 1 at MM 28.5, Little Torch Key, FL 33042. © **800/343-8567** or 305/872-2524. Fax 305/872-4843. www.littlepalmisland.com. 30 units. Winter $840–$1,695 double; off-season $640–$1,595 double. Rates include transportation to and from the island and unlimited (nonmotorized) watersports. Meal plans include 2 meals daily for $125 per person per day, 3 meals at $140 per person. AE, DC, DISC, MC, V. No children 15 and under. **Amenities:** Restaurant; bar; courtesy van from Key West or Marathon airport; concierge; ferry service to and from the mainland; health club; jogging trail; 2 pools; limited room service; spa; extensive watersports equipment/rentals. *In room:* A/C, hair dryer, Internet access, Jacuzzi, minibar, no phone.

INEXPENSIVE

Parmer's Resort ★   Parmer's, a fixture here for more than 20 years, is well known for its charming hospitality and helpful staff. This downscale resort offers modest but comfortable cottages, each of them unique. Some are waterfront, many have kitchenettes, and others are just a bedroom. The Wahoo room (no. 26), a one-bedroom efficiency, is especially nice, with a small sitting area that faces the water. All units have been recently updated and are very clean. Many can be combined to accommodate families. The hotel's waterfront location, not to mention the fact that it's only a half-hour from lively Key West, almost makes up for the fact that you must pay extra for maid service.

565 Barry Ave. (P.O. Box 430665), near MM 28.5, Little Torch Key, FL 33043. © **305/872-2157.** Fax 305/872-2014. www.parmersresort.com. 45 units. Winter $134–$194 double; from $174 efficiency; off-season $99–$129 double; from $129 efficiency. Rates include continental breakfast. AE, DISC, MC, V. From U.S. 1, turn right onto Barry Ave. Resort is ½ mile down on the right. **Amenities:** Bike rental; boat ramp; kayak rental; heated pool. *In room:* A/C, TV.

CAMPING

Bahia Honda State Park ★★★ (© 800/326-3521; www.abfla.com/parks/bahiahonda/bahiahonda.html) offers some of the best camping in the Keys. It is as loaded with facilities and activities as it is with campers. But don't be discouraged by its popularity—this park encompasses more than 500 acres of land, 80 campsites spread throughout three areas, and three spacious and comfortable duplex cabins. Cabins hold up to eight guests each and come complete with linens, kitchenettes, wraparound terraces, barbecue pits, and rocking chairs. For one to four people, camping costs about $36 per site. Depending on the season, cabin prices range from $120 to $160.

Another excellent value can be found at the **KOA Sugarloaf Key Resort** ★★, near MM 20. This ocean-side facility has 200 fully equipped sites, with water, electricity, and sewer, which rent for about $89 a night (no-hookup sites cost about $55). Or you can pitch a tent on the 5 acres of waterfront property. Or stay in a brand new Airstream trailer which sleeps up to four people for about $170 a night. This place is especially nice because of its private beaches and access to diving, snorkeling, and boating; its grounds are also well maintained. In addition, the resort rents travel trailers: The 25-foot Dutchman sleeps six and costs about $150 a day. For details, contact the resort at P.O. Box 420469, Summerland Key, FL 33042 (© **800/562-7731** or 305/745-3549; fax 305/745-9889; www.koa.com).

Where to Dine

There aren't many fine-dining options in the Lower Keys, with the exception of the **Dining Room at Little Palm Island** (p. 290), MM 285, Little Torch Key (© **305/872-2551**), where you'll be wowed with gourmet French Caribbean fare that looks like a meal but tastes like a vacation. You need to take a ferry to this chichi private island, where you can indulge at the exquisite ocean-side restaurant even if you're not staying over.

MODERATE

Mangrove Mama's Restaurant SEAFOOD/CARIBBEAN As the dedicated locals who come daily for happy hour will tell you, this is a true Lower Keys institution and a dive in the best sense of the word (the restaurant is a shack that used to have a gas pump as well as a grill). Guests share the property with stray cats and some miniature horses out back. It's run-down, but in a charming Keys sort of way—they serve beer in a jelly glass. A handful of simple tables, inside and out, are shaded by banana trees and palm fronds. Fish is the menu's mainstay, although soups, salads, sandwiches, and omelets are also good. Grilled-chicken and club sandwiches are tasty alternatives to fish, as are meatless chef's salads and spicy barbecued baby-back ribs. The restaurant is under new ownership, which some say has let the place slip a bit, though they still rock their Sunday brunch with amazing crab Benedict.

U.S. 1 at MM 20, Sugarloaf Key. © **305/745-3030.** www.mangrovemamasrestaurant.com. Main courses $10–$20; lunch $9–$11; brunch $5–$15. MC, V. Daily 11am–3pm and 5:30–10pm.

INEXPENSIVE

Coco's Kitchen ★ CUBAN/AMERICAN This tiny storefront has been dishing out black beans, rice, and shredded beef for more than 10 years. The owners, who are actually from Nicaragua, cook not only superior Cuban food, but local specialties, Italian dishes, and Caribbean choices. Specialties include fried shrimp, whole fried yellowtail, and Cuban-style roast pork (available only on Sat). The best bet is the daily special, which may be roasted pork or fresh grouper, served with rice and beans or salad and crispy fries. Top off the huge, cheap meal with a rich caramel-soaked flan.

283 Key Deer Blvd. (in the Winn-Dixie Shopping Center), Big Pine Key. 🅒 305/872-4495. Main courses $6–$15; breakfast $2–$10. MC, V. Tues–-Sun 7am–3pm. Turn right at the traffic light near MM 30.5; stay in the left lane.

No Name Pub PUB FARE/PIZZA This funky old bar out in the boondocks serves snacks and sandwiches until 11pm on most nights, and drinks until midnight. Pizzas are tasty—try one topped with local shrimp. Or consider a bowl of chili with all the fixings. Everything is served on paper plates. Locals hang out at the rustic bar, one of the Keys' oldest bars, drinking beer and listening to a jukebox heavy with 1980s tunes.

¼ mile south of No Name Bridge on N. Watson Blvd., Big Pine Key. 🅒 305/872-9115. www.nonamepub. com. Pizzas $6–$18; subs $5–$9. MC, V. Daily 11am–11pm. Turn right at Big Pine's only traffic light (near MM 30.5) onto Key Deer Blvd. Turn right on Watson Blvd. At the stop sign, turn left. Look for a small wooden sign on the left marking the spot.

The Lower Keys After Dark

Although the mellow islands of the Lower Keys aren't exactly known for wild night-life, there are some friendly bars and restaurants where locals and tourists gather to hang out and drink. One of the most scenic is **Parrotdise Waterfont,** Barry Avenue near MM 28.5 (🅒 305/872-9989; www.parrotdisewaterfront.com), the only waterfront restaurant between Key West and Marathon. The place is enclosed with windows looking out onto the water where there's a shark pond for those who are curious. Great food (even sushi) is served from 10:30am until 10pm, and the bar closes around midnight. The place even has its own brand of wine, which is currently being marketed in France, of all places. Paradise attracts an odd mix of bikers and blue-hairs daily, and is a great place to overhear local gossip and colorful metaphors. Pool tables are the main attraction, but there's also live music some nights. The drinks are reasonably priced, and the food isn't too bad, either. For another fun bar scene, see the **No Name Pub,** listed above in "Where to Dine."

KEY WEST ★★★

159 miles SW of Miami

There are two schools of thought on Key West—one is that it has become way too commercial, and the other is that it's still a place where you don't have to worry about being prim, proper, or even well-groomed. I think it's a bizarre fusion of both—a fascinating look at small-town America where people truly live by the (off) beat of their own drum, albeit one with a Coach outlet, Banana Republic, Starbucks, and, most recently, a handful of multimillion-dollar condo developments, thrown in to bring you back to reality. The locals, or "conchs" (pronounced *conks*), and the developers here have been at odds for years. This once low-key island has been thoroughly commercialized—there's a Hard Rock Cafe smack in the middle of Duval Street, and thousands of cruise-ship passengers descend on Mallory Square each day. It's definitely not the seedy town Hemingway and his cronies once called their own. Or is it?

Laid-back Key West still exists, but it's now found in different places: the back-yard of a popular guesthouse, for example, or an art gallery, a secret garden, a clothing-optional bar, or the hip hangouts of Bahama Village. Fortunately, there are plenty of these, and Key West's greatest historical charm is found just off the beaten path. Don't be afraid to explore these residential areas, as conchs are notoriously friendly. In fact, exploring the side streets always seems to yield a new discovery. Of course, there are always the calm waters of the Atlantic and the Gulf of Mexico all around.

The heart of town offers party people a good time—that is, if your idea of a good time is the smell of stale beer, loud music, and hardly shy revelers. Here you'll find good restaurants, fun bars, live music, rickshaw rides, and lots of shopping. In recent years, Duval Street has actually struggled to maintain its raw, raucous flavor, as a spate of newer, swankier spots have opened in the spaces that formerly housed raunchy T-shirt and souvenir shops. Key West is still very gay-centric, except during Spring Break. Same-sex couples that walk hand in hand are the norm here; if you're not open-minded and prefer to avoid this scene, look for the ubiquitous rainbow flag hanging outside gay establishments and you'll know what to expect. For the most part, however, the scene is extremely mixed and colorful. If partying isn't your thing, then avoid Duval Street—the Bourbon Street of South Florida—at all costs. Instead, take in the scenery at a dockside bar or ocean-side Jacuzzi. Whatever you do, don't bother with a watch or tie—this is the home of the perennial vacation.

Essentials

GETTING THERE   For directions by car, see "Essentials" (p. 266) for the Upper and Middle Keys and continue south on U.S. 1. When entering Key West, stay in the far-right lane onto North Roosevelt Boulevard, which becomes Truman Avenue in Old Town. Continue for a few blocks and you'll find yourself on **Duval Street ★**, in the heart of the city. If you stay to the left, you'll also reach the city center after passing the airport and the remnants of historic houseboat row, where a motley collection of boats once made up one of Key West's most interesting neighborhoods.

Several regional airlines fly nonstop (about 55 min.) from Miami to Key West. **American Eagle** (© **800/433-7300**), **Continental** (© **800/525-0280**), **Delta** (© **800/221-1212**), and **US Airways Express** (© **800/428-4322**) land at the recently expanded **Key West International Airport,** South Roosevelt Boulevard (© **305/296-5439**), on the southeastern corner of the island.

Greyhound (© **800/231-2222;** www.greyhound.com) has buses leaving Miami for Key West every day for about $35 to $48 one-way and $69 to $93 round-trip. Seats fill up in season, so come early. The ride takes about 4½ hours.

You can also get to Key West from Fort Myers or Marco Island via the **Key West Express** (© **866/KW-FERRY** [593-3779]; www.seakeywest.com), a 155-foot-long catamaran that travels to Key West at 40 mph. The Big Cat features two enclosed cabins, sun seated deck, observation deck, satellite TV, and full galley and bar. Prices range from $85 one-way and $140 round-trip per person.

GETTING AROUND   Old Town Key West has limited parking, narrow streets, and congested traffic, so driving is more of a pain than a convenience. Unless you're staying in one of the more remote accommodations, consider trading in your car for a bicycle. The island is small and flat as a board, which makes it easy to negotiate,

Key West

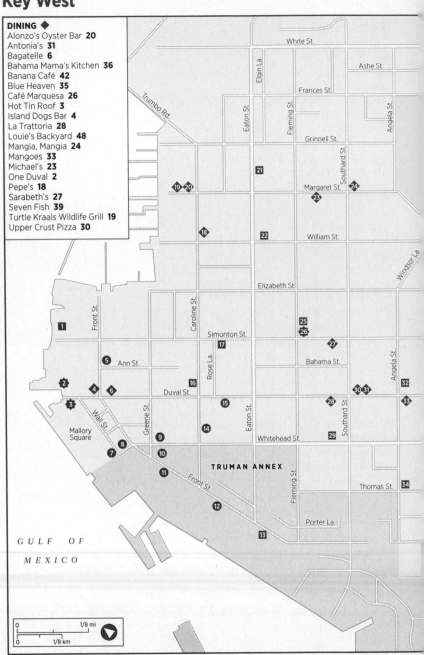

DINING ◆
Alonzo's Oyster Bar **20**
Antonia's **31**
Bagatelle **6**
Bahama Mama's Kitchen **36**
Banana Café **42**
Blue Heaven **35**
Café Marquesa **26**
Hot Tin Roof **3**
Island Dogs Bar **4**
La Trattoria **28**
Louie's Backyard **48**
Mangia, Mangia **24**
Mangoes **33**
Michael's **23**
One Duval **2**
Pepe's **18**
Sarabeth's **27**
Seven Fish **39**
Turtle Kraals Wildlife Grill **19**
Upper Crust Pizza **30**

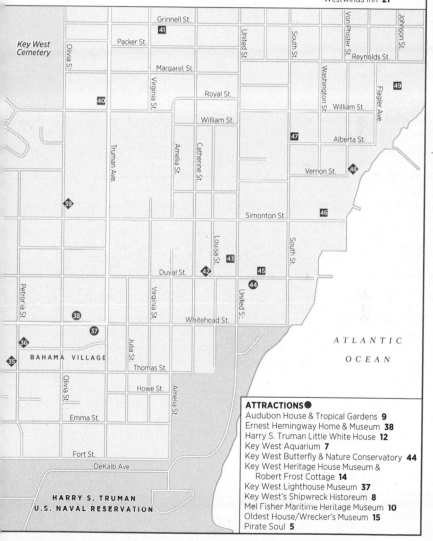

ACCOMMODATIONS ■

Ambrosia Key West **25**
Angelina Guest House **34**
Big Ruby's **29**
Casa Marina Resort
& Beach Club **49**
Curry Mansion Inn **16**
The Gardens Hotel **32**
The Grand **41**

Hyatt Key West Resort &
Marina **1**
Island City House Hotel **22**
Key West International
Hostel & Seashell Motel **47**
La Pensione **40**
Marquesa Hotel **26**
Ocean Key Resort & Spa **3**
Pearl's Rainbow **43**

Pier House Resort &
Caribbean Spa **2**
The Reach Resort **46**
Simonton Court **17**
Southernmost Point
Guest House **45**
Weatherstation Inn **13**
Westin Key West Resort
& Marina **11**
Westwinds Inn **21**

Grinnell St.
41
Packer St.
Key West
Cemetery
Olivia S:
Margaret St.
Virginia St.
Royal St.
40
William St.
United St.
South St.
Von Phister St.
Johnson St.
Reynolds St.
Washington St.
William St.
Flagler Ave.
49
47
Alberta St.
Truman Ave.
Amelia St.
Catherine St.
Vernon St.
48
39
Simonton St.
46
Louisa St.
South St.
43
Duval St.
42
45
Virginia St.
United S:
44
Petronia St.
38
Whitehead St.

ATLANTIC
OCEAN

37
36
Julia St.
35
BAHAMA VILLAGE
Thomas St.
Olivia St.
Howe St.
Amelia St.
Emma St.
Fort St.
DeKalb Ave.

ATTRACTIONS ●
Audubon House & Tropical Gardens **9**
Ernest Hemingway Home & Museum **38**
Harry S. Truman Little White House **12**
Key West Aquarium **7**
Key West Butterfly & Nature Conservatory **44**
Key West Heritage House Museum &
Robert Frost Cottage **14**
Key West Lighthouse Museum **37**
Key West's Shipwreck Historeum **8**
Mel Fisher Maritime Heritage Museum **10**
Oldest House/Wrecker's Museum **15**
Pirate Soul **5**

HARRY S. TRUMAN
U.S. NAVAL RESERVATION

especially away from the crowded downtown area. Many tourists choose to cruise by moped, an option that can make navigating the streets risky, especially because there are no helmet laws in Key West. Hundreds of visitors are seriously injured each year, so be careful and spend the extra few bucks to rent a helmet.

Rates for simple one-speed cruisers start at about $10 per day. Mopeds start at about $20 for 2 hours, $35 per day, and $100 per week. The best shops include the **Bicycle Center,** 523 Truman Ave. (✆ **305/294-4556**); the **Moped Hospital,** 601 Truman Ave. (✆ **305/296-3344**); and **Tropical Bicycles & Scooter Rentals,** 1300 Duval St. (✆ **305/294-8136**). The **Bike Shop,** 1110 Truman Ave. (✆ **305/294-1073**; www.thebikeshopkeywest.com), rents cruisers for $12 per day, $60 per week; a $150 deposit is required.

PARKING   Parking in Key West's Old Town is particularly limited, but there is a well-placed **municipal parking lot** at Simonton and Angela streets, just behind the firehouse and police station. If you've brought a car, you may want to stash it here while you enjoy the very walkable downtown part of Key West.

VISITOR INFORMATION   The **Key West Chamber of Commerce,** 402 Wall St., Key West, FL 33040 (✆ **800/527-8539** or 305/294-2587; www.keywest chamber.com), provides both general and specialized information. The lobby is open daily from 8:30am to 6pm; phones are answered from 8am to 8pm. The **Key West Visitor Center** (✆ **800/LAST-KEY** [527-8539]) is the area's best for information on accommodations, goings-on, and restaurants; it's open Monday through Friday from 8am to 5:30pm, Saturday and Sunday from 8:30am to 5pm. Gay travelers may want to call the **Key West Business Guild** (✆ **305/294-4603**), which represents more than 50 guesthouses and B&Bs, as well as many other gay-owned businesses. (Ask for its color brochure.)

While you're in one of the above offices, be sure to pick up a free copy of *Sharon Wells' Walking & Biking Guide to Historic Key West*. Though I still couldn't find all the spots I wanted to in the Key West Cemetery (p. 298) while using the guide, it was helpful for historic descriptions throughout town. Sharon Wells also leads guided walking tours around the island. For information, call her at ✆ **305/294-8380** or go to www.seekeywest.com.

ORIENTATION   A mere 2×4-mile island, Key West is simple to navigate, even though there's no real order to the arrangement of streets and avenues. As you enter town on U.S. 1 (Roosevelt Blvd.), you will see most of the moderate chain hotels and fast-food restaurants. The better restaurants, shops, and outfitters are crammed onto Duval Street, the main thoroughfare of Key West's Old Town. On surrounding streets, many inns and lodges are set in picturesque Victorian/Bahamian homes. On the southern side of the island are the coral-beach area and some of the larger resort hotels.

The area called Bahama Village is the furthest thing from a tourist trap, but can be a bit spotty at night if you aren't familiar with the area. With several newly opened, trendy restaurants and guesthouses, this hippie-ish neighborhood, complete with street-roaming chickens and cats, is the roughest and most urban you'll find in the Keys. You might see a few drug deals happening on street corners, but they're nothing to be overly concerned about: It looks worse than it is, and resident business owners tend to keep a vigilant eye on the neighborhood. The area is actually quite funky and should be a welcome diversion from the Duvalian mainstream.

Seeing the Sights

Key West's greenest attraction, the **Florida Keys Eco-Discovery Center,** opened in early 2007. Overlooking the waterfront at the Truman Annex (35 E. Quay Rd., 𝄐 305/809-4750), the Center features 6,000 square feet of interactive exhibits depicting Florida Keys underwater and upland habitats—with emphasis on the ecosystem of North America's only living contiguous barrier coral reef, which parallels the Keys. Kids dig the interactive yellow submarine while adults seem to get into the cinematic depiction of an underwater abyss. Free admission. Open 9am to 4pm daily except Sunday and Monday.

Before shelling out big bucks for any of the dozens of worthwhile attractions in Key West, I recommend getting an overview on either of the two comprehensive island tours, the **Conch Tour Train** or the **Old Town Trolley** (p. 302 for both). There are simply too many attractions and historic houses to list. I've highlighted my favorites below, but I encourage you to seek out others.

Audubon House & Tropical Gardens ★★ This well-preserved 19th-century home stands as a prime example of early Key West architecture. Named after renowned painter and bird expert John James Audubon, who is said to have visited the house in 1832, the graceful two-story structure is a peaceful retreat from the bustle of Old Town. Included in the price of admission is a self-guided, half-hour audio tour that spotlights rare Audubon prints, gorgeous antiques, historical photos, and lush tropical gardens. With voices of several characters from the house's past, the tour never gets boring—though it is a bit hokey at times. Even if you don't want to explore the grounds and home, check out the impressive gift shop, which sells a variety of fine mementos at reasonable prices. Expect to spend 30 minutes to an hour.

205 Whitehead St. (btw. Greene and Caroline sts.). 𝄐 **305/294-2116.** www.audubonhouse.com. Admission $10 adults, $6.50 students, $5 children 6–12, free children 5 and under. Daily 9:30am–5pm (last entry at 4:30pm).

East Martello Museum and Gallery Adjacent to the airport, the East Martello Museum is in a Civil War–era brick fort that itself is worth a visit. The museum contains a bizarre variety of exhibits that collectively do a thorough job of interpreting the city's intriguing past. Historic artifacts include model ships, a deep-sea diver's wooden air pump, a crude raft from a Cuban "boat lift," a supposedly haunted doll, and a horse-drawn hearse. Exhibits illustrate the Keys' history of salvaging, sponging, and cigar making. After seeing the galleries (which should take 45–60 min.), climb a steep spiral staircase to the top of the lookout tower for good views over the island and ocean. A member of the Key West Art and Historical Society, East Martello has two cousins: the **Key West Museum of Art and History,** 281 Front St. (𝄐 305/295-6616), and the **Key West Lighthouse Museum** (p. 299). Expect to spend 1 to 2 hours.

3501 S. Roosevelt Blvd. 𝄐 **305/296-3913.** www.kwahs.com/martello.htm. Admission $6 adults, $5 seniors, $3 children 8–12. Daily 9:30am–4:30pm (last entry at 4pm).

Ernest Hemingway Home and Museum ★ Hemingway's particularly handsome stone Spanish colonial house, built in 1851, was one of the first on the island to be fitted with indoor plumbing and a built-in fireplace. It also has the first swimming pool built on Key West (look for the penny that Hemingway pressed into the cement near the pool). The author owned the home from 1931 until his death in

1961, and lived here with about 50 cats, whose descendants, including the famed six-toed felines, still roam the premises. It was during those years that the Nobel Prize–winning author wrote some of his most famous works, including *For Whom the Bell Tolls, A Farewell to Arms,* and *The Snows of Kilimanjaro.* Fans may want to

> **Impressions**
>
> *I've a notion to move the Capitol to Key West and just stay.*
> —President Harry S Truman

take the optional half-hour house tour to see his study as well as rooms with glass cabinets that store certain artifacts, books, and pieces of mail addressed to him. It's interesting (to an extent) and included in the price of admission. If you don't take the tour or have no interest in Hemingway, the price of admission is really a waste of money, except for the lovely architecture and garden. If you're feline phobic, beware: There are cats everywhere. Guided tours are given every 15 minutes, and expect to spend an hour on the property.

907 Whitehead St. (btw. Truman Ave. and Olivia St.). © **305/294-1136.** Fax 305/294-2755. www. hemingwayhome.com. Admission $12 adults, $6 children. Daily 9am–5pm. Limited parking.

Key West Aquarium ★★ ☺ The oldest attraction on the island, the Key West Aquarium is a modest but fascinating place. A long hallway of eye-level displays showcases dozens of varieties of fish and crustaceans. Kids can touch sea cucumbers and sea anemones in a shallow tank. The Touch Tank allows for a hands-on experience with harmless sea creatures and the Atlantic Shores Exhibit features a cross section of a near-shore mangrove environment and a 50,000-gallon tank that's home to a variety of tropical fish and game fish. If possible, catch one of the free guided tours—you can witness the dramatic feeding frenzy of the sharks, tarpon, barracudas, stingrays, and turtles. Expect to spend 1 to 1½ hours here.

1 Whitehead St. (at Mallory Sq.). © **305/296-2051.** www.keywestaquarium.com. Admission $12 adults, $5 children 4–12. Website offers tickets for $1 cheaper. Look for discount coupons at local hotels, at Duval St. kiosks, and from trolley and train tours. Daily 10am–6pm; tours at 11am and 1, 3, and 4pm.

Key West Butterfly & Nature Conservatory ★★ ☺ Housed in a 13,000-square-foot pavilion, this attraction has nature lovers flitting with excitement, thanks to the 5,000-square-foot, glass-enclosed butterfly aviary as well as a gallery, learning center, and gift shop exploring all aspects of the butterfly world. Inside, more than 1,500 butterflies and 3,500 plants, including rare orchids, and even fish and turtles coexist in a controlled climate. You'll walk freely among the butterflies, so if you have even the slightest fear of the creatures, consider twice before entering. Expect to spend about an hour inside.

1316 Duval St. © **305/296-2988.** www.keywestbutterfly.com. Admission $12 adults, $9 seniors, $8.50 children 4–12. Daily 9am–5pm; last ticket sold at 4:30pm.

Key West Cemetery ★★★ 🛉 This funky cemetery is the epitome of quirky Key West: irreverent and humorous. Many tombs are stacked several high, condominium style, because the rocky soil made digging 6 feet under nearly impossible for early settlers. Epitaphs reflect residents' lighthearted attitudes toward life and death. I TOLD YOU I WAS SICK is one of the more famous, as is the tongue-in-cheek widow's inscription AT LEAST I KNOW WHERE HE'S SLEEPING TONIGHT. Pick up a copy of *Sharon Wells' Walking & Biking Guide to Historic Key West* (p. 296). Some of the inscriptions are hard to

GOING, GOING, GONE: WHERE TO CATCH THE FAMOUS KEY WEST sunset

A tradition in Key West, the Sunset Celebration can be relaxing or overwhelming, depending on your vantage point. If you're in town, you must check out this ritual at least once. Every evening, locals and visitors gather at the docks behind Mallory Square (at the westernmost end of Whitehead St.) to celebrate the day gone by. Secure a spot on the docks early to experience the carnival of portrait artists, acrobats, food vendors, animal acts, and other performers trading on the island's bohemian image. But the carnival atmosphere isn't for everyone: In season, the crowd can be overwhelming, especially when the cruise ships are in port. Also, hold on to your bags and wallets, as the tight crowds make Mallory Square at sunset prime pickpocket territory.

A more refined choice is the Westin's **Sunset Deck** ((C) **305/294-4000**), a luxurious second-floor bar on Front Street, right next door to Mallory Square. From the civilized calm of a casual bar, you can look down on the mayhem with a drink in hand.

Also near the Mallory madness is the bar at the **Ocean Key Resort,** at the very tip of Duval Street ((C) **800/328-9815** or 305/296-7701). This long open-air pier serves drinks and decent bar food against a dramatic pink-and-yellow-streaked sky.

For the very best potent cocktails and great bar food on an outside patio or enclosed lounge, try **Pier House Resort and Caribbean Spa's Havana Docks,** 1 Duval St. ((C) **305/296-4600**). There's usually live music and a lively gathering of visitors enjoying this island's bounty. The bar is right on the water and makes a prime sunset-viewing spot.

find even with the free walking-tour guide, but this place is fun to explore. Plan to spend 30 minutes to an hour or more depending on how morbid your curiosity is.

Entrance at the corner of Margaret and Angela sts. Free admission. Daily dawn–dusk.

Key West Heritage House and Robert Frost Cottage   For a glimpse into one of the oldest houses in Key West, check out the Heritage House Museum, the former 1834 home of Jessie Porter, a Key West preservationist who hosted the likes of Robert Frost, Tennessee Williams, Ernest Hemingway, Gloria Swanson, and Tallulah Bankhead. Poet Robert Frost was friends with Porter and used to stay in the cottage out in the garden. Every April, the house hosts the Robert Frost Poetry Festival. Furnished with 19th-century antiques, the house is a fascinating look at 19th- and early-20th-century Key West. Guided tours are informative and entertaining, sort of an antique version of an *E! True Hollywood Story.* Expect to spend 30 minutes to an hour.

410 Caroline St. (C) **305/296-3573.** www.heritagehousemuseum.org. Guided tour $9, self-guided tour $6, children under 12 $3. Mon–Sat 10am–4pm.

Key West Lighthouse Museum ★   When the Key West Lighthouse opened in 1848, it signaled the end of a profitable era for the pirate salvagers who looted reef-stricken ships. The story of this and other area lighthouses is illustrated in a small museum that was formerly the keeper's quarters. It's worth mustering the energy to climb the 88 claustrophobic steps to the top, where you'll be rewarded with magnificent panoramic views of Key West and the ocean. Expect to spend 30 minutes to an hour.

938 Whitehead St. © **305/295-6616.** www.kwahs.com. Admission $10 adults, $9 seniors and locals, $5 children 7-12. Daily 9:30am-4:30pm.

Key West's Shipwreck Historeum   You'll see more impressive artifacts at nearby Mel Fisher's museum, but for the morbidly curious, shipwrecks should rank right up there with car wrecks. For those of you who can't help but look, this museum is the place to be for everything you ever wanted to know about shipwrecks and more. See movies, artifacts, and a real-life wrecker, who will be more than happy to indulge your curiosity about the wrecking industry that preoccupied the early pioneers of Key West. Depending on your level of interest, you can expect to spend up to 2 hours here.

1 Whitehead St. (at Mallory Sq.). © **305/292-8990.** Fax 305/292-5536. www.shipwreckhistoreum. com. Admission $12 adults, $5 children 4-12. Website sells tickets for $1 cheaper. Shows daily every half-hour 9:45am-4:45pm.

Mel Fisher Maritime Heritage Museum ★★   This museum honors local hero Mel Fisher, whose death in 1998 was mourned throughout South Florida and who, along with a crew of other salvagers, found a multimillion-dollar treasure trove in 1985 aboard the wreck of the Spanish galleon *Nuestra Señora de Atocha.* If you're into diving, pirates, and sunken treasures, check out this small museum, full of doubloons, pieces of eight, emeralds, and solid-gold bars (one of them you can lift!). A 1700 English merchant slave ship, the only tangible evidence of the transatlantic slave trade, is on view on the museum's second floor. An exhibition telling the story of more than 1,400 African slaves captured in Cuban waters and brought to Key West for sanctuary is the museum's latest, most fascinating exhibit to date. Expect to spend 1 to 3 hours.

200 Greene St. © **305/294-2633.** www.melfisher.org. Admission $12 adults, $11 students and seniors, $6 children 6-12. Daily 9:30am-5pm. Take U.S. 1 to Whitehead St. and turn left on Greene.

   A Great Escape

Many people complain that Key West's quirky, quaint panache has been lost to the vulture of capitalism, evidenced by the glut of T-shirt shops and tacky bars. But that's not entirely so. For a quiet respite, visit the **Key West Tropical Forest Botanical Gardens** (© **305/296-1504;** www.keywestbotanicalgarden. org), a little-known slice of serenity tucked between the Aqueduct Authority plant and the Key West Golf Course. The 11-acre gardens—maintained by volunteers and funded by donations—contain the last hardwood hammock in Key West, plus a colorful representation of wildflowers, butterflies, and birds. Over 60 endangered botanical species are alive and well here. A genetically cloned tree is one of the many sites at "the only frost-free tropical moist garden in the continental United States." Located at Botanical Garden Way and College Road, Stock Island. Free admission but a donation of $5 per adult, $4 per child (12 to 18) is suggested. Open daily from 8am to sunset. Follow College Road; then turn right just past Bayshore Manor.

literary KEY WEST

Counting Ernest Hemingway and Tennessee Williams among your denizens would give any city the right to call itself a literary mecca. But over the years, tiny Key West has been home—or at least home away from home—to dozens of literary types who are drawn to some combination of its gentle pace, tropical atmosphere, and lighthearted mood (not to mention its lingering reputation for an oft-ribald lifestyle). Writers have long known that more than a few muses prowl the tree-laden streets of Key West.

Robert Frost first visited Key West in 1934 and wintered here for the remainder of his life. In the early 20th century, writers such as John Dewey, Archibald MacLeish, John Dos Passos, Wallace Stevens, and S. J. Perelman were drawn to the island. Even as Key West boomed and busted and boomed again, and despite the island's growing popularity with world travelers, writers continued to move to Key West or to visit it with such regularity that they were deemed honorary "conchs." Novelists Phil Caputo, Tom McGuane, Jim Harrison, John Hersey, Alison Lurie, and Robert Stone were among these.

Of course, one of Key West's favorite sons also earned a spot in the annals of local literary history. Famous for his good-time, tropical-laced music, Jimmy Buffett was also a surprisingly well-received novelist in the 1990s. Although Buffett now makes the infinitely ritzier Palm Beach his Florida home, his presence is still felt in virtually every corner of Key West.

But it is Nobel Prize winner and avid outdoorsman Ernest Hemingway who is most identified with Key West. Much of the island has changed since he lived here from 1931 to 1961. Even the famous Sloppy Joe's bar, which Hemingway frequented mostly from 1933 to 1937, has changed locations (reportedly without closing—customers picked up their drinks and whatever else they could carry from the bar and brought it all down the block to the new location, and service resumed with barely a blink!). Fortunately, the Ernest Hemingway Home and Museum (p. 297) has been lovingly preserved. But to get the best feel for what Hemingway loved most about Key West, visit the docks at Garrison Bight. It is from here that Hemingway and his many famous (and infamous) friends and contemporaries departed for Caribbean ports of call and for sport upon the sea.

Key West pays homage to its literary legacy with the annual Key West Literary Seminar in January. For information, call ℂ **888/293-9291** or visit www.keywestliteraryseminar.org.

Oldest House/Wrecker's Museum ★   Dating from 1829, this old New England Bahama House has survived pirates, hurricanes, fires, warfare, and economic ups and downs. The one-and-a-half-story home was designed by a ship's carpenter and incorporates many features from maritime architecture, including portholes and a ship's hatch designed for ventilation before the advent of air-conditioning. Especially interesting is the detached kitchen building outfitted with a brick "beehive" oven and vintage cooking utensils. Although not a must-see on the Key West tour, history and architecture buffs will appreciate the finely preserved details and the glimpse of a slower, easier time in the island's life. Plan to spend 30 minutes to an hour.

322 Duval St. ℂ **305/294-9501.** Free admission. Daily 10am–4pm.

Pirate Soul ★ ☺ Thanks to Johnny Depp and Disney's *Pirates of the Caribbean,* pirates have never been hotter. This museum is dedicated to everything about the legendary seafaring rogues, featuring more than 500 artifacts from the golden age of piracy, as well as animatronics and interactive exhibits. Among the highlights are the only authentic pirate treasure chest in America, originally belonging to Captain Thomas Tew, and Blackbeard's original blunderbuss. As with any kitschy museum, there's a store where you can buy all sorts of gear, from eye patches to bath products sporting the Jolly Roger. If you find yourself thirsty or hungry, Rum Barrel is the museum's homage to grub and grog. Plan to spend 30 minutes to an arrrrrrrgh, I mean hour.

524 Front St. ℂ **305/292-1113.** www.piratesoul.com. Admission $15 adults, $9 children 6–12. Tickets are cheaper on the website. Mon–Fri 9am–7pm, Sat–Sun 10am–7pm; summer Mon–Fri 9am–5pm, Sat–Sun 10am–5pm.

Organized Tours

BY TRAM & TROLLEY-BUS Yes, it's more than a bit hokey to sit on this 60-foot tram of yellow cars, but it's worth it—at least once. The city's whole story is packed into a neat, 90-minute package on the **Conch Tour Train,** which covers the island and all its rich, raunchy history. In operation since 1958, the cars are open-air, which can make the ride uncomfortable in bad weather. The engine of the "train" is a propane-powered jeep disguised as a locomotive. Tours depart from both Mallory Square and the Welcome Center, near where U.S. 1 becomes North Roosevelt Boulevard, on the less-developed side of the island. For information, call ℂ **305/294-5161** or go to www.conchtourtrain.com. The cost is $29 for adults, $14 for children 4 to 12. Tickets are cheaper on the website. Daily departures are every half-hour from 9am to 4:30pm.

The **Old Town Trolley** is the choice in bad weather or if you're staying at one of the hotels on its route. Humorous drivers maintain a running commentary as the enclosed trolley loops around the island's streets past all the major sights. Trolley buses depart from Mallory Square and other points around the island, including many area hotels. For details, call ℂ **305/296-6688** or visit www.trolleytours.com. Tours are $29 for adults, $14 for children 4 to 12. Tickets are cheaper on the website. Departures are daily every half-hour (though not always on the half-hour) from 9am to 4:30pm.

Whichever you choose, both of these historic, trivia-packed tours are well worth the price of tickets.

BY AIR Proclaimed by the mayor as "the official air force of the Conch Republic," **Island Aeroplane Tours,** at Key West Airport, 3469 S. Roosevelt Blvd. (ℂ **305/294-8687;** www.keywestairtours.com), offers windy rides in its open-cockpit 1940 Waco biplanes that take you over the reefs and around the islands. Thrill-seekers will also enjoy a spin in the company's S2-B aerobatics airplane, which does loops, rolls, and sideways figure-eights. Company owner Fred Cabanas was decorated in 1991, after he spotted a Cuban airman defecting to the United States in a Russian-built MIG fighter. Sightseeing flights cost $90 to $345 for two people, depending on duration.

BY BOAT The catamarans and the glass-bottom boat of **Fury Water Adventures,** 237 Front St. (ℂ **305/296-6293;** www.furycat.com), depart on daytime coral-reef tours and evening sunset cruises (call for times). Reef trips cost $35 per person; sunset cruises are $37 per person. Kids ages 5 through 12 sail on all cruises for $19. Prices are cheaper on the website.

The schooner *Western Union* (© 305/292-9830; www.schoonerwesternunion. com) was built in 1939 and served as a cable-repair vessel until it was designated the flagship of the city of Key West and began day, sunset, and charter sailings. Sunset sailings are especially memorable and include entertainment, cocktails, and a cannon fire. Prices vary; inquire for details.

A new boat tour combines Florida Keys sunsets with delectable Keys cuisine. **Sunset Culinaire Tours** (© 305/296-0982; www.sunsetculinaire.com) is a cruise aboard the vessel *RB's Lady* and includes a tour of Key West harbor as the sun sinks below the horizon, and a three-course gourmet dinner (including beer or wine) prepared by Chef Brian Kirkpatrick. The vessel departs from Sunset Marina, off U.S. 1 at 5555 College Rd., at 5:30pm nightly. Boarding time is 5pm and the cost is $85 per person.

OTHER TOURS Sharon Wells (© 305/294-0566; www.kwlightgallery.com), historian, artist and owner of the KW Light Gallery, leads a slew of great tours throughout the island, focusing on things as diverse as literature, architecture, and places connected with the island's gay and lesbian culture.

For a lively look at Key West, try the **Key West Pub Crawl** (© 305/744-9804; www.keywestwalkingtours.com), a tour of the island's most famous bars. It's given on Tuesday and Friday nights at 8pm, lasts 2½ hours, costs $30, and includes five (!) drinks. Another fun option is the 1-mile, 90-minute **ghost tour** (© 305/294-WALK [9255]; www.hauntedtours.com), leaving daily at 8 and 9pm from the Holiday Inn La Concha, 430 Duval St. Cost is $15 for adults and $10 for children 11 and under. This spooky and interesting tour gives participants insight into many old island legends.

Key West's **Ghosts and Legends Tour** (© 866/622-4467 or 305/294-1713; www.keywestghosts.com) is a fun, 90-minute narrated tour of the island and spirits that don't come in a plastic cup or mug. You'll walk through the shadowy streets and lanes of Old Town, stopping at allegedly haunted Victorian mansions, and learning about fascinating island pirate lore, voodoo superstitions and rituals, a Count who lived with the corpse of his beloved, and other bizarre yet true aspects of this eerie place. Tours depart nightly from the Porter Mansion on the corner of Duval and Caroline streets. Space is limited and reservations are required. Tickets are $18 for adults and $10 for children.

Since the early 1940s, Key West has been a haven for gay luminaries such as Tennessee Williams and Broadway legend Jerry Herman. A trolley tour of **Gay Key West,** created by the Key West Business Guild, showcases the history, contributions, and landmarks associated with the island's flourishing gay and lesbian culture. Highlights include Williams's house, the art gallery owned by Key West's first gay mayor, and a variety of guesthouses whose gay owners fueled the island's architectural-restoration movement. The 70-minute tour takes place Saturday at 10:50am, starting and ending at City of Key West parking lot, corner of Simonton and Angela streets. Look for the trolley with the rainbow flags. The cost is $20 to $25. Call © 305/294-4603 or go to www.gaykeywestfl.com.

For Jimmy Buffett fans, or "parrotheads," as they're also known, **Trails and Tales of Key West** (✆ 305/292-2040) is an amusing, 2-hour guided walking tour in which Key West's finest storytellers share tales of Jimmy Buffett, Captain Tony, Ernest Hemingway, Mel Fisher, and more. The informative and often hilarious guides lead you past the hangouts and other high points of these colorful characters' Key West. Visit Buffett's first house on the island, Shrimp Boat Sound Recording Studio, where the likes of Toby Keith have since recorded. Visit legendary pubs and the historic seaport; plus, hear fascinating stories about the Conch Republic and get some insider tips to the secrets of Key West. This 2-hour tour departs daily at 4pm from **Captain Tony's Saloon,** 428 Greene St., where Buffett used to hang out and perform, and ends at—you guessed it—**Margaritaville Cafe,** on Duval Street. The tour conveniently goes during happy hour. Tickets are $20 for adults, and $10 for children 6 to 12. Bring cash or traveler's checks; no credit cards are accepted. Reservations are required.

Outdoor Activities

BEACHES   Unlike the rest of the Keys, Key West actually has a few small beaches, although they don't compare with the state's wide natural wonders up the coast; the Keys' beaches are typically narrow and rocky. Here are your options: Smathers Beach, off South Roosevelt Boulevard, west of the airport; Higgs Beach, along Atlantic Boulevard, between White Street and Reynolds Road; and Fort Zachary Beach, located off the western end of Southard Boulevard.

A magnet for partying teenagers, **Smathers Beach** is Key West's largest and most overpopulated. Despite the number of rowdy teens, the beach is actually quite clean and looks lovely since its renovation in the spring of 2000. If you go early enough in the morning, you may notice people sleeping on the beach from the night before.

Higgs Beach is a favorite among Key West's gay crowds, but what many people don't know is that beneath the sand is an unmarked cemetery of African slaves who died while waiting for freedom. Higgs has a playground and tennis courts, and is near the minute Rest Beach, which is actually hidden by the White Street pier. The sand here is coarse and rocky and the water tends to be a bit mucky but if you can bear it, Higgs is known as a great snorkeling beach. If it's sunbathing you want, skip Higgs and go to Smathers.

Although there is an entrance fee ($6 per car of 2-8, $4 single-occupant vehicle, $2 pedestrians and bicyclists plus 50¢ per person for Monroe County surcharge), I recommend **Fort Zachary Beach,** as it has a great historic fort, a Civil War museum, and a large picnic area with tables, barbecue grills, restrooms, and showers. Large trees scattered across 87 acres provide shade for those who are reluctant to bake in the sun.

BIKING & MOPEDING   A popular mode of transportation for locals and visitors, bikes and mopeds are available at many rental outlets in the city (p. 296). Escape the hectic downtown scene and explore the island's scenic side streets by heading away from Duval Street toward South Roosevelt Boulevard and the beachside enclaves along the way.

DIVING One of the area's largest scuba schools, **Dive Key West, Inc.,** 3128 N. Roosevelt Blvd. (© **800/426-0707** or 305/296-3823; www.divekeywest.com), offers instruction at all levels; its dive boats take participants to scuba and snorkel sites on nearby reefs.

Key West Marine Park (© **305/294-3100**), the newest dive park along the island's Atlantic shore, incorporates no-motor "swim-only" lanes marked by buoys, providing swimmers and snorkelers with a safe way to explore the waters around Key West. The park's boundaries stretch from the foot of Duval Street to Higgs Beach.

Wreck dives and night dives are two of the special offerings of **Lost Reef Adventures,** 261 Margaret St. (© **800/952-2749** or 305/296-9737; www.lostreefadventures. com). Regularly scheduled runs and private charters can be arranged. Phone for departure information.

Big news for divers in 2009: *The General Hoyt S. Vandenberg,* a 524-foot former U.S. Air Force missile tracking ship, was sunk 6 miles south of Key West to create an artificial reef. For a map of the Florida **Keys Shipwreck Heritage Trail,** an entire network of wrecks from Key Largo to Key West, go to http://floridakeys. noaa.gov/sanctuary_resources/shipwreck_trail/welcome.html.

Also see **Mosquito Coast Outfitters,** under "Kayaking," below.

FISHING As any angler will tell you, there's no fishing like Keys fishing. Key West has it all: bonefish, tarpon, dolphin, tuna, grouper, cobia, and more—sharks, too.

Step aboard a small exposed skiff for an incredibly diverse day of fishing. In the morning, you can head offshore for sailfish or dolphin (the fish, not the mammal), and then by afternoon get closer to land for a shot at tarpon, permit, grouper, or snapper. Here in Key West, you can probably pick up more cobia—one of the best fighting and eating fish around—than anywhere else in the world. For a real fight, ask your skipper to go for the tarpon—the greatest fighting fish there is, famous for its dramatic "tail walk" on the water after it's hooked. Shark fishing is also popular.

You'll find plenty of competition among the charter-fishing boats in and around Mallory Square. You can negotiate a good deal at **Charter Boat Row,** 1801 N. Roosevelt Ave. (across from the Shell station), home to more than 30 charter-fishing and party boats. Just show up to arrange your outing, or call **Garrison Bight Marina** (© **305/292-8167**) for details.

The advantage of the smaller, more expensive charter boats is that you can call the shots. They'll take you where you want to go, to fish for what you want to catch.

 Reel Deals

When looking for the best deals on fishing excursions, know that the bookers from the kiosks in town generally take 20% of a captain's fee in addition to an extra monthly fee. You can usually save yourself money by booking directly with a captain or by going straight to one of the docks.

These "light tackles" are also easier to maneuver, which means you can go to backcountry spots for tarpon and bonefish, as well as out to the open ocean for tuna and dolphinfish. You'll really be able to feel the fish, and you'll get some good fights, too. Larger boats, for up to six or seven people, are cheaper and are best for kingfish, billfish, and sailfish. For every kind of fishing charter you can imagine, from flats and offshore to backcountry and wreck fishing, call **Almost There Sportfishing Charters** (📞 800/795-9448; www.almostthere.net).

The huge commercial party boats are more for sightseeing than serious angling, though you can be lucky enough to get a few bites at one of the fishing holes. One especially good deal is the *Gulfstream III* (📞 305/296-8494; www.keywestpartyboat.com), an all-day charter that goes out daily from 11am to 4:30pm. You'll pay $55 for adults, $52 for seniors, $35 for kids 11 and under, and the price includes rod, bait, tackle, and license. This 65-foot party boat usually has at least 30 other anglers. Bring your own cooler or buy snacks onboard. Beer and wine are allowed.

Serious anglers should consider the light-tackle boats that leave from **Oceanside Marina,** on Stock Island at 5950 Peninsula Ave., 1½ miles off U.S. 1 (📞 305/294-4676). It's a 20-minute drive from Old Town on the Atlantic side. There are more than 30 light-tackle guides, which range from flatbed, backcountry skiffs to 28-foot open boats. There are also a few larger charters and a party boat that goes to the Dry Tortugas. Call for details.

For a light-tackle outing with a very colorful Key West flair, call **Captain Bruce Cronin** (📞 305/294-4929; www.fishbruce.com) or **Captain Ken Harris** (📞 305/731-4907; www.kwextremeadventures.com), two of the more famous (and pricey) captains working these docks for more than 20 years. You'll pay from $750 for a full day, usually about 8am to 4pm, and from $500 for a half-day. For a comprehensive list of Florida Keys fishing guides go to www.ccaflorida.org/guides/keys_guides.html.

GOLF A relative newcomer in terms of local recreation, golf is gaining in popularity here, as it is in many visitor destinations. The area's only public golf club is **Key West Golf Club** (📞 305/294-5232; www.keywestgolf.com), an 18-hole course at the entrance to the island of Key West at MM 4.5 (turn onto College Rd. to the course entrance). Designed by Rees Jones, the course, which was renovated in 2008, has plenty of mangroves and water hazards on its 6,526 yards. It's open to the public and has a new pro shop. Call ahead for tee-time reservations. Rates are $95 per player during off-season and $165 in season, or $70 off-season and $95 in season after 2:30pm, including cart.

KAYAKING Housed in a woodsy wine bar, **Mosquito Coast Outfitters,** 1017 Duval St. (📞 305/294-7178; www.mosquitocoast.net), operates a first-rate kayaking and snorkeling tour every day as long as the weather is mild. The tours depart at 9am sharp and return around 3pm. Included in the $60 price are snacks, soft drinks, and a guided tour of the mangrove-studded islands of Sugar Key or Geiger Key, just north of Key West. The tour is primarily for kayaking, but you'll have the opportunity to get in the water for snorkeling, if you're interested. A new 2-hour tour called the Doggie Paddle Tour allows you to bring your furry friend along.

Shopping

You'll find all kinds of unique gifts and souvenirs in Key West, from coconut postcards to Key lime pies. On Duval Street, T-shirt shops outnumber almost any other business. If you must get a wearable memento, be careful of unscrupulous salespeople. Despite efforts to curtail the practice, many shops have been known to rip off unwitting shoppers. It pays to check the prices and the exchange rate before signing any sales slips. You are entitled to a written estimate of any T-shirt work before you pay for it.

At Mallory Square, you'll find the **Clinton Street Market,** an overly air-conditioned mall of kiosks and stalls designed for the many cruise-ship passengers who never venture beyond this super-commercial zone. There are some coffee and candy shops, and some high-priced hats and shoes. There's also a free and clean restroom.

Once the main industry of Key West, cigar making is enjoying renewed success at the handful of factories that survived the slow years. Stroll through **Cigar Alley** (while on Greene St., go 2 blocks west and you'll hit Cigar Alley, also known as Pirate's Alley), where you will find *viejitos* (little old men) rolling fat stogies just as they used to do in their homeland across the Florida Straits. Stop at the **Conch Republic Cigar Factory,** 512 Greene St. (© 305/295-9036; www.conch-cigars. com), for an excellent selection of imported and locally rolled smokes, including the famous El Hemingway. Remember, buying or selling Cuban-made cigars is illegal. Shops advertising "Cuban cigars" are usually referring to domestic cigars made from tobacco grown from seeds that were brought from Cuba decades ago. To be fair, though, many premium cigars today are grown from Cuban seed tobacco—only it is grown in Latin America and the Caribbean, not Cuba.

If you're looking for local or Caribbean art, you'll find nearly a dozen galleries and shops clustered on Duval Street between Catherine and Fleming streets. There are also some excellent shops scattered on the side streets. One worth seeking out is the **Haitian Art Co.,** 1100 Truman Ave. (© **305/296-8932;** www.haitian-art-co.com), where you can browse through room upon room of original paintings from well-known and obscure Haitian artists, in a range of prices from a few dollars to a few thousand. Also check out **Cuba, Cuba!** at 814 Duval St. (© **305/295-9442;** www. cubacubastore.com), where you'll see paintings, sculpture, and photos by Cuban artists, as well as books and art from the island.

From sweet to spicy, **Peppers of Key West,** 602 Greene St. (© **305/295-9333;** www.peppersofkeywest.com), is a hot-sauce-lover's heaven, with hundreds of variations, from mild to brutally spicy. Grab a seat at the tasting bar and be prepared to let your taste buds sizzle. *Tip:* Bring beer, and they'll let you taste some of their secret sauces!

Literature and music buffs will appreciate the many bookshops and record stores on the island. **Key West Island Bookstore,** 513 Fleming St. (© **305/294-2904**), carries new, used, and rare books, and specializes in fiction by residents of the Keys, including Ernest Hemingway, Tennessee Williams, Shel Silverstein, Ann Beattie, Richard Wilbur, and John Hersey. The bookstore is open daily from 10am to 9pm.

For anything else, from bed linens to candlesticks to clothing, go to downtown's oldest and most renowned department store, **Fast Buck Freddie's,** 500 Duval St. (© **305/294-2007**). For the same merchandise at reduced prices, try **Half Buck Freddie's ★**, 726 Caroline St. (© **305/294-2007**), where you can shop for out-of-season bargains and "rejects" from the main store.

Also check out **KW Light Gallery,** 534 Fleming St. (© **305/294-0566;** www. kwlightgallery.com), for high-quality contemporary photography as well as historic images and other artwork relating to the Keys or to the concept of light and its varied interpretations. The gallery is open Thursday through Tuesday from 10am to 6pm (10am–4pm in summer). Owner/photographer/painter Sharon Wells also gives historic tours of Key West so inquire while you're inside for the inside scoop.

Where to Stay

You'll find a wide variety of places to stay in Key West, from resorts with all the amenities to seaside motels, quaint bed-and-breakfasts, and clothing-optional guesthouses.

Unless you're in town during Key West's most popular holidays—Fantasy Fest (around Halloween), where Mardi Gras meets South Florida for the NC-17 set and most hotels have outrageous rates and 5-night minimums; Hemingway Days (in July), where Papa is seemingly and eerily alive and well; and Christmas and New Year's—or for a big fishing tournament (many are held Oct–Dec) or a boat-racing tourney, you can almost always find a place to stay at the last minute. However, you may want to book early, especially in winter, when prime properties fill up and many require 2- or 3-night minimum stays. Prices at these times are extremely high. Finding a decent room for less than $100 a night is a real trick.

Another suggestion, and my recommendation, is to call **Vacation Key West** (✆ 800/595-5397 or 305/295-9500; www.vacationkw.com), a wholesaler that offers discounts of 20% to 30% and is skilled at finding last-minute deals. It represents mostly larger hotels and motels, but can also place visitors in guesthouses. The phones are answered Monday through Friday from 9am to 6pm, and Saturday from 11am to 2pm. **Key West Innkeepers Association** (✆ 800/492-1911 or 305/292-3600; www.keywestinns.com) can also help you find lodging in any price range from among its members and affiliates.

Gay travelers may want to call the **Key West Business Guild** (✆ 305/294-4603; www.gaykeywestfl.com), which represents more than 50 guesthouses and B&Bs in town, as well as many other gay-owned businesses. Be advised that most gay guesthouses have a clothing-optional policy. One of the most elegant and popular is **Big Ruby's,** 409 Applerouth Lane (✆ 800/477-7829 or 305/296-2323; www.bigrubys.com), located on a little alley just off Duval Street. Rates start at $173 double in peak season and $125 off-season. A low cluster of buildings surrounds a lush courtyard where a hearty breakfast is served each morning and wine is poured at dusk. The all-male guests hang out by the pool, tanning in the buff.

For women only, **Pearl's Rainbow,** 525 United St. (✆ 800/74-WOMYN [749-6696] or 305/292-1450; www.pearlsrainbow.com), is a large, fairly well-maintained guesthouse with lots of privacy and amenities, including two pools and two hot tubs. Rates range from $89 to $359.

VERY EXPENSIVE

The Gardens Hotel ★★★ 🏨 At last, the true Garden of Eden has been located—and it's on Angela Street in Key West. Once a private residence, the Gardens Hotel (whose main house is listed on the National Register of Historic Places) is hidden amid exotic botanical gardens. Behind the greenery is a Bahamian-style hideaway with luxuriously appointed rooms in the main house, garden and courtyard rooms in the carriage house, and one ultrasecluded cottage. Though the place is within walking distance of frenetic Duval Street, you may not want to leave. A pretty, free-form pool is centered in the courtyard, where a Tiki bar serves libations. The Jacuzzi is hidden behind foliage. Guest rooms have hardwood floors, plantation beds with Tempur-Pedic mattresses, and marble bathrooms. Winding brick pathways leading to secluded seating areas in the private gardens make for an idyllic getaway. On Sunday afternoons the hotel features live jazz in the gardens. *Note:* If you plan to party, do not stay here—guests tend to be on the quieter, more sophisticated side.

526 Angela St., Key West, FL 33040. ✆ **800/526-2664** or 305/294-2661. Fax 305/292-1007. www.gardenshotel.com. 17 units. Winter $300–$415 double, $495–$620 suite; off-season $175–$325 double, $225–$395 suite. Rates include continental breakfast. AE, DC, MC, V. **Amenities:** Bar; pool. *In room:* A/C, TV, hair dryer.

It's Not Easy Being a Green Hotel

The **Gardens** is one of the first **"Florida Green Lodging Hotels"** in the Keys, meaning the hotel has installed energy-efficient light bulbs throughout the property, uses all "green" cleaning products, eliminated plastics and Styrofoam use, educates staff and guests of the importance of recycling, and raises room temperatures to 78°F (26°C) when not in use, among other eco-friendly efforts. For more info on the organization and participating hotels, see www.floridagreenlodging.org.

Key West Marriott Beachside Hotel ★★★ Key West's newest luxury resort, this one is right at the entrance to Key West, overlooking the Gulf of Mexico and the only one in town to boast a helicopter pad on the roof for some of the resort's more boldface names. The resort has spacious one-, two-, and three-bedroom suites as well as king bedrooms, all adorned with oversize balconies with waterfront views, open gourmet kitchens, marble Jacuzzi tubs, and, on the third floor, private sundecks. Tavern N Town Restaurant, Key West's culinary destination, features a theater kitchen and a gourmet menu of tapas, pizzas, fantastic steaks, and taste of the island seafood, and a private dining room for up to 16 guests. At the tropical waterfront pool, you'll find available private cabanas, a private tanning beach, and the Blue Bar, a casual dining oasis with always a generous splash of island geniality. Although the resort is located on busy Roosevelt Boulevard, home to chain motels and restaurants, you'll feel like you're in another world once you enter the premises.

3841 N. Roosevelt Blvd., Key West, FL 33040. © **800/546-0885** or 305/296-8100. Fax 305/293-0205. www.keywestmarriottbeachside.com. 222 units. Winter $229 double, $329–$699 suite; off-season $189 double, $289–$429 suite. AE, DC, MC, V. Valet parking $28 per day. **Amenities:** 2 restaurants; 2 bars; free airport shuttle and shuttle to and from downtown Key West; babysitting; moped/bike rental; concierge; water-view fitness center; private helicopter pad; heated pool; watersports equipment/rentals; free Wi-Fi in common areas. In room: A/C, LCD flatscreen TV w/satellite, hair dryer, Internet access, full gourmet kitchen (in suites), washer/dryer (in suites).

Ocean Key Resort and Spa ★★ You can't beat the location of this 100-room resort, at the foot of Mallory Square, the epicenter of the sunset ritual. Ocean Key also features a Gulf-side heated pool and the lively Sunset Pier, where guests can wind down with cocktails and live music. Guest rooms are huge and luxuriously appointed, with living and dining areas, oversize Jacuzzis, and views of the Gulf, the harbor, or Mallory Square and Duval Street. The newly renovated two-bedroom suite is 1,200 square feet and has a full kitchen, three beds, and a large private balcony. The property is adorned in classic Key West decor, from the tile floors and hand-painted furniture to the pastel art. The Indonesian-inspired SpaTerre is perhaps the best in town. The resort's restaurant, **Hot Tin Roof** (p. 318), is one of Key West's best. New to the resort: the Liquid Lounge, a VIP pool lounge featuring private cabanas, dipping pool, whirlpool, and nightclub-style bottle service and music.

0 Duval St. (near Mallory Docks), Key West, FL 33040. © **800/328-9815** or 305/296-7701. Fax 305/292-2198. www.oceankey.com. 100 units. Winter $379–$679 double, $479–$1,149 suite; off-season $239–$439 double, $319–$639 suite. AE, DC, MC, V. **Amenities:** 2 restaurants; 3 bars; babysitting; bike/moped rental; concierge; heated pool; room service; watersports equipment/rentals. In room: A/C, TV, hair dryer, minibar, Wi-Fi.

Westin Key West Resort & Marina ★★   Ideally situated in the heart of Old Town, the Westin Key West Resort & Marina is next to Mallory Square and within walking distance of famous Duval Street. Featuring large, well-appointed rooms with all the modern conveniences and the signature Westin Heavenly Bed, most of the 178 rooms and suites have ocean views and balconies. Bistro 245 serves ample breakfasts and a huge Sunday brunch. Visit the Westin Sunset Pier for the nightly Sunset Celebration, with live performers and outdoor dining. The Westin's sister property, **Sunset Key Guest Cottages, A Westin Resort** ★★★ (© **888/477-7SUN** [7786] or 305/292-5300; fax 305/292-5395; www.sunsetkeyisland.com), features 37 luxurious cottages just 10 minutes by boat from Key West. Check in at the Westin Key West Resort & Marina and take a 10-minute launch ride to the secluded island of Sunset Key, where there is a white sandy beach, free-form pool with whirlpool jets, two tennis courts, and Latitudes Beach Cafe. Cottages are equipped with full kitchens, high-tech entertainment centers, and one, two, or three bedrooms. Private chef and grocery shopping services available upon request. Guests at Sunset Key have access to all the amenities at the Westin Key West Resort & Marina. For a nominal fee, guests of the Westin Key West Resort & Marina can enjoy the beach on Sunset Key; however, access is limited and on a first-come, first-served basis.

245 Front St. (at the end of Duval St.), Key West, FL 33040. © **800/221-2424** or 305/294-4000. Fax 305/294-4086. www.westin.com/keywest. 215 units, including cottages. Winter $399–$550 double, $469–$1,149 suite, $595–$2,225 Sunset Key Cottage, up to 5 people; off-season $229–$459 double, $359–$949 suite, $595–$1,345 Sunset Key Cottage, up to 5 people. AE, DC, DISC, MC, V. Valet parking $20; self-parking $6/hr. ($24 per day). Pets up to 40 lbs. allowed. **Amenities:** 5 restaurants; 3 bars; bike rental; concierge; health club; Jacuzzi; full-service marina; outdoor heated pool; limited room service; watersports equipment/rentals. *In room:* A/C, TV, hair dryer, Wi-Fi.

EXPENSIVE

Casa Marina Resort & Beach Club ★ ☺   This resort has completed a dramatic $44-million renovation to offer a pleasing mix of historic architecture and modern Key West vibe. Supremely located on the south side of the island, spanning more than 1,000 feet of private beach, the Casa Marina features sweeping lawns, a grand verandah, and a new "water walk" leading from the historic lobby to the water's edge. Recently revitalized rooms with sun-soaked balconies overlook the Atlantic and historic Old Town Key West. Elegant artwork and furnishings are complemented by luxurious bedding and soothing earth tones. One- and two-bedroom oceanview suites have stellar views and separate living areas. In addition to the beach itself, there are also two outdoor pools, a full-service spa, and an outdoor restaurant. Nightly movies shown at the pool with free popcorn and snacks cater to families with kids.

1500 Reynolds St., Key West, FL 33040. © **866/397-6342** or 305/296-3535. Fax 305/296-3008. www. casamarinaresort.com. 311 units. Winter $249–$499 double, $349–$799 suite; off-season $149–$399 double, $249–$699 suite. AE, DC, MC, V. **Amenities:** Restaurant; bar; bike/scooter rental; concierge; nearby golf; fitness center; 2 pools; room service; spa; nearby tennis; watersports equipment/rentals. *In room:* A/C, TV, hair dryer, high-speed Internet, minibar.

Curry Mansion Inn ★★ 🏠   This charismatic inn is the former home of the island's first millionaire, a once-penniless Bahamian immigrant who made a fortune as a pirate. Owned today by Al and Edith Amsterdam, the Curry Mansion is now on the National Register of Historic Places, but you won't feel like you're staying in a museum—it's rather like a wonderfully warm home. Rooms are very sparsely decorated, with wicker furniture, four-poster beds, and pink walls—call it Key West minimalism meets Victorian. The dining room is reminiscent of a Victorian dollhouse, with elegant table settings and rich wood floors and furnishings. Every morning, there's a delicious European-style breakfast buffet; at night, cocktail parties are held. There's also a really nice patio, on which, from time to time, there's live entertainment.

511 Caroline St., Key West, FL 33040. © **800/253-3466** or 305/294-5349. Fax 305/294-4093. www. currymansion.com. 28 units. Winter $240–$300 double, $315–$365 suite; off-season $195–$235 double, $260–$285 suite. Rates include breakfast buffet. AE, DC, MC, V. No children 11 and under. **Amenities:** Dining room; bike rental; concierge; pool. *In room:* A/C, TV, minibar.

Hyatt Key West Resort & Marina ★

After an $11-million renovation, the Hyatt is now up to speed with other luxe resorts in the area. Ideally situated on the bay, the Hyatt features a waterfront pool, small beach area, and guest rooms with white porcelain tile floors, flatscreen TVs, and fabulous bathrooms. New spa cabanas allow for outdoor treatments, and a restaurant overlooking the water is great for dinner but spotty on breakfast service. Located right near Duval Street and next door to several lively bars, the Hyatt offers the best of both worlds when it comes to Key West relaxation—and partying. A new signature restaurant called SHOR American Seafood Grill serves great, well, seafood, and the spa is now using a new skin-care line, Amala, which is green-certified.

601 Front St., Key West, FL 33040. © **800/55-HYATT** (4-9288) or 305/809-1234. Fax 305/809-4050. www.keywest.hyatt.com. 118 units. Winter $485–$550 double; off-season $335–$450 double. AE, DC, DISC, MC, V. **Amenities:** Restaurant; bar; private sunbathing beach; fitness center; meeting and conference space; pool; private sailboat; spa; watersports equipment/rentals. *In room:* A/C, plasma TV, hair dryer, minibar, Wi-Fi.

Island City House Hotel ★★

The oldest running B&B in Key West, the Island City House consists of three separate buildings that share a common junglelike patio and pool. The first building is a historic three-story wooden structure with wraparound verandahs on every floor. The warmly outfitted interiors here include wood floors and many antiques. The tile bathrooms could use more counter space, but eccentricities are part of this hotel's charm. The unpainted wooden Cigar House has particularly large bedrooms, similar in ambience to those in the Island City House. The Arch House has newly renovated floors and features six airy Caribbean-style suites. Built of Dade County Pine, this house's cozy bedrooms are furnished in wicker and rattan, and come with small kitchens and bathrooms. A shaded brick courtyard and pretty pool are surrounded by lush gardens where, every morning, a delicious continental breakfast is served. *Note:* For those who have a fear or dislike of cats, there are several friendly "resident" felines who call Island City House home.

411 William St., Key West, FL 33040. © **800/634-8230** or 305/294-5702. Fax 305/294-1289. www. islandcityhouse.com. 24 units. Winter $230–$420 double; off-season $150–$300 double. Rates include breakfast. AE, DC, MC, V. **Amenities:** Babysitting; bike rental; concierge; access to nearby health club; outdoor heated pool. *In room:* A/C, TV, hair dryer, kitchen.

La Mer Hotel & Dewey House ★★★ 🎁

If I were to build a beach house, this is exactly what it would look like. And although it's technically one bed and breakfast, the La Mer Hotel is Victorian-style while the adjoining Dewey House is more quaint and cottagey. Between the two there are 19 rooms, each with a turn-of-the-19th-century feel but with modern amenities including granite wet bars, Wi-Fi, and luxurious linens that may have you lingering in the comfy beds for longer than you'd like. Especially when you look out from your balcony or private patio and check out the views of the ocean. Stunning. Every morning there's a delicious, deluxe continental breakfast of fresh breads, made-to-order waffles, fresh-squeezed juices, and more on the Dewey Terrace overlooking the beach that's shared with La Mer and Dewey House's sister hotel, the more party-hearty Southernmost on the Beach. To keep with the old-school theme, there's a daily afternoon tea service, also included in the rates, from 3:30 to 5:30pm. No need to make sure you stick your pinky up, though. As Old World and luxurious as it is here, it's not even close to being pretentious or stuffy.

506 South St., Key West, FL 33040. ℂ **800/354-4455** or 305/296-6577. Fax 305/294-8272. www. southernmostresorts.com. 19 units. Winter $249–$449 double; off-season $159–$299 double. Rates include continental breakfast, daily afternoon tea, and parking. AE, DISC, MC, V. **Amenities:** Restaurant; bar; beach and pool shared with Southernmost on the Beach; concierge. *In room:* A/C, TV, minifridge, hair dryer, free Wi-Fi.

Marquesa Hotel ★★★ 🎁 The exquisite Marquesa offers the charm of a small historic hotel coupled with the amenities of a large resort. It encompasses four buildings, two pools, and a three-stage waterfall that cascades into a lily pond. Two of the hotel's buildings are luxuriously restored Victorian homes outfitted with plush antiques and contemporary furniture. The rooms in the two newly constructed buildings are even more opulent; many have four-poster wrought-iron beds with bright floral spreads. The bathrooms in the new buildings are lush and spacious; those in the older buildings are also nice, but not nearly as huge and luxe. The decor is simple, elegant, and spotless. The hotel also boasts one of Key West's most elegant restaurants, Café Marquesa.

600 Fleming St. (at Simonton St.), Key West, FL 33040. ℂ **800/869-4631** or 305/292-1919. Fax 305/294-2121. www.marquesa.com. 27 units. Winter $330–$395 double, $495–$520 suite; off-season $220–$290 double, $270–$330 suite. AE, DC, MC, V. No children 11 and under. **Amenities:** Restaurant; bike rental; concierge; access to nearby health club; 2 outdoor pools (1 heated); limited room service. *In room:* A/C, TV, CD player, hair dryer, Internet access, minibar.

Parrot Key Resort ★★★ Parrot Key's waterfront Conch-style cottages, suites, and rooms are the epitome of beachy luxury and are the largest available in Key West. Accommodation options include deluxe king or double queen rooms, deluxe one- and two- bedroom suites, and luxury two- and three-bedroom guest cottages. Guest cottages feature gourmet kitchens and all rooms offer private patio, porch, or balcony, flatscreen TVs, premium cable service, and DVD/stereo systems. All rooms are smoke-free. Situated on 5 acres of award-winning tropical landscaping, the resort boasts four private pools (each in its own sculpture garden setting), private white-sand sunbathing terraces, and the poolside Café Blue and Tiki bar. Minutes from the action on Duval Street, Parrot Key is an idyllic retreat from the neighboring madness.

2801 N. Roosevelt Blvd., Key West, FL 33040. ℂ **305/809-2200.** Fax 305/292-3322. www.parrot keyresort.com. 104 units. Winter $349–$1,199 double; off-season $169–$799 double. AE, DC, DISC, MC, V. **Amenities:** Poolside cafe and Tiki bar; bike rental; concierge; nearby golf; fitness center; outdoor pools; spa services; nearby tennis; watersports equipment rental; free Wi-Fi property-wide. *In room:* A/C, TV, hair dryer.

Pier House Resort and Caribbean Spa ★ If you're looking for something a bit more intimate than the Reach Resort (see below), Pier House is an ideal choice. Its location—at the foot of Duval Street and just steps from Mallory Docks—is the envy of every hotel on the island. Set back from the busy street, on a short strip of private beach, this place is a welcome oasis of calm. The accommodations vary tremendously—no two rooms are alike—from simple business-style rooms to romantic quarters complete with whirlpool tubs. Although every unit has either a balcony or a patio, not all overlook the water. My favorites, in the two-story spa building, don't have any view at all. But what they lack in scenery, they make up for in opulence: Each well-appointed spa room has a sitting area and a huge Jacuzzi bathroom. In 2008, all rooms received a multimillion-dollar renovation that added new and modern furnishings and best of all, bathrooms were redesigned and enlarged, and feature fabulous glass showers and rain showerheads.

1 Duval St. (near Mallory Docks), Key West, FL 33040. © **800/327-8340** or 305/296-4600. Fax 305/296-9085. www.pierhouse.com. 142 units. Winter $309–$529 double, $479–$3,000 suite; off-season $229–$369 double, $389–$2,000 suite. AE, DC, MC, V. **Amenities:** 3 restaurants; 3 bars; babysitting; bike/moped rental; concierge; full-service fitness center and spa; 2 Jacuzzis; heated pool; limited room service; sauna; watersports equipment/rentals. In room: A/C, TV, hair dryer, Internet access, minibar.

The Reach Resort ★★★ Fresh from a $41-million renovation, the boutique-style Reach Resort features gingerbread balconies, tin roof accents, and shaded Spanish walkways characteristic of historic Key West. Newly refurbished guest rooms are large, with modernized decor and custom furnishings that are vibrant and crisp. Every room features comfortable sectional sofas and sliding glass doors that open onto balconies, some with ocean views. Sixty-eight boutique and 10 executive suites are also available. A new pool deck and 450-foot natural-sand beach are the perfect settings to enjoy a massive array of watersports, available right on the premises. The resort is also home to the Manhattan-based Strip House restaurant, which is as delicious as it is gorgeous. Unlike most area resorts which are small-ish, this one seems infinitely larger and, in many ways, worlds away from the rest of Key West.

1435 Simonton St., Key West, FL 33040. © **866/397-6427** or 305/296-5000 for reservations. Fax 305/296-3008. www.reachresort.com. 150 units. Winter $249–$499 double, $299–$549 suite; off-season $149–$399 double, $199–$449 suite. AE, DC, DISC, MC, V. **Amenities:** 2 restaurants; bar; bike rental; concierge; nearby golf; outdoor heated pool; room service; spa; nearby tennis; watersports equipment/rentals. In room: A/C, TV, minifridge, hair dryer, high-speed Internet; minibar.

Simonton Court ★★★ 👔 This is my favorite stay in Key West—too bad it's always booked. Once a cigar factory, Simonton Court features meticulously appointed restored historic cottages and suites amid sparkling pools and luxuriant private gardens. There are several options to choose from: bed-and-breakfast, cottages, guesthouse, mansion, and inn. Some cottages even have their own pools. There's no restaurant here, but the well-informed concierge will help you with reservations anywhere no matter what you crave. What I really crave, however, is a standing reservation here. People love the place so much, they book years in advance. Once you stay here, if you're lucky, you'll understand why.

320 Simonton St., Key West, FL 33040. © **800/944-2687** or 305/294-6386. Fax 305/293-8446. www.simontoncourt.com. 30 units. Winter $260–$400 double in mansion, $480–$515 cottage, $260–$400 inn, $330–$430 manor house, $260–$520 town house; off-season $160–$270 double in mansion, $360–$395 cottage, $160–$270 inn, $220–$320 manor house, $160–$400 town house. Rates include continental breakfast. AE, DISC, MC, V. **Amenities:** Concierge; 4 outdoor pools; Wi-Fi throughout the 2 acres. In room: A/C, TV/VCR/DVD, fridge, hair dryer.

Southernmost on the Beach ★★★ Revamped in 2008, this beachfront hotel—one of very few in Key West—offers 127 rooms, all with views of the Atlantic, a huge oceanfront pool, and lively pool bar. Eighty brand new luxury suites feature flatscreen TVs, iPod docking stations, sleek mahogany furniture, and blue and white decor made to resemble a yacht. Best part about this resort is its location directly on an actually sandy private beach. Grounds have been beautifully landscaped with lush gardens and palm trees. The open-air Southernmost Beach Café is a nice place for lunch or sunset dinner, but the poolside Tiki Bar is where most of the action is. Because of its impressive, beautiful beach Southernmost is the site of many weddings. In addition to its more subdued, romantic sister bed-and-breakfast La Mer Hotel & Dewey House, Southernmost on the Beach has another property across the street, also with a great pool scene, albeit not on the water—the **Southernmost Hotel in the USA,** 1319 Duval St. (© **800/354-4455**), where rates range from $159 to $299 in winter and $99 to $199 in summer.

508 South St., Key West, FL 33040. © **800/354-4455** or 305/295-6550. Fax 305/294-8272. www. southernmostresorts.com. 127 units. Winter $279–$475 double; off-season $159–$299 double. Rates include parking. AE, DC, DISC, MC, V. **Amenities:** Restaurant; bar; beach; bike rental; concierge; health club; pool; spa; watersports equipment rental. *In room:* A/C, TV, minifridge, hair dryer, free Wi-Fi.

Weatherstation Inn ★ 🛄

Originally built in 1912 as a weather station, this beautifully restored, meticulously maintained, Renaissance-style inn is just 2 blocks from Duval Street but seems worlds away. It's situated on the tropical grounds of the former Old Navy Yard, now an exclusive and private gated community. Presidents Truman, Eisenhower, and JFK all visited the station. Spacious and uncluttered, each guest room is uniquely furnished to complement the interior architecture: hardwood floors, tall sash windows, and high ceilings. The large, modern bathrooms are especially appealing. The staff is both friendly and accommodating.

57 Front St., Key West, FL 33040. © **800/815-2707** or 305/294-7277. Fax 305/294-0544. www.weatherstationinn.com. 8 units. Winter $235–$335 double; off-season $180–$245 double. Rates include continental breakfast. AE, DISC, MC, V. **Amenities:** Concierge; outdoor pool. *In room:* A/C, TV/VCR, hair dryer.

MODERATE

Ambrosia Key West ★★ 🛄

Despite countless visits each year to the tiny island of Key West, I discover yet another hidden treasure every time I go back. Ambrosia is one of them, a private compound set on 2 lush acres just a block from Duval Street. Three lagoon-style pools, suites, town houses, and a cottage are spread around the grounds. Town houses have living rooms, kitchens, and spiral staircases leading to master suites with vaulted ceilings and private decks. The cottage, overlooking a dip pool, is a perfect family retreat, with two bedrooms, two bathrooms, a living room, and a kitchen. All rooms, several which recently received major renovations, have private entrances, most with French doors opening onto a variety of intimate outdoor spaces, including private verandahs, patios, and gardens with sculptures, fountains, and pools. The breakfast buffet rocks, with eggs, biscuits, gravy, bacon, sausage, and pretty much anything you'd want. Fantastic service, bolstered by the philosophy that it's better to have high occupancy than high rates, explains why Ambrosia has a 90% year-round occupancy—a record in seasonal Key West.

622 Fleming St., Key West, FL 33040. © **800/535-9838** or 305/296-9838. Fax 305/296-2425. www. ambrosiakeywest.com. 20 units. Winter $279–$609 suite; off-season $179–$389 suite. Rates include breakfast buffet. AE, DISC, MC, V. Off- and on-street parking. Pets accepted. **Amenities:** 3 outdoor heated pools. *In room:* A/C, TV, CD player, fridge, hair dryer, kitchen (in some), microwave, Wi-Fi.

Doubletree Grand Key Resort ★

If you don't mind staying on the quiet "other" side of the island, a 10-minute cab ride away from Duval Street, the Doubletree is a good choice, not to mention an excellent value. An ecologically conscious resort, the pet-friendly hotel has been renovated with eco-sensitive materials as well as an interior created to conserve energy, reduce waste, and preserve the area's natural resources.

Rooms are clean and comfortable, with some looking onto the spacious pool area, which is surrounded by an unsightly empty lot of mangroves and marshes. The resort provides complimentary high-speed Internet access, both wired and wireless.

3990 S. Roosevelt Blvd., Key West, FL 33040. © **888/310-1540** or 305/293-1818. Fax 305/296-6962. www.doubletreekeywest.com. 216 units, with 24 suites. Winter $255–$279 double, $295–$495 suite; off-season $149–$199 double, $239–$379 suite. AE, DISC, MC, V. Valet or self-parking $10. **Amenities:** Restaurant; Tiki bar; lounge; concierge; gym; pool; limited room service. *In room:* A/C, TV, minifridge, hair dryer, Internet access.

Eden House ★ 👜 Owned and operated by Mike Eden for over 34 years, Eden House is a fabulous spot for everyone from budget travelers to those seeking a more private retreat. With a variety of rooms ranging from semiprivate with shared bathrooms to suites with private Jacuzzi, full kitchen, washer, dryer, porch, and private entrance, Eden House does have something for everyone. A free happy hour from 4 to 5pm daily is a great way to meet people, grab a drink and relax amidst the beautifully landscaped grounds complete with waterfalls and porch swings. For those not in the social mood, steal away to a hammock—there are several throughout the property. Other amenities include pool, Jacuzzi, sundeck, and grill area. Owner Eden is hilarious and if you have a chance, chat with him. As he says, "Key West is a bowl of granola. What's not fruits and nuts, is flakes."

1015 Fleming St., Key West, FL 33040. © **800/533-5397** or 305/296-6868. Fax 305/294-1221. www.edenhouse.com. 40 units. Winter $155–$195 semiprivate, $190–$230 private, $230–$330 deluxe, $335–$475 apartment or conch house; off-season $155–$180 semiprivate, $125–$150 private, $175–$240 deluxe, $255–$300 apartment or conch house. MC, V. **Amenities:** Restaurant; barbecue grills; hot tub; garden pool; Wi-Fi. *In room:* A/C, TV/VCR, fridge, hair dryer.

La Pensione ★★ This classic B&B, set in a stunning 1891 home, is a total charmer. The comfortable rooms all have air-conditioning, ceiling fans, and king-size beds. Many also have French doors opening onto spacious verandahs. Although the rooms have no TVs, the distractions of Duval Street, only steps away, should keep you adequately occupied. Breakfast, which includes Belgian waffles, fresh fruit, and a variety of breads or muffins, can be taken on the wraparound porch or at the communal dining table. Recent guests, however, have informed us that service here is not as friendly as it used to be and that the inn's location on U.S. 1 isn't so hot when it comes to the noise and traffic levels.

809 Truman Ave. (btw. Windsor and Margaret sts.), Key West, FL 33040. © **800/893-1193** or 305/292-9923. Fax 305/296-6509. www.lapensione.com. 9 units. Winter $168–$328 double; off-season $118–$168 double. Rates include breakfast. Discount of 10% for readers who mention this book. AE, DC, DISC, MC, V. No children. **Amenities:** Bike rental; outdoor pool; Wi-Fi. *In room:* A/C.

Orchid Key Inn ★ What happens to an old-school motor lodge located smack in the middle of Duval Street? It becomes a new-school, trendy motor lodge complete with wine bar and 24 modern, albeit tiny, rooms. And although it's right in the middle of the action, the Orchid Key Inn is surprisingly a quiet and peaceful place. I actually stayed in the very first room right on Duval and heard hardly any noise. Paths lead you through lush tropical landscapes which surround the rooms and suites. Tranquil waterfalls and water features surround the sundeck, heated pool, and spa, all which are hidden from the main drag. Free daily breakfast and sunset happy hours make it a great place for socializing or just getting your day or party started.

1004 Duval St., Key West, FL 33040. © **800/845-8384** or 305/296-9915. Fax 305-292-4886. www. orchidkey.com. 24 units. Winter $189–$289 king deluxe, $209–$309 1-bedroom suite; off-season $119–$169 king deluxe, $149–$209 1-bedroom suite. Rates include continental breakfast and happy hour. AE, DISC, MC, V. Pets allowed with advance arrangements. **Amenities:** Bar; concierge; Jacuzzi; heated pool. *In room:* A/C, HDTV, hair dryer, MP3 docking station, Wi-Fi.

Seascape ★   This romantic retreat located on a quiet street behind the Hemingway House and within walking distance to the water and the action was built from native pine in the Bahamas in the 1840s and transported by ship to Key West where it was rebuilt in 1889. Fast-forward to 2010 and you have a splendidly renovated, tropical-style inn with turn-of-the-19th-century charm. Rooms are decorated in colorful, tropical decor and have private baths. Most have French doors that open out to a heated pool and Jacuzzi, upstairs sundeck, or lush gardens and courtyard where guests indulge in a delicious champagne continental breakfast. The two-story Havana Suite has a private entrance as well as a kitchenette. A complimentary wine hour takes place nightly.

420 Olivia St., Key West, FL 33040. © **888/765-6438** or 305296-7776. Fax 305/296-6283. www. seascapetropicalinn.com. 5 units. Winter $154–$214 double, $204–$224 suite; off-season $129–$149 double, $169 suite. Rates include champagne breakfast and wine hour. AE, DISC, MC, V. **Amenities:** Jacuzzi; pool. *In room:* A/C, TV, hair dryer, Internet access.

Southernmost Point Guest House ★★ 🛍️ 😊   One of the few inns that actually welcomes children and pets, this romantic guesthouse is a real find. The antiseptically clean rooms are not as fancy as the house's ornate 1885 exterior, but each is unique and includes some combination of basic beds and a hodgepodge of furnishings, such as futon couches and high-back wicker chairs. Room no. 5 is best, with a private porch, ocean view, and windows that let in lots of light. Every unit comes with fresh flowers, wine, and a full decanter of sherry. Mona Santiago, the kind, laid-back owner, provides chairs and towels for the beach, which is just a block away. Guests can help themselves to free wine as they soak in the 14-seat hot tub. Kids will enjoy the backyard swings and the pet rabbits.

1327 Duval St., Key West, FL 33040. © **305/294-0715.** Fax 305/296-0641. www.southernmostpoint. com. 6 units. Winter $125–$200 double, $260–$285 suite; off-season $75–$120 double, $165–$175 suite. Rates include breakfast. AE, MC, V. Pets accepted ($5 in summer, $10 in winter). **Amenities:** Barbecue grills; hot tub; garden pool; Wi-Fi. *In room:* A/C, TV/VCR, fridge, hair dryer.

Westwinds Inn ★   A close second to staying in your own private 19th-century, tin-roofed clapboard house is this tranquil inn, just 4 blocks from Duval Street in the historic seaport district. And although it looks 19th century, it's completely wired into the 21st with wireless Internet and HDTV. Lush landscaping keeps the place extremely private and secluded; at times, you'll feel as if you're alone. Two pools, one heated in winter, are offset by alcoves, fountains, and the well-maintained whitewashed inn, which is actually composed of five separate buildings. Rooms are Key West comfortable, with private bathrooms, wicker furnishings, and fans. All rooms are nonsmoking.

914 Eaton St., Key West, FL 33040. © **800/788-4150** or 305/296-4440. Fax 305/293-0931. www. westwindskeywest.com. 22 units. Winter $185–$220 double, $225–$275 suite; off-season $90–$180 double, $140–$195 suite. Rates include continental breakfast. DISC, MC, V. No children 11 and under. **Amenities:** Bike rental; 2 pools (1 heated); Wi-Fi. *In room:* A/C, TV (in some), kitchenette (in some).

INEXPENSIVE

Angelina Guest House ★★   This former bordello and gambling-hall-turned-youth-hostel-type guesthouse is one of the cheapest in town—and it's conveniently located near a hot hippie restaurant called Blue Heaven (p. 322). Though the neighborhood is definitely urban, it's generally safe and full of character. Accommodations are furnished uniquely in a modest style. Four rooms have private bathrooms. A gorgeous lagoon-style heated pool, with waterfall and tropical landscaping, is an excellent addition. Even better are the poolside hammocks—get out there early, as they go quickly! Even though the Angelina is sparse (perfect for bohemian types who don't mind a little grit), it's a great place to crash if you're traveling on the cheap.

302 Angela St. (at Thomas St.), Key West, FL 33040. © **888/303-4480** or 305/294-4480. Fax 305/272-0681. www.angelinaguesthouse.com. 13 units. Winter $99–$199 double; off-season $69–$139 double. Rates include continental breakfast. DISC, MC, V. **Amenities:** Concierge; outdoor heated pool. *In room:* A/C, no phone.

The Grand Guesthouse ★★ 🎒   Don't expect cabbies or locals to know about this well-kept secret, located in a modest residential section of Old Town, about 5 blocks from Duval Street. It's got almost everything you could want, including a very moderate price tag. Proprietors Jim Brown, Jeffrey Daubman, and Derek Karevicius provide any and all services for their appreciative guests. All units have private bathrooms, air-conditioning, and private entrances. The best deal is room no. 2; it's small and lacks a closet, but it has a porch and the most privacy. Suites are a real steal, too: The large two-room units come with kitchenettes. This place is undoubtedly the best bargain in town.

1116 Grinnell St. (btw. Virginia and Catherine sts.), Key West, FL 33040. © **888/947-2630** or 305/294-0590. Fax 305/294-0477. www.grandkeywest.com. 10 units. Winter $168–$208 double, $228–$268 suite; off-season $98–$148 double, $128–$188 suite. Rates include expanded continental breakfast. DISC, MC, V. Free parking. **Amenities:** Bike/scooter rental; full concierge. *In room:* A/C, TV, fridge, Wi-Fi.

Key West International Hostel & Seashell Motel   This well-run hostel is a 3-minute walk to the beach and Old Town. Very busy with European backpackers, it's a great place to meet people. The dorm rooms are dark, grimy, and sparse, but livable if you're desperate for a cheap stay. There are all-male, all-female, and co-ed dorm rooms for couples. The higher priced private motel rooms are a good deal, especially those equipped with kitchens. Amenities include a pool table under a Tiki roof; bike rentals; cheap food at breakfast, lunch, and dinner; and discounted prices for snorkeling, diving, and sunset cruises. There's also free wireless Internet access throughout the property.

718 South St., Key West, FL 33040. © **800/51-HOSTEL** (514-6783) or 305/296-5719. Fax 305/296-0672. www.keywesthostel.com. 102 units, with 92 dorm beds and 10 motel rooms. Year-round $39 dorm room. Winter $75–$105 motel room; off-season $55–$85 motel room. MC, V. Free parking. **Amenities:** Bike rental; kitchen. *In room:* Motel rooms have A/C, TV, fridge, hair dryer; dorm rooms have A/C only.

Where to Dine

With its share of the usual drive-through fast-food franchises—mostly up on Roosevelt Boulevard—and Duval Street succumbing to the lure of a Hard Rock Cafe and Starbucks, you might be surprised to learn that, over the years, an upscale and high-quality dining scene has begun to thrive in Key West. Just wander Old Town or the newly spruced-up Bahama Village and browse menus after you've exhausted my list of picks below.

If you're staying in a condominium or efficiency, you may want to stock your fridge with groceries, beer, wine, and snacks from the area's oldest grocer, **Fausto's Food Palace.** Open since 1926, Fausto's has two locations: 1105 White St. and 522 Fleming St. The Fleming Street location will deliver with a $25-minimum order (© **305/294-5221** or 305/296-5663).

VERY EXPENSIVE

Café Marquesa ★★★ CONTEMPORARY AMERICAN If you're looking for fabulous, upscale dining (and service) in Key West, this is the place. The intimate, 50-seat restaurant is something to look at, but it's really the food that you'll want to admire. Specialties include macadamia-crusted yellowtail snapper, prosciutto-wrapped black Angus filet, and roast duck breast with red curry coconut sauce. If you're looking to splurge, this is the place.

In the Marquesa Hotel, 600 Fleming St. © **305/292-1919.** Reservations highly recommended. Main courses $21–$39. AE, DC, MC, V. Summer daily 7–11pm; winter daily 6–11pm.

Hot Tin Roof ★★★ FUSION SEAFOOD Ever hear of conch fusion cuisine? Neither did I, until I experienced it firsthand at Hot Tin Roof, Ocean Key Resort's chichi restaurant which transforms South American, Asian, French, and Keys cuisine into an experience unlike any other in this part of the world. The vibrant 3,000-square-foot space features both indoor and outdoor deck seating overlooking the harbor. Live jazz/fusion adds to the stunning environment—it's the epitome of casual elegance. Signature dishes include an irresistible lobster with garlic, chilies, and Cuban mojo sauce; broiled yellowtail snapper with papaya pink shrimp salsa and poppyseed vinaigrette; and chocolate-lava cake that makes this tin roof very hot, to say the least, especially for Key West. If you like truffles, try the polenta fries with truffle dip. It's divine. Last time I ate here, Meryl Streep was sitting next to me with her family, looking as impressed as she was impressive.

In the Ocean Key Resort, 0 Duval St. © **305/296-7701.** Reservations highly recommended. Main courses $20–$40. AE, DC, MC, V. Daily 7:30–11am and 5–10pm.

Louie's Backyard ★★ CARIBBEAN Nestled amid blooming bougainvillea on a lush slice of the Gulf, Louie's remains one of the most romantic restaurants on earth. It's off the beaten path, which makes it even more romantic. Famed chef Norman Van Aken, of Norman's in Miami, brought his talents farther south and started what has become one of the finest dining spots in the Keys. As a result, this is one of the hardest places to score a reservation: Either call way in advance or hope that your hotel concierge has some pull. Try the sensational oyster, sweet corn, and shiitake mushroom pot pie for starters and for a main course, the grilled Berkshire pork chop with beer-braised cabbage and sweet potatoes is to die for. After dinner, sit at the dockside bar and watch the waves crash, almost touching your feet, while enjoying a cocktail at sunset. You can't go wrong with the fresh catch of the day, or any seafood dish, for that matter. The weekend brunches are also great. And a ritual for many in Key West is sunset cocktails at the oceanfront Tiki bar. If you can't stay for dinner, go for lunch; this is one dining experience you won't want to miss. If you're not in the mood for a full-blown meal, consider the restaurant's stellar Upper Deck Lounge, serving tapas including focaccia, bruschetta, carpaccio, roasted clams, flaming Ouzo shrimp, grilled Mongolian barbecued lamb ribs, a daily assortment of cheeses, and pizzas Tuesday through Saturday from 5 to 10pm.

700 Waddell Ave. ☎ **305/294-1061.** www.louiesbackyard.com. Reservations highly recommended. Main courses $30–$40; lunch $10–$20; tapas $5–$15. AE, DC, MC, V. Daily 11:30am–3pm and 6–10:30pm.

Tavern N Town ★ FLORIBBEAN Tavern and Town are two separate eateries within a bi-level space—superstar chef Norman Van Aken, who left here (but left some of his Floribbean influences) in 2008, called it a hyphenated restaurant, with Tavern featuring tapas and small plates and Town a more world-class dining experience, but both equally good. An open theater kitchen shows action, but the real show is on your plate. For starters, consider the BBQ Berkshire pork belly with brioche, corn salsa, arugula, and a BBQ demi sherry "mist." For entrees, the black grouper in a miso ginger or pan-cooked filet of yellowtail are a far cry from Duval Street's chicken fingers and conch fritters. Although it's not as good as when Van Aken was here, it's still worth a splurge.

In the Beachside Resort, 3841 N. Roosevelt Blvd. ☎ **305/296-8100.** Reservations highly recommended. Main courses $19–$32. AE, DC, MC, V. Tavern daily 8am–10:30pm. Town daily 6–11pm.

EXPENSIVE

Antonia's ★★ REGIONAL ITALIAN The food is great, but the atmosphere a bit fussy for Key West. If you don't have a reservation in season, don't even bother. Still, if you don't mind paying high prices for dishes that go for much less elsewhere, try this old favorite. From the perfectly seasoned homemade focaccia to an exemplary crème brûlée, this elegant little standout is amazingly consistent. The menu includes a small selection of classics, linguine with shrimp, delicious, pillowy gnocchi, and *zuppa di pesce* (fish soup). And don't miss the outstanding warm goat cheese soufflé served with pan-seared asparagus, baby green beans, carrots, and Belgian endive over a roasted tomato vinaigrette. You can't go wrong with any of the handmade pastas. And the owners, Antonia Berto and Phillip Smith, travel to Italy every year to research recipes, so you can be sure you're getting an authentic taste of Italy in small-town Key West.

615 Duval St. ☎ **305/294-6565.** Fax 305/294-3888. www.antoniaskeywest.com. Reservations suggested. Main courses $20–$30; pastas $15–$30. AE, DC, MC, V. Daily 6–11pm.

Bagatelle ★★ SEAFOOD/TROPICAL Reserve a seat at the elegant second-floor verandah overlooking Duval Street's mayhem. From the calm above, you may want to start your meal with the zingy conch ceviche or the wasabi tuna pizza with carpaccio-style tuna on crisp flat bread with avocado, arugula, wasabi oil, and ponzu. For main courses, the honey fried lobster tail is something you don't see on many menus, a tempura-battered 7-ounce lobster served with honey butter and wasabi mash that's exceptional. Caribbean faves included Jamaican jerk shrimp skewers and a delicious Jamaican sweet curry chicken. The whole fried snapper is also excellent, but we prefer it up the block at Nine One Five.

115 Duval St. ☎ **305/296-6609.** www.bagatellekeywest.com. Reservations recommended. Main courses $18–$55. AE, DISC, MC, V. Sun–Thurs 11:30am–10pm; Fri–Sat 11:30am–11pm.

La Trattoria ★ ITALIAN Have a true Italian feast in a relaxed atmosphere. Each dish here is prepared and presented according to old Italian tradition. Try the delicious bread-crumb-stuffed mushroom caps; they're firm yet tender. The stuffed eggplant with ricotta and roasted peppers is light and flavorful. Or have the seafood salad of shrimp, calamari, and mussels, which is fish-market fresh and tasty. The pasta dishes are also great—go for the penne Venezia, with mushrooms, sun-dried tomatoes, and crabmeat. For dessert, don't skip the homemade tiramisu; it's light yet full-flavored. The dining room is spacious but still intimate, and the waiters are friendly. Before you leave, visit Virgilio's, the restaurant's resplendent indoor/outdoor cocktail lounge with live jazz until 2am.

524 Duval St. ☎ **305/296-1075.** www.latrattoria.us. Main courses $14–$40. AE, DC, DISC, MC, V. Daily 5:30–11pm.

Mangoes ★★★ FLORIBBEAN   This restaurant's large brick patio, shaded by overgrown banyan trees, is so alluring to passersby that it's packed almost every night of the week. Many people don't realize how pricey the meals can be here because, upon first glance, it looks like a casual Duval Street cafe. Appetizers include grilled shrimp cocktail with spicy mango chutney. Crispy curried chicken and local snapper with passion-fruit sauce are typical among the entrees, but the garlic and lime pinks—a half-pound of Key West pink shrimp seasoned and grilled with a roasted garlic and Key lime glaze—is the menu's best offering by far. Even though it's right on touristy Duval Street, Mangoes enjoys a good reputation among locals and stands out from the rest of the places offering greasy bar fare. For a cool, local, loungey scene, check out the speakeasy-esque back bar inside.

700 Duval St. (at Angela St.). ☎ **305/292-4606.** Reservations recommended for parties of 6 or more. Main courses $15–$30; pizzas $10–$15; lunch $7–$18. AE, DC, DISC, MC, V. Daily 11am–midnight; pizza until 1am.

Michael's ★★★ 🍴 STEAKHOUSE   Tucked away in a residential neighborhood, Michael's is a meaty oasis in a big sea of fish. With steaks flown in daily from Chicago, this is *the* steakhouse for when you're craving meat, from New York strip to porterhouse. Unlike most steakhouses, Michael's exudes a relaxed, tropical ambience with a fabulous indoor/outdoor setting that's romantic but not stuffy. A fantastic fondue menu makes for a tasty snack or even a meal, complemented by an excellent, reasonably priced wine list. Sure, Michael's is on the pricier side, but it's not every day that you can enjoy slabs of beef from Chicago in a warm, tropical setting.

532 Margaret St. ☎ **305/295-1300.** www.michaelskeywest.com. Reservations recommended. Main courses $15–$40. AE, DC, DISC, MC, V. Daily 5–11pm.

Nine One Five ★★★ ECLECTIC   Housed in a restored Victorian mansion, Nine One Five is a cozy, romantic restaurant with such good food that it was selected to host a six-course dinner at the James Beard House in NYC. Two times. The cuisine is simple yet flavorful with everything from Devils on Horseback, bacon-wrapped dates stuffed with garlic and served with a soy ginger dipping sauce, to duck liver pâté. A tapas platter can be enjoyed as appetizer or as a main course up in the restaurant's loft lounge area. For main courses I highly suggest the Thai whole fish with sizzling chili garlic sauce and steamed basmati rice or the duck mole, a pan-seared duck breast and leg of confit with Oaxacan mole sauce and roasted sweet potatoes. Service is seamless and attentive, although if you sit up on the quaint second floor porch you may be there for a while. But that's okay, because this is the kind of place in which you want to linger.

915 Duval St. ☎ **305/296-0669.** www.915duval.com. Reservations recommended. Main courses $18–$34. AE, DISC, MC, V. Mon–Sat noon–3pm; daily 6–11pm; upstairs lounge daily until 2am.

Seven Fish ★★★ 🍴 SEAFOOD   "Simple, good food" is Seven Fish's motto, but this hidden little secret is much more than simple. One of the most popular restaurants with locals, Seven Fish is a chic seafood spot serving some of the best fish dishes on the island. Yellowtail snapper with Thai curry sauce, mahimahi with Dijon cracked pepper sauce, and gnocchi with blue cheese and sautéed fish are among the dishes to choose from. For dessert, do not miss the Key lime cake over tart lime curd with fresh berries.

632 Olivia St. ☎ **305/296-2777.** www.7fish.com. Reservations recommended. Main courses $12–$29. AE, MC, V. Wed–Mon 6–10pm.

MODERATE

Alonzo's Oyster Bar ★ SEAFOOD

Alonzo's serves good seafood in a casual setting. It's on the ground floor of the A&B Lobster House, at the end of Front Street in the marina; if you want to dress up, go upstairs for the "fine dining." To start your meal, try the steamed beer shrimp—tantalizingly fresh jumbo shrimp in a sauce of garlic, Old Bay seasoning, beer, and cayenne pepper. A house specialty is white-clam chili, a delicious mix of tender clams, white beans, and potatoes served with a dollop of sour cream. The staff is cheerful and informative, and the service is very good.

700 Front St. ☎ **305/294-5880.** www.alonzosoysterbar.com. Main courses $15–$25. MC, V. Daily 11am–11pm.

Ambrosia ★ SUSHI

Trendy sushi spot Ambrosia, housed in the Santa Maria condo-turned-hotel, features some of the freshest fish in town. Chef-owner Masa offers you expertly prepared sushi—if you're a fan of tuna, try his *toro* (tuna belly). It's fabulous. Specialty rolls include the Key West, a mix of stone crab, avocado, and smelt roe and the Florida, tempura lobsters wrapped in pink soybean protein. Ambrosia is also a vegetarian hot spot, with excellent tofu dishes.

1401 Simonton St. ☎ **305/293-0304.** Sushi $4–$15. AE, DISC, MC, V. Daily 11am–11pm.

Banana Café ★★★ 🍴 FRENCH

Banana Café benefits from a French-country-cafe look and feel. The upscale local eatery discovered by savvy visitors on the less-congested end of Duval Street has retained its loyal clientele with affordable prices and delightful, light preparations. The crepes are legendary on the island, for breakfast or lunch; the fresh ingredients and French-themed menu bring daytime diners back for the casual, classy, tropical-influenced dinner menu. There's live jazz every Thursday night.

1211 Duval St. ☎ **305/294-7227.** Main courses $6–$15; breakfast and lunch $3–$10. AE, DC, MC, V. Daily 8am–11pm.

Blue Heaven ★★ 🍴 SEAFOOD/AMERICAN/NATURAL

This hippie-run restaurant has become the place to be in Key West—and with good reason. Be prepared to wait in line. The food here is some of the best in town—especially at breakfast, which features homemade granola, tropical-fruit pancakes (owner Richard often makes his pancakes with beer), and seafood Benedict. Dinners are just as good and run the gamut from fresh-caught fish and Jamaican jerk chicken to curried soups and vegetarian stews. Some people are put off by the dirt floors and roaming cats and birds, but frankly, it adds to the charm. The building used to be a bordello, where Hemingway was said to hang out watching cockfights. It's still lively here, but not *that* lively!

305 Petronia St. ☎ **305/296-8666.** http://blueheavenkw.homestead.com/Blue_Heaven_Restaurant Key_West.html. Main courses $10–$36; lunch $6–$15; breakfast $5–$15. DISC, MC, V. Daily 8–11:30am, noon–3pm, and 6–10:30pm, Sun brunch 8am–1pm. Closed mid-Sept to early Oct.

Mangia, Mangia ★ 🍷 ITALIAN/AMERICAN   Locals appreciate that they can get good, inexpensive food here in a town filled with tourist traps. Off the beaten track, this great Chicago-style pasta place has some of the best Italian food in the Keys. The family-run restaurant serves superb homemade pastas of every description, including one of the tastiest marinara sauces around. The simple grilled chicken breast brushed with olive oil and sprinkled with pepper is another good choice. You wouldn't know it from the front, but there's a fantastic little patio dotted with twinkling pepper lights and lots of plants. While you wait for your table, relax out back with a glass of wine— this place is said to have the largest selection in the Keys—or homemade beer.

900 Southard St. (at Margaret St.). ℂ **305/294-2469.** Reservations not accepted. Main courses $10–$30. AE, MC, V. Daily 5:30–10pm.

Pepe's ★ 👔 AMERICAN   This old dive has been serving good, basic food for nearly a century. Steaks and Apalachicola Bay oysters are the big draws for regulars, who appreciate the rustic barroom setting and historical photos on the walls. Look for original scenes of Key West in 1909, when Pepe's first opened. If the weather is nice, choose a seat on the patio under a stunning mahogany tree. Burgers, fish sandwiches, and standard chili satisfy hearty eaters. Buttery sautéed mushrooms and rich mashed potatoes are the best comfort foods in Key West. There's always a wait, so stop by early for breakfast, when you can get old-fashioned chipped beef on toast and all the usual egg dishes. In the evening, reasonably priced cocktails are served on the deck.

806 Caroline St. (btw. Margaret and Williams sts.). ℂ **305/294-7192.** www.pepescafe.net. Main courses $16–$30; breakfast $3–$17; lunch $3–$18. DISC, MC, V. Daily 6:30am–10:30pm.

Sarabeth's ★★ 👔 AMERICAN   An offshoot of the popular New York City breakfast hot spot, Sarabeth's brings a much-needed shot of cosmopolitan comfort food to Key West in the form of delicious breakfasts with Sarabeth's signature home-made jams and jellies. Choose from buttermilk to lemon ricotta pancakes or almond-crusted cinnamon French toast. For lunch, the traditional Caesar salad, burger, or Key West pinks shrimp roll with avocado are all excellent choices. Dinner is simple, but savory, with top-notch dishes from chicken potpie and meatloaf to a divine green-chili-pepper macaroni with three cheeses or meaty shrimp-and-crabmeat cakes. The dining room is cozy and intimate, and it feels like you're eating in some-one's house; a few tables are on a small outdoor patio.

530 Simonton St. ℂ **305/293-8181.** www.sarabethskeywest.com. Main courses $9–$20; breakfast $6–$10; lunch $6–$14. MC, V. Mon 8am–3pm; Wed–Sun 8am–3pm and 6–10pm.

Turtle Kraals Wildlife Grill ★ 👔 ☺ BBQ/SEAFOOD   You'll join lots of locals in this out-of-the-way converted warehouse with indoor and dockside seating, which serves innovative seafood at great prices. Try the twin lobster tails stuffed with mango and crabmeat, stone crabs when in season (Oct–May), or any of the big quesadillas or fajitas. If you're not in the mood for seafood, there's also a BBQ menu created by an award winning pit master from Chicago who presides over an on-premise smoker on which ribs, pork butts, beef brisket, and chicken are slow-smoked for up to 14 hours. Kids will like the wildlife exhibits, the turtle cannery, and the very cheesy menu. Blues bands play most nights and for drinks, the restaurant's roof deck, the Tower Bar, has fabulous views of the marina.

213 Margaret St. (at Caroline St.). ℂ **305/294-2640.** www.turtlekraals.com. Main courses $10–$23. DISC, MC, V. Mon–Thurs 11am–10:30pm; Fri–Sat 11am–11pm; Sun noon–10:30pm. Bar closes at midnight.

White Street Bistro ★★★ 🏚FRENCH   Located on the edge of Old Town Key West, White Street Bistro is one of Key West's best kept secrets. Featuring an exceptionally creative menu and stellar ambience with an intimate dining room and stunning and secluded garden, White Street Bistro is a place you'll want to linger in, especially in the garden or at the indoor zinc-topped bar reminiscent of an elegant 19th-century watering hole. The menu changes often and features moderate prices. Among the specialties, chicken liver pâté, shrimp ceviche, roast lemon chicken with potatoes and vegetables, and a South of France–style pizza with caramelized onions, garlic, and mozzarella that's out of this world. Desserts are also great, including tarte tartin and chocolate mousse, but I especially love the option of ordering a cheese plate with dates and almonds and just hanging out in the garden. Local artists display their works here and musicians perform on certain nights.

1019 White St. ✆ **305/294-1943.** Main courses $9–$12; small plates, salads, and sandwiches $5–$11. AE, DC, MC, V. Mon–Fri 11:30am–2:30pm, Mon–Sat 5:30–9pm.

INEXPENSIVE

Hogfish Bar & Grill ★ 🏚SEAFOOD   A ramshackle, rough-and-tumble seafood bar and grill on Safe Harbor in "downtown" Stock Island (there's no town, just fisheries, boats, and artists and craftsmen working out of shacks and trailers), Hogfish is a popular spot for its namesake sandwich. Similar to grouper, hogfish is a delicious, rare fish with a scallop-like flavor and the sandwich they make out of it here, served on Cuban bread, is so popular it's usually sold out if you don't get there by noon. Other fish sandwiches are available, but it's the "world famous killer hogfish sandwich" that you want to come here for. So get here early. Key West pink shrimp are aplenty here, so peel and eat is another popular pastime while you're waiting for your hogfish. Live music and a lively, salty, bar scene created by locals and tourists alike make Hogfish a quintessential Key West experience. Kids especially like feeding the fish in the harbor.

6810 Front St., Stock Island ✆ **305/293-4041.** www.hogfishbar.com. Main courses $10–$19. AE, DISC, MC, V. Daily 11am–10pm. Take U.S. 1 N. out of Key West and across the Cow Key Channel Bridge. At the third stoplight, bear to the right and onto MacDonald Ave. Follow this for approximately 1 mile and make a right on 4th Ave. (across from Boyd's Campground). Take your next left on Front St. and drive almost to the end—you'll see the Hogfish Bar and Grill on the right.

Island Dogs Bar ★ AMERICAN   This islandy, Tommy Bahama–esque bar is a cool spot to throw back a few while catching a game or a live band. But more importantly is the fare—not your typical bar fare, but delicious burgers, chicken fingers, chicken wings, and, well, you get the picture. Sit at the bar or at one of the few outdoor tables ideally placed for watching the crowds stumble—literally—off Duval Street.

505 Front St. ✆ **305/295-0501.** Main courses $5–$10. AE, DISC, MC, V. Daily 11am–2am.

Upper Crust Pizza ★★ PIZZA   There's nothing better after a day or night of drinking rum runners than chasing them down with a slice or three of this heavenly pizza. The owner hails from Boston and won't tell us his secret to the perfectly crisp, garlicky crust, but as long as he keeps up the good work, we won't bother him for it. All sorts of varieties, from cheese to spinach with goat cheese, are available until the wee hours of the night.

611 Duval St. ✆ **305/293-8890.** www.uppercrustkeywest.com. Pizza $5–$8 slice, $13–$18 pie. AE, DISC, MC, V. Daily 11am–2am.

Key West After Dark

Duval Street is the Bourbon Street of Florida. Amid the T-shirt shops and clothing boutiques, you'll find bar after bar serving neon-colored frozen drinks to revelers who bounce from bar to bar from noon until dawn. Bands and crowds vary from night to night and season to season. Your best bet is to start at Truman Avenue and head up Duval to check them out for yourself. Cover charges are rare, except in gay clubs (see "The Gay Scene," below), so stop into a dozen and see which you like. For the most part, Key West is a late-night town, and bars and clubs don't close until around 3 or 4am.

Captain Tony's Saloon   Just around the corner from Duval's beaten path, this smoky old bar is about as authentic as you'll find. It comes complete with old-time regulars who remember the island before cruise ships docked here; they say Hemingway drank, caroused, and even wrote here. The late owner, Captain Tony Tarracino, was a former controversial Key West mayor—immortalized in Jimmy Buffett's "Last Mango in Paris." 428 Greene St. © **305/294-1838.** www.capttonyssaloon. com.

Cowboy Bill's Honky Tonk Saloon   ["]The Southernmost Country Bar in the USA" features indoor and outdoor bars, pool, darts, video games, 26 TVs, line dancing, live music, and the only mechanical bull in the Keys that gets kicking every Tuesday through Saturday from 10pm until 2am with a special "sexy" bull-riding competition every Wednesday at 11:30pm. Participate or watch but do know that there are webcams catching all the action. And after several dollar Pabst Blue Ribbons, trust me, there's a lot of action going on here. 610½ Duval St. © **305/295-8219.** www.cowboybillskw.com.

Durty Harry's   This large complex features live rock bands almost every night. You can wander to one of the many outdoor bars or head to Upstairs at Rick's, an indoor/outdoor dance club that gets going late. For racy singles or couples, there is the Red Garter, a pocket-size strip club. The hawker outside reminds couples, in case they've forgotten, that "the family that strips together, sticks together." 208 Duval St. © **305/296-4890.** www.ricksanddurtyharrys.com.

The Green Parrot Bar   A landmark Key West watering hole since 1890, The Green Parrot is a locals' favorite featuring stiff drinks, salty drinkers, and excellent live music from bluegrass and country to Afro-punk. 601 Whitehead St. © **305/294-6133.** www.greenparrot.com.

Sloppy Joe's   You'll have to stop in here just to say you did. Scholars and drunks debate whether this is the same Sloppy Joe's that Hemingway wrote about, but there's no argument that this classic bar's early-20th-century wooden ceiling and cracked-tile floors are Key West originals. There's live music nightly, as well as a cigar room and martini bar. 201 Duval St. © **305/294-5717,** ext. 10. www.sloppyjoes.com.

The Gay Scene

Key West's bohemian live-and-let-live atmosphere extends to its thriving and quirky gay community. Before and after Tennessee Williams, Key West has provided the perfect backdrop to a gay scene unlike that of many large urban areas. Seamlessly blended with the prevailing culture, there is no "gay ghetto" in Key West, where alternative lifestyles are embraced and even celebrated.

Although restaurants and businesses welcome visitors without discrimination, nightlife *is* inevitably nightlife. In Key West, the best music and dancing can be found at the predominantly gay clubs. While many of the area's other hot spots are geared toward tourists who like to imbibe, the gay clubs are for those who want to rave, gay or not. Covers vary, but are rarely more than $10.

Two popular adjacent late-night spots are the **801 Bourbon Bar/One Saloon** (801 Duval St. and 514 Petronia St.; $\mathcal{C}$ **305/294-9349** for both), featuring great drag and lots more disco. A mostly male clientele frequents this hot spot from 9pm until 4am. Another Duval Street favorite is **Aqua,** 711 Duval St. ($\mathcal{C}$ **305/292-8500**), where you might catch drag queens belting out torch songs or judges voting on the best package in the wet-jockey-shorts contest.

Sunday nights are fun at La-Te-Da, proper name: **La Terraza de Martí,** 1125 Duval St. ($\mathcal{C}$ **305/296-6706**), the former Key West home of Cuban exile José Martí. This is a great spot to gather poolside for the best martini in town—but don't bother with the food. Just upstairs is the **Crystal Room** ($\mathcal{C}$ **305/296-6706**), with a high-caliber cabaret performance featuring the popular Randy Roberts in winter. For more cabaret-caliber entertainment, check out **The Keys, A Key West Piano Bar,** 114 Duval St. ($\mathcal{C}$ **305/294-8859;** www.akeywestpianobar.com), featuring live music from show tunes and standards to rock and roll. An outdoor garden bar, The Off-Key Bar is the place to be if you happen to be there during a time when a tone-deaf customer takes advantage of the open mic policy.

THE DRY TORTUGAS ★★

70 miles W of Key West

Few people realize that the Florida Keys don't end at Key West, as about 70 miles west is a chain of seven small islands known as the Dry Tortugas. Because you've come this far, you might wish to visit them, especially if you're into bird-watching, their primary draw.

Ponce de León, who discovered this far-flung cluster of coral keys in 1513, named them Las Tortugas because of the many sea turtles, which still flock to the area during nesting season in the warm summer months. Oceanic charts later carried the preface "dry" to warn mariners that fresh water was unavailable here. Modern intervention has made drinking water available, but little else.

These undeveloped islands make a great day trip for travelers interested in seeing the natural anomalies of the Florida Keys—especially the birds. The Dry Tortugas are nesting grounds and roosting sites for thousands of tropical and subtropical oceanic birds. Visitors will also find a historic fort, good fishing, and terrific snorkeling around shallow reefs.

Getting There

BY BOAT **Sunny Days Catamarans** ($\mathcal{C}$ **800/236-7937** or 305/292-6100; www.sunnydayskeywest.com) operates the *Fast Cat,* a high-speed catamaran complete with sundeck and air-conditioning that zips you to and from the Dry Tortugas in two hours. The round-trip fare ($145 for adults, $135 for seniors, $100 for children) includes a continental breakfast; a buffet lunch with cold cuts, fresh veggies, fruits, salads, and unlimited sodas and water; an island tour; and a snorkeling excursion to a shipwreck in 5 to 20 feet of water. The high-speed catamaran leaves Key West for Garden Key at 8am and returns by 6pm. Expect to spend about 4½ hours at Fort Jefferson. The **Dry Tortugas Ferry** (✆ **800/634-0939;** www.fastcat-ferry.com), will also take you there and is cheaper than Sunny Days. During the transit to the park an onboard naturalist will give you an orientation about the area and the national park's surroundings. Passengers also have the option of taking a 40-minute guided tour of Fort Jefferson. Breakfast, lunch, and snorkeling gear are included in the price. Round-trip fares are $109 adults, $99 seniors, and $69 children.

Exploring the Dry Tortugas

Of the seven islands that make up the Dry Tortugas, Garden Key is the most visited because it is where Fort Jefferson and the visitor center are located. Loggerhead Key, Middle Key, and East Key are open only during the day and are for hiking. Bush Key is for the birds—literally! It's a nesting area for birds only, though it is open from October to January for special excursions. Hospital and Long keys are closed to the public.

Fort Jefferson, a huge six-sided, 19th-century fortress, is set almost at the water's edge of Garden Key, so it appears to float in the middle of the sea. The monumental structure is surrounded by formidable 8-foot-thick walls that rise from the sand to a height of nearly 50 feet. Impressive archways, stonework, and parapets make this 150-year-old monument a grand sight. With the invention of the rifled cannon, the fort's masonry construction became obsolete and the building was never completed. For 10 years, however, from 1863 to 1873, Fort Jefferson served as a prison, a kind of "Alcatraz East." Among its prisoners were four of the "Lincoln Conspirators," including Samuel A. Mudd, the doctor who set the broken leg of fugitive assassin John Wilkes Booth. In 1935, Fort Jefferson became a national monument administered by the National Park Service. Today, however, Fort Jefferson is struggling to resist erosion from the salt and sea, as iron used in the gun openings and the shutters in the fort's walls has accelerated the deterioration, and the structure's openings need to be rebricked. As a result, the National Park Service has designated the fort as the recipient of a $15-million face-lift, a project that may take up to a decade to complete.

For more information on Fort Jefferson and the Dry Tortugas, call the **Everglades National Park Service** (✆ **305/242-7700**) or visit www.fortjefferson.com. Fort Jefferson is open during daylight hours. A self-guided tour describes the history of the human presence in the Dry Tortugas while leading visitors through the fort.

Outdoor Activities

BIRD-WATCHING Bring your binoculars and your bird books: Bird-watching is *the* reason to visit this little cluster of tropical islands. The Dry Tortugas, uniquely situated in the middle of the migration flyway between North and South America, serve as an important rest stop for the more than 200 winged varieties that pass through here annually. The season peaks from mid-March to mid-May, when thousands of birds show up, but many species from the West Indies can be found here year-round.

DIVING & SNORKELING   The warm, clear, shallow waters of the Dry Tortugas produce optimum conditions for snorkeling and scuba diving. Four endangered species of sea turtles—green, leatherback, Atlantic Ridley, and hawksbill—can be found here, along with myriad marine species. The region just outside the seawall of Fort Jefferson is excellent for underwater touring; an abundant variety of fish, coral, and more live in just 3 to 4 feet of water.

FISHING   In July 2001, a federal law closed off all fishing in a 90-square-mile tract of open ocean called the Tortugas North and a 61-square-mile tract of open ocean called the Tortugas South. It basically prohibits all fishing in order to preserve the dwindling population of fish (a result of commercial fishing and environmental factors). However, rules have been alleviated and some sport fishing is now allowed in Dry Tortugas. To be safe we recommend a fishing charter such as **Dry Tortugas Fishing Adventures** (© 305/797-6396; www.tortugasfishing.com), which will take you on an impressive 42-foot sport-fishing catamaran into deep water where you'll catch dolphin, tuna, wahoo, king mackerel, sailfish, and an occasional marlin. Trips are overnight and rates are steep: from $3,400 to $3,600 and $1,000 per extra day. If you don't have the money or the time, **Captain Andy Griffiths** (© 305/296-2639; www.fishandy.com) will take you on custom fishing trips out to the Tortugas at $140 per passenger with a minimum of six anglers.

Camping

The rustic beauty of tiny **Garden Key** (the only island of the Dry Tortugas where campers are allowed to pitch tents) is a camper's dream. Don't worry about sharing your site with noisy RVs or motor homes; they can't get here. The abundance of birds doesn't make it quiet, but the camping—a stone's throw from the water—is as picturesque as it gets. Picnic tables, cooking grills, and toilets are provided, but there are no showers. All supplies must be packed in and out. Sites are $3 per person per night and are available on a first-come, first-served basis. The 10 sites book up fast. For more information, call the **National Park Service** (© 305/242-7700)

THE GOLD COAST

13

Named not for the sun-kissed skin of the area's residents, but for the gold salvaged from shipwrecks off its coastline, the Gold Coast embraces more than 60 miles of beautiful Atlantic shoreline—from the pristine sands of Palm Beach to the legendary strip of beaches in Fort Lauderdale.

If you haven't visited the cities along Florida's southeastern coast in the last few years, you'll be amazed at how much has changed. Miles of sprawling grassland and empty lots have been replaced with luxurious resorts and high-rise condominiums. Taking advantage of their proximity to Miami, the cities that make up the Gold Coast have attracted millions of people looking to escape crowded sidewalks, traffic jams, and the everyday routines of life.

Fortunately, amid all the building, much of the natural treasure of the Gold Coast remains. There are 300 miles of Intracoastal Waterway, not to mention Fort Lauderdale's Venetian-inspired canals, and the unspoiled splendor of the Everglades is just a few miles inland.

The most popular areas in the Gold Coast are Fort Lauderdale, Boca Raton, and Palm Beach. While Fort Lauderdale is a favored beachfront destination, Boca Raton and Palm Beach are better known for their country-club lifestyles and excellent shopping. Farther north is the quietly popular Jupiter, best known for spring training at the Roger Dean Stadium and for former resident Burt Reynolds. In between these better-traveled destinations are a few things worth stopping for, but not much. Driving north along the coastline is one of the best ways to fully appreciate what the Gold Coast is all about—it's a perspective you certainly won't find in a shopping mall.

Tourists come here by the droves, but they aren't the only people coming; thousands of transplants, fleeing the increasing population influx in Miami and the frigid winters up north, have made this area their home. As a result, there was a brief construction boom in the existing cities and even westward, into the swampy areas of the Everglades. The boom is at a standstill now, obviously, though you'll still see construction on some homes contracted before the recession, in Broward County, for instance. There has also been a great revitalization of several downtown areas, including Hollywood, Fort Lauderdale, and West Palm Beach. These once-desolate urban centers have been spruced up and now attract more young travelers and families than ever.

Unfortunately, like its neighbors to the south, the Gold Coast can be prohibitively hot and buggy in summer. The good news is that bargains are plentiful from May through October, when many locals take advantage of package deals and uncrowded resorts.

For the purposes of this chapter, the Gold Coast will consist of the towns of Hallandale, Hollywood, Pompano Beach, Fort Lauderdale, Dania, Deerfield, Boca Raton, Delray Beach, Boynton Beach, Jupiter, and the Palm Beaches.

EXPLORING THE GOLD COAST BY CAR

Like most of South Florida, the Gold Coast consists of a mainland and adjacent barrier islands. You'll have to check maps to keep track of the many bridges that allow access to the islands where most tourist activity is centered. Interstate 95, which runs north-south, is the area's main highway. Farther west is the Florida Turnpike, a toll road that can be worth the expense since the speed limit is higher and it's often less congested than I-95. Also on the mainland is U.S. 1, which generally runs parallel to I-95 (to the east) and is a narrower thoroughfare that is mostly crowded with strip malls and seedy hotels.

I recommend taking Florida A1A, a slow oceanside road that connects the long, thin islands of Florida's entire east coast. Although the road is narrow, it is the most scenic and, thus, ushers you into the relaxed atmosphere of these resort towns.

BROWARD COUNTY

23 miles N of Miami

Less exposed than highly hyped Miami–Dade County, Broward County is a lot calmer and, according to some, a lot friendlier than the Magic City. In fact, a friendly rivalry exists between residents of both counties. Miamians consider themselves more sophisticated and cosmopolitan than their northern neighbors, who, in turn, dismiss the alleged sophistication as snobbery and actually prefer their own county's gentler pace.

With more than 23 miles of beachfront and 300 miles of navigable waterways, Broward County is also a great outdoor destination. Scattered amid the shopping malls, condominiums, and tourist traps is a beautiful landscape lined with hundreds of parks, golf courses, tennis courts, and, of course, beaches.

The City of Hallandale Beach is a small, peaceful, oceanfront town just north of Dade County's Aventura. Condos are the predominant landmarks in Hallandale, which is still pretty much a retirement community, although the revamped multimillion-dollar Westin Diplomat Resort (p. 344) is slowly trying to revitalize and liven up the area.

Just north of Hallandale is the more energetic, burgeoning city of Hollywood. Once a sleepy community wedged between Fort Lauderdale and Miami, Hollywood is now a bustling area of 1.5 million people with an array of ethnic and racial identities: from white and African-American to Jamaican, Chinese, and Dominican. (*Money* magazine trumpeted the self-described "City of the Future" as having an ethnic makeup that mirrors what the U.S. will look like by the year 2022.) In 2004, the $300-million

Seminole Hard Rock Hotel & Casino (p. 346) debuted, with a 500-room hotel, spa, and 130,000-square-foot casino. This was exactly what the city needed to kick its slow renaissance up a notch. A spate of redevelopment has made the pedestrian-friendly center along Hollywood Boulevard and Harrison Street, east of Dixie Highway, a popular destination for travelers and locals alike. Some predict Hollywood will be South Florida's next big destination—South Beach without the attitude and traffic jams. While the prediction is a dubious one, Hollywood is definitely awakening from its long slumber. Prices are a fraction of those at other tourist areas, and a quasi-bohemian vibe is apparent in the galleries, clubs, and restaurants that dot the new "strip." Its gritty undercurrent, however, prevents it from becoming too trendy.

Fort Lauderdale, with its well-known strip of beaches, restaurants, bars, and souvenir shops, has really undergone a major transformation. Once famous (or infamous) for the annual mayhem it hosted during Spring Break, this area is now attracting a more affluent, better-behaved yachting crowd. The *Miami Herald* business section discussed the changes in a 2006 article, "Upscale Inn Crowd," which agreed that "the city once famous for Spring Break antics undergoes a broad upgrade of its hotel stock." In fact, Starwood's new W Fort Lauderdale, a 346-room boutique hotel, opened at the end of 2008, as did the swanky Ritz-Carlton. And in 2009, Sir Richard Branson debuted his fleet of Virgin America jetliners in Florida with service from Fort Lauderdale, not Miami, to L.A. and San Francisco with more destinations, but not Miami, to come.

In addition to beautiful wide beaches, Fort Lauderdale, known as the Venice of America, has more than 300 miles of navigable waterways and innumerable canals, which permit thousands of residents to anchor boats in their backyards. Boating is not just a hobby here; it's a lifestyle. Visitors can easily get on the water, too, by renting a boat or by hailing a moderately priced water taxi.

Huge cruise ships also take advantage of Florida's deepest harbor, Port Everglades. The seaport is on the southeastern coast of the Florida peninsula, near the Fort Lauderdale Hollywood International Airport on the outskirts of Hollywood and Dania Beach. And with a $75-million cruise terminal expansion, Port Everglades is on its way to being the busiest cruise port in the world.

Essentials

GETTING THERE   If you're driving from Miami, it's a straight shot north to Hollywood or Fort Lauderdale. Visitors on their way to or from Orlando should take the Florida Turnpike to exit 53, 54, 58, or 62, depending on the location of your accommodations. The **Fort Lauderdale–Hollywood International Airport** is easy to negotiate, and just 15 minutes from both of the downtown areas it services. However, its user-friendliness may not last much longer: Due to its popularity, the airport is still undergoing a $700-million runway expansion and renovation that often renders it just as maddening as any other major metropolitan airport. Completion is expected in 2015. In 2009, Sir Richard Branson introduced his **Virgin America** (© **877/FLY-VIRGIN** [359-8474]; www.virginamerica.com) service from the West Coast to FLL, offering two daily nonstop round-trips from San Francisco International Airport and two daily nonstop round-trips from Los Angeles International Airport.

The airport has wireless Internet access and a fantastic car-rental center where 10 rental companies are under one roof—very convenient. Levels 1 through 4 are home to Alamo, Avis, Budget, Dollar, Enterprise, E-Z, Hertz, National, Royal, and Thrifty. Levels 5 to 9 provide 5,500 spaces for public parking.

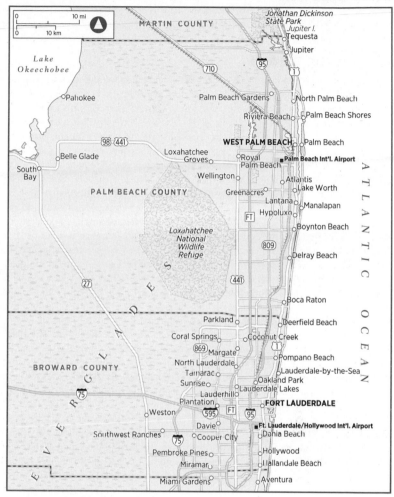

Amtrak (✆ **800/USA-RAIL** [872-7245]) stations are at 200 SW 21st Terrace (Broward Blvd. and I-95), Fort Lauderdale (✆ **954/587-6692**), and 3001 Hollywood Blvd. (northwest corner of Hollywood Blvd. and I-95, Hollywood; ✆ **954/921-4517**).

VISITOR INFORMATION The **Greater Fort Lauderdale Convention & Visitors Bureau,** 1850 Eller Dr., Ste. 303 (off I-95 and I-595 E.), Fort Lauderdale, FL 33316 (✆ **800/22-SUNNY** [227-8669] or 954/765-4466; fax 954/765-4467; www.sunny.org), is an excellent resource for area information in English, Spanish, and French. Call in advance to request a free comprehensive guide covering events, accommodations, and sightseeing in Broward County.

The **Greater Hollywood Chamber of Commerce,** 330 N. Federal Hwy. (at U.S. 1 and Taylor St.), Hollywood, FL 33020 (© **800/231-5562** or 954/923-4000; fax 954/923-8737; www.hollywoodchamber.org), is open Monday through Friday from 9am to 5pm. Here you'll find the lowdown on all of Hollywood's events, attractions, restaurants, hotels, and tours.

Hitting the Beach

The southern part of the Gold Coast, Broward County, has the region's most popular and amenities-laden beaches, which stretch for more than 23 miles. Most do not charge for access and all are well maintained. Here's a selection of some of the county's best, from south to north:

Hollywood Beach, stretching from Sheridan Street to Georgia Street, is a major attraction in the city of Hollywood, a virtual carnival of young hipsters, big families, and sunburned French Canadians who dodge bicyclers and skaters along the rows of tacky souvenir shops, T-shirt shops, game rooms, snack bars, beer stands, hotels, and miniature-golf courses. **Hollywood Beach Broadwalk,** modeled after Atlantic City's legendary boardwalk, is the town's popular beachfront pedestrian thoroughfare, a cement promenade that's 30 feet wide and stretches along the shoreline for 3 miles. A recent makeover added, among other things, a concrete bike path, a crushed-shell jogging path, new trash receptacles, and the relocation of beach showers to each street end (all of are them are accessible for people with disabilities). Popular with runners, skaters, and cruisers, the Broadwalk is also renowned as a hangout for thousands of retirement-age snowbirds who get together for frequent dances and shows at a faded outdoor amphitheater. Despite efforts to clear out a seedy element, the area remains a haven for drunks and scammers, so keep alert.

If you tire of the hectic diversity that defines Hollywood's Broadwalk, enjoy the natural beauty of the beach itself, which is wide and clean. There are lifeguards, showers, restroom facilities, and public areas for picnics and parties.

The **Fort Lauderdale Beach Promenade,** along the beach, underwent a $26-million renovation and looks fantastic. It's especially peaceful in the mornings, when there's just a smattering of joggers and walkers; but even at its most crowded on weekends, the expansive promenade provides room for everyone. Note, however, that the beach is hardly pristine; it is across the street from an uninterrupted stretch of hotels, bars, and retail outlets. Also nearby is a retail-and-dining megacomplex, Beach Place (p. 356), in the throes of its own renovation that will add newer, hipper stores, bars, and restaurants, on Florida A1A, midway between Las Olas and Sunrise boulevards.

On the sand just across the road, most days you'll find hard-core volleyball players who always welcome anyone with a good spike, and you'll find an inviting ocean for swimmers of any level. The unusually clear waters are under the careful watch of some of Florida's best-looking lifeguards. Freshen up afterward in the clean showers and restrooms conveniently located along the strip. Pets have been banned from most of the beach in order to maintain the impressive cleanliness; a designated area for pets exists away from the main sunbathing areas.

Especially on weekends, parking at the oceanside meters is nearly impossible. Try biking, skating, or hitching a ride on the water taxi instead. The strip is located on Florida A1A, between SE 17th Street and Sunrise Boulevard.

Fort Lauderdale

13

THE GOLD COAST | Broward County

Turtle Trail

In June and July, the John U. Lloyd Beach is crawling with nature lovers who come for the spectacular **Sea Turtle Awareness Program.** Park rangers begin the evening with a lecture and slide show while scouts search the beach for nesting loggerhead sea turtles. If a turtle is located—plenty of them usually are—a beach walk allows participants to see the turtles nest and, sometimes, their eggs hatch. The program begins at 9pm on Wednesday and Friday from mid-May to mid-July. Call ℂ **954/923-2833** for reservations. Walks last between 1 and 3 hours. Comfortable walking shoes and insect repellent are necessary. The park entrance fee of $4 to $6 per carload applies.

Dania Beach's **John U. Lloyd Beach State Park,** 6503 N. Ocean Dr., Dania (ℂ **954/923-2833**), consists of 251 acres of barrier island, situated between the Atlantic Ocean and the Intracoastal Waterway, from Port Everglades on the north to Dania on the south. Its natural setting contrasts sharply with the urban development of Fort Lauderdale. Lloyd Beach, one of Broward County's most important nesting beaches for sea turtles, produces some 10,000 hatchlings a year. The park's broad, flat beach is popular for both swimming and sunning. Self-guided nature trails are great for those too restless to sunbathe. Admission to the park is $6 per vehicle of two to eight people, $4 for single occupant, and $2 for pedestrians and bicyclists.

Outdoor Activities & Spectator Sports

BOATING   Often called the "yachting capital of the world," Fort Lauderdale provides ample opportunity for visitors to get out on the water, either along the Intracoastal Waterway or on the open ocean. If your hotel doesn't rent boats, try **Aloha Watersports,** Marriott's Harbor Beach Resort, 3030 Holiday Dr., Fort Lauderdale (ℂ **954/462-7245;** www.alohawatersports.com). It can outfit you with a variety of craft, including jet skis, WaveRunners, and catamarans. Rates start at $65 per half-hour for WaveRunners ($15 each additional rider; doubles and triples available), $70 to $125 for sailboats, $60 to $70 for catamarans, $20 per person per hour for ocean kayaks, $25 an hour for paddleboards or $100 for an hour lesson, and $75 per person for a 15-minute parasailing ride. Aloha also offers a Surfing School ($50—though the waves are hardly rippin' here!) and a Coast Guard class (9am daily), through which adults can obtain their Florida Boaters License for $3. And for the treasure hunters, you can rent a metal detector for $20 per hour.

FISHING   The **IGFA** (International Game Fish Association) **World Fishing Center,** 300 Gulf Stream Way, Dania Beach (ℂ **954/922-4212;** www.igfa.org), is an angler's paradise. One of the highlights of this museum, library, and park is the virtual-reality fishing simulator that allows visitors to actually reel in their own computer-generated catch. Also included in the 3-acre park are displays of antique fishing gear, record catches, famous anglers, various vessels, and a wetlands lab. To get a list of local captains and guides, call **IGFA headquarters** (ℂ **954/927-2628**) and ask for the librarian. Admission is $8 for adults, $5 for seniors and children 3 to 16. The museum and library are open daily from 10am to 6pm. On the grounds is also **Bass Pro Shops Outdoor World,** a huge retail complex set on a 3-acre lake.

GOLF More than 50 golf courses in all price ranges compete for players. Among the best is **Emerald Hills,** 4100 N. Hills Dr., Hollywood (© 954/961-4000; www.theclubatemeraldhills.com), just west of I-95 between Sterling Road and Sheridan Street. This beauty consistently lands on the "best of" lists of golf writers nationwide. The 18th hole, on a two-tier green, is the course's signature; it's surrounded by water and is more than a bit rough. The course is pricey—Friday through Sunday, greens fees start at $150 for tee times after 1pm, and $175 for tee times before noon during high season; Monday through Friday, the fees are $125 before noon and $110 after 1pm. Rates are cheaper during the brutally hot summers.

Another great course is the Howard Watson–designed 18-hole Pembroke Lakes course at the **Pembroke Lakes Golf Club,** 10500 Taft St., Pembroke Pines (© 954/431-4144; www.pcmgolf.com), run by the same management company that runs the Miami Beach Golf Club and the recipient of a $7-million renovation that saw the addition of Paspalum Supreme Grass. Best of all, greens fees are almost rock bottom, ranging from $25 to $55 depending on time and season.

The **Diplomat Golf Resort and Spa,** 501 Diplomat Pkwy., Hallandale Beach (© 954/602-6000; www.diplomatgolfresortandspa.com), is across the Intracoastal from the Westin Diplomat Resort. It has fabulous golf facilities, with 8 acres of lakes and rolling fairways, plus a fantastic delivery service that brings lunch and drinks to your cart. You pay for the services, however, with greens fees of $139 to $179 during high season and $89 to $99 off-season. Twilight fees at 2pm cost from $39 to $89.

For one of Broward's best municipal challenges, try the 18-holer at the **Orangebrook Golf Course,** 400 Entrada Dr., Hollywood (© 954/967-GOLF [4653]; www.orangebrook.com). Built in 1937, this is one of the state's oldest courses and one of the area's best bargains. Morning and noon rates are $17 to $23. After 3pm, you can play for about $13, including a cart. Men must wear collared shirts to play here, and no spikes are allowed.

SCUBA DIVING In Broward County, the best dive wreck is the *Mercedes I,* a 197-foot freighter that washed up in the backyard of a Palm Beach socialite in 1984 and was sunk for divers the following year off Pompano Beach. The artificial reef, filled with colorful sponges, spiny lobsters, and barracudas, is 97 feet below the surface, a mile offshore between Oakland Park and Sunrise boulevards. Dozens of reputable dive shops line the beach. Ask at your hotel for a nearby recommendation, or contact **Neil Watson's Undersea Adventures,** 1525 S. Andrews Ave., Fort Lauderdale (© 954/462-3400; www.nealwatson.com).

SPECTATOR SPORTS Baseball fans can get their fix at the **Fort Lauderdale Stadium,** 5301 NW 12th Ave. (© 954/828-4980; www.theorioles.com), where the Baltimore Orioles play spring-training exhibition games starting in early March; call © 954/776-1921 for tickets. General admission is $10, a spot in the grandstand $14, and box seats $20; admission for kids 14 and under is $4. During the season, the Florida Marlins play just south of Hallandale at **Land Shark Stadium,** near the Dade–Broward County line. Tickets go on sale in January for $4 to $100; call **Ticketmaster** (© 305/358-5885; www.ticketmaster.com) to purchase them.

Pompano Park Racing, 1800 SW Third St., Pompano Beach (© 954/972-2000), has parimutuel harness racing from October to early August. Admission is free to both grandstand and clubhouse.

Wrapped around an artificial lake, **Gulfstream Park Racing and Casino,** at U.S. 1 and Hallandale Beach Boulevard, Hallandale (© **954/454-7000;** www.gulf streampark.com), is pretty and popular, especially after its multimillion-dollar renovation, with a spanking-new casino and restaurants. Large purses and important horse races are commonplace at this recently refurbished suburban course, and the track is often crowded. The most recent renovation has transformed it into a world-class, state-of-the-art facility with shops, bars, higher-end restaurants, 20 luxury suites, private accommodations for top players, and more. It hosts the Florida Derby each March. Call for schedules. Admission and parking are free. From January 3 to April 25, post times are 1:15pm Wednesday through Sunday, and the doors open at 11:30am.

Jai alai, a sort of Spanish-style indoor lacrosse, was introduced to Florida in 1924 and still draws big crowds that bet on the fast-paced action. Broward's only fronton, **Dania Jai Alai,** 301 E. Dania Beach Blvd., at Florida A1A and U.S. 1 (© **954/920-1511**), is a great place to spend an afternoon or evening.

In the sport of ice hockey, the young **Florida Panthers** (© **954/835-7000**) play in Sunrise at the **BankAtlantic Center,** 2555 NW 137th Way (© **954/835-8000**). Tickets range from $15 to $100. Call for directions and ticket information.

TENNIS There are hundreds of courts in Broward County, and plenty are accessible to the public. Many are at resorts and hotels. If yours has none, try the **Jimmy Evert Tennis Center,** 701 NE 12th Ave. (off Sunrise Blvd.), Fort Lauderdale (© **954/828-5378**), famous as the spot where Chris Evert trained. There are 18 lighted clay courts and three hard courts here. Nonresidents of Fort Lauderdale pay $6 per hour before 4pm and $7 after. Reservations are accepted after 2pm for the following day, but cost an extra $3.

ONE IF BY LAND, TAXI IF by sea

Plan to spend at least an afternoon or evening cruising Fort Lauderdale's 300 miles of waterways the only way you can: by boat. The **Water Bus of Fort Lauderdale** (© **954/467-6677;** www. watertaxi.com) is one of the greatest innovations for water lovers since those cool Velcro sandals. A trusty fleet of older port boats serves the dual purpose of transporting and entertaining visitors as they cruise through the "Venice of America." Because of its popularity, the water taxi fleet has welcomed several sleek, 70-passenger "water buses" (featuring indoor and outdoor seating with an atriumlike roof).

Taxis operate on demand and also along a fairly regular route, carrying up to 48 passengers to 20 stops. If you're staying at a hotel on the route, you can be picked up there, usually within 15 minutes of calling, and then be shuttled to any of the dozens of restaurants, bars, and attractions on or near the waterfront. If you aren't sure where you want to go, ask one of the personable captains, who can point out historic and fun spots along the way.

Starting daily at 8am, boats run until midnight 7 days a week, depending on the weather. Check the website for exact times of pickup. The cost is $13 for an all-day pass with unlimited stops on and off and $7 if you board after 7pm. If you want to go to South Beach, it's $33 adults, $30 seniors, and $16 for children 4-11. Tickets are available onboard; no credit cards are accepted.

Seeing the Sights

Billie Swamp Safari ★ Billie Swamp Safari is an up-close-and-personal view of the Seminole Indians' 2,200-acre Big Cypress Reservation. There are daily tours into reservation wetlands, hardwood hammocks, and areas where wildlife (seemingly strategically placed deer, water buffalo, bison, wild hogs, ornery ostriches, rare birds, and alligators) reside. Tours are provided aboard swamp buggies, customized motorized vehicles specially designed to provide visitors with an elevated view of the frontier while they comfortably ride through the wetlands and cypress heads. The more adventurous may want to take a fast-moving airboat ride or trek a nature trail. Airboat rides run about 20 minutes, while swamp-buggy tours last about an hour. A stop at an alligator farm reeks of Disney, but the kids won't care. You can stay overnight in a native Tiki hut for $35 per night if you're really looking to immerse yourself in the culture.

Big Cypress Seminole Reservation, 1½-hr. drive west of Fort Lauderdale. © **800/949-6101.** www.semtribe.com/safari. Free admission. Swamp-buggy tours $25 adults, $23 seniors 62 and over, $15 children 4–12; airboat tours $15 for all ages. Daily 8:30am–6pm. Airboats depart every 30 min. from 9:30am–4:30pm. Swamp-buggy tours leave on the hour btw. 10am and 5pm. Reptile and Critter Shows daily. Day and overnight packages available.

Bonnet House ★★★ This historic 35-acre plantation home and estate, accessible by guided tour only, will provide you with a fantastic glimpse of Old Florida. Built in 1921, the sprawling two-story waterfront home (surrounded by formal tropical gardens) is really the backdrop of a love story, which the very chatty volunteer guides will share with you if you ask. Some have actually lunched with the former resident of the house, the late Evelyn Bartlett, wife of world-acclaimed artist Frederic Clay Bartlett. The worthwhile 1¼-hour tour introduces you to quirky people, whimsical artwork, lush grounds, and interesting design.

900 N. Birch Rd. (1 block west of the ocean, south of Sunrise Blvd.), Fort Lauderdale. © **954/563-5393.** www.bonnethouse.org. Admission $20 adults, $18 seniors, $16 students 18 and under, free for children 6 and under. Call for hours and tour times.

Butterfly World ★ ☺ After moving to Florida from Illinois in 1968, electrical engineer Ronald Boender decided to actively pursue his passion, raising local butterflies at his home and recording data on each. After realizing there was a need for farmed butterflies, Boender set up a company in 1984 and went one step further, building this butterfly house along with the founder of the world renowned London Butterfly House across the pond. Enter Butterfly World, renowned globally for its butterfly farm and research facility as well as its 10 acres of aviaries and botanical gardens. Kids especially love the "bug museum," which features some of the insect world's biggest celebrities—all which kids are able to touch, if they dare, with the help of an expert. There's lots to see here in terms of flitting, fluttery things, so set aside at least 2 hours to, uh, flit around yourself.

Tradewinds Park, 3600 W. Sample Rd., Coconut Creek. © **954/977-4400.** www.butterflyworld.com. Admission $25 adults and seniors, $20 children ages 3–11. Mon–Sat 9am–5pm; Sun 11am–5pm.

Hillsboro Inlet Lighthouse ★ Completed in 1907, the Hillsboro Inlet Lighthouse, which rises 136 feet above water and marks the northern end of the Florida Reef, isn't just any lighthouse. It contains a 5,500,000-candlepower light and is the most powerful light on the east coast of the United States. And there's more history. This lighthouse was also made famous thanks to the most famous of the "barefoot mailmen," carriers of the first U.S. mail route between Palm Beach and Miami. Because there was no paved road on that route, the mailmen had to get through by boat and by walking the sand along the beach. James Hamilton was the most famous of these after disappearing delivering mail on the route just after October 10, 1887, presumably the victim of drowning or an encounter with a hungry alligator while trying to swim across Hillsboro inlet to retrieve his boat from the far side. His body was never recovered. A big trial ensued and his death still remains a mystery today. The original stone statue of the *Barefoot Mailman* by Frank Varga is permanently displayed on the shores of the Hillsboro inlet next to the Hillsboro lighthouse with an inscription dedicated to Hamilton. A fascinating story, that can be told in much more detail with a tour by the Hillsboro Lighthouse Preservation Society, given once every other month, usually on Saturdays. If the tour isn't available, go see it for yourself.

Hillsboro Inlet, off A1A, Pompano Beach. © **954/942-2102.** www.hillsborolighthouse.org. Tours $15. Call for hours and tour times. Take I-95 to Atlantic Blvd. Go east across the Intracoastal and left at Highway A1A for 2 miles to Pompano Beach City Park. Stop at the Hillsboro Inlet bridge's SE corner where there is an excellent view of the Hillsboro Lighthouse. Tours meet on the dock across from Riverside Dr. To get there, go east, cross the Intracoastal and make an immediate left on N. Riverside Dr. Go 1 block to the parking lot. Park and head west to the dock across Riverside Dr.

International Swimming Hall of Fame (ISHOF) ★★★

Any aspiring Michael Phelps (who may or may not donate one of his million gold medals to the museum) or those who appreciate the sport will love this splashy homage to the best backstrokers, front crawlers, and divers in the world. The museum houses the world's largest collection of aquatic memorabilia and is the single largest source of aquatic books, manuscripts, and literature. Among the highlights are Johnny Weissmuller's Olympic medals, Mark Spitz's starting block used to win six of his seven 1972 Olympic gold medals, and more than 60 Olympic, national, and club uniforms, warm-ups, and swimsuits. For those who don't mind getting their feet wet, the ISHOF Aquatic Complex is the only one of its kind in the world with two 50m (164-ft.) pools, a diving well, and a swimming flume.

1 Hall of Fame Dr., Fort Lauderdale. © **954/462-6536.** www.ishof.org. Admission $8 adults, $6 seniors, $4 children 12 and over. Call for hours and tour times.

Museum of Art Fort Lauderdale ★ ☺

A fantastic modern-art facility, the Museum of Art Fort Lauderdale has permanent collections, including those from William Glackens; the CoBrA Movement in Copenhagen, Brussels, and Amsterdam, with more than 200 paintings; 50 sculptures; 1,200 works on paper from 1948 to 1951, including the largest repository of Asger Jorn graphics outside the Silkeborg Kunstmuseum in Denmark; stunning Picasso ceramics; and contemporary works from more than 90 Cuban artists in exile around the world. Traveling exhibits and continuing art classes make the museum a great place to spend a rainy day—or night, on Thursdays, the cafe and wine bar have happy hour from 5 to 7pm. On the third Thursday of every month, museum offers free admission from 5 to 8pm.

1 E. Las Olas Blvd., Fort Lauderdale. © **954/525-5500.** www.moafl.org. Admission $10 adults, $7 seniors and children 6-17, free for children 5 and under. Oct-May daily 11am-5pm, Thurs until 8pm; June-Sept Mon and Wed-Sun 11am-5pm.

Museum of Discovery & Science ★★ ☺

This museum's high-tech, interactive approach to education proves that science can equal fun. Adults won't feel as if they're in a kiddie museum, either. Kids ages 7 and under enjoy navigating their way through the excellent explorations in the Discovery Center. Florida Ecoscapes is particularly interesting, with a living coral reef, bees, bats, frogs, turtles, and alligators. Most weekend nights, you'll find a diverse crowd ranging from hip high-school kids to 30-somethings enjoying a rock film in the IMAX theater, which also shows short, science-related films daily. Out front in the atrium, see the 52-foot-tall *Great Gravity Clock*, the largest kinetic-energy sculpture in the state.

401 SW 2nd St., Fort Lauderdale. © **954/467-6637.** www.mods.org. Admission (includes IMAX film) $16 adults, $15 seniors, $12 children 2–12; without IMAX film $11 adults, $10 seniors, $9 children 2–12. Mon–Sat 10am–5pm; Sun noon–6pm. Movie theater closes later. From I-95, exit on Broward Blvd. E. Continue to SW 5th Ave., turn right; garage is on the right.

Stranahan House ★★★   In a town where nothing appears to date back earlier than 1940, visitors may want to take a minute to see Fort Lauderdale's very oldest standing structure and a prime example of classic "Florida Frontier" architecture. Built in 1901 by the "father of Fort Lauderdale," Frank Stranahan, this house once served as a trading post for Seminole trappers who came here to sell pelts. It's been a post office, town hall, and general store, and now serves as a worthwhile little museum of South Florida pioneer life, containing turn-of-the-20th-century furnishings and historical photos of the area. It is also the site of occasional concerts and social functions; call for details.

335 SE 6th Ave. (Las Olas Blvd. at the New River Tunnel), Fort Lauderdale. © **954/524-4736.** www. stranahanhouse.org. Admission $12 adults, $11 seniors, $7 students and children. Wed–Sat 10am–3pm; Sun 1–3pm. Tours are on the hour; last tour at 3pm. Accessible by water taxi.

Shopping & Browsing

It's all about malls in Broward County and, while most of the best shopping is within Fort Lauderdale proper, other areas are also worth browsing.

Dania is known as the antiques capital of the South because within 1 square mile of Federal Highway, the city has more than 100 dealers selling everything from small collectibles to fine antiques. Parking is best along Federal Highway, on the "row," where Federal Highway meets U.S. 1. For information on "Antique Row," call © **954/924-3627.** Also in Dania is the **Design Center of the Americas (DCOTA),** at the intersection of I-95 and Griffin Road (© **954/920-7997;** www.dcota.com), a 775,000-square-foot interior-design center with furniture showrooms (featuring everything from ultramod to classic), designer studios, and, from time to time, fabulous sample sales. You'll never know who you may see here: just before he got hitched Matt Damon and his then-fiancée (now wife) were there furnishing their zillion-dollar Miami Beach manse.

For bargain mavens, there's a strip of "fashion" stores on Hallandale Beach Boulevard's "Schmatta Row," east of Dixie Highway and the railroad tracks, where off-brand shoes, bags, and jewelry are sold at deep discounts. Hollywood Boulevard also has some interesting shops, with everything from Indonesian artifacts to used and rare books, leather bustiers, and handmade hats. Dozens of shops line the pedestrian-friendly strip just west of Young Circle. The art galleries are clustered along Harrison Street, just east of Dixie Highway.

The area's only beachfront mall, the **Gallery at Beach Place,** is in Fort Lauderdale on Florida A1A just north of Las Olas Boulevard. This 100,000-square-foot giant sports the usual chains, such as Sunglass Hut, as well as chain bars and restaurants such as Hooter's. While views of the ocean are fantastic, the shopping isn't so great, with only about 12 stores, one of them being a CVS Pharmacy.

Other more traditional malls include the upscale **Galleria,** at Sunrise Boulevard near the Fort Lauderdale Beach, and **Broward Mall,** west of I-95 on Broward Boulevard, in Plantation.

If you're looking for unusual boutiques, especially art galleries, head to quaint **Las Olas Boulevard ★**, located west of A1A and a block east of Federal Highway/U.S. 1, off SE Eighth Street, where there are hundreds of shops with alluring window decorations (like kitchen utensils posing as modern-art sculptures) and intriguing merchandise such as mural-size oil paintings. On the edge of the Arts and Science District is **Las Olas Riverfront,** a retail complex on the water with a few restaurants, nightclubs, bars, and boutiques. While it's not worth a trip on its own, if you're in the area, you may want to take a quick stroll there.

For bargains, there's no better place than **Sawgrass Mills,** 12801 W. Sunrise Blvd. (© **954/846-0179**), featuring over 350 name-brand outlets such as Off Fifth and Nordstrom Rack. Nearby is Florida's first ever **Ikea,** 151 NW 136th Ave. (© **954/838-9292;** www.ikea.com), purveyor of all things sleek and Swedish—everything from furniture to meatballs.

Where to Stay

The Fort Lauderdale beach has a hotel or motel on nearly every block, ranging from run-down to luxurious. **Fort Lauderdale Beach Resort Hotel and Suites,** 4221 N. Ocean Blvd. (© **800/329-7466** or 954/563-2521), has clean oceanside rooms starting at about $65. For a cushier stay, look into the **Ritz-Carlton Fort Lauderdale** resort (see below), which opened in May 2007 as a St. Regis and was quickly taken over by the Ritz (see below). Just opened in the fall of 2009 is the $220-million **W Fort Lauderdale Hotel & Residences** (© **954/525-8133**), a boutique-hotel-slash-condominium with ocean views and a very hip and happening bar.

In Hollywood, where prices are generally cheaper, the **Ramada Hollywood Beach Resort,** 101 N. Ocean Dr. (© **954/921-0990;** www.ramadahbr.com), operates a full-service hotel right on the ocean. With prices starting at around $79 in season and discounts for AAA members, it's a great deal. **Marriott Hollywood Oceanfront,** 2501 N. Ocean Dr. (I-95 to Sheridan St. E. to Fla. A1A S.; © **866/306-5453** or 954/924-2202), is a recently renovated beach resort with a fantastic location right on the beach.

Hollywood Beach's reasonable prices may not last much longer, though. In 2010, a developer signed a deal with singer Jimmy Buffett to bring the first ever Margaritaville resort to a city-owned site on the ocean. Plans for the resort include Tiki bars, an amphitheater with free concerts and rates 15 percent higher than area hotels. Despite the deal, Planet Hollywood is said to be fighting for that same land to open a hotel and water park. At press time, the two teams were set to battle it out in a City Hall meeting. If either or both parties win, it could dramatically change the sleepy landscape of Hollywood Beach. Stay tuned.

Extended Stay America/Crossland Economy Studios (© **800/398-7829;** www.extendedstayhotels.com) has four super-clean properties in Fort Lauderdale and offers year-round rates as low as $45 a night and $159 per week. The studios are designed with business travelers in mind: Each includes free local calls, a dataport, a kitchenette, and a well-lit desk.

For rentals for a few weeks or months, call **Florida Sunbreak** (© **800/SUN-BREAK** [786-2732]) or check the annual list of small lodgings compiled by the

Greater Fort Lauderdale Convention & Visitors Bureau (© 954/765-4466). The latter is especially helpful if you're looking for privately owned, charming, affordable lodgings.

VERY EXPENSIVE

The Atlantic Hotel ★★★ Overlooking 23 miles of white sand, the Atlantic is a study in minimal modernity—soothing colors and comfortable, stylish decor. Besides the usual high-tech amenities found in all rooms of this category—flatscreen TVs, wireless Internet—each room has a fully equipped granite kitchen or kitchenette. The Atlantic also has a fantastic award-winning restaurant Trina and a spectacular 10,000-square-foot spa. For those looking to stay here in rock star style, The Penthouse Collection includes five two- and three-bedroom suites, ranging from 3,500 to 4,000+ square feet, some with private elevators. Service is usually stellar, though we've had some complaints of a bit of attitude.

601 N. Fort Lauderdale Beach Blvd., Fort Lauderdale, FL 33304. © **866/318-1101** or 954/567-8020. Fax 954/567-8040. www.atlantichotelfl.com. 124 units. Winter $299–$619 double, $399–$999 suite; off-season $199–$329 double, $499 suite. AE, DC, DISC, MC, V. Valet parking $28. **Amenities:** 2 restaurants; bar; bike rentals; concierge; outdoor heated pool; room service; spa; watersports equipment/rentals. *In room:* A/C, TV, hair dryer, kitchen/kitchenette, microwave, minibar, Wi-Fi.

Harbor Beach Marriott Resort & Spa ★★ ☺ Harbor Beach is loaded with the same amenities as Pier 66 (below), but has a more secluded setting on 16 oceanfront acres just south of Fort Lauderdale's "strip." Everything in this place is huge—from the quarter-mile of private beach to the 8,000-square-foot pool and the $8-million, 22,000-square-foot European spa. Accommodations feature pillow-top bedding, marble, crown molding, and bathrooms with granite vanities, marble flooring, designer lighting, and wraparound mirrors. Most units open onto private balconies overlooking the pool, the city, the ocean, or the Intracoastal Waterway. The hotel's 3030 Ocean is an excellent seafood restaurant and raw bar helmed by Executive Chef Dean James Max with Chef Paula DaSilva as chef de cuisine, a finalist on the ruthless Gordon Ramsey reality show *Hell's Kitchen;* the Riva, a Mediterranean-style oceanfront eatery, is also top-notch. Return guests include many convention groups and families who enjoy the space and great location. The hotel's Surf Club, $45 half-day and $80 full day, includes lunch, provides arts and crafts, watersports and games to keep the young 'uns happily occupied. Speaking of watersports, this hotel has the most comprehensive list, from surfing to parasailing.

3030 Holiday Dr., Fort Lauderdale, FL 33316. © **800/222-6543** or 954/525-4000. Fax 954/766-6152. www.marriottharborbeach.com. 650 units. Winter $345–$659 double; off-season $298–$401 double; year-round from $630 suite. AE, DC, DISC, MC, V. Valet parking $27; self-parking $22. From I-95, exit on I-595 E. to U.S. 1 N.; proceed to SE 17th St.; make a right and go over the Intracoastal Bridge past 3 traffic lights to Holiday Dr.; turn right. **Amenities:** 4 restaurants; 3 bars; babysitting can be arranged; basketball court; bike rentals; children's programs; concierge; health club; outdoor heated pool; room service; European-style spa; 4 clay tennis courts; extensive watersports equipment/rentals. *In room:* A/C, TV, hair dryer, high-speed Internet, minibar, PlayStation capability.

Hilton Fort Lauderdale Beach Resort ★★ The Hilton Fort Lauderdale Beach Resort is a 25-story landmark property located on the shoreline of Fort Lauderdale's famous A1A between the palm-shaded boulevards of Sunrise and Las Olas. Guests enter the resort through a gracious porte-cochere into a dramatic two-story lobby. The sixth floor Sunrise Terrace offers unobstructed views of the Atlantic

Ocean and features an infinity pool and private poolside cabanas and is reminiscent of the deck of a luxury yacht. The resort's commitment to personal service can be experienced through a dedicated beach concierge, kids' poolside program, accommodating staff, and deluxe turndown service. Each of the 374 studios and suites is outfitted with a separate shower and soaking tub, high-definition flatscreen television, kitchen or kitchenette, and private oceanview balcony with expansive views of the Atlantic. The resort features the Spa Q and two distinct dining options including ilios—an upscale signature restaurant of contemporary Mediterranean cuisine—and Le Marche Gourmet Market & Bakery featuring Starbucks drinks, pizzas, paninis, gelatos, and more.

505 N. Fort Lauderdale Beach Blvd., Fort Lauderdale, FL 33404. (✆ **800/HILTONS** (445-8667) or 954/414-2222. Fax 954/414-2612. www.fortlauderdalebeachresort.hilton.com. 374 units. Seasonal from $400 double. AE, DISC, MC, V. **Amenities:** 2 restaurants; concierge; high-speed Internet access; pool; room service; spa. *In room:* A/C, TV, fridge, microwave.

Hyatt Regency Pier 66 Resort & Spa ★★

Set on 22 tropical acres on the Intracoastal Waterway, this resort is best known for its world-class marina and a rooftop lounge that spins every 66 minutes. If you experience vertigo after sitting in the revolving lounge, an invigorating treatment at the hotel's exquisite Spa 66 will help relocate your sense of balance. Equally invigorating are the recreational amenities, which include a three-pool complex with a 40-person hydrotherapy pool, tennis courts, and an aquatic center with watersports. Grille 66 and Bar, a classy, upscale steakhouse, is a welcome addition. A $40-million refurbishment has transformed the lobby, lawn, and remaining guest rooms with a retro modern decor. New lanai guest rooms have cherrywood furnishings and bathrooms with marble floors and granite vanities. All units have flatscreen televisions, wireless Internet access, and balconies with views of the Intracoastal Waterway and the hotel's lushly landscaped gardens.

2301 SE 17th St. Causeway, Fort Lauderdale, FL 33316. (✆ **800/233-1234** or 954/525-6666. Fax 954/728-3541. www.pier66.com. 380 units. Winter $259–$309 double; off-season $130–$200 double; year-round from $1,000 suite. Rates are cheaper on the hotel's website. AE, DC, DISC, MC, V. Valet parking $23; self-parking $19. **Amenities:** 5 restaurants; 3 bars; bike rentals; concierge; 3 pools; room service; spa; 2 lighted clay tennis courts; watersports equipment/rentals. *In room:* A/C, TV, hair dryer, Wi-Fi.

Il Lugano Suite Hotel ★

If you're looking for condo-like accommodations with full kitchens, washer and dryer, and off-the-beaten-path location with Intracoastal views, this place is for you. If you're looking for action, keep moving along. Much like most of South Florida's condos, this hotel seems, well, empty. The only real action to be had is at star chef Todd English's restaurant da Campo Osteria, which brings people in. We can't quite figure out why English chose this random spot for his first So Flo eatery, but nonetheless, it does bring the people. What it doesn't bring is a hotel scene, per se. Yes, there's a tiny bar in the lobby and an even tinier pool out back, but that's about it. If you see a person in the hallways, don't be alarmed, but it is sort of a rare sight. Suites are condo-comfy, but lack any personality. Staff, when they are around, are very accommodating in that they will lead you away from the hotel and point you in the direction of a place where there's actually people. For those curious about the strange little street on which the hotel is situated—if you're not in the mood to walk under the bridge to the water taxi to see signs of life, check out the little jazz bar or the dive bar called, well Dive Bar, and try to figure out what's going on in this bizarre little neighborhood. We're still trying to understand it.

3333 NE 32nd Ave., Fort Lauderdale, FL 33308 ☎ **954/564-4400.** Fax 954/564-4401. www.illugano. com. 105 suites. Winter $299–$899 double, $289–$999 suite; off season $169–$499 double, $159–$599 suite. AE, DC, DISC, MC, V. Valet parking $25. **Amenities:** Restaurant; bar; private beach cabanas; boat rental; fitness center; pool, in-suite spa treatments. *In room:* A/C, TV/DVD, full kitchens, MP3 docking station, washer/dryer, Wi-Fi.

The Ritz-Carlton Fort Lauderdale ★★★   The first and only five-star hotel on Fort Lauderdale Beach, this $160-million property formerly run by St. Regis and now a Ritz-Carlton has elevated the strip to an entirely new level of luxury. The 183 rooms, including 28 private residences and 34 hotel condominiums, all feature views of the Atlantic or the Intracoastal Waterway, have Wi-Fi Internet access, a state-of-the-art DVD theater entertainment system with a 32-inch LCD panel TV, a 13-inch LCD panel TV in each bathroom, Italian linens, designer bath amenities, and a refrigerated minicellar of refreshments. We particularly like chef Christian Claire's restaurant, a stellar Italian grill, and the 5,000-bottle wine vault with nightly wine tastings. The oceanfront pool is nice, yet understated, and the spa is sublime. Some people have complained that service is snooty while others deem it refined and top-notch. What's universal is that this is a welcome departure from the norm for the area. Inside tip: All rooms ending in 10 offer floor-to-ceiling windows and spectacular views!

1 N. Fort Lauderdale Beach Blvd., Fort Lauderdale, FL 33316. ☎ **800/241-3333** or 954/465-2300. Fax 954/465-2340. www.ritzcarlton.com. 192 units. Winter from $399 double; off-season from $209 double; year-round from $600 suite. AE, DC, DISC, MC, V. Valet parking $30; no self-parking. From I-95, exit on I-595 E. to U.S. 1 N.; proceed to SE 17th St.; make a right and go over the Intracoastal Bridge past 6 traffic lights to Castillo St.; turn left. **Amenities:** 2 restaurants; 2 bars; concierge; health club; outdoor heated pool; room service; European-style spa. *In room:* A/C, TV/DVD, hair dryer, minibar, Wi-Fi.

W Fort Lauderdale ★★★   Wow. Until this W (and the one on South Beach, frankly) opened, we thought that if you'd seen one W hotel you'd seen 'em all. Not so. Designed to resemble a sailboat (but we'd say it's more like a sailing yacht), the W is composed of two towers of 23 stories of hotel rooms and residences. In fact, the entire hotel's design was inspired by the sand and sea, its pièce de résistance being the stunning oceanfront pool deck with glass-enclosed stairway allowing guests and residents to literally walk from the ultramodern W Living Room through the pool's inviting waters and onto the pool deck. When you're standing in the hotel's Living Room you can watch swimmers above through slivers in the ceiling, which virtually assures you that no one is going to pee in the pool. Rooms are typically W, sleek and chic, but unlike some of the more urban Ws, these exude that beach house vibe with neutral colors also inspired by sand and sea and gorgeous bathrooms that open into the main living area. And with almost every W, a Bliss Spa, a branch of Rande Gerber's hipper-than-thou Whiskey Blue bar and lounge, Living Room bar, and WET pool bar. Also unique to this W, a culinary offering from Stephen Starr, whose empire includes Buddakan and Morimoto in Philadelphia and New York City, in the form of his latest concept, Steak 954, a sexy, see-and-be-sceney steakhouse. If the W is too sceney for you, consider its more laid back sister hotel up the block, **The Westin Beach Resort, Fort Lauderdale,** 321 N. Fort Lauderdale Beach Blvd.; (tel. **954/467-1111;** www.starwoodhotels.com), the recipient of a multimillion dollar facelift, featuring 433 rooms and an 8,100-square-foot Heavenly Spa.

401 N. Fort Lauderdale Beach Blvd., Fort Lauderdale, FL 33304. ☎ **866/837-4203** or 954/414-8200. Fax 954/414-8250. www.whotels.com/fortlauderdale. 517 units. Winter $305–$515 double, $675–$875 suite;

off-season $220–$340 double, $475–$675 suite. AE, DC, DISC, MC, V. Valet parking $30. **Amenities:** 2 restaurants; 2 lounges; state-of-the-art fitness center; 2 pools; room service; spa. *In room:* A/C, TV, hair dryer, minibar, Wi-Fi.

Westin Diplomat Resort & Spa ★★   The Diplomat is a 1,060-room, full-service beach resort—the only one of its kind in the somewhat desolate area—loaded with amenities. The main building is a 39-story oceanfront tower surrounded by 8 acres of man-made lakes. A gorgeous bridged, glass-bottom pool with waterfalls, private cabanas, and a slew of watersports adds a tropical touch. Rooms are a cross between those in a subtle boutique hotel and in an Art Deco throwback, with dark woods, hand-cut marble, and the 10-layer Heavenly Bed, a Westin trademark, with custom-designed pillow-top mattresses and very cushy down blankets. Dining options are aplenty, from the fine-dining steakhouse to several more-casual places. Diplomat Landing, the hotel's shopping-and-entertainment complex across the street, features shops and a waterfront sports bar. The resort's golf resort and spa is located across the Intracoastal, featuring 60 luxurious guest rooms, yacht slips, a 155-acre golf course, and a world-class spa and tennis club.

3555 S. Ocean Dr. (Fla. A1A), Hollywood, FL 33019. ☎ **888/627-9057** or 954/602-6000. Fax 954/602-7000. www.diplomatresort.com. 998 units. Winter $305–$515 double, $675–$875 suite; off-season $220–$340 double, $475–$675 suite. AE, DC, DISC, MC, V. Valet parking $22. **Amenities:** 8 restaurants; 3 lounges; golf course; health club; 2 pools; room service; spa; 10 clay tennis courts; watersports equipment/rentals. *In room:* A/C, TV/WebTV, fax, hair dryer, high-speed Internet access, minibar.

EXPENSIVE

Lago Mar Resort and Club ★★ ☺   A charming lobby with a rock fireplace and saltwater aquarium sets the tone of this utterly inviting resort, a casually elegant piece of Old Florida that occupies its own, 10-acre lush little island between Lake Mayan and the Atlantic. Guests have access to the broadest and best strip of 500 feet of private beach in the entire city, not to mention a wonderful bougainvillea-lined, 9,000-square-foot swimming lagoon. Lago Mar is very family oriented, with many facilities and supervised activities for children. Service is spectacular. The plush rooms and suites have Mediterranean or Key West influences. A full-service spa offers a wide array of treatments, while the 1,000-square-foot exercise facility may come in handy after you indulge in the hotel's Northern Italian restaurant, Acquario, which is worth a visit even if you don't stay here. A new $15-million six-story wing of one- and two-bedroom ocean-front suites with individual balconies and larger luxurious bathrooms includes a deck of native tropical landscaping and a 5,000-square-foot saltwater lagoon.

1700 S. Ocean Lane, Fort Lauderdale, FL 33316. ☎ **800/524-6627** or 954/523-6511. Fax 954/524-6627. www.lagomar.com. 212 units. Winter $295 double, from $365 suite; off-season $155 double, from $200 suite. AE, DC, MC, V. Free valet parking. From Federal Hwy. (U.S. 1), turn east onto SE 17th St. Causeway; turn right onto Mayan Dr.; turn right again onto S. Ocean Dr.; turn left onto Grace Dr.; then turn left again onto S. Ocean Lane to the hotel. **Amenities:** 4 restaurants; bar; wine room; children's programs during holiday periods; concierge; exercise room; outdoor pool and lagoon; room service; 2 tennis courts; watersports equipment/rentals. *In room:* A/C, TV, hair dryer, high-speed Internet, kitchenette.

Pillars Hotel ★ 📷   It took me awhile to discover this hotel—and apparently that's exactly the point. One of Fort Lauderdale's best-kept secrets, the Pillars transports you from the neon-hued flash and splash of Fort Lauderdale's strip and takes you to a two-story British colonial, Caribbean-style retreat tucked away on the bustling Intracoastal Waterway. Because it has just 22 rooms, you'll feel as if you have the grand house all to yourself—albeit a house with white-tablecloth room service, an Edenistic courtyard with a free-form pool, lush landscaping, access to a water taxi, and a private chef. Rooms are luxurious and loaded with amenities such as flatscreen TVs, DVD players, private-label bath products, ultraplush bedding, and, if you're so inclined, a private masseuse to iron out your personal kinks. The hotel's private restaurant, the Secret Garden, is open only to guests providing gourmet dinner served under the stars and overlooking the Intracoastal. A library area (with over 500 books) is at your disposal, as is pretty much anything else you request here. Not everyone agrees. One reader complained that her room was small, musty, and far from luxurious.

111 N. Birch Rd., Fort Lauderdale, FL 33304. (℃) **954/467-9639.** Fax 954/763-2845. www.pillarshotel.com. 22 units. Winter $285–$355 double, $399–$575 suite; off-season $195–$235 double, $275–$469 suite. AE, DC, DISC, MC, V. Free off-street parking. **Amenities:** Restaurant; 24-hr. concierge; waterfront pool; room service; water-taxi service; free Wi-Fi. *In room:* A/C, TV/DVD, hair dryer, high-speed Internet, minibar.

Riverside Hotel ★★ A touch of New Orleans hits Fort Lauderdale's popular Las Olas Boulevard in the form of this charming, six-story 1936 hotel. There's no beach here, but the hotel is set on the sleepy and scenic New River, capturing the essence of that ever-elusive Old Florida. Guest rooms, outfitted in Mexican tile and wicker furnishings, are spacious and well maintained. Such details as intricately tiled bathrooms and old-style furniture enhance the charm of the otherwise stark building. The best units face the river, but it's hard to see the water past the parking lot and trees. Twelve rooms offer king-size beds with mirrored canopies and flowing drapes. There are also seven elegantly decorated suites with wet bars and French doors that lead to private balconies. The hotel has two restaurants worth trying: Indigo, a fantastic seafood spot (p. 353), and the Grill Room, for Old World elegance.

620 E. Las Olas Blvd., Fort Lauderdale, FL 33301. (℃) **800/325-3280** or 954/467-0671. Fax 954/462-2148. www.riversidehotel.com. 217 units. Winter $229–$279 suite; off-season $139–$185 suite. Special packages available. Online discounts available. AE, DC, MC, V. Valet parking $8–$10. From I-95, exit onto Broward Blvd.; turn right onto Federal Hwy. (U.S. 1); turn left onto Las Olas Blvd. **Amenities:** 2 restaurants; concierge; outdoor pool; limited room service. *In room:* A/C, TV, fridge, hair dryer, high-speed Internet, minibar.

MODERATE

Courtyard Villa on the Ocean ★ Nestled between a bunch of larger hotels, this small historic hotel is a romantic getaway right on the beach. Courtyard Villa has spacious oceanfront efficiencies with private balconies, larger suites overlooking the pool, and full two-bedroom apartments. Accommodations are plush, with chenille bedspreads and carved four-poster beds; fully equipped kitchenettes are an added convenience. The tiled bathrooms have strong, hot showers to wash off the beach sand. Room no. 8 is especially nice, with French doors that open to a private balcony overlooking the ocean. Relax in the hotel's unique heated pool/spa or on the second-floor sun deck. You can also swim from the beach to a living reef just 50 feet offshore. Located on the same street is Courtyard Villa's sister property, Buena Vista Hotel and Beach Club, 4225 El Mar Dr. ((℃) **800/291-3560**), where in-season rates range from $179 to $279 and off-season rates are $99 to $169.

4312 El Mar Dr., Lauderdale-by-the-Sea, FL 33308. (℃) **800/291-3560** or 954/776-1164. Fax 954/491-0768. www.courtyardvilla.com. 10 units. Winter $159–$359; off-season $109–$225. Rates include full breakfast. AE, MC, V. Pets less than 35 lb. accepted with a $200 deposit; must be caged while outside; no pit bulls, Dobermans, or Rottweilers. **Amenities:** Free bike use; Jacuzzi; free laptop use w/Internet access; outdoor heated pool; limited room service; scuba instruction. *In room:* A/C, TV/VCR, hair dryer, kitchenette.

Ocean Sands Resort and Spa ★   What happens to a struggling oceanfront condo/hotel during a recession? The owner gets desperate—or smart—and hires a hospitality company to run the place as a Residence Inn. And that's exactly what happened here. But this isn't your typical Residence Inn. Instead of a vacant condo, it's now a thriving, low-frills hotel catering to travelers on extended stays looking to save money by cooking their own meals in their own kitchenettes instead of ordering room service or eating out. Too lazy to cook? Don't worry, the resort has a full-service restaurant and bar, which makes this Residence Inn unique from the others, as do the two heated pools, aerobics, Pilates, spinning studios, full-service spa, rooftop walking path, putting green, and *free* valet parking. If only more of those vacant condos took this one's lead.

1350 N. Ocean Dr., Pompano Beach FL 33062. ℂ **800/583-3500** or 954/590-1000. Fax 954/590-1101. www.theoceansandsresortandspa.com. 89 units. Winter $159–$189 studio, $229–$449 suites; off-season $159–$189 studio, $269–$319 suite. AE, DC, MC, V. **Amenities:** Restaurant; bar; putting green; fitness center; Jacuzzi; 2 heated pools; spa; rooftop walking path; watersports. *In room:* A/C, TV, hair dryer, fully equipped kitchen, washer/dryer, free Wi-Fi.

Pelican Grand Beach Resort ★ ☺   The Pelican Beach Resort sits on a 500-foot private beach, with 159 oversize accommodations, oceanfront suites with balconies, and a sublimely relaxing, wraparound oceanfront verandah and sun deck with rocking chairs. What also rocks about this place is the zero-entry pool and the Lazy River tubing ride. This is a great, low-key luxury resort, especially for families looking for a relaxing vacation, with all the amenities of a more harried chain resort overwrought with slews of people. The resort is also completely nonsmoking.

2000 N. Ocean Blvd., Fort Lauderdale, FL 33305. ℂ **800/525-OCEAN** (6232) or 954/568-9431. Fax 954/565-2662. www.pelicanbeach.com. 159 units. Winter $299–$349 double, $520 suite; off-season $220–$270 double, $420 suite. AE, DC, MC, V. Parking $24. **Amenities:** Restaurant; ice cream parlor; bar; fitness center; zero-entry pool; sundeck. *In room:* A/C, TV, fridge, hair dryer, high-speed Internet, microwave.

Seminole Hard Rock Hotel & Casino ★★★   The Seminole Indians have created a miniature Vegas within Hollywood, Florida, and it's doing a booming business, especially after the massive, 130,000-square-foot casino added blackjack in addition to thousands of Vegas-style slot machines, baccarat, and all kinds of poker tables that are always packed. The main draw here is the casino, but the guest rooms are surprisingly cushy and swank, with flatscreen TVs, Egyptian-cotton linens, and big bathrooms with massive shower heads; the suites are hyperluxurious. Equally impressive is the 4½-acre lagoon-style pool that's very similar to the one at the Hard Rock in Vegas, with waterfalls, hot tubs, wireless Internet access, and, of course, a bar. There are lots of bars here, especially at the attached entertainment complex, with two clubs open 24/7, as well as restaurants and stores. There's also a food court, or you can choose from several on-site, full-service restaurants, including a swanky steakhouse, Gloria and Emilio Estefan's

---

Anna Nicole & "Room 607"

Anna Nicole Smith died tragically in Room 607 at the **Seminole Hard Rock Hotel** on February 8, 2007. Because the hotel didn't want to create a macabre tourist attraction, they took the room number "out of inventory," meaning the room is still there, but the number has been changed.

Bongos Cuban Café, and a branch of Fort Lauderdale's disco-licious Italian hot spot, Café Martorano (see below). If all this action has you feeling wiped out, there's always the spa, which, in Seminole Hard Rock fashion, is also pretty sizeable.

1 Seminole Way, Hollywood, FL 33314. ℂ **800/937-0010** or 954/327-7625. Fax 954/327-7655. www. seminolehardrockhollywood.com. 481 units. $189–$259 double; $279 luxury room; $650–$2,000 suite. AE, DC, DISC, MC, V. **Amenities:** 18 restaurants; 11 nightclubs and lounges; casino; Jacuzzi; pool; room service; spa. *In room:* A/C, TV, hair dryer, high-speed Internet access, Tivoli sound system w/CD player.

INEXPENSIVE

Backpacker's Beach Hostel   For the young, or for backpackers on a budget, this hostel is a great option, with both dorm beds and private rooms at bargain-basement prices. Clean and conveniently located, the hostel is just 654 feet from the ocean. It features free parking, free phones, free food for self-cooking, free breakfast buffet, and, if you're lucky, free use of the surfboards or in-line skates lying around.

2115 N. Ocean Blvd., Fort Lauderdale, FL 33305. ℂ **954/567-7275.** www.fortlauderdalehostel.com. 12 units. Dorm beds $20 per night, $145 per week; private rooms $55 double. Rates include breakfast buffet. MC, V. **Amenities:** Garden; kiosk with free Internet access; Ping-Pong; sundeck. *In room:* A/C, TV

Hollywood Beach Hotel & Hostel ★ 📷   From the owners of Miami's hotelier to the hipster on a budget (South Beach Group) comes this beachy, kitschy hostel that pays homage to nomadic surfer culture. Rooms—shared female, male, mixed sex, and private—are Key West style, decorated in blues and yellows and featuring bunk beds, queen beds, security lockers, and mini-kitchenettes with microwave, refrigerator, and sink. The main house is where the action is, with full kitchen, living room, outdoor lounge area, deck, Mexican outdoor restaurant, and bar. Located steps from Hollywood Beach, amenities here are exceptional, from free Wi-Fi to free use of surfboards, bikes, and pool tables. Beach access and parking are also free.

334 Arizona Ave., Hollywood Beach, FL 33109. ℂ **954/391-9448.** www.southbeachgroup.com. 24 units. Dorm beds $20 per night, $145 per week; private rooms $55 double. Rates include breakfast buffet. MC, V. **Amenities:** Garden; free Internet access; sundeck. *In room:* A/C, TV.

Sea Downs (and the Bougainvillea) ★★   This bargain lodging is often booked months in advance by return guests (mostly Europeans) who want to be directly on the beach without paying a fortune. The hosts of this super-clean 1950s motel, Claudia and Karl Herzog, live on the premises and keep things running smoothly. All rooms have fully equipped kitchens with fridges, stoves, utensils, and glassware and have been redecorated here and at the Herzogs' other, even less expensive property next door, the 11-unit Bougainvillea. Guests at both hotels share the Sea Downs' pool. All rooms are now nonsmoking.

2900 N. Surf Rd., Hollywood, FL 33019. ℂ **954/923-4968.** Fax 954/923-8747. www.seadowns.com or www.bougainvilleahollywood.com. 12 units. Winter $111–$168 studio, $127–$198 1-bedroom apt.; off-season $88–$144 studio, $106–$144 1-bedroom apt. Weekly discounted rates available. No credit cards. From I-95, exit Sheridan St. E. to Fla. A1A and go south; drive ½ mile to Coolidge St.; turn left. **Amenities:** Concierge; freshwater outdoor pool. *In room:* A/C, TV, Internet access, fully equipped kitchen.

Where to Dine

It took awhile for a more sophisticated, varied epicurean scene to reach these shores, but Fort Lauderdale—and, to some extent, Hollywood—finally has several fine restaurants. Increasingly, ethnic options are joining the legions of surf-and-turferies that have dominated the area for so long. **Las Olas Boulevard** has so many eateries that the city has put a moratorium on the opening of new restaurants on the 2-mile street. And despite the so-called recession, 2009 saw the opening of star chef Todd English's first South Florida restaurant, Da Campo Osteria, and the opening of Morimoto restaurateur Stephen Starr's Steak 954, kicking off a trend of big name, high end restaurants bypassing Miami for Fort Lauderdale for a change.

VERY EXPENSIVE

Café Martorano ★★★ ITALIAN   This small storefront eatery doesn't win any awards for decor or location, but when it comes to food that's good enough for an entire Italian family, Café Martorano, which recently opened to rave reviews in Las Vegas, is one of the best. People wait for a table for upward of 2 hours because the restaurant accepts no reservations and can get away with it. An almost-offensive sound system (playing disco tunes and Sinatra) has a tendency to turn off many a diner, but you don't go to Café Martorano for an intimate dinner. Dining here is like being at a big, fat, Italian wedding, where eating, drinking, and dancing are paramount. The menu changes daily, but regulars can request special off-the-menu items. If you don't ask, you don't get, so open your mouth. Also keep your eyes wide open for such celebrities as Liza Minnelli, James Gandolfini, and Steven Van Zandt, among others, who make it a point to stop here for a meal while in town. A new outpost of the restaurant opened at the Seminole Hard Rock Hotel and Casino.

3343 E. Oakland Park Blvd., Fort Lauderdale. (✆ **954/561-2554.** www.cafemartorano.com. Reservations not accepted. Main courses $12–$58. MC, V. Daily 5–11pm.

Casa D'Angelo ★★★ ITALIAN   Although Fort Lauderdale may be transforming into thoroughly modern 21st-century beach city, Casa D'Angelo remains steeped in old-school, Old World style and service with an impeccable reputation for some of the best Tuscan-style Italian food in South Florida. Don't be intimidated by the 40-plus-page wine list of regional Italian varietals. The waiters here are friendly and knowledgeable and will help guide you through it if need be. As for chef/owner Angelo Elio's cuisine, insert superlative here, but you won't truly understand until you taste some of the handmade pastas—handmade ravioli filled with spinach and ricotta, homemade fettuccine with roasted veal ragu, pappardelle with porcini mushrooms—after a while saying the word *homemade* becomes redundant because, well, it's the standard here. In addition to pastas, there are expertly grilled chops and fresh and simply prepared seafood such as the superb snapper *oreganatta* with sun-dried tomatoes or jumbo prawns sautéed in white wine, garlic, fresh tomato, and imported Ligurian olives which make the word *flavorful* seem like an understatement. A newer sibling opened in Boca Raton at 171 E. Palmetto Park Rd. (✆ **561/996-1234**) which some say is quieter than the original, but the food is just as exceptional.

1201 N. Federal Hwy., Fort Lauderdale. (✆ **954/564-1234.** www.casa-d-angelo.com. Reservations recommended. Main courses $15–$46. AE, DC, DISC, MC, V. Sun–Thurs 5:30–10pm; Fri–Sat 5:30–11pm.

Da Campo Osteria ★★★ ITALIAN   Why star chef Todd English chose to open in this condo-esque hotel off the beaten track is beyond us, but it doesn't matter. Foodies and fans of English's gourmet Northern Italian fare would go through an *Amazing Race*–type challenge to find the place it's that good. Smaller than most of his restaurants, English has carved a cozy niche here and it's not the slivers of Intracoastal views that keep 'em coming back. You'll stop wondering about the bizarre location as soon as a server arrives to prepare tableside mozzarella ($15), which is quite the show on your eyes and taste buds. Choose from a simple olive oil, sea salt, and cracked pepper prep or go for a spicy version with pickled hot pepperoncini peppers or a sweet one with honey spiced walnuts and blonde raisins. But don't fill up too much because entrees are divine. Skip the simple spaghetti and meatballs—as good as it is, there's better in the form of the ricotta ravioli, prepared old-school Bolognese style, the pork Milanese on the bone with olive-caper relish, or the yellowtail snapper marsala. If you insist on having the meatball, which actually does explain why English is where he is and not cooking at Macaroni Grill (not that there's anything wrong with that), you can order one as a side dish for $10. Some people wonder whether to choose Da Campo over the neighborhood's reigning Italian royalty, Café Martorano. We say you can't choose between the two—Da Campo is a refined, gourmet dining experience, while Martorano is like eating your Italian grandma's cooking—in a disco. Depends on your mood, we guess. English has since expanded in South Florida, opening **Wild Olives by Todd English** in Boca Raton, 5050 Town Center Circle (*ⓒ* **561/544-8000;** www.toddenglish.com), and one expected in CityPlace in West Palm Beach in mid-2010.

In Lugano Hotel, 3333 NE 32nd Ave. (btw. Oakland Park Blvd. and NE 34th Ave.). *ⓒ* **954/226-5002.** www.dacampofl.com. Reservations recommended. Main courses $20–$38. AE, DC, DISC, MC, V. Mon-Sat 7am–11pm; Sun 8am–9pm. From I-95, exit at Oakland Park Blvd. Cross the bridge and make a left on NE 32nd Ave. The hotel is straight ahead on the water.

Darrel & Oliver's Cafe Maxx ★★ FLORIBBEAN/NEW WORLD   Despite its bleak location in an unassuming storefront, Darrel & Oliver's Cafe Maxx is one of the best restaurants in Broward County. When it opened in 1984, it was the first restaurant to have an open kitchen, and what a stir that caused! Now, instead of the kitchen, the marvel is what comes out of it. Consider rosemary-rubbed ostrich filet with roasted corn and pumpkin polenta, cranberry blueberry relish, and shaved "drunken" goat cheese; or pan-seared scallops with bacon-braised Brussels sprouts, toasted pine nut polenta, and cranberry balsamic vinaigrette. Yum. But save room for dessert—the coconut sweet potato pie or chocolate ancho flan with prickly pear coulis and candied jalapeño are just two of many diet- and mind-blowing options.

2601 E. Atlantic Blvd., Pompano Beach. *ⓒ* **954/782-0606.** Fax 954/782-0648. www.cafemaxx.com. Reservations recommended. Main courses $9–$49. AE, DC, DISC, MC, V Mon–Thurs 5:30–10:30pm; Fri–Sat 5:30–11pm; Sun 5:30–10pm. From I-95, exit at Atlantic Blvd. E. The restaurant is 3 lights east of Federal Hwy.

Steak 954 ★ STEAKHOUSE   With the exception of the Strip House down in Key West, there aren't many steakhouses that can be called playful, per se. Until restaurant mogul Stephen Starr, of Morimoto fame, decided to open this restaurant at the very playful W Fort Lauderdale. Playful in a sleek and sexy way, Steak 954's menu emphasizes simple flavors of dry-aged meats, but the taste and the scene are anything but simple. While the menu may be steakhouse simple, with steaks, chops, seafood, sandwiches, raw bar, and sides, this is Fort Lauderdale's newest "it" girl, a virtual meat market of seeing and being seen in between stabbing into serious steaks. Taking a cue from Nobu, or should we say Morimoto, the miso-glazed black cod is a great alternative to meat. The restaurant is tops for ambience too—dark woods and bold floral silk wall panels, with the restaurant's centerpiece being a 15-foot-long reef aquarium home to hypnotic jellyfish. Between that and the cocktails, you'll understand what we mean by playful. Don't be too playful, though, and accidentally order the 36-ounce Kobe porterhouse—price tag: $245. That's one expensive play date.

W Fort Lauderdale, 401 N. Fort Lauderdale Beach Blvd., Fort Lauderdale. ⓒ **954/414-8333.** www. steak954.com. Reservations recommended. Main courses $26–$65. AE, DC, DISC, MC, V. Sun–Thurs 7am–10pm; Fri–Sat 7am–11pm; Sun 5:30–10pm.

3030 Ocean ★★ SEAFOOD   The Harbor Beach Marriott signature, casually chic lobby (read: no ocean views) restaurant was always known for good food thanks to Chef Dean Max (who most recently also signed on as creative director of cuisine down in the Keys at Cheeca Lodge) but then its chef de cuisine, Paula da Silva, came in second place on the grueling Gordon Ramsey reality show *Hell's Kitchen.* She didn't need to win to make this place a hit, either. With a focus on seafood and local, seasonal ingredients, da Silva, under Max's direction, sure can cook. But before things get cooking, consider the spicy tuna tartare, a common sighting in many area restaurants, but none as delicious, fresh, and savory as here, diced ahi Gulf tuna served with sesame oil, pickled daikon, yuzu aioli, and orange soy juice. Raw bar selections are plentiful and tempting, but where da Silva shines is, indeed, in the kitchen, *Hell's* or otherwise. Among the standouts: sautéed Florida red snapper with a smooth purée of sweet boniato yam, grilled green onions, and a light cumin-scented orange carrot sauce; and Niman Ranch pork rib chop with organic Yukon purée, baby bok choy, and baby champagne beets, in a divine white truffle honey sauce. Menu changes often and varies by season guaranteeing the freshest ingredients possible. For aspiring future contestants on *Hell's Kitchen,* Chef Max teaches cooking classes and promises to part with some culinary secrets.

Marriott's Harbor Beach Resort & Spa, 3030 Holiday Dr., Ft. Lauderdale. ⓒ **954/765-3030.** www.3030ocean.com. Reservations recommended. Main courses $29–$44. AE, DC, DISC, MC, V. Sun–Thurs 6–10pm; Fri–Sat 6–10:30pm.

EXPENSIVE

Anthony's Runway 84 ★★★ ITALIAN   Meet Anthony, the gregarious owner of this Fort Lauderdale restaurant with an interior all about jet-setting—albeit in the mid- to late '70s—and a bar crafted out of a plane fuselage. Once you meet him, he will introduce your server, whose name is likely to be Tony. Same goes for the bartender. The quintessential, convivial Italian vibe in here (think Travolta in *Saturday Night Fever*) is conducive to one of the most enjoyable meals you'll ever have. The best way to go is—what else?—family-style, in which you'll be able to share lots of dishes such as mussels marinara, fried clams, roasted red peppers in garlic, shrimp parmigiana, an out-of-this-world rigatoni with cauliflower (although it sounds boring, order it no matter what!), and stellar meat and poultry dishes that frequent fliers to Anthony's rave about each time, as if it were their last meal. For the best pizza, try nearby **Anthony's Coal Fired Pizza,** 2203 S. Federal Hwy. (ⓒ **954/462-5555**), which is quickly on its way to becoming a bona fide chain with locations all over South Florida. This one is the original though.

330 S.R. 84, Fort Lauderdale. ⓒ **954/467-8484.** Reservations strongly recommended. Main courses $15–$50. AE, DC, DISC, MC, V. Tues–Thurs and Sun noon–10pm; Fri–Sat 5–11pm.

Eduardo De San Angel ★★★ MEXICAN   Gourmet Mexican is *not* an oxymoron, and for those who don't believe that, take one meal at the sublime Eduardo De San Angel and you'll see how true it is. Chef Eduardo Pria has a masterful way with food, as seen in dishes such as *jaibas rellenas* (fresh Florida blue crab, plum tomatoes, onions, jalapeños, and Spanish green olives baked in a shell with melted jack cheese au gratin and mole poblano) or the ancho chili–flavored crepe filled with *cuitlacoche,* serrano chilies, and onions with melted *asadero* cheese laced with a squash blossom sauce. Fresh flowers and candlelight, not to mention the fact that the restaurant resembles an intimate hacienda, also drive home the fact that this isn't your mom's Old El Paso taco dinner. Beer and wine only.

2822 E. Commercial Blvd., Fort Lauderdale. ℂ **954/772-4731.** www.eduardodesanangel.com. Reservations essential. Main courses $24–$32. AE, DC, DISC, MC, V. Mon–Thurs 11:30am–10:30pm; Fri–Sat 5:30–10:30pm.

Himmarshee Bar & Grille ★ AMERICAN   Located on a popular street of bars frequented by Fort Lauderdale's young professionals, Himmarshee Bar & Grille is known for its scene and cuisine. A mezzanine bar upstairs is ideal for people-watching; outdoor tables are tight, but strategically situated in front of all the street's action. On weekend nights, in particular, it's difficult to get a table. However, if you can deal with cramming into the bar, it's worth a cocktail or two. The wine list is impressive, and the grilled chili–dusted pork chop with boniato-stuffed poblano chili, Monterey Jack cheese, and creamy, spicy corn sauce is really good. Also try the chorizo taquitos as an appetizer. Check out Side Bar, the restaurant's very ski-lodgey bar next door featuring live music and a bustling crowd of young hipsters.

210 SW 2nd St. (south of Broward Blvd., west of U.S. 1), Fort Lauderdale. ℂ **954/524-1818.** www. himmarshee.com. Reservations recommended. Main courses $20–$35. AE, MC, V. Mon–Thurs 11:30am–2:30pm and 6–10:30pm; Fri 11:30am–2:30pm and 6–11:30pm; Sat 6–11:30pm; Sun 6–10:30pm.

Johnny V's ★★★ SOUTHWESTERN   South Florida's favorite so-called Caribbean Cowboy, Chef Johnny Vinczencz, has moved around quite a bit—from South Beach's Hotel Astor (twice!) to Delray Beach's Sundy House. But this Las Olas hot spot looks to be his final stop, and that's good news to all Johnny V's faithful foodies who will travel to the end of the earth to sample some of his barbecue and Caribbean-inspired contemporary cuisine. What that means is, sage-grilled Florida dolphin with rock shrimp plantain stuffing, lobster pan gravy, cranberry-mango chutney, baby green beans and carrots, and a slew of dishes you've likely never seen before Once you've tasted his fare, you'll understand why a herd of hungry folks are extremely happy to have a place to satisfy their cravings for such gourmet grub. Barbra Streisand dined here while in town for her sold-out concerts in 2006 and couldn't stop singing the praises of Johnny V—onstage during her show! She—and Johnny—were *verklempt* (falling over themselves with delight)! Chef Johnny has also opened a new, inexpensive eatery where nothing is over $20, including a delicious Philly cheesesteak sandwich with shaved rib-eye for $11. **Smith & Jones Bar and Grill,** 1313 Las Olas Blvd., will also feature live jazz and blues nightly.

625 E. Las Olas Blvd. ℂ **954/761-7920.** www.johnnyvlasolas.com. Reservations suggested. Main courses $25–$42. AE, DC, MC, V. Mon–Thurs 11:30am–2:30pm and 5:30–11pm; Fri 11:30am–2:30pm and 5:30pm–midnight; Sat 5:30pm–midnight; Sun 5:30–11pm.

Sage French Café and Oyster Bar ★★ FRENCH   A cozy, modern, cacophonous Francophile's dream come true, Sage's Hollywood locale is less bawdier than its Fort Lauderdale one which comes complete with a Moulin Rouge–meets–Fort Lauderdale Strip burlesque show. We prefer the less flashy Hollywood (FL) version because you can concentrate more on the food, which is the true showgirl here, one who wears a lot less makeup than its sister. A far cry from a brassy brasserie, this

Sage features a backlit bar, open grill, shellfish bar, see-through wine cellar, and a Chihuly-esque chandelier straight out of an animated Disney flick. As for the menu, Chef Laurent Tasic has his shellfish flown in daily from Canada, California, or the Chesapeake Bay. The menu isn't all seafood, however, with an unabridged list of crepes, French classic starters including grilled artichoke, chicken liver pâté, escargot, and a hearty French onion soup, and entrees such as a fabulous casoulet, a superb plate of steak *frites,* coq au vin, short ribs Parisienne—Tasic's secret sauce of mystery ingredients along with red peppers and onion demi sauce, and Chef Laurent's meatloaf—ground veal and filet mignon with fresh herbs in a savory mushroom garlic Merlot sauce. Fans of duck rave about the crispy, half roasted duck served with a honey raspberry sauce. For those who want a side of bawdy with their Bourginon, Sage's Fort Lauderdale location is at 2378 N. Federal Hwy., Fort Lauderdale (© **954/565-2299**).

2000 Harrison St., Hollywood. © **954/391-9466.** www.sagecafe.net. Reservations recommended. Main courses $18–$30. AE, MC, V. Sun–Thurs 11am–10pm; Fri–Sat 11am–11pm.

Sunfish Grill ★★★ SEAFOOD   Unlike its fellow contemporary seafood restaurants, the Sunfish Grill chooses to focus on fish, not fusion. Chef Anthony Sindaco is content to leave the spotlight on his fantastic fish dishes, which are possibly the freshest in town, thanks to the fact that he buys his fish at local markets and often from well-known fishermen who appear at his back door with their catches of the day. Chef Tony's tuna tartare is legendary. Chilean sea bass, expertly cooked with roast beef–potato hash, glazed turnips, and crispy parsnip fries in a natural sauce, is wonderful. The best dish, in my opinion, is the truffle-crusted black grouper. But the menu changes often so you never know what you may get here, but whatever it is, it's going to be good. In fact, almost everything at the Sunfish Grill is better than at most seafood restaurants.

2761 E. Oakland Park Blvd., Pompano Beach. © **954/788-2434.** www.sunfishgrill.com. Reservations recommended. Main courses $20–$35. AE, MC, V. Mon–Thurs 6–9:30pm; Fri–Sat 6–10:30pm.

Trina Restaurant ★★★ MEDITERRANEAN   Yes, it's expensive, but the Mediterranean-infused seafood dishes are worth every penny. Try the skewers of diver scallops and braised short ribs with summer truffle reduction and truffled cauliflower or the fire-roasted Chilean sea bass with basil crumbs, white beans, and garlic spinach in a tomato basil broth. Out of this world. Menu changes often so you may find other dishes equally as excellent such as the oven-roasted sea bass with sautéed baby watercress, braised cherry tomatoes, fingerling potatoes, raisins, capers, and Kalamata olives. Reservations here are hard to come by, especially in season, but the Trina Lounge is also a great option, offering lighter—and cheaper—fare with high-style ambience. Although we love the buzz of the indoor dining room, request a table outside overlooking the ocean.

601 N. Fort Lauderdale Beach Blvd., Fort Lauderdale. © **954/567-8070.** www.trinarestaurantand lounge.com. Reservations recommended. Main courses $22–$42. AE, DC, DISC, MC, V. Sun–Thurs 5:30–10pm; Fri–Sat 5:30–10:30pm. Lounge open later.

MODERATE

Cap's Place Island Restaurant ★ 📷 SEAFOOD   Opened in 1928 by a bootlegger who ran in the same circles as gangster Meyer Lansky, this barge-turned-restaurant is one of the area's best kept secrets. Although it's no longer a rum-running restaurant and casino, its illustrious past (FDR and Winston Churchill dined here together) landed it a spot on the National Register of Historic Places. To get here, you have to take a ferryboat, provided by the restaurant. The short ride across the Intracoastal definitely adds to the Cap's Place experience. The food is good, not great. Traditional seafood dishes such as Florida or Maine lobster, clams casino, and oysters Rockefeller will take you back to the days when a soprano was just an opera singer.

2765 NE 28th Court, Lighthouse Point. 954/941-0418. www.capsplace.com. Reservations recommended. Main courses $14–$32. MC, V. Daily 5:30pm–midnight. To get to Cap's Place, motor-launch from I-95, exit at Copan's Rd. and go east to U.S. 1 (Federal Hwy.). At NE 24th St., turn right and follow the double lines and signs to the Lighthouse Point Yacht Basin and Marina (8 miles north of Fort Lauderdale). From here, follow the CAP'S PLACE sign pointing you to the shuttle.

Creolina's Dixie Takeout ★ 🍴 CREOLE You'll find authentic Louisiana Creole cuisine at this small but very popular restaurant that moved from the Riverwalk area in 2008 to nearby suburb Davie when the landlord decided to expand the neighboring bar into the restaurant. Though the new strip-mall locale is hardly idyllic, the prices are—gumbo is offered all day at just $4.50. In addition to Creole, the chef has added Southern classics including country-fried steak, chicken and dumplings, pulled pork, and country-style ribs. Sides include cornbread, greens, black-eyed peas, as well as macaroni and cheese. There is also a terrific New Orleans Sunday brunch. Ask to sit in sassy Rosie's section.

13150 W. S.R. 84, Fort Lauderdale. 954/524-2003. Main courses $5–$20. AE, MC, V. Mon 11am–2:30pm and 5–9pm; Tues–Thurs 11am–2:30pm and 5–10pm; Fri 11am–2:30pm and 5–11pm; Sat 5–11pm; Sun 5–9pm.

Indigo ★ SEAFOOD A popular people-watching spot, Indigo is a reliable seafood restaurant housed in the New Orleans–style Riverside Hotel. The dining room is nice enough, but sit outside and watch the pedestrian parade that is Las Olas Boulevard. Among the menu highlights: pan-roasted Florida snapper, citrus-crusted Florida grouper, and chargrilled pork loin.

In the Riverside Hotel, 620 E. Las Olas Blvd., Fort Lauderdale. 954/467-0671. Reservations accepted for parties of 6 or more. Main courses $10–$36. AE, DC, DISC, MC, V. Daily 7am–9:45pm.

Rustic Inn Crabhouse ★ SEAFOOD A Fort Lauderdale rough and-tumble landmark for more than 50 years, Rustic Inn isn't the place for a romantic, intimate, quiet dinner. The minute you walk into this inn that's more reminiscent of a trailer, you're assaulted by fluorescent interrogation-style lighting and cacophonous banging—a symphony from a packed house of happy diners cracking their crabs with wooden mallets. Although you don't *have* to crack your own crabs—diva Barbra Streisand didn't when she dined here (she requested them already cracked—god forbid she should break a nail!)—it's all part of the experience. Newspaper lines the tables, so prepare to get your hands dirty. Although the restaurant is known for its "world-famous garlic crabs" (and we think they are totally deserving of that lofty tagline), you can also order lobster, pasta, and all sorts of fried fish—even fried alligator (it's chewier than chicken!). The fried clams are especially good, but if you want to gorge yourself, try the Reef Raft, a basket of fried oysters, fried scallops, and fried fish. Dress very casual and prepare to wait awhile for a table; but trust me, it's worth it.

4331 Ravenswood Rd., Fort Lauderdale. 954/584-1637. Reservations not accepted. Main courses $10–$20; crabs are market price. AE, DC, DISC, MC, V. Mon–Sat 11:30am–10:45pm; Sun 2–9:45pm.

Sugar Reef ★★ FRENCH CARIBBEAN   I could go on about this restaurant's priceless ocean view, but the menu of Mediterranean, Caribbean, and French dishes is just as outstanding. A funky fish-shack vibe is bolstered by fresh air wafting in from the Atlantic. Seafood bouillabaisse in green curry and coconut broth and Sugar Reef *pho*—a Vietnamese noodle dish with chicken, shrimp, ginger, and spices—are among the restaurant's most popular dishes. The kitchen puts a savory spin on duck, roasted and topped with sweet-chili-and-papaya salsa. This is not a place you'd expect to find on a beach boardwalk, which makes it all the more delightful.

600 N. Surf Rd. (on the Broadwalk, just north of Hollywood Blvd.), Hollywood. ⓒ 954/922-1119. www. sugarreefgrill.com. Reservations accepted for parties of 6 or more. Main courses $10–$28. AE, DISC, MC, V. Mon 4–10:30pm; Tues–Thurs 11am–10:30pm; Fri-Sun 11am–11pm (sometimes later in winter).

INEXPENSIVE

The Floridian Restaurant ★ 🍴 AMERICAN/DINER   The Floridian, affection-ately known as "The Flo" has been filling South Florida's diner void for more than 63 years, serving breakfast, lunch, and dinner, 24/7. It's especially busy on weekend morn-ings when locals and tourists come in for huge omelets, fresh oatmeal, sausage, and biscuits. Just to prove it's up to par with swanky Fort Lauderdale, the Floridian offers a $300 Fat Cat meal for two that includes steak, eggs, and a bottle of Dom Perignon! While some say the place needs a major cleaning (especially if you sit outside—it's filthy there), others insist that the grit and grime are part of the greasy spoon's charm.

1410 E. Las Olas Blvd., Fort Lauderdale. ⓒ **954/463-4041.** Fax 954/761-3930. Sandwiches $3–$7; breakfast combos $3.50–$8; hot platters $7–$14. No credit cards. Daily 24 hr.

Jaxon's ★ 😊 ICE CREAM   South Florida's best and only authentic old-fash-ioned ice-cream parlor and country store attracts those with sweet tooths from all over the area. Their cravings are satisfied with an unabridged assortment of home-made ice cream served any which way. Kids love the candy store in the front of the restaurant, and adults love the pre–Ben & Jerry's authenticity. For the calorie-con-scious, the sugar-free and fat-free versions are pretty good. Jaxon's most famous everything-but-the-kitchen-sink sundae has countless scoops and endless toppings.

128 S. Federal Hwy., Dania Beach. ⓒ **954/923-4445.** Sundaes $2.75–$7.95. AE, DISC, MC, V. Mon–Thurs 11:30am–11pm; Fri-Sat 11:30am–midnight; Sun noon–11pm.

La Spada's Original Hoagies ★★ SANDWICHES   An institution since 1973, La Spada's is the answer to every sandwich fan whether you call it a sub or a hoagie. That said, we think the so-called sandwich artists at Subway could stand to take a lesson or two on the art that has been so perfected here. The artful arranging of lay-ers of fresh meats piled into a chewy roll with lettuce, tomato, onion, pickles, and their own blend of marinated sweet peppers make us rethink the whole sandwich-artist moniker. Here, they're sandwich scientists.

4346 Seagrape Dr., Lauderdale-by-the-Sea. ⓒ **954/776-7893.** www.laspadashoagies.com. Sand-wiches $6–$11. AE, MC, V. Mon-Sat 10am–8pm; Sun 11am–8pm (open at 10am on game days).

Lester's Diner ★ AMERICAN   Since 1968, Lester's Diner has been serving swarms of South Floridians large portions of great greasy-spoon fare until the wee hours. Try the eggs Benedict and the 14-ounce "cup" of classic coffee, or sample one of Lester's many homemade desserts. The place serves breakfast 24 hours a day and is a Fort Lauderdale institution that attracts locals, club crowds, city officials, and a generally motley, friendly crew of hungry people craving no-nonsense food served by seasoned waitresses with beehive hairdos that contribute to the campy atmosphere. A second Lester's opened in Sunrise, right near Sawgrass Mills and Ikea, at 1399 NW 136th Ave. (© **954/838-7473**).

250 S.R. 84, Fort Lauderdale. © **954/525-5641.** Main courses $5–$15. AE, MC, V. Daily 24 hr.

Le Tub ★★ 🍴 AMERICAN   Hands down, this is one of the coolest, most unpretentious, quintessential pre–swanky South Florida restaurants, if not one of the coolest restaurants, period. Established in 1959 as a Sunoco gas station, Le Tub was purchased in 1974 by a man who personally transformed the place into this waterfront restaurant, made out of flotsam, jetsam, and ocean-bone treasures gathered over 4 years of jogging on Hollywood Beach. But the waterfront location and unique building aren't the only things to marvel at. As you walk in, take note of the hand-painted bathtubs and toilet bowls (it's not at all gross; they're used as planters) lining the walkway. Inside is a divey bar complete with pool table and jukebox; outside seating on the deck is the real gem. Le Tub is famous for its burgers (which *Esquire* magazine and Oprah have declared the country's best, thereby increasing the masses who flock here a millionfold), chili, and seafood, but more appealing than the food is the peaceful, easy feeling exuded by the place.

1100 N. Ocean Dr., Hollywood. © **954/931-9425.** Main courses $6–$17. No credit cards. Daily 10:30am–4am.

Sushi Blues Cafe ★ SUSHI   Before Hollywood was "hot," Sushi Blues Cafe was singing the blues—in a good way, as the only game in town. Now that the area is bustling, it's singing the blues in an even better way, serving up live music 4 nights a week, along with raw fish that's quite good. Garlic- and ginger-studded tuna steak is also fantastic for those who are bored with sushi. Even better, however, is the fact that, for once, a meal at a sushi restaurant where such restaurants are a dime a dozen actually seems like a unique experience. Attached to the restaurant is the Blue Monk Lounge, where cocktails and live music make for a lively scene.

600 N. Surf Rd. (on the Broadwalk just north of Hollywood Blvd.), Hollywood. © **954/922-1119.** Reservations accepted for parties of 6 or more. Main courses $9–$29; sushi rolls $4–$15. AE, DISC, MC, V. Daily 11:30am–2am.

Tarpon Bend ★ SEAFOOD/AMERICAN   This restaurant is one of the few places where the fishermen still bring the fish to the back door. The oysters from the raw bar are shucked to order and are incredible. Try the house specialty, "smoked fish dip"—a kingfish smoked on premises. The seafood kettle, with clams, mussels, shrimp, calamari, and fresh fish simmered in light tomato sauce with grilled veggies and red skinned potatoes, is scrumptious and served in its own pot. There's live entertainment Monday, Wednesday, and Saturday and a full bar. There's another Tarpon Bend in Coral Gables at 65 Miracle Mile (© **305/444-3210**).

200 SW 2nd St., Fort Lauderdale. © **954/523-3233.** Reservations accepted for parties of 6 or more. Main courses $12–$15. AE, MC, V. Mon–Thurs 11:30am–1am; Fri–Sat 11:30am–3am.

The Hollywood & Fort Lauderdale Area After Dark

Fort Lauderdale no longer mimics the raucous antics of *Animal House* as far as nightlife is concerned. It has become hip to the fact that an active nightlife is vital to the city's desire to distract sophisticated, savvy visitors from the magnetic lure of South

Beach. While Lauderdale is no South Beach, it has vastly improved the quality of its nightlife by welcoming places that wouldn't dare host wet-T-shirt or beer-chugging contests. It also lacks the South Beach attitude, which is part of the attraction.

Hollywood's nightlife seems to be in the throes of an identity crisis, touting itself as the next South Beach, while at the same time hyping its image as an attitude-free nocturnal playground. Here's the real deal: At press time, Hollywood nightlife was barely awake, with the exception of a few bars and one struggling dance club. If you're looking for a quiet night out, it's probably your best bet. But don't come too late—after midnight, the city is absolutely deserted.

For information on clubs and events, pick up a free copy of Fort Lauderdale's weekly newspaper *City Link,* or the Fort Lauderdale edition of the *New Times.*

The Culture Room   If you consider rock and heavy metal to be culture, visit the Culture Room and bang your head to local bands. Open nightly from 8pm to 3am. 3045 N. Federal Hwy. (at Oakland Park Blvd.), Fort Lauderdale. (f) **954/564-1074.** www.cultureroom.net. Cover varies.

Elbo Room   Formerly Spring Break central, the Elbo Room has actually managed to maintain its rowdy and divey reputation by serving up frequent drink specials and live bands. Ironically, it was almost torn down until the Penrod family of chic and sleek Nikki Beach fame bought the place to keep it alive. No matter what, it'll always be a beloved dive, though! Open daily from 10am to 2am. 241 S. Atlantic Blvd. (corner of Las Olas Blvd. and Fla. A1A), Fort Lauderdale. (f) **954/463-4615.** www.elboroom.com.

The Gallery at Beach Place   This outdoor shopping-and-entertainment complex, modeled after Coconut Grove's CocoWalk, landed on the legendary "strip" with several franchised bars and restaurants. It's the beachy version of a mall and is popular with a very young set at night. The view of the ocean makes it worth a stop for a drink. Hours vary by establishment; some places are open until 2 or 3am, while others close around 11pm. 17 S. Fort Lauderdale Beach Blvd., Fort Lauderdale. (f) **954/760-9570.**

Harrison's Wine Bar   Dark, cozy, and so comfy that it's hard to get up from the big leather couches, Harrison's attracts a hip crowd that mulls over, sniffs, and sips from more than 100 kinds of vino at reasonable prices. There are also 40 bottled beers. Cheese platters, hummus platters, and panini are available. Open daily from 4pm to 2am. 1916 Harrison St., Hollywood. (f) **954/922-0074.** www.harrisonswinebar.com.

Karma Lounge   Almost too hip for Fort Lauderdale, Karma Lounge boasts a British resident DJ, which, if you know anything about DJs or club music, is a big deal. Progressive house music is the soundtrack for this glammy, orange-and-white ultra-mod spot that's frequented by the dolled-up over-25 set. Open Wednesday through Thursday from 10pm to 3am, Friday and Saturday from 10pm to 4am. 4 W. Las Olas Blvd., Fort Lauderdale. (f) **954/523-7159.** Cover varies.

Mai Kai   Immerse yourself in this fabulous vestige of Polynesian kitsch: hula dancers, fire eaters, and potent drinks served in coconuts. The food, an ambiguous blend of Chinese, Polynesian, and other Asian cuisine, is tasty but overpriced. No matter; it's bound to get cold as you watch the hilarious show, which includes everything from Tahitian classics to Polynesian versions of American hits. A trip to undeniably fun Mai Kai is a must. **Note:** The cocktails cost almost as much as a meal. Open daily from 5pm until midnight. 3599 N. Federal Hwy. (between Commercial and

Oakland Park blvds.), Fort Lauderdale. ☎ 954/563-3272. Reservations required. Shows (2 nightly) are $11 for adults, free for children 12 and under.

The Parrot   Fort Lauderdale's most famous dive bar, The Parrot is a local's and out-of-towner's choice for an evening of beer (16 kinds on tap), bonding, and browsing the bar's gallery of photos of almost everyone who's ever imbibed here since its opening in 1970. Open Sunday through Thursday from 11am to 2am, and Friday and Saturday from 11am to 3am. 911 Sunrise Lane, Fort Lauderdale. ☎ **954/563-1493.**

The Poor House   There's nothing poor about this microbrew hangout, where excellent live music by local bands starts at midnight and goes on well into the wee hours. A friendly, lively, mixed crowd composes a generational cross section where the gap is bridged by a common love of music, cold beer, and good times. Open nightly from 5pm to 2am. 110 SW 3rd Ave., Fort Lauderdale. ☎ **954/522-5145.**

Revolution   Some of today's hottest indie bands play here, but if you're not into live music, fret not because this cavernous place is a dance club, too. Open Thursday to Sunday until 4am. Opening hours and cover charges vary, depending on what band is playing. 200 W. Broward Blvd., Fort Lauderdale. ☎ **954/727-0950.**

Riverwalk   You'll find this outdoor shopping-and-entertainment complex in the heart of downtown Fort Lauderdale, on the sleepy yet scenic New River—as a result of its river site, it has more charm than most such complexes. In fact, if you've got a boat, you can sail here. A host of bars, restaurants, and shops, not to mention a high-tech virtual-reality arcade, the Escape, and a multiplex cinema are enough to keep you occupied for at least a few hours. On weekends, this place is packed. 400 SW 2nd St. (along the New River from NE 6th Ave. to SW 6th Ave.), Fort Lauderdale. ☎ **954/468-1541.**

Seminole Hard Rock Hotel & Casino ★★★   When it comes to nightlife in these parts, some of the hottest lounges and clubs are located within this mega-complex. Among them, Pangaea and Gryphon, opened by a NYC nightlife impresario, and Opium, which—gasp—crossed the county line from Miami and was followed by its faithful disciples of A-listers and club kids spanning the tricounty area. Also here: popular dance club Passion, Murphy's Law Irish Pub, Automatic Slim's, and more. 5707 Seminole Way, Hollywood ☎ **954/581-5454.** Cover charges vary at each venue and range from free to $20.

Shooters   This waterfront bar is quintessential Fort Lauderdale. Inside you'll find nautical types, families, and young professionals mixed with a good dose of sun-burned tourists enjoying the live reggae, jazz, or Jimmy Buffett-style tunes, with the gorgeous backdrop of the bay and marinas all around. Open Monday through Friday from 11:30am to 2am, Saturday from 11:30am to 3am, and Sunday from 10am to 2am. 3033 NE 32nd Ave., Fort Lauderdale. ☎ **954/566-2855.**

BOCA RATON ★★ & DELRAY BEACH ★

26 miles S of Palm Beach, 40 miles N of Miami, 21 miles N of Fort Lauderdale

Boca Raton is one of South Florida's most expensive, well-maintained cities—home to ladies who lunch and SUV-driving yuppies. The city's name literally translates as "rat's mouth," but you'd be hard-pressed to find rodents in this area's fancy digs.

If you're looking for funky, wacky, and eclectic, look elsewhere. Boca is a luxurious resort community and, for some, the only place worth staying in South Florida. Although Jerry Seinfeld's TV parents retired to the fictional Del Boca Vista, Boca is just too pricey to be a retirement community. With minimal nightlife, entertainment in Boca is restricted to leisure sports, excellent dining, and upscale shopping. The city's residents and vacationers happily comply.

Delray Beach, named after a suburb of Detroit, is a sleepy-yet-starting-to-awaken beachfront community that grew up completely separate from its southern neighbor. Because of their proximity, Boca and Delray can easily be explored together. Budget-conscious travelers would do well to eat and sleep in Delray and dip into Boca for sightseeing and beaching only. The 2-mile stretch of beach here is well maintained and crowded, though not mobbed. Delray's "downtown" area is confined to Atlantic Avenue, which is known for restaurants from casual to chic, quaint shops, and art galleries. During the day, Delray is slumbering, but thanks to the recent addition of trendy restaurants and bars, nighttime is a much more animated hotbed of hipster activity. Still, compared to Boca, Delray is much more laid-back, trendy, but hardly as chichi, and a cuter little beach town than sprawling, swanky, suburban Boca.

Essentials

GETTING THERE Like the rest of the cities on the Gold Coast, Boca Raton and Delray are easily reached from I-95 or the Florida Turnpike. Both the Fort Lauderdale–Hollywood International Airport and the Palm Beach International Airport are about 20 minutes away. **Amtrak** (© **800/USA-RAIL** [872-7245]; www.amtrak.com) trains make stops in Delray Beach at an unattended station at 345 S. Congress Ave.

VISITOR INFORMATION Contact or stop by the **Palm Beach County Convention and Visitors Bureau,** 1555 Palm Beach Lakes Blvd., Suite 800, West Palm Beach, FL 33401 (© **800/554-PALM** [7256] or 561/233-3000; fax 561/471-3990; www.palmbeachfl.com). It's open Monday through Friday from 8:30am to 5:30pm and has excellent coupons and discounts. Monday through Friday from 8:30am until at least 4pm, stop by the **Greater Boca Raton Chamber of Commerce,** 1800 N. Dixie Hwy., 4 blocks north of Glades Road, Boca Raton, FL 33432 (© **561/395-4433;** fax 561/392-3780; www.bocaratonchamber.com), for information on attractions, accommodations, and events in the area. You can also try the **Greater Delray Beach Chamber of Commerce,** 64 SE Fifth Ave., half a block south of Atlantic Avenue on U.S. 1, Delray Beach, FL 33483 (© **561/278-0424;** fax 561/278-0555; www.delraybeach.com), but I recommend the Palm Beach County Convention and Visitors Bureau since it has information on the entire county.

Beaches & Outdoor Activities

BEACHES Thankfully, Florida had the foresight to set aside some of its most beautiful coastal areas for the public's enjoyment. Many of the area's best beaches are located in state parks and are free to pedestrians and bikers, though most do charge for parking. Among the beaches I recommend are Delray Beach's **Atlantic Dunes Beach,** 1600 S. Ocean Blvd., which charges no admission to access a 7-acre developed beach with lifeguards, restrooms, changing rooms, and a family park area; and Boca Raton's **South Beach Park,** 400 N. Ocean Blvd., with 1,670 feet of beach, 25 acres, lifeguards, picnic areas, restrooms, showers, and 955 feet of developed beach

Boca Raton & Delray Beach

The Addison **27**
Baja Cafe **25**
Bistro Zenith **16**
Boca Raton Executive
  Country Club **11**
Boca Raton Municipal
  Golf Course **17**
Boca Raton Museum of Art **24**
Boca Raton Resort & Club **28**
Boston's on the Beach **9**
Caldwell Theatre **12**
Crane's BeachHouse **8**
Dada **2**
Daggerwing Nature Center **17**
De La Tierra **7**
Delray Beach Public Beach **9**
Delray Beach Tennis Center **1**
Delux **3**
Elwood's **5**
Falcon House **6**
Gatsby's **29**
Gumbo Limbo
  Environmental Complex **22**
Inn at Ocean Breeze Golf
  and Country Club **14**
Kathy's Gazebo **21**
Mario's of Boca **19**
Max's Grille **24**
Mizner Park **24**
Morikami Museum
  and Japanese Gardens **10**
New York Prime **18**
Old Homestead **28**
Patch Reef Park **15**
Red Reef Park **23**
Sundy House **7**
32 East **4**
The Tin Muffin Cafe **26**
Tom's Place **13**
Town Center Mall **20**
Uncle Tai's **20**

THE GOLD COAST | Boca Raton & Delray Beach

359

south of the Boca Inlet, accessible for an admission charge of $15 Monday through Friday, and $17 Saturday and Sunday. The two beaches below are also very popular.

Delray Beach, on Ocean Boulevard at the east end of Atlantic Avenue, is one of the area's most popular hangouts. Weekends especially attract a young and good-looking crowd of active locals and tourists. Refreshments, snack shops, bars, and restaurants are just across the street. Families enjoy the protection of lifeguards on the clean, wide strip. Gentle waters make it a good swimming beach, too. Restrooms and showers are available, and there's limited parking at meters along Ocean Boulevard.

Spanish River Park Beach, on North Ocean Boulevard (Fla. A1A), 2 miles north of Palmetto Park Road in Boca Raton, is a huge 95-acre oceanfront park with a half-mile-long beach with lifeguards as well as a large grassy area, making it one of the best choices for picnicking. Facilities include picnic tables, grills, restrooms, showers, and a 40-foot observation tower. You can walk through tunnels under the highway to access nature trails that wind through fertile grasslands. Volleyball nets always have at least one game going on. The park is open from 8am to 8pm. Admission is $16 for vehicles Monday through Friday; $18 on Saturday, Sunday, and major holidays.

Also see the description of **Red Reef Park** under "Scuba Diving & Snorkeling," below.

GOLF   This area has plenty of good courses. The best ones that are not in a gated community are **Boca Raton Resort & Club** (p. 363) and the **Breeze Golf and Country Club** (p. 364), formerly known as the Inn at Boca Teeca. Another great place to swing clubs is at the **Deer Creek Golf Club,** 2801 Country Club Blvd., Deerfield Beach (© **954/421-5550;** www.deercreekflorida.com), which also features a 300-plus-yard driving range and practice facility. Rates at the Deer Creek Golf Club are seasonal and range from $45 to $140. However, from May to October or November, about a dozen private courses open their greens to visitors staying in Palm Beach County hotels. This "Golf-A-Round" program is free or severely discounted (carts are additional), and reservations can be made through most major hotels. Ask at your hotel or contact the **Palm Beach County Convention and Visitors Bureau** (© **561/471-3995**) for information on which clubs are available for play.

The **Boca Raton Municipal Golf Course,** 8111 Golf Course Rd. (© **561/483-6100**), is the area's best public golf course. There's an 18-hole, par-72 course covering approximately 6,200 yards, as well as a 9-hole, par-30 course. Facilities include a snack bar and a pro shop where clubs can be rented. Greens fees are $16 to $34 for 9 holes, and $24 to $56 for 18 holes. Ask about special summer discounts.

SCUBA DIVING & SNORKELING   Moray Bend, a 58-foot dive spot about ¾ mile off Boca Inlet, is the area's most popular. It's home to three moray eels that are used to being fed by scuba divers. The reef is accessible by boat from **Force E Dive Center,** 877 E. Palmetto Park Rd., Boca Raton (© **561/368-0555;** www.force-e.com). Phone for dive times. Dives cost $55 to $65 per person with an extra $15 for two tank fills.

Red Reef Park, 1400 N. Ocean Park Blvd. (© **561/393-7974**), a 67-acre oceanfront park in Boca Raton, has good swimming and year-round lifeguard protection. There's snorkeling around the shallow rocks and reefs that lie just off the beach. The park has restrooms and a picnic area with grills. Located a half-mile north of Palmetto Park Road, it's open daily from 8am to 10pm. The cost is $16 per car Monday through Friday, $18 on Saturday and Sunday; walkers and bikers get in free.

TENNIS   The snazzy **Delray Beach Tennis Center,** 201 W. Atlantic Ave. (© **561/ 243-7360;** www.delraytennis.com), has 14 lighted clay courts and five hard courts available by the hour. Phone for rates and reservations.

The 17 public lighted hard courts at **Patch Reef Park,** 2000 NW 51st St. (© **561/367-7090**), are available by reservation. The fee for nonresidents is $5.75 per person per 1½ hours. Courts are available Monday through Saturday from 7:30am to 10pm, and Sunday from 7:30am to dusk; call ahead to see if a court is available. To reach the park from I-95, exit at Yamato Road West and continue past Military Trail to the park.

Seeing the Sights

Boca Raton Museum of Art ★★
In addition to a relatively small but well-chosen permanent collection that's strongest in 19th-century European oils (Degas, Klee, Matisse, Picasso, Seurat), the museum stages a wide variety of excellent temporary exhibitions by local and international artists. Lectures and films are offered on a fairly regular basis, so call ahead for details.

Mizner Park, 501 Plaza Real, Boca Raton. © **561/392-2500.** www.bocamuseum.org. Admission $8 adults, $6 seniors, $4 students, free for children 12 and under. Additional fees may apply for special exhibits and performances. Free on Wed except during special exhibitions. Tues, Thurs, and Sat 10am-5pm; Wed and Fri 10am-9pm; Sun noon-5pm.

Daggerwing Nature Center ★
Seen enough snowbirds? Head over to this 39-acre swampy splendor where birds of another feather reside, including herons, egrets, woodpeckers, and warblers. The trails come complete with a soundtrack provided by songbirds hovering above (watch your head). The park's night hikes will take you on a nocturnal wake-up call for owls at 6pm. Bring a flashlight. A $2-million expansion in 2007 added a 3,000-square-foot exhibit hall, a laboratory classroom, and exciting wet forest and conservation exhibits. Best part about the new addition is the elevated boardwalk over a swamp featuring two trails and an observation tower from which a keen eye can view the abundant plant and animal life including: osprey, woodpeckers, butterflies (including the park's namesake S Ruddy Daggerwing), endangered wood storks, alligators, and a wide variety of bromeliads.

South County Regional Park, 11200 Park Access Rd., Boca Raton © **561/488-9953.** Free admission. Tues-Sun 10am-4:30pm. Call for tour and activity schedule.

Gumbo Limbo Environmental Complex ★★★
If manicured lawns and golf courses aren't your idea of communing with nature, then head to Gumbo Limbo. Named for an indigenous hardwood tree, the 20-acre complex protects one of the few surviving coastal hammocks, or forest islands, in South Florida. Walk through the hammock on a half-mile-long boardwalk that ends at a 40-foot observation tower, from which you can see the Atlantic Ocean, the Intracoastal Waterway, and much of Boca Raton. From mid-April to September, sea turtles come ashore here to lay eggs.

1801 N. Ocean Blvd. (on Fla. A1A btw. Spanish River Blvd. and Palmetto Park Rd.), Boca Raton. © **561/338-1473.** www.gumbolimbo.org. Free admission ($3 donation suggested). Mon-Sat 9am-4pm; Sun noon-4pm.

Morikami Museum and Japanese Gardens ★★★
Slip off your shoes and enter a serene Japanese garden that dates from 1905, when an entrepreneurial farmer, Jo Sakai, came to Boca Raton to build a tropical agricultural community. The Yamato

Colony, as it was known, was short-lived; by the 1920s, only one tenacious colonist remained: George Sukeji Morikami. But Morikami was quite successful, eventually running one of the largest pineapple plantations in the area. The 200-acre Morikami Museum and Japanese Gardens, which opened to the public in 1977, was Morikami's gift to Palm Beach County and the state of Florida. A stroll through the garden is almost a mile long. An artificial waterfall that cascades into a koi- and carp-filled moat; a small rock garden for meditation; and a large bonsai collection with miniature maple, buttonwood, juniper, and Australian pine trees are all worth contemplation. There's also a cafe with an Asian-inspired menu if you want to stay for lunch.

4000 Morikami Park Rd., Delray Beach. ℗ **561/495-0233.** www.morikami.org. Museum $12 adults, $11 seniors, $7 children 6-17. Museum Tues–Sun 10am–5pm; gardens Tues–Sat 10am–5pm. Closed major holidays.

Shopping & Browsing

Even if you don't plan to buy anything, a trip to Boca Raton's **Mizner Park** is essential for capturing the essence of the city. Mizner is the place to see and be seen, where Rolls-Royces and Ferraris are parked curbside, freshly coiffed women sit amid shopping bags at outdoor cafes, and young movers and shakers chat on their constantly buzzing cellphones. Beyond the human scenery, however, Mizner Park is scenic in its own right, with beautiful landscaping. It's really an outdoor mall, with 45 specialty shops, seven good restaurants, and a multiplex. Each shop front faces a grassy island with gazebos, potted plants, and garden benches. Mizner Park is on Federal Highway, between Palmetto Park and Glades roads (℗ **561/362-0606**).

Boca's **Town Center Mall,** on the south side of Glades Road, just west of I-95, has seven huge department stores, including Nordstrom, Bloomingdale's, Burdines, Lord & Taylor, and Saks Fifth Avenue. Add hundreds of specialty shops, an extensive food court, and a range of other restaurants, and you have the area's most comprehensive shopping center.

On Delray Beach's Atlantic Avenue, especially east of Swinton Avenue, you'll find a few antiques shops, clothing stores, and galleries shaded by palm trees and colorful awnings. Pick up the *Downtown Delray Beach* map and guide at almost any of the stores on this strip, or call ℗ **561/278-0424** for more information.

Where to Stay

A number of national chain hotels worth considering include the moderately priced **Holiday Inn Highland Beach Oceanside,** 2809 S. Ocean Blvd., on Florida A1A, southeast of Linton Boulevard (℗ **800/234-6835** or 561/278-6241). Although you won't find rows of cheap hotels as in Fort Lauderdale and Hollywood, a handful of mom-and-pop motels have survived along Florida A1A between the towering condominiums of Delray Beach. Look along the beach just south of Atlantic Boulevard. Especially noteworthy is the pleasant little two-story, shingle-roofed **Bermuda Inn,** 64 S. Ocean Blvd. (℗ **561/276-5288**). The **Delray Beach Marriott,** 10 N. Ocean Blvd. (℗ **561/274-3200;** www.marriottdelraybeach.com) is a popular but expensive stay, directly across from the beach with pool and spa. Rates range from $399 during season to a lot lower in the summer.

Even more economical options can be found in Deerfield Beach, Boca's neighbor, south of the county line. A number of beachfront efficiencies offer great deals, even in the winter months. Try the **Panther Motel and Apartments,** 715 S. A1A

(**954/427-0700**), a clean and convenient motel with rates starting as low as $49 (in season, you may have to book for a week at a time; rates then start at $250).

VERY EXPENSIVE

Boca Raton Resort & Club ★★ ☺   This landmark resort is a sprawling 350-acre collection of oddly matched buildings: the original Cloister (which is undergoing a long, drawn out renovation with some of the old rooms still available at lesser prices and are only a decent option if you don't mind being the only one on an entire floor or you've ever wondered what mustiness smelled like back in 1927); the drab pink 27-story Tower; the renovated Beach Club and Pool Oasis, accessible by water shuttle or bus and featuring three redesigned swimming pools, oceanfront bar, beach access, cabana, modern rooms, and sunning terraces; and Yacht Club, a Venetian-style wing of 112 luxury rooms and suites. Fans of the old-school resort should feel right at home as Old World blends beautifully with New World, modern twists. Everything at this resort, which straddles the Intracoastal, is at your fingertips, but may sometimes require some effort to reach. Thankfully the resort provides transportation shuttles every 10 minutes. Amenities include the grand Spa Palazzo, two 18-hole championship golf courses, a $10-million tennis and fitness center, a 25-slip marina, and a private beach with watersports equipment. The resort's also foodie heaven, with a choice of 10 places to dine including **Morimoto Sushi Bar, Cielo,** Meat Packing District landmark **Old Homestead,** and a bustling branch of NYC's venerable **Serendipity** ice cream parlor.

501 E. Camino Real (P.O. Box 5025), Boca Raton, FL 33432. ℂ **888/495-BOCA** (2622) or 561/447-3000. Fax 561/447-3183. www.bocaresort.com. 1,047 units. Winter $259–$760 double; off-season $169–$329 double. Seasonal packages available. AE, DC, DISC, MC, V. From I-95 N., exit onto Palmetto Park Rd. E. Turn right onto Federal Hwy. (U.S. 1), then left onto Camino Real. **Amenities:** 10 restaurants; 5 bars; indoor basketball court; extensive children's programs; concierge; 2 18-hole championship golf courses; 2 fitness centers; 32-slip marina; 4 pools; room service; spa; 30 hydrogrid tennis courts; watersports equipment/rentals. *In room:* A/C, TV, hair dryer, minibar.

The Seagate Hotel & Spa ★★★   Not everything was a victim of the real estate bust. Take this beachy, Nantucket-y resort that opened in December in a space originally set to be a swanky condo. Located just one block from the beach on Delray's bustling East Atlantic Avenue, The Seagate Hotel & Spa offers you the best of the beach and the city. The best part about the hotel besides its location is the nearby Seagate Beach Club, located less than a mile from the hotel and offering casual and fine dining with gorgeous coastal views, access to watersports equipment rentals, an outdoor swimming pool and free transportation to and from the hotel. Decor is beachy-chic, featuring a 5,000-gallon aquarium in the main lobby and rooms boasting upscale designer furnishings with Egyptian-cotton linens and all the stylish, tranquil neutral tones you'd find in, say, Martha Stewart's beach house. The pool on the actual hotel property is pretty large and tropically landscaped. An on-site restaurant, the Atlantic Grille, offers indoor and terrace seating and seafood, pasta, and steak dishes. The world-class 8,000-square-foot spa has seven treatment rooms and signature treatments including the Hot Shell Massage.

1000 E. Atlantic Ave., Delray Beach, FL 33483. ℂ **877/57-SEAGATE** (577-3242) or 561/665-4800. Fax 561/665-4801. www.theseagatehotel.com. 162 units. Winter $349–$669; off-season $169–$559. AE, DC, MC, V. **Amenities:** Restaurant; bar; beach club with pool; room service; watersports; free Wi-Fi in public areas. *In room:* A/C, TV/DVD, hair dryer, high-speed Internet, MP3 docking station.

Sundy House ★★★   The oldest residence in Delray Beach, Sundy House is a bona fide 1902 Revival-style home that has been restored to its Victorian glory—on the outside, at least. Inside, the four one- and two-bedroom apartments are in a style best described as Caribbean funky or tropical chic, adorned in brilliant colors and outfitted with state-of-the-art electronics, full modern kitchens, and laundry facilities. Six guest rooms known as the Stables are equestrian chic, with rustic appointments in dark woods. While the rooms here are outstanding, it's the surrounding property that garners the most oohs and aahs. Set on an acre of lush gardens, the Sundy House is surrounded by more than 500 species of exotic plants, streams, and parrots, making an escape here seem more Hawaii than Florida. You can even swim with fish in the hotel's swimming pond! The on-site restaurant features exquisite New Florida cuisine, often using fresh fruits and herbs straight from Sundy House's botanical Taru Garden.

106 S. Swinton Ave., Delray Beach, FL 33444. © **877/439-9601** or 561/272-5678. Fax 561/272-1115. www.sundyhouse.com. 11 units. Winter $219–$549 1- or 2-bedroom or cottage; off-season $169–$499 1- or 2-bedroom or cottage. AE, DC, DISC, MC, V. **Amenities:** Restaurant; bar; swimming pond; limited room service. *In room:* A/C, TV/DVD, CD player, hair dryer, kitchen, washer/dryer.

EXPENSIVE

Crane's BeachHouse ★★   If you can't afford your own South Florida beach house—and why bother with all the maintenance, anyway?—Crane's BeachHouse, meticulously run and maintained by husband and wife Michael and Cheryl Crane, is a haven away from home, located just 1 block from the beach and right in the middle of historic Delray Beach. The main draws here are the whimsical, tropical suites, in which every piece of furniture and bric-a-brac is completely original and often crafted by local artists. Although each unit has its own theme—Hawaii, Amazon, Anacapri, and Capetown, for instance—the beds are all the same, in that they are downright heavenly. Lush gardens, a Tiki bar, and a swimming pool leave you with little reason to flee the premises, but when you do, you'll want to return as quickly as possible.

82 Gleason St., Delray Beach, FL 33483. © **866/372-7263** or 561/278-1700. Fax 561/278-7826. www.cranesbeachhouse.com. 27 units. Winter $189–$239 double, $289–$499 suite; off-season $139–$169 double, $199–$299 suite. AE, DC, DISC, V. Free parking. **Amenities:** 2 small outdoor pools. *In room:* A/C, TV/VCR, hair dryer, Internet access, full kitchen, minibar.

INEXPENSIVE

The Inn at Ocean Breeze Golf and Country Club ★   For more than 3 decades, this lodging has attracted golf fanatics who couldn't care less about the small but comfortable rooms, because they're too busy out on the superb 27-hole golf course, open only to members and guests. For the golf widow(er)s, most of the rooms in this three-story motel-style building have balconies or patios from which to watch or signal to their significant others that it's time for dinner.

5800 NW 2nd Ave., Boca Raton, FL 33487. © **561/994-0400.** Fax 561/998-8279. www.theinnatocean breeze.com. 46 units. Winter from $119 double; off-season from $59 double. AE, DC, MC, V. **Amenities:** Restaurant; golf course; fitness center; small pool; 6 tennis courts. *In room:* A/C, TV, free Wi-Fi.

Where to Dine

Boca Raton and its surrounding area is the kind of place where you discuss dinner plans at the breakfast table. Nightlife in Boca means going out to a restaurant. But who cares? This is some of the best dining in South Florida. Delray Beach, on the other hand, has an excellent cuisine and nightlife scene. Best of both worlds.

VERY EXPENSIVE

The Addison ★★★ NEW AMERICAN/CONTINENTAL   Located in Addison Mizner's 1925 office building near his famous Boca Raton Resort, the Addison is one of Boca's most popular—and romantic—restaurants, with a stunning courtyard with a canopy of banyan trees and a setting straight out of a swank Spanish village. The menu ranges from comfort food, including such dishes as fried chicken and barbecued beef short ribs, steaks, and chops, to more nouveau dishes such as corn-crusted soft-shell crab with roasted garlic mash and fennel salad. Service is swift and professional, but people really come here for the ambience.

2 East Camino Real, Boca Raton. ⓒ **561/395-9335.** www.theaddison.com. Reservations recommended. Main courses $16–$37. AE, DC, DISC, MC, V. Sun–Thurs 5–10pm; Fri–Sat 5–11pm.

Cielo ★★★ CONTINENTAL   The nicest thing about the ugly pink tower at the Boca Resort, Cielo (located on the 26th floor), is this restaurant where the Italian-accented continental cuisine is nothing short of exceptional. While it may be hard to ignore the spectacular views from above, once you see what's on your plate, you may notice nothing but. Choose from a decadent, three-course dinner, or opt for a lighter meal of Spanish-style tapas, available at the restaurant's ultramodern bar area complete with loungey cruise ship-esque or Vegas-esque window seating. Whichever you choose, consider as your appetizer the twice-baked cheese soufflé with mushroom, English pea and Parmesan velouté or the tortelli of oven-roasted pumpkin with amaretti biscuit and sage and brown butter emulsion. Entrees are the standouts, including a five-spice organic Irish salmon with beluga couscous, creamy leeks, tomato, and steamed clams or Ellensburg lamb osso bucco of seared breast, creamy polenta, and baby vegetables in a *harissa* jus. Even if you don't eat here, have a drink at the sleek bar. Cocktails are as creative as the food.

501 E. Camino Real (in the Boca Raton Resort), Boca Raton. ⓒ **561/447-3640.** www.bocaresort.com. Main courses $29–$41. AE, MC, V. Tues–Sat 6–10pm; bar 4:30–11pm Tues–Sat.

Kathy's Gazebo Cafe ★★★ CONTINENTAL   An elegant, old-school Continental restaurant with chandeliers and white linen tablecloths, Kathy's white-glove restaurant is an ideal spot for special occasions or culinary nostalgia. The food is superb—the Dover sole is flown in from Holland and prepared with nothing fancier than an almandine or meunière sauce; chateaubriand is also spectacular and, in a city smitten by plain ol' steak and sushi, it's a delicious throwback to simpler, delicious days. Fresh homemade pastries and peach Melba are among the desserts. While jackets aren't commonly required at restaurants in South Florida, you'll want to wear one here just to fit in with the dapper moneyed types who frequent the place.

4199 N. Federal Hwy., Boca Raton. ⓒ **561/395-6033.** www.kathysgazebo.com. Reservations required. Main courses $20–$43. AE, MC, V. Daily 5:30–10pm.

Morimoto Sushi Bar ★★★ SUSHI   A tiny outpost of Iron Chef Masaharu Morimoto's original Philly sushi spot, Morimoto is one of the hottest tickets in Boca and South Florida in general. If you can snag a reservation to this tiny, ultramodern eatery, take it, even if it's at the unfashionably early hour of, say, 5pm. Don't come expecting a huge selection of dishes, either. It's all about the sushi and sashimi and if you're a true fan of both, you won't hesitate to order the Omakase Tasting Menu in which the skilled sushi chef trained by the Iron Chef himself will choose for you.

501 E. Camino Real (in the Boca Raton Resort), Boca Raton. ☎ **561/447-3640.** www.bocaresort.com. Sushi/sashimi $6–$9 per piece, *maki* $6–$14, *omakase* tasting menu $50 and $75 per person. AE, MC, V. Sun–Wed 5–10pm; Thurs–Sat 5–11pm.

New York Prime ★ STEAKHOUSE This South Florida outpost of a South Carolina–based chain is the prime spot for carnivores looking to satisfy their cravings for big, succulent steaks. Fish dishes are also available, including lobsters ranging from 3 to 13 pounds. But excess does not come cheap. In fact, the restaurant brazenly states its case on the menu: "We strive to be the Mercedes of steakhouses by offering the very best . . . but you can't drive a Mercedes for the same price as a Buick." Cute motto, but in terms of consistency, New York Prime is a Pinto. On one night, the food and service are exquisite, while on another, abysmal. Take your chances, though, because if you do hit it on a good night, you won't be disappointed.

2350 Executive Center Dr., Boca Raton. ☎ **561/998-3881.** www.newyorkprime.com. Reservations recommended. Main courses $21–$75. AE, MC, V. Daily 5–11pm.

Old Homestead ★★★ STEAKHOUSE If you're homesick for New York, this branch of New York's oldest meatery is the place to cure your yearnings, especially if money is no object. The 40-porterhouse for two at $46 per person is pricey, but cheaper than a plane ticket to Gotham—and it's worth it. The meat here is divine. Sides are a la carte and outstanding. The hash-brown potato pie and buttermilk onion rings are my favorites, but all sorts of starches and veggies are available at steep prices from $8 to $10 per dish. Seafood is also aplenty, from fresh shucked oysters to Maine lobsters; and for diners who just can't seem to find the ideal chopped salad, the hand-chopped version of blue cheese, olives, mushrooms, bacon bits, eggs, and hearts of palm is a meal in itself.

501 E. Camino Real (in the Boca Raton Resort), Boca Raton. ☎ **561/447-3640.** www.bocaresort.com. Reservations required. Main courses $28–$46. AE, MC, V. Sun–Wed 5–10pm; Thurs–Sat 5–11pm.

EXPENSIVE

Ke'e Grill ★★★ SEAFOOD Owners Jim and Debbie Taube respect the seafood they serve, some of the freshest in all of South Florida, by leaving off the bells, whistles, and soppy sauces found on so many fish dishes these days. Boasting a beautiful, bustling dining room overlooking a tropical garden, Ke'e Grill used to not take reservations until the lines out the door got out of control. Lucky for us they do now, although it's still completely worth the wait. Appetizers include a sensational blue crab cake or perfectly crispy, fried calamari with dipping sauce that's delicious but not even necessary. For entrees, choose from a papaya, roasted garlic, and sweet chili–glazed Chilean sea bass which may sound like a lot going on, but it's flavor in its most simplest form, complimenting the fish like a simple diamond necklace does a plain black dress. Sautéed yellowtail snapper, sautéed yellowfin tuna or crab cakes all come with two side dishes of pasta, rice, veggies, or potato. The house specialty, the Keè Grill [sic] Chioppino is a study in seafood—specifically shrimp, scallops, grouper, clams, mussels, lobster, and pearl pasta in a spicy seafood broth—an all-in-one explanation of why this restaurant serves some of South Florida's finest fish fare.

17940 N. Military Trail, Boca Raton. ☎ **561/995-5044.** Reservations strongly suggested. Main courses $20–$28. AE, DC, DISC, MC, V. Daily 4:30–9:30pm.

Sundy House Restaurant ★★ FLORIBBEAN This restaurant is a stunning place that combines elegant indoor dining and lush tropical outdoor settings with a gastronomic wizardry of fresh fruits, vegetables, and spices grown on the Sundy House's 5-acre farm. Each dish is prepared with palpable precision. Consider the following: pan-roasted Chilean sea bass with garlic broccolini, balsamic marinated plum tomatoes and truffled sweet pea and lobster risotto, or the mojo-seared salmon with Manchego cheese corn arepa, sweet bell peppers, hearts of palm, watercress salad, and papaya chili vinaigrette. Save room for dessert, including a decadent vanilla bean crème brûlée and mandarin orange chocolate torte. A decadent Sunday brunch buffet makes the day before you return to work infinitely more bearable. On the negative side, the service here can be surly and spotty.

In the Sundy House, 106 S. Swinton Ave., Delray Beach. ✆ **561/272-5678.** www.sundyhouse.com. Reservations essential. Main courses $22–$36. AE, DC, DISC, MC, V. Daily 11:30am–2:30pm and 6–10pm; Sun brunch 10:30am–2:30pm.

32 East ★★ NEW AMERICAN The menu changes every day at this popular people-watching outpost of tasty, contemporary American food, with a focus on local, seasonal ingredients and a menu that changes nightly. Among the standouts are sauté of Gulf Coast grouper with hedgehog mushrooms, Cipollini onions, and white beans in butternut squash sherry broth; sauté of Florida dolphin on potato purée with white truffle-mushroom gravy, sugar snap peas, and crispy leeks; and grilled duck breast and radicchio with parsnip-yam purée and pomegranate-Saba brown butter. The buzzing ambience makes 32 East a popular hangout spot for the cocktail set.

32 E. Atlantic Ave., Delray Beach. ✆ **561/276-7868.** www.32east.com. Reservations recommended. Main courses $18–$40. AE, DC, MC, V. Sun–Thurs 5:30–10pm; Fri–Sat 5:30–11pm. Bar until 2am.

Uncle Tai's ★★★ CHINESE Not your average egg-roll-and-lo-mein place, Uncle Tai's, Boca's best upscale Chinese restaurant, offers a savory spin on classics such as garlic chicken and duck with plum sauce. A family-run restaurant, Uncle Tai's is the product of Wen Dah Tai, who studied with master chefs in China, Japan, and the Philippines. Tai wants to make sure you emerge from his restaurant satisfied, and he'll go the extra mile to discourage you from ordering a dish that's less suited to Western palates because it was specially created for the restaurant's many Chinese diners.

5250 Town Center Circle (btw. Glades and Palmetto Park roads), Boca Raton. ✆ **561/368-8806.** www. uncle-tais.com. Reservations suggested. Main courses $15–$50. AE, DISC, MC, V. Sun–Thurs 11:30am–2:30pm and 5–10pm; Fri–Sat 11:30am–2:30pm and 5–10:30pm.

MODERATE

Bova Cucina ★ ITALIAN This extremely popular, bustling Italian bistro keeps Boca's biggest mouths busy with massive portions of great homemade Italian food. The garlic rolls and the pizza are especially worth piping down for. A huge selection of pastas, sandwiches, and entrees is also available and pretty good, but we say stick to the pizzas. Formerly Mario's of Boca, Bova Cucina is part of a huge restaurant conglomeration (whose owner Scott Rothstein was busted and imprisoned in 2010 for a billion dollar Madoff-esque Ponzi scheme) that owns several swanky South Florida steakhouses called **Bova Prime,** with the original being at 401 Las Olas Blvd. in Fort Lauderdale (✆ **954/767-6555;** www.bovaprime.com).

1901 N. Military Trail (at the Holiday Inn, opposite Kings Market), Boca Raton. ✆ **561/392-5595.** www. mariosofboca.com. Reservations not accepted. Main courses $11–$17. AE, MC, V. Daily 7–10:30am; Mon–Thurs 11:30am–10pm; Fri–Sat 11:30am–11pm; Sun noon–9:30pm.

Max's Grille ★ AMERICAN   Max's Grille is a very popular, very good option in Mizner Park, but you'll have to wait to be seated. An exhibition kitchen occupies the back wall of the restaurant, so those diners lucky enough to score a table can watch as their yellowfin tuna steak or filet mignon is seared on a flaming oak grill. There's also a large selection of chicken, meatloaf, pastas, and main-course salads.

404 Plaza Real, in Mizner Park, Boca Raton. ✆ **561/368-0080.** Reservations accepted for parties of 6 or more. Main courses $11–$30. AE, DC, DISC, MC, V. Mon–Thurs 11:30am–3pm and 5–10:30pm; Fri–Sat 11:30am–3pm and 5–11pm; Sun 11:30am–10pm.

The Office ★★ AMERICAN   Ever since he closed his own eponymous eateries in Miami and Fort Lauderdale, Miami's boldface chef Mark Militello couldn't seem to find his place. After a short stint at the hotel formerly known as the Regent Bal Harbour, Militello backed away from the scene for a while until he partnered with restaurateur David Manero (DeVito South Beach) to open The Office in early 2010, a gastropub whose cuisine Militello describes as "modern American casual fare with style." Because it's Militello, however, it's upscale with an emphasis on local growers, products, and seafoods. Think grass-fed pork honey-braised ribs with fennel pollen and celery root apple slaw; "pork and beans"—Niman Ranch pork belly, BBQ-baked butter beans, and crispy leeks; roasted beef marrow with parsley-caper salad; burgers, and spicy Asian chicken wings. Decor is reminiscent of an industrial chic, yet cozy, library. Oh, and there's a selection of 35 to 40 beers. We're all hopped up over this one.

210 E. Atlantic Ave., Delray Beach. ✆ **561/276-3600.** www.theofficedelray.com. Reservations recommended. Entrees $9–$28. AE, DC, MC, V. Daily 11am–11pm.

Taste Gastropub AMERICAN   Is it coincidence that Militello's fellow Mango Gang member and star chef Allen Susser also opens his own gastropub in Delray, of all places? We're not sure, but the more the merrier, as Susser gets beach with his own gastropub which opened in the spring of 2010. Taste features gourmet pub fare from sandwiches and sliders to small plates and creative cocktails with, according to Susser, "a little South Florida flavor—of course." Among the specialties: house-made potato chips with caramelized onion-garlic-chive dipping sauce, oysters with carbonated cucumber gazpacho, jerk chicken lollipops with mango barbecue sauce, peekytoe crab and Kobe beef sliders, Korean-style spareribs, and Julia Child's beef bourguignon. Decor is retro-urban, with couches and communal tables, tapas bar, and exhibition kitchen.

169 NE 2nd Ave. and Pineapple Grove Way, Delray Beach. ✆ **877/418-2783.** http://tastegastropub. com. Reservations suggested. Main courses $10–$30. AE, DC, DISC, MC, V.

INEXPENSIVE

Baja Cafe ★ MEXICAN   A jeans-and-T-shirt kind of place with wooden tables, Baja Cafe serves fantastic Mexican food at even better prices. Although the salsa borders on somewhat sweet, they do have the hottest sauces; if you like spicy, they will be happy to slap plenty on your meal if you request it. This place is located right by the Florida East Coast Railway tracks, so don't be surprised if you feel a little rattling. Live music and entertainment make this place a hot spot for an unpretentious crowd.

201 NW 1st Ave., Boca Raton. ✆ **561/394-5449.** Reservations not accepted. Main courses $6–$15. No credit cards. Mon–Thurs 11:30am–10pm; Fri–Sat 11:30am–11pm; Sun 5–10pm.

Heart Stoppers Sports Grill ★ AMERICAN   This hospital-themed burger joint isn't for everyone with a disclaimer on their menu saying "Overconsumption of our food will definitely lead to obesity, at which point you should consult a physician before starting an exercise program." In addition, the entire place is decked out, if you can call it that, like a hospital with waitresses dressed as nurses, wheelchairs in lieu of regular chairs, and assorted hospital equipment all over the place. It's kind of vile if you ask me, but apparently the medical kitsch is secondary to their menu boasting things like chili chest pain fries and burgers with names like the Heart Attacker and The Ripper, which are wheeled out on a cart attached to an IV bag. If you don't pass out from the food, you may when you receive your bill, delivered in a first-aid box. Actually, you won't. The food is reasonably priced but we couldn't resist. In fact, anyone weighing more than 350 pounds can eat at the restaurant for free. For the daredevils out there, we dare you to take The Heart Stopper Challenge: eat their 3-pound burger and fries and beat the best existing time and you'll replace the current champ on the wall. If not, your picture may end up in their City Morgue. Just like your arteries.

1100 Linton Blvd., Delray Beach. © **561/276-5554.** Reservations not accepted. Burgers $6–$11. AE, MC, V. Daily 11am–11pm.

The Tin Muffin Cafe ★ BAKERY/SANDWICH SHOP Popular with the downtown lunch crowd, this excellent storefront bakery keeps folks lining up for big sandwiches on fresh bread, plus muffins, quiches, and good homemade soups such as split pea or lentil. The curried-chicken sandwich is stuffed with chunks of white meat doused in a creamy curry dressing and fruit. There are a few cafe tables inside and even one outside on a tiny patio. Be warned, however, that service is forgivably slow and parking is a nightmare. Try looking for a spot a few blocks away at a meter.

364 E. Palmetto Park Rd. (btw. Federal Hwy. and the Intracoastal Bridge), Boca Raton. © **561/392-9446.** Sandwiches and salads $7–$14. No credit cards. Mon–Fri 11am–5pm; Sat 11am–4pm.

Boca Raton & Delray Beach After Dark
THE BAR, CLUB & MUSIC SCENE
Atlantic Avenue in Delray Beach has finally gotten quite hip to nightlife and is now lined with sleek and chic restaurants, lounges, and bars that attract the Palm Beach County "in crowd," along with a few random patrons such as Yanni, who has a house nearby. Although it's hardly South Beach or Fort Lauderdale's Las Olas and Riverfront, Atlantic Avenue holds its own as far as a vibrant nightlife is concerned. In Boca Raton, **Mizner Park** is the nucleus of nightlife, with restaurants masking themselves as nightclubs or, at the very least, sceney bars, such as **Gigi's Tavern,** 346 Plaza Real (© **561/368-4488**), and **Dubliner Irish Pub,** 433 Plaza Real (© **561/620-2540**).

Boston's on the Beach This is a family restaurant with a somewhat lively bar scene. It's a good choice for post-sunbathing, super-casual happy hours Monday through Friday from 4 to 8pm, or live reggae on Monday. With two decks overlooking the ocean, Boston's is an ideal place to mellow out and take in the scenery. Open daily from 7am to 2am. 40 S. Ocean Blvd., Delray Beach. © **561/278-3364.**

Dada Dada is a nocturnal outpost of food, drink, music, art, culture, and history. In other words, here you can expect to find neobohemian, arty types lingering in their dark glasses and berets on one of the living room's cozy couches, listening to music, poetry, or dissertations on life. Live music, great food, a bar, an outdoor patio area, and a very eclectic crowd make Dada the coolest hangout in Delray. Open daily from 5:30pm to 2am. 52 N. Swinton Ave., Delray Beach. © **561/330-DADA** (3232).

Delux   Believe it or not, this red-hued dance club on Atlantic Avenue is cooler than some of South Beach's big-shot clubs, thanks to a soundtrack of sexy house music, bedlike seating, and a beautiful crowd in which someone as striking as past patron Gwen Stefani can actually blend in without being noticed. Open Wednesday through Sunday from 7pm to 2am. 16 E. Atlantic Ave., Delray Beach. (*C*) **561/279-4792.**

Dubliner   A bustling, authentic Irish pub that's popular with the young professional set, Mizner Park's Dubliner features traditional pub fare, pints and pints of Guinness, impressive selection of beers on tap, assorted spirits, flatscreens for soccer, rugby, and American sporting events, and live music and DJs. Open 4pm to 2am daily. 435 Plaza Real, Boca Raton. (*C*) **561/620-2540.**

Falcon House   A cozy wine and tapas bar on a side street off the Atlantic Avenue bustle, Falcon House is reminiscent of a bar you'd find in Napa Valley, with an impressive selection of wine and a hip, well-heeled crowd. It's a haven for those who are over the whole hip-hop scene on Atlantic Avenue. Open Monday through Saturday from 5pm to 2am. 116 NE 6th Ave., Delray Beach. (*C*) **561/243-9499.**

Gatsby's   This always-busy bar is singles central, featuring big-screen TVs, microbrews, and martinis. Thursday college nights are especially popular, as are Friday happy hours. Open Monday, Tuesday, and Thursday from 4pm to 2am; Wednesday from 4pm to 3am; Friday from 4pm to 4am; Saturday from 6pm to 4am; and Sunday from 4pm to 3am. 5970 SW 18th St., Boca Raton. (*C*) **561/393-3900.**

THE PERFORMING ARTS

For details on upcoming events, check the *Boca News* or the *Sun-Sentinel,* or call the **Palm Beach County Cultural Council** information line at (*C*) **800/882-ARTS** (2787). During business hours, a staffer can give details on current performances. After hours, a recorded message describes the week's events.

For live concerts, featuring everyone from Dolly Parton to Kelly Clarkson, the **Mizner Park Amphitheater** ((*C*) **866/571-ARTS** [2787]) is the place to see them in an open-air format, under the stars, and, at times, rain. If you're not that big a fan, you'll still hear the concerts from Mizner Park!

The **Florida Symphonic Pops,** a 70-piece professional orchestra, performs jazz, swing, rock, big-band, and classical music throughout Boca Raton. This musical force has entertained audiences for nearly 50 years. Call (*C*) **561/393-7677** for a schedule.

Boca's best theater company is the **Caldwell Theatre,** and it's worth checking out. Located in a strip shopping center at 7873 N. Federal Hwy., this equity showcase does well-known dramas, comedies, classics, off-Broadway hits, and new works throughout the year. Ticket prices are reasonable—usually $34 to $55. Full-time students with ID will be especially interested in the little-advertised student rush: When available, tickets are sold for $5 if you arrive at least an hour early. Call (*C*) **561/241-7432** for details.

PALM BEACH ★★ & WEST PALM BEACH ★

65 miles N of Miami, 193 miles E of Tampa, 45 miles N of Fort Lauderdale

Palm Beach County encompasses cities from Boca Raton in the south to Jupiter and Tequesta in the north. But it is Palm Beach, the small island town across the Intracoastal Waterway, that has been the traditional winter home of America's

Palm Beach & West Palm Beach

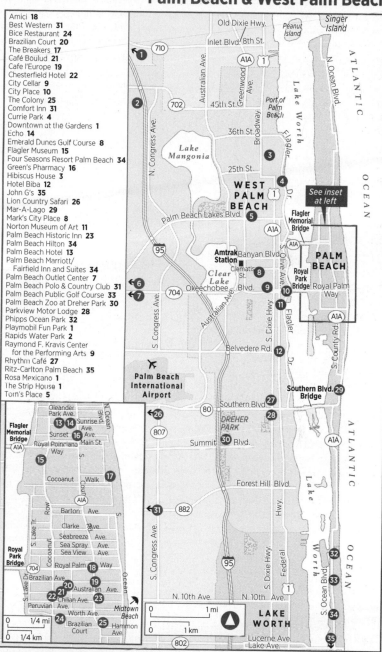

Amici **18**
Best Western **31**
Bice Restaurant **24**
Brazilian Court **20**
The Breakers **17**
Café Boulud **21**
Cafe l'Europe **19**
Chesterfield Hotel **22**
City Cellar **9**
City Place **10**
The Colony **25**
Comfort Inn **31**
Currie Park **4**
Downtown at the Gardens **1**
Echo **14**
Emerald Dunes Golf Course **8**
Flagler Museum **15**
Four Seasons Resort Palm Beach **34**
Green's Pharmacy **16**
Hibiscus House **3**
Hotel Biba **12**
John G's **35**
Lion Country Safari **26**
Mar-A-Lago **29**
Mark's City Place **8**
Norton Museum of Art **11**
Palm Beach Historic Inn **23**
Palm Beach Hilton **34**
Palm Beach Hotel **13**
Palm Beach Marriott/
　Fairfield Inn and Suites **34**
Palm Beach Outlet Center **7**
Palm Beach Polo & Country Club **31**
Palm Beach Public Golf Course **33**
Palm Beach Zoo at Dreher Park **30**
Parkview Motor Lodge **28**
Phipps Ocean Park **32**
Playmobil Fun Park **1**
Rapids Water Park **1**
Raymond F. Kravis Center
　for the Performing Arts **9**
Rhythm Café **27**
Ritz-Carlton Palm Beach **35**
Rosa Mexicano **1**
The Strip House **1**
Tom's Place **5**

aristocracy—the Kennedys, the Rockefellers, the Pulitzers, the Trumps, until recently Bernie Madoff and his unlucky investors, titled socialites, and plenty of CEOs. For a perspective on what it means to put on the ritz, there is no better place than Palm Beach, where teenagers cruise around in their parents' Rolls-Royces while socialites seem to jump out of the glossy pages of society magazines and into an even glitzier real life. It's something to be seen, despite the fact that some may consider it all over the top and, frankly, obscene. But this is not just a city of upscale resorts and chic boutiques. In fact, Palm Beach holds some surprises, from a world-class art museum to one of the top bird-watching areas in the state.

Across the water from Palm Beach proper, or the "island" as locals call it, is downtown West Palm Beach, which is where everybody else lives. Clematis Street is the area's nightlife hub, with a great selection of bars, clubs, and restaurants. City Place is West Palm's version of Mizner Park; shops, restaurants, and other entertainment options liven up this once-dead area. In addition to good beaching, boating, and diving, you'll find great golf and tennis throughout the county. *Note:* Palm Beach's population swells from 20,000 in the summer to 40,000 in the winter. Book early if you plan to visit during the winter months.

Essentials

GETTING THERE If you're driving up or down the Florida coast, you'll probably reach the Palm Beach area by way of I-95. Exit at Belvedere Road or Okeechobee Boulevard, and head east to reach the most central part of Palm Beach.

Visitors on their way to or from Orlando or Miami should take the Florida Turnpike, a toll road with a speed limit of 65 mph. Tolls are pricey, though; you may pay upward of $9 from Orlando and $4 from Miami. If you're coming from Florida's west coast, you can take either S.R. 70, which runs north of Lake Okeechobee to Fort Pierce, or S.R. 80, which runs south of the lake to Palm Beach.

All major airlines fly to the **Palm Beach International Airport,** at Congress Avenue and Belvedere Road (© **561/471-7400**). **Amtrak** (© **800/USA-RAIL** [872-7245]; www.amtrak.com) has a terminal in West Palm Beach, at 201 S. Tamarind Ave. (© **561/832-6169**).

GETTING AROUND Although a car is almost a necessity in this area, a recently revamped public transportation system is extremely convenient for getting to some attractions in both West Palm and Palm Beach. **Palm Tran** (www.palmtran.org) covers 32 routes with more than 140 buses. The fare is $1.50 for adults, 75¢ for children 3 to 18, seniors, and riders with disabilities. Free route maps are available by calling © **561/233-4-BUS** (4287). Information operators are available Monday through Saturday from 6am to 7pm.

In downtown West Palm, free shuttles from City Place to Clematis Street operate Sunday through Wednesday from 11am until 9pm, and Thursday through Saturdays 11am until 11 pm. Allegedly, the shuttles come every 5 minutes, but I'd count on them taking longer. Look for the bubblegum-pink minibuses throughout downtown. Call © **561/833-8873** for details.

VISITOR INFORMATION The **Palm Beach County Convention and Visitors Bureau,** 1555 Palm Beach Lakes Blvd., Ste. 204, West Palm Beach, FL 33401 (© **800/554-PALM** [7256] or 561/471-3995; www.palmbeachfl.com), distributes an informative brochure and answers questions about visiting the Palm Beaches. Ask for a map as well as a copy of the *Arts and Attractions Calendar,* a day-to-day guide to art, music, stage, and other events in the county.

Beaches & Outdoor Activities

BEACHES   Public beaches are a rare commodity here in Palm Beach. Most of the island's best beaches are fronted by private estates and inaccessible to the general public. However, there are a few notable exceptions, including **Midtown Beach,** east of Worth Avenue, on Ocean Boulevard between Royal Palm Way and Gulfstream Road, which boasts more than 100 feet of undeveloped sand. This newly widened coast is now a centerpiece and a natural oasis in a town dominated by commercial glitz. There are no restrooms or concessions here, though a lifeguard is on duty until sundown. A popular hangout for locals lies about 1½ miles north of here, near Dunbar Street; they prefer it to Midtown Beach because of the relaxed atmosphere. Parking is available at meters along Florida A1A. At the south end of Palm Beach, there's a less-popular but better-equipped beach at **Phipps Ocean Park.** On Ocean Boulevard, between the Southern Boulevard and Lake Avenue causeways, there's a lively public beach encompassing more than 1,300 feet of groomed oceanfront. With picnic and recreation areas and plenty of parking, the area is especially good for families.

BIKING   Rent anything from an English single-speed to a full-tilt mountain bike at the **Palm Beach Bicycle Trail Shop,** 223 Sunrise Ave. (© **561/659-4583;** www.palmbeachbicycle.com). Rates are $15 per hour, $29 per half-day (9am–5pm), and $39 for 24 hours, and include a basket and lock (not that a lock is necessary in this fortress of a town). The most scenic route is called the Lake Trail, running the length of the island along the Intracoastal Waterway. On it, you'll see some of the most magnificent mansions and grounds, and enjoy the views of downtown West Palm Beach as well as some great wildlife.

GOLF   There's good golfing in the Palm Beaches, but many private-club courses are maintained exclusively for members' use. Ask at your hotel or contact the **Palm Beach County Convention and Visitors Bureau** (© **561/471-3995**) for information on which clubs are available for play. In the off-season, some private courses open to visitors staying in Palm Beach County hotels. This "Golf-A-Round" program boasts no greens fees; reservations can be made through most major hotels.

The best hotel for golf in the area is the **PGA National Resort & Spa,** Palm Beach Gardens (© **800/633-9150;** www.pga-resorts.com), which features a whopping 90 holes of golf.

The **Palm Beach Public Golf Course,** 2345 S. Ocean Blvd. (© **561/547-0598;** www.golfontheocean.com), a popular public 18-hole course, is a par-3 that was redesigned in 2009 by Raymond Floyd and includes new layout, more holes by the ocean, and, down the road, a state-of-the-art clubhouse. The course opens at 8am on a first-come, first-served basis. Club rentals are available. Greens fees start at $14 to $45 per person depending on time and season.

SCUBA DIVING   Year-round warm waters, barrier reefs, and plenty of wrecks make South Florida one of the world's most popular places for diving. One of the best-known artificial reefs in this area is a vintage Rolls-Royce Silver Shadow, which was sunk offshore in 1985. Nature has taken its toll, however, and divers can no longer sit in the

THE SPORT OF kings

The posh **Palm Beach Polo and Country Club** and the **International Polo Club** are two of the world's premier polo grounds and host some of the sport's top-rated players. Even if you're not a sports fan, you must attend a match at one of these fields, which are on the mainland in a rural area called Wellington. Rest assured, however, that the spectators, and many of the players, are pure Palm Beach. After all, a day at the pony grounds is one of the only good reasons to leave Palm Beach proper. You need not be a Vanderbilt or a Kennedy to attend—matches are open to the public and are surprisingly affordable.

Even if you haven't a clue how the game is played, you can spend your time people-watching. In recent years, stargazers have spotted Prince Charles, Sylvester Stallone, Tommy Lee Jones, Bo Derek, and Ivana Trump, among others.

Dozens of lesser-known royalty keep box seats right on the grounds.

Dress is casual; a navy or tweed blazer over jeans or khakis is the standard for men, while neat-looking jeans or a pantsuit is the norm for women. On warmer days, shorts and, of course, polo shirts are fine, too.

General admission is $15 to $45; box seats cost $75 to $100 but are usually for members only. Call for more information. Special polo brunches are often available too at $85 per person. Matches are held throughout the week. Schedules vary, but the big names usually compete on Sunday at 3:30pm from January to April.

The fields are located at 11809 Polo Club Rd. and 3667 120th Ave., South Wellington, 10 miles west of the Forest Hill Boulevard exit off I-95. Call © **561/793-1440** or 204-5687, or visit www.internationalpoloclub.com for tickets and a detailed schedule of events.

car, which has been ravaged by time and salt water. For gear and excursions, call **The Scuba Club,** 4708 N. Flagler Dr., West Palm Beach (© **561/844-2466;** www.thescubaclub.com).

TENNIS   There are hundreds of tennis courts in Palm Beach County. Wherever you are staying, you're bound to be within walking distance of one. In addition to the many hotel tennis courts (see "Where to Stay," below), you can play at **Currie Park,** 2400 N. Flagler Dr., West Palm Beach (© **561/835-7025**), a public park with three lighted hard courts. They're free and available on a first-come, first-served basis.

WATERSPORTS   Call the **Blue Water Boat Rental,** 200 E. 13th St., Riviera Beach (© **561/840-7470;** www.bluewaterboatrental.com), to arrange sailboat, jet-ski, bicycle, kayak, water-ski, and parasail rentals.

Seeing the Sights

Flagler Museum ★★★   The Gilded Age is preserved in this luxurious mansion commissioned by Standard Oil tycoon Henry Flagler as a wedding present to his third wife. Whitehall, also known as the Taj Mahal of North America, is a classic Edwardian-style mansion containing 55 rooms, including a Louis XIV music room and art gallery, a Louis XV ballroom, and 14 guest suites outfitted with original antique European furnishings. Out back, you can climb aboard the *Rambler*, Mr. Flagler's private restored railroad car. Allow at least 1½ hours to tour the stunning grounds and interior. Group tours are available, but for the most part, this is a self-guided museum.

1 Whitehall Way (at Cocoanut Row and Whitehall Way), Palm Beach. ℭ **561/655-2833.** www.flagler museum.us. Admission $18 adults, $10 ages 13–18, $3 children 6–12. Tues–Sat 10am–5pm; Sun noon–5pm.

Norton Museum of Art ★★★   The Norton is world famous for its prestigious permanent collection and top temporary exhibitions. The museum's major collections are divided geographically. The American galleries contain major works by Hopper, O'Keeffe, and Pollock. The French collection contains Impressionist and post-Impressionist paintings by Cézanne, Degas, Gauguin, Matisse, Monet, Picasso, Pissarro, and Renoir. The Chinese collection contains more than 200 bronzes, jades, and ceramics, as well as monumental Buddhist sculptures. Allow about 2 hours to see this museum, depending on your level of interest. On the second Thursday of every month from 5 until 9pm it's Art After Dark, featuring music, film, special tours with curators and docents, hands-on art activities, a cash bar, and menu options from Café 1451 at the Norton. General admission applies, but it's worth it for an arty night out.

1451 S. Olive Ave., West Palm Beach. ℭ **561/832-5196.** Fax 561/659-4689. www.norton.org. Admission $12 adults, $5 ages 13–21. Mon–Sat 10am–5pm; Sun 1–5pm. Closed Mon May–Oct and all major holidays. Take I-95 to exit 52 (Okeechobee Blvd. E.). Travel east on Okeechobee to Dixie Hwy., then south ½ mile to the Norton. Access parking through entrances on Dixie Hwy. and S. Olive Ave.

Playmobil Fun Park ★★ ☺   For a child, it doesn't get any better than this. The 17,000-square-foot Playmobil Fun Park is housed in a replica castle and loaded with themed areas for imaginative play: a medieval village, a Western town, a fantasy dollhouse, and more. Kids can play with the Playmobil boats on two water-filled tables. Tech-minded youths may get bored, but tots up to age 5 or so will love this place. You *could* spend hours here and not spend a penny, but parents, beware: Everything is available for purchase. There's another Playmobil park in Orlando.

8031 N. Military Trail, Palm Beach Gardens. ℭ **800/351-8697** or 561/691-9880. Fax 561/691-9517. www. playmobil.com. Admission $1. Mon–Sat 10am–6pm; Sun noon–5pm. From I-95, go north to Palm Beach Lakes Blvd., then west to Military Trail. Turn left; the park is about a mile down on the right.

trump's UNREAL ESTATE

No trip to Palm Beach is complete without at least a glimpse of **Mar-A-Lago,** the stately residence of Donald Trump, the 21st century's answer to Jay Gatsby. In 1985, Trump purchased the estate of cereal heiress Marjorie Merriweather Post for a meager $8 million (for a fully furnished beachfront property of this stature, it was a relative bargain), to the great consternation of locals, who feared that he would turn the place into a casino. Instead, Trump, who sometimes resides in a portion of the palace,

opened the house to the public—for a price, of course—as a tony country club (membership fee: $100,000). Rumor has it Trump is selling the place. In the meantime, he continues to make his presence loudly known in Palm Beach.

While there are currently no tours open to the public, you can glimpse the gorgeous manse as you cross the bridge from West Palm Beach into Palm Beach. It's located at 1100 S. Ocean Blvd., Palm Beach.

Nature Preserves & Attractions

Lion Country Safari ★★ ☺ More than 1,300 animals on this 500-acre preserve (the nation's first cageless drive-through safari) are divided into their indigenous regions, from the East African preserve of the Serengeti to the American West. Elephants, lions, wildebeest, ostriches, American bison, buffalo, watusi, pink flamingos, and many other unusual species roam the preserve. When I visited, most of the lions were asleep; when awake, they travel freely throughout the cageless grassy landscape (this can be very scary). In fact, you're the one who's confined in your own car without an escort (no convertibles allowed). You're given a detailed pamphlet with photos and descriptions, and are instructed to obey the 15 mph speed limit—unless you see the rhinos charge (a rare occasion), in which case you're encouraged to floor it. Driving the loop takes slightly more than an hour, though you could make a day of just watching the chimpanzees play on their secluded islands. Included in the admission is Safari World, an amusement park with paddle boats, a carousel, miniature golf, and a baby animal nursery. Picnics are encouraged, and camping is available. The best time to go is late afternoon, right before the park closes; it's much cooler then, so the lions are more active. Though some may consider this a tourist trap, I had a great time.

Southern Blvd. W. at S.R. 80, West Palm Beach. ✆ **561/793-1084,** or 793-9797 for camping reservations. www.lioncountrysafari.com. Admission $26 adults, $23 seniors, $19 children 3–9. Van rental $10 per hour. Daily 9:30am–5:30pm (last vehicle admitted at 4:30pm). From I-95, exit on Southern Blvd. Go west for about 18 miles.

Palm Beach Zoo at Dreher Park ★ If you want animals, go to Lion Country Safari (above). Unlike big-city zoos, this intimate 23-acre attraction is more like a stroll in the park than an all-day excursion. It features about 500 animals representing more than 100 different species. The monkey exhibit and petting zoo are favorites with kids. Stroller and wagon rentals are available. The newest attraction is the Tropics of the Americas, a 3-acre jungle path and complex that immerses guests in the animals, plants, and culture of a New World rainforest. You'll encounter animals such as jaguars, monkeys, giant anteaters, tapirs, bats, birds, snakes, and more. A new Siamang Habitat opened in 2005; it is currently home to a pair of primates known to be the largest species of lesser apes in the world. There are two Malayan tigers at the zoo now—there are only 47 in North America. A baby jaguar cub was born in October of 2008. Mom is one of the zoo's endangered jags. New in 2009, a baby anteater named EO and two baby spider monkeys, a critically endangered species, born in November of that year. Allow at least 2 hours to see all of the sights here.

1301 Summit Blvd. (east of I-95 btw. Southern and Forest Hill boulevards). ✆ **561/547-WILD** (9453). www.palmbeachzoo.org. Admission $15 adults, $11 seniors, $10 children 3–12. Daily 9am–5pm. Closed Thanksgiving.

Rapids Water Park ★ ☺ It may not be on the same grand scale as the theme parks in Orlando, but Rapids is a great way to cool off on a hot day. There are 12 acres of water rides, including a children's area and miniature golf course. A few new attractions opened in 2007, including the Black Thunder, involving a huge dark funnel and water; a Raging Rapids ride; and an aquatic obstacle course. Check out the Superbowl, a tubeless water ride that spins and swirls before dumping you into the pool below, and the Big Thunder, a giant funnel that plunges you down 50 feet in a four-person tube. Claustrophobia, anyone?

6566 N. Military Trail, West Palm Beach (1 mile west of I-95 on Military, btw. 45th St./exit 54 and Blue Heron Blvd./exit 55 in West Palm Beach). ☎ 561/842-8756. www.rapidswaterpark.com. Admission $32 Mon–Fri, $35 Sat–Sun; free for children 2 and under. Parking $10. Mid-Mar to Sept Mon–Fri 10am–5pm; Sat–Sun 10am–6pm.

Richard and Pat Johnson Palm Beach County Museum ★   There's more to Palm Beach history than Donald Trump and well-preserved octogenarians. Opened to the public in March 2008 within the historic 1916 Courthouse in downtown West Palm Beach, the museum has two permanent exhibits—the People Gallery, a tribute to approximately 100 individuals and families who have contributed to the growth of Palm Beach County, and the Place Gallery, featuring models and photographs exploring Palm Beach county's natural environment and the animals and ecology that make it unique.

300 N. Dixie Hwy., West Palm Beach. Entrance is on 2nd floor of courthouse. ☎ **561/832-4164.** www. historicalsocietypbc.org. Free admission. Tues–Sat 10am–5pm; Sun 1–5pm.

South Florida Science Museum ★ ☺   It's hands on at this veteran West Palm science museum, boasting a planetarium, aquarium, interactive galleries, and traveling exhibitions. But the museum got a big boost in 2009 when its Marvin Dekelboym Planetarium became one of only a handful of planetariums in the country to showcase state-of-the-art, full-dome digital projection capability that allows visitors to take a virtual space walk or to explore the realms of the sea. Upgrades also include a new, programmable laser system to continue the popular laser concerts, LED lighting, and Blu-ray high-definition video technology. For those so inclined there's also a mini-golf course, Galaxy Golf, where, for $2 you can putt around the planets.

4801 Dreher Trail N., West Palm Beach (at the north end of Dreher Park). ☎ **561/832-1988.** www.sfsm. org. Admission $9 adults, $7.50 seniors, $6 children. Planetarium shows $4 adults, $2 children in addition to museum admission. Laser shows $5 per person. Mon–Fri 10am–5pm; Sat 10am–6pm; Sun noon–6pm.

Shopping

No matter what your budget, be sure to take a stroll down Worth Avenue, the "Rodeo Drive of the South" and a window-shopper's dream. Between South Ocean Boulevard and Cocoanut Row, there are more than 200 boutiques, posh shops, art galleries, and upscale restaurants. If you want to fit in, dress as if you are going to an elegant luncheon, not the mall down the street.

You'd never know there was ever a recession based on the swarms of shoppers armed with bags from **Gucci, Chanel, Armani, Hermès,** and **Louis Vuitton,** among others. And besides the boldface collection of couturiers there are also a good number of unique, independent boutiques. For privileged feet, **Stubbs & Wooton,** 4 Via Parigi (☎ **561/655-4105**), sells velvet slippers that are a favorite of the loofahed locals. For rare and estate jewelry, **Richter's of Palm Beach,** 224 Worth Ave. (☎ **561/655-0774**), has been specializing in priceless gems since 1893. Just off Worth Avenue is the **Church Mouse,** 378 S. County Rd. (☎ **561/659-2154**), a great consignment/thrift shop with antique furnishings and tableware, as well as lots of good castoff clothing and shoes from socialites who've moved on to the next designers or, worse than that, to the big gala in the sky. This shop usually closes for 2 months during the summer; call to be sure. Oh, and if you plan to put something up for consignment, make sure to use the special "donor's door" (a nice way of saying service entrance) on the south side of the building.

City Place, Okeechobee Road (at I-95), West Palm Beach (✆ **561/820-9716**), is a $550-million, Mediterranean-style shopping, dining, and entertainment complex that's responsible for revitalizing what was once a lifeless downtown West Palm Beach. Among the 78 mostly chain stores are **Macy's, Barnes & Noble, Banana Republic, Armani Exchange, Pottery Barn,** and **SEE** eyewear. Restaurants include a Ghirardelli ice-cream shop; Legal Seafoods; the legendary Tampa-based Cuban restaurant Columbia; Miami Beach, Fort Lauderdale, and Hollywood's Taverna Opa; City Cellar Wine Bar and Grill; Brewzzi; BB King's Blues Club; Blue Martini; and Cheesecake Factory. Best of all is the Muvico Parisian, a 20-screen movie theater where you can wine and dine while watching a feature.

Where to Stay

The island of Palm Beach is the epitome of *Lifestyles of the Rich and Famous* (or, for our younger readers, VH1's *The Fabulous Life Of*), oozing with glitz, glamour, and the occasional scandal. Royalty and celebrities come to winter here, and there are plenty of lavishly priced options to accommodate them. Happily, there are also a few special inns that offer reasonably priced rooms in elegant settings. But most of the more modest places to lay your straw hat surround the island.

A few of the larger hotel chains operating in Palm Beach include the **Palm Beach Fairfield Inn and Suites,** 2870 S. Ocean Blvd. (✆ **800/228-2800** or 561/582-2581), across the street from the beach. In West Palm Beach, chain hotels are mostly on the main arteries close to the highways and a short drive from downtown. They include **Best Western,** 1800 Palm Beach Lakes Blvd. (✆ **800/331-9569** or 561/683-8810), and, just down the road, **Comfort Inn,** 1901 Palm Beach Lakes Blvd. (✆ **800/221-2222** or 561/689-6100). Farther south is **Parkview Motor Lodge,** 4710 S. Dixie Hwy., just south of Southern Boulevard (✆ **561/833-4644**). This 28-room motel is the best of many along Dixie Highway (U.S. 1). With rates starting at about $75 for a room with TV, air-conditioning, and phone (don't laugh, some don't have any), you can't ask for more.

For other options, contact **Palm Beach Accommodations** (✆ **800/543-SWIM** [7946]).

VERY EXPENSIVE

Brazilian Court Hotel & Beach Club ★★★   This elegant, Old World, Mediterranean-style hotel dates from the 1920s and almost looks like a Beverly Hills bungalow. Much like Palm Beach residents, the hotel debuted a new youthful glow after a remake in 2008. The 80 custom-redesigned suites all feature mahogany case goods and crown molding, Provence-style wood shutters, and king-size beds topped with imported linens. Pampered pets under 20 pounds (you know the type: held hostage in Mummy's Gucci bag) receive gift bags full of treats for a (required) one-time $100 pet fee. A large hotel by Palm Beach standards (the Breakers notwithstanding), Brazilian Court sprawls over half a block and features fountains and private courtyards. The only downside? A tiny pool where you feel you have to whisper. To counter the size is stellar poolside service—order drinks or food and voila! A small Jacuzzi hidden from the pool is where shy types and celebs like to hide. Celebrity stylist Frederic Fekkai offers the hotel's premier salon and spa. With the addition of renowned chef Daniel Boulud's hauter-than-thou **Café Boulud** (which provides stellar room service and a great bar scene with live music), Brazilian Court is Palm Beach's number-one place to see and be seen. In 2009, the hotel added the words "beach club" to its name after implementing new amenities such as a chauffeured car to and from a private area of beach complete with food and cocktail service reserved just for hotel guests

301 Australian Ave., Palm Beach, FL 33480. ⓒ **800/552-0335** or 561/655-7740. Fax 561/655-0801. www.thebraziliancourt.com. 80 units. From $550 studio; from $950 1-bedroom suite; from $1,145 2-bedroom suite. Special packages available. AE, DC, DISC, MC, V. Pampered pet fee $100. **Amenities:** Restaurant; concierge; exercise room; library; heated outdoor pool; room service; spa treatments. *In room:* A/C, TV, hair dryer, minibar, Wi-Fi.

The Breakers Palm Beach ★★★ ☺ This 140-acre beachfront hotel is quintessential Palm Beach, where old money mixes with new money, and the Old World gives way, albeit reluctantly, to a bit of modernity. The seven-story building is a marvel, with a frescoed lobby and long, palatial hallways. Plush rooms feature huge bathrooms and views of the ocean or the magnificently manicured grounds. The Mediterranean-style Beach Club features magnificent vistas of the ocean and is reminiscent of a panoramic island escape. After a $15-million beachfront redevelopment project, the Beach Club now features five pools, four whirlpool spas, expansive pool decks, lush tropical landscaping, and lawn space; a 6,000-square-foot rooftop terrace, 20 private, luxury beach bungalows, and 10 pool cabanas for daytime rental, with a dedicated staff of concierges; a beach gazebo; and two restaurants. The 20,000-square-foot oceanfront spa features 17 private treatment rooms for a variety of massages, body wraps, scrubs, and Guerlain skin-care treatments and steam and sauna. Spa treatments fill a 16-page book! A revamp of Florida's oldest existing golf course transformed the Ocean Course into a 6,100-yard, championship-level par-70, and the Breakers Rees Jones Course underwent a $6-million redesign and reconstruction in 2004. Kids aren't neglected either at the impressive Family Entertainment Center, a 6,160-square-foot space that includes an arcade, toddler's playroom, arts-and-crafts area, children's movie theater, and video-game room all filled with the latest in high-tech toys and games. All nine distinct restaurants are fantastic, but don't miss the remarkable Sunday brunch.

1 S. County Rd., Palm Beach, FL 33480. ⓒ **888/BREAKERS** (273-2537) or 561/655-6611. Fax 561/659-8403. www.thebreakers.com. 540 units. Winter $499–$1,340 double, $1,310–$6,100 suite; during the summer season, rooms start as low as $249. AE, DC, DISC, MC, V. Valet parking $20. From I-95, exit Okeechobee Blvd. E., head east to S. County Rd., and turn left. **Amenities:** 9 restaurants; 5 bars; babysitting; bike rentals; children's programs; concierge; 2 championship golf courses; 2 fitness centers; 5 outdoor pools; room service; indoor/outdoor spa; 10 Har-Tru tennis courts; watersports equipment/rentals; 4 whirlpool spas. *In room:* A/C, flatscreen TV/DVD/CD player, hair dryer, minibar, MP3 docking station, PlayStation, Wi-Fi, wireless keyboard.

Four Seasons Resort Palm Beach ★★ ☺ Situated on the pristine Palm Beach oceanfront, Four Seasons is a quiet retreat from Worth Avenue—a pricey cab ride from the hotel. Guest rooms are spacious, with private balconies and lavish bathrooms. The full-service spa is excellent and brand new at 9,000 square feet, featuring nine treatment rooms including a "Man Room," a wet room, spa suite, and full-service salon. The main dining room, known simply as the Restaurant, has recently been updated as a casual seafood oriented eatery with lovely lounge seating on the outdoor terrace where you can just have a cocktail (try their new organic drinks) and a small plate from the restaurant's raw bar. Two other restaurants, the Ocean Bistro—which is sub par for this kind of hotel—and the Atlantic Bar & Grill, round out the dining options. The resort offers a complimentary kids program, and teens will enjoy the game room with Xbox, a pool table, and a large-screen TV.

Meanwhile, parents can entertain themselves in the Living Room, a swank lounge, or at the Restaurant's outdoor lounge.

2800 S. Ocean Blvd., Palm Beach, FL 33480. ☎ **800/432-2335** or 561/582-2800. Fax 561/547-1557. www.fourseasons.com/palmbeach. 210 units. Winter $379–$899 double, from $2,100 1-bedroom suite, from $3,850 2-bedroom suite; off-season $195–$525 double, $1,200 1-bedroom suite, $2,500 2-bed-room suite. AE, DC, DISC, MC, V. Valet parking $25. From I-95, take the 6th Ave. exit east and turn left onto Dixie Hwy. Turn east onto Lake Ave. and north onto A1A (S. Ocean Blvd.); the resort is just ahead on your right. Pets less than 20 lbs. accepted. **Amenities:** 3 restaurants; lounge/outdoor patio; babysit-ting' children's programs; concierge; fitness center; outdoor heated pool; spa; 2 tennis courts; water-sports equipment/rentals; whirlpool. *In room:* A/C, TV/DVD/VCR, CD/MP3 player, fridge, hair dryer, high-speed Internet access, minibar.

The Omphoy Ocean Resort   This 134-room waterfront boutique hotel is the first new resort to open in Palm Beach in 18 years and is owned by the same company that owns the fabulous Brazilian Court. Featuring an open lobby and a minimalist South Beach modern vibe, the stylish Omphoy may be the island's hippest hotel, catering to a younger clientele than many of the area hotels. Rooms feature sleek, high end fur-nishings, plush linens and offer panoramic ocean or Intracoastal views. The resort also features surfside cuisine, by Miami's star chef Michelle Bernstein, and New York–based Exhale Spa, with 5,000 square feet of dedicated spa space with indoor and outdoor treatments combining fitness and movement with spa and healing.

2842 S. Ocean Blvd., Palm Beach, FL 33480. ☎ **561/540-6440.** www.omphoy.com. 134 units. Winter $450–$700 suite; off-season $279–$450 suite. **Amenities:** 2 restaurants; 2 bars; pool; spa; watersports equipment/rentals; free Wi-Fi in business center. *In room:* A/C, TV/DVD.

The Ritz-Carlton, Palm Beach ★★★ ☺   If the Breakers is too mammoth for your taste, consider the Ritz. A lot warmer than the Four Seasons, the Ritz, located on a beautiful beach in a tiny town about 8 miles from Worth Avenue, lacks pretension and feels more like a boutique hotel. A $130-million renovation in 2007 added flatscreen HDTVs, bedside electronic control "pamper panels," and Italian custom mahogany furniture. Oceanfront suites have oceanview stone soaking tubs, a sofa sleeper, two-line phones, and two HDTVs. Two pools are perfect for families and/or ideal for relaxation. The 42,000-square-foot Eau Spa debuted in March 2009, complete with a custom Scrub and Polish Bar, Bath Lounge, Spa Villas with outdoor verdant gardens, and the Self-Centered Garden featuring water massage benches. A casual oceanfront all-day restaurant called Temple Orange features Italian/Mediterranean fare with fresh sea-food. Breeze, the "gourmet" Burger Patio and Bar sits on the ocean's edge; while Stir Bar serves muddled, stirred and mixed cocktails and light bites.

100 S. Ocean Blvd., Manalapan, FL 33462. ☎ **800/241-3333** or 561/533-6000. Fax 561/588-4202. www.ritzcarlton.com. 310 units. Winter $469–$829 double, $829–$1,599 suite, $4,999 presidential suite; off-season $279–$619 double, $639–$969 suite, $2,999 presidential suite. AE, DISC, MC, V. Valet park-ing $28. From I-95, take exit for Lantana Rd., heading east. After 1 mile, turn right onto Federal Hwy. (U.S. 1/Dixie Hwy.). Continue south to the next light and turn left onto Ocean Ave. Cross the Intracoastal Waterway and turn right onto Fla. A1A. **Amenities:** 2 restaurants; bar; bike rental; children's and teen's programs; concierge; fitness center; Jacuzzi; 2 outdoor pools; room service; spa; watersports equip-ment/rentals. *In room:* A/C, flatscreen HDTV/DVD, hair dryer, minibar, Wi-Fi.

EXPENSIVE

Chesterfield Hotel ★★★   Reminiscent of an English country manor, the Ches-terfield in all its flowery, Laura Ashley–inspired glory is a magnificent, charming hotel with exceptional service. Warm and inviting, the Chesterfield is one of the only places in South Florida where the idea of a fireplace (there's one in the hotel's library) doesn't seem ridiculous. Traditional English tea is served every afternoon, including fresh-baked scones, petit fours, and sandwiches. Rooms are decorated with antiques and with bright fabrics and wallpaper. The roomy marble bathrooms are stocked with an array of luxurious toiletries. A small heated pool and courtyard are nice, and the beach is only 3 blocks away, but the real action is inside: The hotel's retro-elegant Leopard Lounge serves decent Continental cuisine, but is better as a late-night hangout for live music, schmoozing, and staring at the local cognoscenti.

363 Cocoanut Row, Palm Beach, FL 33480. Ⓒ **800/243-7871** or 561/659-5800. Fax 561/659-6707. www.chesterfieldpb.com. 52 units. Winter $395–$465 queen, $495–$570 king, $675–$1,585 suite; off-season $175–$249 queen, $259–$319 king, $339–$719 suite. Rollaway bed $15. Packages available. AE, DC, DISC, MC, V. Free valet parking. From I-95, exit onto Okeechobee Blvd. E., cross the Intracoastal Waterway, and turn right onto Cocoanut Row. **Amenities:** Restaurant; lounge; concierge; access to nearby health club; library; heated pool and hot tub spa; room service; Wi-Fi. *In room:* A/C, flat-panel TV, entertainment center w/DVD/CD (in kings/suites only), fridge (in kings/suites only), hair dryer, high-speed Internet access.

MODERATE

The Colony ★★ The sign outside this Palm Beach mainstay should read ROX-ANNE PULITZER SLEPT HERE. She did, actually, for quite a while after her 7-week marriage went bust. For years, the Colony has been a favorite hangout—hideout, perhaps—for old-timers, socialites, and mysterious luminaries. The very old-school bar and lounge features an eclectic mix of no-name lounge and A-list cabaret singers and entertainers, but the people-watching there is priceless as octogenarian sugar daddies proudly and boldly sashay by with bedecked, bejeweled arm candy at least half their age. Beyond that, this Georgian-style hotel is known for its attentive staff, kitschy Florida-shaped pool, floral-decorated guest rooms, and, unfortunately, really small bathrooms. The 39 suites and apartments, not to mention the seven two-bedroom villas with Jacuzzis, are much more lavish—and lavishly priced.

155 Hammon Ave., Palm Beach, FL 33480. Ⓒ **800/521-5525** or 561/655-5430. Fax 561/659-8104. www.thecolonypalmbeach.com. 92 units. Winter $250–$525 double, $600–$1,200 suite; off-season $175 double, $275 suite. AE, DC, MC, V. From I-95, exit onto Okeechobee Blvd. E. and cross the Intracoastal Waterway. Turn right on S. County Rd. and then left onto Hammon Ave. **Amenities:** Restaurant; bar; concierge; heated pool; limited seasonal room service; spa. *In room:* A/C, TV, hair dryer, Internet access.

Palm Beach Historic Inn ★★ Built in 1923, the Palm Beach Historic Inn is an area landmark within a block's walking distance of the beach (chairs and towels are provided for guests of the hotel), Worth Avenue, and several good restaurants. The small lobby is filled with antiques, books, magazines, and an old-fashioned umbrella stand, all of which add to the homey feel of this intimate B&B. In-room wine, fruit, snacks, tea, and cookies ensure that you won't go hungry—never mind the excellent continental breakfast that is brought to you daily. All bedrooms are uniquely deco-rated and have hardwood floors, down comforters, Egyptian-cotton linens, fluffy bathrobes, and plenty of good-smelling toiletries. Here you'll find a casual elegance that's comfortable for everyone. In addition, a baby grand piano and guitars for the musically inclined, as well as videotapes to keep the kids entertained, have been added to the hotel's amenities. *Note:* Smoking is not permitted.

365 S. County Rd., Palm Beach, FL 33480. Ⓒ **561/832-4009.** Fax 561/832-6255. www.palmbeach historicinn.com. 13 units. Winter $185–$345 double, $345–$395 suite; off-season $145–$175 double, $225 suite. Rates include breakfast. Children stay free in parent's room. AE, MC, V. Small pets accepted. *In room:* A/C, TV/VCR, fridge, hair dryer.

13

THE GOLD COAST | Palm Beach & West Palm Beach

INEXPENSIVE

Hibiscus House ★★ 🎁 Inexpensive bed-and-breakfasts are rare in Southeast Florida, making the Hibiscus House, one of the area's first, a true find. Located a few miles from the coast in a quiet residential neighborhood, this 1920s-era B&B is filled with handsome antiques and tapestries. Every room has a private terrace or balcony. The Red Room has a fabulous bathroom with Jacuzzi. The peaceful backyard retreat has been transformed into a tropical garden, with a heated pool and lounge chairs. There are pretty indoor areas for guests to enjoy; one little sitting room is wrapped in glass and is stocked with playing cards and board games. Huge gourmet breakfast portions are as filling as they are beautiful. Make any special requests in advance; owners Raleigh Hill and Colin Rayer will be happy to oblige.

501 30th St., West Palm Beach, FL 33407. ☏ **800/203-4927** or 561/863-5633. Fax 561/863-5633. www.hibiscushouse.com. 8 units. Winter $125–$210 double; off-season $100–$150 double. Rates include breakfast. AE, DC, DISC, MC, V. From I-95, exit onto Palm Beach Lakes Blvd. E. and continue 4 miles. Turn left onto Flagler Dr. and continue for about ½ mile; then turn left onto 30th St. Pets accepted. **Amenities:** Concierge; heated pool. *In room:* A/C, TV, hair dryer.

Hotel Biba ★★ 🎁 Located in the historic El Cid neighborhood, just 1 mile from City Place and Clematis Street, the very cool Biba answers the call for an inexpensive, chic hotel that young hipsters can call their own. Housed in a renovated Colonial-style 1940s motor lodge, Biba has been remarkably updated by de rigueur designer Barbara Hulanicki and features a sleek lobby with the hip hotel bar, and a gorgeously landscaped outdoor pool area with Asian-inspired gardens. Guest rooms are shabby chic, with private patios, mosaic-tile floors, custom-made mahogany furniture, Egyptian-cotton linens, down pillows, and flatscreen TVs. The bold color schemes mix nicely with the high-fashion crowd that convenes here. *A word of advice:* This place is not exactly soundproof. Rooms may be cloistered by fence and gardens, but they're still extremely close to a major thoroughfare. Ask for a room that's on the quieter Belvedere Road, as opposed to those facing South Olive Avenue.

320 Belvedere Rd., West Palm Beach, FL 33405. ☏ **561/832-0094.** Fax 561/833-7848. www.hotelbiba.com. 41 units. $110–$215 double; $200–$300 suite. Rates include breakfast. Online discounts available. AE, MC, V. **Amenities:** Lounge; concierge; outdoor pool. *In room:* A/C, TV, CD player, hair dryer, free Wi-Fi.

Where to Dine

Palm Beach has some of the area's swankiest restaurants. Thanks to the development of downtown West Palm Beach, however, there is also a great selection of trendier, less expensive spots. Dress here is slightly more formal than in most other areas of Florida: Men wear blazers, and women generally put on modest dresses or chic suits when they dine out, even on the oppressively hot days of summer.

VERY EXPENSIVE

Café Boulud ★★★ FRENCH Snowbird socialites rejoiced over the opening of star chef Daniel Boulud's eponymous restaurant in the Brazilian Court hotel. Nonsocialites said, "Figures, another restaurant where we can't afford even a bread crumb." If you're out to splurge, Boulud is ideal, with an exquisite menu divided into four sections—La Tradition (French and American classics), La Saison (seasonal dishes), Le Potager (dishes inspired by the vegetable market), and Le Voyage (world cuisine). The roasted barramundi with squash, pomegranate, and brown butter is superb. There's also a light and somewhat reasonably priced menu offering salads, sandwiches—including possibly the best I've ever had, the BLT with smoked beef brisket, lettuce slaw, Creole mustard, fried green tomatoes, and homemade pickles—and even a cheeseburger if you prefer; try the chickpea fries with *piquillo* pepper ketchup. If star chefs, stuffy socialites, and froufrou cuisine aren't your thing, don't even bother.

In the Brazilian Court, 301 Australian Ave., Palm Beach. (C) **561/655-6060.** www.danielnyc.com. Reservations essential. Main courses $11–$38. AE, DC, MC, V. Daily 9am–10pm.

Cafe l'Europe ★★★ CONTINENTAL   One of Palm Beach's finest and most popular spots, this award-winning, romantic, and formal restaurant gives you a good reason to get dressed up. The enticing appetizers served by a superb staff might include crispy veal sweetbreads, wild mushroom and asparagus, or lobster bisque. Main courses run the gamut from wiener schnitzel with herbed spaetzle to sautéed potato-crusted Florida snapper to roasted rack of lamb. Seafood dishes and steaks in sumptuous but light sauces are always exceptional.

331 S. County Rd. (at Brazilian Ave.), Palm Beach. (C) **561/655-4020.** www.cafeleurope.com. Reservations recommended. Main courses $34–$47. AE, DC, DISC, MC, V. Tues–Sat noon–3pm and 6–10pm; Sun 6–10pm.

Echo ★★ ASIAN   This hyperstylish, sleek eatery is the Breakers hotel's homage to young and hip. The hotel runs the restaurant, even though it's off premises, and it's worth leaving the comfy, upper-crust confines of the Breakers for this resounding Echo. The menu is broken down into categories: earth, wind, fire, water, and flavor, which doesn't do the food any real justice. Sushi bar specialties, such as the *hamachi kama,* grilled *hamachi,* Asian greens, and citrus soy, and the outstanding echo roll with shrimp tempura, cucumber, avocado, and *tobiko* in a sesame soy sheet with superspicy *sriracha* sauce, are two of my favorites. But it's not all sushi. There are Chinese dim sum specialties, too. The dim sum sampler, at $27, feeds two and is an ideal starter or full-blown meal. Then there's the Thai roast duck, and the open-flame wok specialties. There's too much to choose from, but it's all good. Be sure to check out the restaurant's Dragonfly Lounge after dinner. It's a hopping scene, especially by Palm Beach standards.

230 Sunrise Ave., Palm Beach. (C) **561/802-4222.** www.echopalmbeach.com. Reservations essential. Sushi $4–$23. Main courses $18–$60. AE, DC, MC, V. Tues–Sun 5:30–9:30pm.

Michelle Bernstein's at The Omphoy ★★ MEDITERRANEAN   Miami's culinary "it" girl takes on finicky Palm Beach diners with her latest, a restaurant located in a trendy, swanky hotel featuring spectacular water views. Fans of Bernstein's will say this sounds familiar, as Bernstein rose up in the culinary ranks via Azul at Miami's Mandarin Oriental. And while there are similarities, it seems that here, Bernstein is a bit more whimsical than she is down in Miami, with dishes such as shrimp tiradito, her own spin on popcorn shrimp, prepared with a blend of limes, cilantro and spices. Bernstein's channeling of her Judeo-Latino heritage in the kitchen is where she really shines, taking an old fashioned Cuban croquetta and sending it off to the Med where it receives an infusion of feta and spinach instead of the usual ham. Other dishes include the finger lickin' good Michy's Famous Fried Chicken, a Miami import marinated in a mix of buttermilk and tarragon; a bouillabaisse with Latin accents in the form of *sofrito*-flavored broth; and another Michy's signature dish of beautifully braised short ribs. Prices are steep, but worth it—especially if you consider the gas money saved from not having to drive down to Miami for a Bernstein fix.

The Omphoy Ocean Resort, 2842 S. Ocean Blvd. Palm Beach. ☎ **561/540-6444.** www.omphoy.com. Reservations recommended. Main courses $24–$36. AE, DC, DISC, MC, V. Daily noon–2:30pm and 6–10pm.

EXPENSIVE

Amici Ristorante and Bar ★ ✋ ITALIAN   This is one of those restaurants whose scene is tastier than its cuisine. An upper-crusty Palm Beach set convenes here and consistently raves about above-average, overpriced Italian food. The best item on the menu is gnocchi with white truffle oil, fontina cheese, and spinach. Everything else is fairly standard: grilled sandwiches, pastas with rustic sauces, pizzas, grilled shrimp, and fish. Despite its less-than-stellar food, Amici is always crowded and very noisy.

288 S. County Rd. (at Royal Palm Way), Palm Beach. ☎ **561/832-0201.** www.amicipalmbeach.com. Reservations strongly recommended on weekends. Main courses $26–$44; pizzas $15–$18. AE, DC, MC, V. Mon–Thurs 11:30am–3pm and 5:30–10:30pm; Fri–Sat 11:30am–3pm and 5:30–11pm; Sun 5:30–10:30pm.

Bice Restaurant ★★ NORTHERN ITALIAN   Bice's Milanese cuisine far surpasses that of Amici's, but as far as atmosphere, the air in here is a bit haughty, bordering on rude. Servers and diners alike have attitudes, but you'll forget all that with one bite of the juicy veal cutlet with tomato salad or the *pasta e fagioli* (pasta with beans). But for great people-watching and actually nice service, consider the bar where you can linger over a glass of wine and, if the bartender likes you, free pizza, for hours.

313½ Worth Ave., Palm Beach. ☎ **561/835-1600.** Reservations essential. Main courses $20–$40. AE, DC, MC, V. Daily noon–10pm.

MODERATE

City Cellar Wine Bar & Grill ★★ AMERICAN   If the Palm Beach–proper dining scene is too stuffy, head over to City Place to find this yuppie brick-and-pressed-tin enclave where people-watching is at a premium. Despite its all-American appearance, City Cellar offers a varied menu, from pizzas and pastas to steak and sea bass. We love the onion and mushroom soup with pinot grigio and the twin 7-ounce pork chops with potato purée, sweet-and-sour shallots, and a sherry mustard butter. The place is mobbed on weekends, so plan for a long wait that's best spent at the action-packed bar.

700 S. Rosemary Ave., West Palm Beach. ☎ **561/659-1853.** Reservations suggested. Main courses $10–$30. AE, MC, V. Sun–Wed 11:30am–10:30pm (bar until 1am); Thurs–Sat 11:30am–11pm (bar until 2am).

Rhythm Café ★ 🍴 ECLECTIC AMERICAN   This funky hole-in-the-wall is where those in the know come to eat some of West Palm Beach's most laid-back gourmet food. On the handwritten, photocopied menu (which changes daily), you'll always find a fish specialty accompanied by a hefty dose of greens and garnishes. Reliably outstanding is the pork tenderloin with mango chutney. Salads and soups are a great bargain, as portions are relatively large, but there's an extensive menu of appetizers which can be ordered in small or entree form. The kitschy decor of this tiny cafe comes complete with vinyl tablecloths and a changing display of paintings by local amateurs. Young, handsome waiters are attentive, but not solicitous. The old drugstore where the restaurant recently relocated features an original 1950s lunch counter and stools.

3800 S. Dixie Hwy., West Palm Beach. ☎ **561/833-3406.** www.rhythmcafe.cc. Reservations recommended Sat–Sun. Main courses $13–$29. AE, DISC, MC, V. Tues–Sat 6–10pm; Sun (Dec–Mar) 5:30–9pm. Closed in early Sept. From I-95, exit east on Southern Blvd. Go 1 block north of Southern Blvd.; restaurant is on the right.

INEXPENSIVE

Green's Pharmacy ★ 🍴 AMERICAN   This neighborhood pharmacy offers one of the best meal deals in Palm Beach. Both breakfast and lunch are served coffee-shop style, either at a Formica bar or at tables on a black-and-white checkerboard floor. Breakfast specials include eggs and omelets served with home fries and bacon, sausage, or corned-beef hash. The grill serves burgers and sandwiches, as well as ice-cream sodas and milkshakes, to a loyal crowd of pastel-clad Palm Beachers.

151 N. County Rd., Palm Beach. 📞 **561/832-0304.** Fax 561/832-6502. Breakfast $2–$6; burgers and sandwiches $3–$8; soups and salads $2–$8. AE, DISC, MC, V. Mon–Sat 7am–5pm; Sun 7am–3pm.

John G's ★ AMERICAN   This coffee shop is the most popular in the county. For decades, John G's has been attracting huge breakfast crowds; lines run out the door (on weekends, all the way down the block). Stop in for good, greasy-spoon food served in heaping portions right on the beachfront. This place is known for fresh and tasty fish and chips, and its selection of creative omelets and grill specials.

10 S. Ocean Blvd., Lake Worth. 📞 **561/585-9860.** www.johngs.com. Reservations not accepted. Breakfast $3–$10; lunch $4–$15. No credit cards. Daily 7am–3pm. From the Florida Tpk., take the Lake Worth exit and head toward the ocean.

Tom's Place for Ribs ★★ 🍴 BARBECUE   There are two important factors in a successful barbecue: the cooking and the sauce. Tom and Helen Wright's no-nonsense shack wins on both counts, offering flawlessly grilled meats paired with well-spiced sauces. Beef, chicken, pork, and fish are served soul-food style, with corn bread and your choice of sides such as rice with gravy, collard greens, black-eyed peas, coleslaw, or mashed potatoes. There's another very popular branch of Tom's in Boca Raton, at 7251 N. Federal Hwy. (📞 **561/997-0920**).

1225 Palm Beach Lakes Blvd., West Palm Beach. 📞 **561/832-8774.** www.tomsplaceforribs.com. Reservations not accepted. Main courses $9–$26; sandwiches $6–$8. AE, MC, V. Tues–Thurs 11:30am–10:30pm; Fri 11:30am–10pm; Sat noon–10pm.

The Palm Beaches After Dark
THE BAR, CAFE & MUSIC SCENE

In 2008, **Clematis Street,** West Palm Beach's hub of nightlife, also known as the Clematis District, celebrated an immense resurgence, with a slew of new dining destinations, retailers, and nightspots that dot the street from Flagler Drive to Rosemary Avenue, creating a hot spot for a night out, especially on weekends, when yuppies mingle with stylish Euros and disheveled artists.

Over the bridge, it's a completely different world. Palm Beach is much quieter and better known for its rather private society balls and estate parties. With the exception of some restaurants that are more of a scene (such as **Amici,** described above, or **Ta-boo,** reviewed below), Palm Beach nightlife is more likely to entail sipping port at one of the finer hotels such as The Breakers, Colony, Ritz-Carlton, Four Seasons, or Chesterfield.

West Palm Beach

Dr. Feelgood's Rock Bar and Grill   The latest hit from former Mötley Crüe singer Vince Neil, this raucous watering hole features concert decor, fist-pumping rock 'n' roll, booze, beer, and burgers. Ladies night on Thursdays is very popular with the fairer sex and their respective groupies. Open Tuesday, Thursday, and Saturday 8pm to 4am, Friday 5pm to 4am. 219 Clematis St. ☎ **561/833-6500.** Cover for men $10–$20.

E. R. Bradley's   What used to be a swank saloon on the island of Palm Beach is now a friendly, very casual indoor/outdoor bar in downtown West Palm, attracting a mixed crowd. The later-night bar scene is a real draw. If you're hungry, try the "crab bomb," Maryland lump crabmeat baked in a light cream sauce with steamed vegetables. Open Sunday through Wednesday from 8am to 3am, Thursday through Saturday from 8am to 4am. 104 Clematis St. ☎ **561/833-3520.**

Respectable Street Café   This is one of the premier live-music venues in South Florida. In addition to the requisite DJs, the grungy bar features a lineup of alternative-music acts. The plain storefront exterior belies a funky, high-ceilinged interior, decorated with large black booths, psychedelic wall murals, and a checkerboard-tile dance floor. Open Wednesday and Thursday from 9pm to 3am, Friday and Saturday from 9pm to 4am. 518 Clematis St. ☎ **561/832-9999.** Cover $5–$20.

Palm Beach

Cucina Dell'Arte   The locals call it Cucina but we call it the only semblance of, say, South Beach–style seen-and-be-scenery where the median age isn't necessarily pushing 80. Although it's an Italian restaurant, Cucina turns into a lounge and virtual disco later in the evening, often with DJs, and always with local, lively flavor that's less stuffy than the alternatives below. Open daily from 7am to 3am. 257 Royal Poinciana Way. ☎ **561/655-0770.** http://cucinadellarte.com.

Leopard Lounge 🎁   *The Flintstones* meets *Dynasty* at this spotty lounge in the Chesterfield Hotel, in which the carpeting, tablecloths, and waitstaff's waistcoats are all in leopard print. There's live music every night, ranging from Cole Porter to swing. The crowd's a bit older, but younger couples and a celebrity or two often find their way here, which makes for an amusing scene. Open daily from 6pm to 1:30am. 363 Cocoanut Row. ☎ **561/659-5800.**

Ta-boo   Ta-boo is reminiscent of an upscale TGI Friday's (with food that's about on the same level). It caters to a well-heeled crowd, with lots of greenery, a fireplace, and a somewhat cheesy Southwestern decor. But make no mistake, Ta-boo is not about the food: This stellar after-dinner spot is where bejeweled socialites spill out of fancy cars to salsa and show off their best Swarovski jewelry. Find someplace else to eat first. Open Sunday through Thursday from 11:30am to 10pm, and Friday and Saturday from 11:30am to 11pm. 221 Worth Ave. ☎ **561/835-3500.**

THE PERFORMING ARTS

With a number of dedicated patrons and enthusiastic supporters of the arts, this area happily boasts many good venues for those craving culture. Check the *Palm Beach Post* or the *Palm Beach Daily News* for up-to-date listings and reviews.

The **Raymond F. Kravis Center for the Performing Arts,** 701 Okeechobee Blvd., West Palm Beach (☎ **561/832-7469;** www.kravis.org), is the area's largest and most active performance space. With a huge curved-glass facade and more than 2,500 seats in two lushly decorated indoor spaces, plus a new outdoor amphitheater, the Kravis stages more than 300 performances each year. Phone or check the website for a current schedule of Palm Beach's best music, dance, and theater.

FAST FACTS: SOUTH FLORIDA

American Express You'll find American Express offices in Bal Harbour at 9700 Collins Ave. (© **305/865-5959;** Mon–Sat 10am–6pm); and 32 Miracle Mile, Coral Gables (© **305/446-3381;** Mon–Fri 9am–5pm and Sat 10am–4pm). To report lost or stolen traveler's checks, call © **800/221-7282. Universal Travel,** 1425C SE 17th St. (© **954/525-5000**) in Fort Lauderdale offers licensed American Express services.

Area Codes The original area code for Miami and all of Dade County was 305. That is still the code for older phone numbers, but all phone numbers assigned since July 1998 have the area code 786 (SUN). For all local calls, even if you're calling across the street, you must dial the area code (305 or 786) first. Even though the Keys still share the Dade County area code of 305, calls to there from Miami are considered long distance and must be preceded by 1-305. (Within the Keys, simply dial the seven-digit number.) The area codes for Fort Lauderdale are 954 and 754; for Palm Beach, Boca Raton, Vero Beach, and Port St. Lucie, it's 561.

ATM Networks ATMs are as ubiquitous in South Florida as the palm trees. Machines are found on nearly every street corner, in main shopping areas, and, in most cases, in supermarkets and even convenience stores.

Automobile Organizations Auto clubs will supply maps, suggested routes, guidebooks, accident and bail-bond insurance, and emergency road service. The **American Automobile Association (AAA)** is the major auto club in the United States. If you belong to an auto club in your home country, inquire about AAA reciprocity before you leave. You may be able to join AAA even if you're not a member of a reciprocal club; to inquire, call AAA (© **800/222-4357**). AAA is actually an organization of regional auto clubs, so look under "AAA Automobile Club" in the White Pages of the telephone directory. AAA has a nationwide emergency road service telephone number (© **800/AAA-HELP** [222-4357]).

Business Hours Banking hours vary, but most banks are open weekdays from 9am to 3pm. Several stay open until 5pm or so at least 1 day during the week, and many banks feature ATMs for 24-hour banking. Most stores are open daily from 10am to 6pm; however, there are many exceptions. In Miami, shops in the Bayside Marketplace are usually open until 9 or 10pm, as are the boutiques in Coconut Grove. Boutiques on South Beach operate in their own time zone and hours range from 11am to midnight, sometimes earlier, sometimes later. Stores in Bal Harbour and other malls are usually open an extra hour 1 night during the week (usually Thurs). As far as business offices are concerned, Miami is generally a 9-to-5 town. In the Keys, hours are much more leisurely, and often left at the discretion of the proprietors. Call ahead before you go. In Key West, however, hours are similar to those in South Beach. Things are open rather late there. In Fort Lauderdale, hours are typically 9am to 5pm for businesses, but on the "Strip" (Las Olas Blvd. and downtown Fort Lauderdale), shops, restaurants, and clubs tend to stay open into the wee hours, or at least after midnight. Boca Raton, Palm Beach, and the Treasure Coast are entirely different and tend to keep earlier hours, with stores closing between 5 and 6pm and restaurants closing around 11pm, with the exception of those stores and restaurants on Clematis Street.

Car Rentals See "Getting Around," p. 35.

Climate See "When to Go," p. 27.

Currency The most common bills are the $1 (a "buck"), $5, $10, and $20 denominations. There are also $2 bills (seldom encountered), $50 bills, and $100 bills (the last two are usually not welcome as payment for small purchases).

Coins come in seven denominations: 1¢ (1 cent, or a penny); 5¢ (5 cents, or a nickel); 10¢ (10 cents, or a dime); 25¢ (25 cents, or a quarter); 50¢ (50 cents, or a half dollar); the Sacagawea and some presidential gold-colored coins, worth $1; and the rare silver dollar.

For additional information see "Money & Costs," p. 37.

Drinking Laws The legal age for purchase and consumption of alcoholic beverages is 21; proof of age is required and often requested at bars, nightclubs, and restaurants, so it's always a good idea to bring ID when you go out.

Do not carry open containers of alcohol in your car or any public area that isn't zoned for alcohol consumption. The police can fine you on the spot. And nothing will ruin your trip faster than getting a citation for DUI ("driving under the influence"), so don't even think about driving while intoxicated. Drivers suspected to be under the influence of alcohol or drugs must agree to breath, blood, or urine testing under "implied consent laws." Penalties for refusing testing can mean suspension of the driver's license for up to one year. In Florida, the first conviction carries a mandatory suspension of the driver's license for 6 months; for the second offense, 1 year; for the third offense, 2 years. Underage drivers (21 or younger) have a maximum legal blood-alcohol content percentage of .02 percent. Above this amount, they are subject to DUI penalties.

At .20 percent above the legal limit of .08 percent, a driver faces much harsher repercussions. This also applies to drivers refusing chemical testing for intoxication.

As for open-container laws: Open alcoholic containers on public property, including streets, sidewalks, or inside a vehicle are prohibited, though opened bottles of liquor are allowed inside a car trunk. Beer and wine are sold in most supermarkets and convenience stores. Most liquor stores throughout South Florida are closed on Sundays, but liquor stores in the city of Miami Beach are open all week.

Electricity Like Canada, the United States uses 110 to 120 volts AC (60 cycles), compared to 220 to 240 volts AC (50 cycles) in most of Europe, Australia, and New Zealand. Downward converters that change 220 to 240 volts to 110 to 120 volts are difficult to find in the United States, so bring one with you.

Embassies & Consulates All embassies are located in the nation's capital, Washington, D.C. Some consulates are located in major U.S. cities, and most nations have a mission to the United Nations in New York City. If your country isn't listed below, call for directory information in Washington, D.C. (✆ **202/555-1212**) or log on to **www.embassy.org/embassies**.

The embassy of **Australia** is at 1601 Massachusetts Ave. NW, Washington, DC 20036 (✆ **202/797-3000;** www.austemb.org). There are consulates in New York, Honolulu, Houston, Los Angeles, and San Francisco.

The embassy of **Canada** is at 501 Pennsylvania Ave. NW, Washington, DC 20001 (📞 **202/682-1740;** www.canadianembassy.org). Other Canadian consulates are in Buffalo (New York), Detroit, Los Angeles, New York, and Seattle.

The embassy of **Ireland** is at 2234 Massachusetts Ave. NW, Washington, DC 20008 (📞 **202/462-3939;** www.embassyofireland.org). Irish consulates are in Boston, Chicago, New York, San Francisco, and other cities. See website for complete listing.

The embassy of **New Zealand** is at 37 Observatory Circle NW, Washington, DC 20008 (📞 **202/328-4800;** www.nzembassy.com/usa). New Zealand consulates are in Los Angeles, Salt Lake City, San Francisco, and Seattle.

The embassy of the **United Kingdom** is at 3100 Massachusetts Ave. NW, Washington, DC 20008 (📞 **202/588-7800;** www.ukinusa.fco.gov.uk). Other British consulates are in Atlanta, Boston, Chicago, Cleveland, Houston, Los Angeles, New York, San Francisco, and Seattle.

Emergencies To reach the police, ambulance, or fire department, dial 📞 **911** from any phone. No coins are needed. Emergency hot lines include **Crisis Intervention** (📞 **305/358-HELP** [4357]) and the **Poison Information Center** (📞 **800/282-3171**). For crisis emergencies in Broward County, call **First Call for Help** (📞 **954/467-6333**), and in Palm Beach, call **Crisis Line** (📞 **561/930-1234**).

Gasoline (Petrol) At press time, in the U.S., the cost of gasoline (also known as gas, but never petrol), is abnormally high. Taxes are already included in the printed price. One U.S. gallon equals 3.8 liters or .83 imperial gallons. Fill-up locations are known as gas or service stations.

Holidays Banks, government offices, post offices, and many stores, restaurants, and museums are closed on the following legal national holidays: January 1 (New Year's Day), the third Monday in January (Martin Luther King, Jr., Day), the third Monday in February (Presidents' Day), the last Monday in May (Memorial Day), July 4th (Independence Day), the first Monday in September (Labor Day), the second Monday in October (Columbus Day), November 11 (Veterans' Day/Armistice Day), the fourth Thursday in November (Thanksgiving Day), and December 25 (Christmas). The Tuesday after the first Monday in November is Election Day, a federal government holiday in presidential-election years (2008, 2012, and so on).

For more information on holidays see "Calendar of Events" (p. 28).

Legal Aid If you are "pulled over" for a minor infraction (such as speeding), never attempt to pay the fine directly to a police officer; this could be construed as attempted bribery, a much more serious crime. Pay fines by mail, or directly into the hands of the clerk of the court. If accused of a more serious offense, say and do nothing before consulting a lawyer. Here the burden is on the state to prove a person's guilt beyond a reasonable doubt, and everyone has the right to remain silent, whether he or she is suspected of a crime or actually arrested. Once arrested, a person can make one telephone call to a party of his or her choice. International visitors should call their embassy or consulate.

Lost & Found Be sure to tell all of your credit card companies the minute you discover your wallet has been lost or stolen and file a report at the nearest police precinct. Your credit card company or insurer may require a police report number or record of the loss. Most credit card companies have an emergency toll-free number to call if your card is lost or stolen; they may be able to wire you a cash advance immediately or deliver an emergency credit card in a day or two. Visa's U.S. emergency number is 📞 **800/847-2911** or 410/581-9994. American Express cardholders and traveler's check holders should call ✆ **800/221-7282.** MasterCard holders should call ✆ **800/307-7309** or 636/722-7111. For other credit cards, call the toll-free number directory at ✆ **800/555-1212.**

If you need emergency cash over the weekend when all banks and American Express offices are closed, you can have money wired to you via **Western Union** (✆ **800/325-6000;** www.westernunion.com).

Mail At press time, domestic postage rates were 28¢ for a postcard and 44¢ for a letter. For international mail, a first-class letter of up to 1 ounce costs 75¢ (79¢ to Mexico); a first-class international postcard costs 98¢ (75¢ to Canada and 79¢ Mexico). For more information go to **www.usps.com** and click on "Calculate Postage."

If you aren't sure what your address will be in the United States, mail can be sent to you, in your name, c/o General Delivery, at the main post office of the city or region where you expect to be. (Call ✆ **800/275-8777** for information on the nearest post office.) The addressee must pick up mail in person and must produce proof of identity (driver's license, passport, or other). Most post offices will hold your mail for up to 1 month, and are open Monday to Friday from 8am to 6pm, and Saturday from 9am to 3pm.

Always include zip codes when mailing items in the U.S. If you don't know your zip code, visit www.usps.com/zip4.

Newspapers & Magazines The *Miami Herald* is the city's only English-language daily. It is especially known for its extensive Latin American coverage and has a decent Friday "Weekend" entertainment guide. The most respected alternative weekly is the giveaway tabloid called *New Times,* which contains up-to-date listings and reviews of food, films, theater, music, and whatever else is happening in town. Also free, if you can find it, is *Ocean Drive,* an oversize glossy magazine that's limited on text (no literary value) and heavy on ads and society photos. It's what you should read if you want to know who's who and where to go for fun; it's available at a number of chic South Beach boutiques and restaurants. It is also available at newsstands. In the same vein: *Miami Magazine* and *944 Magazine,* also free and available throughout the city.

Passports **For Residents of Australia:** You can pick up an application from your local post office or any branch of Passports Australia, but you must schedule an interview at the passport office to present your application materials. Call the **Australian Passport Information Service** at ✆ **131-232,** or visit the government website at www.passports.gov.au.

For Residents of Canada: Passport applications are available at travel agencies throughout Canada or from the central **Passport Office,** Department of Foreign Affairs and International Trade, Ottawa, ON K1A 0G3 (✆ **800/567-6868;** www.pptc.gc.ca). *Note:* Canadian children who travel must have their own passport. However, if you hold a valid Canadian passport issued before December 11, 2001, that bears the name of your child, the passport remains valid for you and your child until it expires.

For Residents of Ireland: You can apply for a 10-year passport at the **Passport Office,** Setanta Centre, Molesworth Street, Dublin 2 (✆ **01/671-1633;** www.irlgov.ie/iveagh). Those under age 18 and over 65 must apply for a €12 3-year passport. You can also apply at 1A South Mall, Cork (✆ **021/272-525**) or at most main post offices.

For Residents of New Zealand: You can pick up a passport application at any New Zealand Passports Office or download it from their website. Contact the **Passports Office** at ✆ **0800/225-050** in New Zealand or 04/474-8100, or log on to www.passports.govt.nz.

For Residents of the United Kingdom: To pick up an application for a standard 10-year passport (5-year passport for children 15 and under), visit your nearest passport office, major post office, or travel agency or contact the **United Kingdom Passport Service** at ✆ **0870/521-0410** or search its website at www.ips.gov.uk.

Police For emergencies, dial ✆ **911** from any phone. No coins are needed. For other matters, call ✆ **305/595-6263.** The Broward County Sheriff's Office number is (✆ **954/831-8900**); the Palm Beach County Sheriff's Office number is (✆ **561/470-5257**).

Safety See "Crime & Safety," p. 38.

Smoking Smoking is no longer allowed in restaurants. A law passed prohibiting smoking in any establishment that makes the bulk of its money in food sales. Outdoor areas are immune to these laws, and some restaurants have ignored the law and still permit smoking indoors.

Taxes A 6% state sales tax (plus 1% local tax, for a total of 7% in Miami–Dade County [from Homestead to North Miami Beach]) is added on at the register for all goods and services purchased in Florida. In addition, most municipalities levy special taxes on restaurants and hotels. In Surfside, hotel taxes total 11%; in Bal Harbour, 11%; in Miami Beach (including South Beach), 13%; and in the rest of Dade County, a whopping 13%. Food and beverage tax in Miami Beach, Bal Harbour and Surfside is 9%, in Miami-Dade restaurants not located inside hotels it's 8%, and in restaurants located in hotels, 9%. Broward County sales tax is 6% and resort tax is 5%. Sales tax in Palm Beach is 6.5%, while resort tax is 5%.

Telephone & Fax Generally, hotel surcharges on long-distance and local calls are astronomical, so you're better off using your **cellphone** or a **public pay telephone.** Many convenience groceries and packaging services sell **prepaid calling cards** in denominations up to $50; for international visitors these can be the least expensive way to call home. Many public phones at airports now accept American Express, MasterCard, and Visa credit cards. **Local calls** made from public pay phones in most locales cost either 25¢ or 35¢. Pay phones do not accept pennies, and few will take anything larger than a quarter.

Most long-distance and international calls can be dialed directly from any phone. **For calls within the United States and to Canada,** dial 1 followed by the area code and the seven-digit number. **For other international calls,** dial 011 followed by the country code, city code, and the number you are calling.

Calls to area codes **800, 888, 877,** and **866** are toll-free. However, calls to area codes **700** and **900** (chat lines, bulletin boards, "dating" services, and so on) can be very expensive—usually a charge of 95¢ to $3 or more per minute, and they sometimes have minimum charges that can run as high as $15 or more.

For **reversed-charge or collect calls,** and for **person-to-person calls,** dial the number 0 and then the area code and number; an operator will come on the line, and you should specify whether you are calling collect, person-to-person, or both. If your operator-assisted call is international, ask for the overseas operator.

For **local directory assistance** ("information"), dial 411; for long-distance information, dial 1, and then the appropriate area code and 555-1212.

Most hotels have **fax machines** available for guest use (be sure to ask about the charge to use it). Many hotel rooms are even wired for guests' fax machines. A less expensive way to send and receive faxes may be at stores such as **The UPS Store** (formerly Mail Boxes Etc.).

Time Florida, like New York, is in the **Eastern Standard Time (EST)** zone. The continental United States is divided into **four time zones:** Eastern Standard Time (EST), Central Standard Time (CST), Mountain Standard Time (MST), and Pacific Standard Time (PST). Alaska and Hawaii have their own zones. For example, when it's 9am in Los Angeles (PST), it's 7am in Honolulu (HST),10am in Denver (MST), 11am in Chicago (CST), noon in New York City (EST), 5pm in London (GMT), and 2am the next day in Sydney.

Daylight saving time takes effect at 2am the second Sunday in March until 2am the first Sunday in November except in Arizona, Hawaii, the U.S. Virgin Islands, and Puerto Rico. Daylight savings moves the clock 1 hour ahead of standard time.

Tipping Tips are a very important part of certain workers' income, and gratuities are the standard way of showing appreciation for services provided. (Tipping is certainly not compulsory if the service is poor!) In hotels, tip **bellhops** at least $1 per bag ($2–$3 if you have a lot of luggage) and tip the **chamber staff** $1 to $2 per day (more if you've left a disaster area for him or her to clean up). Tip the **doorman** or **concierge** only if he or she has provided you with some specific service (for example, calling a cab for you or obtaining difficult-to-get theater tickets). Tip the **valet-parking attendant** $2 every time you get your car.

In restaurants, bars, and nightclubs, tip **service staff** 15% to 20% of the check, tip **bartenders** 10% to 15%, and tip **valet-parking attendants** $2 per vehicle.

As for other service personnel, tip **cab drivers** 15% of the fare; tip **skycaps** at airports at least $1 per bag ($2–$3 if you have a lot of luggage); and tip **hairdressers** and **barbers** 15% to 20%.

Toilets You won't find public toilets or "restrooms" on the streets in most U.S. cities but they can be found in hotel lobbies, bars, restaurants, museums, department stores, railway and bus stations, and service stations. Large hotels and fast-food restaurants are often the best bet for clean facilities. If possible, avoid the toilets at parks and beaches, which tend to be dirty; some may be unsafe. Restaurants and bars in resorts or heavily visited areas may reserve their restrooms for patrons.

Useful Phone Numbers U.S. Department of State Travel Advisory: ☎ **202/647-5225** (manned 24 hr.).

U.S. Passport Agency: ☎ **202/647-0518.**

U.S. Centers for Disease Control International Traveler's Hot Line: ☎ **404/332-4559.**

Visas For information about U.S. visas go to **http://travel.state.gov** and click on "Visas." Or go to one of the following websites.

Australian citizens can obtain up-to-date visa information from the **U.S. Embassy Canberra,** Moonah Place, Yarralumla, ACT 2600 (☎ **02/6214-5600**) or by checking the U.S. Diplomatic Mission's website at http://canberra.usembassy.gov.

British subjects can obtain up-to-date visa information by calling the **U.S. Embassy Visa Information Line** (☎ **0891/200-290**) or by visiting the "Visas to the U.S." section of the American Embassy London's website at www.usembassy.org.uk.

Irish citizens can obtain up-to-date visa information through the **Embassy of the USA Dublin,** 42 Elgin Rd., Dublin 4, Ireland (☎ **353/1-668-8777**), or by checking the "Consular Services" section of the website at http://dublin.usembassy.gov.

Citizens of **New Zealand** can obtain up-to-date visa information by contacting the **U.S. Embassy New Zealand,** 29 Fitzherbert Terrace, Thorndon, Wellington (☎ **644/472-2068**), or get the information directly from http://newzealand.usembassy.gov.

Weather Hurricane Season runs from June through November. For an up-to-date recording of current weather conditions and forecast reports, call ☎ **305/229-4522.**

Index

See also Accommodations and Restaurant indexes, below.

General Index

A

AAA (American Automobile Association), 387
AARP, 40
The Abbey (South Beach), 223
Accessibility, 39
Accommodations. *See also specific destinations; and Accommodations Index*
  best, 7–10
Actors' Playhouse (Coral Gables), 238
Adrienne Arsht Center for the Performing Arts (Miami), 240
Adventures in Backwater Fishing, 251
Agua Spa at the Delano (Miami), 86
Airboat tours, Everglades National Park, 252
Air Lauderdale (Fort Lauderdale), 30
Air tours, 267, 302
Air travel, 34, 35–36
Alabama Jack's (Card Sound), 266
Alf's Golf Shop (Miami), 220
Alhambra Antiques (Coral Gables), 210
Almost There Sportfishing Charters (Key West), 306
Aloha Watersports (Fort Lauderdale), 334
Amelia Earhart Park (Hialeah), 187
American Automobile Association (AAA), 387
American Express, 387
  Miami, 64
American Watersports (Miami Beach), 194
America the Beautiful Senior Pass, 40
Amtrak, 35, 36
Anhinga Trail (Everglades National Park), 249
Anne's Beach, 267
Antiques and collectibles, Miami, 210
Aqua (Key West), 325
Aquatic Rental Center (Miami), 195
Architectural Antiques (Miami), 210
Area codes, 387

Arroyo, Angel, 237
Art Basel Miami Beach, 31
ArtCenter/South Florida (South Beach), 179
Art Deco District (South Beach), 59, 172–176
Art Deco Weekend (South Beach), 28
Art Deco Welcome Center (South Beach), 174, 176
Art galleries, Miami, 176–178
Atlantic Avenue (Delray Beach), 369
Atlantic Dunes Beach (Delray Beach), 358
ATMs (automated-teller machines), 387
Atrium (South Beach), 213
Audubon House & Tropical Gardens (Key West), 297
Australia, 388, 390, 392
Automatic Slim's (South Beach), 223
Auto Train, 35
Autumn, 28
Aventura, 60, 208, 218
Aventura Mall, 218

B

Bahia Honda State Park, 287–289, 291
Bal Harbour, 59. *See also* Miami Beach
Bal Harbour Shops, 218
Ballet Flamenco La Rosa (Miami), 237, 239
Bally's Total Fitness (Miami), 202
BankAtlantic Center (Sunrise), 336
Bardot (Miami), 223–224
Barnacle State Historic Site (Coconut Grove), 183–184
Barnes & Noble (Miami), 211
Barneys Co-Op (South Beach), 213
Bar 721 (South Beach), 223
Baseball, Broward County, 335
Base USA (South Beach), 213
Bass Museum of Art (South Beach), 179
Bass Pro Shops Outdoor World (Dania Beach), 221, 334
Bayside Marketplace (Miami), 218
Beaches. *See also specific beaches*
  Bahia Honda, 287
  best, 6–7
  Boca Raton/Delray Beach, 358, 360
  Broward County, 332, 334
  Key West, 304
  Miami, 169–172
  Palm Beach area, 373

Belinda's Designs (South Beach), 214
Benini Bug (South Miami), 215
Bernice Steinbaum Gallery (Miami), 176
Bertini European Men's Clothing (Coral Gables), 215
Big Cypress National Preserve, 246
Big Pine and Lower Keys Chamber of Commerce, 287
Biking, 42
  the Everglades, 250
  Key West, 293, 296, 304
  Lower Keys, 288
  Miami, 64, 196–197
  Palm Beach area, 373
Bill Baggs Cape Florida State Park, 187
Billie Swamp Safari (Big Cypress Seminole Reservation), 337
Biltmore Hotel (Miami), golf course, 200
Biltmore Hotel Tour (Miami), 192
Bird-watching, 250, 270, 288, 326
Biscayne Corridor (Miami), 61
  shopping, 208
Biscayne National Park, 257–261
Blue Hole, 288
Blue Moon Outdoor Center (Miami), 194–195
Blue Planet Kayak Tours, 274
Blue Water Boat Rental (Riviera Beach), 374
Boat charters and rentals, Palm Beach area, 374
Boating and sailing (rentals and charters), 42. *See also* Fishing
  Broward County, 334
  Everglades National Park, 252
  Islamorada, 268
  Lower Keys, 288–289
  Miami, 194, 195
  Upper and Middle Keys, 273
Boat Rental Plus (Miami Beach), 194
Boat tours and cruises
  the Everglades, 253
  Key West, 302–303
  Miami, 189–191
Boca Chita Key, 257, 259
Boca Raton, 357–370
  accommodations, 362–364
  beaches and outdoor activities, 358–361
  nightlife, 369–370
  restaurants, 364–369
  shopping, 362
  sights and attractions, 361–362
  traveling to, 358
  visitor information, 358

Accommodations